# Reason and Experience in Mendelssohn and Kant

**Paul Guyer** is emeritus professor of philosophy and humanities at Brown University and the University of Pennsylvania. He is the author, editor, and/or translator of more than thirty books, and was General Co-Editor of the *Cambridge Edition of the Works of Immanuel Kant*. His most recent books with Oxford University Press are *Idealism in Modern Philosophy* (2023, with Rolf-Horstmann) and *Kant's Impact on Moral Philosophy* (2024). Professor Guyer was the recipient of the 2024 International Kant Prize of the Kant Gesellschaft and Fritz Thyssen Foundation. He is a Member of the American Philosophical Society, a Fellow of the American Academy of Arts and Sciences, and a Corresponding Foreign Member of the Academy of Athens.

# Reason and Experience in Mendelssohn and Kant

Paul Guyer

## OXFORD
UNIVERSITY PRESS

Great Clarendon Street, Oxford, OX2 6DP,
United Kingdom

Oxford University Press is a department of the University of Oxford.
It furthers the University's objective of excellence in research, scholarship,
and education by publishing worldwide. Oxford is a registered trade mark of
Oxford University Press in the UK and in certain other countries

© Paul Guyer 2020

The moral rights of the author have been asserted

First published 2020
First published in paperback 2025

All rights reserved. No part of this publication may be reproduced, stored in
a retrieval system, or transmitted, in any form or by any means, without the
prior permission in writing of Oxford University Press, or as expressly permitted
by law, by licence or under terms agreed with the appropriate reprographics
rights organization. Enquiries concerning reproduction outside the scope of the
above should be sent to the Rights Department, Oxford University Press, at the
address above

You must not circulate this work in any other form
and you must impose this same condition on any acquirer

Published in the United States of America by Oxford University Press
198 Madison Avenue, New York, NY 10016, United States of America

British Library Cataloguing in Publication Data
Data available

Library of Congress Cataloging in Publication Data
Data available

ISBN 978–0–19–885033–5 (Hbk.)
ISBN 978–0–19–898982–0 (Pbk.)

Links to third party websites are provided by Oxford in good faith and
for information only. Oxford disclaims any responsibility for the materials
contained in any third party website referenced in this work.

# Table of Contents

*Acknowledgments* — vii
*Abbreviations* — ix

Introduction — 1
  1. Prologue: The Prize Essays — 27

## Part I. Metaphysics and Epistemology

  2. Mendelssohn, Kant, and Proofs of the Existence of God in Kant's Pre-Critical Period — 75
  3. Proofs of the Existence of God in the *Critique of Pure Reason* and *Morning Hours* — 103
  4. Mendelssohn and Kant on the Immortality of the Soul — 142
  5. Mendelssohn, Kant, and Idealism — 167

## Part II. Aesthetics

  6. Mendelssohn's Aesthetics — 205
  7. Kant's Aesthetics — 224
  8. Mendelssohn's and Kant's Aesthetics Compared — 241

## Part III. Religion, Politics, and History

  9. Mendelssohn, Kant, and Enlightenment — 259
  10. Freedom of Religion in Mendelssohn and Kant — 276
  11. Judaism, Christianity, and the Religion of Pure Reason — 302
  12. Mendelssohn, Kant, and the Possibility of Progress — 321

*Bibliography* — 339
*Index* — 349

# Acknowledgments

In some ways, this book has been long in the making. I first heard about Moses Mendelssohn in Sunday school in my Reform synagogue, perhaps around sixth or seventh grade; it was clear that he was a cultural hero for his efforts to bridge the gulf between the Jewish community and their grudging hosts in eighteenth-century Prussia, but it was not made clear to us in our age-appropriate textbook what his specific contributions to either Judaism or the secular culture had actually been. I next encountered Mendelssohn in graduate school, after I had left contact with organized religion behind, when I was studying the historical background to Kant's aesthetics in preparation for my dissertation, and I wrote some pages on Mendelssohn's aesthetics as part of that work. When I rewrote the dissertation as *Kant and the Claims of Taste* (1979) I omitted the pre-Kantian history for reasons of space, but my continuing work on the historical context of Kant's aesthetics kept me in touch with Mendelssohn's aesthetics, and my first published essay on the aesthetics of Mendelssohn and Kant (and Karl Philipp Moritz) was written in 1990 and appeared in my collection *Kant and the Experience of Freedom* (1993). My first attempt at a comparison of the essays the two philosophers contributed to the Royal Prussian Academy of Science's 1762 competition on the prospects for the success of mathematical method in philosophy, in which Mendelssohn's essay took first place and Kant's second, appeared in *Philosophical Topics* in 1991, and was included in my collection *Kant on Freedom, Law, and Happiness* (2000). At some point after that, I began to think that the significance of his interactions with Mendelssohn for Kant was greater than the historiography of philosophy and perhaps Kant himself always recognized, and the idea of a book charting the history of this interaction began to form. The present volume is the result of that thought.

Neither of those earlier papers has been incorporated into the present volume, but several more recent pieces have. I owe thanks to Thomas Höwing, Florian Marwede, and Marcus Willaschek for the invitation to present the paper at a conference on Kant on the highest good at the Johann Wolfgang von Goethe University of Frankfurt am Main that became 4 of this volume; it has previously been published in the volume edited by Thomas Höwing, *The Highest Good in Kant's Philosophy* (Berlin and Boston: Walter de Gruyter, 2016), and thanks are due to Walter de Gruyter for permission to use this material here. The second half of 5 was originally presented at a conference organized by Corey Dyck and Falk Wunderlich and published by them in the volume entitled *Kant and his German Contemporaries, Volume I: Logic, Mind, Epistemology, Science, and Ethics* (Cambridge University Press, 2018); thanks are due to Cambridge University Press for permission to reuse that material here. 11 was originally presented as a plenary lecture at the Multilateral Kant Conference at Hofstra University in 2016, but has not previously been published. All the other material in this volume has been written specifically for it, although an abbreviated version of Chapters 6 and 7 has in the meantime appeared in *Kant and His German Contemporaries, Volume II: Aesthetics, History, Politics, and*

*Religion*, edited by Daniel O. Dahlstrom (Cambridge University Press, 2018). Again, thanks to Cambridge University Press for permission to reuse this material. Dahlstrom's work as a Mendelssohn scholar, especially his translations of Mendelssohn's *Philosophical Writings* and *Morning Hours* (with Corey Dyck), merits the gratitude of all readers of English interested in Mendelssohn.

Apart from what I have already mentioned, much of the material in this volume was written during my tenure as a Daimler Fellow at the American Academy in Berlin from January through May, 2017. I am deeply grateful to the Academy and its staff, especially librarian Yolande Korb, for my selection and for their support of my work in their commodious villa on the right (in both senses of "right") bank of the Wannsee in Berlin. An abbreviated version of Chapters 9 and 10 formed the basis for my public lecture at the Academy of May 2, 2017, and I am grateful to my dear friends Rolf-Peter Horstmann, Jay Wallace, Dina Emundts, Stefan Gosepath, and Sally Sedgwick for their valuable questions on that occasion, and for their companionship and hospitality throughout my stay in Berlin. I am deeply grateful to my wife Pamela Foa for her encouragement of this project at every stage but especially for accompanying me during my fellowship in Berlin in spite of her family's suffering during an earlier period of German history. I am also grateful to the two anonymous referees for Oxford University Press for their detailed and helpful comments. And special thanks to Alex Kwan and Courtney D. Fugate for discovering a number of typographical errors in the original edition of this book.

I dedicate this book to the memory of my teachers Stanley Cavell, Morton White, Robert Nozick, Israel Scheffler, Nelson Goodman, and Hilary Putnam, and to my friends and mentors Lewis White Beck and Maurice Mandelbaum. Although each of these was a very different philosopher from the others and from me, I learned from all of them, and I like to think that each would have found something to interest him in this book.

# Abbreviations

Mendelssohn:
| | |
|---|---|
| J | *Jerusalem* |
| JubA | *Jubliäumsausgabe* |
| LW | *Late Writings (Morning Hours)* |
| PW | *Philosophical Writings* |

Kant:
| | |
|---|---|
| CF | *Conflict of the Faculties* |
| CPJ | *Critique of Power of Judgment* |
| CPracR | *Critique of Practical Reason* |
| CPuR | *Critique of Pure Reason* |
| EAT | *The End of All Things* |
| G | *Groundwork for the Metaphysics of Morals* |
| ID | *Inaugural dissertation (On the Form and Principles of the Sensible and Intelligible World)* |
| ND | *Nova Delucudatio (New Exposition of the First Principles of Metaphysical Cognition)* |
| OPB | *Only Possible Basis for a Demonstration of the Existence of God* |
| PP | *Toward Perpetual Peace* |
| RBMR | *Religion within the Boundaries of Mere Reason* |
| WIE? | *What is Enlightenment?* |
| WOT? | *What Does it Mean to Orient Oneself in Thinking?* |

# Introduction

In November, 1785, Kant wrote to Christian Gottfried Schütz, a professor in Jena and a co-founder of the new *Allgemeine Literaturzeitung*, which would become a major organ for supporters of the Kantian philosophy, with reference to Moses Mendelssohn's newly published *Morgenstunden* (*Morning Hours* or *Morning Lessons*)—which was, unbeknownst to either of the correspondents or to anyone else, about to become Mendelssohn's last major book—the following:

Although the worthy M's book must be regarded in the main as a masterpiece of the self-deception of our reason, insofar as it takes the subjective conditions of our reason's determination of objects in general as conditions of the possibility of these objects themselves, a self-deception whose true character it is no easy task to expose and from which it is not easy to liberate our understanding completely, this book will nevertheless be highly useful—not only for what is said with penetration, originality, and exemplary clarity in its "Preliminary Notions" concerning truth, appearance, and error, things that can be used very well in any philosophy lecture, but also for its second part, which has significant value for the critique of human reason... this extremely penetrating pursuit of our chain of concepts, extending itself until it embraces the whole of reality, provides us with the most splendid occasion and at the same time challenge to subject our faculty of pure reason to a total critique, in order that we may distinguish the merely subjective conditions of its employment from those from which something valid about its objects can be inferred. Pure philosophy must certainly profit from this, even assuming that after a complete investigation illusion intervenes, so that something may appear to be victory over a field of highly remote objects when it is really only (though very usefully) the direction of the subject to objects that are very close by. One can regard this final legacy of a dogmatizing metaphysics at the same time as its most perfect accomplishment, both in view of its chain-like coherence and in the exceptional clarity of its presentation, and as a memorial, never to detract from its worth, to the sagacity of a man who knows and controls the full power of the mode of reasoning that he has adopted, a memorial that a critique of reason, which casts doubt on the happy progress of such a procedure, can thus use as an enduring example for testing its principles, in order either to confirm or reject them.[1]

It is clear from this that Kant regarded Mendelssohn the man with respect. But the passage also suggests that he regarded Mendelssohn's book—fully titled *Morning Hours: Lectures on the Existence of God*—as a careful and, as it would turn out, final

---

[1] Kant to Christian Gottfied Schütz, end of November, 1785; 10:428–9; *Correspondence*, pp. 237–8. Zweig capitalized "Critique of Reason" in his translation, as if referring to the book the *Critique of Pure Reason*, but since all nouns are capitalized in German and Kant does not otherwise mark that he is referring to his book, I use lower case letters to suggest that Kant is referring to the project of a critique of the pretensions of pure reason rather than to his book itself.

statement of the rationalist project of proving the existence of objects, above all the existence of God, by a priori arguments from reason alone, and in that regard useful primarily for demonstrating to philosophy students of the future the impossibility of proving the existence of any object from reason alone, thus of the failure of the rationalist project as a whole. This letter is consistent with, if not the source of, the picture of Mendelssohn that has prevailed in many quarters ever since it was written, namely as a philosopher who produced an elegant and precise statement of a doomed philosophy, a philosophy that in his own words was destined to be destroyed once and for all by the "all-crushing" (*alles zermalmenden*) Kant (*MS, JubA* 3.2:3), never to raise its admittedly lovely head again.

This greatly simplifies the relation between Mendelssohn and Kant, as indeed Kant himself well knew. Kant's recognition that there was more common ground between himself and Mendelssohn than his letter to Schütz might suggest is clear from the opening of the public statement on the controversy between Mendelssohn and his opponent Friedrich Heinrich Jacobi, the controversy known as the *Pantheismusstreit*, that Kant published some months later, in the *Berlinische Monatsschrift* for October, 1786.[2] This is the essay entitled "What Does It Mean to Orient Oneself in Thinking?" Here Kant starts with a cardinal principle of his own philosophy—as he put it in the *Critique of Pure Reason*, that "Without sensibility no object would be given to us, and without understanding none would be thought. Thoughts without content are empty, intuitions without concepts are blind" (A 51/B 75)—and then suggests that Mendelssohn actually agreed with it:

However exalted the application of our concepts, and however far up from sensibility we may abstract them, still they will always be appended to **picture-like** [*bildiche*] representations, whose proper function is to make these concepts, which are not otherwise derived from experience, serviceable for **experiential use**. For how would we procure sense and significance for our concepts if we did not underpin them with some intuition (which ultimately must always be an example from some possible experience)? If from this concrete act of the understanding we leave out the association of the image [*Bild*]—in the first place an accidental perception through the senses—then what is left over is the pure concept of understanding, whose range is now enlarged and contains a rule for thinking in general. It is in just such a way that general logic comes about; and many **heuristic** methods of thinking perhaps lie hidden in the experiential use of our understanding and reason; if we carefully extract these methods from that experience, they could well enrich philosophy with many useful maxims even in abstract thinking.

Of this kind is the principle to which the late Mendelssohn expressly subscribed for the first time, so far as I know, in his last writings (the *Morning Hours*... and the *Letters to Lessing's Friends*...): namely, the maxim that it is necessary to orient oneself in the speculative use of reason (which Mendelssohn otherwise trusted very much in respect of the cognition of supersensible objects, even so far as claiming for it the evidence of demonstration) by means

---

[2] For a description of the *Pantheismusstreit*, see Frederick C. Beiser, *The Fate of Reason: German Philosophy from Kant to Fichte* (Cambridge, Mass.: Harvard University Press, 1987), chapter 3, pp. 93–108. For further description as well as selection from the relevant writings by Mendelssohn and Jacobi, see Gérard Vallée, *The Spinoza Conversations between Lessing and Jacobi: Text with Excerpts from the Ensuing Controversy* (Lanham: University Press of America, 1988).

of a certain guideline which he sometimes called **common sense** or **healthy reason** (in the *Morning Hours*) and sometimes **plain understanding** (*To Lessing's Friends*)

(*WO*, 8:133; *Religion and Rational Theology*, p. 7)

Mendelssohn claimed to ground or "orient" his philosophy in common sense, and Kant did too—after all, his *Groundwork for the Metaphysics of Morals*, also published in 1785, a few months before Mendelssohn's *Morning Hours*, begins with a "Transition from Common Rational to Philosophic Moral Cognition," claiming to derive the categorical imperative from commonsense conceptions of the good will and of duty—and Kant seems to suggest that what is commonsensical is precisely to assume that all concepts, however abstract, must ultimately be linked to some actual experience in order to yield knowledge of the existence of any objects. Thus Kant suggests that Mendelssohn's common sense led him too to recognize that concepts need to be anchored in experience in order to yield knowledge of objects. On this suggestion, Mendelssohn would have gone wrong—departed from common sense—only in excepting a few "supersensible" objects—God, but also, as we will see, human immortality (the subject of Mendelssohn's earlier work from 1767, *Phaedo or on the Immortality of the Soul*)—from this sound principle.

However, this is not quite the criticism of Mendelssohn that Kant makes in "What Does It Mean to Orient Oneself...?" Rather, he continues the passage just quoted thus:

Who would have thought that this admission would not only have a destructive attitude on his favorable opinion of the power of **speculative** reason when used in theological matters (which was in fact unavoidable), but that even common healthy reason, given the ambiguous position in which he left the employment of this faculty in contrast to speculation, would also fall into the danger of serving as a principle of enthusiasm in the dethroning of reason? And yet this happened in the controversy between Mendelssohn and Jacobi...

And then, in what seem quite surprising to a reader not already well-versed in Kant's philosophy, Kant continues that "it was in fact **only** reason—not any alleged sense of truth, not any transcendent intuition under the name of faith, on which tradition and revelation can be grafted without reason's consent"—as Jacobi held—"which Mendelssohn affirmed, staunchly and with justified zeal; it was only that genuine pure human reason which he found necessary and recommended as a means of orientation" (*WO*, 8:133–4; *Religion and Rational Theology*, pp. 7–8). It might seems as if Kant is now taking back the criticism that he had just made of Mendelssohn, insisting that Mendelssohn was justified after all in zealously insisting that the existence of the supersensible—God and immortality—can be known by reason alone. But this is not exactly what he is doing. For the operative word in his previous comment is "speculative:" what he will argue in the rest of the essay is that Mendelssohn was indeed mistaken to think that even though in general existence-claims do need experience as well as concepts nevertheless in the special case of God and immortality "speculative" or *theoretical* reason suffices, when in fact it is only the *practical* use of reason that can justify us in the belief in the existence of God and immortality, as conditions of the possible realization of the highest good: Mendelssohn "retains the merit of insisting that the final touchstone of the reliability of judgment is to be sought in **reason alone**," but "erred here in that he nevertheless trusted speculation to the extent of letting it alone settle everything on the path of demonstration," when it is only "**rational faith**, which rests on a need of reason's use with a **practical** intent... a **postulate** of reason," which can securely ground our belief in God and immortality" (*WO*, 8:140, 142; *Religion and Rational Theology*, pp. 13–14). Neither Kant nor Mendelssohn in fact applies the principle "no knowledge without intuition" or actual experience universally; both allow exceptions in the case of God and immortality—Kant also in the case of human freedom—but while Mendelssohn thinks that in these special cases speculative or theoretical reason can act on its own, for Kant is only practical reason that can so act.

This is an important point in any comparison between the two philosophers, but there is a larger point to be made here. This is that any contrast between Mendelssohn as an unreconstructed pure rationalist (if there ever were one) and Kant as a philosopher who always insists on a synthesis between rationalism and empiricism—always insists that we can know that our concepts are instantiated only on the basis of intuitions, particularly those furnished in sensory perception—is too simple. A blunt statement like this one, found in one of the few direct comparisons of the two philosophers, cannot be accepted: "Mendelssohn as a representative of the Enlightenment is everywhere a *dogmatic* rationalist, but Kant a critical" one.[3] Rather, both philosophers are engaged in a common project of showing that empiricism and rationalism, the first based on *experiences* of objects originating in our sensory experience and the second on *concepts* of objects originating in our own intellect, must go hand-in-hand to furnish any complete *knowledge* of objects, except in a few very special cases where reason can provide knowledge of the existence of objects on its own, although for Mendelssohn that is theoretical reason and for Kant that can be only practical reason. The latter difference between them is pretty obvious—pretty much anyone who had read the *Critique of Pure Reason* carefully could have written Kant's essay "What Does It Mean to Orient Oneself...?" for him. What is more complex is the comparison between them as both synthesizers of rationalism and empiricism. What I shall be arguing in this book is that while we might have thought that Mendelssohn, the heir to Leibniz, Christian Wolff, and Alexander Gottlieb Baumgarten, would be a better rationalist than Kant, while Kant, who was in many ways so impressed with David Hume and was much more explicit than Mendelssohn that "concepts without content are empty" would be the better empiricist, we will find that this is not always true. Rather, Kant, who divides the human intellect into understanding and reason and in turn divides reason into theoretical and practical, often has a richer picture of human intellect or reason as a whole than Mendelssohn does, and can exploit its resources more fully in his analysis of the categories, principles, and ideas of human thought; but Mendelssohn often has a richer picture of the complexity of human experience, including of human emotions and feelings. Thus while Kant may come up with a better model of human knowledge in the abstract, there are areas of philosophy, such as aesthetics and philosophy of religion, where Mendelssohn is at least sometime the wiser philosopher.

---

[3] Walter Kinkel, "Moses Mendelssohn and Immanuel Kant," *Kant-Studien* 34 (1929): 391–409, at p. 401.

To be sure, the distinction between rationalism and empiricism, or more precisely between continental rationalism and British empiricism, has been criticized in recent scholarship.[4] Indeed, it is easy to show that there were strong connections between the two supposedly separate schools. For example, Malebranche had considerable influence on both Berkeley and Hume, and beyond that there was a vigorous rationalist tradition in Britain, which included Cambridge Platonists such as Ralph Cudworth and later philosophers such as Samuel Clarke, while Leibniz himself stated that "We are all mere empirics in three-quarters of our actions... when we expect daylight tomorrow, we act as empiricists, because this has always happened up to the present,"[5] and Wolff clearly drew on Locke as well as on Descartes and Leibniz for his own approach to philosophy. Nevertheless, it is clear that Kant thought that there was a fundamental difference between Leibniz, who "**intellectualized** the appearances," and Locke, who "**sensitivized** the concepts of understanding" (*CPuR*, A 371/B 327), and that these two and their own followers were in turn members of the traditions begun by Plato and Aristotle, respectively: "Aristotle can be regarded as the head of the **empiricists**, Plato that of the **noologists**" (but also "Epicurus can be called the foremost philosopher of sensibility") while "in recent times" Locke "followed the former" and "Leibniz... followed the latter" (*CPuR*, A 853–4/B 881–2)—Kant always regarded Hume, however, as a skeptic rather than an empiricist (A 855/B 883), while he brought up Berkeley only as a representative of the "empirical idealism" to which he opposed his own "transcendental idealism"—and it is equally clear that Kant conceived of his own critical philosophy as undercutting this great historical division by showing that both input from our senses and conceptualization by our understanding is necessary for any genuine knowledge. If Kant set up the distinction between rationalism and empiricism, it was only to knock it down himself. My argument in this book will then be that, although he did not put in precisely the same terms, Mendelssohn too was engaged in the project of reconciling rather than dividing rationalism and empiricism, and that it will be useful to compare his version of this project to Kant's in order to see the strengths and weaknesses of each.

* * *

Thus far, I have been speaking primarily about *comparisons* between Mendelssohn and Kant, both about that which Kant himself made shortly before and after Mendelssohn's death and those that we might make on our own. But these two philosophers also had a long *relationship*, although they met in person only once and exchanged fewer than a dozen letters, and I want to describe this relationship as well as to compare the positions of the two philosophers on a number of issues ranging from metaphysics to aesthetics, philosophy of religion, philosophy of history, and political philosophy. Both philosophers began publishing in 1755, Mendelssohn aged

---

[4] This criticism begins with Louis E. Loeb, *From Descartes to Hume: Continental Rationalism and the Development of Modern Philosophy* (Ithaca and London: Cornell University Press, 1981).

[5] Gottfried Wilhelm Leibniz, "The Monadology," §31, in Leibniz, *Philosophical Papers and Letters*, ed. Leroy E. Loemker, second edition (Dordrecht: D. Reidel, 1969), p. 645.

twenty-six and Kant thirty-one.[6] But Kant's publications in that year were, with one exception, academic exercises necessary for his university career in Königsberg, while the publisher of his one more potentially popular work, the *Universal Natural History and Theory of the Heavens*, went bankrupt and the book was not distributed; Mendelssohn's works, by contrast, were more popular in style and published in Berlin, the center of the German Enlightenment, and quickly earned him wide notice. There is no evidence, however, that Mendelssohn came to Kant's attention at that time, nor is there evidence that Kant came to Mendelssohn's then. But their intellectual paths certainly crossed in the period from 1762 to 1764. In the first of these years, Frederick the Great's Academy of Sciences in Berlin announced an essay competition on the question whether the prospects for certainty in philosophy, specifically "natural theology and morality," are as great as those in mathematics—in other words, what are the prospects for the use of mathematical method in philosophy?—to which both Mendelssohn and Kant submitted entries; and in 1764 the Academy announced the results, with Mendelssohn winning the first prize of fifty gold ducats, and Kant the *accessit*, second place or honorable mention, with no monetary prize but the honor of the publication of his essay alongside of Mendelssohn's. At the same time, Mendelssohn also reviewed Kant's first substantial book, *The Only Possible Basis for a Demonstration of the Existence of God*, published in 1763. It seems natural to suppose that from that time on Mendelssohn was on Kant's radar, or that Kant was often looking over his shoulder at him, and at least to some extent formulating his own philosophical positions in response to Mendelssohn—although hardly exclusively in response to him, since Kant developed his positions in response to all the other leading philosophical positions of his time, and preferred to emphasize the importance of his own work by making more reference to the biggest fish in the philosophical pond—as we have seen, Plato and Aristotle, Leibniz and Locke, and the skeptic Hume—than to some of the more immediate stimuli, or irritants, for his thought, such as Mendelssohn (and other closer contemporaries such as Johann Heinrich Lambert, Johann Georg Sulzer, Christian Garve, and more). Kant does sometimes explicitly argue with Mendelssohn: of course, in the essay directly about the Mendelssohn-Jacobi controversy, but in other places as well, such as his critique of a speculative argument for immortality in the "Paralogisms of Pure Reason" in the *Critique of Pure Reason*, in his critique of Mendelssohn's pessimism about the moral progress of human history in the 1793 essay "On the Common Saying: That Might be Correct in Theory but it is of no use in Practice," and in his critique of historical religions in his main work of 1793, *Religion within the Boundaries of Mere Reason*. I will discuss all of these responses in the chapters that follow. But I will also be arguing that it is instructive to read Kant as if he was both sometimes appropriating and sometimes criticizing ideas of Mendelssohn in places where he is not explicitly mentioned, such as in the aesthetics of the *Critique of the Power of Judgment* and in his argument in the *Religion* that religious practices are no more immune from human

---

[6] I am here skipping over Kant's earliest work, *On the True Estimation of Living Forces* (1747), which did *not* earn him his university degree and which quickly disappeared from view (so that in recent years a first edition of that work has cost as much as fifty percent more than a first edition of the *Critique of Pure Reason*).

subversion than our religious words or symbols are. We will never be able to know if Kant was actually thinking about Mendelssohn in such places, but I will argue, again, that the mere comparison of their positions can illuminate the strengths and weaknesses of each.

It is clear that Mendelssohn was only intermittently engaged with Kant. Mendelssohn had established himself as a philosopher—although as a Jew in eighteenth-century Prussia he could never be a university professor or member of the Academy of Sciences—earlier than did Kant, and thus had already developed many of his own positions by the time Kant became prominent. Moreover, while Kant spent the "silent decade" of the 1770s publishing little, but working away on what would become the massive *Critique of Pure Reason* of 1781, Mendelssohn, after what seems to have been a "nervous debility" or breakdown in 1771 triggered by the demands of the importunate Swiss pastor Johann Christian Lavater that he either refute the truth of Christianity or convert, turned away from philosophy altogether for a decade, devoting himself instead to the translation of and commentary on the Pentatuech and Psalms, and came back to philosophy only in the last few years of his life, with *Jerusalem, or on Religious Power and Judaism* of 1783 and the *Morning Hours* of 1785. The last work, to be sure, both attempts to defend rationalist arguments for the existence of God from Kant's critique but also borrows some important points from Kant, while the former work is not a response to Kant, although Kant's *Religion* a decade later is at least in part a response to it. So insofar as my story is one of influence and criticism, it will be somewhat one-sided, with more emphasis on Kant's relationship to Mendelssohn than on Mendelssohn's to Kant, although for purposes of comparison both authors will receive their fair share of attention.

*    *    *

Before I launch into the detailed exposition and comparison of the views of my two heroes, a brief narrative of their separate lives and moments of direct contact might be useful.

Immanuel Kant and Moses Mendelssohn were born into circumstances that were worlds apart, but in some ways also similar.[7] Kant was born in 1724 in Königsberg, the original capital of Prussia, a bustling Hanseatic trading port, a university town, and one of the most populous cities in the Germany of its time, although almost 400 miles away from Berlin and even further from the rest of Germany, while Mendelssohn was born in 1729 in Dessau, a much smaller town and capital of a much smaller state, although only about seventy-five miles from Berlin; but both were born into religious families of very modest means, although Kant's family were Lutheran Pietists and Mendelssohn's, of course, were Jewish, and for that reason on the fringes of contemporary society. Kant's father was a saddlemaker, his mother the

---

[7] For detailed biographies, see Manfred Kuehn, *Kant: A Biography* (Cambridge: Cambridge University Press, 2001), and Alexander Altmann, *Moses Mendelssohn: A Biographical Study* (Alabama: University of Alabama Press, 1973). For a briefer biography of Mendelssohn, with less detail on his philosophical work, see Shmuel Feiner, *Moses Mendelssohn: Sage of Modernity*, trans. Anthony Berris (New Haven: Yale University Press, 2010).

daughter of a more prosperous one. The child's potential was recognized by the family pastor, who was also the director of the leading school of the city, the *Collegium Fredericianum*, and Kant was a student there from the ages of eight to sixteen, studying Latin above all, but also some Greek, French, mathematics, and modern subjects such as history and geography.[8] Kant then entered the university in Königsberg, the *Albertina* (founded in 1544), where he pursued a range of philosophical and scientific courses. However, he left the university in 1747, at the age of twenty-three, without a degree, having published a scientific work in German, *The True Estimation of Living Forces*, rather than the requisite doctoral dissertation in Latin, and having disagreed in that work with his teacher Martin Knutzen over an important matter of doctrine.[9] His father having died and himself now responsible for the support of his younger siblings, Kant spent the next years as private tutor for several wealthy families in the countryside of Königsberg—the extent of his travels for the rest of his life. His duties left him time to continue his studies, and after returning to Königsberg in late 1754, he was able to submit two Latin treatises, a *Meditation on Fire* and a *New Exposition of the First Principles of Metaphysical Cognition*, which finally earned him his degree and the right to teach at the university as an unsalaried *Privatdozent*, living off of the fees students paid to attend his many lectures. In 1755 he also published the popular work in German, *Universal Natural History and Theory of the Heavens*, in which he explained how the solar system could have arisen out of a nebula of dust in accordance with the principles of Newtonian mechanics. This later became known as the Kant-Laplace hypothesis, although since, as already noted, Kant's publisher went bankrupt before circulating the books, the French astronomer Pierre-Simon Laplace developed his version of the nebular hypothesis two decades later independently from Kant's work. In 1756, Kant published a further Latin dissertation, the *Physical Monadology*, as a prerequisite for an appointment as a salaried professor, which however was not forthcoming at this time. After this burst of publications, Kant continued as a *Privatdozent* with at most local recognition until his next round of publications in 1762 to 1764, when he would reach the age of forty still dependent on student attendance at his lectures.

By that point Moses Mendelssohn, although five years younger, had achieved much wider recognition. He was born in Dessau in 1729 as the son of Mendel Heymann, a synagogue custodian and later scribe, although on his mother's side he was descended from distinguished sixteenth- and seventeenth-century rabbis. He received a traditional Jewish education until the age of fourteen, when his teacher David Fränkel was called to become the chief rabbi in Berlin. Moses followed him—according to legend, on foot—and although without any legal right to residence in Berlin, he was placed in the home of a Jewish family to continue his studies. At twenty, he entered the household of Isaac Bernhard, a silk manufacturer, as a tutor, and later became his bookkeeper, subsequently the manager, and eventually the co-owner of the business. He continued to work in this business his entire life,

---

[8] A contemporary account of the curriculum of Kant's school can be found in Heiner F. Klemme, ed., *Die Schule Immanuel Kants: Mit dem Text von Christian Schiffert über das Königsberger Collegium Fredericianum*, Kant-Forschungen Band 6 (Hamburg: Felix Meiner Verlag, 1994).

[9] See Kuehn, *Kant*, pp. 86–95.

doing his intellectual work in his spare time, and during his lifetime was as widely known for his expertise in textiles as for his accomplishments in both Jewish studies and secular philosophy. His path toward the latter was facilitated first by friendships with several privileged young Jewish men who had received secular education in Berlin and in turn introduced Mendelssohn to it, and then by his friendship with the young men of letters Gotthold Ephraim Lessing, also born in 1729, to whom he was introduced by their mutual friend Aaron Gumpertz, and the slightly younger Friedrich Nicolai, who would become a leading publisher of the Berlin Enlightenment and in particular of the several journals in which Mendelssohn continued his education by reviewing dozens of books in philosophy, literature, and the sciences through the later 1750s and into the 1760s. By the time Mendelssohn met Lessing and Nicolai, he had already learned much of the recent history of European philosophy, especially that of Locke, Spinoza, Leibniz, and Christian Wolff, and had added Latin, French, and English to his German and Hebrew. Already in 1754, the year he met Lessing, Mendelssohn wrote *Philosophical Dialogues*, which were published early in 1755, followed in the same year by *Letters on Sentiments* and an essay "Pope: A Metaphysician!," co-authored with his new friend Lessing, originally for an Academy of Sciences essay competition but then published on their own. These works quickly earned Mendelssohn recognition, and the first two, along with several other essays chiefly on aesthetics published in the next few years, one of which brought Edmund Burke's 1757 work on the beautiful and sublime to the attention of Germany, were collected in the first edition of Mendelssohn's *Philosophical Writings* in 1761—a work that would prove sufficiently popular to go through two more editions in the next decade.[10] During 1755, Mendelssohn also tested his fluency in French by making a translation of Jean-Jacques Rousseau's *Discourse on the Origins of Inequality*, which was published in 1756. Thus by 1761, when Kant was still an obscure lecturer in remote Königsberg, Mendelssohn, just thirty-two years old, had become a major player in the intellectual life of Berlin, the city that was a century away from being the capital of a unified Germany but which under Frederick the Great was the center of the German Enlightenment.

---

[10] Mendelssohn made significant changes between the first edition of the *Philosophische Schriften* and the "improved edition" of 1771, which is the text translated by Daniel O. Dahlstrom in Mendelssohn, *Philosophical Writings* (Cambridge: Cambridge University Press, 1997). No edition of the book appears in the list of books in Kant's library at the time of his death, compiled in 1922 by Arthur Warda from the sale catalogue of the books of Johann Friedrich Gensichen, who had inherited Kant's books. We have no reason to believe that this list represented all the books Kant ever owned, and every reason to believe that Kant had read many books he never owned—he supplemented his income as *Privatdozent* with a job in the university library, and during this period also lived above the town bookstore, with ready access to new publications. But we also have no reason to believe that Kant had any special interest in aesthetics before his logic lectures beginning in 1770 and especially his anthropology lectures beginning in 1772–3, so it seems reasonable to suppose that if Kant made a careful study of Mendelssohn's work in aesthetics, it would only have been around then, and in that case that he would most likely have read the 1771 edition of *Philosophische Schriften*. In any case, I will base my comparison of the two aesthetic theories on that assumption, thus without attention to differences between the 1761 and 1771 editions of Mendelssohn's book.

As already suggested, the careers of Kant and Mendelssohn would finally intersect in the years from 1762 to 1764. During that period Kant returned to public notice with five works. Two were technical essays, "On the False Subtlety of the Four Syllogistic Figures" and "On the Introduction of Negative Quantities into Philosophy," in which he made a major step forward in distinguishing between "logical" and "real" relations, thus preparing the way for his breach with unadulterated rationalism, and one was a little popular book, *Observations on the Feeling of the Beautiful and Sublime*, influenced to some extent by Edmund Burke's *Philosophical Enquiry into the Origin of Our Ideas of the Beautiful and Sublime* of 1757, which Mendelssohn had brought to German attention with a lengthy review. Mendelssohn reviewed both "The False Subtlety" and "Negative Quantities" in Nicolai's journal *Letters concerning the latest Literature*. Mendelssohn was well-schooled in classical logic through his study of the medieval Jewish philosopher Maimonides (1135–1204), whose *Logical Terms*, intended as both "an introduction to logic and a philosophical primer,"[11] he had just published with an introduction and commentary, including a discussion of Maimonides's account of syllogisms.[12] In his review of "False Subtlety," Mendelssohn reported Kant's argument that all syllogisms ultimately turn on syllogisms linking a judgment that connect two concepts to each other to a judgment that connects a concept to one or more objects, or mediate judgments to immediate judgments, and that this in turn implies that "the *higher power of cognition* rests absolutely only on the capacity to judge [*Vermögen zu urtheilen*]" (*JubA* 5.1:660). Mendelssohn thus picked out precisely what would become the linchpin of Kant's eventual transcendental deduction, perhaps even before Kant realized its importance, namely that since all cognition ultimately takes the form of judgment, all objects of our cognition must be conceived in a way that makes them suitable for judgment, thus our concepts of objects must be structured by the "categories" of pure understanding derived from the "logical functions" of judgment (see above all *Critique of Pure Reason*, A 79/B 104).[13] And in his review of "Negative Quantities," in which Kant argued that "real" relations, such as an opposition of forces, are different from "logical" relations, such as assertion and denial of the same predicate of the same object, Mendelssohn recognized that Kant was raising a fundamental question about what real relations and the basis of our knowledge of them are, or, in his words, "if I correctly grasp the sense of the author: what makes a cause a cause, a force a force?" Mendelssohn thus recognized that Kant had raised a fundamental question for the entire program of rationalism, for he had changed the subject "from a logical ground or ground of cognition to that of a real ground." He concluded, in words that would surely have warmed Kant's heart and explained the

---

[11] David Sorkin, *Moses Mendelssohn and the Religious Enlightenment* (Berkeley and Los Angeles: University of California Press, 1996), p. 18.

[12] For the Hebrew text, see *JubA* 14:23–119; for German translation, *JubA* 20.1: 33–175.

[13] See my accounts of Kant's transcendental deduction in *Kant and the Claims of Knowledge* (Cambridge: Cambridge University Press, 1987), Part II, pp. 73–154; "The Transcendental Deduction of the Categories," in Paul Guyer, ed., *The Cambridge Companion to Kant* (Cambridge: Cambridge University Press, 1992), pp. 123–60; and "The Deduction of the Categories: The Metaphysical and Transcendental Deductions," in Paul Guyer, ed., *The Cambridge Companion to Kant's Critique of Pure Reason* (Cambridge: Cambridge University Press, 2010), pp. 118–50.

warmth with which Kant always subsequently addressed or referred to Mendelssohn even when he disagreed with him, "My spirit has found more nourishment" in Kant's "little text" "than in many great systems" (*JubA* 5.1:668–9).

But the two works that clearly brought the two philosophers into contact were, first, Kant's 1763 book *On the Only Possible Basis for a Demonstration of the Existence of God*, in which Kant developed his critique of the ontological argument for the existence of God and replaced it with an argument for the existence of God as the ground of all *possibilities*, still an a priori theoretical argument but a major criticism of Leibnizianism, and developed a new approach to teleology on this basis. Mendelssohn reviewed this book in the *Letters concerning the latest Literature* even before he reviewed the two essays just mentioned, recognizing Kant's famous insistence that "existence is not any predicate or determination of any thing, because God can conceive a merely possible thing in all its individual determinations" (*JubA* 5.1:603), but resisting Kant's critique on the ground that "The Baumgartian definition, although it is only a nominal definition, still seems to be the most distinct and closest to the truth, and having only the flaw that it is merely applicable to the human manner of thinking... Existence, it says, is a thoroughgoing inner determination of everything in a thing that is left undetermined by its essence or the properties that follow from that" (*JubA* 5.1:605), the position he would hold to the end, thus to his final defense of the ontological argument in the *Morning Hours* in response to Kant's repeated criticism of the argument in the *Critique of Pure Reason*. We will examine the controversy between the two philosophers over the ontological argument in Chapters 2 and 3.

For now, I turn to the second major encounter between the two philosophers in this crucial period. In 1762 the Berlin Academy announced a competition on the question whether the prospects for certainty in philosophy are the same as in mathematics, and as previously mentioned, both Kant and Mendelssohn submitted entries to this competition by the deadline of January 1, 1763; Mendelssohn's first prize and Kant's honorable mention were announced later that year, and the two essays were published together the next year. Mendelssohn's essay, an elegant synthesis of his Wolffian philosophy, was naturally preferred by the Wolffian-dominated Academy, but was also a better literary performance than Kant's still tentative steps towards his emerging "critical" philosophy. As the more detailed comparison of the two essays in Chapter 1 will show, the positions of the two philosophers are far from completely apart. Without using Kant's later distinction between analytic and synthetic judgment, Mendelssohn distinguishes between conceptual analyses, which can be known with complete certitude, and judgments about the actual existence of objects, which ordinarily can be made only on the basis of sensory experience and therefore are less than completely certain. However, Mendelssohn recognizes three exceptions to the uncertain empirical status of existential judgments: knowledge of one's own existence, based on the indubitable certainty of the Cartesian *cogito*; knowledge of the exemplification of mathematical formalisms, based on our empirical but nevertheless indubitable experience of space and time; and knowledge of the existence of God, based on the cosmological and ontological arguments. Mendelssohn also includes a brief account of a perfectionist moral philosophy in his essay. Kant also does not yet deploy his subsequent distinction between analytic and synthetic judgments, but foreshadows it by arguing that while mathematics can begin with definitions in philosophy they come only at the end, thus are not available for the demonstration of philosophical analyses but merely sum them up; he then criticizes both the traditional arguments for the existence of God and perfectionist moral philosophy, although as presented by Alexander Gottlieb Baumgarten rather than by Mendelssohn, whose essay was of course not yet available to Kant as he wrote his own. Once the two essays were published, the battle lines were clear: while both philosophers recognized that most of our knowledge emerges from a combination of a priori and empirical elements, they would differ on the status of self-knowledge, mathematical knowledge, belief in the existence of God, and on the foundations of morality. The latter would not figure much in their subsequent interactions, and will therefore not be a topic of this book, but the first three certainly would.

The next chapter will offer a detailed comparison of the two prize essays. There is no evidence that the two philosophers ever directly corresponded about these essays. Their earliest correspondence rather concerns Kant's 1766 book *Dreams of a Spirit-seer, explained by Dreams of Metaphysics*. In this work, unusual in his oeuvre for its arch tone,[14] Kant likened the claims of traditional metaphysicians to know of the existence of immaterial substances and to understand the communion between mind and body and among spiritual substances to the fantastic claims of the Swedish mystic Emmanuel Swedenborg to be able to communicate with spirits, for example to find out from a widow's late husband where his secret correspondence was hidden (2:355), concluding that "pneumatology" is a "fiction, in which reason, stripped of all assistance whatever, seeks its refuge," and can properly be no more than a theory of our "necessary ignorance in respect to a type of being which is supposed to exist," namely spiritual substance (2:352). However, prefiguring his subsequent argument that we can believe on practical grounds that which we cannot claim to know on theoretical grounds, Kant concluded this work with the statement that "there has never existed, I suppose, an upright soul which was capable of supporting the thought that with death everything was at an end, and whose noble disposition has not aspired to the hope that there would be a future," although "it seems more consonant with human nature and moral purity to base the expectation of a future world on the sentiments of a nobly constituted soul than, conversely, to base its noble conduct on the hope of another world" (2:373). On February 7, 1766, Kant sent Mendelssohn a copy along with further copies to be presented to several other important figures in Berlin, including Johann Joachim Spalding, the author of the influential *Die Bestimmung des Menschen*, the philosopher Johann Heinrich Lambert, whom Kant particularly admired, the Academy member Johann Georg Sulzer, and the Academy secretary Samuel Formey (Kant, 10:67–8; *Correspondence*, p. 88). On April 8, Kant responded to the "unfavorable impression" that Mendelssohn had apparently conveyed in an intervening letter, no longer extant. Although he did so respectfully, Kant dug in his heels and reiterated his doubt that it is "really possible to settle questions

---

[14] Although Kant was by no means humorless, and several of his later essays, such as "Toward Perpetual Peace" (1795) and "On a Recently Prominent Tone of Superiority in Philosophy" (1796), also show his satirical side.

about [the] powers of spiritual substances by means of *a priori* rational judgments," that "if these powers are not given in experience, they can only be the product of poetic invention," and thus that "we must decide whether there really are not boundaries imposed upon us by the limitations of our reason, or rather, the limitations of experience that contain the *data* for our reason" (10:72; *Correspondence*, pp. 91–2). At the same time, Kant also wrote that "my suggested treatment will serve a merely negative purpose, the avoidance of stupidity... but it will prepare the way for a positive one" (10:71; *Correspondence*, pp. 90–1). This surely points to Kant's claim in *Dreams* that we must believe on practical grounds what we cannot know on theoretical grounds. This would remain a central part of Kant's response to Mendelssohn's defense of traditional metaphysics, culminating in his critique in "What Does It Mean to Orient Oneself in Thinking" twenty years later. There is no record of a response by Mendelssohn to this letter either, only Mendelssohn's one-paragraph notice of Kant's book in the *Allgemeine deutsche Bibliothek* the following year. Here Mendelssohn wrote simply:

The joking profundity with which this little work is written occasionally leaves the reader in doubt whether Mr. Kant wants to make metaphysics ridiculous or spirit-seeing [*Geisterseherey*] credible. Nevertheless it contains the seeds for important considerations, several new thoughts on the nature of the soul, as well as some objects against the familiar systems, which deserve a more serious treatment. (*JubA*, 5.2:73)

Of course Kant was going to give his ideas the more serious treatment that Mendelssohn requested, although it would take the next decade for him to do so.

I refer to the "silent decade" of the 1770s, during which Kant worked on the *Critique of Pure Reason* that he would finally publish in 1781. The decade of the 1770s commenced with Kant's long-awaited appointment to the chair of Logic and Metaphysics at Königsberg (after some less than savory manipulation by Kant).[15] Following his appointment, Kant presented and published the customary inaugural dissertation, in his case entitled *On the Form and Principles of the Sensible and Intelligible World* (1770). This is a transitional work: here Kant first develops the position that he would subsequently call transcendental idealism, namely, that space and time are the pure forms of our intuition or representation of particular objects, external objects in the case of space and internal states in the case of time, which make possible our a priori knowledge of geometry and arithmetic, but which do not represent the objects of our knowledge as they are in themselves (§§13–15, 2:398–406); but, somewhat surprisingly given the *Dreams of a Spirit-seer* of four years earlier, Kant also held that the "concepts of metaphysics" such as "possibility, existence, necessity, substance, cause, etc." (§8, 2:395) do have a "real use" through which pure reason on its own can give us the knowledge that the world is a whole consisting of contingent beings that are in real relations to each other because of their common dependence upon a single, necessary being: "the UNITY *in the conjunction of substances in the universe is a corollary of the dependence of all substances on one being*. Hence, the form of the universe is testimony to the cause of its matter, and only

---

[15] See Kuehn, *Kant*, pp. 188–9.

*the unique cause of all things taken together is the cause of its entirety*, and there is no *architect of the world who is not also, at the same time, its Creator"* (§20, 2:408). It might seem difficult to distinguish this position from the metaphysical theory of the pre-established harmony defended by Leibniz and Baumgarten, although Kant describes his position as that of a *"generally established* harmony" rather than an *"individually established* harmony" (§22, 2:409), having in mind his position in the *Only Possible Basis* that God builds harmony into his grounding of the *possibilities* or essences of things rather than in his choice of individual substances to exist. One might have thought that Mendelssohn would have celebrated Kant's apparent return to traditional metaphysics in this part of his inaugural dissertation, but that was not what he focused on when he did respond to the work, and in any case, Kant's apparent reversion to traditional metaphysics in the dissertation was not destined to last. Rather, the work of Kant's "silent decade" would consist in his discovering that the kinds of categories he had listed in the dissertation have genuine cognitive use only insofar as they are used to link the forms of our judgment to the objects of our sensibility, thus that the transcendental ideality of the latter carries over the former as well, and that, as already suggested in the *Dreams of a Spirit-seer*, it is only in its practical rather than theoretical use that pure reason can function on its own. This would be the position that Kant would reach in the *Critique of Pure Reason* and henceforth hold without wavering.

Mendelssohn's response to the inaugural dissertation was one of three letters that Kant received in response to the copies of his work that he sent to Mendelssohn, Lambert, and Sulzer to be delivered by the Jewish medical student, Marcus Herz, who had been his "respondent" on the occasion of the public defense of the dissertation. He particularly recommended Herz to Mendelssohn as a co-religionist, and Mendelssohn did indeed take Herz under his wing as a philosopher and later as a doctor, in which capacity Herz became prominent; indeed, Herz would attend Mendelssohn in his final illness fifteen years later. Mendelssohn and Lambert responded to Kant in similar terms: although they could make sense of the transcendental ideality of *space*, the idea that *time* is merely a form of appearance, thus that our own inner states merely *appear* to change, made no sense to them. What could be more real than the succession of our mental states themselves, even if the way in which those states represent objects *other than themselves* might not be veridical? As Lambert put it, "*If time is unreal, then no changes can be real.* I think, though, that even an idealist must grant that changes really exist and occur in his representations...Thus time cannot be regarded as something *unreal*" (letter of October 13, 1770, 10:207; *Correspondence*, p. 116). Mendelssohn made the same point by saying that "Succession is after all at least a necessary condition of the representation that finite minds have," to which Kant would not object, but then by continuing that "finite minds are not only subjects; they are also objects of representations, both those of God and those of their fellows. Consequently it is necessary to regard succession as something objective" (letter of December 25, 1770, 10:115; *Correspondence*, p. 124). Kant would write to Herz, although only six months later and with florid apologies to Mendelssohn and Lambert, that their letters had led him to "a long series of investigations" (letter of June 7, 1771). However, as his famous letter to Herz of February 21, 1772, shows, Kant was worrying not about the objection to the transcendental ideality of time, but about the problem about the relation of intellectual categories to sensible intuitions, a general problem that is independent of the alleged transcendental ideality of the forms of sensible intuitions. Kant would return to the objection to the transcendental ideality of time in the "Transcendental Aesthetic" of the *Critique* when he published it in 1781, and he scratched this itch again in the revisions for the second edition of 1781; with what success, we shall consider when we examine the treatment of idealism by both Kant and Mendelssohn in Chapter 5.

Only in the second edition of the *Critique of Pure Reason*, thus twenty years after the fact, would Kant respond to a central argument of what was Mendelssohn's own major philosophical work of the years between the essay competition of 1762 and Kant's inaugural dissertation of 1770, namely Mendelssohn's 1767 *Phaedo or on the Immortality of the Soul*. This book, Mendelssohn's free adaptation of Plato's dialogue of the same name, in which Socrates's arguments for the immortality of soul to comfort his disciples as he was about to be executed are supplemented with new arguments grounded in modern metaphysics, was widely translated and earned Mendelssohn fame throughout Europe. But the immortality of the soul was precisely the sort of belief that Kant insisted could not be proven on theoretical grounds although it can be defended on practical grounds, so it was bound to become an issue between him and Mendelssohn. Their disagreement on this issue was not explicit in the first edition of the *Critique of Pure Reason*, where Kant criticized theoretical arguments for immortality in the "Paralogisms of Pure Reason," but he would add an explicit criticism of one of Mendelssohn's own central arguments in the revision of the "Paralogisms" in the second edition. The debate over immortality will be the topic of Chapter 4, although there I will also argue that Kant's eventual position on the freedom of the will, as developed only half a dozen years after the death of Mendelssohn in his 1792 essay on "Radical Evil," which would become the first part of *Religion within the Boundaries of Mere Reason* in 1793, would undermine his insistence that belief in our personal immortality is necessitated by practical, that is to say, moral considerations, and that what Kant called the "postulate" of immortality would play a diminishing role in his late works. In other words, on the issue of personal immortality the positions of neither Mendelssohn nor Kant can be defended.

The central metaphysical issue between Mendelssohn and Kant, however, would be neither idealism nor immortality, but that of the possibility of theoretical demonstration of the existence of God. That divided Mendelssohn and Kant in 1763 and still divided them in the period from 1781 to 1785, thus from the publication of Kant's *Critique of Pure Reason* to that of Mendelssohn's *Morning Hours*. This period was marked by a pair of moving letters between Mendelssohn and Kant. To understand these letters, a little more biographical background on Mendelssohn is necessary. In August, 1769, the Swiss pastor Johann Caspar Lavater, who had in fact paid Mendelssohn a friendly visit several years earlier, published a German translation of a work of Christian apologetics by the Swiss naturalist Charles Bonnet. Without approval by Bonnet, Lavater dedicated the translation to Mendelssohn, but in his dedication also challenged him either "to refute...publicly...the *essential* arguments adduced in support of the facts of Christianity" by Bonnet but if he could not, then "to do what prudence, love of truth, and honesty bid," namely convert to

Christianity.[16] Mendelssohn had no intention of doing the latter, but neither did he want to undermine his position as a barely tolerated Jew in Frederick's Prussia by vigorously attacking Bonnet's arguments. It took him nearly a year to compose a response that reproached Lavater for putting him in this position, without taking up his challenge, and to defend Judaism as a religion of tolerance that would not put anyone else in such a position.[17] This in turn led to another year of controversy, with pamphlets by many others as well, that went on into January, 1771, thus just past the period in which Mendelssohn was responding to Kant's inaugural dissertation. All of this led to a "nervous attack" in the early spring of 1771, which, Mendelssohn claimed, recurred any time he "tried to resume even moderate intellectual activity,"[18] and would be used by him as a reason why he could not fully engage with the latest philosophy, including Kant's, for the rest of his life. What exactly this illness was, and whether it was brought on by the dispute with Lavater or had independent physiological causes, obviously cannot be diagnosed at this distance from eighteenth-century sources. Whatever it was, it does seem to have kept Mendelssohn from philosophy throughout the 1770s—his own version of a "silent decade"—although hardly from serious "intellectual activity"—in addition to continuing to conduct the Bernhard silk business successfully, during this period Mendelssohn also produced, partly on his own and partly with others, his German translation and commentary on the Pentatuech and his translation of the Psalms, surely what others would consider serious work even if he found it relaxing.

This means that the sole personal contact between Mendelssohn and Kant took place during the period in which Mendelssohn was not actively producing philosophy. The story of this meeting thus adds nothing to the narrative of the philosophical interaction between the two men, but as a moving story about two human beings it cannot be omitted here. In the summer of 1777, Mendelssohn planned a trip to Memel (now Klaipeda, Lithuania), an important trading port 140 kilometers up the Baltic coast from Königsberg, where his brother-in-law was making a mess of a joint business enterprise. He would be accompanied by his friends Benjamin Veitel Ephraim, the son of one of the leading Berlin Jews, and David Friedländer, a Königsberg native, and they planned to spend a week on Königsberg on the way to Memel. So they did, from July 24 to July 31, 1777, with a further ten-day stop (August 10–20) on the way back. Mendelssohn took the occasion to meet Kant and attended several of Kant's lectures. The writer August Lewald described one of the visits thus (although since he was born only in 1792, he must have been relying on some earlier source): First there was a tumult in the lecture room as the young students noticed the unusual presence of an older, recognizably Jewish man amongst them. They quieted down when Kant entered the room. Then Kant's:

lecture drew their attention to other things, and they were so taken, so absorbed in the sea of new ideas, that they had forgotten about the appearance of the Jew when, at the end of the lecture, he pressed forward through the crowd toward the lectern with a vigor that was in striking contrast to his earlier diffidence. The students had hardly noticed him when the derisive laughter again burst out, but a silent astonishment grew as Kant, after he had

---

[16] See Altmann, *Mendelssohn*, p. 209.
[17] Altmann, *Mendelssohn*, pp. 212–16.
[18] Altmann, *Mendelssohn*, p. 269.

meaningfully contemplated the stranger for a moment, and said a few words to him, pressed his hand heartily and then embraced him. Like a brush fire it went through the crowd: "Moses Mendelssohn! It is the Jewish philosopher from Berlin!" and deferentially the students formed a corridor, through which the two philosophers left the lecture hall hand in hand.[19]

Kant clearly enjoyed his time with Mendelssohn, and wrote to Marcus Herz on the very day of Mendelssohn's departure for Berlin:

Today Herr Mendelssohn, your worthy friend and mine (for so I flatter myself), is departing. To have a man like him in Königsberg on a permanent basis, as an intimate acquaintance, a man of such gentle temperament, good spirits, and enlightenment—how that would give my soul the nourishment it has lacked so completely here, a nourishment I miss more and more as I grow older!... I fear I did not manage to take full advantage of my one opportunity to enjoy this rare man, partly because I worried about interfering with his business here. The day before yesterday he honored me by attending two of my lectures, taking potluck, so to speak, since the table was not set for such a distinguished guest. The lecture must have seemed incoherent to him, since I had to spend most of the hour reviewing what I had said before vacation. The clarity and order of the original lecture were largely absent. Please help me to keep up my friendship with this fine man. (10:212; *Correspondence*, p. 162).

Aside from the touching evidence that Kant's experience in the classroom was not so different from that of the rest of us, the letter gives clear evidence of Kant's enjoyment of Mendelssohn. Alas, it gives us no clue to any philosophical conversations they may have had, and we remain bound to the written record of their publications and correspondence for interpreting their philosophical interaction.

So back to that. Mendelssohn's philosophical work would resume only after 1780, thus in the last half-dozen years of his life, with his two great works *Jerusalem, or on Religious Power and Judaism* (1783) and the *Morning Hours* (1785).

We will come to those in due course. But first, back to the exchange between Mendelssohn and Kant following the publication of the *Critique of Pure Reason*: Kant had asked Marcus Herz to make sure that Mendelssohn would be among the first four people in Berlin to receive a copy of the *Critique* as soon as it appeared in May, 1781, obviously harboring great hopes for Mendelssohn's reception of the book (10:266–7; *Correspondence*, pp. 179–80). In a letter to Herz a few weeks later, Kant expressed his disappointment "at Herr Mendelssohn's putting my book aside; but I hope that it will not be forever. He is the most important of all the people who could explain this theory to the world" (10:270; *Correspondence*, p. 181). We have no record that Mendelssohn himself responded to Kant before April 10, 1783, when he wrote Kant a letter in which he first expressed the hope, apparently based on some false information that he had received, that Kant would visit him in Berlin that summer and then continue on to one of the spas that Mendelssohn himself routinely visited in the summer—an indulgence that hardly fits with everything we know about Kant, and which of course did not happen! He then continued apologetically:

For many years I have been as though dead to metaphysics. My weak nerves forbid me every exertion and I amuse myself with less stressful work of which I shall soon have the pleasure of sending you some samples. Your *Critique of Pure Reason* is also a criterion of health for me.

---

[19] August Lewald, *Ein Menschenleben*, Teil I (Leipzig, 1844), p. 98; cited in *JubA* 24:333.

Whenever I flatter myself that my strength has increased I dare to take up this nerve-juice consuming book, and I am not entirely without hope that I shall still be able to think my way through it in this life. (10:308; *Correspondence*, pp. 190–1)

Kant responded on August 16. He noted first that the rumors of his trip to the baths had "been bandied about locally without my ever having given the least incentive to such conjecture," and said that pleasant as the image of such a trip was, he had long held that what was best for his own health was not to disturb his usual routine. He then went on to say, perhaps somewhat sardonically, that Mendelssohn's feeling himself "dead to metaphysics does not offend me, since virtually the entire learned world seems to be dead to her," but then, sincerely and graciously, that "of course, there is the matter of your nervous indisposition (of which, by the way, there is not the slightest sign in your book, *Jerusalem*" (10:344; *Correspondence*, pp. 201–2), suggesting that Kant had read Mendelssohn's book very soon after its publication. He would come back to *Jerusalem* at the end of the letter, but not before he told Mendelssohn that although the *Critique* was "the product of nearly twelve years of reflection, I completed it hastily, in perhaps four or five months, with the greatest attentiveness to its content but less care about its style and ease of comprehension" (10:345; *Correspondence*, p. 202). This is the remark that later gave credence to the "patchwork theory," the view that alleged tensions in the *Critique* can be explained by the fact that Kant must have patched it together in four or five months because no one could have written all of its 856 pages (plus twenty-two pages of preface) in such a short period—a claim belied by the rate at which Kant churned out books for the next decade.[20] Kant then expressed his continuing hope that Mendelssohn would use his "position and influence in whatever way you think best to encourage an examination of my theses, considering them in the following order"; he then went on to provide a compact statement of the three issues that he himself regarded as most important in the *Critique*:

[i] One would first inquire whether the distinction between analytic and synthetic judgments is correct; whether the difficulties concerning the possibility of synthetic judgments, when these are supposed to be made *a priori*, are as I describe them; and whether the completing of a

---

[20] The patchwork thesis was promoted by Hans Vaihinger in "The Transcendental Deduction in the First Edition of the *Critique of Pure Reason*" in his *Philosophische Abhandlungen* (Halle, 1902), translated in Moltke S. Gram, *Kant: Disputed Questions* (Chicago: Quadrangle Books, 1967), pp. 13–61, at p. 13, and Norman Kemp Smith, *A Commentary to Kant's "Critique of Pure Reason*," second edition (London: Macmillan, 1923), pp. xix–xxv. H.J. Paton argued against the patchwork theory in "Is the Transcendental Deduction a Patchwork?" originally published in the *Proceedings of the Aristotelian Society* in 1930, reprinted in Paton's *In Defence of Reason* (London: Hutchinson, 1951), pp. 65–90, and in Gram, *Disputed Questions*, pp. 62–91. Lewis White Beck also argued against the patchwork thesis on the ground that "Since there is no independent evidence for the existence of multiple manuscripts, the methodology of the patchwork theory requires that these manuscripts be isolated by recutting the text and putting the cuts together in a new order. This can be done only on one assumption: *each stratum or independent manuscript was perfectly consistent in thought and terminology*"; see Beck, *Early German Philosophy: Kant and His Predecessors* (Cambridge, Mass.: Harvard University Press, 1969), p. 469. Or as I once heard him put the point in a lecture, anyone who could have been inconsistent enough to put together inconsistent manuscripts from different periods could also have written something inconsistent in one go. And of course the whole argument depends upon the assumption that Kant *is* inconsistent in crucial parts of the *Critique*, which is itself doubtful.

deduction of synthetic *a priori* cognitions, without which all metaphysics is impossible, is as necessary as I maintain it to be. [ii] Second, one would investigate whether it is true, as I asserted, that we are incapable of maintaining synthetic *a priori* judgments concerning anything but the formal condition of a possible (outer or inner) experience in general, that is, in regard to both its sensuous intuition and the concepts of the understanding, both of which are presupposed by experience and first of all make it possible. [iii] Third, one would inquire whether the conclusion I draw is also correct: that the *a priori* knowledge of which we are capable extends no farther than to objects of a possible experience, with the proviso that this field of possible experience does not encompass all things in themselves; consequently, that there are other objects in addition to objects of possible experience—indeed, they are necessarily presupposed, though it is impossible for us to know the slightest thing about them. If we were to get this far in our investigations, the solution to the difficulties in which reason entangles itself when it strives to transcend entirely the bounds of possible experience would make itself clear, as would the even more important solution to the question why it is that reason is driven to transcend its proper sphere of activity. In short, the Dialectic of Pure Reason would create few difficulties any more. (10:345–6; *Correspondence*, pp. 22–3).

In this lapidary passage, Kant himself summed up what he saw to be most important in his work: first, the distinction between analytic and synthetic a priori cognition and the deduction of the sensible and conceptual forms of synthetic a priori cognition in the Transcendental Aesthetic and Deduction respectively as the conditions of the possibility of all experience, and second the restriction of these forms of experience to objects as we experience them, without the ordinary assumption that these forms also veridically represent the nature of things as they are in themselves, independently of our experience of them—the restriction that allows for the solution of the dialectical paradoxes in which we entangle ourselves when we assume that we can have knowledge of objects through pure reason alone.

There is no evidence of any immediate response to this letter from Mendelssohn; the next, and last surviving, letter from Mendelssohn to Kant is dated October 16, 1785, and is the cover letter with which Mendelssohn sent Kant a copy of his just published *Morning Hours*. This letter seems to say that Mendelssohn had in the end found it impossible to study Kant's book seriously, and instead of responding to Kant's outline of the book reduces Kant's message to a bromide that Kant must have found disappointing:

Though I no longer have the strength to study your profound writings with the necessary concentration, I recognize that our basic principles do not coincide. But I know too that you tolerate disagreement, indeed that you prefer it to blind worship. From what I know of you, the intention of your *Critique* is just to drive blind worship out of philosophy. Apart from that, you permit everyone to have and to express opinions that differ from your own.
(10:413; *Correspondence*, p. 230).

Of course Kant was committed to "permitting" freedom of belief and expression, even on philosophical matters; such freedom is one of the essential "authorizations" included in the "innate right" to freedom, the corollary of our fundamental obligation to recognize the freedom of all, in Kant's "Doctrine of Right" in the *Metaphysics of Morals* he would publish a decade and a half after this letter (1797). And of course Kant wanted to drive "blind worship" out of philosophy, indeed out of human life in general—that would be an essential part of his message in *Religion within the*

*Boundaries of Mere Reason* a decade after he received this letter (1793). But the goal of the *Critique of Pure Reason* is hardly limited to driving blind worship out of philosophy; if that is a fair description of part of what it aims to do, it aims to do so on very particular grounds, namely its proof but also restriction of the validity of the a priori forms of intuition and conceptualization to experience, where there is no need for blind worship of any kind, with the consequent restriction of our knowledge of things as they are in themselves, about which worship would be entirely groundless, combined with the reconstruction of belief in God on practical grounds, where not worship but moral conduct is what is required. But Kant could also have replied that Mendelssohn's recognition that the "basic principles" of the two philosophers "do not coincide" is too blunt. To be sure, as Mendelssohn's *Morning Hours* and Kant's response in "What Does It Mean to Orient Oneself in Thinking?" will show, Mendelssohn's continued faith in the theoretical arguments for the existence of God and Kant's position that belief in God can be founded only in the imperatives of practical reason is a fundamental difference between them. On other issues, however—that on all other matters rationalism and empiricism must be synthesized; that this synthesis inevitably involves some element of idealism; and that the synthesis of rationalism and empiricism can never, following Hume's arguments in the *Enquiry concerning Human Understanding* and the *Dialogues concerning Natural Religion*, include an *empirical* argument for the existence of God, that is, the argument from design—the two philosophers had much in common. Their agreements as well as their disagreements will both concern us.

But before Mendelssohn could publish his response to Kant's critical philosophy in his *Morning Hours* there was the book to which Kant referred in his letter of May, 1783, namely *Jerusalem*. This book, perhaps Mendelssohn's most enduring work, has a complicated pre-history. Throughout the 1770s, Mendelssohn was often called upon by Jewish communities throughout Germany to defend them from repressive charges and legislation; for example, in 1777, the same summer that he visited Kant in Königsberg, Mendelssohn was also called upon to support the synagogue there in its protests against the interference of its government-appointed "inspector," the university professor David Kypke.[21] In 1780, the Jews of Alsace were being harassed by a local anti-Semite, and called for Mendelssohn's help in composing a memorandum to the Council of State to request an amelioration of repressive conditions. Mendelssohn enlisted the cooperation of a non-Jewish Prussian bureaucrat, Christian Wilhelm Dohm, in writing the memorandum. This eventually produced some royal relief, but had the more immediate effect of spurring Dohm to publish a book upon the *Civic Improvement of the Jews* (1781).[22] One main argument of that work anticipates that of John Stuart Mill, made in *The Subjection of Women* (1869):

---

[21] See Altmann, *Mendelssohn*, pp. 307–9; Altmann provides many other examples in the surrounding pages.

[22] Christian Wilhelm Dohm, *Ueber die bürgerliche Verbesserung der Juden* (Berlin and Stettin: Friedrich Nicolai, 1781); for a modern edition with commentary, see Dohm, *Über die bürgerliche Verbesserung der Juden: Kritische und kommentierte Studienausgabe*, ed. Wolf Christoph Seifert, 2 vols.(Göttingen: Wallstein Verlag, 2015).

just as Mill argued that it cannot be soundly inferred from their incapacities in their present repressed circumstances that women are naturally liable to those incapacities, likewise Dohm argued that it cannot be soundly inferred from the present repressed circumstances of the Jews that they are naturally incapable of making all sorts of contributions to society. On the contrary, he argued, a wise polity would recognize that if allowed full civil rights Jews could make many contributions to social and economic flourishing. On a separate point, he also defended the right of rabbis to discipline their congregations, even by excommunication of offending members.[23] Mendelssohn was not about to reject the gift of an argument for extending civil rights to the Jews from a respectable Gentile author, but he clearly did not think that Dohm's pragmatic argument for Jewish rights was an adequate basis, nor did he accept the argument for the use of a coercive sanction such as excommunication within Jewish communities themselves. His first response came in the form of a preface, dated March 19, 1782, to a translation by Marcus Herz of the 1656 *Vindiciae Judaeorum* by Menasseh Ben-Israel, a work that had argued for the readmission of Jews to England during the seventeenth-century Commonwealth, which, under Oliver Cromwell, did indeed reverse their expulsion by Henry II in 1290. This was published as a "supplement" to Dohm's treatise.[24] In his preface, Mendelssohn stated the principle that would become the basis for his argument in *Jerusalem* as well, that "True divine religion arrogates to itself no prerogative over opinion and judgments, nor does it grant or take away any claim to worldly goods besides the power of prevailing and persuading by means of reason and promoting felicity by means of persuasion" (*JubA* 8:18; *Writings on Judaism*, p. 46). Mendelssohn further argued that "Since our opinions do not depend immediately upon our will, no other right belongs to us except the right to investigate them, to subject them to the strenuous test of reason, to delay our judgment in the absence of reason's agreement, and so forth" (*JubA* 8:20; *Writings on Judaism*, p. 47). Therefore no one, whether civil or religious authorities, has the right to try to control anyone else's beliefs by any form of coercion. Mendelssohn would then develop this argument more fully in Part I of *Jerusalem*, published the following year, while in Part II of this work he would defend his continued adherence to Judaism against the objection, made by a journalist, August Friedrich Cranz, and an army chaplain, Daniel Mörschel, that it was a legalistic and coercive religion that violated Mendelssohn's own argument for freedom of religious belief. Mendelssohn's defense, we will see, takes the form of arguing that the many prescribed rituals or *mitzvot* of Judaism are not meant as commandments to be enforced by rewards or punishments but are prescribed to Jews as occasions for reflection on the truths of religion, truths ultimately founded on pure reason, throughout the day, week, and year.

---

[23] Dohm, *Bürgerliche Verbesserung*, Vol. 1, p. 68; see Altmann, *Mendelssohn*, p. 455.
[24] *Manasseh Ben Israel, Rettung der Juden. Aus dem Englischen übersetzt. Nebst einer Vorrede von Moses Mendelssohn. Als ein Anhang zu des Hrn. Kriegsraths Dohm Abhandlung: Ueber die bürgerliche Verbesserung der Juden* (Berlin and Stettin: Friedrich Nicolai, 1782); *JubA* 8:1–71. Translation of selection from Mendelssohn's Preface in Mendelssohn, *Writings on Judaism, Christianity, and the Bible*, ed. Micah Gottlieb (Waltham: Brandeis University Press, 2011), pp. 39–52.

As already noted, Kant praised *Jerusalem* in the conclusion of his letter to Mendelssohn of August 16, 1783, in which he expressed his hope that the Berlin philosopher would support his work. Kant wrote:

> Herr Friedländer will tell you how much I admired the penetration, subtlety, and wisdom of your *Jerusalem*. I regard this book as the proclamation of a great reform, that is slowly impending, a reform that is in store not only for your own people but for other nations as well. You have managed to unite with your religion a degree of freedom of conscience that one would hardly have thought possible and of which no other religion can boast. You have at the same time thoroughly and clearly shown it necessary that every religion have unrestricted freedom of conscience, so that finally even the church will have to consider how to rid itself of everything that burdens and oppresses conscience, and mankind will finally be united with regard to the essential point of religion. For all religious propositions that burden our conscience are based on history, that is, on making salvation contingent on belief in the truth of those historical propositions. (10:347; *Correspondence*, p. 204)

Kant's comment shows that he clearly understood the thrust of the two parts of Mendelssohn's book (although he puts the points in reverse order): that religion is entitled to unrestricted freedom of conscience, so there is no room for coercive enforcement of religious doctrines either by the state or within any church; and that Judaism itself is a religion based upon freedom of conscience. Further, Kant's concluding remark that in religion historical propositions are only a burden upon conscience implies that he shared Mendelssohn's view that true religion is based upon reason alone, the only alternative to historical knowledge.[25] There is no hint of substantive disagreement between Kant and Mendelssohn. And Kant's own eventual work on religion, namely *Religion within the Boundaries of Mere Reason*, published a decade later, would make as explicit as could be that true religion is grounded on pure reason, in Kant's version pure practical reason, not on history nor on revelation. But beneath this general level of agreement there lurk some specific disagreements, and Kant's *Religion* can be regarded at least in part as his belated but considered response to *Jerusalem*. For one, Kant's *Religion* does not include any argument for freedom of conscience or separation of church and state, although Kant certainly makes that argument in many, indeed all of his political writings, and, I will argue, does so in his overtly political writings rather than in his work on religion precisely because for him, unlike for Mendelssohn (and many others), the argument for religious liberty does not depend upon any religious premises but is a purely political—which is to say moral—argument. But second, Kant will overtly disagree with Mendelssohn's interpretation of Judaism, accepting an argument made by many from Spinoza to his own time that the commandments of *Judaism* are not purely religious at all, but the laws of a vanished theocratic state—although, Kant will also insist, individual *Jews*, as human beings, are just as cognizant of the moral law and just as capable of acting from it as anyone else. Further, Kant will reject Mendelssohn's argument that Jewish *practices* are superior to religious formulas and symbols because unlike the latter they

---

[25] Within the Wolffian framework, what we call empirical knowledge was often classified as historical knowledge; see Christian Wolff, *Preliminary Discourse on Philosophy in General* (1728), translated by Richard J. Blackwell (Indianapolis: Bobbs-Merrill, 1963), Chapter One, pp. 3–16, especially pp. 3–4.

are immune to corruption with the objection, based on his own conception of radical evil, that *nothing* human is immune to self-induced corruption—although the freedom that makes corruption possible also means that purity of heart is always *possible* for every human being. We will examine the deep commonalities and the equally deep disagreements between these two great works in philosophy of religion, Mendelssohn's *Jerusalem* and Kant's *Religion within the Boundaries of Mere Reason*, in Part III. Although before we come to that, in Part II we will examine the relation between Mendelssohn's and Kant's aesthetics and specifically their philosophies of art: although Kant does not mention the name of Mendelssohn in the *Critique of the Power of Judgment*, the first half of which expounds his aesthetic theory, he uses a Mendelssohnian idea at least once in the work. But more importantly, Kant's insistence upon keeping emotion out of "pure aesthetic judgment" can be read as a direct response to the centrality of "mixed sentiments" in Mendelssohn's aesthetic theory, developed more than thirty years earlier; so whether or not Kant so intended his work, it will be illuminating to compare the aesthetics of the two philosophers.

Be that as it may, from Kant's point of view, the *Religion*, published seven years after the death of Mendelssohn, was the last act in the lifelong interaction between the two philosophers. Or almost: in Part III of the essay "On the common saying: That may be right in theory but it is of no use in practice," also published in 1793, the same year as the *Religion*, Kant took up a passage from *Jerusalem* in which Mendelssohn, himself arguing against his friend Lessing, had held that it makes no sense to think of the moral progress of the human race as a whole but only of moral progress within individual human lives; Kant argues that we must be able to conceive of the moral progress of the human race, a position he had held since at least his essay on "The Idea of a Universal History" from 1784. How that view comports with the insistence upon freedom of the individual will upon which Kant insists in the *Religion* is a question that we shall examine. But Mendelssohn could not respond to Kant's objection, for by 1793 he was long dead. From his point of view the last act of his dramatic relation with Kant had to be his *Morning Hours*, published in October, 1785, just a few months before Mendelssohn's death on January 4, 1786. This work, like *Jerusalem*, has a complicated history. It purports to be the record of lessons that Mendelssohn gave to his son Joseph (1770–1848) and several friends, his future son-in-law Simon Veit Witzenhausen and Bernhard Wessely, perhaps around the time of Joseph's bar mitzvah and therefore in preparation for it—and if that really happened, then perhaps the lectures were effective, for Joseph was one of only two of Mendelssohn's six surviving children who would resist the lure of baptism as the way to acceptance in the German society of the late eighteenth and early nineteenth centuries.[26] But the philosophical and polemical origins of the work go beyond that

---

[26] Altmann, *Mendelssohn*, p. 98. At the age of twenty-five, Joseph Mendelssohn founded an investment bank that would endure and remain within the family until it was expropriated by the Nazis in 1939, in spite of the fact that his own descendants and those of his brother Abraham (father of Felix and Fanny Mendelssohn Bartholdy), who joined the firm in 1804, had long been Christian. When it came to getting their hands on money, the Nazis would violate their own Nuremburg laws and go back as far as they needed to in order to find Jewish ancestors.

family origin. Part of the aim of the work was to defend the rationalist, a priori arguments for the existence of God from the renewed attack of the "all-crushing" Kant in the *Critique of Pure Reason*—although Mendelssohn would also show that he was prepared to take on board some aspects of Kant's idealism—but not when it came to the existence of God. Another objective of the work was to define Mendelssohn's relation to Spinoza, which would no doubt have been necessary for any Jew who might have come forth as a philosopher in the eighteenth century, but which was particularly necessary for Spinoza because of the claim by Friedrich Heinrich Jacobi that Lessing, Mendelssohn's lifelong friend, had confessed to him what he had never told his dearest friend, namely that he was really a Spinozist. Jacobi (1743–1819), a native of Düsseldorf and a businessman and bureaucrat fourteen years younger than both Mendelssohn and Lessing, claimed to have had conversations with Lessing in 1780, a year before Lessing's death, in which the latter had confessed that Spinozism was the only coherent result of philosophy. Lessing seemed moreover to be happy with this result, which however for Jacobi, fifty years before Søren Kierkegaard would argue the same sort of thing, demonstrated that reason was inadequate to prove the existence of God and that we must instead take a *salto mortale* or leap of faith to believe in God. Mendelssohn and Lessing were put in touch by Elise Reimarus (1735–1805), the daughter of the Hamburg rationalist theologian Samuel Hermann Reimarus (1694–1768), fragments of whose controversial work on deism Lessing had published, and a series of letters passed between them. The story of the interchange between Mendelssohn and Jacobi over what Lessing believed is immensely complicated, but what we need to know here is just that it led to two competing works published in the fall of 1785, Jacobi's *On the Doctrine of Spinoza, in Letters to Mr. Moses Mendelssohn* (Breslau, 1785), published without any notice to or permission from Mendelssohn, and Mendelssohn's *Morgenstunden*, published about the same time.[27] With regard to both Kant and Spinoza, the point of the *Morning Hours* is to defend rational arguments for the existence of a God who is ontologically distinct from his creation from Kant, on the one hand, who disputes the soundness of the arguments, and Spinoza, on the other, who denies the conclusion of the arguments by identifying God with his creation rather than distinguishing him from it. Mendelssohn would further defend Lessing in a pamphlet *To the Friends of Lessing*, which he delivered to his publisher Nicolai on New Year's Eve, catching a cold in the process and dying five days later, so that some blamed Jacobi for his death. Kant, meanwhile, was pressed to take sides in the debate, but got involved only after Mendelssohn had died, arguing in "What Does It Mean to Orient Oneself in Thinking?," as quoted at the outset of this Introduction, that Jacobi was wrong to reject reason in favor of non-rational faith, but that Mendelssohn was wrong to ground his rational arguments for the existence of God in theoretical rather

---

[27] The story of the Mendelssohn-Jacobi debate, or "pantheism controversy," is told in tremendous detail in Altmann, *Mendelssohn*, chapters 7 and 8, pp. 552–759, and more briefly in Frederick C. Beiser, *The Fate of Reason: German Philosophy from Kant to Fichte* (Cambridge, Mass.: Harvard University Press, 1987), chapter 3, pp. 92–108. An account with documents is provided in Gérard Vallée, ed., *The Spinoza Conversations between Lessing and Jacobi: Text with Excerpts from the Ensuing Controversy* (Lanham: University Press of America, 1988).

than pure practical reason. This was the view that Kant would develop at length in the *Critique of Practical Reason*, composed in 1787 for publication the next year, which is thus perhaps his fullest statement on the Mendelssohn-Jacobi debate, although neither name is mentioned in the work.

\* \* \*

This sketch of the history of the interactions between Mendelssohn and Kant, completed only with Kant's publication of *Religion within the Boundaries of Mere Reason* and the essay on "Theory and Practice" in 1793, has shown how over a period of more than thirty years the two philosophers both explicitly and implicitly criticized each other, and sometimes borrowed from each other, on a range of topics. During this period they sometimes circled back to topics—such as the plausibility of idealism and above all the demonstrability of the existence of God—that they had earlier treated. So a strictly chronological treatment of the relationship would involve a lot of doubling back to specific topics, and I will therefore eschew a chronological approach in what follows in favor of one organized around the central topics of their debates. But a topical approach has to follow some sequence as well, and that raises the question whether to address the topics in the order which they arose for one philosopher or the other. Discussing the topics in the order in which Mendelssohn raised them would mean starting with aesthetics, for that is where Mendelssohn first made his mark in the 1750s, before anyone had heard of Kant. But from a Kantian point of view, that would be a strange thing to do, since Kant's systematic treatment of aesthetics comes only late in his career, and as I mentioned Mendelssohn is not even an explicit target of Kant's aesthetic theory, though he may well have been an implicit target. So I will instead organize the topics of the following chapters in an order that is more reflective of the narrative arc of Kant's philosophical career than of Mendelssohn's. There will also be something systematic to be said in favor of the approach I will follow, since it will begin by comparing the metaphysics and epistemologies of the two philosophers, and those would have been considered by them, as well as by any others both before and since, as the foundational disciplines of philosophy.

Specifically, I will proceed as follows. Chapter 1 will compare Mendelssohn's prize-winning entry in the 1762 Prussian Academy competition with Kant's runner-up, in which so many of the issues subsequently debated between them are first raised. Part I, consisting of Chapters 2–5, will then consider the main metaphysical and epistemological issues debated between the two: first the question of the rationality of arguments for the existence of God that preoccupied Kant as early as the *New Exposition of the First Principles of Metaphysical Cognition* of 1755 and Mendelssohn as late as the *Morning Hours* of 1785; then the topic of the immortality of the human soul, which Mendelssohn defended on theoretical grounds in 1767 by an argument that Kant attacked in 1787, but which Kant in turn defended on practical grounds from 1781 to 1788; and finally the argument over idealism that they conducted from Mendelssohn's letter of December, 1770, through both editions of Kant's *Critique of Pure Reason* and Mendelssohn's *Morning Hours* in between those two editions. Part II will then turn to aesthetics, which preoccupied Mendelssohn early in his career and Kant only late in his, but where, as suggested,

Kant's aesthetics can be read as a response to Mendelssohn's whether he intended it that way or not. Finally, Part III will return to the two philosophers' arguments about religion, but now not to the arguments about philosophical theology considered in Part I but rather to their agreements and disagreements about the place of religion in politics and history. This Part will focus on Mendelssohn's *Jerusalem* and Kant's *Religion within the Boundaries of Mere Reason* to the extent that the latter can be considered as a response to the former, but will also examine the argument over the possibility of moral progress for the human species as a whole that Kant conducted with Mendelssohn in the third part of "Theory and Practice."

Throughout, I will let the texts speak for themselves and the philosophers debate in their own terms as much as possible. But the details of the discussion should illuminate two main points. First, both philosophers were heirs to a common, rationalist tradition, and wanted to defend that as far as possible; but while Mendelssohn thought that much of rationalism could be defended on theoretical grounds, for Kant, as he made clear in "What Does It Mean to Orient Oneself in Thinking?" in explicit response to Mendelssohn and more generally in the first two critiques and in many other writings central tenets of rationalism, above all the existence of God and the immortality of the human soul, can be defended only by appeal to the practical use of reason. From our own point of view, two and a half centuries later, we can question whether either of these approaches is convincing. Second, both philosophers, each students of John Locke, Lord Shaftesbury, Francis Hutcheson, and David Hume, as well as of Gottfried Leibniz, Christian Wolff, and Alexander Gottllieb Baumgarten, saw the need to reconcile rationalism with empiricism, and conceived of their approaches to metaphysics and epistemology, to aesthetics, and even to religion in such terms. Here I will suggest that although Kant had more of enduring value to say about the rational *structure* of empirical knowledge and of religious belief, in many ways Mendelssohn was the better empiricist as regards the concrete circumstances of human experience, particularly in the cases of aesthetics and religion.

And this is just to say that both philosophers, the one at the core of any approach to the history of modern philosophy and the other usually left on the periphery, deserve our continued attention.

# 1
# Prologue
## The Prize Essays

## 1. The Competition

In June, 1761, the Royal Prussian Academy of Sciences announced one of its regular essay competitions, the prize to be a gold medallion worth fifty ducats and publication of the winning entry. The question, formulated by member Johann Georg Sulzer, himself a leading aesthetician of the day whose monumental *General Theory of the Fine Arts* would be published a decade later,[1] asked whether metaphysics had the same prospects for certainty as mathematics—in other words, whether the use of the mathematical style of argument in philosophy, popularized by Spinoza in the seventeenth century and Christian Wolff in the first half of the eighteenth, was justified. As recorded in the proceedings of the Academy, the question was "whether metaphysical truths in general and the first principles of natural theology and morality in particular are capable of the same evidence as mathematical truths, and, in case they are not, then of what nature their certainty is, to what degree they can attain this, and whether this degree is sufficient for conviction?"[2] As published, the announcement read:

The Class of Speculative Philosophy herewith proposes the following question for the year 1763: One wishes to know whether the metaphysical truths in general, and the first principles of *Theologiae naturalis* and morality in particular, admit of distinct proofs to the same degree as geometrical truths; and if they are not capable of such proofs, one wishes to know what the genuine nature of their certainty is, to what degree the said certainty can be brought, and whether this degree is sufficient for complete conviction. Scholars of all countries, ordinary members of the Academy only excepted, are invited to examine this question. The prize, consisting of a memorial medal in gold, *Fifty ducats in weight*, will be awarded to the person whose work, in the *judgment of the Academy*, succeeds best of all. Treatises, written in a clear and legible hand, shall be submitted to the permanent secretary of the Academy, Herr Professor [Johann Heinrich Samuel] Formey. Submissions must be made by 1 January 1763; submissions will not be accepted after that date, no matter what excuses may be offered. Authors are requested not to give their names but to choose a motto, attaching a sealed note

---

[1] Johann Georg Sulzer, *Allgemeine Theorie der schönen Künste* (1771-4), second edition, 4 vols. (Leipzig: Weidmann, 1792-4).

[2] Quoted from Dominique Bourel, *Moses Mendelssohn: Begründer des modernen Judentums*, trans. Horst Brühmann (Zürich: Ammann Verlag, 2007), p. 205.

containing their motto, their name, and their address. The judgment of the Academy will be delivered on 31 May 1763 at the public assembly of the Academy.³

The switch from "mathematical" to "geometrical" truth in the final form of the question is revealing: at that time, the only part of mathematics that had been axiomatized was geometry, and the question was whether or not philosophical arguments could be put in deductive form beginning with indubitable definitions and axioms.

Moses Mendelssohn submitted an entry to the competition, apparently some time before the deadline; Immanuel Kant submitted his on December 31, 1762, just under the wire. At least two dozen other entries were also received. The Academy met as promised, on May 26, 1763. "The votes were for a while balanced equally between entries No. XX and XXVIII, but agreement was eventually reached in favor of No. XX, the proviso being made that at the public assembly entry No. XXVIII should be declared to have come extremely close to winning and that it merited the highest praise."⁴ Opening the sealed envelopes revealed that the author of No. XX was Moses Mendelssohn, and that of No. XXVIII Immanuel Kant, and so it was announced at the public meeting of the Academy on June 2 and in the *Berlinische Nachrichten* on June 21. Kant apparently learned of the outcome from the newspaper article. What was unusual and important for Kant was that the Academy decided not just to praise him for having come close to winning, but also to publish his essay along with Mendelssohn's. Kant expressed his pleasure in a letter to Secretary Formey of June 28, 1763, and said that before it was published he would like to add a "supplement" to his essay, "consisting of substantial enlargements and containing a more detailed explanation."⁵ Formey gave him permission to do so, but there is no evidence that Kant ever prepared the supplement, and when the two essays were published the next year, in an edition of 400 copies, Kant's appeared in its original form.⁶ That Kant's essay should only have come in second to Mendelssohn's was no injustice, and that he should have both felt that it needed a supplement and yet have been unable to provide it is no surprise. For Mendelssohn's essay is a polished piece of work, while Kant's is much less so, containing hints of his eventual position but, as he was well aware, needing much more development—indeed, the nearly two more decades of development that would culminate with the *Critique of Pure Reason*. In 1763, Kant was in no position to write the supplement that his essay actually needed.

Mendelssohn's essay is often described as an elegant condensation of Leibnizo-Wolffian rationalism, while Kant's essay, with the benefit of hindsight, is seen as a first indication of his emerging synthesis of rationalism and empiricism. But that assessment is, on one hand, unfair to Mendelssohn, whose philosophical pantheon had always included Locke as well as Leibniz and Wolff, who would write a decade

---

³ *Berlinische Nachrichten von Staats und Gelehreten Sachen*, 23 June 1761; translation from Kant, *Theoretical Philosophy 1755–1770*, p. lxii.
⁴ Kant, *Theoretical Philosophy 1755–1770*, p. lxiii.   ⁵ Kant, 10:42; *Correspondence*, p. 69.
⁶ Bourel, *Mendelssohn*, p. 207.

after his prize essay of Locke's *Essay concerning Human Understanding* and Leibniz's *New Essays concerning Human Understanding* that "these two works alone almost suffice to form a philosophical head if they are studied with the requisite reflection" (*JubA* 3.1:305), and whose prize essay pursues its own synthesis of rationalism and empiricism. On the other hand, this assessment also underestimates how much work Kant would have to do before he arrived at his way of putting the two approaches to philosophy together: while in his prize essay he emphasizes one difference between mathematical and philosophical method, he has no clear view yet of the relation between philosophical concepts and actual experience. What one might say instead is that Mendelssohn's essay provides an example of a synthesizing project upon which Kant would attempt to improve throughout his subsequent work, which he would eventually succeed in doing in some regards but not in others.

This is not to say that Mendelssohn's position in his own essay is completely clear. His opening statement is "that metaphysical truths are capable, to be sure, of the same certainty but not of the same perspicuity [*Faßlichkeit*, literally "graspability"] as geometric truths" (*JubA* 2:272, *PW*, p. 255). His argument is that in all cases certainty follows from the analysis of concepts in accordance with the basic laws of logic, in metaphysics as well as mathematics, and in this way the prospects for certainty is the same in both fields; but while mathematics deals with simple concepts of magnitude, for example, the concept of extension in geometry as a magnitude of co-existing parts, metaphysics deals with more complex concepts of qualities, and for that reason its inferences are less perspicuous. But Mendelssohn also argues that conceptual analyses yield only possibilities, and that these must be anchored in experience to give knowledge of actuality, thus that there is an irremovable experiential or empirical element in the knowledge of reality. In the case of geometry, for example, our general experience of spatial extension anchors its conceptual analyses in reality, and our experience of particular objects gives those concepts specific application. But in fact he does not apply this model of the relation between conceptual analysis and experience exactly to the case of the two philosophical fields about which the Academy specifically inquired, namely natural theology and moral philosophy. Rather, as we will see, Mendelssohn argues that the existence of God can be proven in two ways, both by inference from our indubitable experience of our own existence as contingent being to its necessary ground but also, by means of the ontological argument, from conceptual analysis alone, without any appeal to experience at all; and in the case of morality, he will argue that a purely conceptual argument to the most general principle of morality parallels an argument from the common experience of humankind rather than depending upon the latter, although he will also argue that the derivation of particular obligations from the general principle of morality depends upon empirical knowledge, which however never yields complete certainty about our particular duties. So his argument is actually that in the very special case of the existence of God, metaphysics can actually attain *greater* certainty than any mathematical knowledge of existence can, while in the case of morality although there is a similar step from the conceptual to the empirical in the application of our general concepts, this stage of our thought does not reach the same level of certainty as the application of, say, the geometrical concept of a triangle to a particular triangular object does. So in spite of his opening suggestion that both mathematics and metaphysics rely on conceptual analysis alone, with the difference being merely that metaphysics has to deal with more complex concepts than mathematics does, the bulk of his essay actually describes more complex relations between concepts and experiences and significant differences within philosophy, above all the purely conceptual character of the main argument of natural theology in contrast to the mixed conceptual and empirical knowledge that we have in morality.

Meanwhile, Kant's essay rejects the idea that philosophical knowledge can ever be acquired by strictly logical inferences from antecedent definitions, for although philosophy does analyze concepts, these concepts are given but adequate definitions of them are reached only at the end of analysis, not at the beginning. This differs altogether from mathematics, where we can start from definitions and construct our objects in accordance with them. But Kant is not clear about how philosophical concepts are given. He does not clearly say they are given in experience, but neither does he clearly say they are given in some other way; nor is he clear about what the epistemological status of the definitions from which we can construct objects in mathematics is, and thus about what the relation between the mathematical objects that we construct and the physical objects that we experience with our senses might be. When Kant does eventually develop his theory of mathematical knowledge, we will see, there is a significant difference between his view and Mendelssohn's, but also some striking similarities, suggesting that the arguments of Mendelssohn's essay were not lost on Kant in the further development of his own position. In the case of morality, we will also see that the relation between Mendelssohn's and Kant's is by no means a simple opposition. In his prize essay, Kant actually seems to allow a greater role for experience in the derivation of the most general principle or principles of morality than Mendelssohn does; in his subsequent "critical" period he disallows any role for experience in the derivation of the fundamental principle of morality at all, and thus seems to repudiate his own earlier position; but in his final derivation of particular duties from the fundamental principle of morality in his late *Metaphysics of Morals* (1797) he takes a similar approach to that Mendelssohn had taken thirty-five years earlier, that is, he derives particular duties from general principles by adding in certain empirical assumptions about human nature and human circumstances—but he still tries to avoid the implication of a certain degree of uncertainty about our particular duties that Mendelssohn had drawn from this approach. Once again, in other words, Kant's eventual position both shares certain elements with Mendelssohn's original position while rejecting others. But throughout, both philosophers are attempting to make the relation between conceptual analysis and actual experience precise in both mathematics and philosophy, even while they differ about the details.

The remainder of this chapter will compare the views of Mendelssohn and Kant about the relationship between concepts and experience in mathematics, natural theology, and moral philosophy, and consider how their positions in 1762 point to both differences but also similarities in their later positions, above all in their great works of the 1780s, Kant's *Critique of Pure Reason* and Mendelssohn's *Morning Hours*.

## 2. The Certainty of Mathematics in Mendelssohn and Kant

Since the challenge was to compare philosophical to mathematical method, both Mendelssohn and Kant began by presenting their accounts of the latter. For Mendelssohn, "The certainty of mathematics is based upon the general axiom that nothing can be and not be at the same time" (*JubA* 2:273, *PW*, p. 257), that is, the law of non-contradiction. But of course the law of non-contradiction presupposes some concept to which it can be applied, that is, what it proscribes is the assertion of a proposition of the form "*a* is F" and "*a* is not-F," thus it can only be applied in light of the particular predicates included in concepts. In the case of geometry Mendelssohn holds that its basis is "nothing other than the abstract concept of extension": geometry "derives all its conclusions from this single source...in such a way that one recognizes distinctly that everything maintained in it is necessarily connected by the principle of contradiction with the cultivable [*urbahren*] concept of extension" (*JubA* 2:273, *PW*, p. 257).[7] He suggests how this is supposed to work with an illustration:

> In the concept of extension, for example, there is the inner possibility that a space is limited by three straight lines in such a way that two of them include a right angle. For it follows from the essence of extension that it is capable of many sorts of limitations and that the assumed sort of limitation of one of its level planes contains no contradiction. If one subsequently shows that the concept of this assumed limitation or of a right-angled triangle necessarily entails that the square of the hypotenuse is such-and-such, then it must also have been possible to find this truth originally and implicitly in the initial concept of extension.  (*JubA* 2:272–3, *PW*, p. 257)

In other words, Mendelssohn supposes that the possibility of a right triangle on a single plane follows logically, solely in accordance with the principle of non-contradiction, from the concept of extension, and that the Pythagorean theorem, that the square of the length of the hypotenuse of a right triangle is equal to the sum of the squares of the lengths of the other two sides, follows logically, using nothing other than the principle of non-contradiction, from the concept of a right triangle. "One analyzes the original concept of extension and shows that there is an indissoluble connection between it and certain consequences derived from it and that, without these consequences, it contains an obvious contradiction. In a word, one shows that the original concept that we have of extension is, objectively considered, one and the same with the concepts and implications derived from it" (*JubA* 2:276, *PW*, p. 260). Mendelssohn does not provide any further detail about the contents of the concept of extension from which we could see how these inferences are supposed to work. Is it supposed to be part of the concept of extension that from any point on a plane a straight line can be drawn to any other, so that it automatically follows that there is always a point outside of any given line from which a line can be drawn that intersects the former perpendicularly, thereby creating a right angle? Will that same

---

[7] In his translation, Dahlstrom replaces Mendelssohn's remarkable use of the agricultural term *urbahr*, "arable" or "cultivable," which thus suggests that a concept is something like a field to be plowed, with a second use of the term "abstract," actually "abstracted," for which there is no basis.

assumption about the content of the concept of extension itself suffice to prove that squares can be constructed on each of the sides of a right triangle such that the area of the square constructed on the hypotenuse is equal to the sum of the areas of the squares constructed on the other two sides? An explicit account of the content of the "original concept" of extension would be needed to persuade us of this.

Mendelssohn's larger objective is to show that metaphysical truths can be proved and are certain in the same way as mathematical ones. Above all, he is concerned to show that the existence of God can be proven from the concept of God, and in this case, as we will see, he actually provides a more detailed account of the contents of the "original concept" of God from which we can see how the argument is supposed to work. But before we get to that, there are two points to notice. First, Mendelssohn argues that there are "unextended magnitudes," or "intensive magnitudes," that is, quantities "whose parts neither are next to one another nor follow upon one another" (as in the extensive magnitude of temporal durations) "but rather collapse into one another such as, for example, degrees and their measurements" (JubA 2:278, PW, p. 261), that intensive magnitude has its own mathematics, and that this too rests upon analysis of the concept of magnitude, in this case intensive magnitude. He claims that intensive magnitude is especially important for psychology (Seelenlehre) (JubA 2:277, PW, p. 261), and illustrates this with an example from moral psychology: "moral goodness... consists in a proficiency at fulfilling one's duties perfectly, despite the obstacles and without a sensuous enticement," and can be measured by intensive magnitudes or degrees: "For (a) (1) the greater the proficiency, (2) the more duties, and (3) the more important the duties, (4) the more the obstacles and (5) the stronger the obstacles, and finally (b) the fewer and (6) the weaker the sensuous enticements, the greater is the degree of moral goodness" (JubA 2:280, PW, p. 263). This conception of the measurement of moral goodness shows the influence of Francis Hutcheson's mathematical model for "comput[ing] the Morality of any Action," according to which that is measured by the amount of good any action does for others (the moment of benevolence) adjusted for the abilities of the agent (how easy or difficult it is for the particular agent to produce that good) minus the degree to which the action serves the self-interest of the agent, such that "$M = (B - S) \times A$" (moral goodness of an action = benevolence minus self-interest adjusted for the ability of the agent or degree of difficulty):[8] Mendelssohn is arguing that we need a mathematics of degrees in order to use Hutcheson's formula. Mendelssohn's use of a Hutchesonian idea is striking because, as we will see, Kant also appeals to a central idea of Hutcheson's, although a different one, in his own prize essay; this is interesting not just because it shows the widespread influence of Hutcheson in Germany when these essays were being written, but specifically because of Hutcheson's empiricism: the common use of his ideas shows that neither of our philosophers was conceiving of himself simply as a rationalist, but each was looking for the proper place of empiricism within his own position.

---

[8] Francis Hutcheson, *An Inquiry into the Original of Our Ideas of Beauty and Virtue* (London, 1726), ed. Wolfgang Leidhold (Indianapolis: Liberty Fund, 2008), Treatise II, Section III, paragraph XI, pp. 128–9.

But Mendelssohn's effort to find the proper relationship between conceptual analysis and experience is even more evident if we return to his account of geometry. Empiricism enters into Mendelssohn's account of geometry at two points.[9] One is obvious: the application of geometrical definitions and the theorems they entail to particular, physical objects depends upon the sensory perception of such objects: the conceptual analysis of definitions yields possibilities, but "as soon as we wish to pass from mere possibilities to actualities, an empirical proposition [*Erfahrungssatz*] must be placed at the basis, a proposition which asserts that this or that figure, number, and so forth are actually present." This will be the basis for a fundamental distinction between mathematics and philosophy and the superior certainty of the latter over the former, because whereas in "The entire field of mathematics there is not to be found a single example where one is supposed to be able to infer from merely possible concepts to the actuality of their object" (*JubA* 2:283, *PW*, p. 265), in metaphysics there is one such example, namely the ontological argument. In the mathematical case, "one can trust the testimony of the senses and assume it to be undeniable that this or that basic concept has an object actually at hand," and thus that "implications that have been drawn from this basic concept must be at hand as well" (*JubA* 2:283, *PW*, p. 266), so there is no need to doubt the reliability of the application of geometry (or other branches of mathematics) to actual objects on the basis of sensory experience; but in one metaphysical case, the existence of God, there will be no need to appeal to experience at all for our knowledge of its actuality. Mendelssohn did not say as much in his introduction, but in this case his view is actually that metaphysical certainty is greater than mathematical certainty.

The second, less explicit element of empiricism in Mendelssohn's model of mathematical knowledge is that the basic concept of extension or other basic concepts of mathematics are actually grounded in the "intrinsic constitution of the human senses in general" (*innern Bestimmungen der menschlichen Sinne*) (*JubA* 2:286, *PW*, p. 267), and thus our knowledge that the basic concept is the right one to use must be dependent upon our acquaintance with our own sensibility. Mendelssohn makes this point in the course of his discussion of "practical" or applied mathematics to particular objects, but recognizes that it applies to the general concept or concepts at the foundation of mathematics as well:

But does not this claim expose practical mathematics, if not theoretical mathematics, to the attacks of doubters and idealists who do not trust the senses and regard everything that we perceive by means of them as mere appearances? By no means! They may do this, but then they still must concede that, within the universal delusion, there are constant and variable appearances, and, furthermore, that certain constant appearances are always connected with one

---

[9] The account of Mendelssohn's position on mathematics given by John Callanan in "Mendelssohn and Kant on Mathematics," *Kant Yearbook* 6 (2014): 1–21, is thus misleading. Callanan describes Mendelssohn as supposing that the truth of geometrical propositions is strictly analytic because they can be proven by the analysis of concepts. But he fails to see that for Mendelssohn these concepts themselves are anchored in sensible experience, which is why in Mendelssohn's view only our knowledge of the existence of God is purely conceptual. Callanan goes on to argue correctly that for the mature Kant mathematical proof requires construction and is in that sense not purely analytic, but the most significant difference between the two philosophers is that for Kant mathematical proofs are anchored to experience by *pure* intuition but for Mendelssohn only by *empirical* intuition.

another in such a way that one can never perceive one of them without being sure that, from the proper perspective, one must also perceive the other appearances connected with it. If a figure presents me with all the constant appearances of a triangle and one of its angles has the constant appearance of a right triangle, then I am convinced that the other two angles together must likewise constantly appear to equal a right angle. The mathematician never troubles himself with the true existence of things. He proves either the coherence of ideas or the coherence of appearances. (*JubA* 2:284, *PW*, pp. 266–7)

That we can count on the repeated application of our mathematical definitions and theorems to particular objects presented to our senses is grounded upon the fact that the fundamental concepts of mathematics are grounded in the constitution of our sensibility itself. Our acquaintance with the constitution of our own sensibility is empirical, so mathematics has an empirical foundation as well as empirical applications. In our use of mathematics, this does not cause us any trouble, because the inner constitution of our senses is constant and reliable, and we can ignore the worries of "doubters and idealists"; however, it does mean that for Mendelssohn there is actually *no* mathematical knowledge that is based on conceptual analysis alone.

Mendelssohn's willingness to settle for mere constant appearance as the basis of mathematical knowledge might seem surprising in a supposed rationalist. But it must be remembered that the specific variety of rationalism that looms largest in Mendelssohn's background is that of Leibniz, and Leibniz was famous, especially in the mid-eighteenth century, when such late publications as the *Monadology* and the Leibniz-Clarke correspondence were the best-known of his works, for the view that space and time nothing but *phenomenae bene fundata*, the way in which non-spatial and -temporal relations among non-spatial and -temporal monads appear to those monads who are conscious in the way we are. Leibniz often says that material bodies in space and time are "well-founded phenomena," the ways in which aggregates of non-spatial and -temporal monads appear to us.[10] Space and time themselves, he often says, are "ideal." He reaches this conclusion in two steps. First, he maintains that space and time are relations, of co-existence or succession, among substances, not substances of any kind themselves: "I have said more than once that I hold space to be something merely relative, as time is, that I hold it to be an order of coexistences, as time is an order of successions."[11] But second, these relations are ideal, that is, they appear to us in a way that cannot be the way they really are: "space itself is an ideal thing like time."[12] Now, as we will see in Chapter 5, Mendelssohn will later balk when Kant insists upon the ideality of time as well as of space, and in this regard Kant will actually be the more loyal Leibnizian than Mendelssohn. We will see that there is a further fundamental difference between them, namely that while in his prize essay Mendelssohn is just arguing that the reliable appearance of space and time will suffice for "practical" mathematics or our application of mathematics to objects presented to our senses, and that we can simply remain agnostic whether space and time as they appear to us truly characterize reality, Kant's position beginning in 1770

---

[10] E.g., "Against Barbaric Physics" (1710–16), in *Philosophical Essays*, trans. Roger Ariew and Daniel Garber (Indianapolis: Hackett Publishing Co., 1989), p. 319.
[11] *Leibniz-Clarke Correspondence*, Leibniz's Third Paper, §4; *Philosophical Essays*, p. 324.
[12] *Leibniz-Clarke Correspondence*, Leibniz's Fifth Paper, §4; *Philosophical Essays*, p. 335.

will be the paradoxical one that just because our mathematical knowledge of the forms of space and time possesses the highest level of certainty space and time can be nothing but our own forms of sensibility; they *cannot* be the forms of things as they are in themselves. Kant's eventual position can thus be seen as a rebuff to Mendelssohn's epistemological modesty about applied mathematics, a return to Leibniz's stricter idealism as well as to Leibniz's insistence upon the ideality of time as well as space. Kant's position on this issue will certainly not be Mendelssohn's easy-going empiricism or even pragmatism—that is, the view that we cannot know whether or not our representations of space and time veridically represent things as they are actually are but it also does not matter for the successful use of mathematics, although it would also be misleading to characterize Kant's position as rationalism if by that is meant the position that the real nature of things can be known by reason alone. In that regard, Kant's position will differ from Leibniz's as well, since Leibniz based his own arguments for the ideality of space and time on principles, such as the principles of sufficient reason and the identity of indiscernibles, that Kant regarded as principles of pure reason, and he would criticize Leibniz for thinking that because these principles are principles of pure reason we can use them by themselves to derive knowledge of how things are in themselves.[13]

But all that is for later; what needs to be said now is that what I have just called Mendelssohn's easy-going empiricism about the constant appearance of space and time is certainly not his epistemological attitude toward metaphysics, or at least not to the special case of metaphysical knowledge of the nature and existence of God, of which he holds we can have completely certain knowledge from concepts alone. "Only metaphysics has to identify an example where an inference can be made from a mere possibility to an actuality and it has only a single such example to identify" (*JubA* 2:284, *PW*, p. 266)—but it can identify that example. Before we turn to Mendelssohn's model of metaphysics, however, let us look at Kant's approach to mathematics in his submission to the Academy's competition.

Kant's comparison between mathematical and philosophical method is focused on the point that mathematical definitions are constructed synthetically, by "arbitrary combination," and "the thought of [their] object[s] first becomes possible in virtue of that arbitrary combination" (Kant, *PE*, 2:280; *Theoretical Philosophy 1755–1770*, p. 252), whereas "It is the business of philosophy to analyze concepts which are given in confused fashion, and to render them complete and determinate" (2:278; *Theoretical Philosophy 1755–1770*, p. 250). For example, in geometry we simply define a trapezium as "four straight lines bounding a plane surface so that the opposite sides are not parallel to each other," or "Whatever the concept of a cone may ordinarily signify, in mathematics the concept is the product of the arbitrary representation of a right-angled triangle which is rotated on one of its sides," and then we see "what can be inferred from such" synthetically or arbitrarily formed concepts (2:276, 278; *Theoretical Philosophy 1755–1770*, pp. 248, 250). In philosophy, however "the concept of a thing is always given, albeit confusedly or in an

---

[13] Kant's mature critique of Leibniz is presented in the chapter of the *Critique of Pure Reason* entitled "The Amphiboly of the Concepts of Reflection through the Confusion of the Empirical Use of the Understanding with the Transcendental" (A 260–89/B 326–46).

insufficiently determinate fashion," and "The concept has to be analyzed; the characteristic marks which have been separated out and the concept which has to be given have to be compared with each other in all kinds of contexts; and this abstract thought must be rendered complete and determinate." For example, we will all have a few basic ideas about time from which to begin thinking about it, but to reach a philosophical definition of it "The idea of time has to be examined in all kinds of relations if its characteristic marks are to be discovered by means of analysis; different characteristic marks which have been abstracted have to be combined together to see whether they yield an adequate concept; they have to be collated with each other to see whether one characteristic mark does not partly include another within itself," and so on (2:277; *Theoretical Philosophy 1755–1770*, pp. 248–9). Only when that has been done could we reach a philosophical definition of time, and that philosophical concept would not so much be the basis for further inferences as itself the goal of philosophizing about time.

For Kant the idea that mathematics constructs its objects from its concepts whereas philosophy does not would remain a constant: "**Philosophical** cognition is **rational cognition** from **concepts**, mathematical cognition that from the **construction** of concepts" (*CPuR*, A 713/B 741). But in the prize essay, he does not yet offer any theory either of what constraints there might be on our arbitrary construction of mathematical concepts and their corresponding objects, or from whence the confused and indeterminate concepts that philosophy has to analyze are as he says "given." The contrast between the "ordinary" concept of a cone and the determinate mathematical concept of a cone might suggest that while the latter is arbitrarily constructed the former is given by common sense as expressed by ordinary language, but he certainly does not say enough to make it clear that this is what he means. In any case, that would leave open the question of what constraints there are on the construction of mathematical concepts. But there must be such constraints: after all, although we can construct a trapezium and therefore it is reasonable for us to define it in the way Kant has, Kant would assume that we cannot construct a closed plane figure out of two straight lines (call it a "bipezium"), so there would be no point in arbitrarily defining a bipezium as a plane figure enclosed by two straight lines. But what constrains the possibility of the mathematical figures or objects we can construct and therefore the mathematical definitions that it makes sense for us to synthesize? Kant gives only the barest of hints of an answer to this question:

I notice that there is a manifold in space of which the parts are external to each other; I notice that this manifold is not constituted by substances, for the cognition I wish to acquire relates not to things in space but to space itself; and I notice that space can have only three dimensions, *etc.* Propositions such as these can well be explained if they are examined *in concreto* so that they come to be cognized intuitively; but they can never be proved.

(2:281; *Theoretical Philosophy 1755–1770*, p. 254)

The hint lies in the words "examined *in concreto* so that they come to be cognized intuitively"; but what do these words mean? They could be understood empirically, and in that case they could mean that we constrain our mathematical constructions and definitions by our sensory experience of something that exists independently of our representation of it, or they could mean that the constraint comes from the form of our own sensibility with which we are empirically acquainted—the position that Mendelssohn seems to have had in mind. Beginning in 1770, Kant will argue that we are acquainted a priori with the pure form of our intuition of particular objects, thus that we can examine *in concreto* the pure form of our intuition as well as the particular forms of particular objects; but that theory is very much a new discovery in 1770, perhaps part of the "great light" of the year 1769 (Reflexion 5037, 18:69; *Notes and Fragments*, p. 207). So we must conclude that while Mendelssohn had a clear theory about the relation between mathematics and reality in 1762—mathematical propositions are either definitions or logically derived theorems within a formal system that is anchored to reality by our acquaintance with our own form of sensibility, the inner determination of our senses, and which is applied to particular objects on the basis of our sensory perception of them—Kant has a clear view that mathematical definitions allow the construction of their objects but does not yet have a clear theory about what allows some mathematical definitions but not others. This is one regard in which Kant's essay of 1762 is more tentative than Mendelssohn's. In time, Kant will develop the theory that space and time are the pure forms of all our intuitions, and that we have a priori acquaintance with these pure forms, and that can be taken as both inspired by and as an alternative to Mendelssohn's theory that we have empirical acquaintance with the forms of our own sensibility—but Kant is not there yet in 1762.

The other point about which Kant's essay is unclear is, as noted, the source of the confused and indeterminate philosophical concepts that need to be analyzed. But before we pursue that question further, let us turn back to Mendelssohn and see what his general theory of metaphysical knowledge is.

## 3. Mendelssohn and Kant on Metaphysical Knowledge

Mendelssohn begins the second section of his essay with the assertion that while "Mathematics is a science of magnitudes (*quantitatum*)...philosophy is in general a science of the constitutions [*Beschaffenheiten*] (*qualitatum*) of things." Further, "one may posit that philosophy is *a knowledge of constitutions, based on reason*" (*JubA* 2:286, *PW*, p. 269). Whereas knowledge of many of the qualities studied by the natural sciences, or what, under the name of natural philosophy, could still be considered a part of philosophy in the eighteenth century, is obviously not produced by reason alone but also require the senses, the kinds of qualities studied by metaphysics specifically can apparently be understood by reason alone. Further, Mendelssohn's position is that metaphysics analyzes the concepts of the qualities with which it is concerned, and that in so doing in it can demonstrate its results "with as much certainty as any proposition in geometry" (*JubA* 2:289, *PW*, p. 272):

Just as there is a purely theoretical mathematics which is not based upon any experiential proposition or actual existence and merely shows the coherence of concepts of quantity with one another, so there is a part of philosophy which, all actuality having been set aside, merely unpacks our concepts of the qualities of things and teaches us how to see their intrinsic coherence....Who, then, would want to deny that the concepts of the qualities of things are linked with one another and with other sorts of knowledge and that the latter can be unpacked and derived from the former through undeniable inferences? (*JubA* 2:289, *PW*, p. 271)

Now, in fact, the central claim of Mendelssohn's treatment of metaphysics is going to be that metaphysics is *not* always limited to conceptual analysis with no assertion of actual existence, but that in the unique case of God conceptual analysis alone can also prove his existence. But before we come to that, there is a preliminary question to be considered. For in the first section of his essay, Mendelssohn had held that the mathematics of unextended, intensive quantities applies to qualities. That makes perfectly good sense when it comes to the kinds of qualities accessible to our senses, such as heat and cold, light and dark, and so on, a position with which Kant will agree when it comes to sensation and the "real" that is the "matter of sensation" in the "Anticipations of Perception" in the *Critique of Pure Reason* (A 165–76/B 107–18). And while Mendelssohn had also applied the mathematics of intensive quantities to such a non-sensory quality as moral goodness (*JubA* 2:280, *PW*, p. 262), a quality that is certainly one of the subjects of philosophy, the suggestion that metaphysics is *always* concerned with the analysis of qualities to which the mathematics of intensive quantity or degree can be applied might seem strange. After all, such standard metaphysical concepts as those of substance, causation, or being do not seem to be concepts of qualities with variable degrees of intensity—something either has being or does not, is a substance or is not, is a cause or not. (One event might be the *partial* cause of another, but that is not a matter of degree.) Indeed, metaphysics seems to include concepts of the things that can have qualities as well as concepts of the qualities that they can have, and must include such concepts if it is to prove the existence of some or any thing the concept of which it analyzes.

But this objection, while it seems correct, does not really damage Mendelssohn's approach, for his argument is going to be that God's existence follows from his concept precisely because of the degree that his qualities must have in accordance with his concept, namely the highest or infinite degree. This is already evident in the illustration that immediately follows the passage previously quoted: "Who would dispute, for example, that the following two propositions can be demonstrated with as much certainty as any proposition in geometry, namely, that the necessary substance possesses justice *to the highest degree*, while a contingent substance possesses it only *to a limited degree*? For since justice is a wise benevolence, the highest degree of it must be possessed by the wisest and most benevolent being. Now, the necessary being possesses these properties, and so forth" (*JubA* 2:289–90, *PW*, pp. 271–2; emphasis added). Even if the analysis of the concepts of qualities with degrees of intensive magnitude will not exhaust the contents of metaphysics, the analysis of the implication of possession of certain qualities—positive qualities such as justice—to the highest degree will be the axis on which the metaphysical proof of the existence of God turns.

Before he comes to the case of divine existence, Mendelssohn uses the example of the concept of justice to demonstrate his initial position that although metaphysics can attain as much certainty as mathematics, "The principles of this science cannot be explained as perspicuously" (*JubA* 2:290, *PW*, p. 272). His basis for this claim is that the "intrinsic characteristics of things are bound up with one another so exactly that one cannot define any of them clearly without an adequate insight into the others," and such knowledge cannot come from a distinct grasp of a single, initial definition. Mendelssohn illustrates this claim with the concept of justice again.

In what reads like a capsule summary of a Socratic dialogue, he says that "If one were to say to a beginner, for example, 'justice is a wisely administered benevolence,' he will neither grasp this definition nor see the necessity of making it so complicated"; rather, one will have to further clarify what is meant by will, entitlement, right, and various other concepts before the beginner can understand that justice is not the same as benevolence but that "a person who practices justice lets each individual make use of the permitted means to his happiness" (JubA 2:291–2, PW, p. 272). Once the concepts of justice and of God have been fully analyzed, however, one will be able to see that "justice is a reality and that the Supreme Being must possess it to the highest degree," although that cannot be inferred from the concept of justice alone (JubA 2:292, PW, p. 274).

This last qualification is important, for it means that Mendelssohn's next statement cannot be taken without a crucial exception. Mendelssohn continues:

Moreover, if the philosopher has survived all these difficulties, then he has still discovered nothing but certain kinships [Verwandschaften] among concepts. At that point, however, the important step into the realm of actuality must take place. He must show that the object of his basic concepts, from which he infers these truths, is actually to be encountered, so that he can infer from those truths the actual existence of the consequences. The mathematician, as we have seen, can take this step quite easily. He places the testimony of the senses at the foundation of his practical system and does not worry whether the senses assert truths or mere appearances. (JubA 2:292, PW, p. 274)

But the easy-going attitude toward constant appearances that satisfies the mathematician will not do for the philosopher.

Let us suppose that he has proven that matter cannot think, in other words, that he has demonstrated that our concept of thinking directly contradicts the concept of matter. If he then wants to draw the conclusion that a simple being dwells in us that is different from our body and thinks, then he must show that the concept of matter presupposed by him applies to our visible body and that there is something present in us to which the concept of thinking in the intellect applies... (JubA 2:293, PW, pp. 274–5)

However, he very well may not be able to show the latter on the basis of any sense-perception, constant or not. Likewise, "If he has shown irrefutably that a necessary being cannot exist without being the creator and preserver of all things outside him, then it is still incumbent upon him to prove that such a necessary being exists."

In short, it is not enough for the philosopher if, like the mathematician, he has shown the necessary connection between a subject and its predicate. In addition, he must establish beyond doubt either the existence of the subject or the nonexistence of the predicate so that he can conclude, in the first instance, to the existence of the predicate and, in the second, to the nonexistence of the subject. For we do not owe the philosopher thanks for the mere possibility of something if he does not know how to render it actual. Hence, far more is demanded of the philosopher than of the mathematician. The latter proves merely the possibility of a figure and unpacks the properties and accidents of the figure from this possibility. The philosopher, by contrast, is supposed to demonstrate the actual existence of the subjects in order to be able to conclude to the consequences. It is easy to understand that by this means conviction is made more difficult and the evidence diminished, since nothing can be more difficult for the understanding than the transition from concepts to actualities. (JubA 2:293, PW, p. 275)

However, Mendelssohn's assessment of the epistemology of metaphysics does not end with this aporia. For what he is going to argue is that in the case of the concept of God the actuality of its object, the existence of God, can be proven from the concept alone, and indeed just as perspicuously as any geometrical conclusion. His initial statement that metaphysical knowledge can be just as certain but not as perspicuous as mathematical knowledge actually has to be qualified in the case of the most central proposition of metaphysics.

But before we turn to Mendelssohn's account of the provability of the existence of God, let us look at Kant's account of the prospects for metaphysical cognition in 1762. In spite of Kant's insistence that while in mathematics definitions come first and in metaphysics only at the end, the differences between his and Mendelssohn's conceptions of the character of metaphysical knowledge are not as great as it might at first seem. For where Kant ends up is with the statement that:

> ...metaphysics has no formal or material grounds of certainty which are different in kind from those of geometry. In both metaphysics and geometry, the formal element of the judgments exists in virtue of the laws of agreement and contradiction. In both sciences, indemonstrable propositions constitute the foundation on the basis of which conclusions are drawn. But whereas in mathematics the definitions are the first indemonstrable concepts of the things defined, in metaphysics the place of these definitions is taken by a number of indemonstrable propositions which provide the primary data. Their certainty may be just as great as that of the definitions of geometry. They are responsible for furnishing either the stuff, from which the definitions are formed, or the foundation, on the basis of which reliable conclusions are drawn. Metaphysics is as much capable of the certainty which is necessary to produce conviction as mathematics. The only difference is that mathematics is easier and more intuitive in character. (2:294–6; *Theoretical Philosophy 1755–1770*, p. 269)

Kant agrees with Mendelssohn that all proof is based on deductive inference in accordance with the laws of logic, although in the preceding pages he makes a point of arguing, as he already had for some years, that logic actually requires two principles, the principle of identity that all identities are true and the principle of contradiction that self-contradictory propositions are false (2:294; *Theoretical Philosophy 1755–1770*, p. 268; see also *New Exposition of the First Principles of Metaphysical Cognition* [1755], Proposition II, 1:389, *Theoretical Philosophy 1755–1770*, pp. 7–8). He makes more explicit than Mendelssohn did that formal principles must be applied to some material, that is there must be some marks that can be asserted to be identical or contradictory in particular propositions, but Mendelssohn must have assumed this as well: simply maintaining that something cannot contain one mark and its opposite cannot give you any particular knowledge but asserting that one and the same triangle cannot be both scalene and obtuse does, whether in the eyes of Mendelssohn or Kant. Kant's concluding claim in the present paragraph that mathematics is "easier and more intuitive" in character than metaphysics is the same point as Mendelssohn's claim that mathematics is equally certain as but more perspicuous than metaphysics; and Kant also agrees with one of Mendelssohn's main reasons for arguing this, namely that mathematics uses natural or intuitive signs for its objects while metaphysics uses linguistic signs that are arbitrarily associated with their objects, thus manipulations of the lines and intersections that are geometrical signs yields results that self-evidently apply to the lines and intersections that are the objects of geometry, while the words in which philosophical arguments are constructed have no such direct connections with their objects (Kant, 2:278–9, 291–2, *Theoretical Philosophy 1755–1770*, pp. 251, 265; see Mendelssohn, *JubA* 2:281–3, *PW*, pp. 264–5).

In their prize essays, the chief difference between Mendelssohn and Kant on metaphysics is rather this: whereas Mendelssohn had held that the main reason for the lesser perspicuity of metaphysical cognition is that the concepts of metaphysics are more confused and indeterminate than those of mathematics, thus need more unpacking, Kant instead holds simply that metaphysics has to start from *many more* fundamental and indemonstrable, "material" concepts than does mathematics. Mathematics can begin with very few fundamental, indemonstrable but intuitive concepts, "scarcely capable of analysis at all," as geometry hardly needs much more to begin than the concept of "being next to each other" and can build its definitions upon that, essentially definitions of different ways of points, lines, or areas, can be "next to each other." Metaphysics has to deal with many more concepts: "It is ... evident that there will be uncommonly many such unanalyzable concepts. For it is impossible that universal cognition of such great complexity should be constructed from only a few fundamental concepts." A few philosophical concepts can be analyzed with relative ease into the same fundamental, intuitive concepts that are used in mathematics, for example, "the concepts of *space* [and] *time*," others can be "partially analyzed," such as "the *feelings* of the human soul ... the feeling of the *sublime*, the *beautiful*, the *disgusting*, and so forth,"[14] while "the definitions of *pleasure* and *displeasure*, of *desire* and *aversion*, and of numberless other such concepts, have never been furnished by means of adequate analyses." The fundamental mistake of those who think that metaphysics is as easy as mathematics is "The error ... of treating all such cognitions as if they could be completely analyzed into a few simple concepts ... like the error into which the early physicists fell," who thought that all of matter could be analyzed with a short-list of substances like earth, water, fire, and air or of qualities such as hot, cold, wet, and dry (2:280, *Theoretical Philosophy 1755–1770*, pp. 252–3). Because of the multitude of fundamental concepts that metaphysics needs in comparison to mathematics, which can carry out its constructions of definitions and objects with very few, metaphysics needs to focus on enumerating its fundamental concepts and making sound inferences from them rather than rushing to conclusive definitions of its most complex concepts:

I should like to see drawn up a table of the indemonstrable propositions which lie at the foundation of these sciences [philosophy in general and metaphysics in particular] throughout their whole extent. Such a table would constitute a scheme of immeasurable scope. But the most important business of higher philosophy consists in seeking out these indemonstrable

---

[14] Kant's use of the examples of the beautiful and sublime here suggest that he must already have been thinking about his 1764 book *Observations on the Feeling of the Beautiful and Sublime*, although it is striking that in that work Kant does not actually analyze those concepts but rather prepares the way for his anthropology by focusing on differences in how different genders, national groups, etc. respond to the experiences designated by these concepts.

fundamental truths; and the discovery of such truths will never cease as long as cognition of such a kind as this continues to grow. (2:281; *Theoretical Philosophy 1755–1770*, p. 253)

But there is no possibility that the enumeration of the fundamental concepts of philosophy will reach a conclusion, because "there are infinitely many qualities which constitute the real object of philosophy" (2:282; *Theoretical Philosophy 1755–1770*, p. 255).

Kant's claim is that we do not need to await the (impossible) enumeration of all fundamental philosophical concepts nor the conclusive definition of complex philosophical concepts to achieve secure results in metaphysics. For example, "Without determining what a body is, I nonetheless know for certain that it consists of parts which would exist even if they were not combined together," and even without a conclusive definition of substance, rather merely with "one which has been arrived at by a process of abstraction from the corporeal things which exist in the world," I can safely infer that it must be the parts of bodies rather than their composites that count as substances; just from knowing that two bodies cannot occupy the same space at the same time, I can infer that there must be such a quality as impenetrability, and so on (2:286–7; *Theoretical Philosophy 1755–1770*, pp. 259–60). Kant even helps himself to the prestige of Isaac Newton to defend his conception of philosophical method, likening his view that we can make secure inferences about the connections among particular properties without yet possessing conclusive definitions of philosophical concepts to the great scientist's methodological conviction that if we have successfully discovered "rules in accordance with which certain phenomena of nature occur" then "Even if one does not discover the fundamental principle of these occurrences in the bodies themselves, it is nonetheless certain that they operate in accordance with this law" (2:286; *Theoretical Philosophy 1755–1770*, p. 259).[15]

But what is striking about Kant's conception of metaphysical method in his prize essay is how little he has to say about how we are to go about identifying the fundamental concepts of philosophy. All he has to say is that in metaphysics "by means of certain inner experience, that is to say, by means of an immediate and self-evident inner consciousness," we should "seek out those characteristic marks which are certainly to be found in the concept of any general property" (2:286; *Theoretical Philosophy 1755–1770*, p. 259). What is striking about this statement is that it at least suggests an *empiricist* approach to the discovery of the most basic concepts of metaphysics, much like Mendelssohn's approach to the discovery of the form of our own sensibility; and we shall see that in the case of moral philosophy the Kant of 1762 is prepared to accept this result, even if, as it turns out, this is not the approach he accepts in the case of natural theology—any more than does Mendelssohn. Further, Kant has no organized method for discovering and denumerating the fundamental concepts of metaphysics; it seems we would just discover them as we need them, that

---

[15] This methodological stance was not original to Newton, but already described by Galileo a half-century earlier, for example, in the *Two New Sciences* of 1638, where he wrote that "For the present it suffices our Author [himself] that we understand him to want us to investigate and demonstrate some attributes of a motion so accelerated (whatever be the cause of its acceleration"; cited from Robert Pasnau, *After Certainty: A History of Our Epistemic Ideals and Illusions* (New York: Oxford University Press, 2017), Lecture One, p. 16.

is, as we reflect on particular issues, whether those be the behavior of bodies in space, the nature and existence of God, or the grounds of moral obligation.

In both regards Kant's conception of metaphysical method will profoundly change by the time he writes the *Critique of Pure Reason*. Although Kant will there admit that it is just an inexplicable fact that we discover two forms of intuition in ourselves, space and time, and in one passage carelessly suggest that it is equally inexplicable that we possess not an indefinite or infinite number of fundamental categories of pure understanding, but exactly twelve (*CPuR*, B 145–6), the overarching argument of Kant's *magnum opus* is rather that we can discover that we possess exactly twelve fundamental categories for conceiving of objects from the self-evident "logical functions of judgment," and that from those categories, especially the "relational" categories of substance, causation, and community, we can in turn generate all the further concepts of metaphysics, such as the soul and God, which have no sound theoretical use but can and must be used by reason in its pure practical application.[16] The central argument of the critical philosophy will overturn Kant's conception of the method of metaphysics in his prize essay on these two key points: it will claim that we need to look only to the structure of understanding, in the form of judgment, in order to discover the fundamental categories of our thought, thus it will reject the apparent empiricism of the prize essay; and it will argue that the fundamental concepts of metaphysics can be precisely identified and enumerated. As Kant will put it in the Preface to the first edition of the *Critique of Pure Reason*, "I have to do merely with reason itself and its pure thinking; to gain exhaustive acquaintance with them I need not seek far beyond myself, because it is in myself that I encounter them, and common logic already gives me an example of how the simple acts of reason may be fully and systematically enumerated" (*CPuR*, A xiv).

Kant's mature conception of the method of metaphysics will differ from that of Mendelssohn in his prize essay as well as from his own in his submission, precisely because in spite of Kant's emphasis on the different roles of definitions in mathematics and metaphysics there is actually so little difference between their conceptions of metaphysics at this stage: they both are still working within the framework that was actually common to both rationalism and empiricism, to Locke and Hume as well as to Leibniz and Wolff: philosophy uses logic to analyze concepts that have to be anchored to reality by experience, except (as we are still to see) in the special case of the concept of God. For this reason it would be misleading to characterize Kant's critical approach to metaphysics as just a rejection of Mendelssohn's approach in his prize essay (and still two decades later in his *Morning Hours*); Kant is rejecting his own earlier approach along with Mendelssohn's approach. But by the same token, he will be rejecting Mendelssohn's approach as well as his own.

We will return to the differences between Mendelssohn and Kant that will only be developed in Kant's subsequent work later. For now, let us turn to the special case in which Mendelssohn thinks that we can infer directly from a concept to the actuality of its object. Mendelssohn describes such an inference as an inference from

---

[16] For a lucid account of how Kant thinks the "ideas of pure reason," the central concepts of traditional metaphysics, are generated from the "concepts of pure understanding," see Marcus Willaschek, *Kant on the Sources of Metaphysics* (Cambridge: Cambridge University Press, 2018).

possibility to actuality, and we will see that at this stage of his career Kant too allows for such an inference, although the argument he accepts is not the same as the traditional ontological argument that Mendelssohn endorses.

## 4. Mendelssohn's and Kant's Arguments for the Existence of God

In general, Mendelssohn has argued, knowledge begins with the analysis of conceptual connections in accordance with the fundamental principle of logic, the principle of non-contradiction. The concept of God is no exception, except that in this case, the connections among the predicates in this concept are obvious and inferences are easy:

> [T[he concepts of God and his properties have a wondrous power. They are so intimately connected with one another that one has only to presuppose a single property of God in order to deduce from it everything that we are in a position to know about the Supreme Being. A single chain of inferences combines all perfections of this fecund being. His independence, infinity, immensity, his supremely perfect will, unbounded intellect, and unlimited power, his wisdom, providence, justice, holiness, and so forth are reciprocally grounded in one another in such a way that, without the others, each of these properties would be contradictory.... Let the following definition, for example, be presupposed: God is a being with a supremely perfect will." The supremely perfect presupposes the most perfect intellect and demands the most perfect might. That will consists, furthermore, in the inclination to every possible good and aversion from every possible evil, according to the standards of their goodness and evil. From this follow justice, benevolence, and wisdom.... (JubA 2:297-8, PW, pp. 279-80)

And so on. The concept of God is the paradigmatic subject for purely logical analysis.

As we have already seen, however, by means of conceptual analysis the philosopher ordinarily "has still discovered nothing but certain kinships among concepts," and "the important step into the realm of actuality must take place" (JubA 2:292, PW, p. 274). And ordinarily this further step requires an appeal to sensory experience, even, as we have also seen, in the case of geometry, where conceptual analysis is supposed to be as easy as in the case of the concept of God but where the starting-points of the analysis must be anchored in our experience of the inner determinations of our own senses and where the results of the analysis must be applied to particular objects on the basis of our sensory experience of them. Now, according to Mendelssohn, one style of sound argument for the actual existence of God has this general form, although in this case the experience from which one begins, namely the experience of one's own existence, has the special characteristic of being completely indubitable. But there is also an alternative way to prove the existence of God, from the concept of him alone and without any experiential input; this is unique in all of human cognition, made possible by the unique concept of God as "the supreme and most perfect actuality thinkable." This is of course the ontological argument. Mendelssohn introduces these two alternative ways to argue for the existence of God thus:

> In philosophy one has two different paths by which to arrive at actualities. By the first path, as in practical mathematics, one takes an experiential proposition as one's ground, though it is the

sort of experiential proposition of which we are certain that it is not mere appearance. I have in mind the inner conviction "I think" which, as we will see in what follows, is indubitable and from which it can be inferred with certainty: "therefore I am." It must be possible for the entire philosophical system to be erected on this fundamental principle without relying on any testimony of the external senses. For what the senses perceive of external things is dubious. Only this single, inner sentiment [*Empfindung*] "I think" has the prerogative that one can say of it, with complete certainty, that it is no mere appearance, but rather a genuine reality, as I will show in what follows. (*JubA* 2:294, *PW*, p. 275)

Mendelssohn's use of the term "sentiment" (*Empfindung*) for the experience of one's own existence is striking, for ordinarily this term suggests something highly subjective, like a feeling of pleasure or other emotion (as we would now say), which may not represent anything in an object or even make sense to think of as a quality of an object; but his thought is that while in the case of mathematics even our most constant ways of representing objects might still just be how we represent them and not how they are in themselves, in the case of our experience of ourselves, there is no room for a gap between mere appearance and objective reality—the self just is its experiences, so conversely its experiences are necessarily veridical experiences of it. There is no way that an experience of the self can fail to represent the existence of the self.

Mendelssohn continues:

The second path is extraordinary and without parallel. One steps sure-footedly from the domain of possibility directly to the realm of actuality, indeed of the supreme and most perfect actuality thinkable. In geometry, for example, the two propositions "an equilateral triangle has equally large sides" and "an equilateral triangle has equally large angles" are inseparably joined. The following propositions are just as firmly and indissolubly bound up with one another: "the necessary being is possible" and "the necessary being is actual." If, therefore, I can prove that the necessary being is possible, then I have demonstrated its actuality, and it is well-known that the former can be proven. (*JubA* 2:294, *PW*, pp. 275-6)

As should already be obvious, "We have Descartes to thank for these two transitions from the possible to the actual."

In fact, the account of arguments for the existence of God that Mendelssohn details in the following Section Three of his essay is more complex than this introduction suggests. He will reiterate that "One infers either from the possibility of a necessary being to its actuality or from the undeniable intuitive proposition "I think" to my actuality and from this to the actuality of a necessary being, by means of the principle of sufficient reason" (*JubA* 2:299, *PW*, p. 281). But he will actually proffer two different a priori proofs for the existence of God, one indeed the Cartesian ontological argument, although as amended by Leibniz with the antecedent proof that the concept of God does indeed describe a genuine possibility, the other, however, an argument adopted from Alexander Gottlieb Baumgarten, that the complete determination of the concept of an individual that we find in the concept of God and only in that concept entails its existence. Mendelssohn will also recognize not one but two arguments from our experience to the existence of God, the one to which he has referred but the other, actually a class of other arguments, teleological arguments or arguments from design, which "fall well short of demonstrative certainty" but nevertheless "touch and move the mind" or produce "practical" rather than "theoretical conviction" (*JubA* 2:311–12, *PW*, pp. 291–2). Mendelssohn's recognition of this last class of arguments is important, because Kant will subsequently take a very similar approach to what he labels the "physicotheological" argument. Mendelssohn's description of such arguments as producing "practical" rather than "theoretical" conviction is also strikingly similar to Kant's critical position that belief in freedom, God, and immortality is not theoretically justified but is justifiably postulated by pure practical reason. That Kant will claim in his reckoning with Mendelssohn is his 1786 essay on orientation that Mendelssohn did not properly understand the difference between the theoretical and the practical use of reason suggests that Kant did not think Mendelssohn had anticipated his own position, and indeed Mendelssohn's claim that such arguments can be *emotionally* affecting (*rühren*) without being theoretically adequate is not identical to Kant's argument that in the case of our highest moral goals it would be irrational to *act* without the theoretical possibility even if also theoretically indemonstrable actuality of the necessary conditions of their realization. But even if we have no documentary evidence that Mendelssohn's distinction between theoretical and practical conviction was a source for Kant's later distinction between theoretical and practical grounds for belief, Kant's later critique may also exaggerate the difference between his position and Mendelssohn's own.

Be that as it may, for now let us return to Mendelssohn's text, which next details the two different forms of argument from the concept to the actuality of God that he accepts. Mendelssohn presents the first of these, the ontological argument, in two steps, demonstrating first that the concept of God describes a genuine possibility and then that this concept entails the necessary existence of its object, although the actual order of his exposition reverses this logical order of the steps. The logically first step, proving that the concept of God represents a genuine possibility, follows Leibniz's emendation of Descartes's version of the ontological argument, made in his widely known essay "Meditations on Knowledge, Truth, and Ideas," published in the *Acta Eruditorum* in 1684. Leibniz put the point by writing that "we cannot safely use definitions for drawing conclusions unless we know first that they are real definitions, that is, that they include no contradictions, because we can draw contradictory conclusions from notions that include contradictions, which is absurd."[17] Mendelssohn's way of proving that the concept of God does describe a genuine possibility turns on interpreting contradiction as arising from the inclusion of both a "reality" and a "deficiency" in the same concept, so that the assertion of the reality would contradict the assertion of the corresponding deficiency, or vice versa. But since in the case of God "all realities" and only realities "are affirmed of the most perfect being, all deficiencies are denied in it," "Hence, no contradiction can lie in the concept of it" (*JubA* 2:301, *PW*, p. 282). Thus the concept of God does represent a genuine possibility. The logical second stage of the argument is then to show that its

---

[17] Leibniz, "Meditations on Knowledge, Truth, and Ideas," in Ariew and Garber, *Philosophical Essays*, p. 25. The argument was also made by Alexander Gottlieb Baumgarten in his *Metaphysica* (1739), §807; in Baumgarten, *Metaphysics*, trans. Courtney D. Fugate and John Hymers (London: Bloomsbury, 2013), p. 281.

very possibility entails the actuality of God. This Mendelssohn attempts to demonstrate not in the traditional way, by simply asserting that existence is a perfection and therefore must be possessed by God, which is of course open to the objection that not all existence, for example, that of the devil, is a perfection. Instead, he supposes that there can only be two types of existence, namely contingent existence or necessary existence, and then argues that contingent "existence cannot be part of the most perfect being since it would contradict its essence." Equating contingent existence with dependent existence, that is, existence on something else, and necessary existence with existence that is not dependent on anything else, Mendelssohn continues:

> For everyone sees that an independent existence is a greater perfection than a dependent existence is. Thus, the proposition "the most perfect being has a contingent existence" contains an obvious contradiction. For... it cannot be merely possible, and hence nothing further remains for it but actuality or impossibility. (JubA 2:300, PW, p. 281)

And as it has already been established that the existence of a perfect being contains no contradiction and is thus a possibility, not an impossibility, the only alternative is that it exists, that is, it exists independently and necessarily and not dependently and contingently.[18]

The obvious objection to this argument is that it begs the question, that is, it proves only that if the most perfect being exists then it necessarily exists, or tacitly presupposes throughout that the concept of a most perfect being does have an object. Or such at least is Kant's objection to the ontological argument, put, for example, by objecting that "If I cancel the predicate in an identical judgment and keep the subject, then a contradiction arises... But if I cancel the subject together with the predicate, then no contradiction arises; for there **is no longer anything** that could be contradicted" (CPuR, A 594/B 623). Kant had just made this point in his book on *The Only Possible Basis for a Demonstration of the Existence of God*, which he had completed just before hastily writing his prize essay, and would make it again in the *Critique of Pure Reason*, but he does not make it in the prize essay itself, and indeed actually seems to be in general agreement with Mendelssohn when he says that "Metaphysical cognition of God is... capable of a high degree of certainty in all those areas where no analogon of contingency is to be encountered" (2:297; *Theoretical Philosophy 1755–1770*, p. 271). In any case, let us defer further discussion of the ontological argument and turn now to Mendelssohn's second argument from the concept to the actuality of God.

This is the argument that Mendelssohn borrows from Baumgarten, namely, that the "complete determination" of the concept of an individual entails the actual existence of the individual.[19] Here is how Mendelssohn puts the argument:

> One can convince oneself of the same truth in another way as well. One might simply recall, from the first principles of metaphysics, that a subject matter actually exists as soon as everything determinable in it is in fact determined, that is to say, as soon as it is established

---

[18] See also Baumgarten, *Metaphysics*, §851, p. 291.
[19] Baumgarten equates the existence of God with "the greatest collection of the most and greatest affections compossible in any one being, or the eternal complement of the greatest essence," at *Metapyhsics*, §820, p. 284.

for each concept that *A* can just as well be part of the thing as not, whether the concept is part of the thing or not. Herein lies the characteristic difference between general possible concepts and individual real concepts.... In the case of individual real things... the affirmation or negation of everything that can be affirmed or denied must be established and decided and, conversely, that of which everything down to the most remote relations is established and decided actually exists.... Now the most perfect being cannot receive from something external any determination through which it is supposed to become actual. Thus either it is sufficiently determined by the power of its inner being, or it is indeterminable. That means, either it exists necessarily, or it is absolutely impossible. We have seen from the foregoing that it cannot be impossible, and, hence, it exists necessarily. (*JubA* 2:201, *PW*, pp. 282–3)

By "the foregoing," Mendelssohn refers only to the previous paragraph arguing that the concept of the most perfect being contains no contradiction and thus presents a genuine possibility, not the whole previously expounded ontological argument, so the argument is not simply parasitic on the latter. But it still seems problematic. In particular, the premise that complete determination entails existence can be taken in two ways: if something actually exists, then of course it must be fully determinate and in principle its concept could be too; but conversely, unless we know that a concept is fully determinate, then we might not know that its object actually exists. Mendelssohn assumes that the concept of the most perfect being is fully determinate—after all, it is the concept of something that has *all* possible perfections—but is that really a fully determinate concept? How could we mere humans even know what all possible perfections are? That we have a fully determinate conception of God seems like a weak straw upon which to build an argument, although of course if we already knew that God exists then of course we would know that he is fully determinate and that an *adequate* concept of him must also be so, even if *our* concept of him is not adequate. But it seems presumptuous and theologically controversial to assume that our concept of God is completely adequate.

Kant does not address this argument in his early writings, in either the prize essay or *The Only Possible Proof*. But he does attack such an argument, under the name of the "Ideal of Pure Reason," in the *Critique of Pure Reason*, arguing there that the idea of a completely determinate conception of God goes beyond anything that we can ever actually have and therefore cannot be used as a basis for an argument for the existence of God (*CPuR*, A 571–83/B 599–611). This is often taken as a criticism of Kant's own earlier theoretical argument for the existence of God, expounded in detail in *The Only Possible Basis* and quickly alluded to in his prize essay. But the argument that Kant is later attacking is not identical to his earlier argument and seems closer to what Mendelssohn has in mind in his prize essay. So this argument in the *Critique of Pure Reason* may be a later and implicit criticism of Mendelssohn's earlier work, one of the numerous points at which Kant eventually differentiated his position from Mendelssohn's without saying that this is what he was doing.

In the course of elaborating on his argument from the complete determination of the concept of God to his existence Mendelssohn introduces the principle of sufficient reason to further explicate the contrast between necessary and contingent being: every being must have a sufficient reason, but a contingent being is one that has its sufficient reason in something else on which it depends, while a necessary being is one that contains its sufficient reason within itself. He supposes that the principle of sufficient reason can be deduced from the principle of contradiction, because "it is absolutely impossible that a determination should be [both] true and incomprehensible" (*JubA* 2:204, *PW*, p. 285). Kant does not address the principle of sufficient reason in his prize essay, but in other essays of the same time, indeed ones that Mendelssohn reviewed, he was arguing that "real" relations such as causation are not the same as "logical" relations such as contradiction or non-contradiction, and that the principle of sufficient reason cannot be derived from logical considerations alone;[20] and in the *Critique of Pure Reason* he would ultimately argue that it can be proven only as principle of the possibility of experience, not as a principle valid for anything *überhaupt*, thus it cannot be used to infer from objects of experience to objects beyond the reach of experience (*CPuR*, A 200–1/B 246). But that is exactly the use that Mendelssohn makes of it in his proof of the existence of God from our experience of our own existence. Mendelssohn states this proof concisely:

"Contingent beings must have the reason for their existence indirectly in a necessary being; I am a contingent being; therefore." The minor premise is composed of two assertions: "I exist" and "I am a contingent being." No skeptic, Descartes says, can doubt the truth of these two assertions: for anyone who doubts exists and anyone who does not know everything with certainty is a contingent thing.

The first of the two parts of the minor premise is readily proven, in properly Cartesian fashion:

The skeptic can, indeed, generally be in doubt whether the things outside us are as we imagine them to be or whether they only appear so to us. There is no doubt, however, that we imagine them and that they appear to us to be in one way and not another. This is, therefore, the most undeniable experience on which reason can rely... (*JubA* 2:309, *PW*, p. 289)

Any experience, even the experience of doubt, suffices to prove our own existence, for whether our existence is reduced to experience (we are nothing but things that have experience) or experience is a sufficient condition to establish our existence (we may be more than mere experience, but as long as our existence includes experience then experience is sufficient to establish it). But obviously doubt is also an imperfection, so the self-evident fact that we are capable of doubt proves that we are imperfect beings, therefore contingent beings, therefore beings that must depend upon the existence of something perfect and necessary. So our self-evident but imperfect existence suffices to prove the existence of God in virtue of the principle of sufficient reason and its interpretation as requiring a necessary being as the sufficient ground of any contingent being.

Kant does not consider an argument for the existence of God from our knowledge of our own existence in his prize essay. But his central constructive argument in the *Critique of Pure Reason* will be a variation on Cartesianism: his notion of the transcendental unity of apperception can be considered his replacement for the Cartesian *cogito*, but instead of inferring from what he calls the possibility of

---

[20] See Kant, "Attempt to Introduce the Concept of Negative Magnitudes into Philosophy (1763), 2:165–204, *Theoretical Philosophy 1755–1770*, pp. 205–41; Mendelssohn's review appeared in *Briefe, die neueste Literatur betreffend* XXII, letter 304, 9 May 1765, *JubA* 5.1:663–9.

attaching the "I think" to every one of my representations (*CPuR* B 131–2) to my own existence and from there to the existence of God, Kant will argue from that possibility to the conclusion that all cognition takes the form of judgment and therefore the categories of the understanding must be able to be applied to all objects of cognition—but he will further argue that since cognition also requires intuition, for we human beings sensible intuition, this also means that the categories never apply to anything beyond the form and matter of sensible intuition, thus that we *cannot* infer directly from the form of our own thought to the existence of God. Kant's later strategy of using a Cartesian premise for his own proof of the objective validity but also the limitations on the use of the categories is an alternative to Mendelssohn's return of Cartesianism for proof of the existence of God in his prize essay, although there is no evidence that Kant intended it to be taken as such. But Kant's if anything increased emphasis upon his critique of and alternative to Cartesianism in the second edition of the *Critique*—especially in the new "Refutation of Idealism" (*CPuR* B 274–9) and in the restatement of the "Paralogisms of Pure Reason" (especially the note at B 422–3n)—may have been particularly stimulated by Mendelssohn's renewal of his own Cartesian argument in the *Morning Hours*. Kant's statement in that note that "The 'I think' is...an empirical proposition, and contains within itself the proposition 'I exist'" but "I would not say by this that the I in this proposition is an empirical proposition; for it is rather purely intellectual, because it belongs to thinking in general" (*CPuR* B 423n), so that what can be inferred from it is not the existence of God but the applicability of the categorial forms of thought to our sensible intuitions, can be regarded as a response to Mendelssohn, namely the insistence that what follows from Mendelssohn's characterization of the "I think" as an empirical proposition is not Mendelssohn's argument for the existence of God but Kant's deduction of the categories. We will see in Chapter 4 that Mendelssohn's argument for the immortality of the soul in *Phädon* was very much on Kant's mind in his revision of the "Paralogisms" for the second edition of the *Critique*, but the distinctive characterization of the "I think" as an empirical proposition suggests that Mendelssohn's Cartesian argument from the experience of the self to the existence of God in both the prize essay and the *Morning Hours* was also on Kant's mind at that point.

Mendelssohn's argument leads him to a further reflection on idealism that Kant will also take up, in fact adopt, in the second edition of the *Critique of Pure Reason*. In his initial treatment of mathematics, as we saw, Mendelssohn took a dismissive and agnostic stance to "doubters and idealists": as long as the appearances on which we rely in mathematics are "constant," we simply do not have to care whether they present only the inner determination of our own sensibility or also represent things independent of us as they really are. But now Mendelssohn brings in God to argue for the stronger position that not merely secondary qualities such as color but even what other philosophers regarded as primary qualities such as extension and its properties cannot be genuine realities and must be only appearances, even if constant rather than variable ones. The argument might initially appear to beg the question:

Of the properties of things outside us, we never know with convincing certainty whether they are realities or mere appearances and, at bottom, depend upon negations; indeed, in the case of

some of them, we have reason to believe that they are mere appearances. Thus, we can ascribe none of these properties to the Supreme Being and must absolutely deny him some of them. Belonging to the latter group are all *qualitates sensibile* that we have reason to believe are not to be found outside us as they seem to us thanks to our sensuous, limited knowledge.
(*JubA* 2:309, *PW*, p. 290)

This seems just to slide from the earlier agnosticism about the external reality of (certain) features of appearance to confidence that they are not real, without any additional argument that these properties are only subjective or valid for us, and then to deny them to God on the basis of their unreality. But then Mendelssohn makes a separate argument, although he presents it as merely an inversion of the previous one:

This inference can also be inverted. What does not belong to the Supreme Being cannot be a reality since all realities are his to the highest degree. From this it follows naturally that extension, movement, and color are mere appearances and not realities. For, were they realities, then they would have to be ascribed to the Supreme Being.... But the absurdities and contradictions that follow from this hypothesis force us to exclude extension in general from realities and look upon it as a mere phenomenon. There are realities in nature, to be sure, on which this appearance is based. But these realities are not extended at all, but rather simple... But the appearances which we perceive in those same realities must be absolutely denied the Supreme Being since they depend upon the ineptitude of our knowledge and are not part of things in the way that we perceive them. (*JubA* 2:309-10, *PW*, p. 290)

The last sentence of this quotation seems to make the same argument as before, namely that extension and properties dependent upon it are not real properties because they are merely features of our way of perceiving, which we might have thought was the point to be proven. But the first part of the quotation actually makes a different argument, namely that all and only those properties that pertain to God are genuine realities; extension and such dependent properties as movement (which of course also involves time) obviously cannot be properties of God; and therefore extension (and for that matter time) cannot be genuine realities. Therefore, they can only be features of our imperfect way of perceiving things. This argument does not beg the question whether the constant properties of appearance are also genuine properties of things external to us or just constant properties of appearance, but derives the latter alternative, although from presumed knowledge of the nature of God.

Kant's primary argument for the transcendental ideality of space and time from 1770 on turns on a point that does not figure in Mendelssohn's argument for idealism (which he himself clearly regards as a defense of Leibnizianism). But in the second edition of the *Critique* (B 71-2) Kant will add precisely the argument that Mendelssohn has just made, even though it contradicts his own prohibition against pretense to theoretical knowledge of the existence and nature of God. Whether he should have added that passage or not, it shows Kant's continuing engagement with Mendelssohn.

In any case, Kant's critical scruples about knowledge of God lay far in the future when he was writing his prize essay. For here he advocated a position about the possibility of metaphysical knowledge in natural theology that is in many ways similar to Mendelssohn's. To begin with, he entitles this section of his work "The Fundamental Principles of Natural Theology are Capable of the Greatest Philosophical Certainty." He claims that "the absolutely necessary being is an object such that, as soon as one is on the right track of its concept, it seems to promise even more certainty than most other philosophical cognition" (2:296, *Theoretical Philosophy 1755–1770*, p. 270). He agrees with Mendelssohn that from one predicate of God established with certainty all the others can be readily inferred: "as soon as the existence of the unique, most perfect and necessary Being is established, then the concepts of that Being's other determinations will be established with much greater precision, for these determinations will always be the greatest and most perfect of their kind" (2:297, *Theoretical Philosophy 1755–1770*, p. 271). And, although just months before, in *The Only Possible Basis*, he had rejected the ontological argument on the ground that you cannot go directly from a concept to the existence of its object (2:72–8, *Theoretical Philosophy 1755–1770*, pp. 117–23), he had there offered a novel alternative to a cosmological argument, that is any argument that infers from any contingent existence to the existence of a necessary being, for example, Mendelssohn's argument from one's own contingent existence to the necessary existence of God. Kant's alternative is an argument from the existence of any *possibility* to the necessary existence of an actual ground for that possibility, equated with the existence of a necessary being or God. Kant had worked out the details of such an argument in *The Only Possible Basis* (2:78–83, *Theoretical Philosophy 1755–1770*, pp. 123–8), and then shown in detail how the other predicates of God can be inferred from the predicate of necessary being (2:83–90, *Theoretical Philosophy 1755–1770*, pp. 128–34). In his prize essay, Kant only alludes to his argument:

[T]he metaphysician could first of all ask the question: *is it possible that nothing at all should exist?* Now, if he realizes that, were absolutely nothing at all to exist, then no *existence* would be given and there would be *nothing to think* and there would be no *possibility*—once that is realized, all that needs to be investigated is the concept of the existence of that which must constitute the ground of all possibility. (2:297, *Theoretical Philosophy 1755–1770*, p. 270)

Quite apart from the question of whether Kant's argument in *The Only Possible Basis* is cogent or rather turns on an equivocation between conditional and absolute necessity, no one could have worked out what the argument actually is from this casual equation of thinkability, which might presuppose the existence of a thinker, and possibility, which needs a detailed analysis before it can be seen to entail the existence of anything, let alone of a necessary being. It is entirely understandable that the Academy preferred Mendelssohn's detailed presentation of multiple arguments for the existence of God to Kant's few lines.

Before we conclude this discussion of metaphysics to turn to the discussion of moral philosophy that constitutes the final section of both prize essays, a word about Mendelssohn's final comment on arguments for the existence of God is required. This is his discussion of teleological arguments. I earlier alluded to this group of arguments as a second kind of argument from experience: the argument from the Cartesian *cogito*, interpreted by Mendelssohn as our experience of our own existence, is one style of argument from experience, Mendelssohn's version of a cosmological argument; arguments from the specific character of our experience, interpreted as experience of a world beyond our own consciousness and existence, is the other. Mendelssohn introduces his discussion of this kind of argument with the following remark:

> [T]heology is supposed to be not only convincing, but touching, moving the mind and spurring change in conformity with it. Thus, merely demonstrative grounds of proof are insufficient; instead, the life of knowledge must be inspired by an array of transporting grounds [*überführenden Gründen*]. Here practical conviction departs from merely theoretical conviction. The latter is content with the driest demonstration, with merely distinct knowledge, but the former demands not expressly distinctness and certainty, but above all a living, efficacious knowledge, a strong and lively impression on the mind by means of which we are spurred to manage our action and omission in accordance with this knowledge.
> (*JubA* 2:311, *PW*, pp. 291–2)

Here Mendelssohn the aesthetician meets Mendelssohn the metaphysician: he recognizes that we are moved, including moved to action, not just by rationally sound argumentation but also by emotionally powerful imagery. Mendelssohn's words "*überführenden Gründen*" are better translated as "transporting grounds" than by "cogent reasons," as Daniel Dahlstrom did, precisely because Mendelssohn's point is that the type of arguments he is about to expound do *not* add additional logically compelling *reasons* for the conclusion that God exists but add emotional force to our belief in the existence of God and motivation to act as we believe God would have us act—just as being of divine origin will be argued in the next section to be *one*, though emotionally effective, way of conceiving of the laws of morality. The influence of Baumgarten is also evident in this passage: *vita cognitionis aestheticae*, or the "life of aesthetic cognition," produced from *impetus aestheticus* or "aesthetic inspiration," was for him one of the key features of the experience of the beautiful and the sublime, rendered into German by his disciple Georg Friedrich Meier precisely as being "touching" (*rührend*), the term Mendelssohn uses in the present passage.[21] We will eventually see that this conception of aesthetic impact, although apparently diametrically opposed to Kant's conception of aesthetic "disinterestedness," is a factor in both his aesthetics and his philosophy of religion; the lesson of Mendelssohn and Baumgarten was not lost on him. As I noted earlier, Mendelssohn's introduction of a distinction between theoretical and practical conviction [*Überzeugung*] in this passage might also appear to be an important forerunner of Kant's later distinction between theoretical knowledge and postulates of practical reason. Yet there are also crucial differences between Kant's eventual conception and Mendelssohn's. Mendelssohn treats the arguments he is about to consider as probabilistic, thus as grounding a degree of conviction that falls short of certitude but that makes up for it with emotional force. For Kant, however, belief based on practical considerations should not be placed on the same scale of degrees of cognitive certitude ranging from

---

[21] Alexander Gottlieb Baumgarten, *Aesthetica* (1750–8), ed. Dagmar Mirbach, 2 vols. (Hamburg: Felix Meiner Verlag, 2007), §78, vol. I, pp. 62–3; Georg Friedrich Meier, *Betrachtungen über den ersten Grundsatz aller schönen Künste und Wissenschaften* (1757), in Meier, *Frühe Schriften zur ästhetischen Erziehung der Deutschen*, ed. Hans-Joachim Kertscher and Günter Schenk, 3 vols. (Halle: Hallescher Verlag, 2002), vol. 3, pp. 170–206, at §22, p. 192.

subjective probability or mere "opinion" to knowledge proper; it is an altogether different thing, practical conviction that the conditions of the possibility of moral success can be realized although dependent upon theoretical argument that the possibility thereof cannot be disproven. Further, Kant is careful to insist that practically grounded belief in the possibility of realizing the object of morality and all the conditions thereof is not a *motive* to be moral, but rather a condition for preventing the pure morality of morality from being undermined by a worry about the impossibility of the object of morality.[22] Still, Kant's distinction between theoretical and practical belief is in the same general family as Mendelssohn's distinction between theoretical and practical conviction, and it would not be amiss for us to consider Kant's distinction as a possible improvement on Mendelssohn's whether or not Kant so intended it.

To get back to the matter at hand, however, we need to glance at Mendelssohn's account of teleological arguments for the existence of God. He recognizes three types: "proofs based upon the beauty and order in the visible parts of creation," or more precisely upon our own experience of beauty and order; "proofs based upon the beauty and order in the laws of motion," or what we experience as their beauty and order; and "proofs based upon the deniable purposes in nature, in general, and, in particular, in ordinary and extraordinary natural events, among which the fates of certain states and even the events of individual persons are to be counted. For even these events, if they are considered as a whole, often make evident the wisest of purposes, purposes that have been sustained by wondrous means" (*JubA* 2:312, *PW*, p. 292). Mendelssohn's use of the word "considered" (*betrachtet*) in the last case suggests that the recognition of purpose in nature might not be as immediate as the recognition of beauty and order, and should be ascribed as much if not more to the intellect than to the senses; but even then it must begin from sensory evidence of particular states of affairs. Be that as it may, Mendelssohn allows that "It is not to be denied that these types of proof still lack a great deal for demonstrative certainty." In particular, even if they are allowed, they cannot take us all the way to conviction of the existence of an all-perfect and all-powerful being capable of creation *ex nihilo*, but only to the idea of a demiurge capable of arranging independently given materials into a beautiful world or bending them to its purposes. "[O]ne can nevertheless infer from [them] only that there is a wide and benevolent cause of this order and beauty, not that this all-wise and all-benevolent cause has produced, created everything outside itself from nothing" (*JubA* 2:312, *PW*, p. 292). Our aesthetic response to the world or our ascription of purposiveness to it or systems within it is not enough to ground theoretical conviction of the belief of a perfect being.

This is not an original criticism of arguments from design or purposiveness. Hume had elaborately developed such a criticism in his *Dialogues concerning Natural Religion*. These were drafted by 1751 but were unknown to Mendelssohn in 1762 because they were published only posthumously, in 1779. However, Hume had already stated the premise of the *Dialogues* in his *Enquiry concerning Human*

---

[22] See especially the 1793 essay "On the Common Saying: That May Be Correct in Theory but it is of no Use in Practice," Section I.

*Understanding* of 1748, where he wrote that "When we infer any particular cause from an effect, we must proportion the one to the other, and can never be allowed to ascribe to the cause any qualities, but what are actually sufficient to produce the effect," and had sketched out the argument that nothing we finite creatures can observe in finite nature can justify the inference to an infinite, perfect cause.[23] The *Enquiry* had been translated into German by 1755 in a collection edited by Johann Georg Sulzer, and was very well known to Mendelssohn. Kant was not so cautious about the argument from design in *The Only Possible Basis* (see Sixth Reflection, section 1, 2:123–4, *Theoretical Philosophy 1755–1770*, pp. 164–5), but he would stress the same point in the *Critique of Pure Reason*, arguing that any proof from "the purposiveness and well-adaptedness of so many natural arrangements...could at most establish a highest **architect of the world**, who would always be limited by the suitability of the material on which he works, but not a **creator of the world**, to whose idea everything is subject, which is far from sufficient for the great aim that one has in view, namely that of proving an all-sufficient original being" (*CPuR*, A 626–7/B 654–5); for that, only the ontological proof that a perfect being must exist would suffice—if only it in turn worked. Kant could have come to this recognition through his famous "recollection" (*Errinerung*) of Hume (*Prolegomena*, 4:260), but it could also have been pressed upon him by Mendelssohn. Either way, Kant's eventual attitude toward the psychological effect of the argument from design is strikingly similar to Mendelssohn's account of its emotional impact:

> This proof always deserves to be named with respect. It is the oldest, clearest and the most appropriate to common human reason. It enlivens the study of nature, just as it gets its existence from this study and through it receives ever renewed force.... [It] increases the belief the highest author to the point where it becomes an irresistible conviction.
> (*CPuR*, A 623–4/B 651–2)

The argument from design cannot prove the existence of God as he is properly conceived, and for Kant the ontological proof tries to prove the proper conclusion but fails. For the mature Kant, only the argument on practical grounds that the existence of God is the necessary condition of the realizability of the complete object of morality (the highest good) will be sufficient to justify rational belief in the existence of God. But that argument, like the (failed) traditional a priori arguments, is abstract and dry, and can well be supplemented by the theoretically inadequate but psychologically moving argument from design. And since this argument *is* psychologically powerful, "it would be not only discomfiting but also quite pointless to try to remove anything from the reputation of this proof" (*CPuR*, A 624/B 652). This emphasis on the psychological if not theoretical power of the argument from design is not found in any of Kant's works before his prize essay or in the prize essay itself, but it is found in his works afterwards. It is hard to resist the thought that it might be a legacy of Mendelssohn's essay.

So much for natural theology in the eyes of both authors. The Academy's question also asked specifically about the possibility of certitude in "moral" or moral

---

[23] David Hume, *Enquiry concerning Human Understanding* (1748), ed. Tom L. Beauchamp (Oxford: Clarendon Press, 2000), Section 11, p. 102.

philosophy as well, so let us now turn to our two authors' responses to this part of the challenge. Here we shall find that Mendelssohn describes a complex mix of a priori and empirical elements in morality, that Kant's account of morality in his prize essay also has a strong empirical element in addition to a formal part, and that in spite of Kant's later insistence on the pure apriority of our cognition of the fundamental principle of morality his mature moral philosophy also combines a priori and empirical elements in a way that resembles Mendeslssohn's earlier model.

## 5. Mendelssohn and Kant on the Metaphysics of Morality

In his prize essay, Mendelssohn explicitly expounded a perfectionist approach to moral philosophy in the tradition of Leibniz, Wolff, and Baumgarten. In his, Kant attacked the formal principle of perfectionist morality as vacuous unless accompanied with a material first principle, and in subsequent texts such as the *Groundwork of the Metaphysics of Morals* and the *Critique of Practical Reason* as well as in his classroom lectures on ethics he repeatedly attacked perfectionism as either vacuous or else dependent upon an unstated and empirical conception of human happiness. But Kant's attacks upon perfectionism simplify what is a more complicated relationship between the perfectionist moral philosophy of the rationalist tradition and his own position. Kant's mature moral philosophy retains a strong flavor of perfectionism, both in its general approach to the fundamental principle of morality and specifically in his account of ethics, or non-coercively enforceable duties to self and others. It also retains the two-level structure that we will find in Mendelssohn's model, on which the fundamental principle of morality that can be identified without empirical input although it can also be confirmed with the help of such input has to be applied in light of our empirical knowledge about the specifics of the human condition. This two-level model clearly expounded by Mendelssohn in his prize essay is the division of labor between the *Groundwork for the Metaphysics of Morals* and the *Metaphysics of Morals* that Kant subsequently adopts. But whereas Mendelssohn allows that the indispensable role of empirical input in the derivation of specific duties for human beings means that moral philosophy at this level must tolerate a certain degree of probabilism, uncertainty, or even potentially irresolvable conflicts with regard to our specific duties, Kant will still insist, in spite of the similarity to Mendelssohn in his approach to specifically human duties, that there can be no such thing as a genuine conflict of duties, thus that all such conflicts can be resolved in accordance with a determinate moral principle. In this regard, it is Kant rather than Mendelssohn who is the more fully fledged rationalist.

Mendelssohn devoted a dozen pages of his prize essay to the topic of "evidence in the first principles of ethics" and did not subsequently publish a systematic treatment of the subject, while Kant devoted only three pages of his essay to the topic but subsequently published three systematic works on the subject and lectured on it for many years. So what follows will be a somewhat detailed account of Mendelssohn's treatment of ethics in his essay followed by a briefer account of Kant's briefer treatment in his, supplemented by some anticipatory remarks about the similarities as well as key differences between his later treatment of moral philosophy and ethics and Mendelssohn's. Because there was no later confrontation between Mendelssohn and Kant on the main issues in moral philosophy, the present section will be the main treatment of this topic in the present book.

The most striking feature of Mendelssohn's approach is division between the "general principles of ethics" that "can be proven with geometrical rigor and precision [*Strenge und Bündigkeit*]" and the "derivative laws of nature which prescribe to us what we are to do and leave undone in particular cases," and the "degree of certainty" of which "gradually decreases in practice and descends through all stages of probability to doubtfulness" (*JubA*, 2:315, 322–3, *PW*, pp. 295, 302). Mendelssohn introduces this distinction using a conception of "maxim" similar to that which Kant will later employ:

In every rightful [*rechtschaffenen*] action that a human being undertakes, he silently makes the following rational inference [*Vernunftschluß*]:

Wherever the property A is encountered, my duty requires me to do B.

The present case has the property A; therefore, and so on.

The major premise of this rational inference is a maxim, a general rule of life, which we adopted at some earlier time and which must naturally come to mind on the occasion of the present case. The minor premise is based on a precise observation of the present circumstances and on the conviction that they agree fully with the subject of the major premise, that is to say, with the requisite property A. (*JubA* 2:315, *PW*, p. 295)

Here Mendelssohn appeals to a syllogistic model of practical reason that goes back to Aristotle, and that was widely shared among his contemporaries.[24] But Mendelssohn distinctively calls what others refer to just as the "major premise" (*Obersatz*) of a practical syllogism as a "maxim," the term that Kant will also adopt. Mendelssohn explicitly says that the *minor* premise (*Untersatz*) of a practical syllogism is "based on a precise observation of the present circumstances," so he leaves no doubt that such a premise, of the form "The present case has the property A" or 'I find myself in circumstances of the type A to which my maxim applies," is empirical, thus that whatever uncertainty might infect such an observation must be transferred to my conclusion that I must do B—the conditional that "If I am in A I must do B" need not possess any degree of uncertainty, but the conclusion "I must do B" must inherit any uncertainty that infects my knowledge that I am in A. Anyone who thinks of practical reasoning as a practical syllogism and allows that the minor premise is empirical must allow this result. This by itself does not establish that there must inevitably be *conflicts* at the level of particular duties, but it leaves the door open to that result.

But before we can get to that issue, the question of the status the *major* premise remains. Mendelssohn's remark that the major premise of a practical syllogism is a maxim "adopted at some earlier time" that "naturally comes to mind" in some particular circumstances might suggest that the major premise is also known

---

[24] E.g., by an almost exactly contemporary work, Georg Friedrich Meier, *Allgemeine praktische Weltweisheit* (Halle: Carl Herman Hemmerde, 1764), §7, p. 17.

empirically; surely that the maxim was adopted at some particular earlier time and that it has come to mind in some present circumstance could only be known empirically. But since Mendelssohn has suggested that an agent may "silently," that is, presumably, unconsciously or subconsciously, perform his practical syllogism, he presumably does not actually have to know when he had adopted his maxim. More importantly, even if we do know that a maxim has been adopted at some particular time and could only know that empirically this would not imply that the maxim itself is contingent and only empirically knowable, any more than my recollection that I learned the Pythagorean theorem in my tenth-grade geometry class, which is surely a bit of empirical knowledge, makes my knowledge of the theorem itself empirical. And in fact, what Mendelssohn now argues is that we can come to know at least the *fundamental* principle of morality, on which any more particular maxims must be based, in three different ways: by "observation of the thousandfold desires and wishes, passions and inclinations" that all "human beings have in common" (*JubA* 2:316, *PW*, p. 296), which is clearly empirical knowledge; but the "same natural law" which that observation yields can also "be proven *a priori* from the mere definition [*Erklärung*] of a being with a free will" (*JubA* 2:317, *PW*, p. 297), which would obviously be a non-empirical way of knowing it; and "It can be demonstrated in another way, by the most irrefutable reasons, that this general law of nature," the fundamental maxim of morality yielded by the other two methods "is in keeping with God's aims" (*JubA* 2:318, *PW*, p. 297), and whether the knowledge yielded in this manner would be a priori or empirical would depend upon whether knowledge of God and his aims is a priori or empirical. Mendelssohn's argument about natural theology in the previous section of the prize essay as well as his advocacy of a religion of pure reason in *Jerusalem* twenty years later imply that in his view knowledge of God and his aims is rational, not dependent upon any revelation that might be considered merely empirical, so presumably the third way of coming to know the fundamental maxim of morality is in his view a priori rather than empirical. Thus in Mendelssohn's view there are one empirical and two a priori ways of knowing the fundamental maxim of morality, with the former confirming the latter and vice versa. Here Mendelssohn anticipates the image of common sense and reason ultimately converging, even if they may seem to have temporarily taken divergent paths, which he will present in the *Morning Hours* (Lecture X).

In particular, Mendelssohn argues that each of the three ways of knowing the fundamental maxim of morality leads to the "first" or fundamental "law of nature" "*make your internal and external condition and that of your fellow human being, in the proper proportion, as perfect as you can*" (*JubA*, 2:317, *PW*, p. 296). By the first method, we observe that all the "thousandfold wishes and desires of human beings have in common ... that they all aim at the *preservation or betterment of the internal or external condition of ourselves or of another creature*," even though, of course, we also observe that people widely "substitute apparent goods for their genuine welfare, or mistake the proper proportion" among goods "because they prefer their selfish ego to every other purpose or seek to improve their external condition at the cost of their internal one" (*JubA* 2:316, *PW*, p. 296). That we can infer from our observations that people are always aiming at some perfection of themselves or others even when they are mistaken about what actually perfects the condition of themselves or others, and thus that we can draw a distinction between the intended and the actual outcomes of human actions, presupposes that we can have empirical knowledge about the intentions of others. Mendelssohn has no qualm about this assumption. To him, this assumption and the conclusion that human beings always aim at some perfection of themselves or others, whether they are well- or ill-informed about what constitutes such perfection, seem obvious matters of common sense.

Mendelssohn's second way of coming to know the fundamental principle of morality is supposed to be purely a priori. Here his argument is that "The same natural law can be proven *a priori* from the mere definition of a being with a free will." The argument is that "A being endowed with freedom can choose what pleases him from various objects or representations of objects," and that the basis of the pleasure or satisfaction (*Wohlgefallens*) that will be the ground of such a choice is "the perfection, beauty, and order that he perceives or believes that he perceives in the preferred object." The argument turns on the Wolffian definition of pleasure as the sensory cognition or perception of perfection, on which a feeling of pleasure is a perception of perfection and the perception of perfection produces pleasure.[25] So the argument presupposes a hedonistic psychology, on which the greatest felt or expected pleasure in any situation of choice is supposed to be the decisive reason for action—"order, beauty, and perfection can yield motivating grounds [*Bewegungsgründe*] by which a free being is determined in his choice"—and an explanation of pleasure on which it is always due to the perception of some perfection, real or apparent—"The contemplation of perfection, beauty, and order affords us pleasure, the contemplation of imperfection, ugliness, and disorder affords us displeasure." Mendelssohn finds no problem in linking perfectionism and psychological hedonism: "I understand also the utility and sensuous pleasure that the object promises us since both belong to the perfections of our internal and external condition" (*JubA* 2:317, *PW*, p. 297).

Kant typically associates perfectionist morality with Wolff (*CPracR*, 5:40) or, as we will see in his own prize essay, Baumgarten, and does not mention Mendelssohn's name in his criticism of the doctrine in the prize essay or later. Baumgarten's *Initia philosophiae practicae primae* (*Elements of First Practical Philosophy*) had been published in 1760, and Kant would use it as a text for his lectures in ethics for many years, so it is an obvious source for Kant's conception of perfectionism.[26] But whether or not Kant had Mendelssohn in mind in his later criticism of moral perfectionism, he could have applied his criticism of the doctrine to Mendelssohn as well as to Wolff and Baumgarten, namely that in spite of its use of an apparently pure or in Kant's terms a priori concept, it actually relies upon more specific ends that are given only empirically and that are therefore contingent. As he puts it in the *Critique of Practical Reason*, two decades after the prize essays:

---

[25] Christian Wolff, *Vernünftige Gedancken von Gott, der Welt, und der Seele des Menschen*, neue Auflage (Halle: Renger, 1751), §404.
[26] See Alexander Gottlieb Baumgarten, *Anfangsgründe der praktiken Metaphysik*, Latin and German texts, translated by Alexander Aichele (Hamburg: Felix Meiner Verlag, 2019), especially §§43–9.

Now, if ends must be first given to us, in relation to which alone the concept of **perfection** (whether internal in ourselves or external in God) can be the determining ground of the will; and if an end is an **object** which must precede the determination of the will by a practical rule and contain the ground of the possibility of such a determination—hence as the matter of the will taken as its determining ground—is always empirical; then it can serve as the Epicurean principle of the doctrine of happiness but never as the pure rational principle of the doctrine of morals and of duty (so too, talents and their development only because they contribute to the advantages of life, or the will of God if agreement with it is taken as the object of the will without an antecedent empirical practical principle independent of this idea, can become motives of the will only by means of the happiness we expect from them)... (CPracR, 5:41)

But the force of Kant's criticism depends upon whether, in the *equation* between pleasure or happiness and the perception of perfection, the experience of pleasure is thought of as determining what counts as a perfection, or whether there is thought to be some independent, possibly a priori criterion of perfection, which then by some law of human psychology inevitably produces a feeling of pleasure. That a feeling of pleasure in perfection is the proximate cause of the determination of the will to action does not by itself imply that the criterion of perfection itself is merely empirical; in fact, it had better not be, because in his theory of the feeling of respect as the "incentive" (*Triebfeder*) of *pure* practical reason (CPracR 5:71), Kant suggests that this feeling, which is at least in part a feeling of pleasure (5:73), must be produced by the determination of the will by the moral law but in turn plays a role in the etiology of particular actions (5:75–6); and in the *Metaphysics of Morals* he will state explicitly that "Every determination of choice proceeds **from the representation of a possible action to** the deed through the feeling of pleasure or displeasure, taking an interest in the action or its effect" (MMn, Doctrine of Virtue, section XII, 6:399). So the issue between Kant and the so-called perfectionists cannot be simply whether feelings of or including pleasure are considered to be the proximate cause or action, but rather whether perfection can be defined *only* as that which produces pleasure in us or whether perfection or whatever else might produce the feeling of pleasure—for example, the moral law—can be independently defined, and defined a priori. We will soon see that at the time of his own prize essay Kant certainly did *not* yet think that the object of moral feeling could be or needed to be determined a priori, though he later would, while Wolff and his followers thought that perfection *could* be defined a priori even though it is perceived by means of a feeling of pleasure. So there may be less room between Wolffian perfectionism and Kant's own mature moral theory than initially meets the eye, or than met Kant's eye.

More generally, there is a way in which Mendelssohn's idea that the fundamental principle of morality can be derived from "the mere definition of a being with free will" may have been significant for Kant. This is that in his *Groundwork for the Metaphysics of Morals* Kant himself states that "just because moral laws are to hold for every rational being as such," it is necessary "to derive them from the universal concept of a rational being as such, and in this way to set forth completely the whole of morals, which needs anthropology for its **application** to human beings" (G, 4:412). The idea that the fundamental principle of morality must be derived from the concept of a rational being as such is very similar to the idea that it can be derived from the definition of a being with a free will, although the particular definitions that

Mendelssohn and Kant use are not, at least on the surface, identical: Mendelssohn's definition of a being with a free will is that such a being inevitably chooses a perfection that promises it pleasure, while Kant's definition is that a rational being "has the capacity to act **in accordance with the representation** of laws" (G, 4:412), so that the lawfulness of maxims is a necessary and sufficient condition for moral choice and the moral law is nothing but that a rational being's maxims must have the form of law (G, 4:402, 421). This may seem like a great difference, but as Kant will also argue that a rational being must have an end in view in acting in accordance with its representation of a law, and indeed a necessary end, the difference between the standard form of perfectionism adopted by Mendelssohn and Kant's own position may be more in how the object of choice is conceived, whether as the perfection of the internal and external condition of human beings in general or as the perfection of the will itself, as an ability to act in accordance with law. At least sometimes Kant puts his own position in the place of an "intellectual" perfectionism in his classificatory scheme for moral theories rather than rejecting it altogether.[27]

A second point to note here is Kant's remark that morals needs anthropology for its application to human beings. He will make clear what he means by this only in the *Metaphysics of Morals*, thirty-five years after the prize essays, namely that the fundamental principle of morality valid for all rational beings yields duties for human beings only when it is applied to the specific circumstances of the human condition (*MM*, Introduction, 6:217). This is exactly what Mendelssohn holds in his two-staged model of the derivation of duties in his prize essay, and in that way both authors, Mendelssohn early and Kant late, will recognize that there is an indispensable empirical aspect to the derivation of human duties even if the fundamental principle of morality is universal and necessary and can be known a priori. But before we come to that stage of Mendelssohn's position in his prize essay, we need to complete the discussion of its first stage, the three ways of knowing the fundamental principle of morality. And before turning to the third of Mendelssohn's parallel derivations of the fundamental principle of morality, we should pause over the brief treatment of free will that he appends to his presentation of the second argument.

Mendelssohn suggests that we need to think about freedom of the will from two different standpoints, but conceives of them in a way that is almost diametrically opposed to the position at which Kant will eventually arrive. On the one hand, Mendelssohn claims, the "motivating grounds" that feelings of pleasure in order, beauty, and perfection provide "do not impose any physical coercion on a free being because the latter chooses on the basis of satisfaction and inner efficacy," but on the other hand these motivations "bring with themselves a moral necessity in virtue of which it becomes impossible for a free spirit to find satisfaction in imperfections, in the ugly and disorderly," which can in turn ground obligation because an "obligation is nothing other than a moral necessity to act, that is, to do something or leave it undone. Since a free person is not physically coerced, I can only be bound to will or not will something by being given motivating grounds for it" (*JubA* 2:317–18, *PW*, p. 297).

---

[27] See Kant's *Lectures on Ethics*, Moral Philosophy Collins, 27:254. For further discussion, see my "Kantian Perfectionism," in Guyer, *Virtues of Freedom: Selected Essays on Kant* (Oxford: Oxford University Press, 2016), pp. 70–86.

Mendelssohn does not define exactly what he means by "moral necessity" here, and the historical use of the phrase "moral certainty" to mean something like not theoretically certain but sufficient to act upon would not seem to be what he means.[28] It is not clear that the phrase means anything different than "obligatory," thus that the sense in which it is "impossible" for a free agent to find satisfaction in what is less than the greatest perfection available to him is just that "each free being is ethically compelled" but not physically "compelled to determine himself in his choice... in accordance with the rule of perfection, beauty, and order," or in accordance with the fundamental "natural law" or principle of morality "*Make the internal and external condition of yourself and others, in appropriate proportion, as perfect as you can*" (JubA 2:318, *PW*, p. 297). The picture then seems to be that it is completely clear, at least in general terms, what morality requires of us (in the second stage of his theory Mendelssohn will argue that is not true at the level of particular duties), but left indeterminate by the natural world and its laws whether any particular agent will actually fulfill the demands of morality in any particular circumstances. At the same time, it is not clear what any agent could want to do more than create the greatest possible perfection and hence pleasure in any situation, so the only explanation for why an agent might fail to comply with obligation or moral necessity would seem to be the intellectualist explanation, that is, that he acted for the sake of apparent rather than actual perfection, thus did not intend to do wrong but did not correctly understand what was required.

Kant's eventual position is the opposite of this, in that it does not allow any indeterminacy in the natural causation of conduct but also treats such determinism as a necessary feature of mere appearance and locates freedom of the will at a deeper level of reality, where the agent has the radical freedom to choose between good and evil without simply mistaking evil for apparent good. But it will take Kant three more decades from the period of the prize essays to arrive at this position, which does not become completely clear to him until 1792, when he published the essay on radical evil that would become the first section of *Religion within the Boundaries of Mere Reason* the next year. Thus brief and unsatisfying as Mendelssohn's discussion of freedom of the will may have been, after seeking for an alternative to it for thirty years, Kant came up with a position that has plenty of problems of its own.

The problem of free will is not going to be solved here, so let us turn to the last of Mendelssohn's three parallel arguments for the fundamental principle of morality, his theological argument. Here Mendelssohn argues that a perfect and therefore benevolent God can only have intended that we humans also do what we can to make the world, above all our own condition and that of others, perfect. Thus "It can be demonstrated in another way, on the most irrefutable grounds, that this general law of nature," namely the moral principle that we ought to make the internal and external condition of ourselves and others as perfect as we can, "is in keeping with God's aims [*Absichten*],"

and that I conform to the great final purpose [*Endzweck*] of creation and become an imitator of the divinity whenever I render a creature, myself or another, more perfect. As soon as one

---

[28] See Pasnau, *After Certainty*, Lecture 2.

assumes that a God, who cannot act without the wisest of intentions, has produced the world, no proposition in Euclid can be proven with more rigor than this one, that the cited law of nature must have been the will of God. Can the wisest and most benevolent being have any other aim than the perfection of creatures? Can he therefore want anything other than that we should orient our free actions in conformity with this aim?—As little as that the tangent should touch the circle at more than one point. (*JubA* 2:318, *PW*, pp. 297-8)

The reference to Euclid and the geometrical example tie the present argument back to the Academy's question whether natural theology and morality can be as certain as mathematics and geometry; the answer is that morality certainly can insofar as it depends upon natural theology, which is in turn as certain as geometry.

Over the coming years, Kant will develop a number of criticisms of what he calls theological morality (as contrasted to his eventual moral theology), but the deepest and most relevant of them here is that this style of argument is actually parasitic upon an independent conception and derivation of the moral law—such as Mendelssohn's own preceding derivation of the moral law from the mere concept of a free agent. For since we have no direct experience of God, how could we determine our conception of what would be willed by a perfect being except from our own antecedent conception of what is morally right? As Kant would put the point in his lectures on ethics in the next decade,

[W]e know the divine will through our reason. We conceive of God as possessing the holiest and most perfect will. Now the question is, which is the most perfect will? We are shown this by the moral law, and thus we have the whole of morality. We now say that the divine will is in accordance with the moral law, and that is why His will is the holiest and most perfect. We therefore recognize the perfection of the divine will from the moral law. God wills everything that is morally good and appropriate, and that is why His will is holy and most perfect. What is in fact morally good, is shown to us by morality.

(Kant, *Moral Mrongovius*, 27:1425; *Lectures on Ethics*, p. 68)

Since we have no experience of God, our conception of him can only be drawn from our own reason, and our conception of the moral law that he wills for us can only be drawn from our own conception of the moral law, formulated by our own pure practical reason. In Kant's eyes, Mendelssohn's third argument for the fundamental principle of morality could add nothing to his second argument. (Kant follows the passage just quoted with an argument, in the great tradition of Shaftesbury's *Moralists*, that if we think that the existence of the divine will would add *motivation* for compliance with the moral law to that which arises from our own heart, it could only be the motivation of hope of reward or fear of punishment, which does not "better the heart" and could not be pleasing to God. Mendelssohn, who once started a translation of Shaftesbury's work [see *JubA* 6.2:213-23], fully agrees with this point, as he will later make clear in *Jerusalem*.)

Kant's and perhaps Mendelssohn's own subsequent reservations about the third of the his arguments for the fundamental principle of morality aside, Mendelssohn sums up the first stage of his moral philosophy with a different use of the term "maxim," meaning now not the principle of morality itself but rather a method or strategy for discovering it. In the first sense, there is only one fundamental maxim of morality, but in the second sense three: "We have laid three different maxims as the foundation: 1) *consider the one thing on which the inclinations of all agree;* 2) *recognize that you are a being endowed with free will;* 3) *recognize that you are the property of God.* All three basic maxims lead to the common conclusion: *Make yourself and others perfect.*" He then initiates the second phase of his exposition with a statement that might be misleading: "The concepts of moral philosophy are therefore fruitful and coherent enough [to be] a theoretical system, and within this theory we can develop all our particular duties, rights, and obligations from a single universal law of nature" (*JubA* 2:321, *PW*, p. 300). Mendelssohn can mean that the universal law of perfection is a necessary condition for deriving our particular duties but not that it is a sufficient condition, in the way in which the single concept of extension is supposedly not only necessary but also sufficient to discover all the properties of possible geometrical figures. For, he continues, "It is the same in applied ethics [*ausübenden Sittenlehre*] as in every other practical science. Every practical syllogism grounds its minor premise in the constitution of a particular case, which cannot be known to us otherwise than through experience" (*JubA* 2:322, *PW*, p. 301). More fully, Mendelssohn argues that what should be our motivation can be known without further information and hence without any room for the uncertainty of empirical knowledge from the fundamental principle of morality alone, or its several versions: "These apply more to the inclinations of our heart than to our external actions. They prescribe to us what we should love and what we should shun, and they leave it to the subordinate law of nature to direct our actions and omissions.... Revere the creator! Love virtue, flee vice! Control your passions, submit your desires to reason!" These are "inferences which entail the utmost conviction... that leave no room for doubt,... that are as certain as the most valid rational inference" (*JubA* 2:232, *PW*, pp. 301–2). But when it comes to the "subordinate law of nature" or the "derivative laws of nature which prescribe to us what we are to do and leave undone in particular cases," then these rest on further, empirical knowledge about the human condition and what needs to be done in order to make it more perfect, and since empirical knowledge is never completely certain and indeed comes in a range of degrees of certainty, "then the degree of certainty" of the laws prescribing particular duties, rights, and obligations "gradually decreases in practice and descends through all levels of probability down to doubtfulness" (*JubA* 2:323–4, *PW*, p. 302)—and presumably no amount of careful research can ever climb all the way back up from probability to certitude.

Mendelssohn does not detail what sort of empirical information is necessary to determine our duties in particular cases. He does assume that actions chosen as means to perfection are chosen because of their expected consequences, but also assumes that we can never have completely adequate knowledge of all the eventual consequences of any of our actions. "Only an all-seeing eye can see the causes, consequences, proportions, and contingencies of an actual event with perfect certainty," and we humans never have all-seeing eyes. Without offering any examples, Mendelssohn assumes that we all understand the difference between "higher" and "lower" duties, and that we can generally assume that fulfillment of a "lower" duty must give way to that of a "higher" one, so that "The most praiseworthy action, the most deserving work can become a sin if we simultaneously neglect a higher duty, whose obligatoriness is more important." But apparently "higher duties can at times stand in the way of... the general rules of life that are to be applied in cases at hand." "We are bound to do not the good but the best," but it is beyond our cognitive capacities always to determine what "the best" is, thus "*conscience and a fortunate sense of truth (bon sens)*... must take the place of reason in most situations" (*JubA* 2:324–5, *PW*, pp. 302–3). That is, we must try to do our best, not settle just for some good, but we will never have any guarantee that we really are doing the best possible. Mendelssohn goes on to describe several ways in which we can work to improve our moral results, in a way reminiscent of David Hume's conditions for improving the taste of art critics in his influential essay "Of the Standard of Taste" (1757).[29] "Ethics puts in our hands the means of maintaining the harmony of the lower powers of the soul with reason." These can be summed up under four headings: "1) *The accumulation of motivating grounds*," or making sure that we are bringing all the relevant motivations to bear in any particular case; "2) *practice*" (the most Humean of the conditions), for "the more we reflect on certain reasons and the more we derive motives for our actions from them, the livelier the impression is why they leave on the mind" but also, presumably, the better we will become at understanding the consequences of acting on our various motivations; "3) *agreeable sentiment*," by which Mendelssohn has in mind supporting "rational grounds" with "beauty and grace," or using "the fine arts [to] wrest the imagination's approval" of what the intellect proposes; and "4) *intuitive knowledge*" rather than abstract, that is, transforming "universal rational grounds through examples as it were into sensory concepts" (*JubA* 2:237–8, *PW*, pp. 305–6). Mendelssohn's list is a mixed bag, but it recommends methods that in fact would tend to improve both one's understanding of possible actions in particular situations and their likely consequences as well as one's motivation for performing the best actions that appear to be available to one in such circumstances. Neither improved understanding nor improved motivation can ever guarantee that one will fact discover and perform the most perfect action that an all-seeing eye could discover and a perfect will perform. A practical ethics or system of specific duties, rights, and obligations for humans will always be imperfect. But humans should also be judged by human standards, so the most that can be asked of humans is that they conscientiously strive for the best or greatest contribution to the perfection of themselves and others that they can foresee, not they should do what only God could actually do.

Kant will subsequently object to any form of consequentialism that it entails precisely the kind of uncertainty that Mendelssohn explicitly recognizes to be unavoidable at the second, applied or practical stage of ethical theory. But in his final statement of his own ethical theory in the *Metaphysics of Morals* Kant will deploy the same distinction between the pure principle of morality valid for any rational being and the specific duties that entails for human beings in the conditions of human life that Mendelssohn has laid out, and it is not clear how exactly Kant could expect to exclude the uncertainty that comes from the limits of human empirical knowledge. Kant seems to think that he can, and insists that there can

---

[29] David Hume, *Essays Moral, Political, and Literary*, ed. Eugene F. Miller, revised edition (Indianapolis: Liberty Fund, 1987), pp. 226–49, at pp. 237–41.

never be a conflict of duties, only a conflict of grounds of duty, thus, apparently, that human beings can always determine what is in fact the right thing to do in any particular circumstances (*MM*, Introduction, section III, 6:224). But why he is so confident of this is not explained.

But that is an issue that arises only much later in Kant's career, in what could well have been intended as a rebuttal of Mendelssohn's probabilism about particular duties. Kant's treatment of ethics in his prize essay is of course not a rebuttal of anything in Mendelssohn's essay since he had not yet seen that when he wrote his own essay. His discussion there does not in fact address the level of particular duties at all. But it does introduce an empiricist element into Kant's account of the general principle of morality, which would itself become a target of his later criticism. So let us now look at Kant's treatment of moral philosophy in his prize essay. Like his treatment of knowledge of the existence of God, this is brief: again, not much more than three pages. In these three pages, Kant makes three points.

First, he introduces the distinction between hypothetical and categorical imperatives, although he does not yet use that terminology, insists that moral obligations and the moral law must be categorical, although not with that word, and argues that while hypothetical imperatives state the means to some end that is contingent, moral obligation must be "subordinated to an end which is necessary in itself." Thus, he states that although "every **ought** expresses a necessity of action," there are two senses of "ought": "either I ought to do something (as a **means**) if I want something else (as an **end**) and make it actual"—this form of "ought" is expressed in what Kant will subsequently call a hypothetical imperative; "or I **ought immediately** to do something else (as an **end**) and make it actual"—the latter is expressed by what Kant will later call a categorical imperative, although the terminology that Kant uses in the prize essay is that the "former may be called the necessity of the means (*necessitas problematica*), and the latter the necessity of the ends (*necessitas legalis*)." Kant will continue to call hypothetical imperatives "problematic" (*G* 4:415) meaning by this that they express the solution to a problem—how best to achieve some end—but where the adoption of that end and thus the need to use the means to it is optional. Here he puts that by stating that the "necessity of the means" merely "specifies as prescription as the solution to the problem concerning the means I must employ if I am to attain a certain end"; but problematic necessities are not genuine obligations at all, merely "recommendations to adopt a suitable procedure, if one wishe[s] to attain a given end." If the ends are contingent, then of course the adoption of certain means "as the condition of certain ends" is also contingent. Genuine obligations, in contrast, must be "subordinated to an end which is necessary in itself" (2:298; *Theoretical Philosophy 1755–1770*, p. 272). This is an important statement, because it suggests that the difference between hypothetical and categorical imperatives is not that the former are dependent upon ends and the latter do not involve ends at all, but rather that the former express the means to contingent ends whereas the latter and thus all genuine moral obligation involve some or one necessary end, and the fundamental task of moral theory would be to identify such a necessary end for all human beings. This will fit Kant's later strategy in the *Groundwork* of identifying humanity as an end in itself as the "ground of a possible categorical imperative" (*G* 4:428), but Kant will sometimes appear to muddle his strategy in the later work by suggesting that a (more precisely, the) categorical imperative is not connected to any end at all, and he seems to do that in the prize essay too by following the last statement quoted with the remark that a genuine moral law, whatever it might be, whether "I ought to advance the total greatest perfection" or "I ought to act in accordance with the will of God," must, "if it is to be a rule and ground of obligation, command the action as being immediately necessary and not conditioned upon some end" (2:298–9; p. 272). The suggestion that moral obligation depends upon no end at all seems to contradict the previous statement that moral obligation depends upon a necessary rather than contingent end. However, if one reads the later *Groundwork* carefully, one will see that Kant at least twice says that "The categorical imperative would be that which represented an action as objectively necessary of itself, without reference to *another* end," or as "objectively necessary without reference to some purpose, that is, even apart from any *other* end" (*G*, 4:414, 415, emphasis added). These formulations are compatible with the idea that the categorical imperative and the moral obligations that follow from it are not dependent upon any contingent ends, but that they are grounded in a necessary end.

As mentioned, this is the strategy that Kant ultimately develops in the *Groundwork*, but he does not clearly develop it in the still tentative prize essay. He only hints at it with his next step, which is to introduce a distinction between the *formal* and *material* first principles of morality. As Kant had argued in the case of metaphysics that "material first principles of human reason" must be subsumed under "formal first principles" in order to derive any knowledge from the latter— the principles of identity and non-contradiction must be applied to some concepts in order to yield any results (2:295, p. 268)—so in the case of morality the rule "perform the most perfect action in our power" may well be the "first **formal ground** of all obligation **to act**" and the proposition "abstain from doing that which will hinder the realization of the greatest possible perfection is the first **formal ground** of the duty to **abstain from acting**," but these will need some material—presumably, some determinate account of what constitutes the perfection that is in our power to produce or hinder—in order to yield any specific obligations. Moreover, Kant assumes that just as the material first principles of metaphysics, concepts such as body or divisibility, are "indemonstrable"—not derivable from any more basic concepts, because then they would not be first principles after all, so must this be true of material first principles in morality. In Kant's words, "just as, in the absence of any material first principles, nothing flowed from the first principles of our judgments of the truth, so here no specifically determinate obligation flows from these two rules of the good unless they are combined with indemonstrable material principles of cognition" (2:299, p. 273). Kant does not say there is anything incorrect about the formal principles of moral perfectionism or suggest any alternative formal principle, let alone one that could determinate our duties by itself; he merely states that these principles cannot yield practical cognition of our obligations by themselves, but need some determinate conception of perfection or the good in order to tell us what it is we should be maximizing or preventing from being minimized. Whether this would be a damaging criticism of Mendelssohn, who as we saw says that it is the "internal or external condition of ourselves and others" that should be perfected, or to other perfectionists such as Wolff and Baumgarten, is another question. Mendelssohn's characterization is brief, to be sure, and could plausibly still be criticized as too abstract or formalistic; Wolff however provides a detailed account of the intellectual and volitional capacities of human beings and of the external conditions or resources that promote the use of such capacities that fills in the formal requirements of maximizing or minimizing harm to these capacities, and Mendelssohn could simply have been relying on his readers to know the details of the Wolffian account.[30]

Kant's subsequent criticism of perfectionism will be that its material principles depend upon empirical knowledge of what is good or, what for it is the same, what makes people happy,[31] and thus cannot yield truly general results. But he could not have made that criticism yet in his prize essay, for here, and this is the third point of his discussion of morality, what is good is given by experience, in particular, "the faculty of experiencing the **good** is feeling." As he puts it, "now, just as there are unanalyzable concepts of the true, that is to say, unanalyzable concepts of that which is encountered in the objects of cognition, considered by themselves, so too there is an unanalyzable feeling of the good (which is never encountered in a thing absolutely but only relatively to a being endowed with sensibility" (2:299, p. 273)—that is, what is good is what makes the likes of us feel good, thus what is to be promoted rather than hindered is what makes human beings feel better rather than worse. The empirical nature of this determination of the material first principles of practical cognition could not be made clearer than by Kant's further statement that "the judgment 'This is good' will be completely indemonstrable," that is, not derived from anything else, but is simply "an immediate effect of the consciousness of the feeling of pleasure combined with the representation of the object." Kant makes the empiricist character of the starting-point of his moral philosophy c.1762 further evident with this statement of allegiance: "those principles, which as postulates contain the foundations of all other practical principles, are indispensable. Hutcheson and others have, under the name of moral feeling, provided us with a starting-point from which to develop some excellent observations" (2:300, p. 274).

Now Francis Hutcheson's position, expounded in his early *Inquiry concerning the Original of our Ideas of Virtue or Moral Good*, was that we have an immediate feeling of approbation toward the perception of benevolence in other people, or "as soon as any Action is represented to us as flowing from Love, Humanity, Gratitude, Compassion, a Study of the Good of others and a Delight in their Happiness, although it were in the most distant Part of the World, or in some past Age, we feel Joy within us, admire the lovely Action, and praise its Author."[32] More precisely, we have this feeling of approbation when we believe that a person's action in behalf of the happiness of another or others was undertaken without any "Self-Interest" on his own part: "We never call that Man benevolent, who is in fact useful to others, but at the same time only intends his own interest, without any desire of, or delight in, the

---

[30] These are spelled out in Wolff's German ethics, *Vernünfftige Gedancken von der Menschen Thun und Lassen, zu Beförderung ihrer Glückseeligkeit*, fourth edition (Frankfurt and Leipzig: n.p., 1733), e.g., Cap. 3, §154, pp. 86–92.
[31] As even the full title of Wolff's work suggests.
[32] Francis Hutcheson, *Inquiry into the Original of Our Ideas of Beauty and Virtue*, Treatise II, Section I, paragraph II, p. 91.

Good of others";[33] our moral approbation depends not only on the intended outcome of an action, but on the purity of its motivation, a point that will of course become of tremendous importance to Kant. And actually, just as Kant will eventually hold that the predispositions toward both morality and self-love are present in every human being, and being morally worthy consists in the subordination of self-love to the moral law, not, *per impossibile*, in the elimination of all self-love, Hutcheson had previously held that "as all Men have Self-Love, as well as Benevolence, these two principles may jointly excite a Man to the same Action," and our moral approbation depends upon which of these is preponderant in his motivation, to be measured by whether his benevolence could have motivated his action even in the absence of self-love.[34] Further, Hutcheson supposes that the degree of benevolence that can be attributed to a person or his intention can be measured by the amount of happiness his action would produce (if successful as intended): "that Action is best, which procures the greatest Happiness for the greatest Numbers; and that, worst, which, in like manner, occasions Misery."

This is of course the classical formulation of utilitarianism, which Kant seems to be endorsing by his appeal to Hutcheson for the material first principle of morality that is to give content to its formal principles. The equally classical objection to utilitarianism is that it ignores the difference among persons, that is, does not care whether the greatest happiness for the greatest number is produced by providing a lot of happiness for a few people or a little happiness for a lot of people; but this would be an unfair criticism of Hutcheson. He assumes that in many cases the number of persons who can be affected by an agent may be fixed, in which case the agent should strive to produce more happiness for those persons, and in other cases the amount of happiness the agent can produce may be fixed, in which case he should strive to affect more people; but he also says that "the Dignity, or moral Importance of Persons," by which he means their own capacity to increase the happiness of others, "may compensate Numbers."[35] How the increase in happiness intended by the benevolent agent is distributed among persons is not indifferent. Be all this as it may, Kant's eventual criticism of utilitarianism and of perfectionism as ultimately a form of utilitarianism, is not that it is indifferent to the difference among persons, but that its conception of happiness is ultimately empirical: what counts as happiness for each person, thus what is to be promoted under the name of the perfect or good, can only be determined empirically. Thus the goal of increasing happiness is subject to the epistemic limitations, or uncertainty, of all empirical knowledge. Further, there can even be conflicts between what clearly would make different persons happy, as in Kant's famous example of one thing that would make two different people, namely King Francis I of France and Emperor Charles V of the Holy Roman Empire, happy, namely sole position of Milan, but where in virtue of the nature of the good involved, sole possession, they cannot both have it (*CPracR*, 5:28). As we saw, Mendelssohn recognized that the entry of empirical conditions into the second stage of moral theory, at which particular duties are derived from the most general maxim or "law of

---

[33] Hutcheson, *Inquiry*, Treatise II, Section II, paragraph III, p. 103.
[34] Hutcheson, *Inquiry*, Treatise II, Section II, paragraph III, p. 104.
[35] Hutcheson, *Inquiry*, Treatise II, Section III, paragraph VIII, p. 125.

nature," would allow uncertainty and even conflict in the determination of our particular obligations. Kant's eventual objection would not have come as a surprise to him, although he would not have seen it as an objection to the combination of a priori principles and empirical conditions of application in moral theory, only as the inevitable outcome of that unavoidable combination. Whether Kant's eventual argument that such uncertainty and conflict can be avoided, a criticism of his own position in 1762 as well as of the position of Mendelssohn, can succeed is a question for another day.

In other words: Kant concludes his prize essay with the remark that

> [A]lthough it must be possible to attain the highest degree of philosophical certainty in the fundamental principles of morality, nonetheless the ultimate fundamental concepts of obligation need first of all to be determined more reliably. And in this respect, practical philosophy is even more defective than speculative philosophy, for it has yet to be determined whether it is merely the faculty of cognition, or whether it is feeling (the first inner ground of the faculty of desire) which decides its first principles. (2:300, pp. 274–5)

Kant will subsequently conclude that it is a faculty of cognition, namely reason itself, that will decide on the fundamental principle of morality. In this he would find no difference with Mendelssohn, who thought that the fundamental principle of morality could be derived from strictly logical analysis of the concept of a being with a free will, although the results of that analysis could be confirmed by common sense or observation of widespread human beliefs and practices on the one hand and by appeal to God's intentions on the other. Yet Mendelssohn also held that the fundamental principles of morality have to be applied to the circumstances of human life as we know them empirically, and recognized that this would inevitably entail some degree of uncertainty in the determination of our particular duties in particular circumstances. In his final work on moral philosophy, Kant would accept Mendelssohn's two-stage model of moral theory, the a priori determination of the fundamental principle of morality at the first stage but the derivation of specific duties for human beings from that at the second stage only with the addition of some basic but empirical knowledge about the human condition, but hold that we could nevertheless avoid uncertainty and in particular conflicts of duties at that stage. Whether he could pull that off remains a question.

## 6. Conclusion

Many points of both initial agreement and developing disagreement between Mendelssohn and Kant come up in the comparison of their two brief prize essays. Before we turn to more detailed comparisons of their continuing debates in metaphysics, aesthetics, philosophy of religion, and more, a summary of the results of this comparison might be helpful.

Throughout, the issue for both philosophers was how properly to combine a priori and empirical elements in their models of metaphysics and morality. The question set by the Academy was whether metaphysics and morality have the same prospects for certainty as mathematics, so both philosophers had to begin with an analysis of the prospects for certainty in mathematics itself. For Mendelssohn, a branch of mathematics such as geometry can be considered a formal system that can be logically analyzed with complete certainty, but that has to be grounded in the experience of our own forms of sensibility and that has to be applied to particular objects of our sensory experience; thus the a priori is limited by the empirical at these two points. Kant argued only that mathematics can construct its own definitions and objects in a way that philosophy cannot, but left open the question of where mathematics gets the materials for its definitions and constructions in the first place. He would later adopt Mendelssohn's suggestion that mathematics must begin with the forms of our own sensibility, but insist that we have a priori rather than merely empirical knowledge of the forms of our sensible intuition. However, he would also accept Mendelssohn's view that we need empirical knowledge of the presence of particular objects to get knowledge of actuality rather than mere possibility from mathematics. Their positions on the nature of mathematical knowledge are not divided on every issue, and each involves both rationalist and empiricist elements.

In philosophy, both philosophers held that we can analyze metaphysical concepts, but that this yields only knowledge of possibilities that have to be anchored to reality in some way. Mendelssohn held that in almost all cases this requires empirical knowledge afforded by our senses, but that in the special case of God we can know his existence from his concept alone, by means of the ontological argument, but also by inference from our experience of our own existence supported by the principle of sufficient reason. By the time the prize essays were published, Kant had already criticized the ontological argument in *The Only Possible Basis for a Demonstration of the Existence of God* and he would repeat that criticism twenty years later in the *Critique of Pure Reason*, but he accepted his own argument for God as the necessarily actual ground of all possibility from the *Only Possible Basis*. As we will subsequently see, he silently rejected this argument in the *Critique of Pure Reason* while explicitly rejecting the argument that Mendelssohn had also made from the complete determination of the concept of God to his existence, although without attaching Mendelssohn's name to this argument. Mendelssohn would defend his arguments for the existence of God in his final work, the *Morning Hours*.

Finally, in morality, Mendelssohn proposed a two-staged model, arguing for a priori knowledge of the fundamental principle of morality that can be empirically confirmed but for an unavoidable empirical element, knowledge of the actual circumstances of human existence, at the stage at which particular rights and obligations are derived from the most general principle of morality. Kant argued that morality has to begin with two kinds of principles, not one—a formal principle of maximizing perfection but a material principle that would tell us what perfection actually is—but at the early stage we have been considering seemed to endorse an entirely empiricist approach to the latter, the question of what is actually good for human beings. Later Kant would insist that the fundamental principle of morality is universal and necessary, for all rational beings, and that our knowledge of it must therefore be entirely a priori, but would also accept Mendelssohn's view that empirical information must enter into the derivation of our particular duties from that principle while trying to avoid Mendelssohn's acceptance of uncertainty about and possible conflict among those duties. So in morality too there are both rationalist and empiricist elements in the positions of each philosopher, in Kant's case both early and later.

Mendelssohn did not publish any further treatise on moral philosophy, and Kant did not mention Mendelssohn's name in his subsequent critiques of perfectionism nor in his adoption of what is in fact Mendelssohn's two-staged model for the derivation of our particular duties. So even though it could nevertheless be illuminating to read much in Kant's mature ethics as a response to Mendelssohn, in the remainder of this book I will not say more on this subject than what I have suggested in the previous section. Instead, I will now turn to the continuing interaction between Mendelssohn and Kant on several central topics of metaphysics, namely the existence of God, the reality of the external world, and the immortality of the human soul.

# PART I
# Metaphysics and Epistemology

As our two philosophers did not address their common topics in the same order during their careers, and both repeatedly recurred to many of their topics throughout their careers, a straightforwardly chronological exposition of their works would be repetitive and confusing. So we need to choose the overall rather than fine-grained narrative arc of the career of one of our philosophers or the other to structure this book, and I have chosen to follow the arc of Kant's career. Thus I will discuss first the metaphysical and epistemological topics on which Kant focused during the first part of his career, through the publication of the first edition of the *Critique of Pure Reason* in 1781 and to which Mendelssohn returned, only many years after his prize essay, in his final book, the *Morning Hours* of 1785. Then I will turn to aesthetics, with which Mendelssohn began his career, on which Kant lectured in his courses on logic and anthropology from the early 1770s until he retired, but in which his theory took its final form only with the publication of the *Critique of the Power of Judgment*. Finally, I will discuss issues about religion, politics, and history that concerned Mendelssohn especially in his penultimate book, *Jerusalem*, in 1783, and which Kant first broached in his 1784 essay "Idea for a Universal History from a Cosmopolitan Point of View" but which preoccupied him chiefly in the final decade of his career, beginning with the his essay on "radical evil" in 1792 which he then incorporated into *Religion within the Boundaries of Mere Reason* in 1793. But within these three main parts of the book, the order of discussion will sometimes be determined by Mendelssohn as well. Thus in this first Part, I will begin with their debate over the possibility of theoretical proofs for the existence of God, which as we saw in the Prologue concerned both philosophers in their prize essays of 1762, but which also concerned Kant in a series of works from 1755 to 1763, which centrally concerned him in the *Critique of Pure Reason* and which again concerned Mendelssohn, after years away from metaphysics, in the *Morning Hours*. I will then turn to the topic of the immortality of the human soul, which Mendelssohn defended in his *Phaedo* of 1767, and belief in which Kant criticized on theoretical grounds but defended on practical grounds in a series of texts from the two editions of the *Critique of Pure Reason* to *Religion within the Boundaries of Mere Reason* in 1793 and beyond. Finally, Part One will turn to the topic of idealism, on which Mendelssohn criticized Kant in 1770 and which continued to be an issue between them in the first *Critique* and *Morning Hours*. Part Two will begin with Mendelssohn's work in aesthetics, which came early in his career, primarily from 1755 to 1761 although with some later revisions, and will then compare Kant's mature position in aesthetics in the *Critique of the Power of Judgment*, although that was published only three decades later, to Mendelssohn's position. Part Three will focus on issues concerning religion other than the metaphysical question of the possibility of proving the existence of God, especially the issue of religious pluralism that is a central topic in Mendelssohn's *Jerusalem* and toward which Kant takes a complicated position in his *Religion*. This Part will also examine their competing positions on the nature of enlightenment and on the possibility of moral progress in human history.

The use of the term "epistemology" in the title of this Part, it might be noted, is an anachronism. This term is a nineteenth-century coinage, and our two eighteenth-century philosophers would have considered most of what will be discussed in this Part to fall into "metaphysics," divided in the tradition of Christian Wolff within which both were educated into "general metaphysics" or ontology and the "special metaphysics" of "rational psychology," in which the immortality of the soul would be proven, "rational cosmology," concerning the metaphysics of the natural world, and "rational theology," in which the existence of God would be proven. Some aspects of one issue debated between Kant and Mendelssohn under the rubric of idealism, namely whether time as well as space could be a mere artifact of the human way of representing things, could also be subsumed under "rational cosmology" and thus considered a metaphysical issue; but by subsequent lights the general question of what we can *know* about the external world on the basis of our own *representations* of it is an epistemological issue, indeed *the* epistemological issue, and I have included the term "epistemology" in the title of this Part to indicate that I will be discussing the two philosophers' positions on this general issue as well.

# 2
# Mendelssohn, Kant, and Proofs of the Existence of God in Kant's Pre-Critical Period

## 1. From Idea to Reality

The ontological argument purports to infer the existence, indeed the necessary existence, of God from the concept of God. At least that is how we now describe it. Descartes presents it as inferring the necessary existence of God from the *essence* of God, as we can infer properties of triangles from the essence of the triangle: its triangularity. If the argument is described in Descartes's terms, the battle is already halfway won: an essence is not something obviously mental, in the mind of the subject trying to make the argument, so if you are already presupposing the extramental existence of essences, including the essence of God, it will not seem like much of a step to allow another instance of extramental existence, that of God himself. Or including his existence within his essence will not seem problematic if his essence is already something that exists beyond our own thought of it. But if the argument is described as inferring the existence of God from the *concept* of God and *concepts* are thought of as mental, in the mind of the subject or subjects trying to make the argument, then how you could infer extramental existence from something entirely mental is a much greater challenge, perhaps an insuperable challenge.[1]

Over the course of eighteenth-century philosophy, a sea change occurred, precisely that of replacing the notion of essence with that of concepts, thus changing the starting-point for all philosophical argumentation from something extramental to something mental.[2] Perhaps this change already began with Locke's revision of

---

[1] Rogelio Rovira defends Mendelssohn's version of the ontological argument precisely because it is "based not on the mere *concept* of God, perhaps arbitrarily constructed, but on the unique case of the divine *essence* as adequately, although not exhaustively, conceived by us"; "Mendelssohn's Refutation of Kant's Critique of the Ontological Proof," *Kant-Studien* 108 (2017): 401–26, at p. 408. My point in these chapters is precisely that such a defense would leave Kant (and other moderns) completely unmoved, given their irreversible shift from talk of essences to talk of concepts.

[2] In his classical work, *Der Ontologische Gottesbeweis* (Tübingen: J.C.B. Mohr [Paul Siebeck], 1960), Dieter Henrich argued that Descartes put the ontological argument back on the table for modern philosophy by reviving Anselm's argument after criticisms by Thomas Aquinas had diminished its popularity in the later middle ages. However, Henrich does not emphasize the difference between Descartes's formulation of the argument as beginning from the essence of God and later versions as beginning from the idea of God, thus that the modern form of the argument did not emerge until the end of the seventeenth century.

Cartesianism, and especially with Locke's complex thought about essence, in which essences that we can know are interpreted as nominal essences—clearly human mental constructs—while real essence is left as an unknowable surd of extramental reality.[3] The change did not happen without a fight, for Leibniz's notion of complete concepts as the basis for all true predications, formulated in the same years (1670s and 1680s) in which Locke was writing his *Essay*, recognized the mental character of concepts but precisely because of their completeness placed them in the mind of God rather than of human beings, a God whose existence Leibniz thought could readily be proved from the non-contradictory possibility of his own concept. One might propose that it was Leibniz's recognition of Locke's thoroughgoing humanization of concepts that led him to identify Locke as the major proponent of the modern philosophy, the only one of his contemporaries worthy of a book-length refutation.[4] One could also argue that the triumph of the mentalization and humanization of concepts over the course of the eighteenth century was not complete, and that absolute idealism, particularly in its Hegelian form, represented nothing less than an attempt to think of concepts once again as more than human and subjective, certainly supra-individual if not exactly extramental. But that development will remain beyond the purview of this book.[5]

The question of how to get beyond the mere idea of God once it is transformed from an extramental essence to a mental concept is particularly salient in the long give-and-take over the possibility of proving the existence of God that took place between Mendelssohn and Kant. In his prize-winning "Essay on Evidence," as we have seen, Mendelssohn recognized that the fundamental issue in proving the existence of God, indeed in philosophy in general, is how we can get beyond our own concepts, understood as mental representations, to the existence of something external and extramental. In all cases except that of the existence of God Mendelssohn recognized, indeed insisted, that we can only get from concept to existence through experience, and even in the case of God he held that there was one route that starts from our experience of our own existence. But he held that there is also a sound argument from the concept of God to his existence, and until his final major work, the *Morgenstunden* or *Morning Hours*[6] of 1785, he defended the

---

[3] See Locke's *Essay concerning Human Understanding* (1690), Book Three.

[4] I refer here of course to Leibniz's *New Essays concerning Human Understanding*, the manuscript that Leibniz had completed but out of a scrupulous concern for fairness shelved when he received the news of Locke's death in 1704. It was not published until 1765, thus perhaps reigniting interest in the issue of the difference between the older and newer understanding of concepts right at the start of the period I am about to describe. The *New Essays* were first published in Leibniz, *Œuvres philosophiques latines et françoises*, ed. Rudolf Eric Raspe (Amsterdam and Leipzig, 1765); English translation in G.W. Leibniz, *New Essays on Human Understanding*, transl. Peter Remnant and Jonathan Bennett (Cambridge: Cambridge University Press, 1981). Leibniz's clearest expositions of his notion of complete concepts as the basis of all true predications can be found in two works from 1686, the paper "Primary Truths" and the longer "Discourse on Metaphysics," but both of these were published only long after the lifetimes of both Mendelssohn and Kant, "Primary Truths" not until 1905.

[5] With what success is questionable; on this question, see Frederick C. Beiser, *German Idealism: The Struggle against Subjectivity, 1791–1801* (Cambridge, Mass.: Harvard University Press, 2001), especially the Conclusion.

[6] As both recent translations have it, though I think "Morning Lessons" would be better. See Moses Mendelssohn, *Morning Hours; Lectures on God's Existence*, trans. Daniel O. Dahlstrom and Corey Dyck

ontological argument as well as a version of the cosmological argument. In the *Morning Hours*, Mendelssohn rejected any argument based on the laws of probabilistic reasoning that suffice for all other human claims about the existence of external objects, but he also developed an additional argument from the *incompleteness* of all human thought to the necessity of a *complete* thought of all reality, and thus to a complete, perfect thinker of all reality.

By contrast, Kant's career in philosophy began with the recognition that the ontological argument was doomed by the mental character of all our concepts, thus including the concept of God, and to this he quickly added the claim that the other traditional proofs of God, any version of the cosmological argument as well as any version of an argument from design, depend upon the ontological argument to get all the way to the existence of a being that is both necessary and perfect. Further, although in his first decade as a publishing philosopher Kant tried to substitute for the ontological argument an argument from the existence of any kind of *possibility* whatsoever to a necessary and perfect being as the ground of all possibility, by the time he wrote the *Critique of Pure Reason* he recognized that we could argue only from the *human representation* of possibility and that this could never be complete enough to entail the existence of a genuinely necessary and perfect being. However, in his "critical" period, beginning with the *Critique of Pure Reason* and continuing through his two further critiques, the *Critique of Practical Reason* and the *Critique of the Power of Judgment*, Kant developed an argument for the rationality of belief in the existence of God (along with freedom and the immortality of the human soul) based on *practical* rather than theoretical grounds, that is, as the necessary conditions of the possibility of our compliance with the demands of morality, and as we have seen, in his 1786 essay "What Does it Mean to Orient Oneself in Thinking?" he marked his moral argument for the existence of God, or as he would come to call it his account of "practico-dogmatic" knowledge of the existence of God, as his fundamental difference with Mendelssohn. Although he did not explicitly say so, Kant would certainly have rejected Mendelssohn's description of him as the "all-crushing [*alleszermalmenden*] Kant" (*JubA* 3.2:3, *LW*, p. 3) precisely on this ground: for Kant his practical argument, although only this argument, could put our belief in the existence of God on a secure, rational foundation. In this regard, Kant was as much of a rationalist as Mendelssohn, although his rationalism was practical rather than theoretical.

We can also see the difference between the two philosophers as a difference in their responses to idealism. Mendelssohn recognizes what we might think of as the modernist dilemma, that we must succeed in thinking about the world from within the circle of our own thoughts, allows that what Charles Sanders Peirce a century later would call "abductive" argument—inference to the best explanation—can carry us to the constant appearances of external objects but not to their inner nature, but insists that in the unique case of God we can argue from his concept alone to his real nature and existence. Kant's transcendental idealism allows him to say only that our thought begins with representations by which we are "affected" by "things in

---

(Dordrecht: Springer, 2011) and Mendelssohn, *Last Works*, trans. Bruce Rosenstock (Urbana: University of Illinois Press, 2012).

themselves" about which we can say nothing more than that they do so affect us, and certainly does not allow us to say that any of those things are or are themselves grounded in any perfect and necessary being, or that we can have theoretically adequate knowledge of the nature and existence of God. Again, Kant allows, indeed insists, that we can postulate the existence of God and determine his predicates on practical grounds, and therefore as characterized only in the terms necessary for morality, thus as the author of laws of nature consistent with the requirements of the moral law and perhaps as an omniscient and omnibenevolent judge of human motivation, but not as a perfect being in general. As we will see in Chapter 4, this approach may even have been inspired at least in part by Mendelssohn's argument for the immortality of the human soul in his *Phaedo*. But it is also an attempt to show the function of the *idea* of God *within the structure of human belief* rather than an argument that leads beyond the confines of such thought, as Kant made clear in his final attempts at a restatement of transcendental idealism in his uncompleted *Opus postumum*, where he claims that God is not a substance but an idea, which means *our* idea, although by then his provocation was more likely the emerging star Schelling rather than the long-dead Mendelssohn.[7] Be that as it may, Kant's practical postulation of the existence of God remains within the confines of his transcendental idealism and is in this sense a thoroughly modernist approach to the question of the existence of God. And ultimately, in the very last pages of the *Morning Hours*, Mendelssohn perhaps concedes the point.[8]

The history of the relation between Mendelssohn's and Kant's arguments about the existence of God is involuted. Kant already re-interpreted the Cartesian argument as one from the *concept* rather than *essence* of God in his first philosophical publication, the *New Exposition of the First Principles of Metaphysical Cognition* of 1755, and in that work also already made his criticism, fatal to that form of the argument, that you can *think* whatever you want without that proving the existence of anything beyond your thought; but there he also suggested his alternative metaphysical or theoretical strategy of inferring the existence of God as the ground of any possibility. There is no evidence that this little academic exercise in Königsberg, prepared as part of Kant's qualifications as a lecturer, ever came to the notice of Mendelssohn, occupied in Berlin as he was in 1755 with his own earliest work in aesthetics. Thus Mendelssohn's defense of the ontological argument in his entry for the Berlin Academy of Sciences competition on the question of whether the mathematical method can work in "natural theology and morality," as the question was phrased, does not appear to have been written in response to Kant's work of 1755,

---

[7] For references and discussion, see my "The Unity of Nature and Freedom: Kant's Conception of the System of Philosophy," originally in Sally Sedgwick, ed., *The Reception of Kant's Critical Philosophy* (Cambridge: Cambridge University Press, 2000), pp. 19–53, reprinted in my *Kant's System of Nature and Freedom: Selected Essays* (Oxford: Clarendon Press, 2005), pp. 277–313.

[8] Alexander Altmann concluded his sympathetic account of Mendelssohn's proofs of the existence of God by quoting Mendelssohn saying at the end of *Morning Hours* that "a man is [not] capable of more than the pursuit of convictions and actions according to human powers" (JubA 3.2:154) and says that "Mendelssohn seems to have guessed, and rightly so, that there was common ground between him and Kant as far as ultimate beliefs were concerned"; see "Moses Mendelssohn's Proofs for the Existence of God," in Altmann, *Essays in Jewish Intellectual History* (Hanover: University Press of New England, 1981), pp. 119–41, at pp. 136–7. But if Mendelssohn had really understood how much common ground there was between him and Kant, he could not in good conscience have called Kant "all-crushing."

and of course Mendelssohn could not have seen Kant's entry in the Academy competition while writing his own. In any case, Kant's entry gives only a very brief statement of his critique of the ontological argument (2:297). However, in his 1763 book on *The Only Possible Basis for a Demonstration of the Existence of God*, which appeared between the submission of the Berlin prize essays and their publication, Kant restated and more fully developed both his critique of the ontological argument and his new argument from possibility to its ground in necessary being, and since Mendelssohn devoted four of the *Letters concerning the Latest Literature* to Kant's book in April 1764, we know that Kant's arguments were on Mendelssohn's radar screen by then. However, Mendelssohn did not address an extensive philosophical work to the issue for another twenty years, and by then he had the first edition of Kant's *Critique of Pure Reason* to face as well, in which Kant not only renewed his attack on all the traditional arguments for the existence of God but tacitly withdrew his own new argument of 1755 and 1763 and subtly undermined an additional argument that Mendelssohn had added in his prize essay: the argument that the complete determination of the concept of God by itself entails his existence. In the work in which Mendelssohn did finally return to the question of arguments for the existence of God twenty years after the prize essay, namely the *Morning Hours*, I propose, Mendelssohn acknowledged Kant's argument for the dependence of the other traditional arguments for the existence of God upon the ontological argument, and for that reason undertook both to defend the ontological argument but also to devise an entirely new argument, immune from Kant's criticism of his own earlier innovation. But Kant did not see any need to strengthen his critique of the ontological argument in the second edition of the first *Critique*, and he dismissed Mendelssohn's own new argument in a brusque note in his own copy of the first edition without publishing it in the second, perhaps out of respect for the by then dead Mendelssohn, or perhaps just because revisions for the second edition stopped with the first main part of the Transcendental Dialectic, the "Paralogisms of Pure Reason," and did not reach as far as the discussion of proofs for the existence of God in the third part, the "Ideal of Pure Reason."

Since we have no indication that Mendelssohn knew Kant's early *New Exposition*, I will begin my own exposition by reviewing Mendelssohn's arguments for the existence of God in the prize essay (already discussed in the previous chapter). I will then describe Kant's twofold strategy in the *New Exposition* and *Only Possible Basis*, as well as Mendelssohn's review of the work. The next chapter will review Kant's position in the *Critique of Pure Reason* and then consider Mendelssohn's *Morning Hours* as a response to Kant's *Critique*. Finally, we can examine Kant's brief response to Mendelssohn's new argument in his late work, consider how Kant restated his idealist approach to God in his final writings, and note that in the last pages of *Morning Hours* Mendelssohn too seems to have given in to what we can call a subjectivist or internalist approach to *belief* in the existence of God.

## 2. Mendelssohn's Prize Essay

If we take recognition of the mental nature of concepts as a paradigmatically modern premise of philosophy and inference from the mental to the extramental as the paradigmatic challenge for modern philosophy, then Mendelssohn's "Essay on Evidence" is a paradigmatically modern work of philosophy. His question throughout is how we get from the circle of our ideas to existence beyond them, or from the analysis of conceptual possibilities to the assertion of extramental actuality. It is not enough for the philosopher to discover "certain kinships among concepts"; "the important step into the realm of actuality must also take place" (*JubA* 2:292, *PW* p. 274). In the case of God, even if the philosopher "has shown that a necessary being cannot exist without being the creator and preserver of all things outside him, it is still incumbent upon him to prove that such a necessary being exists" (*JubA* 2:293, *PW*, p. 275). In other words, like Locke and Hume before him and Kant after, Mendelssohn draws a firm distinction between the analysis of concepts on the one hand and the assertion of the existence of objects satisfying the analyzed concepts on the other. This is what Kant would come to call the distinction between analytical judgments explicating the contents of concepts and synthetic judgments asserting the existence of objects for those concepts or the objective reality of such concepts (see *CPR* A 6–10/B 10–14, A 84/B 117). But with or without Kant's terminology, the fundamental question for metaphysics in this period is how we get from the concept of God, the contents of which are readily analyzed, to the existence of God.

As we saw, Mendelssohn saw no problem in the relation between concepts and reality in the case of mathematics. He held the characteristically modern position that mathematics begins with the "necessary connection of concepts," for example in geometry "one analyzes the original concept of extension and shows that there is an inseparable connection between it and certain consequences derived from it" (*JubA* 2:277, *PW*, p. 260), and then one shows that, as a matter of fact, the concepts involved apply well enough to certain "constant appearances" to allow us to use them in practice. But the "mathematician never troubles himself with the true existence of things. He proves either the coherence of ideas or the coherence of appearances" (*JubA* 2:284, *PW*, p. 267). Mathematicians are content to apply the results of their conceptual analyses to constant "appearances"—Mendelssohn equates the German word *Erscheinung* with the Greek and Latin terms *phaenomenon* and *apparentia*—because their interest in necessity and certainty is satisfied by the necessity and certainty of the analytical connections among their concepts; it is useful to us that at least some of these mathematical concepts turn out to apply well to at least some of our experiences, but the mathematician has no interest in claiming that this is necessary. Mendelssohn is a formalist about pure mathematics but an empiricist about applied mathematics. Nor does he feel the compulsion of Descartes to prove that a benevolent God makes it necessary in some way that our clear and distinct mathematical concepts do apply to our experience; the constant appearance that they do is enough for our purposes.[9]

By the time of his inaugural dissertation in 1770 and that of the first *Critique* in 1781, Kant will dispute both sides of Mendelssohn's view of mathematics, holding that analysis is *not* sufficient to prove all the theorems of mathematics and that

---

[9] Descartes's strategy in the *Meditations on First Philosophy* (1641) is to prove that there exists a benevolent God who guarantees the veracity of our clear and distinct ideas, which, as the Sixth Meditation makes clear, are paradigmatically our mathematical ideas, not our ordinary ideas of sensory qualities such as color, temperature, and so on.

mathematics *does* apply necessarily to our experience.[10] But that is not our concern now. The point now is rather that Mendelssohn himself makes clear that this model of mathematical knowledge of actuality cannot apply in the case of God. This is because although we can, according to him, fully analyze the concept of God, we cannot apply that concept to any appearances, even constant ones, *within* our experience, and even if we could, that would not be enough to establish the *necessary* existence of God, which, however, is the sort of existence that we do attribute to God. About the analysis of the concept of God, Mendelssohn sees no difficulty. Indeed, he claims that:

> [T]he concepts of God and of his properties have a wondrous power. They are so intimately connected with one another that one has only to presuppose a single property of God in order to deduce from it everything that we are in a position to know about the Supreme Being. A single chain of inferences combines all the perfections of this fecund being. His independence, infinity, immensity, his wisdom, providence, justice, holiness, and so forth are reciprocally grounded in one another in such a way that, without the others, each of these properties would be contradictory... Let the following definition, for example, be presupposed: "God is a being with a supremely perfect will": The supremely perfect will presupposes the most perfect intellect and demands the most perfect might. That will consists, furthermore, in the inclination to every possible good, and aversion to every possible evil... From this follow justice, benevolence, and wisdom. Since God possesses all these perfections without limits, he is infinite, and, consequently, singular. Since no finite thing can be the reason for his existence and no infinite thing exists outside him, he has the reason for his existence in himself; therefore he is independent and necessary.   (*JubA* 2:297–8, *PW*, pp. 279–80)

A central part of Kant's criticism of the traditional arguments for the existence of God, that is, his insistence of the dependence of the other arguments upon the ontological argument, is, as we will see, based upon the claim that perfection implies necessary existence but necessary existence by itself does not imply perfection; so Kant will in fact reject Mendelssohn's claim that any predicate of God implies all the others. Kant's eventual insistence that our belief in God is grounded only on practical considerations will also mean that the concept of God may be determined only by the moral predicates of justice, benevolence, and wisdom. But our immediate concern is with Mendelssohn's own question: how are we to get beyond the analysis of the concept of God, complete as it may be, to a justified assertion of the existence of God? What consideration can substitute for the merely empirical and contingent fact of constant appearance that suffices for mathematics?

Mendelssohn's answer to this question in the prize essay, as we saw, consists of two main parts, a defense of the ontological argument, that is, the argument that the concept of God itself entails his existence, which itself consists of two parts, and a version of the cosmological argument, that is, the argument from the contingent existence of one being to the necessary being of another, which, in light of Mendelssohn's claim that any predicate of God entails all the others, will suffice for a proof of his existence: "One infers either from the possibility of a necessary being to

---

[10] Of course, Kant is concerned with the branches of mathematics known in his own time, such as arithmetic, algebra, and geometry, not with some of the more exotic branches of subsequent mathematics that might not claim to have empirical applications.

its actuality or from the undeniable intuitive proposition 'I think' to my actuality and from this to the actuality of a necessary being, by means of the principle of sufficient reason" (*JubA* 2:299, *PW*, p. 281; see also *JubA* 2:298–9, *PW*, p. 289). Mendelssohn acknowledges the Cartesian provenance of both forms of argument, although his specific versions of them differ from those of Descartes and show the intervening influence of Wolff and Baumgarten. We will review his versions of the ontological argument first, both because he expounds them first in his own text and because the critique of the ontological argument is central to Kant's own contemporaneous thought about the issue.

Mendelssohn's first version of the ontological argument begins with the concept of God as a necessary being. His argument begins with the recognition that in most cases one cannot infer the existence of an object from the mere concept of it, but claims that the concept of God is a special case, in which we can infer existence from the mere concept. The argument begins with the claim that there are only two alternatives to existence in general, namely either impossibility or else mere possibility. In the first case, that of impossibility, "the determinations intrinsic" to the concept of the object concerned "must be contradictory, that is, the same predicate must be at the same time both affirmed and denied of the subject [*Vorwurfe*]"; in the case of mere possibility, the concept can "of course contain no contradiction, but on the basis of [it] it cannot be conceived why the thing should exist rather than not exist" (*JubA* 2:300, *PW*, p. 281). However, the concept of a necessary being does not contain any contradictions, so it does not describe an impossibility, because— although here Mendelssohn just switches from the concept of a necessary being to that of a perfect being, as his initial claim about the connection among all the predicates of God allows him to do—"all realities are affirmed of the most perfect being, and all deficiencies are denied it" by its concept, and realities cannot conflict with one another, only a reality and the negation or deficiency of it can.[11] Hence a perfect being is clearly not impossible, and "Whoever says 'the most perfect being contains a contradiction' contradicts himself" (*JubA* 2:300, *PW*, p. 282). So that leaves the question of whether the existence of a necessary being could be a mere possibility. But here Mendelssohn argues that merely possible existence "is not a possibility intrinsic" to a thing that has such existence, "nor part of its essence nor even of one its properties, and, for this reason, is a mere contingency (*modus*), the actuality of which can only be conceived on the basis of another actuality. Such an existence is, accordingly, not independent but dependent [*abhängig, nicht*

---

[11] This step in Mendelssohn's proof is ultimately derived from Leibniz's argument that the Cartesian proof that the most perfect being exists must be preceded by a proof that the most perfect being is possible, which in turn consists in the argument that the perfections of God are positive predicates that cannot conflict with one another. Leibniz clearly states the argument in notes for discussion with Spinoza from November, 1676, see Gottfried Wilhelm Leibniz, *Philosophical Papers and Letters*, ed. Leroy E. Loemker (Dordrecht: D. Reidel, 1969); Mendelssohn would have been familiar with Leibniz's concise statement of the argument in the *Monadology* (1714), §45, in *Philosophical Papers and Letters*, p. 647. The premise is also asserted by Baumgarten: "All realities are truly positive, and no negation is a reality. Therefore, if all realities are indeed maximally joined together in a being, no contradiction would ever arise from them…" (*Metaphysica*, §807). Kant's argument in his little essay of 1764 on "The Introduction of Negative Quantities into Philosophy" disputes the assumption that "real" qualities cannot conflict with one another and threatens this version of the ontological argument, as Mendelssohn recognized.

*selbständig*]." But "everyone sees that an independent existence is a greater perfection than a dependent existence is," and thus that merely dependent "existence cannot be part of the most perfect being since it would contradict its essence." So the existence of the necessary being cannot be merely possible existence, and since its impossibility has already been excluded, "nothing further remains for it" but "actuality" (*JubA* 2:300, *PW*, p. 281).

This conclusion could be reformulated as the conditional that if the necessary being exists then it necessarily exists, since its existence can be neither impossible nor merely contingent, and in this form it would be wide-open to the objection that you can put whatever you want into a concept, even necessary being, without that proving that the concept has objective reality; and this is a version of Kant's objection to any ontological argument. But before we consider that, we have to consider Mendelssohn's second version of the ontological argument as well as his version of the cosmological argument. Mendelssohn's second version of the ontological argument is also suggested by Baumgarten,[12] although Mendelssohn applies it to the case of God in a way that Baumgarten does not, at least not explicitly. Baumgarten states that "something possible is either determined with regard to all the affections that are also compossible in it, or not," that is, for any predicate or its opposite compossible with the other predicates of the thing, it is determinate which—the predicate or its opposite—is true, and he says that "The former is an ACTUAL BEING" (*Metaphysica*, §54).[13] He further states that although universals are not fully determinate, that is, general concepts do not determine everything about the particulars that fall under them, (§148), "Singular beings are internally entirely determined, and hence are actual" (§152). That is, he holds not just that anything actual is fully determinate—an actual extended object, for example, cannot be of indeterminate size, but must have some determinate size or other, and so on for every other "compossible" predicate of it—but also that anything fully determinate is actual. Mendelssohn takes up this argument in the following way:

> One might simply recall, from the first principles of metaphysics, that something [*eine Sache*] actually exists as soon as everything determinable in it is in fact determined... Herein lies the difference between general possible concepts and individual real concepts. In the former, neither the affirmation nor the negation of several determinacies is established, but is undecided, and they can be determined in one manner as well as another. In the case of individual real things, by contrast, the affirmation or negation of everything that can be affirmed or denied must be established and decided and, conversely, that of which everything down to the most remote relations is established and decided, actually exists... Now the most perfect being cannot receive from something external any determination through which it is supposed to become actual. Thus, either it is sufficiently determined by the power of its inner being, or it is indeterminable. That means, either it exists necessarily, or it is absolutely impossible. We have seen from the foregoing that it cannot be impossible, and, hence, it exists necessarily. (*JubA* 2:301, *PW*, pp. 282–3)

---

[12] See Altmann, "Mendelssohn's Proofs," p. 130.

[13] Translations are from Alexander [Gottlieb] Baumgarten, *Metaphysics: A Critical Translation with Kant's Elucidations, Selected Notes, and Related Materials*, ed. Courtney D. Fugate and John Hymers (London: Bloomsbury, 2013).

Mendelssohn has said that this argument is "another way" from the previous one, but the last sentence seems to derive its exclusion of the impossibility of the necessary being, leaving only the necessity of its existence, from the former, so it is not clear that this is a completely independent version of the ontological argument. In any case, it seems to beg the question. If it is already agreed that a necessary being exists, then it follows that it is both completely determined and that its determination cannot come from anything else, for then it would be dependent on the latter and contingent as far as its own determinations are concerned. But, one would suppose, all that would follow from the *concept* of a completely determinate necessary being is that *if* such a thing exists then none of its determinations can depend on anything outside itself. But that is a merely analytic truth, just an analysis of the concept of a necessary being. It is not an argument.

We will see that Kant explicitly rejects an argument of this sort. But before we turn to Kant, we still have to consider Mendelssohn's version of a cosmological argument, which he claims to be both independent of and more readily accessible than the ontological argument (*JubA* 2:300, *PW*, p. 281). Mendelssohn's basic idea is that the representation "I think" purports to represent nothing but the act of thought itself, which obviously has to take place no matter what is thought, thus "it is not mere appearance, but rather a genuine reality"; and "I am" "can be inferred" from this "with certainty" because it adds nothing to the original representation other than the unquestionable supposition that an act is an accident of a substance. An "entire philosophical system" can "be erected on this fundamental principle without relying on any testimony of the external senses" (*JubA* 2:294, *PW*, p. 275), thus any argument from one's own existence to the existence of God will not transmit the contingency of sensory information to the existence of God, which would be fatal. But the argument is nevertheless an argument from a contingent existence to a necessary one. The argument turns on the principle of sufficient reason, "That everything must have a reason for its determination," which Mendelssohn takes to be "an absolutely necessary truth" (*JubA* 2:308, *PW*, p. 288). He equates the necessity of a reason or ground for any being with the ultimate existence of a necessary being as the ground, not by any mere slip of the tongue, but because a being that needed something other than itself to ground or explain its existence would not be a sufficient reason for what it in turn grounds or explains after all. Only "if the existence of no other subject is required in order to infer the predicate from the conditions of the existing subject" is the latter a necessary and sufficient ground. Yet, Mendelssohn also stresses, because the contingent being has the sufficient reason for its existence located in something other than itself, it may be relatively necessary, that is, necessary in relation to its ground, but is not itself absolutely necessary; it preserves its status as a contingent being, "necessary only under the condition that God might want to create and preserve" it (*JubA* 2:304, *PW*, p. 285). Mendelssohn then applies these considerations to the contingent but indubitable existence of oneself: "The second principle is this: Contingent beings must have the reason for their existence indirectly in a necessary being; I am a contingent being; therefore" a necessary being must exist as the sufficient condition of my own existence. "The minor premise is composed of two assertions: I exist; I am a contingent being. No skeptic, Descartes says, can doubt the truth of these two assertions; for whoever doubts exists and anyone who does not know everything with certainty is a contingent thing" (*JubA* 2:309, *PW*, p. 289).

This argument turns on one consideration that Descartes himself uses in his first proof of the existence of God, in the third *Meditation*, namely his knowledge of his own imperfection,[14] but it does not precisely follow the further progress of that argument, which is that in order to know my own imperfection I must have an idea of a perfect being and that because I can only have an idea with such (infinite) "objective" reality if it has a cause with an equal (infinite) degree of "formal" reality, my idea of God can only have been caused by the existence of God. But Descartes's principle that every degree of objective reality must have a cause in an equal degree of formal reality might itself be regarded as a form of the general principle of sufficient reason, and to that extent Mendelssohn's argument is Cartesian in spirit.[15] Mendelssohn does not follow Descartes in deriving an epistemological premise from the case of the *cogito*, namely the principle that everything that is clear and distinct must be true, which Descartes uses to undergird his own statement of the ontological argument in the fifth *Meditation*. Mendelssohn allows his versions of the ontological argument to stand on their own without additional epistemological accreditation.

The principle of sufficient reason is of course itself a fundamental object of Kantian critique: he will ultimately argue that it can be demonstrated only as a principle of the possibility of experience, not as a principle that can take us beyond experience. In this way he will undercut Mendelssohn's use of the principle in the argument from the *cogito* to the existence of God, although it would be a stretch to argue that his attack on the extra-experiential use of the principle is specifically aimed at Mendelssohn. It is aimed at the entire rationalist tradition. Before we turn to Kant, however, there is one last point in Mendelssohn's prize essay that I will here consider more fully than in the previous chapter, namely his critique of the teleological argument or argument from design. This is very similar to that which Kant will include both in the 1763 *Only Possible Basis* and in the 1781 *Critique of Pure Reason*, although here we must be dealing with a parallel between the views of the two philosophers rather than with an influence of either on the other, since Kant published the *Only Possible Basis* before he saw Mendelssohn's essay. Mendelssohn's way of putting the point in his essay is to argue that arguments from design offer "extremely probable conclusions" but "still lack a great deal for demonstrative certainty." He distinguishes three kinds of such argument, namely "proofs based upon the beauty and order in the visible parts of creation," "proofs based upon the beauty and order in the laws of motion," which explain behavior of visible parts of nature but are not themselves visible, and "proofs based upon the undeniable purposes of nature, in general, and, in particular, in ordinary and extraordinary natural events, among which the fates of certain states and even the events of individual persons are to be counted." He does not deny that we may make legitimate inferences about the causes of such kinds of beauty and

---

[14] Descartes puts this point by saying that I am self-evidently a finite being rather than an infinite being, so my own "formal reality" is not equal to and adequate to explain the infinite "objective reality" contained in my idea of God. See Descartes, *Meditations on First Philosophy*, Third Meditation, in *The Philosophical Writings of Descartes*, trans. John Cottingham, Robert Stoothof, and Dugald Murdoch (Cambridge: Cambridge University Press, 1984), vol. 2, pp. 28–31.

[15] Alexander Altmann traces Mendelssohn's simplification of the cosmological argument from the *cogito* to the influence of Wolff, *Metaphysica* §928ff, §942ff. See Altmann, *Moses Mendelssohns Frühschriften zur Metaphysik* (Tübingen: J.C.B. Mohr [Paul Siebeck], 1969), p. 310.

order, even in the last case, although Kant will devote considerable scrutiny to that sort of case in the *Only Possible Basis*. But Mendelssohn does say that in:

> What concerns beauty and order (not to mention the fact that it first has to be demonstrated that they are not necessary but contingent)...one can nevertheless infer from this only that there is a wise and benevolent cause of this order and beauty, not that this all-wise and all-benevolent cause has produced, created everything outside itself from nothing. Perhaps God found himself confronted with a chaos, as some of the ancients dreamed, into which he put order and beauty. Perhaps he merely prescribed orderly and harmonious laws to the disorderly movement to be found in this chaos. These objections can be answered, I admit, but not with the triumphant force with which one can defend a genuine demonstration.
>
> (*JubA* 2:312, *PW*, p. 292)

Such an objection was common property by the middle of the eighteenth century: not only was Kant to make the same sort of criticism in 1763, but Hume had done so in his *Dialogues concerning Natural Religion*, already drafted by 1751, although not published in English until 1779 and German in 1781 and thus not available to either Mendelssohn or Kant when they were making their criticisms of the teleological argument—although to be completely parallel to Hume, Mendelssohn should not have slipped from allowing a "wise and benevolent cause" of the order we observe in nature to an "all-wise and all-benevolent cause," since that is precisely the slide that Hume blocks. Nevertheless, Mendelssohn is clear enough that the teleological argument is not philosophically adequate, not part of the metaphysics that can attain the same level of certainty as mathematics, although, like Kant, he is respectful of such an argument as appealing and moving for ordinary people rather than philosophers. He continues that "These kinds of proof...possess far greater eloquence than the demonstration itself. By their liveliness they make a much greater impression upon the mind, awakening the soul to dynamic decisions and producing the practical conviction that should be our foremost purpose in contemplating divine properties" (*JubA* 2:313, *PW*, p. 293).

This remark is not a throw-away. It is an expression of Mendelssohn's early and enduring recognition that our sensible and emotional side is as important an aspect of our being as our rational side, as long as the deliverances of the former are compatible with the latter. It is in his aesthetics that Mendelssohn makes most clear the physical, perceptual, intellectual, and emotional complexity of the human response to the world, but that recognition is at work in his metaphysical philosophy of religion as well. We will subsequently see that in this regard Kant is closer to Mendelssohn when it comes to religion than in the case of aesthetics.

But that is all for later. For now, let us turn to Kant's critique of traditional philosophical or natural theology, first in his early writings through the *Only Possible Basis* and then in the *Critique*. In this examination, we can see how Kant criticized Mendelssohn. Then we can consider how Mendelssohn tried to respond to Kant in the *Morning Hours*.

## 3. Kant: From the *New Exposition* to the *Only Possible Basis*

In the Latin treatise entitled the *New Exposition of the First Principles of Metaphysical Cognition*, which earned him the *venia legendi* or the right to lecture at the university in Königsberg in September, 1755, Kant introduced both the critique of the ontological argument and the new argument for the existence of God as the ground of all possibility that he would expound more fully in the German book on *The Only Possible Basis for a Demonstration of the Existence of God* in 1763. The later work adds an extensive defense of a refined conception of teleological judgment from its blanket rejection by such opponents as Hobbes and Spinoza, which Kant will refine further, once transcendental idealism is in place, in the *Critique of the Power of Judgment* of 1790. Before that, the *Critique of Pure Reason* will continue the criticism of the ontological argument, supplemented by an argument that the other traditional arguments for the existence of God depend upon the ontological argument and thus fail with it. The *Critique* will precede Kant's restatement of the three traditional arguments with a criticism of an argument for God as the "ideal of pure reason" that is unnamed and directed against unnamed targets, but that undercuts both the argument offered by Baumgarten and Mendelssohn from the complete determination of the concept of God to his existence as well as Kant's own argument for the existence of God as the ground of the sum total of possibility. In this section, I will examine Kant's position in the works of 1755 and 1763, and also look at Mendelssohn's response to the latter work in the *Letters concerning the Latest Literature* in 1764. The next chapter will examine Kant's arguments in the *Critique of Pure Reason*, to which Mendelssohn attempts to respond in *Morning Hours*. Mendelssohn did not comment on Kant's account of teleological judgment in the *Only Possible Basis*, and he died four years before Kant published his critical revision of that account in the *Critique of the Power of Judgment*. So I will not discuss Kant's revised teleology here.[16]

The *New Exposition* presents the criticism of the ontological argument before presenting Kant's own alternative. The treatise begins by defining the concept of a "determining ground," technically an "antecedently" determining ground, as that which determines why a concept includes one predicate rather than its contrary (*ND*, Proposition IV, 1:391–2). A consequently determining ground would be a reason for accepting a proposition that is not what makes the proposition true in the first place, in other words a *ratio cognoscendi* that is not a *ratio essendi*. Kant then accepts what is essentially a version of the principle of sufficient reason, namely "Nothing is true without an [antecedently] determining ground," on the basis of the argument that "Every true proposition indicates that the subject is determinate in respect of a predicate," which requires the exclusion of the contrary of that predicate, which, Kant claims, will not occur "if no concept is present which conflicts with the opposite which is to be excluded." Thus "there is something in every truth which determines the truth of the proposition by excluding the opposite predicate," and this is its determining ground. Thus, Kant concludes that there is a determining ground for every truth (*ND*, Proposition V, 1:393). This would not be an adequate argument for the principle of sufficient reason, since what excludes the inclusion of one predicate in a concept is simply the inclusion of its contrary, not a further reason for the latter. But Kant rejects the ontological argument for a different reason, which does not depend

---

[16] But see my "Kant's Reformed Teleology," in Jeffrey McDonough, ed., *Teleology*, in *Oxford Philosophical Concepts* (New York: Oxford University Press, 2020), pp. 186–218.

upon the principle of sufficient reason. He starts with the ambiguous claim that "To say that something has the ground of its existence within itself is absurd": does this mean that a *thing* or the *concept* of a thing cannot contain the ground of the existence of the thing, or the concept of such a ground? However, Kant quickly makes clear that he is talking about concepts, and about the attempted inference from concept to existence. He allows that an internal contradiction in a *concept* makes it impossible to think of its object as existing, and thus a concept the opposite of which would be self-contradictory makes it necessary for us to *think* of its object as existing. But, he argues, we cannot go from this to an actual assertion of the existence of any object. Thus Kant argues as a "scholium" to this proposition against the claim that "God has the ground of his existence posited in Himself" by offering an argument that the *concept* of God cannot be the ground of the *existence* of God. Then comes Kant's first statement of his critique of the ontological argument, which was written years before Mendelssohn's first version of the ontological argument in his prize essay but applies to it too. Since this is the basis for so much of Kant's subsequent thought, it is worth quotation in full:

> I find, indeed, the view repeatedly expressed in the teachings of modern philosophers that God has the ground of his existence posited in Himself. I find myself unable to support this view. To these good men it seems, namely, somehow rather hard to deny that God, the ultimate and most complete principle both of grounds and of causes, should contain within Himself the ground of Himself. Thus they maintain that, since one may not assert that there is a ground of God which is external to Him, it follows that He contains concealed within Himself the ground of Himself. But there could scarcely be anything more remote from sound reason than this. For when, in a chain of grounds, one has arrived at the beginning, it is self-evident that one comes to a stop and that the questioning is brought to an end by the completeness of the answer.

Here Kant is rejecting the kind of argument that Mendelssohn made when the latter claimed that since the existence of God is not self-contradictory but also cannot be a contingent existence grounded in something outside of himself, it must be a necessary existence grounded within himself. Kant's initial explanation of what makes this "remote from sound reason" may not be clear. But he goes on to make his fundamental claim that it is of no avail to infer whatever you want from a concept, including the existence or even the necessary existence of its object, unless you already assume that the object and not just the concept exists; in other words, any argument from mere concept to actual existence is going to be question-begging:

> Of course, I know that appeal is made to the concept itself of God; and the claim is made that the existence of God is determined by that concept. It can, however, easily be seen that this happens ideally, not really. Form for yourself the concept of some being or other in which there is a totality of reality. It must be conceded that, given this concept, existence has also to be attributed to this being. And, accordingly, the argument proceeds as follows: if all realities, without distinction of degree, are united in a certain being, then that being exists. But if all those realities are only conceived as united together, then the existence of that being is also only an existence in ideas. The view that we are discussing ought, therefore, rather to be formulated as follows: in framing the concept of a certain Being, which we call God, we have determined that concept in such a fashion that existence is included in it. If, then, the concept which we have conceived in advance is true, then it is true also that God exists. I have said these things, indeed, for the sake of those who support the Cartesian argument.

> (*ND*, Proposition VI, Scholum, 1:394–5)

The crucial statements are, first, that no matter what you put into a concept, this is "ideal" not "real," true in or of our ideas but not, just because of what we have included in our concept, true of any object beyond our ideas, and, second, that inferences from a concept, even inferences to existence, are of no avail unless it is antecedently assumed that the concept "is true," that is, has an object. You cannot prove that a concept has an object except by assuming that the concept has an object; thus, any such argument is question-begging.

Kant's argument here does not turn on what is often thought to be the key but controversial premise of his later critique of the ontological argument, namely, that existence is not a predicate. Here Kant allows that existence might be a proper predicate in a *concept*, but that this proves nothing because the inclusion of any predicate in a concept proves nothing unless it is already assumed that the concept has an object. This should be kept in mind when considering Kant's subsequent claim that existence is not a real predicate, which he in any case qualifies to allow that existence can grammatically occupy the position of a predicate in a well-formed sentence. The later claim that existence is not a real predicate should be considered not as the premise of Kant's argument but as its conclusion. The argument itself should be considered an epistemological or maybe a semantic argument, but not a syntactic one: unpacking the contents of a concept cannot yield knowledge about any object unless it is already assumed that the concept has an object. In Kant's terminology, the inclusion of any predicate in a concept cannot be a *consequent* determining ground or *ratio cognoscendi* for a claim about an *object* because the existence of an object for the concept would already have to be assumed for the concept to give any knowledge about an object. For that reason as well the inclusion of any predicate in a concept cannot by itself point to the existence of an *antecedent* determining ground for that predicate because it would again have to be assumed in addition that the concept has an object for there to be any truth about objects rather than mere ideas that needs an antecedent determining ground. The point remains throughout the simple one that a concept cannot yield knowledge of anything except its own contents in the absence of the additional assumption that it has an object. So the concept itself cannot prove that.[17]

Throughout this paragraph, Kant speaks solely of the *concept* of God and never, as did Descartes, of the *essence* of God.[18] He is himself assuming that the ontological argument is supposed to begin from a concept of God, and simply pointing out that concepts are nothing but ideas; ideas not in the objective, Platonic sense of extramental forms but in a subjective, Lockean sense: mental states of subjects. He has no

---

[17] Thus Allen Wood's objection that neither Kant nor modern logicians such as Frege and Russell ever succeeded in arguing that existence is not a predicate is moot. Wood cites more favorably Caterus's objection to Descartes that "Even if it is granted that the very name of a being of highest perfection implies its existence, it still does not follow that this existence itself is something actual *in rerum natura*, but only that the concept of existence is inseparably conjoined with the concept of a highest being"; Allen W. Wood, *Kant's Rational Theology* (Ithaca: Cornell University Press, 1978), pp. 110–12, citing from *First Set of Objections* (in *Philosophical Writings*, vol. 2, p. 72; Wood used an earlier translation). But this is precisely Kant's real point, which does not turn on the claim that existence is not a predicate.

[18] See Descartes, *Meditations on First Philosophy*, Fifth Meditation; in *Philosophical Writings*, vol. 2, p. 46.

reservations about this identification, and once concepts are equated with ideas it is self-evident that concepts themselves can prove nothing but connections among ideas, not the existence of anything beyond ideas. The critique of the ontological argument is just a corollary of the "new way of ideas," as the modern way of thinking of concepts was named by the opponents of Locke.[19] Kant's argument is not an argument within traditional logic or metaphysics; it is the paradigmatic argument of modern epistemology.

Kant makes the premise of his argument clear in his conclusion to the *Only Possible Basis*, in which he argues that there are really only two possible a priori arguments for the existence of God: the ontological argument and the alternative that he is introducing. The way in which he presents his critique of the former makes plain that he can understand the Cartesian notion of essence only from the point of view of his own mentalistic conception of concepts.[20] In the so-called Cartesian proof:

[O]ne begins by thinking the concept of a possible thing, in which one imagines that all true perfection is united. It is now assumed that existence is also a perfection of things. The existence of a Most Perfect Being is thus inferred from the possibility of such a Being. One could draw the same inference from the concept of anything which was merely imagined to be the most perfect thing of its kind. One could, for example, infer the existence of a most perfect world from the mere fact that such a world can be thought.[21] Without entering into an elaborate refutation of this proof, which is to be found in other philosophers, I would merely refer the reader to the explanation given at the beginning of this work, namely, that existence is not a predicate at all, and therefore not a predicate of perfection either. Hence, it is in no wise possible to infer from a definition, which contains an arbitrary combination of various predicates used to constitute the concept of some possible thing, the existence of this thing, nor, consequently, the existence of God either. (*OPB*, 2:156–7)

As before, the claim that existence is not a predicate to which Kant refers is not so much a premise of his critique as it is a description of it. The basic critique is just that once essence is understood as a concept, and likewise possibility is understood as a concept and definition is likewise understood as of a concept, and a concept itself is understood as mental, it is clear that you can think anything you want without the mere fact of your thinking it making anything true except that you are thinking it. Kant's exposition makes it clear that a concept is a subject's way or act of thinking, and this makes his point self-evident in a way that talk about essence might not.

---

[19] See John W. Yolton, *John Locke and the Way of Ideas* (Oxford: Clarendon Press, 1956). It might be noted here that Leibniz's conception of complete concepts existing in the mind of God is also objectivist rather than subjectivist, and a fundamental difference between him and Locke. Insofar as Leibniz's version of the ontological argument used this conception of concepts, it would of course be question-begging too, presupposing that God exists before proving that he does.

[20] It may be noted here that in his objections to Descartes's *Meditations*, Thomas Hobbes had retained the use of the term "essence" but equated essence with a "mental image"; see *Third Set of Objections*, in Descartes, *Philosophical Writings*, vol. 2, p. 136.

[21] This is a classical objection to the inference from God's perfection to his existence, raised by Pierre Gassendi in the *Fifth Set of Objections* to the *Meditations* (Descartes, *Philosophical Writings*, vol. 2, pp. 225–6, but originally raised in the eleventh century by an "otherwise unknown Benedictine monk named Gaunilo" against Anselm's version of the argument; see Thomas Williams, "Gaunilo," in *Encyclopedia of Philosophy*, second edition, ed. Donald M. Borchert, 10 vols. (Farmington Hills: Thomson-Gale, 2006), vol. 4, pp. 33–4.

This simple point might be obscured by the terminology with which Kant dresses up his critique in the *Only Possible Basis*, where he argues, as his summary has reminded us, that "Existence is not a predicate or a determination of a thing" and that existence is rather something that is "posited" of a concept rather than included within it. But Kant's basic point remains the same as in the *New Exposition* and in the conclusion to *Only Possible Basis*. This is immediately evident in his explication of the opening claim that "Existence is not a predicate." Kant writes:

> This proposition seems strange and absurd, but it is indubitably certain. Take any subject you please, for example, Julius Caesar. Draw up a list of all the predicates which may be thought to belong to him, not excepting even those of space and time. You will quickly see that he can either exist with all these determinations, or not exist at all. The Being who gave existence to the world and to our hero within that world could know every single one of those predicates without exception, and yet still be able to regard him as a merely possible thing which, in the absence of that Being's decision to create him, would not actually exist. Who can deny that millions of things which do not actually exist are merely possible from the point of view of all the predicates they would contain if they were to exist. (*OPB*, 2:72)

The argument does not begin with an assumption that existence is not a predicate. It simply reminds us that no matter how fully you specify the contents of a concept it remains a separate question whether any object answers to that concept, or whether the concept has an object, and infers that existence is not a predicate from that observation. In fact, what Kant is doing is subtly showing his Leibnizo-Wolffian predecessors and contemporaries, including Baumgarten and Mendelssohn, that they cannot have their cake and eat it too; that is, they cannot treat existence as an ordinary predicate that can be included within concepts and yet model God as choosing from among concepts of possible worlds and their inhabitants which (the best, of course) should exist. Concepts, even completely determined ones, have to leave the question of existence open; complete determination does not after all imply existence, even if existence implies complete determination. Insofar as that is a general claim about concepts, it has to apply to the concept of God as well.

Kant makes it clear that this is not an argument about grammar, because in ordinary usage the term "existence" (*Dasein*) can be put in the predicate-place of a sentence without confusion. But he says that in this case what is going on beneath the surface of the utterance is that existence is being predicated *of* the concept rather than being included *in* the concept. Existence is not a predicate to be included in a concept; rather, a concept can itself be predicated of something that exists if there is reason beyond the concept itself to do so:

> Nonetheless, the expression "existence" is used as a predicate. And, indeed, this can be done safely and without troublesome errors, provided that one does not insist on deriving existence from merely possible concepts, as one is accustomed to doing when one wants to prove absolutely necessary existence. For then one seeks in vain among the predicates of such a possible being; existence is certainly not to be found among them. But when existence occurs as a predicate in common speech, it is a predicate not so much of the thing itself as of the thought which one has of the thing. For example: existence belongs to the sea-unicorn (or narwhal) but not to the land-unicorn. This simply means: the presentation of a sea-unicorn (or narwhal) is an empirical concept; in other words, it is the representation of an existent thing. (*OPB*, 2:72)

The existence of narwhals is not settled by conceptual analysis; it is settled by empirical observation, which allows us to predicate the concept *narwhal* of an object actually observed. From this, Kant infers that in no case can a concept be predicated of an object on the basis of anything merely included within the concept itself. If a concept cannot be predicated of an object on the basis of observation, as the concept of God could not be, then something other than observation will be required, but it will still be something other than the mere concept itself.

Kant makes the same point with the term "positing" (*Position oder Setzung*), or more precisely, with a distinction between "relative" and "absolute" positing. Relative positing is merely another name for the inclusion of a predicate within a concept: "something can be thought merely relatively, or, to express the matter better, it can be thought merely as the relation (*respectus logicus*) of something as a characteristic mark of a thing." To relatively posit a predicate is merely to say that it is included in a concept, even to relatively posit omnipotence of God is merely to say that the concept of omnipotence is included in the concept of God: "If I say: 'God is omnipotent' all that is being thought is the logical relation between God and omnipotence, for the latter is a characteristic mark of the former. Nothing further is being posited here." But absolutely positing a concept is saying that the concept, with all the marks or predicates that are included within it, is true of some object, or that some object exists for the concept: "If what is considered is not merely this relation" (of a predicate to a subject-concept) "but the thing posited in and for itself, then this being is the same as existence." Thus to absolutely posit is to posit that there is an object for a concept, which cannot be done on the basis of the concept itself and whatever is relatively posited within it. Even in the case of God, then, "Whether God is, that is to say, whether God is posited absolutely or exists, is not contained in the original assertion at all," that is, not contained within the concept of God or the explication of what it relatively posits. There is no new argument here, turning on some antecedent notion of positing or contrast between relative and absolute positing; rather, the contrast between relative and absolute positing is being introduced as a new description of what Kant has already argued, from the very contrast between concepts and objects as well as from the rationalists' own conception of creation as God's choice from among possible worlds which to bring into existence. Kant drives home this polemical point in his continuation of the present passage, in which he says that when God utters "His almighty '*Let there be*' over a possible world, He does not grant any new determinations to the whole which is represented in His understanding. He adds no new predicate to it. Rather, He posits the series of things absolutely and unconditionally, and posits it with all its predicates..." (*OPB*, 2:73-4). In Kant's view, the rationalists had actually accepted his distinction between concept and object all along, and were simply never entitled to the ontological argument.[22]

---

[22] Kant's point was anticipated by Gassendi in his critique of Descartes's version of the ontological argument. Gassendi wrote: "you place existence among the divine perfections... In fact, however, existence is not a perfection in God or in anything else; it is that without which no perfection can be present.... its existence is that in virtue of which both the thing itself and its perfections are existent, and that without which we cannot say that the thing possesses the perfections or that the perfections are possessed by it... if

On this basis, Kant also rejects the argument in Baumgarten that Mendelssohn would adopt as his second version of the ontological argument in the prize essay. First Kant blows off Wolff: "*Wolff's* definition of existence, that it is a completion of possibility, is obviously very indeterminate. If one does not already know in advance what can be thought about possibility in a thing, one is not going to learn it from *Wolff's* definition" (*OPB*, 2:76).[23] That is, if by treating existence as the "completion" or "complement" to possibility Wolff just means that an assertion of existence adds something to everything that is contained within a concept, namely the assertion that the possibility represented by the concept actually obtains, then there is nothing in his view to oppose Kant's own. Kant then continues:

*Baumgarten* introduces the concept of thoroughgoing internal determination, and maintains that it is this which is more in existence than in mere possibility, for it completes that which is left indeterminate by the predicates inhering in or issuing from the essence. But we have already seen that the difference between a real thing and a merely possible thing never lies in the connection of that thing with all the predicates which can be thought in it. Furthermore, the proposition that a possible thing, regarded as such, is indeterminate with respect to many of its predicates, could, if taken literally, lead to serious error. For such indeterminacy is forbidden by the law of excluded middle which maintains that there is no intermediate between any two predicates which contradict each other. It is for example impossible that a man should not have a certain stature, position in time, age, location in space, and so forth.

But, to rephrase Kant's next sentence, this kind of determinacy is to be found as much in the concept of a possible thing as it is in that of an existent thing; the difference between the possible and the actual is not that the concept of the latter is more determinate than the concept of the former, but that the concept of the latter has an actual object and that of the former does not. Of course Kant agrees that the concept of something's essential properties does not determine all its possible properties; the concept *man*, for example, determines certain things about an organism, but not, say, whether it is bald or not. But that is just a feature of general concepts: they are not and cannot be fully determinate in the way that the thought—for Kant, ultimately an intuition—of an individual can and must be. But that remains true whether we are talking about actual or merely possible individuals: we are not conceiving of an individual if we are not conceiving of something fully determinate, yet any mere conception of an individual, no matter how complete, leaves open whether such an individual actually exists. The actual existence of an individual implies the complete determinacy of its concept, but the complete determinacy of a concept does not imply that it actually has an object. Once again, anyone who believes that God has chosen the best of all possible worlds from among fully determinate conceptions of alternative possible worlds has no choice but to accept that—the rationalist cannot accept both that God chooses from among completely determinate concepts of individuals and yet that the complete determinacy of a concept by itself entails existence.

---

a thing lacks existence, we do not say it is imperfect, or deprived of a perfection, but say instead that it is nothing at all" (*Fifth Set of Objections*, in Descartes, *Philosophical Writings*, vol. 2, pp. 224–5.

[23] The reference is to Wolff, *Philosophia prima* (1730), §174, or *Vernünfftige Gedanken von Gott, der Welt, und der Seele des Menschen* ("German Metaphysics," 1720), §14.

Kant's exposition of his critique of the ontological argument in the *Only Possible Basis* thus merely adds some terminology to his original critique in the *New Exposition* and drives home his argument that the rationalists cannot maintain their picture of creation unless they accept his distinction between concept and extra-conceptual existence. So let us now look at Kant's own new, positive argument for the existence of God, which is intended to be consistent with his claim that the existence of God can never be derived from the mere concept of Him.

Kant's new argument is that the possibility not of God but of anything and everything else depends upon the existence, indeed the necessary existence, of God. It thus differs from a cosmological argument because it starts from the possibility rather than the actuality of anything, and from an ontological argument because it does not start from the concept of God. The premises of the argument are that "Possibility is only definable in terms of there not being a conflict between certain combined concepts; thus the concept of possibility is the product of a comparison," and that "in every comparison the things which are to be compared must be available for comparison, and where nothing at all is given there is no room for either comparison or, corresponding to it, for the concept of possibility." From these premises Kant infers that "nothing can be conceived as possible unless whatever is real in every possible concept exists and indeed exists absolutely necessarily." Kant further infers that this necessarily existing reality must be unitary because if it were divided then each part of it would be limited in some contingent way, contrary to the supposition of its necessity. "It is, accordingly, a requirement for their absolute necessity that they should exist without limitation, in other words, that they should constitute an Infinite Being." Thus "a God, and only one God," is "the absolutely necessary principle of all possibility" (*ND*, Proposition VII, 1:395). The existence of God is not derived from his own concept but from any possibility whatsoever. Kant's argument is thus different from the ontological argument but also from any cosmological argument, such as Mendelssohn's, which derives the necessary existence of God from any contingent *existence* or actuality; Kant's derives it from any *possibility*.

The final steps of the argument are thus that the ground of all possibility must be infinite in the sense that it is the ground of *all* possibility and that it must be unitary because if it were divided, each part of it would be contingent rather than necessary. The first step of the argument is that all possibility presupposes something real or actual, which we might explicate by saying that it is only in relation to something actually determinate that we can even conceive any particular possibility; for example, that we can conceive of some particular color as possible, or conceive it as possible that some particular object have some particular color, requires at least that objects or colors be actual. Kant's argument is not Berkeley's "master" argument in the *Principles of Human Knowledge*, where he argues for his idealism that we cannot conceive of anything existing unconceived because after all *we* are conceiving of that which is supposed to be unconceived.[24] So it is not open to the objection to Berkeley's argument that we cannot conceive of something existing unconceived

---

[24] George Berkeley, *A Treatise concerning the Principles of Human Knowledge* (1710), §23; in *The Works of George Berkeley, Bishop of Cloyne*, ed. A.A. Luce and T.E. Jessop (London: Thomas Nelson and Sons, 1949), vol. 2, p. 50.

without conceiving of this possibility, but that this does not entail that something might nevertheless exist unconceived without our being able to conceive that. We might grant Kant's first premise. The problem in his argument seems rather to lie with his second premise, the claim that any possibility presupposes not just some actuality or being but some *necessary* being. This conclusion seems to depend upon a modal fallacy, that of inferring from a proposition like "Necessarily, any possibility presupposes some actuality" to one like "Any possibility presupposes some necessary actuality." Such an inference is not allowed by the rules of modal logic. The coherence of the rest of Kant's argument would become moot.

That Kant mishandles modal logic seems to be confirmed by his restatement of his new argument in the *Only Possible Basis*. Here he begins by observing that "Anything which is self-contradictory is internally impossible" (*OPB*, 2:77). Nobody will deny that, nor think that very much follows from it, and it neither takes us nor requires us to go beyond the realm of concepts: a concept that is internally contradictory cannot have an object, but it is only possible that a concept that avoids internal contradiction does have an object. That is what Kant will later call merely logical possibility, not real possibility. His stronger claim comes when he states that:

> It is clear from what has now been adduced that possibility disappears not only when an internal contradiction, as the logical element of impossibility, is present, but also when there exists no material element, no *datum*, to be thought. For then nothing is given which can be thought. But everything possible is something which can be thought, and the logical relation pertains to it in accordance with the principle of contradiction.
>
> Now, if all existence is cancelled, then nothing is posited absolutely, nothing at all is given, there is no material element for anything which can be thought; all possibility completely disappears. (*OPB*, 2:78)

Again, the thought seems to be that something is possible only relative to something that is actual. Indeed, even an assertion of mere logical possibility, that is, mere non-self-contradiction, requires that some concept be given which, as a matter of fact, does not contain any contradictory predicates. Kant then seems to concede that "it cannot be said that the negation of all existence involves an internal contradiction"; it seems that the possibility that nothing at all exist does not violate mere logic, that is, the law of non-contradiction. But, Kant next says, "to say that there is a possibility and yet nothing real at all is self-contradictory. For if nothing exists, then nothing which could be thought is given either, and we contradict ourselves if we still wish to say that something is possible." That is, even the possibility of non-existence depends upon some existence, so we cannot say that complete non-existence is possible after all. This might be to confuse "It is possible that nothing is possible," which is non-committal about the existence of anything (except the one asserting it), with "It is necessary that nothing is possible," which would seem harder to assert without assuming some necessity and therefore contradicting oneself, since necessity surely entails possibility. But perhaps the clearer confusion lies in Kant's next stab at the argument, in which he says that "That, by means of which all possibility whatever is cancelled, is absolutely impossible, for the two expressions are impossible ... Thus, when all existence is denied, then all possibility is cancelled as well. As a consequence, it is absolutely impossible that nothing at all should exist," which will in turn entail that something necessarily exists, or that a necessary being exists (*OPB*, 2:79). Here Kant seems to confuse the *definition* of impossibility as the cancellation of possibility (of the possibility of that which is impossible, that is) with the *substantive impossibility* of the cancellation of possibility. That is, instead of confining himself to the definition of the impossibility (of some *p*) as the non-possibility that not-*p*, Kant asserts that non-possibility (of unspecified *p*) is itself impossible. Thus whatever it takes to ground possibility, namely a being that unites all reality in itself, is necessary.

Perhaps it would be simplest to say that Kant might be entitled to his premise that any possibility presupposes some reality, but that to get from there to the necessary existence of some (or all) reality we have to presuppose that some possibility is itself necessary: We cannot validly infer from "Necessarily, any possibility presupposes some reality" that "Some reality necessarily exists," but we can validly infer from "Necessarily, any possibility presupposes some reality" *and* "Some possibility necessarily exists" that "Some reality necessarily exists." So Kant is trying to motivate the acceptance of "Some possibility necessarily exists." But he seems to be doing that just by playing with the definition of impossibility. That does not seem persuasive.[25]

Be that as it may, at this stage of his career Kant is content with his argument, and goes on from there to argue that once the reality of the concept of a necessary being has been established as the ground of any possibility, then it can further be demonstrated that the necessary being is unique, simple, immutable and eternal, a mind, and therefore not merely "a god" (*OPB* 2:89) but God.

Returning to the Cartesian proof in his concluding summary of his argument, Kant briefly adds a point that will become much more prominent in the *Critique of Pure Reason*, namely that the other traditional arguments for the existence of God in some way depend upon the ontological argument. Here he considers what he will call in the *Critique* and what we now, following him, call the cosmological argument, but what he here calls "the proof employing the rules of causal inference." This is the argument that the existence of anything contingent implies the existence of something necessary, which as we have seen Mendelssohn deploys beginning from the contingent existence of oneself. But Kant takes it up from Wolff. He admits "that the argument is valid as far as the proposition: *If something exists, then something else also exists which does not itself depend on any other thing*," and as he takes for granted that something exists, perhaps more than one thing, he also admits "that the existence of some one or several things, which are not themselves the effects of something else, is well established." He is also willing to allow the further proposition that "this independent thing"—all of sudden, there is just one—"is *absolutely necessary*," although this inference "has to employ the principle of sufficient reason, which is still contested." Kant does not explain how the inference depends on the principle of sufficient reason, but presumably the thought is, as in Mendelssohn, that as long as

---

[25] F.E. England regarded Kant's argument as his own version of an ontological argument, but it would seem better to reserve that term for the traditional argument from the essence or concept of God. In any case, England then said that "Kant's case here stands or falls with his doctrine of the absolutely necessary ground of contingent reality," which would make the argument a form of the cosmological rather than ontological argument. See F.E. England, *Kant's Concept of God: A Critical Exposition of its Metaphysical Development together with a Translation of the* Nova Delucidatio (London: Macmillan, 1929), p. 55.

a chain of reasoning reaches only a cause that still needs to be explained by something other than itself, the chain is not complete or sufficient; only a being that is absolutely necessary, or depends on nothing other than itself for its existence, can be a complete and sufficient reason for everything else. But the real problem with the causal proof, Kant now maintains, is not with the step from contingent existence to absolutely necessary existence, but from that to the "qualities of supreme perfection and unity." He claims that necessary existence could be inferred from supreme perfection "that in which all reality is, exists necessarily"—but that supreme perfection cannot be inferred solely from necessary existence (all quotes from *OPB*, 2:157–8). Of course, the ontological argument starts from the concept of a supremely perfect being, so it could make the desired connection between supreme perfection and necessary being, and supplement the causal argument—if only it were sound, which, however, Kant has argued it is not: the *concept* of supreme perfection is not enough to entail existence because no concept is. Kant's own argument, however, that God is the ground of all possibility, is supposed to establish that he is supremely perfect, since he is the ground of all possibility because he contains all positive reality.

Kant next turns to what he here calls the cosmological argument, although it is what he will later call the "physico-theological" argument, that is, the argument from design; in the *Only Possible Basis* Kant uses the term "physico-theology" for teleology in general but not specifically for the argument for the existence of God from the evidence of design in nature (e.g., *OPB*, 2:116, 123). Kant does not explicitly argue that this so-called cosmological argument, i.e., the later physico-theological argument, depends on the ontological argument in the same way that what he here calls the causal argument, i.e., the later cosmological argument, does, but he could, for his point is precisely that it does not suffice to prove the existence of a supremely perfect being, and an additional proof is needed for that. That will be the role that he assigns to the doomed ontological argument in the *Critique of Pure Reason*, which will in turn doom both arguments that depend on it. Here Kant just concludes that "either no strict proof of the existence of God is possible at all, or the proof must be based on the argument we have adduced above" (*OPB*, 2:162), namely his own argument from possibility to the necessary existence of God.

But before we get to the *Critique*, let us pause over Kant's consideration in the *Only Possible Basis* whether the existence of God can be "inferred *a posteriori* from the unity perceived in the essences of things" (*OPB*, 2:93), his general description of any argument from design. This discussion is as interesting for what it tells us about Kant's eventual qualified defense of teleological judgment in the third *Critique* as for the question of possible proofs of the existence of God, and also includes a restatement of his model for the mechanical genesis of the solar system from his 1755 *Universal Natural History and Theory of the Heavens*. Much of this material lies beyond the purview of the present study, but it is worth noting that in the course of this discussion Kant distinguishes between three ways in which there might seem to be "unity," which he here equates with "adaptiveness and natural harmony," in nature. There might be adaptive consequences in the very possibilities of things, in laws of nature that are not inherent in the very possibilities of things, or as consequences of the particular selection and arrangement of objects with which God institutes the creation (*OPB*, 2:96). He argues that while traditional "physico-theology regards all the perfection, harmony, and beauty of nature as contingent and as an arrangement instituted by wisdom," that is, by God's wise and benevolent choice, it is surely more philosophical to suppose that "many of these things issue with necessary unity from the most essential rules of nature" (*OPB*, 2:118), that is, from the very possibilities of things that are grounded in God. That is, we do not have to think of God as first creating a world of particular objects and then imposing perfection, harmony, and beauty upon them in a second act; since we have to think of God as the ground of all possibility, we can think of him as having established a set of possibilities with desirable consequences from the outset. Kant expresses this point by saying that "Unity is derived from a Wise Being, but not through His wisdom" (*OPB*, 2:119). The usefulness of this "revised method of physico-theology" (*OPB*, 2:123) is that even with our interest in the usefulness or advantageousness of nature to ourselves, it will focus our research on the "necessary unity of nature," for example the basic structure of both inorganic matter and organic beings, rather than on merely "*contingent* connections of the world" (*OPB*, 2:126). In spite of this "revised method of physico-theology," however, Kant is careful not to overemphasize the value of an argument *from* evidence of order in the world *to* the existence of God. His claim is that the revised method of physico-theology follows from the argument that God is the ground of all possibility, not that an argument for the existence of God follows from evidence of design. In light of Kant's later classification of arguments for the existence of God (and Mendelssohn's usage as well), Kant's presentation of his position might be confusing, because although he later calls an argument from apparent design to the existence of God the "physico-theological" argument and calls what he is here calling "physico-theology" just "teleology," in the *Only Possible Basis* he calls an argument *from* apparent design *to* the existence of God a "cosmological" proof.

Kant's rejection of an argument from apparent adaptiveness in nature to God's wisdom would seem to be a rejection of a fundamental tenet of Leibnizianism, namely that by his will God chooses the best alternative from among the possibilities offered by his intellect. This is an argument that Mendelssohn will defend in *Morning Hours*. Nevertheless, what Kant has to say about such a proof is entirely consistent with what Mendelssohn was saying about it in his prize essay at the same time that Kant was publishing the *Only Possible Basis*, and with what Kant himself will later say about the physico-theological proof in the *Critique of Pure Reason*:

[I]n spite of all its excellence, this mode of proof will never be capable of mathematical certainty or precision. It will never establish more than the existence of some incomprehensibly great Author of the totality which presents itself to our senses. It will never be able to establish the existence of the most perfect of all possible beings.

This is because of the *restrictive* application of the principle of sufficient reason upon which Kant insists, even conceding the truth of the principle in general: "we cannot infer the existence of more or greater properties in the cause than what we find necessary in order to understand the degree and constitution of the effects arising from that cause—assuming, that is, that the only reason we have for supposing that this cause exists is that afforded us by the effects" (*OPB*, 2:160). Nevertheless, Kant adds:

If... one is looking for accessibility to sound common sense, vividness of impression, beauty, and persuasiveness in relation to man's moral motives, then the advantage must be conceded to the cosmological proof [that is, here, the argument from design]. It is doubtless more important, while also convincing sound understanding, to inspire man with noble feelings, which are richly productive of noble actions, than to instruct him with carefully weighed syllogisms, so that the demands of a subtler speculation are satisfied. (*OPB*, 2:161)

Kant could not have been influenced by Mendelssohn's prize essay while writing the *Only Possible Basis*, but like Mendelssohn he recognizes the persuasive force of the argument from design for sensible as well as rational creatures like ourselves. To be sure, the positions of the two philosophers are not identical: Mendelssohn recognizes the rational value of the ontological and cosmological arguments and the empirical, psychological value of the argument from design; Kant rejects those two arguments and replaces them with his own argument from possibility to necessary existence, but also recognizes the empirical value of the argument from design. Nevertheless, in this way both philosophers are attempting to make a place for both the rational and the empirical in their philosophical theology, while recognizing that empirical considerations alone can never suffice to establish the existence of a perfect and necessary being.

## 4. Mendelssohn's Response to the *Only Possible Basis*

As previously mentioned, Mendelssohn reviewed Kant's book in four of the *Letters concerning the latest Literature* in April, 1764 (more precisely, two letters each in two parts). He devoted as many pages in the *Letters* to only a few other works—one, the poems of Frederick the Great (*JubA* 5.1:187-199) and another, a new translation of Milton's *Paradise Lost* (*JubA* 5.1:390-407)—so this alone suggests the importance he attached to Kant's work. Yet he was not moved by it either to surrender the Baumgartian version of the ontological argument that he advocated in his prize essay or to accept Kant's new argument from possibility to actuality. Mendelssohn devotes the two parts of the first letter to Kant's critique of the ontological argument and his alternative. He begins by recognizing Kant's attempt to turn Leibniz's idea of God's choice of the best of all possible worlds against the ontological argument: according to Mendelssohn, Kant says that "Existence is not a predicate or determination of any thing, for God can conceive of a merely possible thing in all of its individual determinations that it could have in accordance with its possible relations to other things and yet it could still be not actual but merely possible." Rather, "existence is the absolute positing [*Position*] of a thing, and distinguishes itself thereby from any predicate, which as such is always posited merely relative to another thing." This sounds like an accurate report of Kant, but notice that Mendelssohn either unwittingly or subtly excludes God from Kant's distinction between complete determination and actual existence, leaving the door open to his own argument that in the case of God, but only in that case, complete determination does imply actuality, since the concept of God is completely determined as the being possessing all perfections, including existence. Mendelssohn also puts Kant's point in slightly different terms from Kant's own by saying that "logical being is very different from real [*eigentlichen*] being. The former merely expresses the relation of a predicate to a subject, whether the subject exists or not; the latter by contrast does not express a relationship but posits [*setzt*] the whole thing itself" (*Letters concerning the Latest Literature*, No. 280, part 1, 26 April 1764, *JubA* 5.1.603). Kant had allowed that an existential assertion could be understood as expressing a relation, namely the relation of the whole subject-concept with all its predicates to something that actually exists, but this was his attempt to accommodate the deep structure of thought to the surface structure of language, and failing to notice it does not compromise Mendelssohn's report. He accurately enough reports Kant's treatment of concepts—except, at least implicitly, the concept of God—as expressions of mere possibility within which existence cannot be contained but to which existence must be added: "In mere possibility the thing [*Sache*] itself does not exist, but there are only posited mere relations of something to something in accordance with the law of contradiction, and it remains that existence is not really any predicate of any thing" (*JubA* 5.1.604).

But Mendelssohn subtly twists Kant's argument with his next restatement. He says that "The merely possible is for us humans nothing more than a representation of our understanding," thereby associating Kant's argument more closely with the kind of Berkeleian argument earlier mentioned, which Kant had not intended. Mendelssohn thereby subjectivizes possibility more explicitly than Kant has done, that is, makes it something mental, something existing in our own minds. Thus a possibility becomes a conjunction of properties that *we* "consider as an inseparable whole," that is "our subject," and that we "*posit absolutely in a logical sense* when we would represent the object," and an "*absolute positing* [*Setzung*] in the logical sense must also take place in the case of merely possible things." "Absolute logical positing [*Position*]" or the positing of the possibility is still to be contrasted with the "*absolute positing of the thing*" itself (*JubA* 5.1.604), the assertion of its existence, and Mendelssohn is not denying Kant's claim that the existence of any thing cannot be derived directly from its concept. But by equating possibilities with concepts or representations in our own minds, he is preparing the way for a different route from possibilities to the existence of God than Kant's, namely from possibility to the actuality of our own minds to the necessary existence of God, as in his own version of the cosmological argument.

Mendelssohn does not go down this different route immediately. The first objection that he makes is that although there is a "shimmer of truth" in what he takes to be Kant's definition of truth (*Definition* at 5.1.604, *Erklärung* at 5.1.605), it is still "so weak and so enveloped in darkness that it is difficult to perceive it correctly." It is clear enough that existence is not supposed to be a "predicate of the thing [*Sache*] but something that pertains to the whole thing [*Ding*]," but what that addendum is supposed to be, Mendelssohn claims, is still not clear. And he claims that what he now explicitly calls the "Baumgartian definition" of existence, even though it is "only a nominal definition, is the clearest and closest to the truth, although it has the flaw of being applicable only to the human manner of thought," and this is that "existence is...the thoroughgoing inner determination of that in a thing which is left undetermined through its essence or the properties flowing from that" (*JubA* 5.1.605), that is, the complete determination of all of the both essential and accidental properties of a thing. However, Mendelssohn does not acknowledge that Kant has argued precisely that the Leibnizo-Wolffian-Baumgartian model of creation as choice among possible worlds allows, indeed requires, that concepts of *possible* objects still be fully determinate, thus that although existence implies complete determinacy, by the rationalists' own lights complete determinacy cannot imply existence. So there is no successful criticism of Kant here.

However, there is a subtle criticism of Kant in Mendelssohn's next comment. He does not fasten on what I have claimed to be weaknesses in modal logic in Kant's argument. He does say this:

But [Kant's] entire proof seems to come down only to this: that we humans could not think anything, and could perceive neither agreement nor contradiction among our representations, if we had first not received the representations themselves from real things. The inner possibility of things is for us nothing more than the agreement of two representations that we have. These representations are original impressions [*Abdrücke*] of real objects. If there are no real objects, then we also cannot have any representations. If we have no representations, then neither agreement nor contradiction among them can take place. If this does not take place, then there is also no internal possibility. No, that would be a leap in reasoning: all that follows is that in that case we would not perceive internal possibility. (*JubA* 5.1.606)

Mendelssohn takes Kant's argument to be that there have to be outer objects in order *for us* to have *representations* of qualities and thereby of possibilities, and protests that it is a leap to conclude that there must *be* outer objects in order for there to *be* possibilities as contrasted to our representations of them. This takes Kant's argument to be intended as a refutation of idealism, which it is not, although as we will see in Chapter 5, the question of idealism would become an issue between Mendelssohn and Kant beginning in 1770. Kant's new argument in *Only Possible Basis* was not intended to be an argument about the conditions of our representation of possibility—a proto-transcendental argument—but an argument that the existence of a necessary being is the condition of the existence of any possibilities *tout court*. That Mendelssohn takes Kant to be inferring from our *representations* of possibility to external *objects* further explains why, in the following letter (No. 280, conclusion, 3 May 1764), he claims that Kant has not succeeded in showing that the condition of possibility is a *single* "final real ground of all *other* possibility" (*JubA* 5.1.607): of course if Kant were just thinking that we have to get *representations* of possible qualities from external objects, he would have no immediate reason to deny that we get *different* representations of qualities from *different* external objects. But that is not the argument that Kant was making at all.

But Mendelssohn's misinterpretation of Kant was hardly accidental. For having introduced into the interpretation of Kant's argument the assumption that *we* do in fact *represent* possibilities and have to begin any argument for God or anything else from our own representations of possibility, he could have argued that the first thing that the representation of possibility proves is the existence of *oneself*, as a representer of possibility, and then argued that the most natural way to prove the existence of God is to argue that his existence is the necessary condition of our own—and this is precisely what Mendelssohn *did* argue in his prize essay. In other words, though without saying so, Mendelssohn seems to be interpreting Kant's argument in such a way as to make his own proof of the existence of God seem more inviting than Kant's.

Perhaps that is why he ultimately still feels secure in defending this proof two decades later in the *Morning Hours*, even when, as we will see, Kant has given up on his own new proof. Or maybe the fact that Kant had to surrender his new proof convinced Mendelssohn that he had been right to stick by his own version of the cosmological argument, from the contingent existence of the self to the necessary existence of God, all along.

Before we turn to the *Critique of Pure Reason* and the *Morning Hours*, however, a brief comment on the second pair of letters (*Letters concerning the Latest Literature*, Letter 281, parts 1 and 2, 3 and 10 May 1764, JubA 5.1.609–16) is called for. Mendelssohn is generally receptive to Kant's revised method of physico-theology, and agrees that it is both better science and better religion to think that God achieves as many of his intentions as possible naturally, through the uniform operation of natural laws, rather than supernaturally, by intervening in their operation (5.1.611). He notices Kant's own concern that "many operations in nature," among them "the generation of plants and animals," "cannot be explained by simple laws of nature," or "mechanical rules" (5.1.612). Mendelssohn does ask whether Kant "has not thrown his entire system overboard with this remark," the system "through which he rightly grounds the cognition of the wisdom of God on the connection of effects and causes in nature" (5.1.613). The problem of how organic life can fit in to a unitary science of nature would continue to obsess Kant into the third *Critique* and to the end of his life, when he was still trying to comprehend the possibility of a genuine science of organic nature in the uncompleted *Opus postumum*.[26] Mendelssohn's challenge sounds as if it could have been a spur to Kant's continued concern with this issue, but Mendelssohn did not return to this issue in later writings, nor did Kant ever mention Mendelssohn's name in connection with it, so there is no evidence for assigning this remark much responsibility for Kant's lifelong recurrence to the problem of the organic.

That being said, let us now turn to the further development of Kant's thought about proofs of the existence of God.

[26] On Kant's attempts to understand the nature of organic life up through the *Opus postumum*, see Reinhard Löw, *Philosophie des Lebendigen* (Frankfurt am Main: Suhrkamp Verlag, 1980), pp. 154–90; Vittorio Mathieu, *Kants Opus postumum*, edited by Gerd Held (Frankfurt am Main: Vittorio Klostermann, 1989), pp. 212–24; Ernst-Otto Onnasch, "The Role of the Organism in the Transcendental Philosophy of Kant's *Opus postumum*," in Ina Goy and Eric Watkins, eds., *Kant's Theory of Biology* (Berlin and Boston: Walter de Gruyter & Co., 2014), pp. 239–55; and Ina Goy, *Kants Theorie der Biologie: Ein Kommentar, eine Lesart, eine historische Einordnung* (Berlin and Boston: Walter de Gruyter & Co., 2017).

# 3
# Proofs of the Existence of God in the *Critique of Pure Reason* and *Morning Hours*

## 1. Kant: *Critique of Pure Reason*

In the Preface to the second edition of the *Critique of Pure Reason*, Kant famously says that he has "had to deny **knowledge** in order to make room for **faith**." That is, he has argued that there can be no theoretical or "speculative" proof of the existence of God, human freedom, or human immortality, but at the same time no theoretical disproof of any of these either, and that leaves room for belief in them on practical grounds. As he says, he "cannot even **assume God, freedom, and immortality** for the sake of the necessary practical use of my reason unless I simultaneously **deprive** speculative reason of its pretension to extravagant insights" (*CPuR*, B xxix–xxx). Our concern in this chapter is just with arguments for the existence of God. Regarding that, this passage tells us that Kant's thought in the *Critique* is divided into two main parts, the criticism of theoretical or speculative arguments for the existence of God and the adumbration of the practical argument for the rationality of belief in his existence, although the latter will be more fully developed in the second *Critique*, the *Critique of Practical Reason* published in 1788. The latter work was completed in 1787, thus in the year following Mendelssohn's death, and although Mendelssohn's name is not mentioned in it, the debate over the basis of the rationality of belief in the existence of God that was taking place between Mendelssohn and Friedrich Heinrich Jacobi at the time of Mendelssohn's death must have been one of the spurs for Kant's continued elaboration of his conception of belief founded in practical rather than theoretical reason: as "What Is Orientation in Thinking?," published the year before Kant wrote the second *Critique*, clearly shows, Kant conceived that as a middle way between Mendelssohn's continued adherence to theoretical arguments for the existence of God and Jacobi's post-Tertullian and proto-Kierkegaardian leap of faith into belief in God without benefit of rational argument at all.

In addition to the division of the approach to arguments for the existence of God in the first *Critique* into two main parts—the critique of theoretical arguments for that existence and the proposal of a practical argument—the critique of theoretical arguments is itself divided into two parts. These are, first, a restatement of the critique of the traditional arguments already provided in the *Only Possible Basis*, now labeled the ontological, cosmological, and physico-theological instead of onto-logical, causal, and cosmological arguments, but also a criticism of the premise of the new argument that Kant himself had put forth in the *New Exposition* and the *Only Possible Basis* as well as of the argument from the complete determinacy of the concept of God to his existence that Baumgarten and Mendelssohn had offered. Kant prefaces his repetition of his previous criticism with this new criticism, so we will consider that first.

Like all but a few scrupulous philosophers, Kant does not seem to have liked admitting that he had changed his mind, and does not say that he is criticizing his own previous argument. He does not in fact directly address the kinds of modal problems that I have attempted to suggest, nor does he directly address Mendelssohn's account of the argument, whether that was just a misinterpretation or a subtle way for Mendelssohn to shine favorable light on his own cosmological argument for the existence of God. Kant does set up his critique in a way that could make it appear to be a critique solely of the argument that Mendelssohn took over from Baumgarten, based on the idea that the complete determination of the concept of an individual suffices to establish its existence. But the criticism that Kant offers undercuts his own argument as much as the Baumgarten-Mendelssohn one, and seems to have been intended to do so; for Kant never repeats that argument, and his rejection of theoretical proofs of the existence of God is a blanket objection, leaving no hole for his own previous argument to squeeze through.

Kant's critique of theoretical arguments for the existence of God is part of the Transcendental Dialectic of the *Critique of Pure Reason*, in which he undermines all of the speculative arguments of traditional metaphysics. After an introductory "book" identifying the ideas of pure reason and explaining how they are derived from the legitimate inferential functions of theoretical reason through the premise that "when the conditioned is given, then so is the whole series of conditions... which is itself unconditioned, also given" (A 307–8/B 364), which expresses the natural ambitions of human reason but exceeds the limits of what can be presented and confirmed by human sensibility, the second book of the Dialectic is divided into three chapters.[1] The first, the Paralogisms of Pure Reason, is devoted to undermining traditional arguments for the immortality of the human soul, which Kant subsumes under the rubric of "rational psychology"; belief in human immortality, Kant will argue, can only be rationalized on practical grounds. We will discuss the debate between Kant and Mendelssohn on immortality in Chapter 4. The second chapter of the second book of the Dialectic, the Antinomy of Pure Reason, tackles a number of issues in "rational cosmology," including whether or not the world is infinitely extended and divided and whether it is a contingent existent dependent upon a necessary being (which discussion might well have been saved for the third chapter),[2] but is also where Kant demonstrates the

---

[1] On Kant's derivation of the ideas of pure reason from the ordinary functions of reason, see Marcus Willaschek, *Kant on the Sources of Metaphysics* (Cambridge: Cambridge University Press, 2018).

[2] Early drafts of the Transcendental Dialectic show that Kant originally intended to discuss all of its issues in a single chapter of antinomies, thus that the division into three chapters was a late change; the inclusion of the fourth antinomy in the Antinomy chapter in spite of the fact that Kant addresses it in his critique of the cosmological argument in the next chapter is obviously a hold-over from this original plan. See R 4757, 17:703–5, *Notes and Fragments*, pp. 184–6, in which Kant shows that in 1775–6, he already had his earlier argument for the existence of God as the ground of all possibility in his sights; R 4759, 17:708–11,

insufficiency of theoretical arguments both for and against the reality of human freedom and a necessary being, leaving those to be affirmed only on practical grounds. Finally, theoretical arguments for the existence of God are properly saved for the third chapter of the second book of the Dialectic, with the practical argument in behalf of the rationality of belief in God reserved for the Canon of Pure Reason in the Transcendental Doctrine of Method, the second and concluding main division of the whole *Critique of Pure Reason*. Kant entitles the chapter on the theoretical arguments for the existence of God "The Ideal of Pure Reason." He explains this title in a brief introductory section: "ideas" of pure reason "contain a certain completeness that no possible empirical cognition ever achieves," but an "ideal" of pure reason is an idea of completeness "not merely *in concreto* but *in individuo*, i.e., as an individual thing which is determinable, or even determined, through the idea alone" (A 568/B 596). The thought of all possible perfections, which of course we cannot derive from mere experience, would be an idea of pure reason; but the thought of a single entity that possesses all possible perfections would be an ideal of pure reason. That is, of course, the thought of God, so the thought of God is not merely an idea of pure reason but an ideal of pure reason. Kant makes the ultimate practical goal of his argument clear following this explanation, when he adds that "human reason contains not only ideas but also ideals, which do not, to be sure, have a creative power like the **Platonic** idea, but still have **practical** power (as regulative principles) grounding the possibility of the perfection of certain **actions**" (A 569/B 597). In speaking of the (or a) Platonic idea as having a creative power, he must be thinking in terms of a Neo-Platonic conception of such an idea, in which particulars actually emanate from the idea, and he certainly will hold no such theory; in referring to a practical ideal as a regulative principle he must be thinking not merely of the moral law, which is itself singular but applies to indefinitely many actions, but also of the moral goal of a realm of ends, which is indeed a complete individual. But all this is just a promissory note at this point in Kant's exposition.

Kant then criticizes the assertion of the existence of a "transcendental ideal" or *prototypon transcendentale* in the second section of the chapter. He begins with the Baumgartian conception of determination, which he expounds in the following way. A *concept* is made determinate by choosing between every predicate that might be included in it and its contradictorily opposed predicates; by "might be included" I mean that, for example, the choice between "reproduces asexually" and "reproduces sexually" has to be made for any concept of an organism, but it does not have to be made for things that do not reproduce at all, such as rocks or tires. "Every **thing**, however, as to its possibility, further stands under the principle of **thoroughgoing determination**; according to which, among **all possible** predicates of things, insofar as they are compared with their opposites, one must apply to it" (A 571–2/B 599/ 600); that is, in order to specify completely the concept of an individual, whether actual or merely possible, we would have to choose one from all possible pairs of

---

*Notes and Fragments*, pp. 187–9; and R 4849, 18:5–8, *Notes and Fragments*, pp. 192–4. For discussion of these texts, see "The Unity of Reason: Pure Reason as Practical Reason in Kant's Early Conception of the Transcendental Dialectic," in Guyer, *Kant on Freedom, Law, and Happiness* (Cambridge: Cambridge University Press, 2000), pp. 60–95.

opposed predicates, not just from a predetermined subset of them. Thus, to determine the character of an individual, we have to determine whether it is a substance or not, if a substance whether it is a finite substance or not, if a finite substance whether it is spiritual or physical (assuming those are contradictorily opposed), if a physical substance whether it is inorganic or organic, if organic whether it reproduces sexually or asexually, if asexually whether by buds or spores, and so on, and on, and on, until the conception of the thing is differentiated from that of any other possible thing. So, as Kant says, the thoroughgoing determination of a thing "considers every thing... in relation to **the whole of possibility**, as the sum total of all predicates of things in general; and by presupposing that as a condition a priori, it represents every thing as deriving its own possibility from the share it has in that whole of possibility" (A 572/B 600). The "transcendental presupposition" of the "complete concept" of any thing is that "of the material **of all possibility**, which is supposed to contain a priori the data for the **particular** possibility of every thing" (A 573/B 601).

So far Kant has not criticized what is a presupposition not only of the Baumgartian-Mendelssohnian conception of the determination of concepts of particulars but also of the Leibnizian conception of complete concepts of particulars,[3] as well as of his own earlier argument for the existence of God. Nor has he yet restated that argument. In his next moves, he comes close to doing the latter. First he states that the idea of the "**sum total of all possibility**" "becomes the concept of an individual object that is thoroughly determined merely through the idea, and then must be called an **ideal** of pure reason" (A 573-4/B 601-2). This might be regarded as an analytical truth, a mere matter of definition, simply saying that insofar as we think of all possibility as comprising a "sum total" we are thinking of it as if it constituted a single object. This object would not obviously be God. However, Kant now moves to the concept of God in a way reminiscent of his original argument. He further explains that possibilities are sometimes represented through "a being," that is, through the affirmation of a predicate, but sometimes as a "non-being," that is, through the negation of a predicate (A 574/B 602). That makes it possible to conceive of the sum total of possibilities as "transcendental substratum," "an entire storehouse of material from which all possible predicates can be taken," which is nothing other than the idea of an "All of reality (*omnitudo realitatis*)" (A 575-6/B 603-4). That is, any possibility can be reached from a sum total of *positive* qualities plus the act of negation. Negations of predicates, in turn, can be considered "nothing but **limits**, which they could not be called unless they were grounded in the unlimited (All)."

So far, we are still in the realm of the logic of concepts, not of theology. But we can think of the argument from these considerations to the idea of God as being completed by the natural thought that a being that has all but only *positive* predicates cannot be identical to any being *in* the world, which is always characterized by both affirmations and negations, or even to the world itself, of which the latter is also true. Such a being must be distinct from every particular object, and can only be the ground of them and the world they comprise. Kant writes:

---

[3] See for example Leibniz, *Discourse on Metaphysics*, §13; in *Philosophical Papers and Letters*, ed. Loemker, pp. 310-11, or *Philosophical Essays*, ed. Ariew and Garber, pp. 44-6.

All manifoldness of things is only so many different ways of limiting the concept of the highest reality, which is their common substratum, just as all figures are possible ways of limiting infinite space. Hence the object of reason's ideal, which is to be found only in reason, is also called the **original being** (*ens originarium*); because it has nothing above itself it is called the **highest being** (*ens summum*), and because everything else, as conditioned, stands under it, it is called the **being of all beings** (*ens entium*). (A 578–9/B 606–7)

While ordinary possibilities, or actual objects, might antecedently be thought of as if they were carved out of the sum total of possibilities, once the sum total of possibilities is thought of as consisting only of positive predicates, it becomes different than any other possibility, and can be conceived of as God. "Rather, the highest reality would ground the possibility of all things as a **ground** and not as a **sum total**" (A 579/B 607).

This comes close to the argument of Baumgarten and Mendelssohn: the concept of God is the concept of the sum total of all positive predicates, or perfections, as such this concept is completely determinate, and as completely determinate it entails the existence of its object. But it also shares a premise with Kant's argument from 1755 and 1763, namely, that *there is such a thing as the sum total of possibilities*, which has to be grounded in the necessary existence of God, but which is distinct from the sum of *positive* possibilities that constitute the concept of God himself. And it is this assumption, which is common to both arguments, rather than the further steps in either argument, that Kant now questions. For what Kant now says is that "It is self-evident that with this aim—namely, solely that of representing the necessary thoroughgoing determination of things—reason does not presuppose the existence of a being conforming to the ideal, but only the idea of such a being" (A 577–8/B 605–6). Even more bluntly, he continues the passage quoted in the previous paragraph by stating that "all of this does not signify the objective relation of an actual object to other things, but only that of an **idea** to **concepts**, and as to the existence of a being of such preeminent excellence it leaves us in complete ignorance" (A 578–9/B 606–7). Kant states that "if we pursue this idea so far as to hypostatize it, then we will be able to determine the original being through the mere concept of the highest reality as a being that is singular, simple, all-sufficient, eternal, etc., in a word, we will be able to determine it in its unconditioned completeness through all its predications," which is the move of the Baumgarten-Mendelssohn argument, but then launches the criticism that applies to his own earlier argument as well as the Baumgarten-Mendelssohn one, namely that this use of the transcendental idea of the sum total of either possibilities or positive realities:

> would already be overstepping the boundaries of its vocation and its permissibility. For on it, as the **concept** of all reality, reason only grounded the thoroughgoing determination of things in general, without demanding that this reality should be given objectively, and itself constitute a thing. This latter is a mere fiction, through which we encompass and realize the manifold of our idea in an ideal, as a particular being; for this we have no warrant, not even for directly assuming the possibility of such a hypothesis... (A 580/B 608).

In other words, we are never actually given the sum total of either of all possibilities or of all positive predicates or realities; those are just ideas, indeed, just *our* idea, as Mendelssohn's review of the *Only Possible Basis* had in fact suggested. Actually forming a complete conception of all possibilities would be a necessary condition for completely determining the concept of any finite individual, and forming a complete conception of all positive predicates would be the necessary condition for a complete concept of God, both of which are natural aims of human reason; but in neither case are we entitled to think that we could actually complete such a task, so we cannot infer the existence of God as its ground from a complete conception of the sum total of all possibilities or of all positive realities.

Kant's point here is not his objection to the ontological argument that we should never confuse the existence of a concept with the existence of a thing, no matter how much we include in the content of the concept. It is rather the separate criticism that the idea of the complete determination of the concept of *any* individual object, contingent or necessary, finite or infinite, is only ever a regulative principle that we can approach but never complete, so of course the idea of the complete sum of possibilities from which the determination of the concept of the individual is drawn, by affirmation and negation, can be only a regulative principle or ideal, never something that is completely given. Kant allows that we can form our representations of the particular figures of objects in space "as different ways of limiting infinite space," and that we might thus be tempted to suppose that we can form concepts of objects in general by "limiting the concept of the highest reality." But he holds that it is only a "natural illusion" for us to transfer the idea of limiting space to the idea of limiting reality in general. For "in fact no other objects except those of sense can be given to us, and they can be given nowhere except in the context of a possible experience; consequently, nothing is an object **for us** unless it presupposes the sum total of all *empirical* reality as condition of its possibility." This is why it is an illusion to "regard as a principle that must hold of all things in general that which properly holds only of those which are given as objects of our senses" (A 582/B 610, italics added). That is, we are just not entitled to carry over a procedure that we can perform within our experience—that of carving out or constructing objects within space- to a realm that we do not experience. Fair enough. In fact, Kant could have gone further, and argued on his own premises that we are never actually given infinite space in its entirety, only the possibility of indefinitely extending our experience of space, so that the idea that even within experience we carve out objects from the sum total of spatial possibility is also an illusion. Perhaps Kant does not say this because he is somewhat confused about the case of space itself, and does say in the Transcendental Aesthetic that "Space is represented as an infinite **given** magnitude" (B 40). But in fact, Kant's ground for saying this is only that any particular space can be represented as part of a larger space (A 25/B 39), which does not imply that we are ever actually given a complete representation of infinite space. In any case, Kant's general position is that we can never actually complete an infinite synthesis. That should apply to the case of the synthesis of an infinitude of possibilities or realities as well as to that of an infinitude of spaces or places.[4]

---

[4] For a fuller version of the argument in this paragraph, see my "The Infinite Given Magnitude and Other Myths about Space and Time," in Ohad Nachtomy and Reed Winegar, eds., *Infinity in Early Modern Philosophy* (Cham, Switzerland: Springer, 2018), pp. 181–204.

Although he could have made this further point, Kant is content to rest his case on his general distinction between representations and objects. He thereby tacitly accepts Mendelssohn's criticism of his original argument from possibility to its ground, which was that the only *immediate* ground that possibility needs is our own representation of it. But by making that criticism, Mendelssohn was in fact undercutting the ground for his own resistance to Kant's criticism of the ontological argument, which basically makes the same point. So let us now see how Kant restates that criticism and all that rests on it in the *Critique of Pure Reason*.

Kant's further exposition is somewhat confusing, because he begins Section Three of Chapter Three of the "Ideal of Pure Reason" with what looks like an outright *endorsement* of the *cosmological* argument. He states that "the natural course taken by every human reason, even the most common, although not everyone perseveres in it," is simply to presuppose "the immovable rock of the absolutely necessary" to make sure that "no room is left over for any further **Why?**" That is, to suppose that "If something, no matter what, exists, then it must also be conceded that something exists **necessarily**. For the contingent exists only under the condition of something else as its cause, and from this the same inference holds further all the way to a cause not existing contingently and therefore necessarily without condition" (A 584/B 612). The immediate problem that Kant raises for this "natural" tendency of thought is that it needs to "look around" for an *informative* concept of this necessary being, that is, a positive concept of it rather than the merely negative concept that it is, well, not contingent. Then he says that "among all concepts of possible things the concept of a being having the highest reality would be best suited to the concept of an unconditionally necessary being" (A 586/B 614). Kant continues that "It cannot be disputed that this concept has a certain cogency if it is a matter of making **decisions**, that is, if the existence of some necessary being is already conceded, and if one agrees that one must take sides on where one is to place it, for then one can make no more suitable choice" (A 587/B 615). This could make it sound as if the argument from contingent to necessary existence is acceptable, and only needs to be supplemented with the idea that the necessary being is also the being with the highest reality, the "All without limits," that is, the perfect being, God. In other words, it looks as if the first cogent argument needs to be supplemented with a second, the *converse* of the traditional ontological argument, that is, an argument that the necessarily existing being is also the perfect being rather than that the perfect being necessarily exists.

However, Kant next restates his by-now standard criticism of the ontological argument, then argues that the cosmological argument needs the ontological argument to make the transition from necessary being to perfect being but that its dependence on the ontological argument, which purports to prove necessary existence, renders the cosmological argument entirely otiose and leaves it entirely dependent upon the ontological argument, which is in fact invalid (and then makes a similar claim about the physico-theological argument as well). This seems puzzling in light of the apparent acceptance of the first phase of the cosmological argument as "natural." What seems missing is an argument that this initial phase is not in fact sound. However, Kant has already provided that argument in the fourth Antinomy, or at least an argument that we cannot make a cognitively sound inference from contingent being to necessary being *within* the limits of *experience* and can only *think* but not *know* that such a being obtains beyond experience, among things in themselves. He does not repeat that argument in the present chapter, but he must be presupposing it. His apparent revival of the first phase of the cosmological argument must be intended to ease the eventual transition to the *practical* argument for the existence of God—note its use of the word "decisions"—but Kant's complete position about the *theoretical* value of the cosmological argument must be that it is doubly dependent upon the ontological argument—dependent on it not only for the proof that the necessary being is also the perfect being but likewise for the proof that a necessary being exists in the first place—and since the ontological argument is completely unsound, so must be the cosmological argument. Kant does not want to destroy every vestige of its naturalness, since its form must be kept alive for the practical argument for the rationality of belief in God, but he does want to gut it of all theoretical value.

In light of this background, we must first consider Kant's repeated critique of the ontological argument; then show how the fourth Antinomy has already sufficiently weakened the cosmological argument to render it doubly and not just singly dependent upon the ontological argument; and then look at Kant's repeated critique of the physico-theological argument.

(i) *The ontological argument.* The *Critique of Pure Reason* is famous for the statement that "**Being** is obviously not a real predicate" (A 598/B 626), and defenders of the ontological argument ever since have tried to show that this is not so obvious after all. But, as earlier, Kant is using this terminology only to redescribe a conclusion already reached on what he takes to be more intuitive grounds, as he makes clear when he says that "I would have hoped to annihilate this over-subtle argumentation," that is, the ontological argument itself, "without any digressions through a precise determination of the concept of existence, if I had not found that the illusion consisting in the confusion of a logical predicate with a real one (i.e., the determination of a thing) nearly precludes all instruction" (A 598/B 626). In other words, some are tempted to defend the ontological argument by the fact that ordinary language allows "existence" or "exists" to occupy the predicate-place in a grammatically acceptable utterance, and that tendency has to be countered by distinguishing between the surface grammar of a merely "logical" predicate and the deep structure of "real" predication. But, as before, the intuitive argument that you cannot simply prove that something exists by analyzing its concept but have to first show that the concept has an object, thus rendering any proof of existence from the concept circular, comes first.

Kant thus opens the section (Section 3) on the ontological argument by saying that "From the foregoing one easily sees that the concept of an absolutely necessary being is a pure concept of reason, i.e., a mere idea, the objective reality of which is far from being proved by the fact that reason needs it" (A 592/B 620), "objective reality" again being Kant's term for a concept having an object. Kant then states the fundamental objection to the ontological argument, not mentioning Descartes's *name* until the end of the section but using Descartes's *example* to make his target perfectly clear; and of course Mendelssohn had explicitly associated his own presentation of the ontological argument with that of Descartes:

If I cancel the predicate in an identical judgment and keep the subject, then a contradiction arises; hence I say that the former necessarily pertains to the latter. But if I cancel the subject together with the predicate, then no contradiction arises; for there **is no longer anything** that could be contradicted. To posit a triangle and cancel its three angles is contradictory; but to cancel the triangle together with its three angles is not a contradiction. It is exactly the same with the concept of an absolutely necessary being. If you cancel its existence, then you cancel the thing itself with all its predicates; where then is the contradiction supposed to come from? Outside it there is nothing that would contradict it, for the thing is not supposed to be externally necessary; and nothing internally either, for by cancelling the thing itself, you have at the same time cancelled everything internal. God is omnipotent; that is a necessary judgment. Omnipotence cannot be cancelled if you posit a divinity, i.e., an infinite being. But if you say, **God is not**, then neither omnipotence nor any other of his predicates is given; for they are all cancelled together with the subject, and in this thought not the least contradiction shows itself. (A 594–5/B 622–3)

The basic argument is just that once you have included certain predicates within a concept, then of course you cannot deny them of that same concept without contradiction; but a mere concept, and therefore nothing in a mere concept, ever forces you to assert that it has an object. You cannot deny that a triangle must have three angles, for that is included in the very definition of a triangle, as a tri-angle; but you can perfectly well deny that any triangles exist, at least until one is put before your eyes, in which case your hand is forced not by the concept but by experience (empirical intuition), or by your mind's eye (pure intuition). You can put whatever you want into a concept of God, you can put infinitude into it and from that infer omnipotence, or vice versa (as Mendelssohn did), you can put possessing all perfections into your concept, but that avails you nothing if all you have is a mere concept, not an object—and of course God cannot be put before your eyes, or even before pure intuition, the way a triangle can.

Kant next put his point in his language of analytic and synthetic judgment, although the point has already been made without this language. If you have included "the concept of existence, under whatever disguised name," then of course you can assert existence, but only as an "illusory victory," a "mere" or even "miserable tautology," or an "analytic proposition," in which case "with existence you add nothing to your thought of the thing; but then either the thought that is in you must be the thing itself," which would of course be a blasphemous account of God, "or else you have presupposed an existence as belonging to possibility, and then inferred that existence on this pretext from its inner possibility." Or, using Kant's term "positing," "you have already posited the thing with all its predicates in the concept of the subject *and assumed it to be actual*, and you only repeat that in the predicate" (A597/B 625, emphasis added). None of this depends upon antecedent acceptance of a technical distinction between analytic and synthetic propositions or of a technical concept of positing. It just depends upon recognizing the basic difference between what is contained in a concept and the separate question of whether the concept has an object or objective reality. If you accept that distinction—and Kant cannot imagine how you could not—then you cannot accept the ontological argument. The distinction between analytic and synthetic propositions or between merely thinking a concept and positing that it has an object can be regarded as defined on the basis of this distinction, not vice versa.

Likewise, Kant's claim that "**Being** is obviously not a real predicate" follows from his basic argument rather than serving as its premise. Earlier, Kant had tried to accommodate the surface structure of ordinary language, in which "exists" or "existence" is sometimes used as a grammatical predicate of a concept, by saying that in such cases the concept is really being predicated of something existent rather than existence being predicated of a concept. Here he takes a slightly different tack. He says that in its ordinary, "logical use it"—that is, the term "being"—is in fact not a predicate but a copula. "The proposition **God is omnipotent** contains two concepts that have their objects," that is, their *intended* objects, namely "God and omnipotence; the little word **is** is not a predicate in it, but only that which posits the predicate **in relation** to the subject." If in its ordinary use linking two concepts "is" is not a predicate, Kant then infers, in the case in which it is used without a trailing predicate, for example in the proposition "**God is**, or there is a God," well, it is still not a predicate, but rather just a verbal expression of the fact that "I add no new predicate to the concept of God, but only posit the subject in itself with all its predicates, and indeed posit the **object** in relation to my **concept**" (A 598-9/B 626-7)—which of course I cannot do on the basis of the concept itself, but must do on some other basis. "Is" or "exists" or "existence" is not a predicate of the concept in this case because it is never a predicate. If Kant were to return to his earlier analysis, he could now add to it that "is" is always a mere copula, in the case in which we say that some existing thing is an instance of some concept as in any other, and that as a copula expressing the relation between a concept and one of its marks "is" can be employed on the basis of the concept alone, but as a copula expressing the relation between the concept and an actual object it must be used on the basis of some independent knowledge of the object, whether by acquaintance as in sense-perception or otherwise, and not on the basis of the concept. But instead of elaborating this point thus, Kant instead returns to his basic argument with his homely example of a hundred possible dollars (*Thaler*): the difference between a hundred possible dollars and a hundred actual dollars is not that the concept of the latter has an additional predicate in contrast to the concept of the former, in which case the difference between them would be like the difference between the *concept* of a hundred dollars and the *concept* of a hundred and one dollars. The difference between them is that in one case you just have the idea of a hundred dollars and in the other case you actually have a hundred dollars in your pocket or your bank account. "[I]n my financial condition there is more with a hundred actual dollars than with the mere concept of them" (A 599/B 627). This is not an argument that depends upon the claim that being is not a real predicate; it is an example of Kant's basic distinction between concept and object, which can, if you like, be explicated with the treatment of "is" as always a mere copula, sometimes between concepts and sometimes between a concept and an object, but in the latter case never simply on the basis of the former case. Kant repeats the basic argument at the end of the section, finally naming his chief target: "Thus the famous ontological (Cartesian) proof of the existence of a highest being from concepts is only so much trouble and labor lost, and a human being can no more become richer in insight from mere ideas than a merchant could in resources if he wanted to improve his financial state by adding a few zeros to his cash balance" (A 602/B 631). The difference between mere ideas and objects remains, whether the latter be dollars or God.

(ii) *The cosmological argument.* Kant next argues that the cosmological argument depends on the ontological argument not just for its transition from necessary to perfect being but in fact for its proof of necessary being as well, and thus fails completely along with the ontological argument. Thus he says that "it is really only the ontological proof from mere concepts that contains all the force of proof in the so-called cosmological proof; and the supposed experience," of some object or other, whether any external object or just oneself, as in Mendelssohn's version, from which the cosmological argument is supposed to begin, "is quite superfluous—perhaps leading us only to the concept of a necessary being but, not so as to establish this concept in any determinate thing" (A 607/B 635).[5] This is puzzling in light of Kant's apparent openness to the "naturalness" of the cosmological argument in Section Two of the Ideal and also in light of his statement at the beginning of the present Section Five that the cosmological argument "was used only to provide more determinate acquaintance with something of which one was already convinced or persuaded on other grounds that it must exist, namely, the necessary being" (A 603/B 631). Such statements seemed to suggest that the argument from the contingent existence of anything to the necessary existence of something was sound, and that a further argument was necessary only to prove that the necessary being is also the perfect being, not just *ens necessarium* but *ens realissimum*. But if we keep in mind that Kant had already shown, at least to his own satisfaction, in the fourth Antinomy of the second chapter of the Transcendental Dialectic, that there could be no sound theoretical inference from contingent existence to necessary existence, then his procedure in the present section makes more sense: the "natural" acceptance of the first phase of the cosmological argument is in fact a "natural illusion," so the argument would really have to depend on the ontological argument for its proof of the necessary existence of God as well as for its proof that he is the *ens realissimum*. Without the ontological argument, it can prove nothing except again the obvious, that we have certain ideas.

So a quick review of the fourth Antinomy is in order.[6] Kant presents it as the conflict between the thesis that "To the world there belongs something that, either as a part of it or as its cause, is an absolutely necessary being" (A 452/B 480) and the antithesis that "There is no absolutely necessary being existing anywhere, either in the world or outside the world as its cause" (A 453/B 481). The argument for the thesis depends upon the use of the principle of sufficient reason and the assumption that the only truly sufficient reason for anything conditioned is something unconditioned—the underlying assumption questioned throughout the Transcendental Dialectic: "every conditioned that is given presupposes, in respect of its existence, a complete series of conditions up to the unconditioned, which alone is absolutely necessary" (A 452/B 480). Without an unconditioned, thus necessary existence, the chain of conditions for conditioned would never end, and there would never be a sufficient reason for anything conditioned after all—precisely what Mendelssohn asserted. Kant explicitly labels this the "**cosmological**" proof (A 456/B 484). The argument for the antithesis is that "a beginning that is unconditionally necessary, and hence without a cause...conflicts with the dynamic law of the determination of all appearances in

---

[5] For discussion of whether the ontological argument renders the cosmological argument completely otiose, see Wood, *Kant's Rational Theology*, pp. 123–30.

[6] For a critical account of the fourth Antinomy, see Jonathan Bennett, *Kant's Dialectic* (Cambridge: Cambridge University Press, 1974), pp. 240–3.

time" (A 453/B 481), that is, the principle of the Second Analogy of Experience, that "All alterations occur in accordance with the law of cause and effect" (B 232), thus that every event in time must have an antecedent cause in time—ad infinitum. Now, this entails that we can have no experience of an absolutely necessary being in time, as an uncaused cause, thus that the thesis's attempt to infer to the existence of an absolutely necessary being *as a part of the world* must fail. To this extent, the antithesis is true and the thesis false. However, it does not suffice to prove what the antithesis also claims, namely that there can exist no absolutely necessary being *outside the world*, or, technically, while it may suffice to prove that there can be no absolutely necessary *cause* outside the world, because the world includes everything in time and a cause is by definition an event in time, it does not suffice to prove that there cannot be an absolutely necessary *ground* of the world but outside the world. It leaves that possibility for the thesis open. But at the same time, since all genuine knowledge requires intuition as well as concept, and by this point in the argument of the *Critique* Kant is treating time not just as the form of inner sense but as the form of all intuition, outer intuition included, the impossibility of a temporal intuition of the unconditioned or absolutely necessary existence means the impossibility of knowledge of such a being. We can *conceive* it but not *know* it. The most we can say is that the existence of a necessary being outside the temporal domain of experience is *not impossible*:

> But here it is not at all the intent to prove the unconditionally necessary existence of any being, or even to ground the possibility of a merely intelligible condition of existence in the world of sense on it; rather, just as we limit reason so that it does not abandon the thread of the empirical conditions and stray into **transcendent** grounds of explanation which do not admit of any exhibition *in concreto*, so on the other side we limit the law of the merely empirical use of the understanding, so that it does not decide the possibility of things in general, **nor** declare the intelligible, even though it is not to be used by us in explaining appearances, **to be impossible.** (A 562/B 590)

But all of this is just to say that we can *think* of an unconditioned and absolutely necessary being as the ground of any and all conditioned existence—that is to say, think of it *as possible*—but we cannot know it to exist. The difference between mere concept and actual existence goes hand in hand with the difference between conceivability and knowledge. (At the same time, we cannot know that a necessary being outside of the series of appearances does *not* exist. That we cannot use the limits of sensibility to limit the *ideas* of reason was always as much a part of Kant's conception of the dialectic as that we cannot have *theoretical knowledge* from reason that outstrips the limits of sensibility; see, for example, ID, Section 5, 2:410-19).

With this in the background, we can better understand Kant's argument in Section Five of the Ideal of Pure Reason that the cosmological argument depends wholly and not just partly on the ontological argument, for Kant's claim in the Antinomy has been that the cosmological argument cannot prove more than the conceivability or possibility of an absolutely necessary existence. Kant's exposition begins with what is in fact Mendelssohn's version of the cosmological proof starting from my knowledge of my own existence, as presented in the prize essay:

> It goes as follows: If something exists, then an absolutely necessary being also has to exist. Now I myself, at least, exist, therefore an absolutely necessary being exists. The minor premise

contains an experience, the major premise an inference from an experience in general to the existence of something necessary. Thus the proof really starts from experience, so it is not carried out entirely a priori or ontologically; and because the object of all possible experience is called "world," it is therefore termed the **cosmological** proof. (A 604-5/B 632-3)

The argument seems to have the epistemological advantage of starting from experience, so that whatever follows from it will be accredited by experience. Then it attempts to proceed from its proof of necessary being to the further proof that this necessary being is the perfect being or *ens realissimum* by what is not so much the ontological proof as its converse, an argument that necessary existence implies perfect being rather than that perfection implies necessary existence:

> Now the proof further infers: The necessary being can be determined only in one single way, i.e., in regard to all possible predicates, it can be determined by only one of them, so consequently it must be **thoroughly** determined through its concept. Now only one single concept of a thing is possible that thoroughly determines the thing *a priori*, namely that of an *ens realissimum*: Thus the concept of the most real being is the only single one through which a necessary being can be thought, i.e., there necessarily exists a highest being. (A 605-6/B 633-4)

This argument is somewhat opaque: it is not clear where the premise that a necessary being can be determined only by a single predicate and therefore must be thoroughly determined by that predicate—a job for which only the predicate of *ens realissimum*, a being that contains all reality—is suitable, is coming from. In fact, Kant must be assuming a typical rationalist assumption, one that we saw at work in Mendelssohn, that a necessary being must be self-determined, because if it were determined by anything other than itself it would be dependent on that other and therefore contingent, and then equating being determined by multiple predicates with being determined by something outside itself and therefore with being contingent rather than necessary. But even if this equation is problematic, that is not the real problem with this completion of the cosmological argument. The problem is still that it cannot successfully take us outside of the circle of our ideas. Our idea of conditioned being takes us to the idea of unconditioned being, and our idea of unconditioned or necessary being takes us to the idea of perfect being or the *ens realissimum*. But as the Fourth Antinomy has already shown, all that is just conceiving of possibility, not actuality. That is why Kant now argues that the cosmological argument depends not on the *converse* of the ontological argument, that necessary being must be perfect being, but on the ontological argument itself, that perfect being must be necessary being. That purports to take us beyond the circle of our own ideas in a way that would apparently circumvent the limitation revealed by the fourth Antinomy. Of course, this refuge has already been shown to fail too.

The twist occurs in this passage:

> [T]he cosmological proof avails itself of... experience only to make a single step, namely to the existence of a necessary being in general. What this being might have in the way of properties, the empirical ground of proof cannot teach; rather, here reason says farewell to it entirely and turns its inquiry back to mere concepts: namely, to what kinds of properties in general an absolutely necessary being would have to have... Now reason believes it meets with these requisites solely and uniquely in the concept of a most real being, and so it infers: that it is the absolutely necessary being. But it is here that one presupposes that the concept of a being of the

highest reality completely suffices for the concept of an absolute necessity in existence, i.e., that from the former the latter may be inferred—a proposition the ontological proof asserted, which one thus assumes in the cosmological proof and takes as one's ground, though one had wanted to avoid it.... Thus it is really only the ontological proof from mere concepts that contains all the force of proof in the so-called cosmological proof; and the supposed experience is quite superfluous—perhaps leading us only to the concept of a necessary being, but not so as to establish this concept in any determinate being. (A 606–7/B 634–5)

The claim that the cosmological proof derives all its force from the ontological proof would make no sense if the cosmological proof had really established the existence of a necessary being and all that remained to be added was a proof that the necessary being is also a perfect being. But in fact the fourth Antinomy has shown, in different language, that the cosmological proof can only lead to the concept of a necessary being, not to knowledge of the existence of such a being. Nothing remains but to turn to the ontological proof not just for the equation of the necessary being with the *ens realissimum* but also for the proof that the latter necessarily exists. But that proof has already been shown to be a failure, so the cosmological proof cannot stand either on its own or together with the ontological argument. "Thus the second way that speculative reason takes in order to prove the existence of the highest being is not only deceptive like the first, but it even has this further blameable feature in it, that it commits an *ignoratio elenchi*, promising to put us on a new footpath, but after a little digression bringing us back to the old one, which for its sake we had left behind" (A 609/B 637).

(iii) *The physico-theological proof.* Finally, Kant claims that the physico-theological proof depends upon the cosmological proof, which however has been shown to depend on the failed ontological argument. The claim that the physico-theological proof depends upon the cosmological proof may seem surprising. The physico-theological proof appears to be that the design that we observe in the world, which certainly goes beyond what can be produced by human agency, must be produced by a greater than human agency, and that since any merely comparative measure of the greatness by which this agency exceeds human agency—such as "**very great**, or 'astonishing' or 'immeasurable power' and 'excellence'"—would be indeterminate, "only relative representations, through which the observer (of the world) compares the magnitude of the object with himself and his power to grasp it," the only alternative is to assign it unlimited reality: "Where it is a question of the magnitude (perfection) of a thing in general, there is no determinate concept except that which comprehends the whole of possible perfections, and only the All (*omnitudo*) of reality is thoroughly determinate in its concept" (A 628/B 656). One would think that the objection to such an argument would be that even if the only fully determinate concept of a greater than human power would have to be that of an *ens realissimum*, we still are not justified in claiming to know anything determinate about this agency, thus in claiming to know that it is an *ens realissimum* or *omnitudo*.

But that is not the objection that Kant makes. Instead, he presents the argument as turning on the *contingency* of the organization of the world, "the contingency of the form, but not of the matter, i.e., of substance, in the world ... that the things of the world would in themselves be unsuited for such an order and harmony in accordance with universal laws if they were not in **their substance** the product of a highest wisdom" (A 627/B 655). This could actually be read in a way consistent with Kant's "revised method of physico-theology" in the *Only Possible Basis*: according to Kant's argument there, the purposive organization of the things in the world will appear contingent if thought of as added on to the essence of such things, but it should be understood as inherent in the very set of possibilities for nature that God has grounded, and so the inference should be not to a God who imposes order and purposiveness on an antecedent set of possibilities or possible substances but to a God who creates possibilities or substances with order inherent in them. But Kant does not reprise or criticize that argument. Instead, he now simply interprets the physico-theological argument as another argument from contingent to necessary existence:

> After one has gotten as far as admiring the magnitude of the wisdom, power, etc., of the world's author, and cannot get any further, then one suddenly leaves this argument carried out on empirical grounds and goes back to the contingency that as inferred right at the beginning from the world's order and purposiveness. Now one proceeds from this contingency alone, solely through transcendental concepts, to the existence of something absolutely necessary, and then from the concept of the absolute necessity of the first cause to its thoroughly determinate or determining concept, namely that of an all-encompassing reality. Thus the physico-theological proof, stymied in its undertaking, suddenly jumps over to the cosmological proof, and... this is only a concealed ontological proof... (A 629/B 657)

And we know how the ontological proof fares. All of this is to say that although it initially looks as if we could prove the existence of a real being through the ontological proof but then have to turn to the ontological proof to fully specify the nature of this being as an *ens realissimum*, which will in turn make that being into necessary being, in fact the argument is just an inference from contingent to necessary existence, which cannot give us knowledge of such existence, so we have to turn to the ontological argument for all its force. In other words, the physico-theological argument turns out to be just another way of making the contingency of the existence of which we do have knowledge obvious, but it has no more ability than any other argument from contingency to get past the idea of a necessary being to the actuality of a necessary being. It has to rely on the ontological argument to do that, but the ontological argument cannot do that.

Kant's criticism of the physico-theological argument is not directed against Mendelssohn; as we saw in our discussion of the latter's prize essay, Mendelssohn also rejects the argument from design. The use of the concept of contingency in the presentation of the argument from design may instead go back to Wolff.[7] But in spite of this criticism, Kant maintains the earlier insistence of Mendelssohn as well himself that "This proof always deserves to be named with respect. It is the oldest, clearest, and the most appropriate to common human reason." In particular, Kant argues that

---

[7] See Christian Wolff, "On the method of demonstrating the existence of God from the order of nature," in *Marburg Leisure Hours* (1730), cited by Johann August Eberhard, *Preparation for Natural Theology* (1781), §28, trans. Courtney D. Fugate and John Hymers (London: Bloomsbury, 2016), pp. 27–8. Kant used this text for his lectures on rational theology, but since it was published only in 1781, it would not have been his source for his reconstruction of the physico-theological argument published in the same year. However, he could well have been directly familiar with Wolff's earlier presentation.

"It enlivens the study of nature, just as it gets its existence from this study and through it receives ever renewed force. It brings in ends and aims where they would not have been discovered by our observation itself, and extends our information about nature through the guiding thread of a particular unity whose principle is outside nature" (A 623/B 651). This anticipates the argument of the Appendix to the Transcendental Dialectic and the Critique of the Power of Teleological Judgment in the third *Critique*, although in both of those places Kant will stress that this idea is heuristic and regulative. But Kant's main point in the *Critique of Pure Reason* is that the idea of a highest being which "remains for the merely speculative use of reason a mere but nevertheless **faultless ideal**... whose objective reality cannot of course be proved" by the "whole of human cognition" may nevertheless be justified as part of a "moral theology that can make good this lack" (A 641/B 669). So let us conclude this study of Kant's attitude toward proofs of the existence of God in the first *Critique* with a brief account of its first presentation of Kant's moral theology, which would continue to occupy him for another decade and more, and which in the essay on "Orientation" he would insist upon as the fundamental difference between Mendelssohn and himself.

(iv) *Moral Theology*. Kant clearly regarded his moral theology as his crowning, positive contribution to philosophy: it occupies the place of honor in each of the three critiques and, as previously noted, he presents it as the fundamental difference between Mendelssohn and himself in "What Does it Mean to Orient Oneself in Thinking?," his public statement on the Mendelssohn-Jacobi dispute of 1785. As earlier suggested, Kant's moral theology would have given him good reason to reject Mendelssohn's characterization of him in *Morning Hours* as "all-crushing"; in Kant's own view, as expressed in the revised Preface for the second edition of the first *Critique*, he had limited knowledge, of the existence of God as well as of freedom and immortality, only in order to make room for faith or belief (*Glaube*) in these based on the demands of practical reason. Kant's most extensive expositions of his conception of rational belief were presented in the second and third critiques as well as in further work of the 1790s, such as his uncompleted drafts for another Prussian Academy essay competition, on the question of what progress metaphysics has made in Germany since the times of Leibniz and Wolff.[8] All this was to come after the death of Mendelssohn and Kant's reckoning with him in the "Orientation" essay, so it will not be discussed in detail in this book. Here a brief account of the preliminary version that Kant offered already in the first edition of the *Critique of Pure Reason*, the only one that Mendelssohn knew, will have to suffice.

The central argument of Kant's moral theology is that the existence of God is a necessary condition for the realizability of the highest good as the complete object of morality, that is, what morality commands us to attempt to achieve, so that since attempting to achieve what morality commands is rational only if we can *believe* it to be realizable, that is, possible, it must be rational for us to *believe* in the existence of

---

[8] These drafts are printed at 20:259–351, and translated by Peter Heath in Kant, *Theoretical Philosophy after 1781*, edited by Henry Allison and Peter Heath (Cambridge: Cambridge University Press, 2002), pp. 349–424.

God as the condition of its possibility.⁹ The argument thus consists of several steps, first that morality commands the effort to realize the highest good; second, that the possibility of the highest good depends upon the existence of God; and then the assumption that it is only rational for us to attempt to do something if it is rational for us to believe in the satisfaction of the condition or conditions of its possibility. But throughout Kant also wants to stress that the existence of God is the necessary condition of the realizability of the *object* of morality, not the necessary condition or the source of the moral law itself. Kant reminds us of this, the anti-voluntarism that is characteristic or even definitive of the Enlightenment, at the end of the Second Section of the Canon of Pure Reason in the Transcendental Doctrine of Method, entitled "On the ideal of the highest good, as a determining ground of the ultimate end of pure reason" (A 804/B 832):

> But now when practical reason has attained this high point, namely the concept of a single original being as the highest good, it must not undertake to start out from this concept and derive the moral laws themselves from it, as if it had elevated itself above all empirical conditions of its application and soared up to an immediate acquaintance with new objects. For it was these laws alone whose **inner** practical necessity led us to the presupposition of a self-sufficient cause or a wise world-regent, in order to give effect to these laws, and hence we cannot in turn regard these as contingent and derived from a mere will, especially from a will of which we would have had no concept at all had we not formed it in accordance with those laws. So far as practical reason has the right to lead us, we will not hold actions to be obligatory because they are God's commands, but will rather regard them as divine commands because we are internally obligated to them. (A 819/B 846–7)

Kant's assumptions are that we have no determinate concept of divinity apart from our concept of morality, so any concept of morality that we might attempt to derive from an independent conception of divinity would be arbitrary and contingent, not necessary, and that we do have an immediate acquaintance with the moral law of a kind that we could not have of the characteristics or existence of God. Kant's premise that we have immediate acquaintance with the moral law will be developed in the *Groundwork for the Metaphysics of Morals* in the form of the "common rational cognition of morals" from which Kant sets out in its first Section and in the *Critique of Practical Reason* in the form of the "fact of reason." It underlies the first *Critique*'s argument that there can be "a source of positive cognition ... in the domain of pure reason" only in the case of practical reason, thus that there can be a "canon" of pure reason, "a sum total of the *a priori* principles of the correct use of certain cognitive faculties in general" (A 796/B 824) only in the case of practical reason, but it is not otherwise further developed in the *Critique*.

As it turns out, Kant's idea that morality commands the highest good and that God is the condition of the possibility of the highest good will also need much further

---

⁹ This is of course a simplification of the complex evolution of Kant's thought about the highest good from the first *Critique* to the 1793 essay "On the Common Saying: That May be Correct in Theory but it is of no Use in Practice." For a fuller account, see "Kantian Communities: The Realm of Ends, the Ethical Community, and the Highest Good," in Paul Guyer, *Virtues of Freedom: Selected Essays on Kant* (Oxford: Oxford University Press, 2016), pp. 275–302, and Paul Guyer, *Kant on the Rationality of Morality* (Cambridge: Cambridge University Press, 2019).

development after its preliminary statement in the first *Critique*. But let us look at the version of the argument that Kant does provide in this text, since that was the one familiar to Mendelssohn and to the early respondents to the doctrine.

There are two parts to Kant's argument, namely, that morality commands the effort to realize the highest good, and that God, actually God plus human immortality, are the conditions of the possibility of the realization of this highest good. There may be tension between these two parts of Kant's argument. One line of thought is that whatever morality commands must be possible, because of the principle that if morality commands that "actions ought to happen, they must also be able to happen," but that in particular morality commands that certain actions ought to happen *in nature* and that they must therefore be able to happen *in nature*. That is, morality commands not just that we form certain intentions, as it were just in mental space, but that we attempt to act on these intentions in the physical world in space and time. This means that a "special systematic kind of unity, namely the moral," must be possible in nature, although "the systematic unity of nature **in accordance with speculative principles of reason** could not be proved" (A 807/B 835), and that for this unity to be possible its grounds "must be inseparably connected a priori to the inner possibility of things, and thereby lead...to a **transcendental theology** that takes the ideal of the highest ontological perfection as a principle of systematic unity, which connects all things in accordance with universal and necessary laws of nature, since they all have their origin in the absolute necessity of a single original being" (A 816/B 844). In other words, Kant's earlier argument to the existence of God as the ground of all possibility is recast in a practical key, now becoming the argument that we must believe that the possibility of realizing the goal of morality is inherent in the possibility of things as such, which can only be conceived by positing God as the ground of such possibility. Kant states that "this moral theology has the peculiar advantage over the speculative one that it inexorably leads to the concept of a **single, most perfect**, and **rational** primordial being, of which speculative theology could not on objective grounds give us even a **hint**, let alone **convince** us," for it is only "from the standpoint of moral unity" that we have any justification for believing that the "necessary law of the world" lies in a "single supreme will" that is "omnipotent, so that all of nature and its relation to morality in the world are subject to it; omniscient, so that it cognizes the inmost dispositions and their moral worth"; and "omnipresent, so that it is immediately ready for every need that is demanded by the highest good for the world" (A 814–15/B 842–3).

What is missing from this argument, however, is an explanation of why morality, which is not directly concerned with happiness (A 807/B 835), nevertheless commands a world in which "a system of happiness proportionately combined with morality can also be thought as necessary" (A 809/B 837). Kant several times equates morality, that is, the individual realization of morality, with *worthiness* to be happy, and thus supposes that morality should be accompanied with happiness as if it is a self-evident principle of reason that worth should get its due. But this just assumes the equation of morality with worthiness to be happy, and does not fully explain why "in an intelligible world, i.e., in the moral world, in the concept of which we have abstracted from all hindrances to morality (of the inclinations), such a system of happiness proportionately combined with morality can also be thought as necessary, since freedom, partly moved and partly restricted by moral laws, would itself be the cause of the general happiness," or be "self-rewarding" (A 809/B 837). In particular, this equation explains neither why morality would be *self*-rewarding rather than worthiness to be happy being *externally* rewarded, nor why the happiness with which morality rewards itself should be *general* rather than just the happiness of the morally virtuous agent.

An answer to these questions is implied a few years later by Kant's *Groundwork*, for if morality requires that everyone be treated as ends in themselves and therefore also that the particular ends that they set be regarded as ends for all (insofar as they are compatible with the first condition) (G 4:433), and if happiness is equated with the realization of ends, then in requiring the realization of the maximum of ends compatible with each other and with the status of all persons as ends in themselves morality would actually command the greatest happiness possible in the world, even though the binding force of morality is not based on any individual agent's mere desire for happiness. And if what morality commands must be possible if it is to be rational for us to seek to realize it, then we could see why we should have to suppose that the very possibility of nature itself must include the possibility of both human morality and human happiness, and why we might have to attribute that possibility to the author of possibility as such.

Thus far we have seen a gap in Kant's exposition of his argument. But there is also a tension between the argument as thus filled out with a central idea of the *Groundwork* and another line of thought that Kant emphasizes in the *Critique*, namely that individuals who are *worthy* of happiness ought to be able to *expect* happiness, but that if they cannot expect it *in this life* because of the less than complete compliance with the demands of morality by other human beings, then they must be able to expect it from a just and benevolent judge in a *future* life. Thus Kant claims that the "system of self-rewarding morality is only an idea, the realization of which rests on the condition that **everyone** do what he should," a condition that is obviously *not* always fulfilled in the natural world as we know it from experience, and that in the face of this indisputable fact the only way for the moral individual to maintain "the necessary connection of the hope of being happy with the unremitting effort to make oneself worthy of happiness" is to be able to believe in a "**highest reason**," "an intelligence, in which the morally most perfect will, combined with the highest blessedness, is the cause of all happiness in the world, insofar as it stands in exact relation with morality (as the worthiness to be happy)" (A 810/B 383):

> Now since we must necessarily represent ourselves through reason as belonging to such a world, although the senses do not present us with anything except a world of appearances, we must assume the moral world to be a consequence of our conduct in the sensible world; and since the latter does not offer such a connection to us, we must assume the former to be a world that is future for us. Thus God and a future life are two presuppositions that are not to be separated from the obligation that pure reason imposes on us in accordance with principles of that very same reason. (A 810–11/B 838–9)

The moral individual must be able to hope for his own well-deserved happiness, not in order to be motivated to be moral in the first place but perhaps to maintain his "resolve and realization," his realization of what morality requires and his resolve to do it (A 813/B 841). If he cannot expect it in his normal, earthly life span of three score and ten and from his own resources, then he must be able to expect it an a "future life," if necessary of immortal duration, and if not from the nature that is visible in this life than from a God who is efficacious in the afterlife.

The problem with this argument is not only that it raises doubts about Kant's commitment to the purity of moral motivation, as his contemporary critic Christian Garve would charge,[10] but also that its promise of the realization of the highest good in a *future* life undercuts Kant's argument that God must be posited as the ground of the possibility of *nature* because the object of morality must be able to be realized *in nature*. Only if Kant's argument for the rationality of belief in the existence of God is the latter, further, can he reasonably claim that practical reason provides what speculative or theoretical reason could not, namely a justifiable conception of *nature* as a systematic domain that can yield to systematic scientific investigation. Kant clearly commits himself to such a "revised method of physico-theology" in the Canon:

> But this systematic unity of ends in this world of intelligences, which, though as mere nature can only be called the sensible world...also leads inexorably to the purposive unity of all things that constitute this great whole, in accordance with universal laws of nature, just as the first does in accordance with universal and necessary moral laws, and unifies practical with speculative reason...All research into nature is thereby directed toward the form of a system of ends, and becomes, in its fullest extension, physico-theology. (A 815–16/B 843–4)

This connection cannot be made if morality requires us to think of a *supernatural* realm and a God who is efficacious *there*; it could work only if morality requires us to think of the *natural* realm as one the systematic laws of which can make the realization of the object of morality possible in ways that science can study.

Kant would ultimately resolve this in favor of the conception of God as the author of the systematic order of nature rather than of a supernatural conjunction of morality and happiness, not in the *Critique of Practical Reason* in 1788 but by the *Critique of the Power of Judgment* in 1790 and the essay on "Theory and Practice" of 1793; but even prior to resolving that issue, he makes it clear that what his practical argument for a moral theology yields is rational *belief* (*Glaube*), not *knowledge* (*Erkenntnis*). The third section of the Canon distinguishes three different degrees of affirmation or assent, *Fürwahrhalten*, or what we might think of as propositional attitudes, namely "opinion" (*Meinen*), "knowing" (*Wissen*), and "believing" (*Glauben*) (A 820/B 848). To have an opinion is to take something to be true "with the consciousness that it is subjectively **as well as** objectively insufficient," that is, to consider that something might be true while knowing there is not adequate evidence for it and that one's own inclination to affirm it rests on something other than such evidence. To assert that one knows something is to take it to be true and that one has adequate evidence for it, as we say now to hold that it is a justified true belief. But to believe something, in Kant's usage, is to hold that one has *good* reason to affirm it even though that is not *objectively* sufficient evidence for its truth, presumably that it

---

[10] See Kant's 1793 essay "On the common saying: That may be correct in theory but it is of no use in practice," Section I.

does not actually *entail* its truth (A 822/B 850). That may seem a strange category, for we might equate good reasons to believe a proposition with sufficient evidence for its truth. But Kant's view is that if we have good, indeed compelling reason to *act* in a certain way—for example, as morality commands—and if it would be reasonable to act that way only if a certain condition were satisfied, then we have good reason to *believe* that this condition is satisfied even if we do not have *other*, theoretically adequate evidence that it is. Because this belief is based on the condition of rationality for action, Kant also calls it "pragmatic belief" (A 824/B 852). This is the category to which he assigns morally grounded belief in the existence of God: we recognize that we do not have adequate theoretical evidence or argument for this existence, but we also recognize that we are commanded to act in a way that only such belief can make rational, so we hold that belief in the face of that recognition. As Kant also puts it, "the conviction is not **logical** but **moral** certainty, and, since it depends on subjective grounds (of moral disposition) I must not even say 'It is morally certain that there is a God,' etc., but rather 'I am morally certain,' etc." (A 829/B 857). Presumably the second "etc." just saves Kant from repeating the end of the sentence, but the first "etc." suggests that this caution applies to the belief in immortality as well as to that in God. Regarding both we have to adopt the complex cognitive state of recognizing that we have and must have inadequate theoretical evidence for their affirmation but that we also have and must have adequate practical grounds for believing in them. Ordinarily we cannot adopt the complex epistemic state of affirming that something is the case but yet that our evidence for it is inadequate—ordinarily we cannot say that "It is raining but I don't have adequate evidence for believing that it is raining"— but in this case, Kant holds, we can and indeed must accept that we have adequate practical grounds for affirming what we know we have inadequate theoretical grounds for affirming.

Kant would seek other ways to express this complex attitude as time went on. But that would take us well past his relation to Mendelssohn. For now, let us turn to Mendelssohn's response to the *Critique of Pure Reason* in the *Morning Hours*.

## 2. Mendelssohn's *Morning Hours*

It would be misleading to suggest that Mendelssohn's last major work is only a response to Kant's *Critique*. It is not only a defense of Mendelssohn's own earlier arguments for the existence of God from the attack by the "all-crushing Kant" but also an attempt to keep belief in God from collapsing into the pantheism of Spinoza, as Mendelssohn's beloved but departed friend Gotthold Ephraim Lessing was being accused by Friedrich Heinrich Jacobi of having done. Indeed, many discussions of *Morning Hours* focus entirely on Mendelssohn's complex argument about Spinozism, which consists of an argument that finite mind and matter cannot be mere modes of God combined with a defense of Lessing as having adopted only the "refined" ethical attitudes of Spinoza.[11] The debate with Jacobi was of profound

---

[11] For an example, see Bourel, *Moses Mendelssohn*, ch. XI. Frederick C. Beiser devotes most of his chapter on Mendelssohn in *The Fate of Reason: Germany Philosophy from Kant to Fichte* (Cambridge, Mass.: Harvard University Press, 1987), pp. 92–108, to the "pantheism" dispute with Jacobi, offering only

importance to Mendelssohn, raising as it did the specter of earlier attempts to persuade him that he should give up his Judaism and accept Christian faith.[12] But his commitment to defending theoretical arguments for the existence of God, which in his mind rose above the divide between Judaism and Christianity, against the criticisms of Kant, was certainly of equal importance to him.

*Morning Hours, or Lectures on the Existence of God*, so named because it purports to report a series of Bar Mitzvah lessons Mendelssohn held for his son Joseph and two other young men during the morning hours, "those few hours of the day when my spirits are generally bright," begins with an apparently modest forward. Mendelssohn states that he is himself too frail to raise the fortunes of speculative philosophy after the attack to which it has been recently subject, especially from an increasingly fashionable materialism, and says that such a task "awaits stronger powers, or the profundity of a *Kant* who, one hopes, will with the same spirit rebuild once more what he has torn down." He purports to have had only the "limited goal of leaving behind for my friends and those who follow after me an accounting of what I have held to be true in regard to the subject of these reflections," namely, the existence of God. Yet he also says that he intended to introduce his son "without delay to the rational knowledge of God" by conversing about "the truths of natural religion" (*LW* 3–5; *JubA* 3.2.3–5). This suggests that he was not reporting just what he believed, but what he believed to be true. Nor does he simply leave the task of rescuing the proof of the existence of God to some future work of Kant. On the contrary, the work concludes with an impassioned defense of the ontological argument from Kant's criticism. Thus even though much of the work has other targets, including a reconstruction of Leibniz's argument for the existence of God on the basis of a new defense of the principle of sufficient reason and a critique of Spinoza's collapse of the distinction between divine and mundane substance, there can be no doubt that Mendelssohn also conceived his book, which begins with his famous reference to the "all-crushing Kant" and ends with his defense of the ontological argument, as an antidote to Kant.

In particular, we can see Mendelssohn as responding to Kant in the following way. In the first of the two parts of *Morning Hours*, Mendelssohn conducts an elaborate dialogue with idealism, in which he ends up arguing that we have good reason to believe in the existence of objects external to our own ideas although in the ordinary case we cannot say more about such objects than that they cause the kinds of ideas we have of them. We can see this as a qualified acceptance of Kant's transcendental idealism—qualified, because it is not based on Kant's insistence on the transcendental ideality of space and time, which at least in the case of time had been an issue between the two philosophers since 1770—and as in turn influencing Kant's

---

three pages to Mendelssohn's response to Kant's idealism and defense of the ontological argument. Altman provides a more balanced account, dividing his chapter on the *Morning Hours* between a detailed account of Mendelssohn's attempt to answer Kant on both of those points (*Moses Mendelssohn*, pp. 671–86) and of his defense of Lessing in response to Jacobi (pp. 686–98). As Altmann points out, "Only three of the seventeen lectures" that comprise the *Morning Hours* "dealt with Spinozism or pantheism...notwithstanding the fact that the book was originally announced as a rebuttal of the *AllEiner*, i.e. of those who believed that All was One (*Hen kai Pan*)" (p. 672).

[12] See Altmann, *Moses Mendelssohn*, p. 702.

"Refutation of Idealism" in the second edition of the *Critique of Pure Reason* (as I will suggest in Chapter 5).[13] At one point we can also see Mendelssohn taking on board the results of Kant's "Antinomies of Pure Reason" and accepting that a defensible conception of God must avoid ascribing ordinary temporal properties to him. Turning to the specific question of whether we are justified in ascribing objective reality to our idea of God, Mendelssohn defends his version of the cosmological argument from our certainty of our own existence even though Kant had rejected that in the *Critique*, but accepts Kant's argument that the full force of the cosmological argument depends upon the ontological argument. However, he then attempts to defend the ontological argument by accepting Kant's general position that existence is posited of a concept rather than a predicate within a concept is generally true—but not in the case of the concept of God.[14] We will see whether Kant would have been impressed with Mendelssohn's defense.

(i) *Morning Hours*, Part One *Knowledge of External Objects and the Principle of Sufficient Reason*. We will discuss Mendelssohn's dialogue with idealism in Chapter 5, so we will not review Part One, entitled "Epistemic Groundwork concerning Truth, Appearance, Error," in much detail here. But several points should be noted. Underlying the whole argument is the view that philosophy must proceed by describing the "unimpaired capability of our mind" but that it would make no sense to try to argue further for the reliability of that unimpaired capability; we must simply rely upon it. Thus, we must simply accept that "*Truth is all knowledge [Erkenntniß (sic)] insofar as its basis is the unimpaired capability of the mind; untruth, on the contrary, is knowledge insofar as it has suffered an alteration due to an impairment in, or the reduction of, our unimpaired power*" (*LW* 30, *JubA* 3.2. 34, Mendelssohn's emphasis; to avoid tautology in the first clause of this statement and incoherence in the second, "knowledge" or *Erkenntnis* must be understood as mental representation that may be true rather than such as is already known to be true). Mendelssohn has no intention of being caught in the circle of trying to use our own faculties to prove that our faculties are reliable. In particular, Mendelssohn argues that we have no choice but to accept as true, first, propositions the denial of which would be self-contradictory, but also that we have no choice but to accept our natural tendency to suppose that there are external causes for repeated sense-impressions or patterns of coherence among the impressions of our different senses. We cannot deny that we have thoughts or that we who have thoughts are something, but we also cannot deny that at least some of our thoughts represent something other than themselves and ourselves: "Just as I myself am not merely a thought that changes but a thinking being that endures, so we are

---

[13] Frederick Beiser represents a common view that Mendelssohn's treatment of idealism in *Morning Hours* is directed against Kant (*Fate of Reason*, pp. 105–6. Altmann argues that Mendelssohn's position is close to Kant's, and even borrows Kant's concept of the thing in itself (*Moses Mendelssohn*, p. 675). I will argue that the latter is correct, although I will argue in Chapter 5 that while Mendelssohn is content with a probabilistic argument for our knowledge of the existence of objects distinct from our representations of them (except in the case of God), Kant's "Refutation of Idealism," added to the second edition of the *Critique*, quite possibly in response to Mendelssohn's *Morning Hours*, aims at an *a priori* argument for the same conclusion.

[14] See also Altmann, *Moses Mendelssohn*, p. 684.

permitted to believe that our various representations are not only representations within us but also pertain to external things, things that are different from us and are the anterior cause of our representations" (*LW* 12, *JubA* 3.2.14). For example, "When in so many different ways and under such different conditions the repeated perceptions of [a] surface are in concord, we may then conclude that an object outside of us exists that contains within itself the ground for this concord." More generally, "our right to draw this conclusion and to use it in other types of argument that we call induction and analogy" (*LW* 17, *JubA* 3.2.19) is grounded in the natural tendency of our unimpaired mental powers to engage in such reasoning. Thus, "the representation we have of material beings, as extended, capable of motion, and impenetrable, is not the consequence of some weakness or impairment of ours, but rather... this representation arises from the unimpaired powers of our mind... it is not merely subjectively true, but is rather the objective truth" (*LW* 50, *JubA* 3.2.58). Yet, Mendelssohn insists, "One lets oneself be deceived and led astray by empty words if one wants to understand more... by the expression 'to be extended,' or 'to be capable of motion,' or 'to be impenetrable'" than that "This material original [*materielle Urbild*] arouses in us the idea of extension, motion, shape, impenetrability, and so on" (*LW* 51, *JubA* 3.2.59). One can say nothing more about external objects than that they have the power to give us the ideas of themselves that they do.

As far as Mendelssohn is concerned, this is a sufficient account of the truth of our belief in external objects, but it only proves this conclusion with what we might call a high degree of subjective probability. He does not attempt to use this argument directly to establish the existence of God, however, precisely because it falls short of complete certainty. Thus in Part Two of the *Morning Hours* he explicitly abjures any attempt to infer that "There is a sensible world that is actually outside us, so therefore there is an actually existing God outside of us as well as the world itself" (*LW* 69, *JubA* 3.2.78). "The agreement of the inner and outer senses, the agreement of all the senses, even the agreement of all people and all living beings in the known world, although all this may lead common sense to accept the actuality of the external world and would be quite justified in doing so; all this does not completely dispel doubt with the persuasive force of a strict geometric definition" and therefore cannot be used to prove the existence of God with such persuasive force. Instead, Mendelssohn argues, the existence of God should be proven from the fact of one's *own* existence because that possesses "the highest degree of certitude" (*LW* 74, *JubA* 3.2.84). In light of this, the note that Kant appended to the end of the "Critique of all speculative theology" in his copy of the *Critique of Pure Reason*—

Whether, if there is no demonstration of the existence of God, there is not at least a great probability. This is not at all worthy of the object[,] also not possible on this path. Probability in the absolutely necessary is contradictory.

All necessity of a thing as a hypothesis is subjective, namely a need of reason of [our] speculation. (Erdmann CLXXXI, AA 23:43; *CPR* ed. Guyer and Wood, p. 589)

—should be taken not as a criticism of Mendelssohn, but as expressing agreement with him that the existence of God can only be proven a priori, not empirically; of course, Kant would add that the only possible a priori proof is from practical, not theoretical reason.

Before we turn to Mendelssohn's renewed attempt to start the cosmological argument from the indubitable premise of his own existence, however, we should acknowledge the different note on which he does end Part One of the *Morning Hours*. This is his famous introduction of the "pleasure-sensing" "faculty of approbation" (*Billigungsvermögen*) between the mental faculties of knowledge on the one hand and desire on the other (*LW* 54, *JubA* 3.2.62). To this faculty Mendelssohn attributes the pleasure that accompanies recognition of the truth and the displeasure that accompanies falsehood, each characterized as the "formal" side of cognition accompanying its "material" side, and the *Billigungsvermögen* becoming in the bargain a faculty for either approbation or disapprobation. But the faculty can also function independently of knowledge; in this case leading in the direction of desire for or aversion toward something that does not exist rather than pleasure or displeasure in something known to exist. In this context Mendelssohn makes a distinction between knowledge and approbation that parallels one between theoretical and practical reason that Kant makes, both of which anticipate the distinction in "directions of fit" that G. E. M. Anscombe was to make nearly two centuries later:[15]

[C]ognition as well as the faculty of approbation are, as you know from psychology, expressions of one and the same power of the mind, but they are distinct in regard to the goal toward which they strive. The first moves out from things and ends up in us; the second, however, takes the opposite route, starting out from ourselves and taking aim at things that are outside us... The drive for cognition... posits as its starting point that the truth is unchanging, and it seeks to bring the mind's concepts into harmony with it. The goal of its activity is objective truth... But this is not the way that the drive toward approbation is expressed. Once this is set in motion, its goal is not in us but in the things found outside us, and it undertakes to actualize in the outside such effects as are in harmony with our faculty of approbation, with our feeling of satisfaction, and with our wishes. The first drive seeks to refashion the human being in accordance with the nature of things, the second to refashion things according to the nature of the human. (*LW* 54, *JubA* 3.2.64)

The faculty of approbation is a bridge between cognition and desire—or perhaps Mendelssohn should better have said, as he does in this passage, the *drive* to approbation is a bridge between drives to cognition and to desire, since, as the good Wolffian that he still is, Mendelssohn believes that at bottom, all our mental capabilities are expressions of a single underlying faculty of representation. What is striking about Mendelssohn's introduction of this faculty, however, is that its relevance to the question of a sound argument for the existence of God is not immediately apparent. What Mendelssohn does immediately use it for is an explanation of certain features of (human) aesthetic response, which to this point has not been a topic of the *Morning Hours* at all: the differences between cognition, approbation, and desire explain how we can have emotional response to fictions, things that we know not to be true, on the one hand, but on the other hand also not actually desire those objects, or how we can even have positive pleasure in something that we would not desire to be actual (*LW* 55–7, *JubA* 3.2.64–6). But the introduction of this faculty will have implications for Mendelssohn's position on arguments for the existence of

---

[15] See G.E.M. Anscombe, *Intention* (Oxford: Blackwell, 1957).

God. Explicitly, Mendelssohn will argue that since we have to attribute a faculty of approbation to ourselves it is also natural for us to include it in our conception of God, and this will be a necessary step in conceiving of God's creation as the result of an approbation of the best of all possible worlds, in other words, a valuable supplement to Leibniz's conception of creation and a response to Spinoza's attempt to conceive of God in completely non-anthropomorphic terms. But Mendelssohn's distinction between approbation on the one hand and both cognition and desire may also be a tacit response to Kant's doctrine that we must believe in what we take to be the necessary conditions of what we must attempt to do: that we *approve* of a wise, just, and benevolent God is no argument for the existence of such a being. Mendelssohn does not mention Kant's name in this context, nor in the *Critique of Practical Reason* will Kant mention Mendelssohn's name in responding to the objection that he has reduced belief in the existence of God to mere wish-fulfillment, imagined satisfaction of an inclination or desire.[16] However, Mendelssohn does use his distinction among faculties in the opening lecture of Part Two of *Morning Hours* to criticize an argument by Johann Bernhard Basedow (1724–90) (who had established the progressive school *Philanthropinum* in Mendelssohn's hometown Dessau, although thirty years after Mendelssohn's departure) that we can have a "duty to believe" in the existence of God. According to Basedow, Mendelssohn reports, "If there is a proposition ... that is so linked to the happiness of humanity that without the truth of this proposition no happiness is possible, then we are obligated to accept the proposition as true and to give it our enthusiastic assent," but Mendelssohn recognizes no such duty "in regard to belief when truth is to be distinguished from falsehood" because that "confuse[s] the two faculties that we took such pains to distinguish ... mistaking a reason for approbation for a reason to claim knowledge" (*LW* 62, *JubA* 3.2.69). Now Kant had publicly supported Basedow's educational project in essays published in 1776 and 1777 (2:447–52),[17] and Mendelssohn might have intended to take a quiet swipe at Kant by criticizing Basedow,[18] especially since Basedow's argument turns on the role of God as the necessary condition for *happiness* and Kant's presentation of the argument from the condition of possibility of the realization of the highest good in the *Critique of Pure Reason* had also focused on the necessity of both God and immortality as conditions for the realization of happiness in proportion to worthiness of it. And Kant might have taken this argument as a criticism of himself, for in the *Critique of Practical Reason* he makes it clear that at least immortality is necessary (necessarily believed in, that is) as a condition for the completion of *virtue* or *worthiness to be happy*, not happiness itself—although God still figures as the condition of the possibility of happiness (*in nature*). But whether or not Mendelssohn intended his argument against Basedow as a tacit criticism of Kant or whether Kant took it that way, by his distinction between approbation and actual

---

[16] See Kant *CPracR*, 5:143n. The objection was made by Thomas Wizenmann (1759–87), in "An den Herrn Professor Kant, von dem Verfasser der Resultate Jacobi'scher und Mendelssohn'scher Philosophie," *Deutsches Museum* (1787): 116–56. Wisenmann was a protégé of Jacobi, who cared for him as he was dying of tuberculosis.
[17] Translated by Robert Louden in Kant, *Anthropology, History, and Education*, pp. 100–4.
[18] See Beiser, *Fate of Reason*, p. 97.

cognition Mendelssohn was clearly attempting to keep the argument for the existence of God firmly on cognitive or theoretical territory, not on Kant's practical ground.

(ii) *Morning Hours, Part Two: The Arguments for the Existence of God.* After the opening critique of Basedow, which we have just considered, Mendelssohn turns to the traditional arguments for the existence of God. He considers three forms of argument, although having already demonstrated the limits of the argument from design in the prize essay, that is not one of them. Instead, he considers two versions of the cosmological argument, which he calls the a posteriori type of proof, and the ontological argument, which he calls the a priori proof (*LW* 70, *JubA* 3.2.78). The two types of cosmological argument would be the inference to the existence of God from the existence of external objects, that is, objects other than oneself, and that from one's consciousness of one's own existence. We have already seen that Mendelssohn regards the certitude of the first of these premises as more than sufficient for our ordinary purposes but not sufficient for proof of the existence of a necessary being: "since the first type of proof for the existence of God rests on the foundation of the actual existence of a material world, this proof at least seems to thereby suffer some weakening of its persuasive force by virtue of the doubts brought against its foundation" (*LW* 73, *JubA* 3.2.82); so Mendelssohn does not pursue it further. Instead, he focuses on the version of the cosmological argument that would infer the existence of God from one's consciousness of one's own existence, as he had in the prize essay. But the program of Mendelssohn's defense of this argument, which extends over much of Part Two of *Morning Hours*, has been much complicated by the years intervening since the earlier essay. Mendelssohn weaves criticism of Spinozism and defense of Leibnizianism into it, but above all tries to render it immune from Kantian doubts by criticizing some Kantian positions but also taking others on board, although in both cases without mentioning Kant's name. He starts with an explanation of the contingency of one's own existence that is actually a restatement of the criticism of Kant's transcendental idealism with regard to the appearance of the self that he had originally made in 1770 (which we will discuss in Chapter 5). He then uses what is clearly the result of Kant's analysis of the antinomies of pure reason to explicate the relation between the temporal and contingent self and an atemporal and necessary God. He also tries to transform what is clearly Kant's own earlier argument for the existence of God as the ground of all *possibility* to argue that all the *actuality* of my own existence, precisely since *I* cannot know it all, must be grounded in the God's own thought. This new argument has the anti-Spinozistic consequence that God must be conceived of as an intelligence, but might also be read as Mendelssohn's attempt to answer Kant's argument that the cosmological argument ultimately depends on the ontological argument for its proof of an *ens realissimum*, because in Mendelssohn's view only the latter could think all actuality.[19] Mendelssohn then

---

[19] This new argument might be considered an anticipation of Hegel's conception of absolute knowing in the *Phenomenology of Spirit* (1807) and as a forerunner of the American idealist Josiah Royce's (1855-1916) "argument from error," in which Royce argues that since truth must be knowable but there is so much we do not know, there must be an omniscient mind that does know what we do not. See Royce, *The Religious Aspect of Philosophy: A Critique of the Bases of Conduct and Faith* (Boston: Houghton, Mifflin, 1885), ch. XI, pp. 384-435.

attempts to defend the ontological argument from what are unmistakably Kant's criticisms even though Kant's name is not mentioned. But in the end, he settles for an account of the existence of God as *something that humans or other rational beings must think* that appears similar to Kant's theory of the *idea* of God as an inevitable *idea* of pure reason. But the fundamental difference remains that Mendelssohn characterizes the idea of God as necessary for human thought on theoretical grounds, while Kant insists that our belief in this idea can be based only on practical grounds.

Mendelssohn's development of his preferred version of the cosmological argument begins with the following statement:

> For the fact that I myself am a changeable being is something the most stubborn of skeptics would find it hard to dispute. And if in reflecting upon myself I am conscious that changes are transpiring with me, this, too, cannot be subject to doubt. As they relate to myself, the subjective and the objective coincide, appearance and truth do not mutually exclude each other. What I experience immediately cannot be mere delusion but must actually transpire within me, and also, as far as it relates to myself, it cannot be taken from me as an object. So my existence as well as my changeability are beyond all doubt. (*LW* 74, *JubA* 3.2.84)

Mendelssohn's argument that both my existence and the change in time of my states are "beyond all doubt" is beyond question Cartesian in inspiration. He clearly invokes Descartes in saying that "The inference *I think, therefore I am* must even be granted by the solipsist, as more than one has been brought to see" (*LW* 74, *JubA* 3.2.84). But the claim is also reminiscent of Mendelssohn's response to Kant's initial statement of transcendental idealism in his inaugural dissertation, fifteen years earlier than *Morning Hours*. In a letter to Kant written at Christmas, 1770, after Mendelssohn had received a copy of the dissertation through Kant's former student Marcus Herz as a go-between, Mendelssohn had written:

> For several reasons I cannot convince myself that time is something merely subjective. Succession is after all at least a necessary condition of the representation that finite minds have. But finite minds are not only subjects; they are also objects of representations, both those of God and those of their fellows. Consequently it is necessary to regard succession as something objective.
>
> Furthermore, since we have to grant the reality of succession in a representing creature and in its alterations, why not also in the sensible object, the model and prototype of representations in the world? (Mendelssohn to Kant, 25 December 1770, 10:115; *Correspondence*, p. 124)

Mendelssohn did not directly address Kant's argument for the transcendental ideality of space as well as time from the apriority of our knowledge of them (*ID* §§14.5, 15.D, 2:400–1, 403–4), nor did he object to Kant's assertion of the transcendental ideality of space. His argument in Part One of *Morning Hours* that all we can know for sure about external objects beyond that they exist is that they have the power to give us certain kinds of ideas is in fact compatible with the transcendental ideality of space. But he always objected to Kant's view that the temporal appearance of the self to itself could be any kind of illusion, because here there is no distinction between the representation and the object, so that if our representations appear to us to be in time, the passage of time in which they appear to us must be real. In the passage from the letter of 1770 he puts that point by saying that anyone who truly represents the inner life of a human being, whether that be God or another human, must represent it as temporal. As he also puts it in the *Morning Hours*, "The idealist merely denies the actual existence of an object that would serve as the original behind these true images" (*LW* 77, JubA 3.2.86), but since in the case of one's own representations as objects of thought there is no distinction between the images and their objects—their objects are not "behind" them—there is no room for idealism. But in the *Morning Hours* Mendelssohn is happy to accept that the genuine temporality of our own existence does demonstrate the *contingency* of this existence and of the change of its states, because precisely that contingency will be the premise for a proof of the existence of a *necessary* being as the ground of any contingent one. (We will return to Mendelssohn's criticism of Kant and Kant's attempt to reply in the *Critique of Pure Reason* in Chapter 5.)

Before he gets to the main proof, Mendelssohn seems to use the reality of change or temporal succession in our own representations just to suggest an anti-Spinozistic, pro-Leibnizian argument:

You have here a simple method for arguing from my own existence to the existence of an unchangeable being that has the best as its intention and freely brings it into existence. If time has changed nothing in the material aspect of the representations and can only alter their formal aspect, then the reason for the change that I perceive within me is not in their conceivability, but in their relative goodness and perfection. Insofar as they are objects of cognition, their relation to time is unchangeable. It is only insofar as they are objects of approbation that their relation to time can be different at different moments. But if goodness and perfection are to be the reason why something is actual, one must presuppose a being who finds pleasure in goodness and perfection and for whom they can serve as incentives to action. For now, let this much suffice concerning this method of proving the existence of God. I will deal with it more fully below. (*LW* 76, JubA 3.2.85–6)

The idea here is that the criterion of conceivability, that is, the law of non-contradiction, cannot explain why the representations of a thinking being change in the way they do: thinking $p$ at one time and $not$-$p$ at another would be consistent with the law of non-contradiction, but so would be thinking $p$ at one time and then thinking $p$ again at another time. Something else is needed to explain why there is change in the representations of a thinking being, why it represents or thinks $p$ at one time but something else at another time. This can only be what Mendelssohn here calls the "formal" side of the mental state, its perfection or imperfection, and then the argument is that ultimately only God's approbation or disapprobation of creatures being in one mental state or another at any given time explains the change in their mental states; their own states of approbation and disapprobation might go some distance toward explaining the changes in their mental states, but the ultimate explanation of the approbations and disapprobations of creatures would have to be God's approbations and disapprobations. This is an example of Mendelssohn using his recognition of the faculty of approbation to recast the Leibnizian theory that the only possible explanation of the actual world is that God chooses it as the best of all possible worlds, thus his defense of Leibnizianism from a Spinozistic refusal to conceive of God in anthropomorphic terms as having a faculty of approbation and disapprobation.

Although central to Mendelssohn's larger program in the *Morning Hours*, this might not seem to be part of his argument with Kant. As we will soon see, it is actually central to his argument with Kant as well. The argument with Kant continues by making several concessions to him but yet maintaining the ultimate soundness of both the cosmological and the ontological proofs. The first concession to Kant, or better the first exploitation of a Kantian resource, comes in Mendelssohn's use of the result of Kant's analysis of the antinomies of pure reason. Having insisted upon the reality of our own representations as a temporal series, Mendelssohn recognizes that he is faced with the problem that Kant has constructed in the antinomies, namely that it is not possible to represent either a temporal series that has a first moment or one that is genuinely endless or infinite. But this is precisely a reason for positing a being outside of the temporal series altogether, an unchanging God that is the ground of changing creatures. Mendelssohn does not name Kant in this discussion, but the reference seems unmistakable:

Various philosophers believed that they were able to demonstrate that a series without beginning is indeed logically conceivable but that it cannot ever come into actuality. They made use of the following reasons.

Concerning a series without end, they said, it is obvious that it could never become actual, because its endlessness consists precisely in that it will never be complete—in other words, that it must always be extended further... Both that which has no beginning and that which has no end require an eternity for their actual existence, and eternity cannot ever have come to pass. We must therefore admit a beginning of things that itself needs no further beginning—in other words, a necessary being whose existence is not dependent upon efficient causes and whose duration [*Dauer*] is not a temporal series [*Zeitfolge*] without beginning, but is rather a *timelessness* [*Zeitlosigkeit*], an unchanging eternity... Only [in] the contingent events of the world do we recognize a past and a future time. (*LW* 82, *JubA* 3.2.92–3).

A timeless necessary being does not need an antecedent cause in time but can serve, in lieu of any cause at a first moment in time, as the ground of the infinite series of the temporal, ourselves included. So Mendelssohn thinks that a timeless necessary being is the inevitable result of Kant's antinomies.

Of course, Kant had argued that the *idea* of a timeless ground outside of the temporal series is the resolution of the (dynamic) antinomies, and that his transcendental idealism makes the possibility of such a ground *conceivable*, but for Kant this did not amount to *knowledge* of the reality of such a being (see, e.g., A 562–4/B 590–2). Whence Mendelssohn's confidence that Kant's antinomy actually yields *knowledge* of the reality of a timeless necessary being? His confidence in the inference from the contingent being of the temporal, of which our own experience is the indubitable example, to the necessary being of a timeless reality, rests, as it did in the prize essay, on his continuing confidence in the principle of sufficient reason. Our own existence with its temporal change of states is real, and Mendelssohn argues there can be only two grounds for any feature of anything real: it would be a contradiction with the concept of the thing to deny it that feature, for although it is not entailed by the concept of the thing, it would be incompatible with the best of all possible worlds and thus with God's creation of the actual world based on his approbation of it as the best of all possible worlds for the object not to have that property:

[S]ome philosophers have inferred the existence of that which is necessary and unchanging from the existence of that which is contingent, and quite appropriately... [O]ne can truly assert of a subject A that it possesses actual existence only insofar as it has some connection with this predicate, either because it cannot be conceived except as having actual existence, or because under certain circumstances it has become the thing that is best, and therefore, in just the way it is and in no other way, it had to have become the object of an act of approbation. The Leibnizians call this the principle of sufficient reason, and therefore they say that everything that is actual must have a sufficient reason...Now in the case of a contingent being we do not find this reason in the being itself. A contingent being's existence cannot be made comprehensible simply by the fact that its existence is conceivable. And its existence can just as little be made comprehensible by virtue of the proximate causes of its existence if these causes are themselves contingent...Since, therefore, contingent beings actually do exist, there must be a necessary being that contains in itself the reason for all contingent things, but whose own reason for existing is not found outside itself, but is found in its inner possibility.   (*LW* 84-5, *JubA* 3.2. 95-6)

Making the Leibnizian provenance of his proof even clearer, Mendelssohn further states that "the existence of contingent being is not due to the fact that its dependence upon the necessary being makes its nonexistence inconceivable," for if "this were the case, it would itself have to be necessary and unchangeable," although the proof begins with the fact of the changeability of contingent being, namely, our own being. Rather, "its dependence on the necessary being is to be sought for in the fact that it has become an object of this being's power of approbation" (*LW* 85-6, *JubA* 3.2.96-7). The necessary being's approbation of any possible contingent being, though no doubt in view of its relation to all other possible contingent beings, is the necessary and sufficient reason for the existence of that contingent being, for example, you or me. The contingent being does not exist because its own concept is inconsistent with nonexistence, because in that case it would be necessary; and even though its existence is grounded in the approbation of the necessary being, that does not make its existence a logically necessary consequence of the conjunction of its own concept and the concept of the necessary being, because the approbation of the necessary being is freely granted, so it would not be a logical inconsistency were it withheld. Mendelssohn further emphasizes both that the approbation of any particular contingent being is granted only in its relation to the best of all possible worlds and that this approbation is freely granted several pages later when he writes that "The ground for my existence must therefore be sought in a free cause, which has recognized and approved of me now and here as belonging to the series of the best and thereby been moved to bring me to actuality" (*LW* 88, *JubA* 3.2.100). Of course, conceiving of the necessary being as having a faculty of approbation and of freely creating that of which it approves is a Leibnizian way of thinking, not a Spinozistic way. Mendelssohn's argument leads him to attribute further anthropomorphic properties to God as well: "Choice of what is best presupposes cognition of it, and so this being possesses the power of cognition. Equally certain is it that this necessary being must also have the power of approbation, desire and aversion, reason and will, for without these properties both the choice and the production of the best are completely inconceivable" (*LW* 87, *JubA* 3.2.99).

None of this will change Kant's view that the principle of sufficient reason cannot be used to infer *knowledge* of a necessary being from knowledge of contingent beings, since it can be demonstrated only as a condition of the possibility of *experience*—that is the result of the Second Analogy of Experience, where Kant explicitly asserts that "the principle of sufficient reason is the ground of possible experience, namely the objective cognition of appearances with regard to their relation in the successive series of time" (A 200-1/B 246). The principle of sufficient reason, once proven, can be used to connect appearances with relative necessity, not to get outside the series of appearances to an absolutely necessary ground. It is thus one of the central results of the entire *Critique* that the principle of sufficient reason cannot ground a sound theoretical inference to the existence of anything outside of the series of temporal events, and if that means that the series of temporal events must always remain incomplete, so be it. On this point, there is no room for compromise between Kant and Mendelssohn. Thus Kant saw no point to moderate his criticism of theoretical proofs of the existence of God in the second edition of the first *Critique*, although as we saw he did emphasize his practical proof of the existence of God (and freedom and immortality) in the new Preface for that edition. Perhaps that was his response to Mendelssohn's hope in the Preface to the *Morning Hours* that Kant would rebuild what he would crush.

In spite of the cold shoulder that he could have anticipated that Kant would give to his revived cosmological argument from his consciousness of his own existence, Mendelssohn does not merely persist with it but actually tries to support it with an argument that seems to be intended as an analogy to Kant's own "only possible basis for a demonstration of the existence of God"—which Kant himself had at least implicitly jettisoned in the first edition of the *Critique*. Further, this argument could be intended as a response to Kant's claim that the cosmological argument depends upon the ontological proof, even though Mendelssohn is going to defend the latter as well. After two lectures (XIII and XIV) in which he presents at length the anti-Spinozistic, specifically anti-pantheistic implications of his argument, Mendelssohn puts it in a form reminiscent of Descartes's argument in the third *Meditation* that even his own doubts, as a mental imperfection, prove the existence not only of himself but of God, because he could not recognize his own imperfection unless he had a—truthful—idea of the perfection of God. Mendelssohn puts this by saying that "The consciousness of myself as it is bound up with the complete ignorance of everything that does not fall within the circle of my cognitive powers is the most telling proof of my extra-divine substantiality," but also that "God's mind in truth holds within itself the most precise measure of my powers" (*LW* 104, *JubA* 3.2.118), that is, of the limitation of my powers in comparison to his. (Although one might have thought that the sheer fact of one's doubt would have been sufficient proof of one's imperfection even in the absence of a truthful idea of any being that is more perfect in being free from doubt, that is, any idea with more of a basis than the mere insertion of a negation in front of one's thought of one's own imperfection.) Then, after a further lecture (XV) in which he defends Lessing from the charge of Spinozism—his original purpose in writing *Morning Hours*—by arguing that Lessing never departed from the theology of Leibniz (and Shaftesbury) (*LW* 113, *JubA* 3.2.128) and that it could only have been his admirable sympathy for a persecuted underdog that would have led him to declare himself a Spinozist to Jacobi (*LW* 116, *JubA* 3.2.132), Mendelssohn returns to the main argument with an "Attempt at a New Proof for the Existence of God from the Incompleteness of Self-Knowledge"

(*LW* 120, *JubA* 3.2.138). This title (for Lecture XVI) is reminiscent of Kant's title for the *Only Possible Basis*, and the argument that Mendelssohn now adds to his cosmological proof is also reminiscent of Kant's argument in that work and the earlier *New Exposition*. As already suggested, this argument also seems intended to rebut Kant's claim that the cosmological argument, even if it sufficed to prove the existence of a *necessary* being, does not suffice to prove a *perfect* being or *ens realissimum*. Mendelssohn does not explicitly address the objection that Kant had made in the *Critique* to his own earlier argument, but we will see how he at least might have thought that his new argument could sidestep this criticism.

The argument that Mendelssohn now proposes is this. To his previous certainty of his own existence, he adds the following reasonable thought: "Besides the immediate sensation [*Empfindung*] of my own existence, which, as we have seen, is secure from every possible doubt, I must further accept the following perception as indubitable: I am not merely that which I distinctly know about myself, or, which is to say much the same: More belongs to my existence than that of which I have conscious insight." Who could deny this, the reasonable alternative to Descartes's preposterous claim that in being certain that he thinks he knows everything that is essential to his proper self?[20] Mendelssohn takes this claim to mean that not only is there more *possibility* in himself than he distinctly knows but also more *actuality*, but this is still hard to dispute. We might regard this as a variant of his claim that we know our own existence to be contingent, namely, that what we know about ourselves is also contingent, because there is certainly more that is true of us than the particular things we happen to know about ourselves. Mendelssohn then constructs his new proof of the existence of God on the back of Kant's, arguing that not merely *possibility* but *actuality* must be grounded in divine thought: "not only must everything that is possible be conceived of as possible by some thinking being, but also...everything that is actual must be conceived of as actual by some thinking being. That which no thinking being represents in his mind as possible is not in fact possible, and, what is more, that which is not conceived of as actual by any thinking being cannot in fact be actual" (*LW* 123, *JubA* 3.2.142). Since I clearly am not the one who thinks of all the actualities in myself of which I am unaware, "then it palpably follows that there must exist a being that represents to itself everything that belongs to my existence in the most distinct, purest and thorough manner... Therefore there must exist a thinking being, an understanding, that thinks in the most perfect manner the totality of all possibilities as possible, the totality of all actualities as actual" (*LW* 124, *JubA* 3.2.143-4). Mendelssohn further clarifies that although further possibilities can be conceived by any finite being once it has assigned to itself or any other object some possibilities (*LW* 125, *JubA* 3.2.144), the unknown *actualities* cannot become known in this way—that would be contrary to the initial hypothesis—so they must be known by God.

The point of this argument is precisely to break out of the circle of mere concepts by arguing that even though I can form the *concepts* of further possibilities from the

---

[20] Descartes, *Meditations on First Philosophy*, Second Meditation, *Philosophical Writings*, vol. 2, pp. 19-22.

concepts of the possibilities that I do know, because they are actual, I obviously cannot know the *actualities* that I do not know—but someone or some being must. Our own concepts of ourselves or any other ordinary objects are not adequate to "match up" to our own or their actualities, and we thus cannot use our own concepts to "match up" (*übereinstimmen*) to these objects; but these actualities must be captured by the concepts of some being, if not us then God.

Mendelssohn was clearly impressed with this argument, and the five continuous pages that he devotes to it are as much or more than he devotes to any other discrete argument in the *Morning Hours*. And perhaps it might even be thought that it could withstand Kant's criticism in the *Critique* of his own argument from *possibility* to its ground, because while Kant's objection to that is that the idea of the sum-total of possibilities is just that, a mere idea that we have no reason to suppose is ever fully realized, not in the mind of God any more than in the mind of any human being, surely the sum-total of *actuality* in, for example, myself, *is actual*, even though I do not know it all—so if someone must know any actuality in order for it to be actual, then that someone must be someone other than me. Further, as Mendelssohn expounds the argument, he may well be signaling that this version of the cosmological argument is sufficient to prove the existence of a not merely necessary but also perfect being, and that it thereby answers Kant's claim that the cosmological argument cannot do that, which renders it dependent upon the ontological argument to reach that result, which in turn renders it superfluous. The basis for this suggestion is Mendelssohn's claim that the being necessary to cognize the actualities in ourselves that you or I cannot cognize must be capable of cognizing not only that but the uncognized actuality of all beings, and must therefore be a perfect or infinite intellect, and must have perfect faculties of approbation and will as well in order to approve of the best possible world and to will it into existence. Even in the actuality of a mere mote of dust, let alone in that of a conscious being:

[T]here lie infinitely many facets that cannot be comprehended in perfect clarity, whether in their extent or in their intensity, by the combined cognitive power of all contingent beings... Therefore there must exist a thinking being, an understanding, that conceives in the most perfect manner the totality of all possibilities as possible, the totality of all actualities as actual. This means that the thinking being represents all of these things to itself in their most complete unfolding possible, in their *coordination* as well as *subordination*, in the most distinct, complete, and thorough manner. *There is an infinite understanding, and so on.*

(*LW* 124, JubA 3.2.143)

The words "and so on" presumably refer to the other attributes of the necessary being, the perfection of its faculty of approbation and will. Thus Mendelssohn says a few pages later, "the fact that insight cannot exist without activity, nor cognition without approbation or disapprobation, nor infinite understanding without the most perfect will, has already been sufficiently expounded in the preceding." Thus Mendelssohn can conclude that "We have therefore in this way a new systematic [*wissenschaftlichen*] proof of the existence of God from the imperfection of our own self-knowledge" (*LW* 127, JubA 3.2.146–7). This proof, at least in Mendelssohn's view, does not need any supplementation from the ontological argument or elsewhere to demonstrate the perfection of God in all his attributes as well as his necessary being.

However, there are two obvious problems with the argument. For one, the justification for the premise that every actuality must be thought is unclear. It might even be question-begging; if there is a God that is anything like any traditional conception of God, namely omniscient, then of course that God must know everything actual, whether any finite being does or not. But that presupposes that there is a God, and does not prove that there is. The second problem is that the argument seems to be open to the same objection that both Kant and Mendelssohn himself had always made to the standard argument from design, namely that it cannot obviously prove the existence of a truly infinite cause. The argument may well be designed to avoid Kant's objection to his own argument in *Only Possible Basis* that *we* cannot fully conceive of the ideal of infinite possibility for which God is supposed to be the ground. But it will not be sufficient to prove a truly *infinite* or infinitely perfect being unless it assumes that each finite being has an infinite number of properties or at least that there is an infinite number of finite beings even if each has only a finite number of properties. As we just saw, Mendelssohn does seem to assume that any finite being has an infinite number of properties that are actual but unknown to him, and which can and must be known by an infinite being perfect in understanding and all its other faculties. But he does not actually argue that each finite being has an infinite number of properties, or in the alternative that there is an infinite number of finite beings each with a finite number of properties. (The latter alternative might seem to have the benefit of avoiding any risk that in their own infinitude contingent beings might end up being too much like God, although that pantheistic conclusion has in fact been precluded by the starting-point of the present argument, namely the *imperfection* of the self-knowledge of contingent beings.) The argument may thus be missing a premise.

Mendelssohn certainly does not worry that the argument is missing a premise. Nevertheless, he thinks that the existence of God can also be proven by the more traditional ontological argument in spite of the "all-crushing" Kant's objections to it. Let us conclude the present chapter with examination of Mendelssohn's attempt to rescue the ontological argument. We will see that in spite of his clear attempt to refute Kant's objection to the argument, the interpretation of its conclusion with which Mendelssohn ends up may not be entirely un-Kantian in spirit.

Mendelssohn begins by calling Descartes's attempt to prove the existence of God from the mere concept of him, "to travel from the conceivability of that which is necessary to its actual existence," "audacious and unprecedented." Ordinarily, Mendelssohn says, "one argues from possibility to possibility or from actuality to actuality" (*LW* 129, *JubA* 3.2.148); the final form that he has just given to the cosmological argument, for example, has taken the form of an argument from actuality to actuality. But he claims that the uniqueness of Descartes's inference from the possibility—conceivability—of God to his actuality "is here precisely the mark of truth": since there can be an inference from conceivability to actuality only in the case of a necessary being and there can be only one necessary being, there can be only one exception to the ordinary rule of inference. Mendelssohn hastens to add that Descartes's proof needs Leibniz's well-known preliminary argument that the concept of God is non-contradictory, but that this is easily demonstrated from the fact that only "positive predicates" are attributed to God, that is, "of the necessary being all realities are affirmed in the highest degree, and all negative ones are removed from it," and that in the concept of God "there can thus be nothing contradictory that might cause us to be concerned" (*LW* 129–30, *JubA* 3.2.149–50).

Having dispensed with this issue, Mendelssohn turns to Kant's objection. He does not mention Kant's name, but puts the objection in unmistakably Kantian terms. To his own confidence that "the pure, systematic argument for the existence of God" is "not standing unshakably before us," Mendelssohn writes:

By no means, say some opponents of this type of proof; you are still building, as usual, on a foundation whose strength you have not properly investigated. You have arbitrarily formed for yourselves an abstract concept and heaped upon it all the properties you can properly think of. We certainly do not dare to deny you the freedom to do this, and we let the concept stand. But no sooner have you done this than you surreptitiously try to manufacture its existence, saying: to make the package complete, we must also take this other property and give the concept an actual existence. Isn't this procedure rather underhanded?"

(*LW* 131, *JubA* 3.2.150)

The language is more colorful than some of Kant's, but the general charge of building without proper investigation of the foundation and the specific charge that the ontological argument works by just unpacking what has been arbitrarily packed into a concept are of course Kant's objections. Mendelssohn's first response to the Kantian objection, however, is that the construction of the concept of God is not arbitrary: "First, abstract concepts are not merely arbitrary. They must at least contain truth, and this truth does not depend upon our arbitrary will [*Willkühr*]." Here Mendelssohn is relying upon the fundamental premise of his epistemology stated in Part One of *Morning Hours*, namely that truth is simply what is delivered by the unimpaired operation of our cognitive powers. Ordinarily, of course, it is precisely the natural and unimpaired operation of our cognitive powers that produces concepts that are themselves real in our minds but whose objects have only "ideal existence," concepts that are merely "modifications of myself" and "can be an object of thought without my attributing to [them] an existence in actuality." But, Mendelssohn claims, this is not so in the case of the concept of the necessary being: "The necessary being, by contrast, can either not be thought, not have any truth as a modification of myself, or else I must at least think it as actually existent... We have merely to demonstrate the conceivability of this concept and we are immediately forced to think of such a being as actually existing" (*LW* 131, *JubA* 3.2.151). Now this statement is just the beginning of Mendelssohn's response to Kant, but we might conclude that he has already given the game away by claiming merely that we cannot but *think* of the necessary being as existing, not that the necessary being cannot but exist. But before we conclude this, let us see how he continues.

He does this by next taking up Kant's claim that existence is not a predicate that can properly be included within a concept but something that can only be posited of a concept.

Precisely here is the trick, cry our opponents. In order to call [the necessary being] into existence [*Daseyn*], you take existence [*Existenz* here and in the remainder of the passage] to be a property of the thing that belongs among all its possible properties... Because in speech we predicate existence of a thing like the [other] properties of the thing, because we say a thing is actual just like we say a number is even or a figure is round, you assume that existence has the same nature as the other properties and marks of things and erect your inference on this presupposition. But this presupposition itself cannot be conceded. Existence is no mere property, no addendum, no supplement, it is rather the positing [*Position*] of all properties and marks of the things, without which they remain mere abstract concepts.

(*LW* 132, *JubA* 3.2.152)

Mendelssohn's response is simply to accept Kant's claim that in spite of ordinary usage existence is not a proper predicate or mark, "not a property but the positing of all the properties of a thing, or something inexplicable but known to us all" (*LW* 133, *JubA* 3.2.152), but nevertheless to hold that even though "I can leave out existence [now *Daseyn* again] from the concept of something contingent without thereby annulling [*aufzuheben*] the concept... in the case of the necessary being, I cannot separate existence from the idea without annihilating the idea itself. I must think concept and thing [*Sache*] together, or else just let the concept go" (*LW* 133, *JubA* 3.2.152–3). In other words, Mendelssohn recognizes Kant's distinction between predication and positing, but holds that the concept of a necessary being forces us to posit the existence of its object. This is just how the "undiminished power of our thought" works (*LW* 135, *JubA* 3.2.155).

We can readily imagine that Kant was not impressed with this response, that he would have said "Well, then, just let it go, or at least recognize that you have formed an idea that has great heuristic and practical value but for which you have no theoretical ground to posit an object." Perhaps trying to strengthen his position, Mendelssohn reverts to a traditional version of the argument: You can have the ideas of the affirmative marks of contingent objects, which however are not of the highest degree, and leave out the affirmative mark of existence without contradiction. The idea of the "necessary being, by contrast, unites all affirmative marks and properties in the highest degree. One of them is not thinkable without all the others. Hence the infinite being without the affirmative predicate of existence [*Daseyns*] is something contradictory" (*LW* 134, *JubA* 3.2.154). Here Mendelssohn is just falling back on the traditional treatment of existence as a predicate that cannot be left out of the concept of the perfect or most real being, and ignoring Kant's objection.

But Mendelssohn's deepest response may actually be to accept Kant's own conclusion, at least in spirit if not in letter. He follows this statement of the traditional version of the ontological argument thus:

[T]he affirmative proposition: The necessary being is actually present, must be assumed by every thinking being, is a consequence of the positive power of thought, and thus *truth*. And now the victory for our side will be complete. For what more could we wish than to prove that the proposition: the *most perfect being is really present* is a consequence of our positive power of thought, and thus not merely subjective but objective, irrefutable truth? The assurance that all thinking beings, by means of their power of thought, agree in a proposition of reason, gives the highest conviction of its truth. What all rational beings must think thus and not otherwise is thus and not otherwise true. Whoever demands more than this conviction seeks something of which he has no concept... (*LW* 135, *JubA* 3.2.155)

In other words, all that any argument can prove is that if we *think* one thing we must also *think* something connected to it. If we *think* of a perfect being, we must *think* of it as existing. But that is still not the same as it actually existing, although of course any further evidence or argument for its existence will just be further reason for us to *think* of it as existing. That is why it will be futile to ask for something more, but also why we can never get beyond the circle of our thoughts by mere argument.

For all his maneuvers, Mendelssohn's argument ends where it began, with the insistence upon the truthfulness of the positive powers of our thought. He does not risk falling into the Cartesian circle of trying to prove that God validates our clear and distinct ideas by means of an argument that presupposes that our clear and distinct ideas of God are true; he takes it as given that what flows from the purely positive powers of our thought is true, and that this suffices to prove the existence of God. At one level, Mendelssohn's position that the thought of the existence of the necessary and perfect being is an inescapable product of the "positive power of thought" may not seem very different from Kant's conclusion that the idea of God is an inevitable product of pure reason. But their positions are certainly not identical, for Mendelssohn seems to have in mind what Kant would call the theoretical power of thought while Kant's position is that belief in the existence of God is ultimately justified practically, by its practical value in the conduct of science and in moral conduct. Yet either way, the argument is that the *idea* of God is natural and valuable to us. Mere argument can never prove more than that.

Mendelssohn's Kantian response to Kant was his last word on arguments for the existence of God. He died a few months after publishing *Morning Hours* and before Kant got around to replying to the copy that Mendelssohn had quickly sent him—according to legend, from a cold he caught while delivering his final broadside against Jacobi to his publisher. But the debate was not over, for several months after that Kant published his essay "What Does It Mean to Orient Oneself in Thought?" and two years later the *Critique of Practical Reason*, and both of these might be seen as continuing the argument with Mendelssohn in the form of the argument that it is only the positive power of our *practical* rather than *theoretical* reason that justifies our belief in the existence of God. We touched upon the essay on orientation in the introduction to this volume. And while Kant's extensive presentation of his practical argument for belief in the existence of God and immortality (along with freedom) in the *Critique of Practical Reason* may in fact have been stimulated by his argument with Mendelssohn, indeed his new term "the primacy of practical reason" can be seen as following directly from the essay on orientation, his only reference to Mendelssohn in the second *Critique*, in the critical elucidation of his own conception of freedom (5:101), hardly suggests that Mendelssohn was the chief target of the book. Kant might not have wished to associate his new *Critique* with the dying embers of the debate between Mendelssohn and Jacobi, or he might have felt that his doctrine of the primacy of practical reason was sufficiently his own property that he did not need to give Mendelssohn any special credit for stimulating his expanded treatment of it. But whatever the case, Kant did explicitly respond to Mendelssohn on two other central metaphysical issues, the immortality of the soul, which Mendelssohn argued for in his 1767 *Phaedo*, and transcendental idealism, which had been an issue between them since 1770. Therefore, the next two chapters will be devoted to those two issues.

# 4
# Mendelssohn and Kant on the Immortality of the Soul

## 1. Introduction

Mendelssohn consistently identified the three core items of belief for a rational religion as the existence of God, providence, and the immortality of the human soul, while for Kant the three postulates of pure practical reason, in his terms also the core of "religion within the boundaries of mere reason," are the existence of freedom, immortality, and God. We have already discussed the views of the two philosophers on arguments for the existence of God, and since for both the idea of God is that of a just and benevolent author of nature, we have tacitly discussed their views on providence as well (although we will return to their competing views on the possibility of moral *progress* for the human race in its natural history in the final chapter of this book). That leaves immortality. Their views on that subject, including what Kant may have borrowed from Mendelssohn and the tension within Kant's own extended thought on this matter, will be the subject of the present chapter.

In *Jerusalem*, his return to philosophical writing a dozen years after his "nervous debility" of 1771 and two years after Kant's *Critique of Pure Reason*, Mendelssohn writes that the "fundamental principles on which all religions agree, and without which felicity is but a dream, and virtue itself ceases to be virtue," are "God, providence, and a future life" (*Jerusalem* p. 63, JubA 8:131). The "universal *religion of mankind*," not just Judaism, *could* have been expressed if on Mount Sinai God had spoken "I am the Eternal, your God, the necessary independent being, omnipotent and omniscient, that recompenses men in a future life according to their deeds" (*Jerusalem* p. 97, JubA 8:164), thereby asserting his own existence, human immortality, and his justice or providence—but God did not need to assert that on Sinai, because it was and is "placed beyond all doubt by human reasoning," and without such reasoning anyone on the holy mountain "could have been stunned and overwhelmed by the great and wonderful manifestations, but he could not have been made aware of what he had not known before" (*Jerusalem* p. 98, JubA 8:165). Kant, for his part, consistently identified belief in our own freedom, the existence of God, and our own immortality as the three postulates of pure practical reason and as the basis for a religion within the boundaries of mere reason, tacitly including providence in his list by means of his argument that the latter two, God and immortality, are rationally affirmed as conditions of the possibility of the highest good, his version of what providence would bring about. In contrast to Mendelssohn, Kant held that "Judaism as such, taken in its purity, entails absolutely no religious faith" precisely because "no religion can be conceived without faith in a future life" and in his view Judaism included no such faith (*RBMR*, 6:126), although it is not clear what evidence Kant thought he had for this claim and it would be easy to providee evidence both from Jewish liturgy and the history of Jewish philosophical writing to prove the opposite.[1] We will return to this issue as well later in this book.

Kant includes our own freedom among the three postulates of pure practical reason, indeed as the premise of the other two (*CPracR*, 5:3-4, 5:132), while Mendelssohn does not list freedom among the three core concepts of the universal religion of reason. Not that Mendelssohn does not have a conception of human freedom or of its importance—he clearly presupposes the fact of human freedom in supposing that God justly recompenses humans for their deeds—but he does not devote a great deal of effort to developing an account of freedom, instead adopting the standard Leibnizian line that freedom is simply acting in accordance with one's representation of the best, without need for any violation of determinism in the form of liberty to choose between good and evil uncompromised by past history—one's own or that of the whole world. As he writes in *Morning Hours* (Lecture XII): "I recognize neither for humanity nor divinity any other freedom except that which depends upon cognition and choice of that which is best. The power to know, to approve, and to choose this best thing is true freedom, and the idea that there is a power to act contrary to this knowledge, this approbation, and this choice is, in my understanding of the matter, an utter absurdity" (*LW* p. 87, *JubA* 3.2:98). Kant himself had defended this Leibnizian understanding of human freedom against Christian August Crusius early in his career (*Nova Delucidatio*, Proposition IX, 1:400-5), but after a long struggle, culminating in the first two Parts of *Religion within the Boundaries of Mere Reason*, decisively rejected it, although it took all the machinery of transcendental idealism, with its distinction between the prevalence of determinism at the phenomenal level of our experience but room for radical freedom at the noumenal level of our existence, to make this rejection possible.[2] However, as he develops his own view, Kant never presents the nature of freedom as a major issue between himself and Mendelssohn, apparently always having Leibniz in his sights, although he does once mention Mendelssohn as one of those who because "they insist on regarding time and space as determinations belonging to the existence of things in themselves" cannot "avoid fatalism of actions" and who in particular would "flatly allow both" space and time, and therefore determinism, "to be conditions necessarily belonging only to existence of finite and derived beings but not to that of

---

[1] Steven Nadler provides clear evidence of a traditional Jewish belief in immortality in Saadia Gaon and Gersonides in "Theodicy and Providence," in *The Cambridge History of Jewish Philosophy* (vol. 1): *From Antiquity through the Seventeenth Century* (Cambridge: Cambridge University Press, 2009), pp. 619-58, at pp. 625, 643. Personal immortality is not generally considered to be part of Biblical Judaism, however; indeed, T.M.Rudavsky states that "Jewish theology presents no clearly elaborated views either on the relationship between body and mind, or on the nature of the soul," and suggests that the view enters into medieval Jewish philosophy through Neo-Platonism and Aristotelianism; see *Jewish Philosophy in the Middle Ages: Science, Rationalism, and Religion* (Oxford: Oxford University Press, 2018), p. 208 and Chapter 8 more generally.

[2] For an account of the evolution of Kant's thought about freedom, see Paul Guyer, *Kant*, second edition (London: Routledge, 2014), pp. 245-65.

the infinite original being" (*CPracR* 5:102). (As we will see in Chapter 5, it is not so clear that Mendelssohn takes spatiality to be a property of external reality and human beings as they are in themselves, but he does defend the reality of time, starting with the successiveness of our own experience, against the transcendental idealism of Kant.)

So although Mendelssohn and Kant disagree about the nature of human freedom, Kant does not appear to make much of an issue of that disagreement. Yet although they both do recognize immortality as a core belief of the religion of reason, Kant does take issue with Mendelssohn's argument for immortality. What we shall find is that their difference takes the same form as did their difference about arguments for the existence of God: while both recognized that to be a rational belief for all human beings and a core of a universal religion of reason, Mendelssohn held that this belief can be defended by one or in fact several theoretical arguments, while Kant held that it could be defended only on practical grounds; likewise, we shall see in this chapter that Mendelssohn defended theoretical argumentation for human immortality, while Kant soundly criticized such argument and instead held that belief in immortality can be defended only on practical grounds. Neither, of course, could present any empirical grounds in favor of belief in immortality, but in his *Religion* Kant did give an account of the role that the *idea* of immortality plays in our moral experience.

But the issue of freedom will rear its head in connection with Kant's practical defense of immortality. In the *Critique of Practical Reason*, the premise of Kant's argument from morality to immortality is that human beings need the prospect of a life without end in order to believe that they have sufficient opportunity to perfect the "complete conformity" of their "disposition" with the "principles of practical reason" (*CPracR* 5:122). But the implication of his radical conception of freedom in the *Religion* is in fact that human beings are free to undergo a "change of heart" and convert from evil to good *at any time* in their *natural* lives. This undercuts the need for a postulate of immortality. So freedom will become an issue in this chapter after all. Furthermore, one of Kant's final disputes with Mendelssohn, in his 1793 essay "On the common saying: That may be correct in theory but it is of no use in practice," will be a dispute over the possibility of collective moral progress in the history of humankind. That will not be overtly a dispute about freedom, but at bottom it is—and one in which Mendelssohn may have a clearer grasp of the implications of the kind of radical individual freedom to which Kant is by then committed than Kant himself does. So the issue of freedom may be more important to Mendelssohn than his trinity of God, providence, and immortality suggests, and there may be more of a debate between him and Kant on this issue than Kant lets on, certainly in the *Critique of Practical Reason*, written as soon after Mendelssohn's death as it was. We will return to this issue in the last part of this chapter and in Part Three of this book. But for now we will focus on what was obviously an issue between them, namely the rationality of our belief in our own immortality. This is not much of an issue in present-day philosophy, and it might seem of purely historical interest to devote a chapter to it. But as it is another arena in which the dispute on the proper method of philosophy played out between Mendelssohn and Kant, it will repay a look.

Mendelssohn's book *Phaedo, or on the Immortality of the Soul* appeared in 1767. In spite of the rapid and widespread popularity of the book, Kant did not refer to it at that time. Nor did he refer to it in the first edition of the *Critique of Pure Reason*, although the section of the "Transcendental Dialectic" entitled the "Paralogisms of Pure Reasons" included a critique of rationalist arguments for the immortality of the soul in general. In the revised version of the Paralogisms in the second edition of the *Critique*, however, Kant explicitly criticized Mendelssohn's argument for the immortality of the soul in the second of the three dialogues that comprise *Phaedo* (which is prefaced with a "Character of Socrates" and begins as if it were a translation of the Platonic dialogue of the same name), an argument that turns on the supposed impossibility of a continuous change from existence to non-existence. This criticism of the argument is Kant's only explicit reference to *Phaedo* or any other work by Mendelssohn in the first *Critique*.[3] Nevertheless, two central ideas of the first *Critique* are reminiscent of ideas that Mendelssohn expounds in *Phaedo* even if they cannot be proven to be due to Mendelssohn. One striking idea in Mendelssohn's work is his conception of the soul as the source of all combination, a lemma in his proof of the simplicity of the soul. This could be taken to foreshadow Kant's view that all synthesis is due to the understanding, expressed in the premise of the revised version of the "Transcendental Deduction of the Pure Concepts of the Understanding" in the second edition of the *Critique of Pure Reason* that "all combination... is an action of the understanding" (*CPuR*, B130), although Mendelssohn does not identify combination or synthesis with judgment and thereby pave the way for Kant's proof of the objective validity of the categories as conditions for the application of judgment—thus Mendelssohn does not prefigure Kant's detailed account of the internal structure of human understanding and of experience insofar as it consists in judgment about intuition, the centerpiece of Kant's reconciliation of rationalism and empiricism. A second striking feature of Mendelssohn's work is his argument in its third dialogue that the soul must be immortal because the full development of all its potential or capacities, thus its capacities for both happiness and virtue, would take forever and God would not have given the soul such potential without also giving it adequate time for its development. This argument foreshadows Kant's treatment of the postulate of immortality in the Canon of Pure Reason in the *Critique of Pure Reason*, which turns on the need for immortality to perfect our virtue as well as our happiness. Kant's argument for the postulate of immortality may have been inspired by Mendelssohn's, or both philosophers may have been inspired by Johann Joachim Spalding's *Vocation of Mankind* (*Bestimmung des Menschen*), which was first published in 1748 but became particularly influential in a new edition of 1764, thus shortly before Mendelssohn published his *Phaedo* and just as Kant's thought

---

[3] In the "Elucidation" of the section on time in the Transcendental Aesthetic, Kant responds to several "insightful men" who had criticized his transcendental idealist theory of time as originally expounded in the inaugural dissertation of 1770. The "insightful men" who had communicated their objections to Kant by letter included Mendelssohn (letter of December 25, 1770, 10:113–16, as well as Johann Heinrich Lambert (letter of October 13, 1770, 10:103–10), and Johann Georg Sulzer (letter of December 8, 1770, 10:111–13), but Kant does not mention Mendelssohn (or the others) by name in his response. We will discuss this issue in the following chapter.

about moral philosophy was getting underway.[4] A central idea of Spalding's work, stated to be sure without any metaphysical or epistemological reservations, is that "eternity" is "only the continuation and completion of what I have begun in the regular direction and activity of my spirit; it merely gives me more opportunity and space for the further development [*Ausbildung*] of the qualities [*Eigenschaften*] with which I here pursue the obligations in my situation and circumstances, thoughtfulness, honesty, diligence."[5]

Kant's thought about immortality has a complex history. In the *Critique of Practical Reason*, Kant restricts the argument for the rationality of our belief in our immortality to the practical ground that we need to be able to think that we have adequate time for the perfection of our moral disposition, leaving our confidence in the possibility of happiness in accordance with that moral disposition to rest on the postulate of the existence of God as the author of nature. In the 1790s, however, Kant sometimes seems to omit any argument for the postulate of personal immortality altogether, often reducing the postulates of pure practical reason to the single postulation of God as the ground of the possibility of the realization of morality in nature, while at other times he seems to revert to an argument closer to that of the first *Critique* than to that of the second, arguing that we need to believe in immortality in order to believe in the possibility of the complete realization of the highest good but not specifically in order to believe in the possibility of the perfection of our virtue. One point I want to make in this chapter is that Kant has good reason for this second shift, because the conception of freedom of the will that he finally reached in 1792–93, in *Religion within the Boundaries of Mere Reason*, undercuts any thought that the perfection of our virtue or at least of our will need take any time at all, let alone eternity. A second point I will make is that in many works of the 1790s—although this view had been anticipated in the 1784 essay on "The Idea of Universal History from a Cosmopolitan Point of View"—Kant argues that the perfection of morality can be expected only in the complete history of the human *species* precisely because human *individuals* are mortal rather than immortal. This argument would make most sense if Kant had simply dropped the postulate of personal immortality.

In the third section of the 1793 essay on theory and practice, Kant makes another explicit reference to Mendelssohn, presenting his theory that the human species is capable of perpetual moral progress as an alternative to what he takes to be Mendelssohn's view that human history is an endless cycle of progress and regress. Ironically, in what appears to be Kant's most enthusiastic endorsement of the inevitability of the moral progress of the human species, or at least the inevitability of its progress towards the external condition of justice, namely the 1795 pamphlet *Towards Perpetual Peace*, Kant adds an afterthought that, likewise in light of his account of human freedom in the *Religion*, undercuts any thought of a *guarantee* of moral progress, namely the necessity of "moral politicians" for the establishment of

---

[4] On the "History of the Success" of Spalding's work, its "editions, pirated editions, translations, and chief reviews," see Laura Anna Macor, *Die Bestimmung des Menschen (1748–1800): Eine Begriffsgeschichte* (Stuttgart-Bad Canstatt: Frommann-Holzboog, 2013), pp. 100–9.

[5] Johann Joachim Spalding, *Die Bestimmung des Menschen*, ed. Wolfgang Erich Müller (Waltrop: Hartmut Spenner, 1997), p. 86.

republics and of their peaceful international federation, who however can never be guaranteed to do the right thing because no human being can ever be guaranteed to do the right thing. Thus Kant ends up coming closer to the position of Mendelssohn that he had rejected in "Theory and Practice" as "abderitism," the position that humans may simply oscillate between moral progress and regress, at least insofar as he gives up any idea that the moral progress of the human species can ever be regarded as guaranteed. The revolution in Kant's thinking about freedom in the 1790s thus creates problems not only for his long-standing commitment to the postulate of personal immortality but also for his faith in the inevitable progress of the human species as well.

But however the relation between Kant's conviction of human freedom and his belief in human immortality might turn out, the difference remains that for Kant we could possibly affirm immortality only on practical grounds, while Mendelssohn remains convinced that there is a sound theoretical argument for it. So let us begin with that fundamental difference.

## 2. The Argument of *Phaedo*

*Phaedo* was not only the sole work by Mendelssohn to which Kant explicitly refers in the *Critique of Pure Reason* but also one of his most popular and successful works altogether, one that enjoyed four authorized editions and many other reprints in Mendelssohn's lifetime, was quickly translated into Dutch, French, Italian, Danish, Russian, and English,[6] and made his reputation throughout Europe.[7] Mendelssohn presents his work as an updating of Socrates's deathbed argument for the immortality of the soul in Plato's *Phaedo* that will employ the best resources of recent philosophy. The work begins with an encomium to Socrates, which is followed by three dialogues that, following Plato's model, report the discussion that took place on Socrates's final day of life. In the first section, where Mendelssohn still follows Plato closely, Socrates tries to reassure his friends that death is nothing to be feared because in death the soul will be liberated from the body and the obfuscations of the senses, but his auditors will not be comforted by this thought until Socrates proves that the soul actually survives the dissolution of the body. At that point Mendelssohn starts putting his own arguments into the mouth of Socrates. The remainder of the first dialogue is taken up with the argument that nothing simple can really go out of existence, because that would require a discontinuous change from being to non-being although all change in nature except for the mere rearrangement of parts in something complex is continuous rather than discontinuous. Thus "The soul cannot eternally perish, for the last step, no matter how long it might be postponed, would always be a jump from being to nothingness, which can be grounded neither in the

---

[6] The first English translation of *Phädon* was by Charles Cullen, under the title *Phædon; or, the Death of Socrates* (London: J. Cooper, 1789). There is a recent translation by Patricia Noble (New York: Peter Lang, 2007). Translations here are my own.

[7] Mendelssohn discussed the project with Lessing as early as December, 1760, and was moved to complete it by correspondence with his friend Thomas Abbt concerning Spalding's *Vocation of Man*. See Altmann, *Moses Mendelssohn*, pp. 140–58. Bourel's chapter on the *Phaedo* (*Moses Mendelssohn*, pp. 225–78) presents more detail on Spalding and Mendelssohn's exchanges with Abbt.

essence of an individual thing nor in its whole interconnection" (*JubA* 3.1:73). But this argument is sound only if the soul truly is simple, and the second dialogue is devoted to the proof of this crucial lemma. The central argument is that there can be no combination or unification of any manifold without an act of unification by thought, and that this itself cannot be the product of anything composite, on pain of an infinite regress. Thus Mendelssohn's Socrates argues that "Order, balance, harmony, regularity, in general all relations that require an apprehension and comprehension [*Zusammennehmen und Gegeneinanderhalten*] of the manifold are effects of the faculty of thought... And once this is conceded, this faculty of thought itself, this cause of all comparison and comprehension, cannot possibly arise from these its own actions... thus I cannot place the origin of this faculty of representation in a whole that consists of... separate parts" (*JubA* 3.92–3). Thus among our parts "there must be at least a single one [*ein einziges*] which unifies and comprehends all these cognitions, desires and inclinations, everything that is to be encountered in our soul" (*JubA* 3.1:96), and "There is therefore in our body at least a single substance that is not extended, not composite, but is simple, has a power of representation, and unites in itself all our concepts, desires and inclinations" (*JubA* 3.1:97). This completes Mendelssohn's argument for the simplicity and therefore the indestructability of the soul.

In his comment on Mendelssohn in the second edition of the Paralogisms, Kant objects that Mendelssohn's proof turns on assigning to the soul only extensive rather than intensive magnitude, which could be destroyed not by the separation of parts but "by gradual remission of all its powers (hence, if I may be allowed to use this expression, by elanguescence)" (*CPR* B 414). This seems not to address Mendelssohn's claim that there can be no discontinuous change from being to non-being, which is supposed to apply precisely to those cases of change that are not mere dispersions of parts of extensive magnitudes. Although Mendelssohn had not used the term "intensive quantity," Kant is nevertheless simply denying what Mendelssohn had asserted.

However, Kant's larger argument in the Paralogisms, that the formal unity of mental acts, and in particular the logical simplicity of the representation of the self through the unanalyzable expression "I," does not imply the simplicity of the underlying source of thought, whatever that might be, although it was already formulated in the first edition of the *Critique* without explicit reference to Mendelssohn, nevertheless bears precisely on Mendelssohn's overall argument: that the act of thought is simple, the point on which Mendelssohn insists, does not imply that its source is simple. In Kant's words, "it is not at all possible through this simple self-consciousness to determine the way I exist, whether as substance or as accident" (*CPR* B 420; see also A 381–2, A 399–400, and B 406–10).[8]

---

[8] The most detailed study of Kant's critique of Mendelssohn's argument that I have seen is Ulrich Pardey, "Über Kants Widerlegung des Mendelssohnschen Bewieses der Beharrlichkeit der Steele," *Kant-Studien* 90 (1999): 257–84. The gist of Pardey's argument is that Kant's refutation of Mendelssohn fails because even if a discontinuous change is possible, for example from having a sensation of red to not having one, something has to persist through such a change, namely the consciousness of red at one point and of its absence at another, and that can only be the seat of consciousness itself, namely the soul. Actually,

Yet it might also seem that Mendelssohn's insistence that all combination must be due to thought could have made a deep impression on Kant, for that is certainly presented without demur as the primary premise of the Transcendental Deduction in the second edition of the *Critique* (*CPR* §15, B 129–30), and in a text as late as the 1792–5 drafts on the *Real Progress of Metaphysics* Kant argues, in Mendelssohnian terms, that "That [the human being] is not solely a body can ... be rigorously proved, since the unity of consciousness, which must necessarily be met with in every cognition (and so likewise in that of himself) makes it impossible that representations distributed among many subjects should constitute unity of thought" (*RPM* 20:308). Thus we might think of the larger argument of the Transcendental Deduction and the Paralogisms together as both an assimilation and a critique of Mendelssohn: Mendelssohn was right to recognize that all combination or synthesis is due to thought, indeed to a unitary act of thought, but he failed to recognize that thought always takes the form of judgment, thus he failed to deduce the categories, and he was wrong to think that the simplicity of the act of thought—or at least the simplicity of the concept "I" that Kant was prepared to recognize—implies the simplicity of the thing that thinks. Thus he was wrong to think that it could be used as a premise in a sound theoretical proof of the immortality of the soul.

Of course, the conclusion that Kant draws from his critique of Mendelssohn's and all "rationalist" arguments from the simplicity to the immortality of the soul, just like the conclusion he draws from his subsequent critique of all rationalist arguments for the existence of God, is not a *disproof* of the point in question, but rather the impossibility of *either* proof or disproof, thus the impossibility of deciding the question on any *theoretical* grounds. Kant claims that "the strictness of critique, by proving the impossibility of settling anything dogmatically about an object of experience beyond the bounds of experience, performs a not unimportant service for reason regarding this interest, in securing it likewise against all possible assertions of the contrary"(*CPR* B 424). And the interest to which he refers is of course the *practical* interest of belief in immortality as a condition of the possibility of a human being fulfilling the demands of morality: the "refusal of our reason to give an answer to those curious questions," whether the soul is material and mortal or immaterial and immortal, is "reason's hint that we should turn our self-knowledge away from fruitless and extravagant speculation toward fruitful practical uses" (*CPR* B 421).

In spite of Kant's rejection of his argument from simplicity to immortality, however, Mendelssohn's further argument in the third Dialogue of *Phaedo* actually provides a model for Kant's account of the practical belief in immortality, indeed for the two different accounts of such belief that Kant offers in the first and second critiques. Having proved in the second Dialogue that the soul is immortal, in the

---

Pardey need not have invoked this example; Kant's argument in the First Analogy of Experience is that no genuine substance can enter into or go out of existence (*CPR* A 182/B 244), thus all that Kant needs to argue is that Mendelssohn has not sufficiently proved that the soul is a genuine substance at all. That is of course what the larger argument of the Paralogisms section in both editions attempts to do. But Pardey is right to argue that Kant's claim that Mendelssohn simply overlooked the possibility that the soul has intensive magnitude is false, as our examination of Mendelssohn's introduction of the mathematics of intensive magnitude into the philosophy of mind in the prize essay showed.

third Socrates is pressed by his friends to prove that "*God has not destined us to eternal misery*," that is, that eternal existence promises eternal happiness and not eternal misery (*JubA* 3.1:102). He responds with an argument, not to be found in Plato, which he says will appeal to God's benevolence rather than to his cognition. The argument is that we cannot have been given powers that we are not destined to develop fully, or that are destined to disappear without a trace, like "foam upon water or the flight of an arrow through the air" (*JubA* 3.1:106–7). Rather, Socrates argues, we can be confident that our powers are destined to reach their goals or at least to make unending progress toward them, thus "we can assume with good ground that this progress toward perfection, this increase, this growth in inner perfection, is the destiny [*Bestimmung*] of rational beings, thus also the highest final goal [*Endzweck*] of creation" (*JubA* 3.1:114). But foremost among our capacities is our capacity for happiness, foremost among our goals happiness itself, and therefore we can be sure that we are destined not to eternal misery but to eternal happiness or at least unending progress toward it. Socrates waxes eloquent:

Is it fitting for wisdom, to bring forth a world in which the spirits that it places there...could be happy and...yet to withdraw eternally from these spirits the capacity for contemplation and happiness?...Oh no, my friends! providence has not given us a longing for eternal happiness in vain; it can and will be satisfied...Thus here below we serve the regent of the world by developing our capacities; thus we will also in that [eternal] life continue under his divine protection to practice in virtue and wisdom continually making ourselves more perfect and industrious in fulfilling the series of divine aims that stretch before us into the infinite.

(*JubA* 3.1:114–15)

In this passage, Mendelssohn's Socrates goes beyond the challenge posed by his friends of proving that eternal existence would not be eternal misery, for he here sets not one but two goals for us, the perfection of our happiness and the perfection of our virtue, the latter understood as the fulfillment of our duties to God, above all (following Christian Wolff as well as Jewish tradition) the admiration of God's own perfection, thus that he has argued that the soul needs and has infinite time to realize both goals or to come ever closer to them.[9] This is why I earlier suggested that in his first treatment of the postulate of immortality in the first *Critique* Kant adopts Mendelssohn's argument *in toto*, while in the second *Critique* he rather adopts it for the case of virtue. But in work after the second *Critique*, I will argue, while sometimes continuing to base an argument for immortality on its necessity for the realization of happiness, Kant abandons what is basically his adaptation of Mendelssohn's suggestion that we need to believe in immortality in order to believe in the possibility of perfecting our virtue. As I suggested, this is because the revision of his conception of freedom that Kant undertakes in the *Religion* obviates the need for such a doctrine.

---

[9] In my allusion to Wolff, I am thinking of his argument in his teleology that "The chief intention for the world is that from that we [human beings] should recognize the perfection of God," and that everything else in the world is meant to support us in this activity; see *Vernünftige Gedancken von der natürlichen Dinge*, Chapter II, §8, p. 6; in my reference to Jewish tradition, I am thinking not of the obligation of Jews to fulfill God's numerous commandments about observances but of the contents of such prayers as even the mourner's *Kaddish*, which consists of little but praise of the glory of God.

## 3. Kant's Initial Assimilation of Mendelssohn's Conception of Immortality

The highest good and the doctrine of postulates of pure practical reason grounded upon it are in many ways the culmination of Kant's philosophy. They are treated at the conclusion of each of his three critiques, in the Canon of Pure Reason in the first *Critique*, in the Dialectic of Pure Practical Reason in the second, and in the Doctrine of Method in the Critique of the Teleological Power of Judgment in the third. Yet Kant's conception of the highest good and certainly his argument for its necessity are sufficiently obscure that even after those three discussions he still had to return to it in the first section of the 1793 essay on "Theory and Practice," in the contemporaneous Preface to *Religion within the Boundaries of Mere Reason*, in the 1794 essay on "The End of All Things," and in the drafts for the essay competition on the real progress of metaphysics. For present purposes I will suggest only that at least some of the obscurity surrounding Kant's idea is occasioned by the fact that he suggests two different derivations of it, often in the same work. On one approach, it would seem that the natural end of practical reason—call it prudential or empirical practical reason—is one's own happiness, while everyone's pure practical reason calls for observance of the moral law by both themselves and others; thus the combination of those two aspects of practical reason naturally proposes and morally allows the complete realization of one's own happiness within the boundaries of the moral law, a condition that Kant equates with worthiness to be happy. This approach would leave any one agent's concern for the happiness of others to follow from his use of pure rather than empirical practical reason, that is, to follow from the moral law, and it is not immediately obvious how the moral law imposes on each a concern for the *happiness* of all—although part of what Kant suggests on this approach is that the natural interest of each in his own happiness must be satisfied so that one's resolve to be moral not be weakened (*CPR* A 813/B 841), which might lead—although Kant does not explicitly say this—not only to an indirect duty to promote one's *own* happiness in order to reduce temptations to immorality for the benefit of one's own morality (*MM* 6: 388) but likewise to an indirect duty to promote the happiness of others so that *their* resolve to be moral will not be weakened. Were there to be such a duty towards others it would of course be in addition to a direct duty to assist others in need of help in order to realize their ends, as explicated in the illustrations of the first two formulations of the categorical imperative in the *Groundwork* (*G* 4:423, 430) or in the form of the imperfect duty of virtue to promote the happiness of others asserted in the *Metaphysics of Morals* (*MS*, 6:385, 387–8.)

However, Kant already hints at another approach in the Canon of the first *Critique* when he says that in a "moral world," that is, the natural world as it would be if we "abstracted from all hindrances to morality (of inclinations)," "a system of happiness proportionately combined with morality" would be "necessary" because "freedom, partly moved and partly restricted by moral laws, would itself be the cause of the general happiness, and rational beings, under the guidance of such principles, would themselves be the authors of their own enduring welfare and at the same time that of others" (*CPR* A 809/B 837). The connection between freedom and happiness that is presupposed here may be understood if we think of freedom as the freedom *to set ends* and of happiness as the condition that follows from the *realization of ends*. If we conceive of morality as prescribing the maximally intra- and interpersonally consistent use of the freedom to set ends, as Kant suggests we should in his *Lectures on Ethics* (*LE Collins*, 27:346; *LE Kaehler*, 178–80), then what would result from freedom so exercised under ideal conditions, in which all hindrances to morality—at least those coming from human inclinations themselves—were removed, and in which all hindrances to the realization of ends freely set—at least those stemming from humans themselves—would likewise be removed, would be the greatest possible realization of ends for all and thus the greatest happiness for all possible in accordance with and as a product of morality, again at least as far as the effects of human motivations, or "plagues" that mankind invents "for itself, "such as "the oppression of domination" and the "barbarism of war," rather than non-human forces such as hurricanes or pestilence are concerned (*CPJ* §83, 5:430)?[10] Although Kant already suggests the second approach in the first *Critique*, he does not unequivocally adhere to it in later works, suggesting the first approach, which separates the ends of empirical and pure practical reason but recombines them in the composite idea of the highest good, in the second *Critique* and even in the Preface to the *Religion*, where he implies that our interest in happiness as part of the highest good is a "natural need" rather than a need of pure reason (see *CPracR* 5:110–11, and *RBMR* 6:5).

But my concern here is not the basis for Kant's doctrine but rather its application in the form of the postulates of pure practical reason, in particular the postulate of immortality, although it would be nice if one could argue that it was Kant's eventual resolution of his ambivalence about the foundation of his own doctrine that led to his eventual de-emphasis of this postulate: that is, if Kant had ever made it completely clear that the need for the happiness component of the highest good comes not from a promise of one's own eventual happiness as a condition of one's continuing resolve to be moral but rather from the need for the possibility of the eventual happiness of the human species as a condition of the rationality of working to promote the freedom of members of the species to set their own ends, then it would also have become self-evident that there would be no need for a promise of personal immortality—at least for the sake of the eventual realization of the happiness of a virtuous and worthy individual in the face of a corrupt world that deprives him of the happiness he is due during his natural life. The texts in which Kant emphasizes only the necessary possibility of the moral progress of the human species as a whole are certainly compatible with this way of grounding the idea of the highest good as the complete collective object of morality rather than as a promise of individual happiness, although what Kant most clearly retracts is only the second *Critique*'s argument

---

[10] In some of his earliest remarks on moral philosophy, the notes he wrote in his own copy of the 1764 *Observations on the Feeling of the Beautiful and Sublime*, Kant suggests that it is only the domination of our wills by the wills of others and not the restriction of our wills by non-human nature that we find morally offensive (e.g., 20:93). It similarly seems to be compensation for the obstacle to individual happiness created by the immorality of other humans that happiness in personal immortality is meant to provide in the *Critique of Pure Reason* (A 810/B 838). Perhaps by means of his argument throughout his mature works that we must postulate God as the author of nature—without any restriction—in order to conceive of the possibility of the highest good Kant means that we must believe in the eventual remission of non-human as well as human obstacles to happiness (individual or collective), but he never says this explicitly.

that personal immortality must be postulated as the condition of the possibility of the perfection of personal virtue. Once he does that, however, he has moved away from Mendelssohn's position even once that had been transformed into a mere postulate of pure practical reason.

Be their later fates what they may, as I suggested, we might regard Kant's diverging arguments for the postulate of immortality in the first and second critiques as his separation and adaptation of the two capacities to be realized in eternity according to Mendelssohn's Socrates in *Phaedo*. In the Canon of Pure Reason in the first *Critique*, Kant most clearly suggests that the individual agent needs to be able to believe in the eventuality of his own happiness in spite of the immorality of others around him and the damage that their immorality might do to his own prospects for happiness in order to maintain his resolve to be moral. What Kant argues is that there does not appear to be a causal connection between the individual's worthiness to be happy in the "world of appearances" and his actual happiness, which depends in good part not on himself but on the actions of others, so we must postulate that this connection will be established in a "world that is future for us." Both "God and a future life are two presuppositions that are not to be separated from the obligation that pure reason imposes on us" (CPR A 810–11/B 838–9), although God seems to be necessary in order to ensure that even in that future life happiness will indeed be the consequence of virtue, that is presumably virtue in the *present* life or "world of appearances." "Without a God and a world that is now not visible to us but is hoped for, the majestic ideas of morality" would be "objects of approbation and admiration but not incentives for resolve and realization because they would not fulfill the whole end that is natural for every human being and determined *a priori* and necessarily through the very same pure reason" (CPuR A 813/B 841). It is not part of Mendelssohn's argument in *Phaedo* that the promise of eventual realization of our natural happiness is a necessary condition for maintaining our resolve to be moral, but it is part of his argument that because our capacity for happiness is part of our natural endowment and we must believe that our natural endowment can eventually be fulfilled, even if not in the natural world, we must believe that Providence or God intends that capacity to be fulfilled. Kant's argument in the Canon and Mendelssohn's inference to our realization of happiness in eternity share the assumption that our interest in happiness is both natural and properly accommodated by morality.

In the second *Critique*, by contrast, Kant argues that we must believe in immortality in order to believe in the possibility of perfecting our virtue and worthiness to be happy, not our happiness, thus picking up the other strand of Mendelssohn's argument. Kant's argument now is that "*complete conformity* of dispositions with the moral law is the supreme condition of the highest good" and required of us, but that such complete conformity, or "*holiness*," is "a perfection of which no rational being in the sensible world is capable at any moment of his existence," so we must instead assume the possibility of "an *endless progress* toward that complete conformity," which is in turn "possible only on the presupposition of the *existence* and personality of the same rational being continuing *endlessly* (which is called the immortality of the soul)" (CPracR 5:122). Kant's argument here is that we must have adequate opportunity to perfect our moral vocation, and this seems similar to Mendelssohn's claim that God would not have given us the capacity for virtue unless he has also given us a future life with the possibility of "continuing to practice" and perfect "virtue and wisdom under his divine guidance" (*JubA* 3.1:114), a future life in which "all conflicts of obligations, all collisions of duties, which could send a limited being into doubt and uncertainty, will find their irrevocable resolution" (*JubA* 3.1:118).[11]

In justifying the postulation of immortality on the practical rather than theoretical ground that we must able to believe that is possible for us to perfect our moral disposition or virtue, Kant actually seems to be hewing more closely to Spalding's original argument in the *Vocation of Humankind* than did Mendelssohn, for Spalding had argued that it is precisely the perfection of our virtue rather than of our happiness that is our vocation. He argued that neither sensory nor even intellectual pleasure can be the proper goal of human beings, because neither of these offers any enduring satisfaction and both run afoul of our inherent suspicion of selfishness; instead, only the development of a moral disposition, which Spalding defines in terms clearly influenced by the British moral-sense school as "natural sympathy with the pain of another" combined with "an effective drive to help the same,"[12] can produce an enduring satisfaction. As Spalding puts it, "this enjoyment [*Mitgenuß*] of the gratifications of others is an extremely treasureable reward for the effort with which I have attempted to make the suffering around me less and to transform it into pleasure."[13] And if helping to transform the suffering of others into their pleasure, rather than striving directly for my own pleasure, is what I should do, then I must *be able* to do it: "There has never been a case in which I have been conscious in my inmost of a genuine obligation that was really impossible for me"[14]—whatever else Kant may or may not have learned from Spalding, here the principle that "ought implies can" is clearly stated, and, as it so often seems, Kant may simply have taken this principle for granted precisely because it was so clearly affirmed by this immensely influential author. Under the rubric of "Religion," Spalding then argues that our moral task is given to us by God, and that "What really makes me something significant is only that I am sensitive to order, that I ascend to its origin, and that I can be conscious of my voluntary concordance with it, the origin of everything good, in my dispositions [*Gesinnungen*] and intentions. That is the greatness and dignity [*Würde*] of my human nature."[15] Spalding here introduces terminology that Kant would certainly adopt—*Gesinnung*, *Würde*—although his position here might

---

[11] Altmann treats this as the main argument of the third dialogue of *Phaedo*. It seems to me rather subsidiary to the main argument that a benevolent creator would have given us adequate opportunity to perfect both our virtue and our happiness.

[12] Johann Joachim Spalding, *Die Bestimmung des Menschen: Die Erstausgabe von 1748 und die letzte Auflage von 1794*, ed. Wolfgang Erich Müller (Waltrop: Hartmut Spenner, 1997), pp. 49–50. Bourel points out that Spalding translated Shaftesbury early in his career, confirming the influence on him of the moral-sense school; see *Moses Mendelssohn*, p. 240, and pp. 240–4 for a good account of Spalding's book. For a more extensive account of Spalding's work and its influence on Mendelssohn and Kant, as well as Schiller, Herder, and others, see Laura Anna Macor, *Die Bestimmung des menschen (1748–1800): Eine Begriffsgeschichte*, Monographien zur Philosophie der deutschen Aufklärung, Band 25 (Stuttgart-Bad Cannstatt: Frommann-Holzboog, 2013). For an account of the influence of Spalding on later figures, especially Fichte, see George di Giovanni, *Freedom and Religion in Kant and His Immediate Successors: The Vocation of Human Kind 1748–1800* (Cambridge: Cambridge University Press, 2005).

[13] Spalding, *Bestimmung*, p. 50.   [14] Spalding, *Bestimmen*, p. 62.

[15] Spalding, *Bestimmung*, p. 73.

come closer to divine-command morality than Kant would like. However, under the title of "Immortality," the final chapter of Spalding's work, he argues in a way that clearly anticipates Kant's argument for the postulate of immortality in the second *Critique*. Actually, he argues in a way that anticipates the complexity and ambivalence of Kant's own argument. First Spalding argues that the morally good soul must be able to expect the due reward for her virtue: he asks rhetorically, "Could the immutable rules of approbation allow that a soul that is as it should be forever be robbed of the naturally happiest consequences of its inner rectitude?" and also speaks of a "most perfect proportion" between virtue and its reward (and presumably its opposite), a way in which Kant often introduces his conception of the highest good.[16] Next, in a way that anticipates the metaphysical argument of Mendelssohn's second dialogue, which Kant in turn has rejected, Spalding argues that because the self is simple, not composed of any parts, it must be "always the same,"[17] thus the same at one moment of ordinary experience and at another, and also the same at one moment of worthy action and at another in which that action is rewarded. But finally Spalding makes the argument that Kant takes over for his postulate in the second *Critique*, namely that I must have as long as it takes to perfect my virtue, which is indeed forever. Spalding writes that in order to be "a upright citizen already in this world,"

I must at the same time work for eternity. This is only the continuation and fulfillment [*Fortsetzung und Vollführung*] of that which I begin here in the well-ruled direction and activity of my spirit; it merely gives me more opportunity and space for the further development of the qualities with which I here pursue my obligations in my situations and circumstances, such as thoughtfulness, honesty, and diligence.[18]

Spalding's argument is not a strictly theoretical or metaphysical argument, but neither does he qualify it by calling it practical rather than theoretical. He wholeheartedly supposes that we must be granted eternal life in order to fulfill our moral task, which is endless.

Kant of course transposes this argument into a practical key. But that does not automatically spare him problems. For one, endless existence naturally is not and cannot be observed in the sensible world, so presumably this endless or immortal existence must be possible for us in another or future world, as the first *Critique* had said, yet it would certainly take some fancy footwork to assign this *endless* existence to our *noumenal* selves, for those are supposed by Kant to be altogether *atemporal*. In order to escape such a difficulty, in the essay on "The End of All Things," which followed *Religion within the Boundaries of Mere Reason* by one year, Kant will suggest that the image of endless time is only our way of *representing* something that is not temporal at all.[19] But there are other problems with Kant's adoption of

---

[16] Spalding, *Bestimmung*, pp. 80–1.   [17] Spalding, *Bestimmung*, p. 82.
[18] Spalding, *Bestimmung*, p. 86.
[19] See Kant, *EAT*, e.g., 8:328. It might seem as if endlessness follows directly from the atemporality of things in themselves. But all that Kant would be entitled to argue is that we cannot *represent* any cessation of existence of a thing in itself temporally, because we cannot represent anything about things in themselves temporally, and not that things in themselves might not cease to exist in some way that we cannot represent.

Spalding's and Mendelssohn's idea that we have an infinite life in which to perfect our virtue. One problem is immediately apparent, namely that Kant's argument for the postulate of the existence of God turns on the necessity of believing in "a supreme cause of nature having a causality in keeping with the moral disposition," a "cause of all of nature" that "is to contain the ground of the correspondence of nature not merely with a law of the will of rational beings but with the representation of this *law*, so far as they make it the *supreme determining ground of the will*" (CPracR, 5:125). The problem is that after Kant's initial worry that there is no apparent causal connection between virtue and happiness, he introduces belief in God as "a cause of all nature, distinct from nature," to explain how we can believe in the possibility of a causal connection between virtue and happiness *within nature* when he just has argued that the perfection of the moral will or of virtue is *not* something that we can expect within nature. So there is no reason why we should have to believe that happiness can be the consequence of virtue *within nature*, thus no reason to postulate a God who is the cause of harmony between virtue and happiness *within nature*. It would even seem that on this account the realization of happiness, as something that is to take place within nature, would have to run *ahead* of the perfection of virtue, as something that can take place only in an endless, clearly non-sensible, non-phenomenal, and at least in that sense non-natural life, that is, a world that is not a *Sinnenwelt*. This seems incoherent, putting the cart before the horse.

But an even more serious problem lies in Kant's assumption that the perfection of human virtue or our worthiness to be happy is equivalent to *holiness*, a condition toward which we could only endlessly progress and thus never attain in our natural life. We might well think that what morality requires of us is unremitting commitment to the moral law no matter what conflicting temptations we experience, but not a kind of holiness that consists in never experiencing any temptations contrary to morality at all. At least in the *Religion*, Kant defines the kinds of holiness possible for human beings simply as "the universal and pure maxim of the agreement of conduct with the law, as the germ from which all good is to proceed," a "change of heart which must be possible because it is a duty." Kant does not say that this requires the humanly impossible elimination of temptation in the form of inclination (*RBMR*, 6:66–7). All that is morally demanded of human beings, one should think, is that they override contrary inclinations in order to act as morality requires whenever and as often as they need to in their ordinary, phenomenal, and therefore temporal lives, not that they become something other than they are, creatures who have no inclinations contrary to morality, which might indeed seem to take forever. Kant gives us no reason to think that human beings are incapable of fulfilling *this* demand in their natural or normal lives; on the contrary his transcendental idealist theory of the will seems intended to explain precisely how human beings can really be free, thus free to subordinate all inclination and self-love to the moral law, while nevertheless appearing to be in time and therefore appearing to be causally determined. Transcendental idealism is not a promise of the freedom to be truly moral in some future life, but an account of how, despite appearances, we are already so free in our natural life. Kant's postulate of an unnatural immortality in the second *Critique* thus seems to rest on a demand for an unnatural holiness that is not otherwise part of his account of the demand of morality and our freedom to fulfill it—that is, indeed, in tension with it.

I would suggest that Kant came to recognize this point after the publication of the *Critique of Practical Reason*, and thus retracted the argument from Spalding and Mendelssohn that belief in immortality is necessary for us to have the opportunity to perfect our virtue. I would also suggest that his recognition of this point combined with his enduring faith in the possibility of moral progress may well have led him to increased emphasis on the possibility of moral progress in the human species rather than human individuals in the final decade of his work, although he had already introduced that theme in the critical decade. Paradoxically this will lead him to downplay the significance of individual freedom in his final dispute with Mendelssohn, the argument with Mendelssohn over the possibility of the moral progress of the human species that Kant makes in the final section of the 1793 essay on "Theory and Practice," seven years after the death of his target.

## 4. Kant's Diminution of the Postulate of Personal Immortality

Kant's final decade of work began with the *Critique of the Power of Judgment*, written in 1788–9 and published in the spring of 1790. Here Kant clearly enunciates the premise of the doctrine of the postulates of pure practical reason as he had developed it in the preceding two critiques, stating that "a final end cannot be commanded by any law of reason without reason simultaneously promising its attainability, even if uncertainly" (*CPJ* §91, 5:471n.), although the entire argument of the third *Critique* essentially reassigns the conception of nature as a realm in which we can realize our moral goals and which we must believe to have been authored by God to make this possible from reason to reflective judgment.[20] But even though in the third *Critique* Kant continues to mention immortality along with the existence of God "as the conditions under which alone we can, given the constitution of our (human) reason, conceive of the possibility" of the highest good as the "effect of the lawful use of our freedom" (*CPJ* §91, 5:470), he offers no explicit reason why we must postulate immortality in addition to the divine authorship of nature in order to conceive of the possibility of the highest good. Even more striking, in *Religion within the Boundaries of Mere Reason*, the first Part of which was published two years after the third *Critique* in the *Berlinische Monatsschrift* and the whole of which was published in book form the following year, and which is the work in which we might most naturally expect to find Kant defending the rationality of belief in immortality as well as in the existence of God, we find that his treatment of the highest good is restricted to its Preface and makes no reference to immortality at all, while in the body of the work, although Kant does not explicitly reject the possibility of personal immortality, he undercuts any argument that personal immortality is necessary for the perfection of our virtue.[21] Instead, he argues that because of our

---

[20] See my "Reason and Reflective Judgment: Kant on the Significance of Systematicity," originally *Noûs* 24 (1990): 17–43, reprinted in my *Kant's System of Nature and Freedom: Selected Essays* (Oxford: Clarendon Press, 2005), pp. 11–37.

[21] It is striking that James DiCenso's recent *Kant's Religion within the Boundaries of Mere Reason: A Commentary* (Cambridge: Cambridge University Press, 2012) contains no reference to the concept of

sensible, thus temporal nature, it is natural for us to *represent* even our successful moral conversion only as progress, but he specifically says that even though this progress can be cut off at any time, by the natural fact of death, God can still recognize the perfection of our moral conversion *in our natural, finite life spans* even if we ourselves cannot. Indeed, he goes even further and suggests at least once that our image of eternity is really only our way of representing the fact that we are faced with the choice between evil and good as long as we live, however long that happens to be. Kant thus essentially reverses his own and Mendelssohn's earlier representation of immortality as the necessary condition for the realization of our moral perfection into a representation of our inescapable freedom to choose good *or* evil that can be exercised in our normal lives even though we ourselves are not in an epistemic position to be certain of our success or failure in moral choice.

In a footnote to the Preface to *Religion* that is almost as long as the Preface itself, Kant presents the challenge presented by the concept of the highest good as explaining how "The proposition, 'There is a God, there is a highest good in the world'… is to proceed (as proposition of faith) simply from morality," as "a synthetic a priori proposition."(*RBMR* 6:6n.). He then proceeds to explain in what sense the command to seek to realize the highest good can be regarded as a synthetic a priori proposition. He argues that "One's own happiness is the subjective ultimate end of rational beings belonging to the world (they each *have* this end by virtue of their nature which is dependent upon sensible objects)." Thus, though Kant does not explicitly state this, the proposition that any rational agent does seek its own happiness would be a synthetic a posteriori proposition. "But that every human being ought to make the highest possible *good* in the world his own *ultimate end* is a synthetic practical proposition a priori, that is, an objective-practical proposition given through pure reason" (*RBMR* 6:6–7n.), precisely because it commands something that goes beyond merely natural desire or inclination. So far, this explains the synthetic a priori status only of the command to seek the realization of the highest good, not of the proposition linking that commandment to the conditions of its possibility, and it does not explain precisely why reason commands that each be concerned with the happiness of all. Kant says nothing to address the latter omission, but he does conclude his note by adding that:

But now, if the strictest observance of the moral laws is to be thought of as the cause of the ushering in of the highest good (as end), then, since human capacity does not suffice to effect happiness in the world proportionate to the worthiness to be happy, an omnipotent moral being must be assumed as ruler of the world, under whose care this would come about, i.e., morality leads inevitably to religion. (*RBMR* 6:7–8n.)

Kant does not explicitly say that the proposition that there is a sufficient cause for the realization of the highest good is synthetic a priori, but it is a causal claim, therefore synthetic, and it is obviously not a posteriori, so he must be assuming that it will be equally obvious that it is synthetic a priori, even if it is a matter of rational faith,

---

immortality at all. DiCenso does not discuss the passages from Part Two of the *Religion* I am about to discuss, which might seem to suggest Kant's continuing commitment to the postulate of immortality but which, as I will argue, do not.

not theoretical speculation, and so his initial question will have been answered. But the point I want to emphasize is that in this account of necessary belief in the conditions of possibility of realization of the highest good, there is no reference to personal immortality at all.

Indeed, as I suggested, Kant actually undermines any need for belief in personal immortality in the *Religion*. This takes place in several steps. First, although Kant does not abjure holiness of will as the perfection of the moral vocation of human beings, as already mentioned he subtly revises his conception of holiness in a way that disconnects it from immortality. While he may previously have conceived of holiness of will as the absence of all inclination, something that can never be expected to occur in phenomenal human existence, in *Religion* he carefully defines holiness as "*holiness of maxims* in the compliance to one's duty," further, as "recovery" (because we are all born with a disposition to the good, even though we also have a tendency to evil and have apparently chosen to act upon it) "of the *purity* of the law, as the supreme ground of all our maxims, according to which the law itself to be incorporated into the power of choice, not merely bound to other incentives, nor indeed subordinated to them (to inclinations)" (*RBMR* 6:46). That is, Kant does not define holiness as consisting in the *elimination* of inclinations, but only as the thoroughgoing *subordination* of them or any maxims they would suggest to the moral law as one's fundamental maxim—and this is something that, because of the transcendental freedom of the human will, any human being can achieve at any time, not something that has to be deferred to some future life. With this account of holiness combined with the conception of radical freedom to which Kant has committed himself in the *Religion*, there is no need of immortality for the perfection of virtue (or worthiness to be happy), nor does Kant suggest that there is.

In the second Part of the *Religion*, however, which describes "the battle of the good against the evil principle for dominion over the human being" (*RBMR* 6:57), Kant introduces what might look like a reference to personal immortality after all. In one passage, Kant clearly refers to personal immortality only in the subjunctive. He argues that the radical character of human freedom allows for complete conversion from good to evil within the natural life span of human beings, which allows the inference that *if* there is an afterlife that moral conversion will continue to hold. He writes here:

> For a human being who from the time of his adoption of the principles of the good and throughout a sufficiently long life henceforth has perceived the efficacy of these principles on what he does, i.e., on the conduct of his life as it steadily improves, and from that has cause to infer, but only by way of conjecture, a fundamental improvement in his disposition, can yet also reasonably hope that in this life he will no longer forsake his present course but will rather press in it with ever greater courage, since his advances, provided that their principle is good, will always increase his *strength* for future ones; nay, if after this life another awaits him, that he will persevere in it (in all appearances under different circumstances, yet according to the very same principle) and come ever closer to his goal of perfection, though it is unattainable; for, on the basis of what he has perceived in himself so far, he can legitimately assume that his disposition is fundamentally improved. (*RBMR* 6:68)

This passage emphasizes, first, that humans can convert to pure morality during their natural lives although they cannot be sure that they have done so, an uncertainty that Kant sometimes presents as due to the empirical and thus contingent fact that one can often do the morally right thing out of the motive of self-interest, which is very good at hiding itself (see G 4:407), but which of course also follows necessarily from the transcendental idealist supposition that the choice of fundamental maxim is noumenal rather than phenomenal. Kant then goes on merely to state that *if* there is an afterlife, such a person might have the same degree of confidence that his moral conversion will continue there too, but this is hardly an assertion, even on practical grounds, that there is an afterlife.[22] It might be objected that the last sentence in this passage implies only the possibility of continued progress toward conversion, not of the completion of conversion; I would rather suggest that the final reference to a fundamental improvement of disposition implies the possibility of complete conversion, although Kant may also be worrying about the possibility of relapse even from complete conversion.

A preceding passage, however, seems actually to assert that there is an afterlife. Carefully read, however, this passage continues Kant's epistemic theme, arguing only that because of our uncertainty about our own moral conversion, we *represent* our lives as endless, but that God, who is not subject to our epistemic limits, can know that we really have undertaken moral conversion in our natural lives: Kant writes here:

According to our mode of estimation, [to us] who are unavoidably restricted to temporal conditions in our conceptions of the relationship of cause to effect, the deed, as a continuous advance *in infinitum* from a defective good to something better, always remains defective, so that we are bound to consider the good as it appears in us, i.e., according to the *deed*, as at each *instant* inadequate to a holy law. But because of the *disposition* from which it derives and which transcends the senses, we can think of the infinite progression of the good towards toward conformity to the law as being judged by him who scrutinizes the heart (through his pure intellectual intuition) to be a perfected whole even with respect to the deed (the life conduct). And so notwithstanding his permanent deficiency, a human being can still expect to be *generally* well-pleasing to God, at whatever point in time his existence be cut short.

(RBMR 6:67)

In this intricate passage, Kant makes two different suggestions. One is the general point that because of our restriction to phenomenal self-knowledge we can never be certain of our complete conversion from evil to good because of the noumenal and thus hidden character of that conversion. The other is that because outwardly good actions could always be performed from self-love rather than respect for the moral law, even if our conversion from the evil to the good fundamental maxim were complete we could not tell this from even the best actions, and we might thus represent our conversion only as progress *in infinitum*, not as ever complete. But

---

[22] In his commentary on *Religion*, Stephen R. Palmquist uses the subjunctive in writing that people who have not made an effort at moral conversion "cannot rationally hope that, if granted another life in some after-death state, they would suddenly start to improve at that stage"; *Comprehensive Commentary on Kant's* Religion within the Bounds of Bare Reason (Chichester: Wiley Blackwell, 2016), p. 187. But he does not emphasize that in this Part of *Religion*, Kant writes of a human afterlife *only* in the subjunctive, and that his doctrine of the possibility of conversion from evil to good at any time actually obviates the need for any postulate of immortality.

either way, Kant goes on to imply that our conversion or choice of good fundamental maxim *can be completed* in our natural or phenomenal lifetime, *before whatever point in time it is cut short*, and that God can know what our choice was even if we ourselves cannot. There is thus no argument for a postulate of personal immortality here; rather there is an argument for the possibility of complete moral conversion within the natural, finite human life span. Even if he does not reject belief in immortality itself, Kant has thus rejected the connection between moral perfection and immortality suggested by Spalding and Mendelssohn and then adopted by himself in the second *Critique*.

Kant makes a further suggestion about the significance of the idea of immortality for us. If transcendental freedom means that a human is free to convert from evil to good at any point in his life, such a being must also be free to relapse or convert back from good to evil at any point as well—even though we cannot cognize noumenal choice temporally, it would be a mistake to infer that we get to make only *one* noumenal choice, for that itself would be an illegitimate importation of temporality into our conception of the noumenal.[23] In fact, it is already part of Kant's model of choice in *Religion* that every human being can make at least *two* free choices, that is, two tokens of free choice—first the free choice to be evil, for as imputable evil must be the product of choice (*RBMR* 6:21n. and 6:37), and then (or "then," in scare-quotes), the free choice to be good. But if any human gets at least two noumenal choices, in spite of the non-temporality of the noumenal, then there is no reason why she cannot have more than two; in fact, a human retains freedom of choice at every moment of her life (whatever non-representable and "inscrutable" form this must take at the noumenal level), and thus always has the power to choose good even though she has previously chosen evil, *or evil even if she has previously chosen good*. In a way, our moral conversion is imperfect precisely because our freedom is, on Kant's account, perfect. Kant puts both this point and the previous point that he is not actually affirming immortality by adding that "without any necessity to presuppose *dogmatically*, as an item of doctrine, that an eternity of good or evil is the human lot also objectively" (*RBMR* 6:69). "Eternity" might seem to imply immortality, but Kant's remark that we do not need to presuppose it dogmatically means that he is not actually asserting it. Thus there is no reason to think that Kant is taking back his previous remark that human life might be cut short at any time without the individual knowing of his own conversion while God does. Instead, this just seems to be a way of describing how we represent our moral condition to ourselves: as long as we live, we are confronted with the choice between good and evil, we are never relieved of that choice no matter how well we have chosen in the past, and perhaps given our notorious inability to imagine our own deaths we represent this condition to ourselves as eternal. But in *Religion* Kant has not argued that human life is immortal, only that human freedom is inescapable.

---

[23] This mistake would be of the same sort as assuming that because we cannot count things in themselves using our ordinary spatio-temporal forms of differentiation, there can only be one thing in itself, a mistake that Schopenhauer makes but that Kant does not. See for example Arthur Schopenhauer, *On the Basis of Morality*, §22, p. 251.

I think that Kant is making a similar point in the opening pages of the essay on "The End of All Things," which was published in the *Berlinischer Monatsschrift*, by now moved to Goethe's Jena in Saxony-Anhalt in order to escape Prussian censorship, two years after the first Part of the *Religion*. Here Kant begins by arguing that we cannot think of eternity as a continuation of ordinary time and thus cannot think of change as possible if we have once passed through the judgment day to eternity; so we must suppose that the moral character that we have adopted by the end of our natural life, good or evil, will remain fixed for eternity. But this is not meant as an argument that we actually will or even must believe that we will somehow endure in a changeless eternity; it is rather meant to suggest simply that we must make every effort to attain moral perfection within our earthly lives, "For we see nothing before us now that could teach us about our fate in a future world except the judgment of our own conscience, i.e., what our present moral state, as far as we are acquainted with it, lets us judge rationally concerning it" (*EAT* 8:330). When it comes to moral improvement, there's no time like the present.

## 5. The Immortality of the Species rather than the Person

Even in the *Religion*, Kant continued to hold that belief in immortality is both natural and a mark of true religion. For example, that Judaism neither promises nor commands a belief in immortality is part of Kant's argument that in its original form it was the statutory law for the civil condition of a particular people, not a religion based on universally valid ethical law—even though "it can hardly be doubted that the Jews subsequently produced, each for himself, some sort of religious faith which they added to the articles of their statutory faith" (*RBMR* 6:126).[24] But he had reduced the endless progress of human individuals to immortality to a mere way of representing both our imperfect knowledge of our own conversion and even more importantly our need to choose between evil and good as long as we live. Yet even in his final decade Kant found it difficult to give up entirely on a more substantive idea of endless progress, so he transferred this possibility from the human individual to the human species.

To be sure, Kant had been concerned with the moral progress of the species while he was still concerned also to defend the rationality of belief in personal immortality: notably, the Second Proposition of the 1784 essay "Idea for a universal history from a cosmopolitan point of view" had stated that "*In the human being* (as the only rational

---

[24] Upon hearing a first version of this chapter, Stephen Palmquist suggested that in a note to the second edition of *RBMR* at 6:166, Kant defended Mendelssohn against the calls for his conversion to Christianity, originally made by Johann Caspar Lavater in 1770 and then repeated in a review of the first edition of *Jerusalem* by August Friederich Cranz, on the ground that Mendelssohn's personal addition of belief in immortality, attested precisely by *Phaedon*, to the articles of statutory Jewish faith, obviated the need for any such conversion. That seems to me a reasonable implication of the whole argument of the *Religion*, but not the point of the note at 6:166, which says only that Mendelssohn thought that if the "yoke of external observances" were removed from Judaism, the "yoke of a profession of faith in sacred history" would remain. Kant does not explicitly say that the second yoke includes belief in immortality.

creature on earth), *those predispositions whose goal is the use of his reason were to develop completely only in the species, but not in the individual.*" Even though this piece was composed between the first and second critiques, thus while Kant continued to emphasize the postulate of personal immortality, Kant's rationale for it emphasized the *mortality* of individual human beings:

> Reason itself does not operative instinctively, but rather needs attempts, practice and instruction in order gradually to progress from one stage of insight to another. Hence every human being would have to live exceedingly long in order to learn how he is to make a complete use of all his predispositions; or, if nature has only set the term of his life as short (as has actually happened), then nature perhaps needs an immense series of generations, each of which transmits its enlightenment to the next, in order finally to propel its germs in our species to that stage of development which is completely suited to its aim. (*IUH* 8:19).

Perhaps Kant had in mind some subtle difference between the perfection of human reason and the perfection of human virtue. Perhaps he had in mind the perfection of theoretical and prudential reason rather than the perfection of pure practical reason, which as we have just seen he would argue a decade later in the *Religion* is available to everyone at all times. Perhaps in this popular essay he was only talking about the phenomenal human being, not the noumenal human being. Be all that as it may, in this essay he was clearly focused on progress in the human species because of the obvious mortality of individual human beings.

After what I have suggested is the turning point of the third *Critique*, Kant returned to the question of the possibility of progress on the part of humanity as a whole. One revealing passage occurs in the third part of the *Religion*, where Kant argues that "The human being ought to leave the ethical state of nature in order to become a member of an ethical community" (*RBMR* 6:96). Whether his argument here is that the realization of the highest good can never be brought about by a single individual, but only by the human species as a whole, or only that an individual's efforts at virtue and toward the realization of the highest good can always be weakened by the influence of others unless all human beings are members of an ethical community, there is in either case no need to postulate personal immortality, although there is need to posit the existence of God as the condition of the possibility of human cooperation and thus of an ethical community itself:

> Now, we have here a duty *sui generis*, not of human beings toward human beings but of the human race toward itself. For every species of rational beings is objectively—in the idea of reason—destined to a common end, the promotion of the highest good as a good common to all. But, since this highest good will not be brought about solely through the striving of one individual person for his own moral perfection but requires rather a union of such persons into a whole toward that very end, toward a system of well-disposed human beings in which, and through the unity of which alone, the highest moral good can come to pass... We can already anticipate that this duty will need the presupposition of another idea, namely, of a higher moral being through whose universal organization the forces of single individuals, insufficient on their own, are united for a common effect. (*RBMR* 6:98)

There is no hint of a postulate of personal immortality here, only an argument for faith in a divinely grounded possibility of the human cooperation that would be necessary for humankind ultimately to realize its highest good.

Another text from the 1790s in which the postulate of personal immortality gives way to faith in the possibility of the progress of the human species is the essay on "Theory and Practice," published at the same time as the *Religion*. This essay begins with a response to Christian Garve's objection that Kant's doctrine of the highest good has undermined the purity of his moral philosophy itself by making the promise of personal happiness the *motivation* to morality. Kant responds that the highest good is only meant to be the *object* of morality, that is, its goal, not its ground, although as the object of morality its realization must be possible if the attempt to be moral is to be rational. He argues further that the happiness with which the highest good is concerned is not individual or "selfish" happiness but "universal happiness combined with and in conformity with the purest morality throughout the world" (*TP* 8:279–80). In the course of this response to Garve, Kant says, perhaps not entirely disingenuously, that "It is not as if the universal concept of duty first gets 'support and stability' only on the presupposition" of both God and a future life, "that is, gets a sure basis and the requisite strength of an *incentive*, but rather that only in the ideal of pure reason does it also get an *object*" (*TP* 8:279); his point here is that if morality ultimately commands us to seek universal happiness, then we must also be able to believe that universal happiness is ultimately possible. We do not need to have a promise of our own happiness and thus of our own immortality in order to retain our incentive to be moral, he is saying—although that is precisely what the first *Critique* had maintained. The second part of "Theory and Practice" provides a preliminary statement of Kant's philosophy of right, to be more fully expounded four years later in the first half of the *Metaphysics of Morals*. The third part raises the question "Are there in human nature predispositions from which one can gather that the race will always progress toward what is better and that the evil of present and past times will disappear in the good of future times?"

Kant argues for an affirmative answer to this question, and explicitly presents his position as an alternative to the position he ascribes to Mendelssohn, not in *Phaedo* but in *Jerusalem*, which is that while individuals may make moral progress, "the human race as a whole make[s] small oscillations, and it never takes a few steps forward without soon afterward sliding back twice as fast into its former state" (*TP* 8:307).[25] The heart of Kant's position is that it is the duty of each human being not to realize the highest good in his own lifetime but to make the best contribution that he can to the moral progress of the species. His explication of his position clearly assumes human mortality:

I shall therefore be allowed to assume that, since the human race is constantly advancing with respect to culture (as its natural end) it is also to be conceived as progressing toward what is better with respect to the moral end of its existence, and that this will indeed be *interrupted* from time to time but will never be *broken off*. I do not need to prove this presupposition; it is up to its adversary to prove [his] case. For I rest my case on my innate duty, the duty of every

---

[25] Kant quotes from *Jerusalem*, Section II, pp. 44–7; the passage may be found in Mendelssohn, *Jerusalem* pp. 94–5, JubA 8:160–2. Mendelssohn seems to be arguing that the moral oscillation of the human race is precisely the condition that gives human individuals the freedom to be moral on their own, with the "appropriate means" to so doing that God has granted to every human at every time and place (*Jerusalem* p. 93, JubA 8:160).

member of the series of generations—to which I (as a human being in general) belong and am yet not so good in the moral character required of me as I ought to be and hence could be—so as to influence posterity that it becomes always better (the possibility of this must, accordingly, also be assumed), and to do it in such a way that this duty may be legitimately handed down from one member [in the series of] generations to another ... however uncertain I may always be and remain as to whether something better is to be hoped for the human race, this cannot infringe upon the maxim, and hence upon its presupposition, necessary for practicable purposes, that it is practicable. (*TP* 8:308–9)

This passage is important because it clearly distinguishes between the natural and the moral end of human beings, so that the claim that it makes upon the assumption of human mortality explicitly applies to the latter and not to the former. With equal clarity Kant then applies his standard premise for a postulate of pure practical reason—ought implies can, i.e., what is morally necessary must be possible or practicable—to the moral duty of each human being "so to influence posterity that it becomes always better." What we must assume to be possible is that each individual can be motivated to make his proper contribution to the morality of future generations and that human nature allows for the influence of past and present generations upon future ones. This is very different from any assumption of the possibility of personal immortality; it is precisely what must be assumed to make the moral progress of the species possible in the absence of personal immortality.

In this passage, Kant thus clearly argues that all that we must postulate in order to make possible the moral progress of the species is the possibility of the moral influence of human individuals on their successors; this replaces the postulate of personal immortality. Kant takes the burden of proof to be on (the late) Mendelssohn to disprove this possibility, not to be on himself to prove it. Does he go even further in his response to Mendelssohn's position by arguing that the moral progress of the human race is not just possible but *necessary*? He seems to do precisely this in several places, one the essay on the "Idea of Universal History" previously discussed and another, the 1795 pamphlet *Toward Perpetual Peace*. In the culminating Ninth Proposition of the former Kant speaks of a "consoling prospect into the future ... in which the human species is represented in the remote distance as finally working itself upward toward the condition in which all germs nature has fully placed in it can be fully developed and its vocation here on earth can be fulfilled" (*IUH* 8:30). In the latter Kant speaks, for example, of the "*guarantee* (surety)" offered by "the great artist nature ... from whose mechanical course purposiveness shines forth visibly, letting concord arise by means of the discord between human beings even against their will" (*PP* 8:360–1). However, Kant cannot mean by such remarks more than that nature, including human nature, contains mechanisms that make moral progress *possible*, and that *can* be used as means for moral progress by properly motivated human beings. This is clear from his statement in the essay on history that since the masters of human beings who will devise and enforce the laws that will make their subjects behave, or make crooked timber grow straight, are themselves only human, the problem of right can be solved only if such rulers have "correct concepts of the nature of a possible constitution, great experience practiced through many courses of life[,] and beyond this a good will that is prepared to accept" the former: all the mechanisms of nature are only *necessary conditions* for justice, and there is never a *sufficient* condition without a good will (*IUH* 8:23). It is likewise clear in *Towards Perpetual Peace* from the First Appendix, which argues that "the concept of right would be an empty thought" without a "*moral politician*," one who "will make it his principle that, once defects that could not have been prevented are found within the constitution of a state or in the relation of states, it is a duty, especially for heads of state, to be concerned about how they can be improved a soon as possible and brought into conformity with natural right" (*PP* 8:372). Again, without a good will on the part of those in power there is no sufficient condition for justice (which I am assuming is part of morality).[26] And while it may be difficult to reconcile this conclusion with Kant's talk of a guarantee of right from nature in *Perpetual Peace*, it is entirely consistent with Kant's claim in the history essay that we must be able to have a prospect of a natural "condition in which all germs nature has fully placed in it *can be* fully developed and its vocation here on earth *can be* fulfilled" (emphasis added), for this is a straightforward application of Kant's principle that ought implies can, which is always consistent with his conception of the radical freedom of human beings. And nothing less than the possibility that human beings can always employ or subvert the mechanisms of nature would be.

Does this conclusion bring Kant's position closer towards Mendelssohn's after all? It does not bring Kant back toward the argument for the practical postulate of personal immortality as a condition of the perfection of personal virtue into which he had transformed Mendelssohn's metaphysical conviction in the second *Critique*; he is still claiming only that it must be possible for mortal human beings to make their individual contributions to the progress of the human race. But it might bring Kant closer to Mendelssohn's position that human history is an "oscillation," for he cannot say more than that it must be *possible* for human politicians to play their special role in realizing human progress. It would hardly be compatible with his theory of human freedom as well as with his or anyone else's observation of human history to hold that human politicians always *will* play that role well. In this way, the distance between Kant's philosophy of history and Mendelssohn's may not be as great as it seems to Kant himself, even though the difference in their metaphysics of immortality is ultimately very great indeed.

We will return to this issue in Part Three, in which we will examine Mendelssohn's and Kant's views on how the religion of reason might actually manifest itself in human history further. For now, we will leave aside further discussion of human freedom, God, and immortality, and instead turn to a different metaphysical issue that both brought our two philosophers together yet divided them—and which is of course relevant at least to Kant's defense of human freedom—namely, the issue of idealism.

---

[26] I defend this assumption elsewhere, including "The Twofold Morality of *Recht*," *Kant-Studien* 107 (2016): 34–63.

# 5
# Mendelssohn, Kant, and Idealism

## 1. Introduction

This chapter will examine Kant's and Mendelssohn's complex interaction on the subject of idealism. The short version of this relationship is that Kant thinks that our belief in the reality of external objects needs a philosophical foundation, which, paradoxically, can only be provided by the theory that space and time are not features of things as they really are, but only of things as they appear to us. This is the position he sums up in the slogan that empirical realism presupposes transcendental idealism. Mendelssohn's position is that we cannot guarantee that our spatial representation of the world represents it as it really is, but neither do we need to guarantee this for the ordinary purposes of life and scientific inquiry—while he also thinks it is impossible to doubt the reality of time at any level. Kant's position is thus a complex blend of empiricism and metaphysics, while Mendelssohn tries to make do with a more purely empiricist approach. But this is a simplified version of what we will now see is a more involuted history.

Kant's defense of the possibility of the existence of God, human freedom, and human immortality, and thus the possible rationality of our belief in these, ultimately on practical grounds, all depend on his doctrine of transcendental idealism. This is his view that spatiality and temporality, as well as causality—which Kant defines as succession according to a rule, thus as involving temporality, but which also presupposes determinate spatial relations, and which thus depends upon both time and space—are necessary features of our representation of things, or their appearances, but not features of things as they are themselves at all. In his prize essay, Mendelssohn argued that the truth of geometry depends only on constant features of our sensible representation of the world, and had also argued that God cannot be spatio-temporal, so he might seem to have anticipated Kant's transcendental idealism. Moreover, Mendelssohn argues in *Morning Hours* that there is no point to asking what ordinary external objects *are* beyond *how they affect us*, and that too might suggest that he ultimately accepts Kant's transcendental idealism rather than rejecting it, as he is often said to do. However, that would simplify what is a more complicated story. For while there is a significant similarity in the way in which both philosophers accept certain aspects of idealism while at the same time accepting what Kant calls "empirical realism," the reliability of our ordinary beliefs about external objects as long as the claims of these beliefs, as beliefs about how things reliably appear to us, are properly understood, there are also two deep differences between them. For one, even while apparently being open to Kant's transcendental idealism about *space*, Mendelssohn explicitly rejects Kant's transcendental idealism about *time*. Second, while being amenable to or even first suggesting certain aspects of idealism, Mendelssohn does not accept Kant's *transcendental* idealism. For Kant, the adjective "transcendental" means that the noun to which it is applied (form of intuition, category, principle, mental capacity or "faculty") is a condition of the possibility of knowledge (*CPR* B 40), and Kant's transcendental idealism about space and time argues that the non-spatiality and -temporality of things as they are in themselves is a condition of our a priori knowledge of the applicability to all appearances of the mathematics that describes the structure of space and time; as we will see, Kant *denies* the spatiality and temporality of things as they are in themselves precisely in order to *guarantee* our a priori knowledge of the mathematical structure of appearances. Mendelssohn, however, is content with a kind of epistemic *modesty* that is sometimes but falsely attributed to Kant himself, namely that we simply cannot know and it is pointless to ask whether the same structures that are evident in our sensory experience of objects are really true of those objects as they are in themselves. Here the supposed rationalist might be considered to be the purer empiricist.

These two fundamental differences emerge in several episodes from 1770 to 1787. The first episode is well-known: Mendelssohn was one of three Berlin philosophers who received copies of Kant's inaugural dissertation, his first statement of transcendental idealism, in the fall of 1770, and who all wrote letters to Kant in which they rejected his position that "*Time is not something objective and real*," but is only "the subjective condition which is necessary, in virtue of the nature of the human mind, for the coordinating of all sensible things in accordance with a fixed law" (*ID*, §14.4, 2:400). Kant did not immediately answer these letters, but in the first edition of the *Critique of Pure Reason* he acknowledged the objection as one "that must naturally occur to every reader who is not accustomed to these considerations" (A 36–7/B 53), and then defended himself against what is in fact Mendelssohn's version of the objection. Kant does not name the "insightful men" who first raised the objection, and of course Mendelssohn's letter would not have been known to the public in 1781, but it has long since been clear to whom Kant was responding.

The second episode is less well-known, but what I will argue here is that Kant's inclusion of a "Refutation of Idealism" in the second edition of the *Critique*, which Kant prepared in 1786 and was published in 1787, may well be a response to Mendelssohn's own discussion of idealism in his last book, the *Morning Hours* published in 1785, in which he in turn had attempted to respond to Kant's attack upon a priori arguments for the existence of God in the first edition of the *Critique*. This is not the story that is usually told about Kant's Refutation of Idealism; it is rather usually understood as a final attempt to lay to rest the charge of Berkeleianism or subjective idealism that had been leveled against Kant in the first major review of the *Critique*, the review written by the "popular philosopher" Christian Garve but redacted by the Göttingen empiricist J.H. Feder and published in 1782. But Kant had already responded to that review in the *Prolegomena to Any Future Metaphysics* in 1783, arguing that contrary to standard idealism—what Kant calls "subjective" and "empirical" idealism—his transcendental idealism does not deny the *existence* of objects that exist independently of our representations of them but only denies that such objects *are as we represent* them to be, and he further suggests in the second edition of the *Critique* that the Transcendental Aesthetic, with its proof that space is the *necessary* form of our representation of external objects, is an adequate response to what he took to be Berkeley's argument that the idea of space is incoherent rather than a necessary condition of our experience. (Berkeley did not deny the reality of time, so Kant does not present the transcendental ideality of time as a response to Berkeley.) The Refutation of Idealism has a different target, namely *Cartesian* skepticism about the existence of external objects (*CPR* A 367–9, B 274–5), and I suggest that Kant's reason for this addition may well have been the prominence that Mendelssohn, unlike Garve and Feder, gave to the threat of Cartesian skepticism in the *Morning Hours*. But Kant did not think that Mendelssohn's answer to Cartesian doubt is strong enough. Mendelssohn himself would have been particularly sensitive to the threat of Cartesian skepticism precisely because of the favorable light that he shines, as we have seen, on Descartes's argument from our certainty of our own existence to the existence of God and on the ontological argument—he would have wanted to make sure that his reliance on these Cartesian arguments was not undercut by Cartesian skepticism. And the proposal that Kant's Refutation of Idealism is actually responding to Mendelssohn rather than to the charge of Berkeleianism would make sense of the structure of the new section, in which Kant actually takes over Mendelssohn's *empirical criteria* for particular beliefs in external objects but undergirds them with a *transcendental argument* for the necessity of belief in external objects in general that complements his previous *transcendental* argument that space and time are not properties or relations of things as they are in themselves: Kant's transcendental argument is meant to replace Mendelssohn's merely inductive, probabilistic argument for the existence of external objects. Thus, even though Kant refers to Mendelssohn by name only once in the *Critique*, in the criticism of his argument for the immortality of the soul in the second edition of the "Paralogisms of Pure Reason" that we discussed in the last chapter, one of the most important additions to the second edition, the Refutation of Idealism, may also have been a response to Mendelssohn. Mendelssohn's *Morning Hours*, his ensuing debate with Jacobi, and his recent death were obviously much on Kant's mind as he revised the *Critique* during 1786, and the new Refutation of Idealism as well as the revised Paralogisms reveal how much Kant was thinking about Mendelssohn.

In this chapter, I will first discuss Mendelssohn's objection to Kant's doctrine of the transcendental ideality of time in the inaugural dissertation and Kant's belated response to this criticism in the first edition of the *Critique of Pure Reason*. I will then consider the Refutation of Idealism in the second edition of the *Critique* as Kant's response—partly an appropriation and partly a repudiation—to Mendelssohn's own response to idealism in the *Morning Hours*.

## 2. Mendelssohn, Kant, and the Transcendental Ideality of Time

Kant's dissertation *On the Form and Principles of the Sensible and Intelligible Worlds*, composed, defended, and published in 1770 on the occasion of his long-awaited appointment to the chair in logic and metaphysics at the "Albertina" university in Königsberg,[1] offered his first statement of the distinction between intuitions as representations of particular objects and concepts as representations of kinds of objects as well as his first statement of the argument that both intuitions and concepts have their characteristic forms, namely the "formal principles" of space and time in the first case and concepts of understanding "inherent in the mind" such as "possibility, existence, necessity, substance, cause, etc." in the second (*ID* §8, 2:395). Kant also offered his first version of the position that intuitions and therefore their forms, space and time, "do not express the internal and absolute quality of objects" (*ID* §11, 2:397), the position that he would subsequently entitle "transcendental idealism," although at this point he held that the concepts of the understanding *do* have a "*dogmatic*" use (*ID* §9, 2:395), in which they give us genuine knowledge of the existence of God and of the dependence of all other substances on God (*ID* Section 4, §§16–22). He would subsequently reject this position in favor of the view that these pure concepts can give us knowledge only when applied to intuitions, and because of that, their necessary application to mere appearances also does not give us *knowledge* of the "real and objective" qualities of objects, but only "ideas" of objective reality, ideas that have valuable and indispensable theoretical and practical roles but still do not amount to knowledge. Our concern here, however, will only be with Kant's argument that space and time are the forms of all intuition but as such only the form of phenomena, the way things appear to us, and not of the "objective and real," "internal and absolute" qualities of objects, and then with Mendelssohn's response to this position.[2]

In particular, we will focus on the case of time, which in both the dissertation and the *Critique* Kant argues is strictly parallel to the case of space but which Mendelssohn objects is importantly different. Interestingly, while in the *Critique* Kant treats the case of space first and then bases his arguments about time on that (leading many modern commentators on the *Critique* to focus on the case of space and just wave their hands in the direction of time), in the Inaugural Dissertation Kant makes the case for the transcendental ideality of time first. Kant offers no explanation for this, but since the transcendental ideality of space will be the basis for Kant's argument for the existence of synthetic a priori knowledge in geometry while the transcendental ideality of time will subsequently be the basis for his argument for the possibility of free human will, perhaps the order of topics in the dissertation reflects

---

[1] Kant, *De Mundi Sensibilis atque Intelligibilis Forma et Principiis* (*On the Form and Principles of the Sensible and Intellectual Worlds*) (1770), translated in Kant, *Theoretical Philosophy 1755–1770*, trans. David E. Walford in collaboration with Ralf Meerbote (Cambridge: Cambridge University Press, 1992), pp. 373–416. The not entirely flattering story of Kant's appointment to the chair is told in Manfred Kuehn, *Kant: A Biography* (Cambridge: Cambridge University Press, 2001), pp. 188–9. The "respondent" or spokesman for Kant's dissertation at its oral presentation and defense on August 21, 1770, was Marcus Herz, a Jewish student of medicine at Königsberg who had attended Kant's lectures and who would become Kant's go-between with Mendelssohn as well as the recipient of Kant's letters reporting his progress during the 1770s on what would become the *Critique of Pure Reason*. Herz would become a famous doctor and medical theorist in Berlin.

[2] For more detailed discussion of the inaugural dissertation, see Guyer, *Kant and the Claims of Knowledge* (Cambridge: Cambridge University Press, 1987), pp. 11–20, and Guyer, *Kant*, second edn. (London: Routledge, 2014), pp. 32–6.

the greater importance Kant ultimately gave to practical rather than theoretical philosophy.[3] Be that as it may, Kant's discussion does begin with the case of time, and it is that is which Mendelssohn objected, so that is where we will begin.

Kant's argument begins with a general claim that needs careful interpretation. He defines "Whatever, as object, relates to our senses [as] a phenomenon" (*ID* §12, 2:397), and asserts that "although phenomena, properly speaking, are aspects of things and not ideas, nonetheless cognition of them is in the highest degree true" (*ID* §11, 2:397). By this Kant means two different things. First, "in so far as they are sensory concepts or apprehensions," phenomena "are, as things caused, witnesses to the presence of an object, and this is opposed to idealism," that is, ordinary idealism, what he would later call subjective or also material idealism, in other words, Berkeleian idealism, which denies that anything except minds and their representations exist. Rather, those representations that Kant calls phenomena are always supposed to be caused in us by something other than themselves and ourselves, and are witnesses to the existence of those objects. But second, since "Truth in judging consists in agreement of a predicate with a given subject," and phenomena, as "representations of a subject and a predicate[,] arise according to common laws... they thus furnish a foothold for cognition which is in the highest degree true" (2:397). That is, although phenomena are true in the sense of being witnesses to the real existence of objects other than themselves, (all the rest of) our true judgments about them do not depend on any direct comparison between our representations and such objects, but rather on connections *among our representations* made in accordance with the laws of representation—the basic forms or principles of which, Kant is about to argue, are given by space and time and their structures.

However, this fact by itself is *not* meant as an argument that space and time as the forms of intuition do not reveal the internal and absolute qualities of the objects to the existence of which phenomena testify. Kant may be thought to begin the argument of the ensuing section of the dissertation, its equivalent of the *Critique*'s Transcendental Aesthetic, with a "short argument to idealism,"[4] namely, that any form of representation, as subjective, is inherently distorting. But this is not quite what Kant goes on to say. Instead, he states that "whatever the principle of the form of the sensible world may, in the end, be, its embrace is limited to *actual things*, in so far as they are thought capable of *falling under the senses*": this excludes "immaterial substances, which are already as such, by definition, excluded from the outer senses," and "the cause of the world," that is, God, which, as outside the world, "cannot be an

---

[3] Desmond Hogan has argued that it was actually Kant's resolution of the problem of free will rather than his theory of mathematical knowledge that prompted transcendental idealism; see. e.g., "Three Kinds of Rationalism and the Non-Spatiality of Things in Themselves," *Journal of the History of Philosophy* 47 (2009): 355–82. I have not been convinced, but in the inaugural dissertation Kant does at least place his argument for the transcendental ideality of time, which has mathematical import but will also subsequently be used to resolve the problem of free will, before his argument for the transcendental ideality of space, which has only mathematical import.

[4] This term is Karl Amerik's; see Ameriks, "Reinhold and the Short Argument to Idealism," *Proceedings of the Sixth International Kant Congress*, ed. G. Funke and T. Seebohm (Washington, 1989), vol. 2, part 2, pp. 441–53; "Kant, Fichte, and Short Arguments to Idealism," *Archiv für Geschichte der Philosophie* 72 (1990): 63–85, and "Kant and Short Arguments to Humility," in Ameriks, *Interpreting Kant's Critiques* (Oxford: Clarendon Press, 2003), pp. 135–57.

object of the senses" (*ID* §13, 2:398), but this by itself does not say that the two forms of intuition, space and time, in any way distort or fail to correspond to the reality of the things that are capable of being presented to or detected by our senses. By itself, it just says that the forms of intuition do apply to those things that are capable of being presented to our senses but do not apply to those things that are not capable of being presented to our senses. Any argument that space and time are the forms of all of our representation of objects that are presented to our senses but are *only* the forms of our *representations* of those objects, not of those objects as they are in themselves, is yet to come.

But come it does, in the course of Kant's detailed discussion of time and space in the next two sections. As mentioned, he discusses time first. His discussion is divided into six points: (1) "*The idea of time does not arise from but is presupposed by the senses*"; (2) "*The idea of time is singular* and not general"; (3) "Therefore, *the idea of time is an intuition*"; (4) "*Time is a continuous magnitude*"; (5) "*Time is not something objective and real,* nor is it a substance, nor an accident, nor a relation. Time is rather the subjective condition which is necessary, in virtue of the nature of the human mind, for the co-ordinating of all sensible things in accordance with a fixed law"; and (6), "although *time,* posited in itself and absolutely, would be an imaginary being, insofar as it belongs to the immutable law of sensible things as such, it is in the highest degree true"; from all of which follows (7), "Time, therefore, is an absolutely first *formal principle of the sensible world*" (*ID* §14, 2:398–402). Here (1) corresponds to the first two points that Kant makes in the 1781 Transcendental Aesthetic (A 30–1/B 46), (2) and (3) to the fourth and fifth points of the later text (A 31–2/B 47–8), and Kant's present point (4), asserting the continuity of time, is not included in the later Transcendental Aesthetic. Kant's present points (5), (6), and (7) correspond to the "Conclusions from these concepts" in the later Transcendental Aesthetic, while point (3) of the later text, that the "*a priori* necessity" of the representation of time "grounds the possibility of apodictic principles of the relations of time" (A 31/B 46), is not stated in the dissertation. This is a crucial omission, for as we will see, although more clearly from Kant's discussion of space than of time in the dissertation, his transition from points (1) through (3) to (5) to (7), that is, his transition from the claims that our *representation* of time has the character of an intuition to the claim that *time itself* is not a real thing or quality of things but is *nothing but our representation of it* depends, at least in part, on this missing point.

Kant's first point, as stated, is that the "idea of time" (*Idea temporis,* but with "idea" here used in Locke's general sense of "whatsoever is the Object of the Understanding, when a Man thinks... whatever it is, which the Mind can be employ'd about in thinking," that is, any content that comes before the mind, not in Kant's later technical sense)[5] does not "arise from but is presupposed by the senses" (2:398). The basis for this claim is that this idea is presupposed by any representation of things, more precisely states of things, as successive or simultaneous: it could not be abstracted or "generated" from multiple representations because they would have to

---

[5] See Locke, *Essay concerning Human Understanding,* Book I, Chapter I, 8; ed. Ph.H. Nidditch (Oxford: Clarendon Press, 1975), p. 47. In the *Critique of Pure Reason,* Kant will introduce his special sense of "ideas" as concepts of the "unconditioned" formed by pure reason (*CPR* A 322–3/B 378–9).

be represented as successive or simultaneous in order to be represented as multiple in the first place. Thus, Kant argues, we must already have the representation of time in order to represent the ideas of particular states of objects from which the general idea of time might be abstracted. This argument is directed against the kind of empiricist account of the generation of the idea of time from the succession of particular ideas that can be found in Locke and Hume.[6] Whatever its force, it clearly concludes only that we must have an a priori representation of time as the form for the representation of particular states of things, not that time is *nothing but* this representation or its form. Kant's second and third claims, that the idea of time is singular and, therefore, an intuition, are subject to the same restriction. The basis for claim (2) is that "no time is thought of except as a part of the same one boundless time" (2:399), so even though we can have ideas of particular times, particular moments or durations of time (e.g., now, today, this week), these are really only ideas of particular points or stretches in a single, all-embracing time, considered in relation to each other within that all-embracing time. For this reason, "you conceive all actual things as situated *in* time, and not as contained *under* the general concept of time, as under a common characteristic." Here Kant presupposes the definitions given in his contemporaneous logic lectures and later included in the *Critique*, namely that a concept is always properly a general representation, which *subsumes* particulars as its *instances* on the basis of their possession of the mark or marks singled out by the concept, while an intuition is a unique or singular representation that contains more particular representations as its *parts*. Thus, while 1770 or 1781 or 2018 might be considered instances of the concept *year* or even of a more general concept *periods of time*, they are properly represented as *parts* of a single, all-embracing time, perhaps beginning at 4004 BC as according to Bishop Ussher or about 14 billion years ago according to contemporary cosmologists, but in Kant's view necessarily "boundless," since any region of time we can represent is always contained in a yet larger one. But again, this is all a claim about how we *represent* time, that we *represent* it as a boundless particular, and therefore the claim that our *representation* of it is an intuition rather than a general concept. Nothing thus far says that time is *nothing but* this intuition or the form of this intuition.

Why then does Kant hold the view that time is *nothing but* the form of our own intuition? Following the discussion of the continuity of motion and therefore of time in (4), he offers two kinds of arguments in (5). The first is that the "relations or connections" of "substances and "accidents" that "confront the senses" themselves "contain nothing which tells us whether they are simultaneous with or successive to each other, apart from their positions in time, and those positions have to be determined as being either at the same or at different points in time" (*ID*, §14.4,

---

[6] Locke thinks of our idea of duration as a "simple mode" formed from repetition of our experience of particular successions: "we have our Notion of *Succession and Duration* from this Original, viz., from Reflection on the Train of *Ideas*, which we find to appear one after another in our own Minds" (*Essay*, Book II, Chapter XIV, §4, p. 182. Hume supposes that our "idea of time" is "deriv'd from the succession of our perceptions of every kind, ideas as well as impressions, and impressions of reflection" on our internal states "as well as of sensation" of external objects (*A Treatise of Human Nature*, Book I, Part 2, Section 3, paragraph 6; edn. David Fate and Mary J. Norton, 2 vols. [Oxford: Clarendon Press, 2007], vol. 2, p. 28).

2:400). In other words, not only does the mere recognition of succession or simultaneity presuppose a background intuition of the form of time, but also the actual determinate relations of succession and simultaneity among particular objects and their states ("substances and accidents") have to be worked out within the overarching framework of time given by that background intuition. This is a premise of immense importance for Kant's future work, for it underlies the arguments for the indispensability of the concepts of substance, causality, interaction, and external existence itself that he will develop in the Analogies of Experience and Refutation of Idealism in the *Critique of Pure Reason*—with the development of the idea of the Analogies being one of the central accomplishments of the "silent decade" that would follow the publication of the inaugural dissertation in 1770 and result in the publication of the *Critique* in 1781, and the Refutation constituting the chief addition that Kant would make to the *Critique* in 1786.[7] But this observation by itself does not prove the transcendental ideality of time. It supposes that we are not immediately given the determinate temporal relations of the objects of our experience and their states but must work them out, in some way not yet specified, but this does not entail that these relations are nothing but subjective constructs—the premise is entirely compatible with the supposition that what we are doing when we construct these relationships is *discovering* and *reconstructing* relationships that do exist independently of our representation of them but are not immediately given to us in some epistemically direct and self-evident way. For example, if I have to work out the sequence of the reigns of two rulers from centuries ago on the basis of evidence that one was the son of the other or one killed the other, and thus his reign must have succeeded that of the other, I am reconstructing the succession of their reigns which is not immediately given to me on the basis of some evidence that is immediately given to me, but I am not *creating* this succession: we suppose that it really happened, and would have been what it was even if no one now could reconstruct it.[8] The epistemic fact that temporal relationships must be reconstructed does not entail any ontological fact that they are mere constructions.

Without admitting any deficiency in his argument to this point, Kant nevertheless tries to supplement it with a further argument that is at least in part ontological. The clearly ontological part of this argument, which he will maintain in the *Critique*, directed there as here against "English philosophers," that is, Newtonians, is that the metaphysical conception of objectively real time as "some continuous flux within existence" that is yet independent of "any existent thing," some sort of supersubstance in addition to ordinary substances, is absurd (*ID* §14.4, 2:400). Kant then adds an argument, directed against "Leibniz and his followers," that the idea of time as a relationship that supervenes on existing things, our conception of which "is abstracted from the succession of internal states," not only leaves out any account of how we would obtain the idea of simultaneity, but also "betrays itself by the vicious circle in the commonly accepted definition of time" (2:401). It is not clear what point

---

[7] For all of these claims, see Guyer, *Kant and the Claims of Knowledge*, parts I, III, and IV.

[8] In his course on Kant's *Critique* at Harvard in the spring of 1967, Robert Nozick referred to Kant's theory of time-determination as his "family circle method of dating," although he did not use fratricidal royal families as his example.

this might be supposed to make beyond the already argued (1)—that the recognition of a multiplicity of instances from which an idea of time might be abstracted already presupposes a background idea of time—but Kant does add that "In this way, all the certainty of our rules is completely destroyed." This may be an allusion to the epistemological point that Kant makes against the Leibnizians in the *Critique*, namely that if our knowledge of the form of time is based on our experience of particulars, it can only be empirical and contingent, not a priori and necessary (*CPR* A 40/B 57). Kant does not unpack this claim in the dissertation's discussion of time, but he does more in the discussion of space. Here he renews the attack upon the "English," now arguing that the idea of space as a "boundless *receptacle* of possible things" is an "empty fabrication," and then argues that the Leibnizian approach casts "geometry down from the summit of certainty," thrusting "it back into the rank of those sciences of which the principles are empirical." His claim is that "if all the properties of space are merely borrowed by experience from outer relations, then there would only be a comparative universality to be found in the axioms of geometry, universality such as is obtained by induction, that is to say, such as extends no further than observation" (*ID* §15.D, 2:403–4). The implication is that genuine universality and necessity, since they cannot be known by induction, can only be known by acquaintance with an a priori intuition.

However, even this does not fully explain why space, or by analogy time, must be *nothing other* than our a priori intuition of it. For that, Kant will need a further argument, which he provides only in the Transcendental Aesthetic of the *Critique* and in the *Prolegomena to Any Future Metaphysics*, namely that even if we can have genuinely a priori knowledge of the formal or structural relations possible *within* our own forms of intuition, if we were to suppose that the same sort of relations were also really present in objects existing independently of us, *that* fact and thus the fact of agreement *between* our forms of intuition and objective reality would be contingent rather than necessary; the only way to avoid this outcome, Kant then supposes, is to deny objective reality to spatial and temporal relations altogether. This is the argument Kant will make in the *Critique*, for example, by means of this rhetorical question:

> If there did not lie in you a faculty for intuiting *a priori*; if this subjective condition regarding form were not at the same time the universal *a priori* condition under which alone the object of this (outer) intuition is itself possible; if the object ([e.g.,] the triangle) were something in itself without relation to your subject: then how could you say that what necessarily lies in your subjective conditions for constructing a triangle must also necessarily pertain to the triangle in itself? ... If, therefore, space (and time as well) were not a mere form of your intuition that contains *a priori* conditions under which alone things could be outer objects for you, which are nothing in themselves without these subjective conditions, then you could make out absolutely nothing synthetic and *a priori* about outer objects. (*CPR* A 48/B 65–6)

The obvious reply to this argument is that we do *not* know that any specific mathematics *necessarily* applies to external objects, that is, objects that exist external to and independently of our representation of them, and therefore do not have to reduce such objects to our representations of them in order to explain our a priori knowledge of such a necessity. We may have a priori knowledge of necessary relations within some formal system that we have conceived—whether that is analytical, as for example Frege and Russell supposed about arithmetic, or synthetic, as Frege allowed but Russell denied about geometry—but our knowledge that such a system also applies to external objects could be empirical knowledge of a contingent fact. In that case there would be no argument for the transcendental ideality of space and time, and without that no argument for transcendental idealism at all.

Kant's argument for the transcendental ideality of space and time in the inaugural dissertation was thus incomplete, and were it to have been extended along the lines suggested in the *Critique*, it would be vulnerable to this objection unless proven otherwise. Mendelssohn does not raise this objection to the argument of the inaugural dissertation, perhaps because he had already defended the assumptions from which the objection to Kant's eventual argument arises in his prize essay of half a dozen years earlier (as we saw in Ch. 1). That is, he had there defended the commonsense view that we can have a priori knowledge of the relations within a formal system but only empirical knowledge that any particular formal system applies to objective reality. Because his own assumptions about the combination of empirical evidence with mathematical analysis were so different from Kant's eventual position, it is hardly surprising that Mendelssohn did not divine the basis of Kant's argument, nor that he would not have been sympathetic to it if he had. And perhaps he did not feel the need to restate this position in what was meant as a friendly letter to Kant. Be that as it may, instead of objecting that Kant's argument for the transcendental ideality especially of space is inadequate, Mendelssohn raises a substantive objection specifically to Kant's thesis of the transcendental ideality of time.

So let us now turn directly to Mendelssohn's objection. At Kant's direction, Marcus Herz, after the defense of Kant's inaugural dissertation returning to his hometown of Berlin in order to continue his medical studies, had delivered copies of the dissertation to the three prominent Berlin philosophers, Johann Heinrich Lambert (1728–77), the polymath who among other accomplishments had proved the irrationality of $\pi$ and whose philosophical work *Neues Organon* had led Kant to entertain thoughts of collaborating with him in the mid-1760s; Johann Georg Sulzer (1720–79), now best remembered for his monumental encyclopedia of aesthetics, the *Allgemeine Theorie der schönen Künste* of 1771–4, but then a central figure at the Academy of Sciences who contributed to many areas of philosophy; and of course Mendelssohn, who took a great interest in his young co-religionist and would promote what turned out to be his very successful medical career in Berlin. All three quickly wrote to Kant with their thanks but also with some criticisms. And indeed all three homed in on the same issue, namely Kant's denial of objective reality to space and time, but especially to time.

Sulzer's letter was the briefest and most laudatory, criticizing only one "small detail." This was not such a small detail, for what he objected to was Kant's rejection of the Leibnizian account of space and time. His objection was that "Duration and extension are absolutely simple concepts, incapable of analysis, but, as I see it, concepts having genuine reality," while "Time and space, on the other hand, are constructed concepts which presuppose the concept of order."[9] That is, he was willing to concede that our representations of space and time as a whole are mental

---

[9] Johann Georg Sulzer, letter of December 8, 1770, 10:111–13, at 112.

constructs, but only because he held them to be constructed on the basis of our experience of particular relations of duration and extension, the objective reality of which he saw no reason to doubt. Since Kant had barely hinted at his epistemological argument for denying reality to any relations of duration or extension, Sulzer could hardly be blamed for sticking to his guns on this issue. In any case, he alleged to have "at present... little time and... little mental dispositions to work on abstract matters of that sort," and instead concluded with his fervent hope that Kant would soon publish a "Metaphysics of Morals," since such a work would be "of the highest importance, given the present unsteady state of moral philosophy." Perhaps Kant took Sulzer's encouragement to heart, but it would be fifteen years before he would publish the *Groundwork for the Metaphysics of Morals* and another dozen before he published the actual *Metaphysics of Morals*. Sulzer died in 1779 and would live to see neither of these works.

Lambert wrote a much more detailed letter. After some opening niceties, he referred to Kant's distinction between the senses and the understanding as two sources of knowledge, but raised what he called the "question of *generality*, namely, to what extent these two ways of knowing are so completely *separated* that they *never come together*."[10] Kant's general position in the dissertation was in fact that sensibility and understanding are two separate sources of knowledge with two distinct objects, the objects of the senses being phenomena and those of the understanding noumena, although at one point Kant had mentioned in passing that the "fundamental properties" of the "concepts" of space and time "constitute *the underlying foundations upon which the understanding rests*, when, in accordance with the laws of logic and with the greatest possible certainty, it draws conclusions from the primary data of intuition" (*ID* §15 Corollary, 2:405); but in spite of this passing remark, it was precisely to this question that Kant would devote so much of his effort in his decade of work on the *Critique of Pure Reason*, although neither there nor elsewhere did he credit Lambert, who had been dead for four years by the time the *Critique* was published, with having raised it. (And whether Kant had successfully solved this question remained a burning issue for many post-Kantian philosophers, beginning with Salomon Maimon; but that is another story.)[11] Having raised this question, Lambert then turned to the issue of time. He first discussed the question of whether time could be defined, concluding that it cannot be—but then distinguished the impossibility of defining time from any denial of its *reality*. He stated that:

All changes are bound to time and are inconceivable without time. *If changes are real, then time is real*, whatever it may be. *If time is unreal, then no change can be real*. I think, though, that

---

[10] Letter from Johann Heinrich Lambert, October 13, 1770, 10:103–10, at 105.
[11] Maimon alleged in his *Essay on Transcendental Philosophy* (1790), trans. Nick Midgley, Henry Somers-Hall, Alistair Welchman, and Merten Reglitz (London: Continuum, 2010) that once having separated intuitions and concepts, Kant had no way to reconnect them. For discussion, see Samuel Atlas, *From Critical to Speculative Idealism: The Philosophy of Solomon Maimon* (The Hague: Martinus Nijhoff, 1964); Frederick C. Beiser, *The Fate of Reason: German Philosophy from Kant to Fichte* (Cambridge, Mass.: Harvard University Press, 1987), ch. 10; and Paul Franks, *All or Nothing* (Cambridge, Mass.: Harvard University Press, 2005). The debate continues among Kant scholars as that between "conceptualism" and "non-conceptualism"; for various contributions, see Dennis Schulting, ed., *Kantian Nonconceptualism* (London: Palgrave Macmillan, 2016).

even an idealist must grant at least that changes really exist and occur in his representations, for example, their beginning and ending. Thus time cannot be regarded as something *unreal*.

He conceded to Kant that "It is not a substance," holding instead that it is a "finite determination of duration, and like duration, it is somehow real in whatever this reality may consist"[12]—in other words, even if we cannot say precisely what time is, we have been given no reason to doubt its reality. After several pages on space, Lambert returned to the issue of time, observing that "If changes have reality, then I must grant it to time as well. Changes follow one another, begin, continue, cease, and so on, and all these expressions are temporal." We might put his general point by saying that the change of our representations shows that *temporality* is real even if we cannot neatly put *time* as such into any existing ontological category. This is a fundamental objection to Kant, although, in a concessionary mood, Lambert concludes by saying that:

If you can instruct me otherwise, I shall not expect to lose much. Time and space will be *real* appearances, and their foundation an existent something that truly conforms to the appearance just as precisely and constantly as the laws of geometry are precise and consistent. The language of appearance will thus serve our purposes just as well as the unknown "true" language.[13]

This is very close to the part of Kant's subsequent position that he will call "empirical realism" as opposed to transcendental idealism, although unlike Lambert, Kant will argue that commitment to empirical realism with regard to space and time and everything formed by them depends on transcendental idealism. It is also close to the position Mendelssohn had already adopted in his prize essay and, as we will see, to the position that he will adopt fifteen years later in the *Morning Hours*. But Kant does not credit Lambert with the recognition of empirical realism any more than he credits him with the question about how sensibility and understanding work together rather than separately, Lambert does not credit Mendelssohn's prize essay with an early statement of his position, and we have no reason to suppose that Mendelssohn ever knew Lambert's personal letter to Kant. But however they came to it, Lambert, Mendelssohn, and Kant would all agree on empirical realism with regard to time (and space), that is, with the claim that whatever their ultimate ontological status, they may be used with complete confidence as the foundations of all empirical knowledge. But only Kant would argue that such empirical realism rests on the truth of transcendental idealism—only he demanded more than empirical certification for the framework of all empirical knowledge.

So now at last we come to Mendelssohn's letter, dated Christmas day of 1770 (of course not a holiday for Mendelssohn). Mendelssohn began with the customary niceties and also a reference (one of his earliest) to his "nervous infirmities" which "make it impossible for me of late to give as much effort of thought to a speculative work of this stature as it deserves," a limitation on his efforts to read the *Critique of Pure Reason* that Mendelssohn would repeat a dozen years later.[14] Then he made a

---

[12] Lambert, letter of October 13, 1770, 10:107. [13] Lambert, letter of October 13, 1770, p. 110.
[14] See letter from Mendelssohn, April 10, 1783, 10:308, and *MS*, 3–4, *JubA* 3.2.3–4. At the time of writing his first letter to Kant, Mendelssohn had just been through his nerve-wracking debate over Johann

point about the difference between Shaftesbury's conception of a moral sense and the Epicurean conception of "sensual pleasure" as a moral motive that Kant would always later recognize as the distinction between "physical feeling" and "moral feeling," although as usual without any acknowledgement of Mendelssohn having pointed it out to him.[15] Finally, Mendelssohn too turned to the question of time. He wrote:

> For several reasons I cannot convince myself that time is something merely subjective. Succession is after all at least a necessary condition of the representations that finite minds have. But finite minds are not only subjects; they are also objects of representations, both those of God and those of their fellows. Consequently it is necessary to regard succession as something objective.
>
> Furthermore, since we have to grant the reality of succession in a representing creature and in its alterations, why not also in the sensible object, the model and prototype of representations in the world?[16]

Lambert's version of the objection had proceeded in two steps, first asserting that if any change is real then time is real and then adding that change of or in representations is real. Mendelssohn collapses Lambert's two steps into one but then adds another of his own: First he directly asserts that the change of representations is real and therefore so is time, but then he adds that if change in representations is real, there is no reason to question that change and therefore time or at least temporality (he does not draw a distinction between them as for example Sulzer had suggested) in the external objects represented by our representations is also real. But either way, the basic objection is the same: how could time be unreal when the change and thus succession of our representations is clearly real?

Kant did not reply to any of these letters, although in a letter to Herz on June 7, 1771 he worried that Lambert and Mendelssohn (no mention of Sulzer) must think poorly of him for his incourtesy and begged Herz to explain that he was thinking too hard about their objections to reply yet. A year later he was still thinking about the problem of the reality of time, as is evidenced by his most famous letter to Herz, that of February 21, 1772. In this letter, he tells Herz that he is working on a book to be entitled *The Limits of Sensibility and Reason*, and then briefly outlines contents that would eventually be covered only by all three critiques rather than by the single critique that he was then planning (not referred to under its eventual title until a letter to Herz of August 20, 1777).[17] He first tells Herz that he is working on the question of how concepts of the understanding known a priori can apply to sense perceptions although they are neither abstracted from them nor constitute them— the form that Lambert's question about the cooperation rather than separation of

---

Caspar Lavater's challenge that he either disprove the truth of Christianity or convert; see Altmann, *Moses Mendelssohn*, pp. 194-263, and Bourel, *Moses Mendelssohn*, pp. 279-318. Whether the nervous debility that Mendelssohn alleged to keep him from working as hard at philosophy as he had previously done was brought on by the "Lavater" affair or was an independent pathology will never be known.

[15] Mendelssohn, letter of December 25, 1770, 10:113-16, at 10:114; for Kant's observance of this distinction, see *Lecture on Ethics*, Collins, 27:253, and *CPracR*, 5:40.

[16] Mendelssohn, letter of December 25, 1770, 10:115.

[17] Letter to Herz, August 20, 1777, 10:211-14, at 213.

sensibility and understanding has taken, although Kant does not yet mention Lambert's name. After mentioning a review of Herz's own little book *Betrachtungen aus der spekulativen Weltweisheit*,[18] an attempt to synthesize the views of Herz's two mentors Kant and Mendelssohn (a review by none other than the Göttingen professor Feder, whose review of the *Critique of Pure Reason* would later so annoy Kant),[19] Kant says that "A single letter from *Mendelssohn* or *Lambert* means more to an author in terms of making him reexamine his theories than do ten such opinions from superficial pens."[20] Kant then raises the question about the objective reality of both space and time. He says that "the second misunderstanding," that is, about time, "seems to be the most serious objection that can be raised against" his system, and credits it to Lambert rather than Mendelssohn. But he formulates the objection with the directness of Mendelssohn's version: "It runs like this: Changes are something real (according to the testimony of inner sense). Now, they are possible only if time is presupposed; therefore time is something real that is involved in the determination of things in themselves." Kant then tries to rebut the objection about time by appeal to the case of space:

> Then I asked myself: Why does one not accept the parallel argument? Bodies are real (according to the testimony of outer sense). Now, bodies are possible only under the condition of space; therefore space is something objective and real that inheres in the things themselves. The reason lies in the fact that it is obvious, in regard to outer things, that one cannot infer the reality of the object from the reality of the representation, but in the case of inner sense the thinking or the existence of the thought and the existence of my own self are one the same. The key to this difficulty lies herein. There is no doubt that I should not think my own state under the form of time and that therefore the form of inner sensibility does not give me the appearance of alterations. [Kant means: It cannot be doubted that I think my own state under the form of time and that the form of inner sensibility gives me the appearance of alterations.] Now I do not deny that alterations have reality any more than I deny that bodies have reality, though all I mean by that is that something real corresponds to the appearance. I cannot even say that the inner appearance changes, for how would I observe this change if it did not appear to inner sense?

Then Kant refers to a thesis from Baumgarten, that "What is absolutely impossible is neither hypothetically possible nor impossible, for it cannot be considered under any condition," and implausibly takes this to license his claim that "the things of the world are objectively or in themselves neither in one in the same state at different times nor in different states, for thus understood they are not represented as in time at all."[21] For this to make any sense, Kant's argument would have to have been that the idea of objective time is absolutely impossible, i.e., incoherent, thus the question of whether external objects are really in time cannot even arise. He has not argued this. He does put his finger on what is bothering Lambert and Mendelssohn, however, namely that while in the case of space we naturally think of ourselves with our representations on the one hand and their objects on the other as

---

[18] Markus Herz, *Betrachtungen aus der spekulativen Weltweisheit*, ed. Elfriede Conrad, Heinrich P. Delfosse, and Birgit Nehren (Hamburg: Felix Meiner Verlag, 1990).
[19] See *Correspondence*, p. 138n9.  [20] Letter to Herz, February 21, 1772, 10:128–35, at 10:133.
[21] Letter to Herz of February 21, 1772, 10:134.

ontologically and numerically distinct, and thus can at least make sense of the idea of the representation having or representing properties that its object does not actually have, in the case of representations of inner sense, that is, representations of our own representations, we do not think of a numerical or ontological difference between the ourselves and our representations on the one hand and what our representations represent on the other, so there is no room for the thought that what is a feature of our representations could fail to be a property of their objects. That is, our representations have temporal features—they change—but insofar as our representations in inner sense are just representing themselves, there is no second object that could lack the property of change and therefore temporality that they so obviously have: "the existence of the thought and the existence of my own self are one and the same." But in spite of recognizing the point, Kant just insists that he can grant reality to alteration in representations or thoughts but deny that alteration is a real property of any "things in the world... objectively," including the self. He seems to understand the objection of Lambert and Mendelssohn, but still thinks he can assert a blanket distinction between the properties of appearances and properties of things in themselves, even in the case of the self.

This does not seem like much of an answer; perhaps that is why Kant did not send it directly to Lambert or Mendelssohn. And the issue clearly continued to bother Kant, for he explicitly returned to it in the *Critique of Pure Reason*, there noting, as already mentioned, that "insightful men have so unanimously proposed one objection" to the transcendental ideality of time "that I conclude that it must naturally occur to every reader who is not accustomed to these considerations" (A 36–7/B 53). The question now is whether Kant does any better in responding to this natural and insightful objection than he did in 1772.

Kant's first response in the *Critique of Pure Reason* to the enduring question about the transcendental ideality of time is essentially to take up Lambert's concession that empirical realism about time is enough while digging in his heels against the doubt of both Lambert and Mendelssohn whether it makes sense to deny time "absolute reality." He formulates the objection accurately, in particular in a way that recognizes that it arises from the difference between the other-referring character of representations of objects with spatial properties and the self-referring character of our representation of our own, changing mental states, as "Alterations are real (this is proved by the change of our own representations, even if one would deny all outer appearances together with their alterations). Now alterations are possible only in time, therefore time is something real" (A 36–7/B 53). But he then replies that he can "admit the entire argument," because he does not deny that "Time is certainly something real, namely the real form of inner intuition. It therefore has subjective reality in regard to inner experience, i.e., I really have the representation of time and <my> determinations in it" (A 37/B 53–4, "my" added in second edition). But nobody has denied that we *experience* our own states as changing and temporal; the question has been rather whether we *could* experience our representations in this way *if those very same representations*—not a distinct set of external objects—*were not really temporal*. On this Kant simply digs in his heels: the "empirical reality" of time "remains as a condition of all our experience. Only absolute reality cannot be granted to it according to what has been adduced above" (A 37/B 54), that is, according to the arguments about time, which Kant would divide in the second edition of the *Critique* into the "metaphysical" and "transcendental" expositions of the concept of time, that parallel those earlier made in the inaugural dissertation. But Kant adds nothing new to his previous arguments, just reiterating that time "is nothing except the form of our inner intuition. If one removes the special condition of our sensibility from it, then the concept of time also disappears, and it does not adhere to the objects themselves; rather merely to the subject that intuits them" (A 37–8/B 54). The distinction between subject and object at least makes sense in the case of space, and leaves room for the possibility that properties of the subject need not be properties of the object; but since in the case of our own representations they are more like *parts* of the subject than *separate* from it, it remains unclear how genuine features of the representations could also not be genuine features of the subject "that intuits them." At least anyone who thinks the cases of the spatiality of outer objects and the temporality of inner sense are not strictly analogous, as Lambert and Mendelssohn if not Sulzer did, would not be moved by Kant's answer here. One thing that Kant might have argued is that just because time is the necessary and inescapable form of inner sense or of all our representation of ourselves, of course we cannot escape it and form any coherent representation of ourselves in non-temporal terms, so to that extent his critics are right—but that implies nothing about what we are really like. Then Kant could at least have cut the ground out from under the criticism. Perhaps that is what he thought—but he does not quite say it. So the debate over the reality of time seems to end in a stand-off.

Two further arguments that Kant made can be read as answers specifically to the second part of Mendelssohn's objection in the letter of Christmas day, 1770, that is, his comment that "finite minds are not only subjects; they are also objects of representations, both those of God and those of their fellows. Consequently it is necessary to regard succession as something objective." The first of these comes in an addition to the second edition of the *Critique*, showing that even then not only did the general question of idealism continue to worry Kant but the original objections to the transcendental ideality of time, and specifically Mendelssohn's, likewise continued to bother him. This addition is the last of the General Remarks that Kant adds to the second-edition version of the Transcendental Aesthetic, where he argues, presumably against Mendelssohn's claim that the properties of finite minds, including the temporality of their representations, must be real because God represents them, that one must be "careful to remove the conditions of time and space from all of [God's] intuition" because if one does not, then "as conditions of all existence in general they would also have to be conditions of the existence of God" (B 71). That is, Kant appears to argue, if we allow objective reality to our temporality, and allow God correct knowledge of everything about us, as of course we must, then we must not only allow God correct knowledge of the temporality of representations but also ascribe temporality to him, which is theologically impermissible. But even leaving aside the general question of whether the Kant who argues that God is only an idea of our own reason should be allowing himself such an appeal to the real nature of God, there seems to be a *non sequitur* here, an inference from God's knowledge of our temporality to God's own temporality. To be sure, I have been arguing in behalf of Lambert and Mendelssohn that there is no *non sequitur* in the inference from *our* representation of changing states to the objective reality of *our* temporality, but that is because there is no ontological gap between our representations and our selves; but in the case of God, except perhaps on a Spinozistic understanding that none of our protagonists would want to endorse, there presumably *is* an ontological gap between our representations and God's representation of our representations: they cannot be identical on the pain of our being identical with God, so there is at least room for God representing features of our representations that are not features of his own representations, just as there is room in the case of our own representation of objects in space for those objects to lack features that our representations of them have. And that is precisely the position that Mendelssohn had taken in his prize essay, when he argued that God could know how we humans sensibly represent things without himself representing them in that way or being subject to the conditions of sensibility (*PW* pp. 290–1, *JubA* 2:309–10). Kant's response does not seem to be a sound response to Mendelssohn's objection, although to be sure Mendelssohn cannot use a claim about how God represents us as a premise in an argument for the objective reality of the specific features of his representation of us, since neither Mendelssohn nor anyone else has direct access to God's representation of us.

The other point I have in mind is that Kant's treatment of the third Paralogism of Pure Reason in the first edition of the *Critique* could be regarded as an attempt to respond to Mendelssohn's remark that "finite minds" are "objects of representations" for "their fellows," that is, for other human beings. His point is presumably that it is objectively correct for us to represent not only ourselves but each other as undergoing objectively real change of representations. Kant agrees that "another," for whom I am "an object of outer sense... originally considers **me** as **in time**" while in my own "apperception **time** is properly represented only **in me**" (A 362). The second part of this statement is problematic, for Kant's full position would appear to be that my *empirical* representation of myself includes my changing representations and the *empirical reality* of time even though from a *transcendental point* of view I, or the philosopher in me, recognizes that time is just "in me," that is, a feature of my way of representing myself. But that point aside, Kant could be conceding to Mendelssohn that we represent each other as in time without admitting that this is any objection to the transcendental ideality of time, for surely his position is that time is just a subjectively real condition of *all* human perception. That *you* represent me or my inner states—to which of course you have only inferential access, hypothesizing that they accompany my directly observable outer states such as speech or other actions—as in time would not, for Kant, make them any more objectively real than *my* own representation of them in time would, since time is as much a merely subjective feature of *your* way of representing the world as it is of *my* way of representing the world, including myself.

This would be a correct response to Mendelssohn, if indeed Kant intended it as such. But of course it is also only a defense of Kant's position from that particular remark of Mendelssohn's, not a response to the more fundamental point of both Mendelssohn and Lambert that in the case of one's own representations there is not the gap between representation and its objects that makes the idea of transcendental idealism at least coherent. Nothing Kant says in the *Critique* seems to resolve this worry.

These attempts to address the worry of Lambert and Mendelssohn about the transcendental ideality of time were included in the first edition of the *Critique of Pure Reason*, so we can see Kant's inaugural dissertation, the criticism of it by Mendelssohn (and Lambert) a few months later, and Kant's response a decade later as part of a single protracted episode, the first stage of his response to Mendelssohn on the question of idealism. As I suggested at the outset of this chapter, we may well think that Kant's addition of the "Refutation of Idealism" refutation to the second edition was a second episode in his response to Mendelssohn on idealism, spurred by Mendelssohn's own response to the threat of Cartesian skepticism in the *Morning Hours*, in turn necessitated by the latter's use of other Cartesian tropes, namely the cosmological argument from the certainty of one's own existence and the ontological argument. One aspect of Kant's refutation seems strongly influenced by Mendelssohn's approach, namely his reliance on empirical criteria for the confirmation of specific claims about particular external objects. But there is also a substantial difference between the two approaches, namely that Kant proposes a transcendental argument for the necessity of belief in the reality of external objects but also tries to reconcile the belief in their reality with his commitment to the transcendental ideality of their spatiality. Mendelssohn obviously did not attempt the latter, since he never shared Kant's commitment to transcendental idealism. Nor is his approach to the reality of external objects a transcendental argument, based on the conditions of the possibility of our experience in general; it is a probabilistic argument for the reliability of our senses. Let us now see what Mendelssohn's final approach to the reality of external objects is and how Kant's differs.

## 3. Mendelssohn's Refutation of Idealism in the *Morning Hours*

Mendelssohn's *Morning Hours*, published in 1785, thus after Kant had already defended himself against the charge of Berkeleianism in his *Prolegomena to Any Future Metaphysics* in 1783, has, as we have already seen, a complex program. Mendelssohn attempts to defend the versions of the cosmological and ontological arguments that he had already offered in the prize essay against Kant's criticism of them in the first edition of the *Critique of Pure Reason*, although he does not defend the straightforward argument from design, which Kant had called the physico-theological argument, having himself criticized it in the prize essay. He instead offers a Leibnizian argument that the existence of the world must be a product of the choice of the best possible world by God. This argument is based on the introduction of a divine *Billigungsvermögen*, or faculty of approbation, which is understood in analogy with the human faculty of approbation that shows itself in various contexts including that of disinterested aesthetic satisfaction; Mendelssohn's introduction of the human version of this faculty has been held to be a stimulus for Kant's addition of a faculty of judgment that is a source of disinterested aesthetic pleasure midway to the faculties of cognition and desire, although in Mendelssohn's argument the faculty of approbation is clearly not intended to be any sort of novelty but is rather intended to be something non-controversial from which an inference to the nature of God can be made, and in any case Kant had long distinguished our free response to the beautiful from our interested responses to the agreeable and the good. At the same time, Mendelssohn's work also contains a critique of Spinozism and a defense of his late friend Gotthold Ephraim Lessing from Friedrich Heinrich Jacobi's claim that Lessing had confessed to him but not to Mendelssohn that he was himself a Spinozist; Mendelssohn objects to Spinoza that it is only common sense that God has created a world external to rather than identical to himself, but also argues that even if Lessing had been attracted to the metaphysics of Spinoza his morals would have remained unshaken by any such metaphysical *jeux des esprits*.

But all of this is preceded, in Part One of the work, with an "Epistemic Groundwork, Concerning Truth, Appearance, and Error," which lays down various premises for the arguments for the existence of God, including the introduction of the divine *Billigungsvermögen* in analogy to the human. Mendelssohn offers a general theory of knowledge and a response to idealism as he defines it, following Christian Wolff and Alexander Gottlieb Baumgarten, in contrast to materialism, as the view that there exist only minds or spirits and their ideas or representations.[22] Mendelssohn operates from within a Cartesian conception of the primacy of self-acquaintance but defends the adequacy of our grounds for belief that there is something other than minds and their ideas, or dualism, along the same lines as Baumgarten had, but subject to the proviso that *although we have adequate grounds to be confident of the existence of non-mental external objects, we can know them only as we represent them, or only as having the "powers" to cause us to represent them in our typical ways*. In his words, "When I tell you what effect a thing has or how it can be affected by something else, do not ask what it is. When I tell you what concept to use in order to categorize a thing, then the further question, What is this thing in and of itself? has no good reason to be asked" (Lecture VII, *LW* p. 52, *JubA* 3.2:60).

This statement sounds as if it could have come from Kant's exposition of his own transcendental idealism. In what follows, I make two points about the relations between Mendelssohn's and Kant's refutations of idealism. First, although Kant's addition of an explicitly labeled "Refutation of Idealism" to the second edition of the *Critique of Pure Reason* has usually been thought of as a continuation of his objection in the *Prolegomena to Any Future Metaphysics* (1783) to the charge that his position is no different from Berkeley's that had been made in the infamous Garve-Feder review of earlier that year, in fact Kant's target in the "Refutation" is Cartesianism, not Berkeleianism, and Kant may have been prompted to take on this new target by the prominence of Cartesianism in Mendelssohn's *Morning Hours*, the publication of which intervened between the *Prolegomena* and Kant's work on the new edition of the *Critique*.[23] Specifically, Kant's list of the empirical criteria for knowledge of the

---

[22] Daniel O. Dahlstrom offers a critical survey of Mendelssohn's epistemology in *Morning Hours* in "Truth, Knowledge, and 'the Pretensions of Idealism': A Critical Commentary on the First Part of Mendelssohn's *Morning Hours*," *Kant-Studien* 109 (2018): 329–51. He is not impressed with Mendelssohn's response to Humean skepticism or to idealism. He does not contrast Mendelssohn's empiricist-friendly account with Kant's transcendental defense of empirical realism, as I will do here.

[23] This suggestion was previously made by Corey W. Dyck in "Turning the Game against the Idealist" and Rainier Munk in "What is the Bond?," in Munk, ed., *Moses Mendelssohn's Metaphysics and Aesthetics* (Dordrecht: Springer, 2011), pp. 159–82 and 183–202. As Munk notes (p. 191n20), that Kant's Refutation

existence of external objects in the notes to the "Refutation," which comes after all in the exposition of the "postulate for [empirically] cognizing the **actuality** of things" (*CPR* A 225/B 272),[24] is so similar to Mendelssohn's that it might plausibly be regarded as a reference to it. But this brings me to my second, philosophical point, which is that in spite of the similarity between Mendelssohn's and Kant's general epistemological positions consisting in the fact that both insist that we have knowledge of the existence of external objects while denying that we know anything of their nature beyond how we represent them, Kant calls his position itself a form of idealism, which Mendelssohn does not, namely "transcendental idealism." This designation signals two fundamental points of difference between the two philosophers. On the one hand, while Mendelssohn is content with the truism that of course we can only represent things as we represent them and cannot know of them anything else than that in conjunction with our own cognitive constitution they cause us to represent them in this way, Kant goes further and actually asserts that things as they are in themselves *are not* spatial and temporal—that is Kant's own *idealism*.[25] On the other hand, Kant also precedes his Mendelssohnian exposition of the empirical criteria for actuality with an a priori and anti-Cartesian proof that the possibility of *self*-knowledge is dependent upon belief in the independent existence of enduring *objects*, and such an argument, which does not occur to Mendelssohn, is what makes Kant's idealism a *transcendental* idealism. Reflection upon what is common to Mendelssohn's and Kant's positions on knowledge of external objects thus also clarifies what divides them, namely Kant's transcendental arguments for the non-spatio-temporality of things in themselves and nevertheless for the necessity of belief in external objects. Mendelssohn's and Kant's positions on things in themselves may initially seem similar, but what divides them is Mendelssohn's epistemological modesty versus Kant's radical insistence upon both what we cannot know about things in themselves and what we must know about them. Again, Mendelssohn is content with an empiricist attitude toward external objects (much like Locke's), while Kant strives for a philosophically more complex position.

## 4. Mendelssohn's Modest Epistemology

Mendelssohn's epistemology is a commonsensical combination of themes from Descartes and Locke, no doubt anticipated by Wolff's use of both of those sources as well, with Baumgarten's refutation of idealism in turn restricted by Lockean

---

was aimed at Mendelssohn was previously observed by Benno Erdmann in the nineteenth century (*Kants Kriticismus* [Leipzig: Leopold Voss, 1878], p. 118) and Dietmar Heidemann (*Kant und das Problem des metaphysischen Idealismus* [Berlin: Walter de Gruyter, 1998], p. 46n78). In spite of their agreement that Kant's Refutation takes up Mendelssohn's approach to idealism in *Morning Hours*, however, Dyck and Munk actually disagree on Kant's response: Dyck argues that Kant is attempting to refute Mendelssohn's criticism of him, while Munk argues that Kant largely accepts Mendelssohn's approach ("What is the Bond?," p. 191). I will side with Dyck in this debate, arguing that Kant rejects Mendelssohn's way of defanging Kant's transcendental idealism, although for a reason Dyck does not bring out.

[24] The discussion of the postulate of actuality extends from A 225/B 272 to A 226/B 279, with the "Refutation of Idealism" and its accompanying three notes inserted at B 274–9.

[25] This is the key point on which I disagree with Dyck, who does not offer such an interpretation of Kant's transcendental idealism.

epistemological modesty. We will first consider Mendelssohn's general epistemology as it leads up to a justification of our confidence in the existence of external objects, and then at the Lockean restriction he places upon the Baumgartian refutation of idealism that he otherwise accepts.[26] Mendelssohn's larger point in this entire discussion is that our belief in the existence of God *cannot* and *need not* be justified by the merely empirical reasoning and ordinary psychology that grounds our beliefs about external objects, so Mendelssohn is hardly an empiricist when it comes to belief in the existence of God. But as we have already considered his a priori arguments for the existence of God, here we will focus on his empiricist account of our knowledge of ordinary and lesser objects.

In his overall epistemology, as I have just said, Mendelssohn combines rationalist and empiricist themes (as indeed did all so-called empiricists themselves). At the beginning of the third lecture in *Morning Hours*, he summarizes this epistemology as follows:

The sum of our knowledge can be divided into three classes: (1) Sensory knowledge, or the direct awareness we have of changes that transpire within us when we see, hear, feel, and so forth; or when we experience pleasure or pain; or when we have a desire for or aversion to something; or when we judge, conclude, hope, fear, and so on. All of this I place in the column of direct knowledge stemming from the outer and inner senses, although the added reflections, consideration, and refinements of reason are so often and so intimately connected to the senses that the boundaries separating them cannot anymore be recognized. (2) Knowledge of what is logically conceivable, or in other words, those judgments and conclusions that can be derived from the immediate knowledge of the senses by the proper use of our understanding; the thoughts into which we analytically dissolve those feelings; *rational knowledge*. And (3) knowledge of the *actual world* outside of us, or in other words, the perceptions that we have because we find ourselves in a physical-actual world in which we undergo changes and also bring them about. (*LW* p. 24, *JubA* 3.2:28)

In the preceding two lectures, Mendelssohn had expounded the first two parts of this list in the opposite order. First, in a manner reminiscent of rationalism but also of the empiricism of Locke and Hume, who were also rationalist in their acceptance of knowledge founded on "relations of ideas" even while contrasting it to knowledge of "matters of fact," Mendelssohn had argued that "thoughts as they may be or may not be of things that are conceivable" can be divided into those that are grounded in the analysis of concepts alone, such thoughts being "true if their properties do not subvert one another" and false if they do (Lecture I, *LW* p. 10, *JubA* 3.2:11), and those that are grounded in "deductions," which display "the possibility or impossibility of uniting in a single thought without contradiction certain concepts and their properties" (*LW* p. 11, *JubA* 3.2:12); Mendelssohn thus marks the difference between analytical truths grounded on the non-contradictoriness of single concepts and those grounded on the logical forms of more complex arguments—a difference that goes unmarked in Kant's own account of analyticity. But in either case, Mendelssohn

---

[26] For an account of Mendelssohn's appeal to common sense, an important theme in the *Morning Hours*, see Munk, "What is the Bond?," p. 201.

claims, "truths of this type possess the common characteristic of being necessary and unchanging, and they are therefore time-independent" (*LW* p. 11, *JubA* 3.2:13).

Having argued that the sphere of what is conceivable or possible is defined by contradiction-free single concepts or conjunctions of concepts, Mendelssohn then argues that the "more narrowly drawn" "sphere of actuality" must be grounded on an additional principle beyond the "law of contradiction": "not everything that is not-self-contradictory and is therefore conceivable has for this reason established its claim to be actualized" (*LW* p. 12, *JubA* 3.2:13). Here is where his Cartesianism as well as his Lockeanism come into play. He argues that "Each human being is himself the first source of what he knows; one must therefore take oneself as one's point of departure when one wants to give an accounting of what one knows and what one does not know"; this commonsensical point continues with the unmistakably Cartesian argument that not only are "The first things of whose actuality I am assured...my thoughts and representations," but also "I myself, therefore, who am the subject of [these] alteration[s], possess an actuality that is not merely ideal, but real" (*LW* p. 12, *JubA* 3.2:13–14). That is, if I am certain of the existence of my thoughts, which I indubitably am, then I must also be certain of the existence of the substance in which they inhere as accidents, namely, myself. As he subsequently says, "Descartes correctly posits as the foundation of all further reflection the proposition *I think, therefore I am*. If my inner thoughts and feelings are actually within me, if the existence of these alterations of my very self cannot be merely illusory, then we must acknowledge the *I* to which these alterations occur. Where there are alterations, there must be present a subject that suffers these alterations" (Lecture VI, *LW* p. 38, *JubA* 3.2:43). This invocation of Descartes's *cogito* could well have returned the French philosopher to the forefront of Kant's mind as he worked on the second edition of the *Critique*, where Descartes suddenly returns to prominence not only in the "Refutation of Idealism" but also in the restatement of the "Paralogisms of Pure Reason," which previously had been aimed at more immediate targets such as Leibniz and his followers. Kant's attack upon Descartes in these additions to the second edition of the *Critique of Pure Reason* could have been intended as signals of his dispute with his contemporary Mendelssohn.[27] However, what is of immediate interest is Mendelssohn's analysis of the "threefold way" that we have of looking at actuality: we consider not only (1) the "thought whose actuality we have called ideal and that is merely an alteration" and (2) "the thing that thinks or the enduring substance in respect of which the alteration happens" but also (3) "the thing that is the object of thought, or is the anterior cause of the thought, to which we are in many cases inclined to ascribe a real existence." It is at this point that we ask "But how are we assured that these things outside of us also have an actual existence and are something more than mere thoughts within us?" (Lecture I, *LW* p. 13, *JubA* 3.2:14).

To answer this question, Mendelssohn constructs an elaborate argument that is partly Lockean and partly original. The Lockean part is that although we are "aware that our senses occasionally deceive us," we nevertheless place confidence in them when we "find agreement or concord among our various senses. For every additional

---

[27] Munk treats the two "addenda" on Descartes in precisely this way; "What is the Bond?," pp. 190–1.

sense that suggests the existence of some object, we grow more confident in believing in its actuality" (Lecture I, *LW* p. 13, *JubA* 3.2:15). The original part—or perhaps a Humean part, if Hume is to be taken, at face-value, as *explaining* rather than *questioning* our practice of induction[28]—is that "the degree of our certainty" about the connection between our concordant sensory observations and an external cause of them "grows, and when the number of such cases is very large... the degree of our certitude is hardly distinguishable from what we feel when something seems self-evidently obvious," that is, obvious from the law of contradiction alone (Lecture II, *LW* p. 22, *JubA* 3.2:25). Sensory concord combined with induction are thus supposed to provide us with a degree of assurance of the existence of external objects practically equivalent to what we have in the case of analytic, necessary truths.[29] To both parts of this argument Mendelssohn then adds a Cartesian argument that although we may be momentarily deluded about external existence in dreams, "The ideas of the waking individual, however, are images of things outside of us that are actually present, appearing according to the rules of the order in which they are actually produced outside us; they all belong to a common world," and we can be confident of this because "as more senses come to confirm our belief that we are seeing the presentation of [the object itself], as we see it from various distances and through manifold media, the more certain is our conviction in the object's actual existence" (Lecture VI, *LW* p. 47, *JubA* 3.2:53-4). In particular, while I may be left entirely to my own devices when dreaming, in waking life my own claims to knowledge of external existence can be corroborated by others: "as more people come to agree with me in finding things to be as I find them, the greater becomes my certainty that the cause of my belief does not lie in my particular constitution" (*LW* p. 48, *JubA* 3.2:54), although it does lie in the human constitution in general.

Once having argued in this way for knowledge of actual existence, Mendelssohn makes the interesting observation, which seems to parallel Kant's conception of the metaphysics of nature in his *Metaphysical Foundations of Natural Science* published in the following year, that natural science is actually a combination of empirical and analytical, contingent and necessary truths: "The researches of Newton, Galileo, and others combine... laws of nature that have come to be accepted by us" on the basis of these factors "with the whole realm of logically conceivable truths governed by the law of contradiction—that is, they combine the physical laws concerning bodies and weight with the principles of mathematics and logic" (Lecture II, *LW* p. 22, *JubA* 3.2:25)—with the key difference, however, that while for Mendelssohn *general* logic,

---

[28] Hume's *Enquiry concerning Human Understanding* (1748), with its "skeptical solution" to its "skeptical doubts" about the rationality of induction in fact offering a naturalistic explanation of our belief in its reliability, had been known in Germany, and to Mendelssohn, since the publication of a collection of Hume's works edited by Sulzer in 1755. On the large issue of whether Hume should be read as a skeptic or a naturalist, see, e.g., Norman Kemp Smith, *The Philosophy of David Hume* (London: Macmillan, 1941), and Barry Stroud, *Hume* (London: Routledge & Kegan Paul, 1977).

[29] Dyck emphasizes an argument that we (that is, any one of us) can derive confirmation in our beliefs about external objects from our agreement with other people ("Turning the Game," pp. 167-8). Such an argument, although Mendelssohn does make it, is patently question-begging, at least if other people are included among the external objects the existence of which the Cartesian self has to prove—as they famously were for the skeptical poseur of the First Meditation, who worried that there might not be other men beneath the appearances of cloaks.

above all the law of non-contradiction that grounds analysis, is all that needs to be added to empirical evidence to yield our knowledge of the laws of nature, while for Kant the laws of *transcendental* logic, the synthetic a priori principles of empirical judgment grounded upon the categories, also have to be added. This is a fundamental difference between the attempts of the two philosophers to find the right balance between rationalism and empiricism, to be sure. But the important point for us now is that Mendelssohn is happy to describe what takes us from our indubitable knowledge of our own mental states to our confidence in the existence of external objects as mechanisms of human psychology, although not conceived of as transcendental psychology. Immediately following the passages just quoted he says in general terms that "it follows from the very nature of human understanding that we resist ascribing an observed concord among things to mere chance, but we always search for a cause whenever we discern harmony and concord within diversity... Our belief can, as we have seen, reach such a level of conviction as to be nearly indistinguishable from what we take to be self-evidently obvious." (*LW* p. 23, *JubA* 3.2:26). But a few pages earlier, he had explicitly described the source of our conviction of the existence of external objects as a matter of human psychology:

This affective aspect of our knowledge is really a matter for the science of psychology and character. As soon as we are dealing with the knowledge of the sort of things whose actuality is possible but not necessary, the quality of our knowledge is mixed. In part it consists in the immediate experience of something or a sensory perception that arises within us by itself; and in part it consists in the comparison of these perceptions and the mental work we do when we notice similarities among them or when we see their underlying general principles. The principles may either be grounded in reason or in an induction whose level of conviction depends upon how perfect or imperfect—that is, complete or incomplete—is the evidence that supports it. (*LW* p. 19, *JubA* 3.2:21)

Strikingly, Mendelssohn feels no need to follow either Descartes or Locke in arguing that God underwrites the reliability of human psychology; his position seems rather to be simply that there is no possibility of resisting the human psychology of belief-formation.[30] Under the circumstances he has described, of sensory concordance and repeated experience, the idea of external existence simply "forces itself upon our well-functioning sensory apparatus and...will not admit of being gainsaid" (Lecture V, *LW* p. 40, *JubA* 3.2:45). This is a conclusion that is closer to Hume than to either Locke or Descartes.[31]

However, Mendelssohn then insists that all that we have come to have an adequate degree of confidence in by means of the psychological mechanisms he has described is that there are external objects that have the powers to produce in us the kinds of ideas that they do, and not anything more about them. His use of the Lockean term

---

[30] As Dyck points out, Mendelssohn goes further and argues that (what I am calling) the human psychology of belief-formation is a "positive power for thinking in the soul," which can be counted upon to deliver truth ("Turning the Game," pp. 171–2). Again, although Mendelssohn does take this approach, it seems question-begging against skeptical idealism: how does he decide what tendencies of the mind are "positive powers" rather than mere "incapacities" of the soul?

[31] See the famous conclusion to Book I of Hume's *Treatise of Human Nature* (Book I, Part IV, Section 7).

"power" here is unmistakable. Locke had observed that we are not "to wonder, that *Powers make a great part of our complex* Ideas *of Substances*," although he had based this claim on the fact that our ideas of the secondary qualities of objects "are those, which in most of them serve principally to distinguish Substances one from another, and commonly make a considerable part of the complex *Idea* of the several sorts of them,"[32] while allowing that our ideas of primary qualities do actually resemble, at least in kind, the actual, internal properties of external objects. Mendelssohn, however, extends Locke's point to all the qualities of objects: what we know of objects, no matter how well we know them, beyond the simple fact that they exist, is how they present themselves to us, or what ideas in us they have the power to evoke. For example, an example clearly borrowed from Hume:

> The color and feeling of bread has been so often observed to be connected with a certain taste and a certain effect upon the nourishment of our body that we are justified in believing that both sets of properties are the consequences of the inward nature of the bread, and that with any given piece of bread we see and feel we may expect the same taste and the same nourishing effect. The inward nature by virtue of which bread produces the effects we ascribe to it we call its "power." (Lecture II, *LW* p.22, *JubA* 3.2:25)[33]

No matter how much we know about the bread or about anything else, what we know is what powers it has to produce ideas in us, not what it is in itself, independently of such powers. In more general terms, "we know nothing more about the body itself than what it does or suffers, and...apart from a thing's doings and sufferings nothing further about it can be conceived." (Lecture VII, *LW* p. 52, *JubA* 3.2:60). Mendelssohn presents this conclusion as trivially true, not depending upon any special reason to deny that our ideas match up to reality but rather as following from the simple fact that however much knowledge of objects we are acquiring, we are always simply acquiring new ideas or concepts of those objects. You might ask:

> "What is the original lying behind all sensible qualities after you take away from it all the effects it may have upon sensate beings?" I answer, "That is something that cannot be asked about, because it must lie outside any concept, and therefore, given the terms of the question, the original cannot be an object of knowledge. You are looking for a concept that would actually be no concept, and therefore something contradictory. Here we are standing at the limits of knowledge, and every step that we want to take further is a step into the void that can lead to no goal." (*LW* p. 52, *JubA* 3.2:60-1)

It is not that there is anything particular that we do not know about objects, any particular aspect of them that is blocked from our grasp; it is just that, truistically, whatever we know about objects is what *we know* about them. The limits of our knowledge are not an impairment or defect of any kind, but just this fact: "We only

---

[32] John Locke, *An Essay concerning Human Understanding*, Book II, Chapter XXIII, §8; in the edition by P.H. Nidditch (Oxford: Clarendon Press, 1975), p. 300.

[33] Hume talks about how we form our expectation of "nourishment and support" from our past experience of eating bread without knowing anything about its "secret powers" in *Essay concerning Human Understanding*, Section 4, Part 2; in the edition by Tom L. Beauchamp (Oxford: Clarendon Press, 2000), pp. 29–30. As already suggested, Mendelssohn would have been familiar with this passage from Sulzer's edition of Hume.

say that the representation we have of material beings, as extended, capable of motion, and impenetrable, is not a consequence of some weakness or impairment of ours, but rather that this representation arises from the unimpaired power of our mind and that it is common to all thinking beings" (Lecture VI, *LW* p. 50, *JubA* 3.2:58). It is not misleading for us to ascribe properties as we represent them to objects and not just to ourselves, for objects really do have the powers to arouse in us the sensory ideas and the concepts they do arouse: "This material original arouses in us the idea of extension, motion, shape, impenetrability, and so on. Therefore, this original itself is extended, capable of motion, impenetrable, and able to assume certain figures." But it is a mistake, one that we might even say we are led to by the form of our language, to think that in saying the latter we are saying anything more than the former, anything more than that the objects do arouse these ideas in us: "One lets oneself be deceived and led astray by empty words if one wants to understand something more than that by the expressions 'to be extended,' or 'to be capable of motion,' or 'to be impenetrable'"(Lecture VII, *LW* p. 51, *JubA* 3.2:59). This, we might say, is the anodyne truth of idealism, or an indisputable form of epistemological modesty.

Mendelssohn actually makes this statement in a defense of "dualism" against "idealism." This is because he understands idealism not as the simple doctrine that after all no matter what we know of things what we know of them is what we know, but rather as the doctrine that there exists nothing but minds, and dualism conversely as the doctrine that there exists objects in addition to minds. He firmly accepts the latter, but subject to the proviso that we cannot know anything of these objects beyond how they appear to us. This is his restriction to Alexander Gottlieb Baumgarten's refutation of idealism.

Mendelssohn describes the idealist, to be distinguished from the "absurdity of the egoist," as one who "admits to the existence of thinking beings besides himself and who does not arrogate to his humble self alone the merit of being the sole substance that has a purchase on reality." There is room for a distinction between subjectivity and objectivity, or illusion and empirical truth, within idealism, because the idealist can distinguish "the subjective sequence of things that is true only in him, from the objective sequence of things that is commonly shared by all thinking beings." Even so, idealism is to be distinguished from dualism, the position that "there are both physical and psychical substances," with the proviso, however, that although the agreement among different subjects in the way they represent physical objects points "to a common source of the agreement located outside us," nevertheless these objects are "not entirely like what they seem to us to be, for the limitations of our cognitive faculty alter the way they come to be represented" (Lecture VI, *LW* p. 49, *JubA* 3.2:56). This restriction is the consequence of the trivial fact that we can only represents things as we represent them, and is the one criticism Mendelssohn has to make of Baumgarten's refutation of idealism. Mendelssohn does not refer explicitly to Baumgarten, only to "philosophers" who "have also tried to use" the principle that due to his faculty of approbation God creates only the best of all possible worlds "to demonstratively persuade the idealists of the groundlessness of their opinion" (Lecture XII, *LW* p. 91, *JubA* 3.2:103). But the argument he then expounds is unmistakably that Baumgarten had directed against the idealists in his

*Metaphysica*. There Baumgarten defined the idealist as "Whoever admits only spirits in this world,"[34] and then argued, on the basis of the previously demonstrated premise that only the most perfect of possible worlds exists together with the definition that "the *most perfect world* embraces as many (1) simultaneous, (2) successive, and (3) as great beings as are compossible in the best world,"[35] that:

even if there is only one non-intellectual monad possible in itself that is compossible with spirits in the world, whose perfection either subtracts nothing from the perfection of the spirits, or does not subtract from the perfection of the spirits so much as it adds to the perfection of the whole, then the IDEALISTIC WORLD, such as is posited by the idealist, is not the most perfect.[36]

In other words, a world that contains both psychical and physical objects, to use Mendelssohn's terms, has more variety and thus more perfection than a world that contains only the former, and is therefore the kind of world God would have created in preference to the former. Baumgarten then adds the requirement that perfection does not consist in sheer numbers or numbers of kinds of things, but also in the greatest possible rather than any lesser harmony among them: "*In the most perfect world there is the greatest universal nexus,* harmony, and agreement that is possible in a world";[37] he does not explicitly say so, but presumably this harmony includes that between minds and non-mental objects in virtue of which the former represent the latter—that could at least be an implication of Baumgarten's subsequent defense of a "UNIVERSAL PRE-ESTABLISHED HARMONY" that includes the "INTERACTION OF MUNDANE SUBSTANCES."[38] Mendelssohn then combines these two steps, that the most perfect world includes two kinds of substances rather than one and the harmony in virtue of which one can represent the other, in the argument that he attributes to the philosophers opposed to idealism:

A configuration of the interconnection among things in which matter, as the object of representation, actually exists must necessarily be more perfect than a configuration in which sensory qualities have no external object. In the latter configuration there is only a harmony among the representations within the minds of thinking beings, insofar as these representations are images that contain truth, but in the former configuration, the representations of thinking beings not only harmonize among themselves, but they also harmonize with the objects that are actually found outside themselves, objects that are the originals behind the represented images... Greater harmony is greater perfection... Since God only brings to actuality that which is most perfect, the world that He created is not only ideational, but it also contains matter, as is required for the greatest degree of harmony.
(Lecture XII, *LW* p. 91, *JubA* 3.2:103)

This assumes that both greater number of kinds and greater harmony are more perfect rather than less, and that among the kinds of harmony necessary for the best of all possible worlds is that in virtue of which "representations within the minds of thinking beings" harmonize with and therefore represent "the objects that are

---

[34] Alexander Gottlieb Baumgarten, *Metaphysics* (fourth edition, 1757), translated and edited by Courtney D. Fugate and John Hymers (London: Bloomsbury, 2013), §402, p. 176.
[35] Baumgarten, *Metaphysics*, §437, p. 183.    [36] Baumgarten, *Metaphysics*, §438, p. 183.
[37] Baumgarten, *Metaphysics*, §441, p. 183.    [38] Baumgarten, *Metaphysics*, §448, p. 185.

actually found outside themselves." The second stage of this argument might also be considered a translation of Descartes's argument that a benevolent God would not fail to create external objects that correspond to our tendency to believe in them insofar as that is irresistible to our best efforts not to believe it into the Leibnizo-Baumgartian idiom of the best of all possible worlds.[39] When he then places his restriction on the Baumgartian refutation of idealism, Mendelssohn is thereby also criticizing Descartes's own form of representationalism, which held on the basis of divine benevolence that we can confidently assert that our (clear and distinct) ideas are both *caused by* and *resemble* external objects,[40] by arguing that the proof entitles us to hold that there are physical substances in addition to our ideas of them but not to assert that our ways of representing them are anything more than just that, namely our ways of representing them. In Mendelssohn's words:

> You see for yourselves, however, that these arguments can support only the existence of an object corresponding to our representations of material things, but it remains undecided how far the subjective aspect of our sensory cognition interferes with and is transformed together with that cognition into the presentation of material qualities as appearances [*Erscheinungen*]. In sensory cognition one can unquestionably find truth. But we find this truth combined with semblance [*Scheine*], we find the original combined with a perspective, and our senses alone cannot separate one from the other. (*LW* p. 91, *JubA* 3.2:103)

Indeed, Mendelssohn uses Kant's own terminology, the word *Erscheinungen*, to make his point that although we can appeal to God and his faculty of approbation to prove the existence of physical objects, we ultimately cannot say more about them than that they affect us in certain typical and to be sure intersubjectively reliable ways. The basic insight of idealism places a restriction on the refutation of idealism.

Mendelssohn's response to the threat of Cartesian skepticism is thus remarkably reminiscent of Hume's position on induction, and thus strikingly empiricist, especially in contrast to his proofs for the existence of God. As we will now see, Kant takes over Mendelssohn's image of our method for confirming our particular beliefs about external objects, but tries to provide a transcendental foundation for our empirical realism.

## 5. Kant's Transcendental Idealism and Transcendental Refutation of Idealism

That even such a friend of common sense as Moses Mendelssohn recognized that we are entitled to assert the existence of things distinct from our own minds and their representations but cannot say more about them than that we represent them in certain ways may help explain why Kant was basically dumbfounded by the

---

[39] See René Descartes, *Meditations on First Philosophy*, Sixth Meditation, in *Oeuvres de Descartes*, edited by Charles Adam and Paul Tannery, revised edition, 12 vols. (Paris: Vrin/CNRS, 1964–76), vol. VII, p. 79–80; in *The Philosophical Writings of Descartes*, edited by John Cottingham, Robert Stoothoff, and Dugald Murdoch, 3 vols. (Cambridge: Cambridge University Press, 1984–91), vol. II, p. 55.

[40] See Descartes, *Meditations*, Third Meditation, *Oeuvres* VII 39, *Philosophical Writings* II 27 (where these two aspects of correspondence are defined as the eventual target of proof although not yet proven).

resistance to his own distinction between things as they are in themselves and the way they appear to us—a distinction which, as he asserted in his *Groundwork for the Metaphysics of Morals*, published the same year as Mendelssohn's *Morning Hours*, even "the commonest understanding can make."[41] And, as I suggested earlier, the empirical criteria for assertions of the actual existence of external objects that Kant provides in the notes to his own "Refutation of Idealism" are basically the same as Mendelssohn's, and were perhaps even inspired by Mendelssohn's recently published account. Nevertheless, there are two fundamental differences between Kant's refutation of idealism and Mendelssohn's, both of which may be connoted by Kant's designation of his own position as *transcendental* idealism. On the one hand, Kant does not modestly think that we are merely limited by our own way of representing things to ignorance about their real nature, but brazenly *denies* that things as they are in themselves are really spatio-temporal.[42] On the other hand, he does not underwrite the empirical criteria for external reality with a theological argument of the Leibnizo-Baumgartian kind, but supports them with a paradigm transcendental argument that empirical consciousness of the existence of objects distinct from our representations is a necessary condition of our empirical consciousness of our representations themselves, even if, of course, we cannot cognize those objects as they are in themselves. In other words, for all their affinities, the difference between Mendelssohn's and Kant's responses to idealism is precisely that, for better or worse (and I will say what I mean by that in due course), Kant's is transcendental, and Mendelssohn's is not. Kant tries to provide a transcendental foundation for empirical realism that Mendelssohn does without.

First, let us stipulate to the resemblance between the two positions on the question of the empirical criteria for particular assertions of actual external existence. Like Mendelssohn, Kant holds that from the general fact that he will allege as the basis of his own refutation of idealism, namely "that the existence of outer objects is required for the possibility of a determinate consciousness of our self ... it does not follow that every intuitive representation of outer things includes at the same time their existence, for that may well be the mere effect of the imagination (in dreams as well as delusions)"; but like Mendelssohn, Kant holds that, once underwritten in general,

---

[41] Kant, *Groundwork for the Metaphysics of Morals*, Section III, 4:450; in Kant, *Practical Philosophy*, edited and translated by Mary J. Gregor (Cambridge: Cambridge University Press, 1996), p. 98.

[42] I have been arguing for this interpretation of Kant's transcendental idealism for a long time. See my *Kant and the Claims of Knowledge* (Cambridge: Cambridge University Press, 1987), Part V; "The Rehabilitation of Transcendental Idealism?," in Eva Schaper and Wilhelm Vossenkuhl, eds., *Reading Kant: New Perspectives on Transcendental Arguments and Critical Philosophy* (Oxford: Basil Blackwell, 1989), pp. 140–67; and "Transcendental Idealism: What and Why?," in Matthew C. Altman, ed., *The Palgrave Kant Handbook* (London: Palgrave Macmillan, 2017), pp. 71–90. For equally long, this interpretation has been unpopular; see especially the work of Henry Allison, including "Transcendental Idealism: A Retrospective," in his *Idealism and Freedom: Essays on Kant's Theoretical and Practical Philosophy* (Cambridge: Cambridge University Press, 1996), pp. 3–26, and "Transcendental Realism, Empirical Realism, and Transcendental Idealism," in his *Essays on Kant* (Oxford: Oxford University Press, 2012), pp. 67–83. More recently, scholarly opinion is swinging in my direction; see Lucy Allais, *Manifest Reality: Kant's Idealism and his Realism* (Oxford: Oxford University Press, 2015). My chief difference with Dyck's interpretation is that although he states that for Kant, unlike Mendelsohn, "the question regarding the constitution of things in themselves [is] a meaningful one" ("Turning the Game," p. 177), he does not link this claim to a specific interpretation of transcendental idealism.

particular assertions of external existence may be based on empirical, commonsensical criteria: "Whether this or that putative experience is not mere imagination must be ascertained according to its particular determinations and through its coherence with the criteria of all actual experience" (*CPR* B 278–9). The criteria of all actual existence are spelled out in the "Postulates of Empirical Thinking in General," very much along the lines of Mendelssohn's distinction between criteria for possibility and for actuality: for Kant, "Whatever agrees with the formal conditions of experience (in accordance with intuitions and concepts)," that is, in his terms, with the pure forms of intuition and the categories of pure concepts of the understanding, "is **possible**," while "That which is connected with the material conditions of experience (of sensation), is **actual**."[43] Since his subsequent discussion makes clear that external objects can be "connected" to sensations with particular causal laws, as for example the existence of a magnetic field can be connected to our "perception of attracted iron filings" by the laws of magnetism,[44] Kant's criteria for actuality are essentially the same as Mendelssohn's, although again for Mendelssohn the only a priori constraint on the possibility of objects of experience is the logical law of non-contradiction, while for Kant experience is constrained by the a priori forms of both intuition and understanding, and thus rests upon synthetic a priori principles as well as upon the logical principle of analysis (see especially *CPR* A 150–8/B 189–97).

But then Kant's combination of his refutation of empirical idealism with his own transcendental idealism takes two very different turns from Mendelssohn's. First, instead of confining himself to the anodyne observation that we can only represent things as we represent them, or even to the stronger claim, hinted at in Mendelssohn's critique of Baumgarten, that we *cannot tell* whether our way of representing things through our senses *may* distort their real nature, Kant argues that things as they are in themselves *cannot be* spatial and temporal. This is the conclusion of the "Transcendental Aesthetic." As Kant plainly says, under the rubric "Conclusions from the above concepts" following (what he separated in the second edition of the *Critique* as) the "metaphysical" and "transcendental" expositions of the concept of space:

Space represents no property at all of any things in themselves nor any relation of them to each other, i.e., no determination of them that attaches to objects themselves and that would remain even if one were to abstract from all subjective conditions of intuition. For neither absolute nor relative determinations can be intuited prior to the existence of the things to which they pertain, thus be intuited *a priori*. (*CPR* A 26/B 42)

*Mutatis mutandis*, he says the same thing about time (*CPR* A 32–3/B 49). As the quotation suggests, Kant holds that the non-spatiality and non-temporality of things in themselves, or the transcendental ideality rather than transcendental reality of space and time, follows from the very fact that we have a priori knowledge of space and time. In the preceding metaphysical and transcendental expositions, he had in fact argued that we have two levels of a priori knowledge about space and time: we have general a priori knowledge that all objects must be perceived in a single, infinite

---
[43] Kant, *Critique of Pure Reason*, A 218/B 265–6; p. 321.
[44] Kant, *Critique of Pure Reason*, A 226/B 273; p. 326.

space and/or time, and we have more particular a priori knowledge of the synthetic propositions of geometry and arithmetic, which describe space and time in detail. The question is, why should such a priori knowledge both general and particular imply that the things that appear to us in space and time are *not* themselves spatial and temporal? That is, if things can *only* appear to us as in space and time, why shouldn't we think that the things that *do* appear to us in space and time *actually are* spatial and temporal? The answer is that Kant holds that whatever is known a priori is known to be such as it is known to be *universally and necessarily*, and that the only explanation for anything being *necessarily* as it is known to be is that *we make it to be such*, a condition that is satisfied by our *representations* or the way things *appear to us* but not by things as they are in themselves. That this is the *nervus probandi* of Kant's argument for the transcendental ideality of space and time is signaled in two key passages, one in the "Transcendental Aesthetic" and one in the *Prolegomena to any Future Metaphysics*. In the former, Kant says that if you were to assume that an object other than your representations has the spatial properties that you represent it as having, for instance if you were to assume that the thing that you represent as a triangle is a triangle independently of your so representing it, thus if you were to deny that the "subjective condition regarding form were...at the same time the universal *a priori* condition under which alone the object of this (outer) intuition were itself possible," then you could not "say that what necessarily lies in your subjective conditions for constructing [e.g.] a triangle must also necessarily pertain to the triangle in itself" (CPR A 48/B 65). In other words, while you can suppose that your *representations* necessarily have the spatial (or temporal) properties you represent them as having, if *objects other than your representations* had these properties you could only suppose that they have them *contingently*, and the universality of your claim to necessity and therefore a priori knowledge would thereby be undermined. Kant says this even more clearly in the *Prolegomena*, when he says that if it were attributed to things in themselves then "The space of the geometer would be taken for mere fabrication and would be credited with no objective validity, because it is simply not to be seen how things would have to agree necessarily with the image that we form of them by ourselves and in advance" (PFM 4:287). In Kant's view, the possibility of our a priori knowledge of space and time and of the synthetic propositions describing their structure implies the transcendental ideality of space and time.[45]

An obvious response to Kant's argument is that we do not have the kind of a priori knowledge that he supposes, that we may have a priori knowledge of relationships within a mathematical system, knowledge that is analytic or even, if you like, synthetic in the sense of needing to be proven by construction rather than by mere deduction, but that any knowledge that we have that a mathematical system or formalism actually *applies* to any existing objects is empirical and thus its truth in regard to such objects is contingent, not necessary at all, in which case we have no reason to deny that it really is true of such objects. This is of course the position of common sense, and it was also Mendelssohn's position: it is implicit in *Morning*

---

[45] For more detail, see *Kant and the Claims of Knowledge*, pp. 354-69.

*Hours* in Mendelssohn's characterization of the science of Galileo and Newton as applying conceptual truths to sensory experience, and as we saw it was spelled out more fully in his prize essay twenty years earlier when he wrote that "the highest degree of certainty is only to be found in pure, theoretical mathematics. As soon as we make use of a geometrical truth in practice, that is, as soon as we wish to pass from mere possibilities to actualities, an empirical proposition must be placed at the foundation, a proposition which asserts that this or that figure, number, and so forth are actually present" (*PW*, p. 265, *JubA* 2:283). Kant was aware of this position and was rejecting it in his "Transcendental Aesthetic," but there is no evidence that Mendelssohn was moved by Kant's alternative, nor is it obvious that we should be—it makes a strong assumption about the scope of the necessity of the truths of mathematics that is not obviously justified. So Kant's reason for going beyond Mendelssohn's modest observation that we can only represent things as we represent them and beyond that cannot say more than that they exist and affect us is not very good.

This means that Kant need never have taken on the burden of reconciling his transcendental idealism with the empirical realism that he also wants to defend. Of course this was not his own view of the matter, so let us see how he did attempt to achieve this reconciliation. As already mentioned, the 1782 Garve-Feder review of the first *Critique* had raised Kant's hackles by associating his form of idealism with Berkeley's: "One basic pillar of the Kantian system rests on these concepts of sensations as mere modifications of ourselves (on which **Berkeley**, too, principally builds his idealism) and of space and time."[46] Kant had responded to this charge in the *Prolegomena*, already underway as a popularization of the *Critique*, with the explanation that what he "called idealism did not concern the existence of things (the doubting of which, however, properly constitutes idealism according to the received meaning), for it never came into my mind to doubt that, but only the sensory representation of things, to which space and time above all belong; and about these last ... I have only shown: that they are not things (but mere modes of representation), nor are they determinations that belong to things in themselves" (following which Kant suggests that perhaps it would be less confusing if he called his doctrine "critical" rather than "transcendental idealism") (*PFM* 4:293). Kant also says that the *Critique* already supplies the "proper antidote" to the "mystical and visionary idealism of Berkeley." In fact, Kant had not explicitly mentioned Berkeley in the first edition of the *Critique*, but his comment on Berkeley in the introduction to the second-edition "Refutation of Idealism" shows us that he took Berkeley to have argued that space is "something that is impossible in itself" (*CPR* B 274), and thus the "antidote" to Berkeley can have consisted in nothing other than his own proof that space and time are actually *necessary* rather than impossible or even merely contingent—from which, however, his own version of idealism, denying not the

---

[46] [Christian Garve, edited by Johann Feder], "*Critique of Pure Reason* by Immanuel Kant. 1781." *Zugabe zu den Göttingschen Anzeigen von gelehrten Sachen* (January 19, 1782): 40–8; translation from Brigitte Sassen, editor, *Kant's Early Critics: The Empiricist Critique of the Theoretical Philosophy* (Cambridge: Cambridge University Press, 2000), pp. 53–8, at pp. 53–4.

reality of things in space and time but only the reality of their spatiality and temporality, had followed.

Berkeley thus dispatched, what remained for Kant was the "problematic idealism" of Descartes (*CPR* B 274). Kant had already mentioned this in the *Prolegomena*, under the name of "the empirical idealism of *Descartes*," where he had rather surprisingly said that "this idealism was only a problem, whose insolubility left everyone free, in *Descartes*'s opinion, to deny the existence of the corporeal world, since the problem could never be answered satisfactorily" (*PFM* 4:293)—a remark that can only be explained by the supposition that Kant summarily dismissed Descartes's theological solution (in *Meditations* III through VI) to the skeptical threat he had raised (in *Meditation* II), as of course he had to do given his rejection of theoretical arguments for the existence of God. Kant then returns to the debate not with Berkeley but with Descartes in the second-edition "Refutation of Idealism," which I have suggested might be better explained by the renewed prominence of Descartes in Mendelssohn's *Morning Hours* than by lingering resentment over the charge of Berkeleianism. In particular, the Refutation's strategy of arguing that "the determination of my existence in time is possible only by means of the existence of actual things outside me, as the condition of time-determination" (*CPR* B 275), can be seen as directed against Mendelssohn's strategy of, first, accepting the Cartesian inference that my consciousness of my own ideas as "modifications" immediately proves the existence of the enduring substance that has them (*Morning Hours*, Lecture I, LW p. 12, JubA 3.2:14), and then underwriting the inductive causal inference to external objects causing those modifications not by appeal to God but simply by appeal to the inevitable operations of the unimpaired human psyche. As he explains in his comments on the Refutation, Kant actually accepts the Cartesian *cogito* argument that "the representation **I am**, which expresses the consciousness that can accompany all thinking...immediately includes the existence of a subject in itself," but he argues that this is "not yet any **cognition**" of this subject, because for to this "there belongs, besides the thought of something existing, intuition, and in this case inner intuition, i.e., time, in regard to which the subject must be determined" (*CPR* B 277). That is, the premise of the Refutation is that we do not know just *that* our subject exists (although, as the "Paralogisms of Pure Reason" later explains, in knowing this we do not know that a *substance* exists), but that we know the *determinate temporal order* of our own representations—"I am conscious of my existence as determined in time," the Refutation begins (*CPR* B 275), that is, as it is determined in time. Kant's argument against Mendelssohn as well as the explicitly named Descartes is then that we cannot just take the order of our own experiences in time to be immediately given without any sort of conditions and then infer the existence of external objects from those experiences, but rather that our consciousness of the temporal order of our own experiences *presupposes* consciousness of the existence of enduring "objects in space outside me" (*CPR* B 275). The argument for this claim is then Kant's transcendental as opposed to Mendelssohn's empirical argument for the existence of external objects, the real nature of which, however, Kant agrees with Mendelssohn we do not know, although, as we saw, because of the transcendental argument from the very necessity of our representing them as spatial and temporal rather than from the mere observation that we can only represent things as we represent them.

To be sure, both what Kant's Refutation is supposed to prove and how it is supposed to work have remained controversial. This is hardly the place to defend answers to these questions in detail, so I will only summarize what I have argued elsewhere.[47] What Kant aims to prove in the Refutation is precisely the position he defines in the *Prolegomena*, namely, that there really are things that exist other than our own representations (and the minds that have them), in other words, things in themselves, although the very property by which we represent the independent existence of these things, namely their distance in space from our own bodies, is an artifact of the way we represent them, not a property of them as they are in themselves. My favorite piece of evidence for this interpretation remains one of Kant's new versions of the Refutation from 1790, one of a number of drafts he wrote in connection with a visit to Königsberg that summer by his former student Johann Gottfried Karl Christian Kiesewetter (1766–1819), then living in Berlin, where he says that the possibility of temporal determination "lies in the relation of representations to something outside us, and, indeed, to something which is not in turn merely inner representation, that is, form of appearance, thus, to something which is something in itself [*Sache an sich*]"—a phrase that Kant never, to my knowledge, uses to refer to mere representation.[48] The harder question is how Kant reaches this conclusion. My interpretation has been that he tried two different strategies, without ever deciding between them: one on which he argued that time-determination always needs something enduring, therefore something other than representations, which we represent spatially because that is our way of representing independence from our own representations, even though it is just our way of doing that;[49] the other is to argue directly that time-determination requires space, e.g., the motion of objects in space, and space itself is something that endures in a way that representations do not, even though, again, that we represent space the way we do is an artifact of our own way of representing.[50] Either way, Kant wants to argue that the representation of something as enduring in space is a necessary condition of our assigning a determinate temporal order to our own, non-permanent representations, and if we turn around and conceive of the thing that endures in space as itself nothing

---

[47] I originally presented my interpretation in "Kant's Intentions in the Refutation of Idealism," *Philosophical Review* 92 (1983): 329–83, and expanded it in *Kant and the Claims of Knowledge*, Part IV. For alternative approaches, see Paul Abela, *Kant's Empirical Realism* (Oxford: Clarendon Press, 2002), pp. 182–213, and Dina Emundts, "The Refutation of Idealism and the Distinction between Phenomena and Noumena," in Paul Guyer, ed., *The Cambridge Companion to Kant's Critique of Pure Reason* (Cambridge: Cambridge University Press, 2010), pp. 168–89.

[48] Kant, Reflection 6312, 18:612; in Kant, *Notes and Fragments*, edited by Paul Guyer, translated by Curtis Bowman, Paul Guyer, and Frederick Rauscher (Cambridge: Cambridge University Press, 2005), p. 357.

[49] See especially Reflection 6313, 18:615; *Notes and Fragments*, p. 359: "I cannot know time as antecedently determined, in order to determine my own existence therein... Now in order to determine that empirically, something which endures must be given..."

[50] See, e.g., Reflection 5653, labeled "Against material idealism," 18:308, *Notes and Fragments*, p. 282: "Permanence is intrinsic to the representation of space, as Newton said... [the representation of space] is the representation of something permanent."

but a representation, then we strip it of the very permanence that we need—"My representations cannot be outside me, and an external object of representations cannot be in me, for that would be a contradiction."[51] Yet this result must be held together with the recognition that although the things I use for determining the temporal order of my own empirical consciousness must be considered to be independent of me, their spatiality cannot be, but must instead be considered to be an artifact of my human way of representing independence.

Thus Kant ends up only partly in the same place as Mendelssohn. Unlike Mendelssohn, he does not merely modestly insist that we can only represent things as we represent them, but insists that the non-spatiality and non-temporality of things in themselves follows from the very necessity of our knowledge of space and time. Like Mendelssohn, he argues that we must believe in the existence of things distinct from our representations of them, yet not as a mere matter of reliable human psychology, but as a very condition of the possibility of empirical consciousness or the determination of the temporal order of our experience of itself. I myself do not place much stock in the former argument, and would rather rest with Mendelssohn's epistemological modesty on this point; but I have always found the latter argument compelling, or at least would if only I could be sure exactly how it goes. But opinions on this differ. What is clear is that when it comes to our knowledge of external objects, as opposed to our knowledge of the existence of God, Mendelssohn is much more an empiricist than he is a rationalist, and it is Kant who defends a sort of rationalism, though the very special sort embodied by his transcendental logic and transcendental psychology, which aims to show that empirical knowledge has not merely analytic but also synthetic a priori foundations.

We have now seen how the debate between Mendelssohn and Kant over proofs for the existence of God, proofs for the immortality of the human soul, and the possibility of knowledge of the external world occupied the two philosophers from the time of their prize essays in the early 1760s to Mendelssohn's death in 1786 and Kant's publication of the second edition of the *Critique of Pure Reason* in the following year. We have seen how with regard to the first two topics Kant sought to replace Mendelssohn's more traditional theoretical rationalism with his own practical rationalism, while with regard to the last Kant took over elements of Mendelssohn's empiricism but tried to ground empiricism in transcendental philosophy. We will now turn from metaphysical issues to two other areas that occupied each of our philosophers and on which they can be interpreted as either implicitly or explicitly debating with one another. These are the fields of aesthetics, in which Mendelssohn had first made his reputation in the 1750s but in which Kant made his major statement only in 1790, thus after the death of Mendelssohn, and the further topic of the place of religion in human society and history, in which Mendelssohn made his major statement in his *Jerusalem* of 1783 and to which Kant responded in his *Religion within the Boundaries of Mere Reason*, a decade later and so again after the death of Mendelssohn. (I say "the place of religion in human society and history" rather than simply "philosophy of religion" because we have already considered the

---

[51] Kant, Reflection 6314, 18;620; *Notes and Fragments*, pp. 361–2.

extensive debate between the two philosophers over natural theology or the proofs of the existence of God in their earlier works and we will not be returning to that subject.) We will consider these two topics in the order in which Kant rather than Mendelssohn took them up, thus we will turn next to aesthetics and then in Part Three of this book to Kant's response to Mendelssohn's *Jerusalem* in his *Religion* and other essays of the 1790s.

# PART II
# Aesthetics

Mendelssohn made his mark with his early publications in aesthetics, beginning with the *Letters on the Sentiments* in 1755, an essay on the *Main Principles of the Fine Arts and Sciences* in 1757, other essays collected with these two in the first edition of his *Philosophical Writings* in 1761 (revised in 1771), and numerous reviews of works in literature and many other fields published in the journals that he edited with his friends Lessing and Friedrich Nicolai throughout this period.[1] He was only twenty-six when he published the *Letters on Sentiments*. Kant was already forty when he published his *Observations on the Feeling of the Beautiful and Sublime* in 1764, intended primarily as an advertisement for his lecture courses on physical geography and later anthropology, and although he did regularly address questions in aesthetics, above all the nature of the beautiful and of judgments of taste, in his logic and anthropology lectures from the early 1770s onwards, his influential publication in aesthetics came only in 1790, when he was sixty-six and Mendelssohn had already been dead for four years. This was the "Critique of the Aesthetic Power of Judgment," the first half of what turned out to be his third and last critique, the *Critique of the Power of Judgment*. Unlike Kant's earlier *Observations*, this quickly became a popular and influential book, for its defense of teleological thinking about nature as well as for its aesthetic theory, and, unlike Mendelssohn's work, has been a staple of courses in philosophical aesthetics throughout the world ever since.

It might be expected that the young Mendelssohn would have hewed closely to the rationalism of his models such as Leibniz, Christian Wolff, and Alexander Gottlieb Baumgarten, while Kant, publishing on aesthetics only deep into his maturity, would have been able to draw on a wider experience of the arts and construct an aesthetic theory deeply responsive to such an experience. In fact, the young Mendelssohn, on

---

[1] Daniel O. Dahlstrom translated the revised 1771 edition of Mendelssohn's *Philosophische Schriften* as *Philosophical Writings* (Cambridge: Cambridge University Press, 1997), although his translation includes several items, such as the prize essay, that were not included in Mendelssohn's book. The *Jubiläum Ausgabe* reprints the earlier as well as later editions of Mendelssohn's work. There is no reason to believe that a response to Kant had anything to do with Mendelssohn's revisions for the 1771 edition, and although there is no record of either edition of Mendelssohn's work being in Kant's library at the time of his death, the fact that Kant addressed issues in aesthetics in his lectures only beginning in the 1770s makes it reasonable to assume that he would have used the later edition of Mendelssohn's work if he was directly responding to Mendelssohn at all. Be that as it may, I shall rely on the second edition of *Philosophische Schriften* and the translation of it in what follow.

his own and through his extensive work as a reviewer, had already acquired an extraordinary mastery of literature, drama, music, and other arts, and, although working within a conceptual framework derived from his rationalist predecessors, was able to find room for a wide range of aesthetic experiences and values within this framework and to give full weight to the perceptual, cognitive, and emotional dimensions of our experience of art. Kant, by contrast, although his central conception in aesthetics, the idea of the free play of our cognitive powers in aesthetic experience, is an enduring contribution to the field, took a much more restrictive review of the proper objects of taste and properly aesthetic dimensions of aesthetic experience, and only late in his work and perhaps grudgingly recognized some of the complexity of aesthetic experience that Mendelssohn had celebrated. Mendelssohn combined his rationalist theory with a healthy empiricism toward the variety of actual aesthetic experience,[2] while Kant's search for an a priori principle in aesthetics that could parallel those he had found in epistemology and morality limited his conception of aesthetic experience, although in the end perhaps his good sense at least occasionally broke out of the limits of his theory. So at least I shall argue in this Part, divided into the present chapter on Mendelssohn's aesthetics and the following chapters, which will first expound Kant's aesthetics and then compare the two.

---

[2] The two most extensive surveys of Mendelssohn's aesthetics in recent literature are Frederick C. Beiser, *Diotima's Children: German Aesthetic Rationalism from Leibniz to Lessing* (Oxford: Oxford University Press, 2009), ch. 7, and Anne Pollok, *Facetten des Menschen: zu Anthropologie Moses Mendelssohns* (Hamburg: Felix Meiner Verlag, 2010), ch. II, sections 2 and 3. According to Beiser, Mendelssohn's "task was to defend aesthetic rationalism against the new irrationalist currents of the age," such as the "new empiricist aesthetics of Dubos and Burke" (p. 196), which he accomplished by defending "Wolff's definition of pleasure as an intuition of perfection... a form of cognition involving an implicit act of judgment" (p. 202), while according to Pollok, "Mendelssohn aimed... at a balance between reflection and passion" (p. 118) and at a "bridge between the two poles of rationalistic and empiricistic theses" (p. 154) and at a "critique of the dominant one-sidedness" in which "the currently represented thesis in rationalism and empiricism, rational and empirical psychology, medicine, and metaphysics would not be presented separately but in their mutual, fruitful interaction" (p. 170). The view of Mendelssohn's aesthetics to be presented here will be much closer to Pollok's than to Beiser's, which is overly impressed with the rationalist language rather than empiricist substance of the work. For my earlier assessment of Beiser's book, see my review in *Philosophical Review* 121 (2012): 285–90.

# 6

# Mendelssohn's Aesthetics

Mendelssohn claims that "the essence of the fine arts and sciences consists in an artful, sensuously perfect representation or in a sensuous perfection represented by art" ("Main Principles," *PW* 173, *JubA* 1:431). Kant insists that "The judgment of taste is entirely independent from the concept of perfection" (*CPJ* §15, 5:226).

Mendelssohn claims that "Through different senses, poetry, rhetoric, beauties in shapes and sounds penetrate our soul and dominate all our inclinations. They can make us happy, then sad at will. They can arouse our passions and tame them in turn, and we willingly submit to the power of the artist who has us hope, fear, become irate, be soothed, laugh, and then pour out our tears" ("Main Principles," *PW* 170, *JubA* 1:428). Kant states that "Taste is always still barbaric when it needs the addition of **charms** and **emotions** for satisfaction, let alone if it makes these into the standard for its approval" (*CPJ* §5:223).

It is hard to imagine two more diametrically opposed sets of statements. Kant's rejection of the concept of perfection and the role of emotions in response to and judgment of art appears to be a repudiation of everything to which Mendelssohn is committed. Perhaps it was intentionally directed at Mendelssohn as well. The first edition of Mendelssohn's *Philosophical Writings*, in which he collected his main essays on aesthetics from the 1750s—namely the letters "On Sentiments" and the essays "On the Main Principles of the Fine Arts and Sciences" and "On the Sublime and Naïve in the Fine Sciences," and added to them, a "Rhapsody," further developing his themes—had appeared in 1761, with no obvious repercussions in Kant's work of that decade, in particular, with no obvious influence on Kant's attempt to write a popular work on aesthetic themes, his *Observations on the Feeling of the Beautiful and Sublime* of 1764. But a second edition of Mendelssohn's essays appeared in 1771,[3] just one year before Kant began regularly discussing issues of aesthetics within the framework of his lectures on anthropology; so even though Kant's attack upon a theory of beauty as a "perfection" of objects might seem to have been aimed at the rationalist aesthetics of Alexander Gottlieb Baumgarten and his disciple Georg Friedrich Meier and his attack upon the importance of emotions in our response to art might be thought to have been aimed at the empiricist aesthetics of Henry Home, Lord Kames (the second and last volume of Baumgarten's *Aesthetica* having appeared in 1758 and Kames's *Elements of Criticism* in 1762, with a German

---

[3] Anne Pollok's work on Mendelssohn's aesthetics is sensitive to his revisions. In addition to her chapter in *Facetten des Menschen*, see also "Beautiful Perception and its Object: Mendelssohn's theory of mixed sentiments reconsidered," *Kant-Studien* 109 (2018): 270–85.

translation quickly following),[4] it would not be implausible to suppose, although it cannot be proven, that Kant's emerging aesthetic theory, many features of which were well in place by the mid-1770s, was in fact tacitly aimed at Mendelssohn.

Whether or not Kant's aesthetic theory and especially his theory of fine art was primarily directed against Mendelssohn, it will be illuminating to read the two theories in contrast with one another. From such an approach two main points will emerge. On the one hand, even though the conceptual frameworks or what we might call the "meta-aesthetics" of the two theories seem to differ so greatly, Mendelssohn using the language of perfection and Kant rejecting it, in many ways the difference between their analyses of both aesthetic experience and of fine art are not so great as initially appears. In particular, Kant's puzzling contrast between our response to the *representation* of objects and to their *existence*, which he uses to explain his revival of what was in fact Francis Hutcheson's nearly forgotten conception of disinterestedness, may perhaps be his revision rather than rejection of Mendelssohn's own contrast between the perfection of sensuous representation and the sensuous representation of perfection.[5] But Mendelssohn uses his contrast between perfections of representation and of objects above all to explain the mixed *sentiments* that we have in response to the successful—beautiful and/or sublime—artistic representation of unhappy events—Mendelssohn's theory of mixed sentiments is his solution to the raging mid-eighteenth century debate about why we take pleasure in tragedy—while Kant often seems to insist upon the exclusion of sentiment from the proper response to beauty altogether. Thus in this case the disagreement between them seems to be substantive rather than verbal.

Yet Kant's theory of *fine art* in particular is closer to Mendelssohn's than initially appears, and given his view of the typical subject-matter of art, which is by no means as devoid of content as he may initially make it appear, Kant's exclusion of "charm and emotion" from the proper response to art may seem unwarranted and unsustainable. Kant's reasons for his rejection of charm and emotion are by no means trivial—his initial exclusion of them comes in the Analytic of the Beautiful, where he is focused above all on the possibility of intersubjective or "universal subjective validity" in aesthetic response and no doubt regards charm and emotion as sources of idiosyncrasy and interpersonal disagreement, and his overall suspicion of them is

---

[4] Henry Home, Lord Kames, *Elements of Criticism, in Three Volumes* (London and Edinburgh: A. Millar, A. Kincaid, and J. Bell, 1762); sixth edition (1785), ed. Peter Jones, 2 vols. (Indianapolis: Liberty Fund, 2005); the first German edition is Heinrich Home, *Grundsätze der Kritik, aus dem Englischen übersetzt*, 3 vols. (Leipzig: Dyck, 1763-6).

[5] Beiser insists that "the Kantian interpretation of Mendelssohn is shamelessly biased, not to mention anachronistic" (*Diotima's Children*, p. 199). He cites no authorities for a "Kantian interpretation" of Mendelssohn's aesthetics, though he does cite some for the view that he was an "essentially transitional figure between the old rationalism of Wolff and the new subjectivism of Burke, Dubos, and Kant" (p. 198). No one would consider Mendelssohn a transitional figure to Du Bos, whose chief work in aesthetics (*Réflexions critique sur la poésie et sur la peinture*, 1719) was published ten years before Mendelssohn was born! Be that as it may, what I shall be arguing in this Part is that Kant's central, if you will "subjectivist" concept of the free play of imagination and understanding as the basis of aesthetic response is closer to Mendelssohn's concept of aesthetic pleasure as grounded in the activity of our intellectual and approbative faculties than his "perfectionist" language might initially suggest. If anything, this will be a Mendelssohnian interpretation of Kant rather than a Kantian interpretation of Mendelssohn.

no doubt connected to his concern to ground *morality*, more precisely its *fundamental principle*, in reason rather than emotion and his hope that aesthetics can support the cause of morality without being reducible to it. Mendelssohn is not as obsessed with the necessity of agreement in aesthetics as Kant is, nor does his approach to morality draw such a rigid distinction between reason and emotion as Kant's does. In the end, Mendelssohn's recognition of the role of emotions in our response to art and his lesser concern for interpersonal agreement in matters of taste may be more realistic than Kant's position. And in the end, that is, in his final work in moral philosophy, without giving up in the least on his view that the fundamental principle of morality must be grounded in pure reason alone, Kant recognizes the vital role that a variety of *moral* feelings must play in the real-world *implementation* of morality, and he could have been more tolerant of emotions as an essential part of our response to art without having to surrender the hope that our experience of art and our aesthetic experience more generally can support the cause of morality.

In this chapter, I will expound key elements of Mendelssohn's theory of aesthetic experience and art. In the next, I will show how Kant both expropriates key elements of Mendelssohn's approach and rejects others. Then we will be in position to draw up a balance-sheet between the two approaches.

Mendelssohn's first essay in aesthetics, although not exclusively in aesthetics, was the *Letters On Sentiments*, published in 1755. The twenty-six-year-old author was only a dozen years removed from his arrival in Berlin as an unknown Jewish youth, but by this time had added literary German, French, English, Latin, and Greek to his vernacular Yiddish and scholarly Hebrew, had mastered a wide range of both classical and contemporary literature in these languages, had become friends with Lessing, Nicolai, Thomas Abbt, and other promising young men in Berlin literary and publishing circles, and was ready to weigh in on the lively issues of the day. Mendelssohn is often thought of as an adherent of the Leibnizo-Wolffian philosophy, and in many ways he was, but he was by no means uncritical, and "On Sentiments" begins by repudiating a central idea of standard Leibnizo-Wolffian aesthetics, namely that pleasure, including aesthetic pleasure, can be fully characterized as a clear but confused cognition of some objective perfection.[6] This view is presented by one of Mendelssohn's characters, Euphranor, who states that "*Beauty rests, in the opinion of every philosopher, on the indistinct representation of a perfection*" ("On Sentiments," second letter, *PW* 12, *JubA* 1:240). But Euphranor is corrected by the older and wiser Theocles,[7] who writes back that it will not do to attempt to explain the pleasure we take in beauty in merely negative terms, as due to a mental limitation like indistinctness, but that "the pure gratification of the soul must be grounded in the positive powers of our soul and not in its incapacity, not in the limitation of these original powers" (Fourth Letter, *PW* 19, *JubA* 1:248). Theocles also argues that we must explain what perfections of objects are perceived in the experience of beauty, not simply take refuge in the unexplained term "perfection":

---

[6] See also Pollok, *Facetten des Menschen*, p. 167.

[7] This is the name Mendelssohn uses in the later editions of the letters for the character previously called "Palemon."

I contemplate the object of the pleasure, I reflect upon all sides of it, and strive to grasp them directly. Then I direct my attention at the general connection among them; I swing from the parts to the whole. The particular distinct concepts recede as it were back into the shadows. They all work on me but they work in such a state of equilibrium and proportion to one another that the whole alone radiates from them, and my thinking about it has not broken up the manifold, but only made it easier to grasp. (Third Letter, *PW* 15, *JubA* 1:243)

It is true that there is something indistinct in our perception of the parts of a beautiful object, Theocles concedes, but that is not the end of the story: The indistinctness of the perception of the parts is only an accommodation to our, admittedly limited, powers of comprehension that makes it possible for us to grasp the whole. The latter is a positive accomplishment, and pleasurable for that reason. In language that Mendelssohn does not tend to repeat, but that may well have been decisive for Kant, the grasp of the whole is actually assigned to the human faculty of *imagination* (*Einbildungskraft*): Speaking of the sublime as well as the beautiful, Theocles states that "The imagination is able to confine the smallest and the largest object to the appropriate limits by extending the parts as far as possible or drawing them together until we are able to grasp the requisite manifold all at once" (Third Letter, *PW* 15, *JubA* 1:243).

Theocles expands upon these statements in subsequent letters. In the Fifth Letter, he makes the still general statement that "The sameness, the oneness in a manifold [*Die Gleichheit, die Einerley im Mannigfaltigen*] is a property of the beautiful object. They must exhibit an order or otherwise a perfection which appeals to the senses and, indeed, does so effortlessly" (*PW* 22, *JubA* 1:250). But as he continues, he differentiates aspects of the perfection of the object that are grasped by the imagination as a positive power of the soul. In the Eleventh Letter, Theocles argues that the source of pleasure is "threefold," including "*sameness [das Einerley] in the manifold*, or beauty, *harmony [Einhelligkeit] in the manifold*, or intellectual perfection, and finally *the improved condition of the state of our body*, or sensuous gratification [*Lust*]" (*PW* 48, *JubA* 1:280). In this remark, Mendelssohn is essentially distinguishing a property that makes the grasp of a whole by the senses easy, and is thus a perfection of perception relative to the powers of our senses and imagination; a perfection that is grasped by the intellect, something that we might think is a perfection in its own right, something valuable in the object; and a third factor, not previously mentioned, the beneficent effect of aesthetic perfection on the *body* of the perceiver or subject, a "feeling of the improved condition of the body," something explained as the pleasing stimulation and harmonization of the nerves and fibers of the body in the perception of something beautiful.[8] Actually, what Mendelssohn describes is a two-way traffic

---

[8] This is an aspect of aesthetic perception emphasized in Part IV of Edmund Burke's *Philosophical Enquiry into the Our Feelings of the Beautiful and Sublime*, although that would be published only in 1757 and read (in English) and reviewed by Mendelssohn then, two years *after* the publication of "On Sentiments." Pollok stresses Mendelssohn's emphasis on interaction between the mental and the physical (*Facectten des Menschen*, pp. 172–8), although she does not include Burke among his possible sources for this emphasis, stressing instead his criticism of the Swiss physiologist Charles Bonnet (pp. 174–5). Bonnet would have been on Mendelssohn's mind at least during the 1771 revision of his *Philosophical Writings* because of his role in the Lavater contretemps of the previous year; see Altmann, *Moses Mendelssohn*, pp. 209–34, and Bourel, *Moses Mendelssohn*, pp. 279–318. Beiser discusses the influence of Burke on

between the mental and the physical, in which one aspect of the feeling of pleasure in a beautiful object is actually a perception of the beneficial effects of the perception of the object on our sense organs and the rest of our body, but in which the more mental cognition of perfection, that is, the recognition of some perfection by the intellect, not by the senses, has a beneficial effect on the body as well. The traffic is two-way: "If now it is true, in addition, that each sensuous rapture, each improved condition of the state of our body, fills the soul with the sensuous representation of a perfection, then every sensuous representation must also, in turn, bring with it some well-being of the body." A beautiful representation arranges "the fibers of the brain into an appropriate tone," and the "brain communicates this harmonious tension to the nerves of the other parts of the body, and the body becomes comfortable; the human being acquires a pleasant emotion"—or vice versa (Twelfth Letter, *PW* 53, *JubA* 1:285). This aspect of Mendelssohn's model is interesting because Kant is at such pains to keep the merely physiological, what he calls the "agreeable" (*das Angenehm*) out of properly aesthetic response, for which he will in turn be criticized by his own student Herder.[9] But before we turn to Kant, there is much more to say about Mendelssohn, beginning with his further expansion of the model thus far introduced in the essay on the "Main Principles of the Fine Arts and Sciences," the supplementary "Rhapsody" first added to the letters on the sentiments in 1761, and in a number of other texts.

The "Rhapsody" clarifies the twofold nature of representation, that is, that a representation represents an object other than itself but that is itself a state of the mind (and, as we just saw, of the body as well), with potential for perfection and hence for pleasure in each respect.[10] "Each individual representation stands in a twofold relation," Mendelssohn writes, "related, at once, to the matter before it as its object (of which it is a picture or a copy) and then to the soul or the thinking subject (of which it constitutes a determination" ("Rhapsody," *PW* 132, *JubA* 1:384).[11] A representation can be enjoyed then because it *represents* a perfection in an object,

---

Mendelssohn's theory of mixed sentiment at *Diotima's Children*, p. 211. See also Aaron Koller, "Mendelssohn's Response to Burke on the Sublime," in Reinier Munk, ed., *Moses Mendelssohn's Metaphysics and Aesthetics* (Dordrecht: Springer, 2011), pp. 329–50.

[9] Herder, *Kalligone* (1800). For discussion of Herder's critique of Kant's aesthetics, see my *A History of Modern Aesthetics*, 3 vols. (Cambridge: Cambridge University Press, 2014), vol. 1, pp. 509–26.

[10] Mendelssohn's twofold deployment of the concept of perfection is stressed by Pollok, *Facetten des Menschen*, p. 198. In spite of Beiser's objection to views according to which Mendelssohn's "first aesthetic writings make perfection an attribute of the object, his later writings make it an attribute of the subject's perception of the object" (*Diotima's Children*, p. 198), he himself writes as if Mendelssohn's recognition that the "principle of perfection is applicable as much to the subject as to the object of the representation" is a revision of his original theory (p. 212).

[11] That a representation has dual intentionality, simultaneously representing both an object other than itself and the self that has it, is often thought to be the innovation of Karl Leonhard Reinhold in his *Versuch einer neuen Theorie des menschlichen Vorstellungsvermögens* (*Essay toward a new Theory of the human Faculty of Representation*) (1789), ed. Ernst-Otto Onnasch, 2 vols. (Hamburg: Felix Meiner Verlag, 2012), who in turn influenced Fichte and subsequent German idealists. But the basic principle is already present in Mendelssohn's "Rhapsody," though presented in Leibnizo-Wolffian language. Mendelssohn's distinction could in turn be traced back to Descartes's distinction between the "formal" and "objective" reality of an idea, the former what it has as a state of a cognitive subject and the latter its representing an object distinct from the subject; see *Meditations on First Philosophy*, Third Meditation.

some content to which we attach a positive valuation, but also because it *is* itself a perfection, because there is something enjoyable about it as a state of mind apart from what it represents. Mendelssohn further explains our pleasure in the representation itself as due to its engagement of *two* positive powers of the soul, namely "the mental powers of knowing and desiring," or the abilities to know an object on the one hand and to approve or disapprove of it on the other, to evaluate it as either good or evil (*PW* 133, *JubA* 1:385). We enjoy the successful exercise of our cognitive capacity, and we enjoy the successful exercise of our conative or approbative faculty.[12] (In his last work, the *Morning Hours* of 1785, Mendelssohn will separate desire from approbation, or the *Billigungsvermögen*, but here he lumps them together.)

Mendelssohn puts his point about the involvement of the "positive powers" of the soul as broadly as possible in a 1757 review of Mark Akenside's 1754 "poem in three books" *The Pleasures of Imagination*. As his title suggests, Akenside still works with the tripartite division of aesthetic properties under the general headings of the "sublime, the wondrous" or novel, and "the beautiful" that Joseph Addison had canonized in his 1712 essays under the same title in *The Spectator*.[13] Under the impact of Edmund Burke, who argued the same year that Mendelssohn published his review of Akenside that the pleasure of novelty does not last,[14] this tripartite distinction was to give way to the twofold distinction between the beautiful and the sublime that we will find in Kant. But Mendelssohn indicates his own approbation of the inclusion of novelty as a basic aesthetic property by writing that "The *wondrous* or the *novel* is destined to gratify human beings by promoting the growth of their perfection, and involves all the capacities that slumber in their souls" (*JubA* 4:95–117, at 100).[15] And the involvement of both our cognitive capacities and our capacities for desire, approbation, and disapprobation in aesthetic response is the abstract framework within which Mendelssohn makes the point, obvious to him and perhaps to most people, that emotions make up a great part of our response to art and even to nature. He states this with particular clarity in the sixty-sixth of the *Letters concerning the Latest Literature*, in a series of letters on the work of Johann Georg Sulzer, this one on the topic of "ideal beauty," a topic in Sulzer that would later prove of

---

[12] Alexander Rueger, "Enjoying the Unbeautiful: From Mendelssohn's Theory of 'Mixed Sentiments' to Kant's Aesthetic Judgments of Reflection," *Journal of Aesthetics and Art Criticism* 67 (2009): 181–9, interprets Mendelssohn's account of our pleasure in the "unbeautiful" solely in terms of our second-order enjoyment of the exercise of our mental activity in judging the object even when the object is judged to be perfect rather than imperfect (p. 185). This interpretation does not adequately account for the possibility of a directly positive enjoyment of the form of the object by our *cognitive* powers combined with a complex response by our approbative or conative faculties, combining disapproval of the object (as represented) with approval of our own judgment, thereby accounting for the mixed character of a "mixed sentiment,"

[13] Joseph Addison and Richard Steele, *The Spectator*, Nos. 411–22, June 21–July 3, 1712; for discussion, see *A History of Modern Aesthetics*, vol. 1, pp. 63–73.

[14] See Edmund Burke, *A Philosophical Enquiry into the Origin of Our Ideas of the Sublime and Beautiful* (1757, second edn. 1759), ed. Paul Guyer (Oxford: Oxford University Press, 2015, Part I, section I, p. 27.

[15] Akenside's work is *The Pleasures of Imagination: A Poem in Three Books* (London: R. Dodsley, 1754); Mendelssohn's review appeared in the *Bibliothek der schönen Wissenschaften und der freyen Künste*, 2. Band, 1. Stuck (October, 1757): 91–124.

importance to Kant.[16] Here Mendelssohn remarks that "The aim of drama is to represent the actions and mental inclinations [*Gemüthsneigungen*] of humans in accordance with life, and to arouse social passions [*Leidenschaften*]. Its ideal beauties are thus those characters that are best suited to the attainment of these goals, and see! the perfectly virtuous characters are by no means these." The argument is that our own passions, as audience, are best aroused by imperfect characters, great but flawed, who "provide more opportunity for actions, who arouse strong passions, whose invention has cost the poet a greater effort of the spirit" (*JubA*, 5.1:98–101, at 99). Mendelssohn continues this argument in an interesting way. Asking how "imitations" can interest us, he says that the artist "takes the illusion so far that we believe ourselves to see the thing itself, not the imitation," and then argues that it is the arousal of our emotions that puts us in this state—"Only how is this happy deception to be achieved? Only through the artful arousal of passions. Only these are more powerful than the senses, and seduce the soul into taking the deceptive representations for real" (*JubA* 5.1:99–100).[17] In other words, it is not a strictly cognitive state of illusion that produces emotions in response to art; it is the powerful emotions aroused by artistic representations that can induce a cognitive state of belief in what is in fact only fiction.[18] We will see in a moment that Mendelssohn's view of the cognitive state created by fiction is a little more complicated than this, for he really holds that the conviction in the reality of the characters that goes along with our emotional response to them is compatible with an underlying recognition of the fact that they are fictions. But now our concern is only with his assumption that art is aimed at and does arouse a wide range of human emotions.

Another place where this is evident is in the essay "On the sublime and naïve in the fine sciences," also included in the 1761 *Philosophical Writings*. Here Mendelssohn first characterizes the effect of immensity, what Kant would subsequently call the "mathematical sublime," in emotional terms. "The *magnitude* captures our attention... The *immensity* arouses a sweet shudder that rushes through every fiber of our being... All these sentiments blend together in the soul, flowing into one another, and become a single phenomenon that we call *awe*." Mendelssohn assumes that the experience of the sublime can be created by art, adding that "Accordingly, if one wanted to describe the sublime in terms of its effect, then one could say: *It is something sensuously perfect in art, capable of inspiring awe*" ("Sublime and Naïve," *PW* 195, *JubA* 1:458). But more to the present point, he goes on to describe the effect of sublime characters, or their depiction, rather than immense objects, something closer to but not identical to what Kant will call the "dynamical sublime." Such characters will produce a complex of emotions: "If we love the object of which we are in awe or if it deserves our sympathy because of an undeserved agony, the awe alternates with the more familiar sentiment in our mind. We wish, hope, and fear for

---

[16] In these letters, Mendelssohn is writing about Sulzer's early *Kurzer Begriff aller Wissenschaften und andern Theile der Gelehrsamkeit*, second edn. (Leipzig: Langenheim, 1759) (first edition, 1745). Mendelssohn would later own the first edition of Sulzer's *Allgemeine Theorie der schönen Künste*, 2 vols. (Leipzig: Weidmann, 1771–4).
[17] *Briefe, die neuste Litteratur betreffend*, No. 66 (8 November 1759), 4. Band, pp. 285–92.
[18] See Pollok, *Facetten des Menschen*, pp. 200–3.

the object of our love or our sympathy and admire his or her great soul that is beyond such hope and fear" (PW 198–9, JubA 1:462). The sublime characters themselves (that is, the depicted characters) may be beyond hope and fear, but we, the audience, are not; the purpose of the depiction of such characters is precisely to arouse a wide range of human emotions in us. This is, Mendelssohn assumes throughout his work, a fundamental aim of art.

In particular, Mendelssohn's division of the positive powers of the soul that are engaged by artistic representations into the cognitive and the evaluative allows him to explain our pleasure in the aesthetic representation of objects that in reality would be unpleasant. First, "many a representation can have something pleasant about it although, as a picture of the object, it is accompanied by disapproval and a feeling of repugnance"; and second, even when we disapprove of the object, we can approve or take pleasure in our disapproval of the object, or enjoy the proper exercise of our faculty of approbation and disapprobation (PW 132, JubA 1:384). That is, we can disapprove of the object of a representation, say a represented tragedy or crime, approve of the representation of it, because it is beautiful (or sublime) in the way already analyzed in the letters, and also approve of our disapproval of the object, as a proper exercise of our faculty of approbation and disapprobation. So although we can sometimes both approve of the object and enjoy the representation of it, we can also disapprove of the object, enjoy our representation of it, and enjoy our disapprobation of it, and the sum of the latter two enjoyments can easily outweigh the pain of the first disapprobation. This is what Mendelssohn calls "mixed sentiment," and it is the key to our enjoyment of tragedy. "On the side of the object and in relation to it, we feel, to be sure, discontent and disfavor in the intuitive knowledge of its deficiencies. But on the side of the mind's projection, the soul's powers of knowing and desiring are engaged, that is to say, its reality is enhanced and this must of necessity cause pleasure and satisfaction [Lust und Wohlgefallen]" (PW 136, JubA 1:389).[19]

Mendelssohn's explanation of our pleasure in tragedy, most fully developed in his correspondence with Lessing and Nicolai in 1756 and 1757,[20] is actually more complicated than this, explaining that our pleasure is most intense when misfortune befalls a person of whom we can approve and who thereby most strongly engages our sympathy, but we will not need to go into that to develop our contrast with Kant, since he does not take up the paradox of tragedy at all in the third Critique. Rather, we can note here that Mendelssohn's account of the mixed emotions induced by art leads to the introduction of the concept of what later became known as "aesthetic distance,"[21] but as a condition specifically of the possibility of mixed sentiment: we have to be not too close to the object, in which case our awareness of the object will

---

[19] On Mendelssohn's theory of mixed sentiments, see Pollok, Facetten des Menschen, pp. 178–90, and my "Mendelssohn's Theory of Mixed Sentiments," in Munk, ed., Moses Mendelssohn's Metaphysics and Aesthetics, pp. 259–78.

[20] Gotthold Ephraim Lessing, Moses Mendelssohn, and Friedrich Nicolai, Briefwechsel über das Trauerspiel, ed. Jochen Schulte-Sasse (Munich: Winkler Verlag, 1972). See Beiser, Diotima's Children, pp. 206–10, and Pollok, Facetten des Menschen, pp. 142–53.

[21] See Edward Bullough, "'Psychical Distance' as a Factor in Art and as an Æsthetic Principle," British Journal of Psychology 5 (1912): 87–118, reprinted in Bullough, Æsthetics: Lectures and Essays, ed. Elizabeth M. Wilkinson (Stanford: Stanford University Press, 1957).

totally dominate our awareness of our representation of it, nor too far from the object, in which case our awareness of our own representation will dominate our awareness of the object—in order to enjoy a mixed sentiment, we have to be able to remain aware of both object and representation. We have to make sure that "subject and object" do not "collapse, as it were, into one another" (PW 134, JubA 1:386).[22] In the case of a natural object, this might mean that we might need to maintain a certain distance from an object, say a bizarre insect or fish, in order not to be overwhelmed by its proximity and to be able enjoy inspecting it; in the case of art, this might mean that we need to maintain a certain distance from the actors in a play in order not to respond to them simply as the real persons that they are rather than to the characters they are presenting. And aesthetic distance is not created just by physical distance, that is, the inches or feet between the object and the observer. It can be created by a variety of means: by the medium of artistic representation, by the proscenium arch and its conventions, and so on. Thus:

> Another means of rendering the most terrifying events pleasant to gentle minds is the imitation by art, on the stage, on the canvas, and in marble, since an inner consciousness that we have an imitation and nothing genuine before our eyes moderates the strength of the objective disgust and, as it were, elevates the subjective side of the representation... The difference between the material of the imitation and the material of nature, the marble and the canvas are the most obvious sensed features which, without damaging the art, call the attention back from the illusion whenever necessary. (PW 138–9, JubA 1:390–1)

A characteristic feature of artistic representation is the way in which it puts an object before our own mental representation (the painting is one representation, our representation of the painting another) yet allows us to have both the represented object and the features of the representation in mind, and to respond to both as appropriate.

Mendelssohn's contrast between representation and what is represented also leads to an emphasis on *form* as well as *content* in art that is clearly intended as a criticism of what he regards as the excessive emphasis on content and thus the excessive intellectualism of Baumgarten's approach to aesthetics. In the essay on the "Main Principles," Mendelssohn presents his position by means of a subtle combination of Wolff's formulation of the basic idea of aesthetics with Baumgarten's. Part of the relevant passage was quoted at the outset of this chapter. Mendelssohn begins with the Baumgartian statement that "We have now found the universal means of pleasing our soul, namely, the *sensuously perfect representation*." This is reminiscent of Baumgarten's definition of poetry in his earliest work, the master's thesis *Meditationes philosophicae de nonnullis ad poema pertinentibus* of 1735, as "sensuously perfect discourse," and would seem to emphasize the sensory aspects of art, not

---

[22] Gertrud Koch has appealed to Mendelssohn in support of the view that we can be engaged with what is presented, in the case she is discussing in a film, as if it were real, without losing our background awareness that it is not; as she puts it, we can have "illusion" without "deception" (*Illusion without Täuschung*). This is a step in her larger argument that although illusion was driven off the agenda of many arts over the course of the twentieth century, it has reentered contemporary artistic aims through the medium of film. See Gertrud Koch, *Die Wiederkehr der Illusion: Der Film und die Kunst der Gegenwart* (Berlin: Suhrkamp, 2016); on Mendelssohn, see pp. 50–4.

just its content.[23] The combination of Wolffian and Baumgartian formulae that follows would seem to have the same implication: as Mendelssohn continues, "And since the final purpose of the fine arts is to please, we can presuppose the following principle as indubitable: the essence of the fine arts consists in an artful, sensuously perfect representation or in a sensuous perfection represented by art" ("Main Principles," *PW* 172–3, *JubA* 1:431). The first part of this disjunction emphasizes the perfection of the representation, the second of that which is represented, although itself as an object accessible to the senses. This potentially allows a role for both the beauty of the representation and the value of what is represented in the overall explanation of our pleasure in art, the framework that allowed Mendelssohn his theory of mixed sentiments. But in explicitly writing about the Baumgartian approach, Mendelssohn accuses it of excessive focus on content alone, or excessive intellectualism. In a review of Georg Friedrich Meier's *Extract from the First Principles of all Fine Arts and Sciences* (*Auszug aus den Anfangsgründen aller schönen Künste und Wissencahften*) of 1757, an abridgement of Meier's three volume *First Principles* published in 1748–50 and described by Meier himself as based entirely on Baumgarten's as yet unpublished Latin work, Mendelssohn first objects that the Baumgarten approach is not sufficiently general but really applies only to "poetry and eloquence." He writes that:

Aesthetics should really contain the *science of beautiful cognition* in general, the *theory of all fine arts and sciences*; all of its explanations and doctrines must therefore be general enough to be applied to every fine art in particular. For example, if one explains in general aesthetics what the *sublime* is, then the explanation must be able to be applied as well to the sublime style of writing as to sublime contour in painting and sculpture, sublime passages in music and sublime architecture.

He continues:

If one explains what *beauty in objects* is, then this explanation must resemble a general algebraic formula to which one has only to add some further determinations in order to be able to more closely explain the different kinds of beauty in thoughts, in language, in figures, lines, and motions, and finally in tones and colors. This is rightly demanded of an *aesthetics*, a *theory of beauty in general*.

He then complains that if one considers "the aesthetics of Professor *Baumgarten*, or the *First Principles* of Herr Meier (for the latter is nothing but an extended development of the former), then it seems as if in the whole plan of the work they have had only the fine sciences, i.e., poetry and eloquence, in view" (*JubA* 4:196–201, at 197–8).[24] The crucial point here is the contrast between thought on the one hand and lines, figures, colors, and tones on the other. The former can clearly stand for the content of a work, whether a poem or a painting, while the latter can stand for the sensorily accessible properties of both artistic representations and the mental

---

[23] Alexander Gottlieb Baumgarten, *Meditationes philosophicae de nonnullis ad poema pertinentibus/ Philosophische Betrachtungen über einige Bedindungen des Gedichtes*, ed. Heinz Paetzold (Hamburg: Felix Meiner Verlag, 1983), §IX, pp. 10–11.

[24] The review of Meier's *Auszug* was originally published in the *Bibliothek der schönen Wissenschaften und der freyen Künste*, 3. Band, 1. Stuck (June, 1758): 130–7.

representations of artistic representations, both in cases where these two have intellectual content but also in cases such as (instrumental) music or architecture where it is much harder to maintain that the object has and pleases in virtue of intellectually accessible content at all. The charge against Baumgarten and Meier is that in spite of their claims to generality they focus only on intellectual content of the kind most characteristic of poetry (from which indeed all their examples are drawn), standing in for literature more broadly. Far from being a slavish follower of these rationalists, Mendelssohn is emphasizing here, within the sphere of aesthetics, the roles of both sensory form and intellectual content, and in this regard anticipating the general distinction between but insistence upon both intuition and content that would become the basis for Kant's theory of knowledge.[25]

The same point is made in the "Main Principles," although without the polemical context. Here Mendelssohn states that:

[E]verything capable of being represented to the senses as a perfection could also present an object of beauty. Belonging here are all the perfections of external forms, that is, the lines, surfaces, and bodies and their movements and changes; the harmony of the multiple sounds and colors; the order in the parts of a whole, their similarity, variety, and harmony; their transposition and transformation into other forms; all the capabilities of our soul, all the skills of our body. ("Main Principles," *PW* 172, *JubA* 1:431)

Anything that can count as a perfection that can be presented *to or through* the senses can engage the powers of our soul and produce aesthetic pleasure. This can include particular sensory properties, such as sounds and colors, perceived by the senses; relations among such properties, such as variety and harmony, which we might say are perceived and transformed by the imagination; and content, represented characters, actions, or more abstract ideas, cognized by our cognitive capacities and approved or disapproved by our faculty or faculties of desire and approbation and disapprobation. Mendelssohn's account of potential aesthetic properties is inclusive rather than restrictive.

As we will see, Kant's account of the proper objects of taste initially appears opposed to but as restrictive as that of Baumgarten, although in the opposite way, focused on form to the exclusion of all else instead of content to the exclusion of all else; but we will see that this impression is not sustained by Kant's account of fine art, which is closer although not identical to Mendelssohn's in its breadth. But before we can turn to Kant, there is a further point about Mendelssohn's account of aesthetic pleasure to be made.

Yet another dimension of perfection and thus of potential enjoyment in Mendelssohn's model is artistry, the originality and skill with which an artistic representation is made and accomplishes everything that it does accomplish. This is emphasized in the essay on "The Main Principles of the Fine Arts and Sciences."

---

[25] Luigi Cataldi Madonna, "The Eighteenth-Century Rehabilitation of Sensitive Knowledge and the Birth of Aesthetics: Wolff, Baumgarten and Mendelssohn," in Munk, *Moses Mendelssohn's Metaphysics and Aesthetics*, pp. 279–97, presents Mendelssohn as a popularizer of Baumgarten's view without mentioning this criticism, which is that Baumgarten and Meier have not adequately recognized the full range of sensory qualities that can enter into aesthetic experience.

Having explained how we take pleasure in both the perfections of represented objects and the perfections of the representations of them, and reminded us that it is this distinction that explains the possibility of mixed sentiments (*PW* 173, *JubA* 1:432), Mendelssohn continues:

> Added to this in the imitations of art is the artist's perfection that we perceive in them. For all works of art are visible imprints of the artist's abilities which, so to speak, put his entire soul on display and make it known to us. The perfection of spirit arouses an uncommonly greater pleasure than mere similarity, because it is more excellent and far more complex than similarity. It is more excellent to the degree that the perfection of a rational being is more sublime than the perfection of inanimate things, and it is also more complex because many of the soul's abilities, and, frequently, diverse skills of the external limbs as well, are required for a beautiful imitation. (*PW* 174, *JubA* 1:433).

It takes exceptional qualities of both mind and body to produce a good work of art, and we admire and enjoy these as perfections as well as admiring and enjoying the perfections depicted by the work of art and the perfections of the depiction. In the *Republic*, Socrates famously derided artistic representations, arguing that better ones could more easily be produced by holding a mirror up to nature;[26] Mendelssohn's argument is that artistic representation reveals perfections in addition to those of the representation itself, namely those of the artist himself. "We find more to admire in a rose painted by Huysum than in a river's reflected image of this queen of the flowers," he adds. His general theory of the compound character of our pleasure in art would allow for a more extended answer to Socrates: even if the reflection of an object in a river or a mirror were in some way more accurate than an artistic representation of the object, and to that extent more perfect and enjoyable, nevertheless the sum total of pleasure in the work of art, including our pleasure in the skill of the artist and everything that goes along with that—for example, the layer of content or meaning that a work of art can have but a purely natural object cannot, as when a painted flower is intended as a symbol of something but a natural flower or its natural reflection is not, can be greater than our pleasure in the merely natural object. (Of course, Mendelssohn adds, our admiration for the creator of nature itself, namely God, should "inflame" our pleasure in the beauty of nature "to the point of ecstasy"; *PW* 174–5, *JubA* 1:433).[27]

Mendelssohn thus recognizes at least four forms of perfection as sources of pleasure in his overall model of our response to art: the perfection of what is represented; the perfection of the representation as recognized by the positive powers of our soul; the perfection of our bodily condition associated with the previous form of perfection; and the perfection of the artist who has produced it, in the case of artistic representation. Mendelssohn's discussion of the additional perfection of the artist can further be connected to a discussion of genius that is only broached in the letters on sentiments but is pursued further in some of his reviews. In the fourth letter, before admonishing Euphranor that the pure gratification of the soul must be

---

[26] Plato, *Republic*, Book X, 596d–e.

[27] Pollok also discusses Mendelssohn's recognition of our enjoyment of artistry itself; *Facetten des Menschen*, p. 204.

grounded in the positive powers of the soul, Theocles had touched upon the function of rules for poetic composition and, presumably, for other forms of art. He is arguing that trying to explain our response to art solely in terms of indistinctness would undermine the importance of artistic rules. But he is also delimiting the role of rules in the production of art. Thus he holds that:

> The rules are preparations by means of which the poet should be putting himself and the object to be worked over into a state where the beauties are shown in their most flattering light. As *preparations* they can be enormously useful to the virtuoso, but in the heat of the work they must not disturb him... At this moment he must take care not to have his rules all too distinctly before his eyes. They are not supposed to put a rein on his imagination, but rather are supposed to show it the way only from a distance and to call it back when it is in danger of losing itself. Then they can set the lesser genius to the side of the greater genius and teach the poet what his spirit was perhaps too small to discover.
> ("On Sentiments," Fourth Letter, *PW* 18–19, *JubA* 1:246–7)

Mendelssohn introduces the terms "genius" and "imagination" causally in this passage, putting no great theoretical weight upon them, but he still suggests that artistic accomplishment cannot be based solely on following rules, helpful as they can be in various ways, but requires an element of inspiration. Although we no doubt have a degree of admiration for the effort that goes into formulating or learning rules, surely our admiration for the kind of inspiration that cannot be reduced to rules is greater. Mendelssohn does devote a letter explicitly to what he recognizes as the current topic of genius in the ninety-second of the *Letters concerning the Latest Literature*, which discusses another recent work by Sulzer. Here he reports with approval Sulzer's analysis of genius into three components, namely "*Wit* and *acuity*, or the capacity [*Vermögen*] for perceiving in objects a great crowd of relations and connections, as it were taking them in with a glance... a thorough *power of judgment* [*Beurteilungskraft*], for assessing the *importance of the relations*, and selecting those which lead most securely, comfortably, and agreeably to the end"; and "*clarity* [*Besonnenheit*], or presence of mind (*contenance, ou présence d'esprit*), which leads the soul to the attention that it loves, to the preservation of freedom, even in the greatest heat of imagination" (*JubA* 5.1.166–71, at 168–9).[28] Mendelssohn adds that "an artist can often have chosen the best means, and yet without help of this important property remain mediocre." Perhaps judgment is a capacity that can be taught and improved with rules, but without wit and clarity of mind, which are more like innate gifts than acquired talents, nothing great will result. If judgment is connected to rules, then rules might be able to function as necessary conditions for the production of successful art, but not as sufficient conditions. For that, natural gifts are also required.

Mendelssohn also discusses genius in the essay on the sublime and naïve. Here he has been discussing admiration or awe (*Bewunderung*) as an emotion directed at immensity and power in nature or great strength in human character, in the case of art in depicted human character, but he then turns to awe directed at artistry itself.

---

[28] *Briefe, die neueste Literatur betreffend*, 6. Band (3 April 1760): 211–24. Mendelssohn refers to *Sammlung vermischter Schriften zur Beförderung der schönen Wissenschaften*, Band 2, Stuck 1.

He posits that "If in his work the artist wants to convince *us* in visible and sensuous fashion of the perfection that *he* possesses to a high degree, then he must direct his attention to the finest and greatest beauties capable of animating his imagination" ("Sublime and Naïve," *PW* 214, *JubA* 1:477, emphases added). He then notes that "fine brushstrokes," in the example of painting, and the "toil and care" necessary to produce them and, we might add, the rules that need to be followed in order to execute them, are no doubt necessary to produce a successful painting, but they are not what trigger our admiration and awe. Rather, "Awe is a duty [*Zoll*] we owe on the extraordinary gifts of the soul. These gifts are called genius in the strictest sense." In other words, genius is manifested in the inspiration of the work of art, not in the effort of its execution. Indeed, if "the insignificant attendant circumstances including the final execution of a picture, which to be sure belongs to the painting but does not constitute an essential part of it, show all too clearly the diligence and effort that they cost the artist," then we "subtract as much from the genius" that we ascribe to the artist "as we attribute to the diligence" (*PW* 215, *JubA* 1:477). Genius is located in imagination and inspiration, not in diligent rule-following, and so the work of the genius must look effortless to us, or the appearance of effort diminishes the impression of genius.[29]

Mendelssohn makes another comment in the essay on the sublime and naïve—although without using the word "genius"—that should also be noted. Here he writes that "In the representation of the sublime ... the artist must devote himself to a naïve, unaffected expression which allows the reader or observer to think more than is said to him. Thus his expression must always remain intuitive, and, where possible, be traced back to individual cases, so that the mind of the reader is awakened and inspired to reflect" ("On the Sublime and Naïve," *PW* 200, *JubA* 1:462). This brief remark evinces Mendelssohn's recognition that the audience's response to a work of art must be active, not passive, that it must be an exercise of the power of the soul of members of the audience to reflect, and that a successful work of art satisfies this requirement at least in part by suggesting more than it explicitly states. Kant will clearly take up this thought in his general theory of the relation between the work of the artist and the response of the audience, and specifically in his theory of aesthetic ideas as containing the "spirit" of art.

Kant will not explicitly recognize our admiration of artistry as itself one of the sources of our pleasure in art, but Mendelssohn's account of genius, perhaps together with Sulzer's account which he discusses, has significant similarities to Kant's. In particular, we will see that Kant echoes both of the points that Mendelssohn has just made. But before we start counting the similarities and differences between Mendelssohn's and Kant's aesthetics, there are two more topics to be considered, namely Mendelssohn's distinction between beautiful or fine arts and sciences, and especially his attitude toward the importance of agreement in matters of taste.

---

[29] Beiser's discussion of Mendelssohn's treatment of genius emphasizes entirely the role of reflection in mastering inspiration, rather than the genius's inspiration itself; see *Diotima's Children*, pp. 230–3, especially pp. 232–3. This is another example of his excessively rationalistic interpretation of Mendelssohn's aesthetics.

Thus far, I have used the hendiadys "beautiful" or "fine arts and sciences" or "beautiful sciences and liberal arts" (as in the name of Nicolai's journal) without explanation. (Both "beautiful" and "fine" translate *schön*.) To the contemporary ear, it might seem as if these phrases are loose and repetitive, a redundant way of referring to the arts in general. The same might be thought of the French phrase with which Mendelssohn associates the distinction in German between fine arts and sciences, namely that between *"beaux artes & belles lettres"* ("Main Principles," *PW* 178, *JubA* 1:437). In fact, for Mendelssohn and many other eighteenth-century writers, the distinction was informative: as he explains, the term "beautiful" or "fine sciences" refers to "poetry and rhetoric," or perhaps more generally fiction (*Dichtkunst*) and eloquence (*Beredsamkeit*), while the expression "fine arts" (the natural way for us to translate *schöne Künste*) refers to painting, sculpture, architecture, music, and dance (*PW* 179, *JubA* 1:438). Because Mendelssohn's concept of the fine arts subtends music and dance, which is usually performed to music, we cannot quite equate his conception of the fine arts with our own, for in contemporary usage, for example in the names of museums or galleries, the term subtends the visual arts, primarily painting and sculpture, with architecture and the decorative arts being problematic cousins because they need to answer to considerations of function and possibilities of movement as well as to the pleasures of the eye. But the main question is: why are the arts grouped under these two headings in this way? One thought that might occur is that it is because the fine arts are representational or imitative (mimetic), which would explain why dance and music, at least on a certain interpretation, are included along with the visual arts as fine arts, while poetry and other forms of literature are not. But that is not how Mendelssohn explains the distinction. Instead, on his account all the arts are representational—we have seen him assume that in everything we have discussed—but the difference between the two groups is that the "beautiful sciences" employ "artificial" or "arbitrary" signs, "perceptible sounds and letters," that designate their objects by convention, while the "fine arts" "make use of natural signs above all," signs that are naturally connected to their objects rather than connected by conventions (*PW* 178–9, *JubA* 1:437–8).[30] A poem consists of letters that arbitrarily designate certain sounds combined into words that arbitrarily designate certain objects combined into sentences and stanzas according to various syntactical and poetic conventions. But painting, sculpture, music, and the other fine arts are comprised by signs that naturally "have an effect on either the sense of hearing or the sense of sight" that is much like that which their objects naturally have (*PW* 179, *JubA* 1:438). Actually, natural signs exploit a variety of connections: an area of yellow pigment on a canvas may be a natural sign of a sunflower because it looks like a sunflower, while an area of gray pigment on a canvas may be a natural sign of a fire because it looks like (has the same or a close enough effect on our visual system as) smoke, and smoke is in turn causally connected with and thus a natural sign of fire. But the connection of the words "sunflower" and "smoke," in English, with their objects, is conventional or arbitrary, as

---

[30] Mendelssohn's use of this distinction is widely discussed. See, e.g., Alexander Altmann, *Moses Mendelssohns Frühschriften zur Metaphysik* (Tübingen: J.C.B. Mohr (Paul Siebeck), 1969), pp. 288–94; Pollok, *Facetten des Menschen*, pp. 212–20; and Gideon Freudenthal, *No Religion without Idolatry: Mendelssohn's Jewish Enlightenment* (Notre Dame: University of Notre Dame Press, 2012), pp. 34–8.

is obvious from the fact that the words for those objects in other languages are different. The distinction between natural and artificial signs is, of course, hardly original with Mendelssohn; it goes back to Leibniz,[31] and before him to St. Augustine,[32] and before him to Plato,[33] and has been made by many others before or since. But Mendelssohn's use of it to divide the arts into two groups is, if not unique to him, characteristic of eighteenth-century aesthetics. As we have also seen, both Mendelssohn and Kant used this distinction in their contrasts between the methods of mathematics and philosophy in their prize essays.

The use of the distinction in the case of the arts has consequences. One is that works in the arts that employ natural signs will be more immediately accessible to everyone than works employing artificial signs: a (reasonably naturalistic) painting of a sunflower will call up the idea of a sunflower to anyone who has ever seen one, or ever seen a flower at all, while a poem using the word "sunflower" will be intelligible only to a speaker of English, and will have to be translated to be accessible to others. Mendelssohn makes this point only indirectly, saying that "Expression in painting, sculpture, architecture, music, and dance does not presuppose anything arbitrary in order to be understood" and only "Very rarely appeals to the consent of human beings in order to designate this or that object" (*PW* 179, *JubA* 1:438). The main point that he wants to make is rather that while poetry or other literature has the advantage of being able to represent anything, because we can come up with words for anything, the other arts have more restricted possibilities of representation, because each medium can use only a specific range of natural signs and thus represent only more specific kinds of objects. Thus "The poet can express everything of which our soul can have a clear concept," while each of the fine arts "must content itself with that portion of natural signs that it can express by means of the senses," that is, by means of the particular sensory signs it employs, thus, two-dimensional visual signs in the case of painting, three-dimensional visual signs in the case of sculpture (and tactile ones, if only the guards would let you touch the sculptures), auditory signs in the case of music, and so on, each of which can represent only a range of reality (*PW* 178–9, *JubA* 1:438). But, as if to compensate, the effects of natural signs, since they are so much like the effects of their object, may be more immediate and intense, in particular their effect on our emotions, which Mendelssohn has held to be the essential aim of all the arts. Natural signs may "storm our minds" more directly and more intensely than artificial signs (*PW* 184, *JubA* 1:444).

---

[31] In the form of the distinction between "intuitive" and "symbolic" cognition; see "Meditations on Knowledge, Truth, and Ideas" (1684), in Loemker, ed., *Philosophical Papers and Letters*, pp. 291–5, at p. 292. For a version closer to Mendelssohn's time, see Georg Friedrich Meier, *Excerpt from the Doctrine of Reason* (1752), trans. Aaron Bunch (London: Bloomsbury, 2016), §236, p. 54.

[32] St. Augustine, *de Doctrina Christiana*, Book II; see R.A. Markus, "St. Augustine on Signs," *Phronesis* 2 (1957): 60–83, reprinted in R.A. Markus, ed., *Augustine: A Collection of Critical Essays* (Garden City: Doubleday, 1972), pp. 61–91, at p. 75, and B. Darrell Jackson, "The Theory of Signs in De Doctrina Christiana," in Markus, ed., *Augustine*, pp. 92–147, at pp. 96–8.

[33] Plato, *Cratylus*, 435a–e (although Socrates gets around to admitting that some names do not resemble their objects in any way only after a long argument with many examples that many names are based on some sort of resemblance with their objects, even if we sometimes do not know what that is because the name has been borrowed from a foreign language).

Mendelssohn devotes quite a few pages to considering the effects of combining both artificial and natural signs and multiple kinds of natural signs in various complex art forms. For example, "Music stands in a natural connection with the live performance of the fine sciences" (*PW* 185, *JubA* 1:445), that is, music often has a text, and the performance of such music will "express the strong, the heroic, the terrifying, the fearful, and the tender"—a wide range of human emotions—by the artificial signs of the text (which will have to be translated for speakers of languages other than the original) but also by the natural signs of the music, "by suitable inflections in the voice, by rising and falling, shortening, pausing and beginning more quickly," all presumably auditory effects naturally rather than artificially connected with the expression of various emotions. Because of the greater emotional impact of the natural signs of the music than of the artificial signs of the text, Mendelssohn further argues, in case of conflicts between purely musical and purely poetical rules, the latter may have to give way to the former to make sure that emotional impact is maximized (*PW* 187, *JubA* 1:447; as we have already seen, rules are in any case useful but not sacrosanct for Mendelssohn). Dance can also accompany poetry, or poetry and music, as in an opera ballet (*PW* 188, *JubA* 1:449), and painting can be combined with poetry, as when the inscription "*Et in Arcadia ego*" appears in the famous painting of Poussin (*PW* 189, *JubA* 1:450). And, although Mendelssohn does not say so, painting, sculpture, and architecture can also be combined with poetry, music, and dance in the case of opera; the theoretical foundations for a conception of opera as a *Gesamtkunstwerk* were laid a century before Richard Wagner coined that term.

Mendelssohn expressly states that he is offering only a sketch of a system of the arts, not a fully elaborated system (*PW* 177, *JubA* 1:436). We will see that Kant makes the same disclaimer, while sketching a system of the separate and combined arts very similar to Mendelssohn's. But before we finally turn to Kant, one last point about Mendelssohn: he does not place the same emphasis on the necessity of possible consensus in our response to and judgment of works of art, or aesthetic objects more generally, that Kant does, and if that concern functions as a constraint on what Kant will allow as proper objects of taste, it does not do so for Mendelssohn. This is not to say that Mendelssohn does not recognize the expectation of consensus in matters of taste at all. But whereas so many other writers of the period place the question of consensus or a "standard of taste" at the forefront of their work in aesthetics—Hume, of course, in the 1757 essay of that title, published in the same year as Mendelssohn's essay on "The Main Principles," and Kant, of course, in his "Analytic of the Beautiful," but also Burke in the "Introduction on Taste" prefaced to the second edition of his book on the beautiful and sublime in 1759, Alexander Gerard in his *Essay on Taste* also published in 1759,[34] and so many others—Mendelssohn touches upon it only in passing, and does not let it determine the direction of his own

---

[34] Alexander Gerard, *An Essay on Taste, with Three Dissertations on the same Subject by Mr. De Voltaire, Mr. D'Alembert, and Mr. De Montesquieu* (London and Edinburgh: A. Millar, A. Kincaid, and J. Bell, 1759); third edition (1780), with *Observations concerning the Imitative Nature of Poetry*, ed. Walter J. Hipple, Jr. (Delmar, NY: Scholars' Facsimiles and Reprints, 1963). This was translated into German; Gerard also published an *Essay on Genius* (1774), which was translated into German in 1776, and which was a target for Kant's discussion of genius in the *Critique of the Power of Judgment*.

arguments. In fact, the supposed problem of consensus in taste does not come up at all in the writings on aesthetics that Mendelssohn considered important enough to reprint in the volume of his *Philosophical Writings*, that is, the letters on sentiments, the essay on the main principles of the fine arts and sciences, and the essay on the sublime and naïve, or in the "Rhapsody" that he added to them. The premise that human minds all work much the same way that Kant would make into the centerpiece of his attempt to provide a "deduction" of judgments of taste may be assumed at the outset of the essay on the main principles: when Mendelssohn writes that "Each rule of beauty is at the same time a psychological discovery. For, since it contains a prescription of the conditions under which a beautiful object can have the best effect on our mind, it must be possible for the rule to be derived from the nature of the human spirit and explained on the basis of its properties" ("Main Principles," *PW* 169, *JubA* 1:427), he is no doubt assuming that "the nature of the human spirit" is pretty much the same in all human beings, thus that the rules of beauty derivable from human psychology are valid for all. But he does not explicitly argue this, and again as we have seen he does not place too much emphasis on the value of rules of beauty.

One place where the question of the universality of taste does come up is in a review of a translation of and commentary upon Charles Batteux published by Carl Wilhelm Ramler (1725–98) in 1758. Here Mendelssohn writes:

The criticism of Mr. *Batteux* are fine, and display a very delicate taste. But since this writer [Batteux] draws his examples, apart from the ancients, only from the finest heads among his own people, since he does not seem to know, or want to know, the writings of foreigners, it seems to us that his taste is somewhat too tender, and almost spoiled. One must take into account not only the genius of his own people, but the genius of different peoples, if one wants to arrive at the universal taste [*dem allgemeinen Geschmacke*], which recognizes and admires the true beauty among all possible forms and costumes. (*JubA* 4:249–62, at 253).[35]

So here Mendelssohn does assume that genuine taste is universal and genuine beauty universally valid or accessible. But this does not lead him, here or in any of his main writings, to restrict the proper objects of taste, for example to exclude either colors or tones on the one hand or emotions on the other because people might disagree about them. Perhaps he simply assumes that people do not disagree in their sensory and emotional responses very much, indeed that they are much more likely to disagree about their abstract ideas than about these basic human responses. But he does not feel the need to make a case for this assumption.

Kant's position on this matter is quite different; his aesthetic theory is driven by his need to secure the possibility of consensus in judgments of taste and his conception of the conditions under which this can reasonably be demanded and the restrictions these conditions impose upon ordinary assumptions about proper objects of aesthetic experience. This might be thought of as a kind of rationalism in aesthetic

---

[35] Review of *Einleitung in die schönen Wissenschaften, nach dem Französischen des Herrn Batteux, mit Zusätzen vermehrt von C.W. Ramler*, 4 vols. (Leipzig: Weidmann, 1758), in *Bibliothek der schönen Künste und freyen Wissenschaften*, 3. Band, 2. Stuck (October, 1758): 341–61.

theory, perhaps excessive rationalism. As we will see, however, Kant is ultimately driven to a more expansive conception of the experience of art, so in the end his conception of such experience has some commonalities with Mendelssohn's more empirically based account of our experience of art, although perhaps not enough. If either philosopher's aesthetic theory can be convicted of excessive rationalism, it will be Kant's, not Mendelssohn's.

# 7
# Kant's Aesthetics

A brief overview of Kant's aesthetic theory will allow us to see where it really differs from Mendelssohn's and where, by contrast, the difference is less than meets the eye. One difference to note at the outset is that while Mendelssohn's writings in aesthetics concern themselves with our response to the arts (as we saw, with what he calls the fine arts and sciences) from the outset, Kant's aesthetic theory is not initially or exclusively a theory of the reception or production of art at all. Rather, Kant begins with an account of our judgments about the beautiful and the sublime in *nature*, recognizes the beauty of art as a special, more complex case of beauty while suggesting that human art cannot produce the experience of sublimity, and adds a theory of the production of art and a sketch of a system of the arts only at the end of his exposition. But because my concern here is the relation between Mendelssohn's philosophy of art and Kant's, I will focus from the outset on the account of the reception and production of art that Kant builds within his framework without further discussion of the fact that for Kant the judgment of art is only a special, more complex case of aesthetic judgment in general.

This approach can be justified by the fact that Kant's exposition of his theory of judgments of taste in the "Analytic of the Beautiful" in the "Critique of the Power of Aesthetic Judgment" in the *Critique of the Power of Judgment*, published in 1790, is actually the final form of thoughts he had been presenting since he began lecturing on what he called "anthropology" in 1772–3,[1] and in those lectures Kant discussed primarily the case of art. The "Analytic of the Sublime" has less of an obvious history

---

[1] Kant used the chapter on "Empirical Psychology" from Baumgarten's *Metaphysics* as the required text for his anthropology lectures, which he gave from 1772–3 until his retirement, as lectures for student fees, in addition to the lectures on logic and metaphysics required by his chair. Baumgarten divided his chapter into sections on cognition, the feeling of pleasure and displeasure, and the faculty of desire, and touched upon his own views in aesthetics twice, in the section on cognition under the heading of the "faculty of invention" (*facultas fingendi*, *Dichtungsvermögen*) (*Metaphysics*, §§589–94) and in the section on pleasure and displeasure (§§655–62), where he defined beauty as *"perfectio phaenomenon"* or "the perfection that is observable by taste in the broader sense." Correspondingly, Kant would touch upon topics in aesthetics twice during the anthropology course. The relevant material is to be found especially in the transcriptions named "Collins" (1772–3), "Friedländer" (1775–6), "Pillau" (1777–8), "Menschenkunde" (1781–2), "Mrongovius" (1784–5), and "Busolt" (1788–9), all in volume 25 of the *Akademie* edition (1997); "Friedländer" and "Mrongovius" are translated in their entirety in Kant, *Lectures on Anthropology*, ed. Allen W. Wood and Robert B. Louden (Cambridge: Cambridge University Press, 2012). For discussion of the development of Kant's aesthetics in his anthropology lectures, see my "Beauty, Freedom, and Morality: Kant's *Lectures on Anthropology* and the Development of his Aesthetic Theory," in Brian Jacobs and Patrick Kain, eds., *Essays on Kant's Anthropology* (Cambridge: Cambridge University Press, 2003), pp. 135–63, and "Play and Society in the Lectures on Anthropology," in Robert R. Clewis, ed., *Reading Kant's Lectures* (Berlin and Boston: Walter de Gruyter, 2015), pp. 223–41.

in Kant's earlier lectures, but that will not be our focus here. In the published editions of the third *Critique* the "deduction of judgments of taste" and theory of fine arts appear as a continuation of the "Analytic of the Sublime," but Kant had actually intended them to constitute a separate, third "book" of the "Critique of the Power of Aesthetic Judgment";[2] Kant's attempt at a deduction of judgments of taste is new, since until the end of 1787 he had rejected the idea that judgments of taste have any a priori foundation at all,[3] but some of the ideas on art that he presents in the published book can also be found in those lectures. The development of Kant's account of judgments of taste therefore took place closer in time to the original publication of Mendelssohn's work in aesthetics and especially to the republication of this work in the 1771 edition of his *Philosophical Writings* than might appear; and even though Kant never mentions the name of Mendelssohn in his 1790 text—but then again, although Baumgarten is certainly a target of Kant's aesthetics,[4] neither does he address his criticism of perfectionism in aesthetics in the third *Critique* (*CPJ*, First Introduction, section VIII, 20:226-32; §15, 5:226-9) explicitly to Baumgarten, although he had acknowledged Baumgarten's attempt to found a science of aesthetics in the *Critique of Pure Reason* (*CPuR* A 21/B 35-6n.)—it is hard not to see Mendelssohn as the target of many of the positions that Kant takes. In any case, it should help to see both what is novel and what is less than novel in Kant's account, as well as what is persuasive and what is less persuasive, by comparing it with Mendelssohn's. In spite of the long gestation of Kant's theory, we can consider his ideas in the form and the order in which he presents them in the 1790 work.

Since Kant wrote the published version of the Introduction only after completing the body of the text, we can proceed through the four "moments" of the Analytic of the Beautiful and supplement them with material from the Introduction.[5] Kant begins with the claims that a judgment of taste is "aesthetic," that is, based on the subjective feeling of pleasure in its object (*CPJ* §1, 5:203-4) but yet "without any interest," usually abbreviated by commentators as "disinterested," which he explicates by stating that it is concerned only with the judge's response to the *representation* of the object of aesthetic judgment and not to its *existence*: "If someone asks me whether I find the palace that I see before me beautiful . . . One only wants to know whether the mere representation of the object is accompanied with satisfaction in me, however indifferent I might be with regard to the existence of the object of this representation" (§2, 5:204-5). It is noticeable that although throughout the Analytic of the Beautiful Kant will claim that only judgments of natural beauty are "pure," his

---

[2] See *CPJ*, Editor's Introduction, pp. xliii-xliv.
[3] See *CPJ*, Editor's Introduction, pp. xiii-xiv, xx-xxii.
[4] For discussions of Baumgarten's aesthetics (in English), see Mary J. Gregor, "Baumgarten's *Aesthetica*," *Review of Metaphysics* 37 (1983): 357-85, and Guyer, *A History of Modern Aesthetics*, vol. 1, pp. 318-40.
[5] On the late composition of the published Introduction, see *CPJ*, Editor's Introduction, pp. xl-xli. For my detailed discussion of the four "moments" and of the relations among them, see my *Kant and the Claims of Taste* (Cambridge, Mass.: Harvard University Press, 1979; second edition, Cambridge: Cambridge University Press, 1997), chs. 4-6; see also Donald W. Crawford, *Kant's Aesthetic Theory* (Madison: University of Wisconsin Press, 1974), chs. 2 and 5; Henry E. Allison, *Kant's Theory of Taste* (Cambridge: Cambridge University Press, 2001), chs. 3-7; and Eli Friedlander, *Expressions of Judgment: An Essay on Kant's Aesthetics* (Cambridge, Mass.: Harvard University Press, 2015), Part I.

first *example* is actually a work of art, indeed from the complex art of architecture, where one and the same object both has a use and can yet be judged purely aesthetically, for its beauty. Kant thereby introduces the idea that beauty is a matter of how we *experience* and *judge* an object, not something the object has independently of our experience and judgment of it.

In their independence from interest, Kant claims, judgments of taste about beauty differ from judgments about the "agreeable" and the "good," both of which are connected with interest in the existence of the object. A judgment that something is agreeable, e.g., that this glass of wine tastes good, is dependent entirely upon physiological contact with the object, in this case upon smelling and tasting it (I was going to say drinking it, but the wine-taster may not swallow everything she tastes!), and in this sense it is dependent upon the actual existence of the object, and also generates an interest in the existence of like objects: Having found this glass of wine good, I will (likely) want to taste it again and thus have (more of) it available to me—that is, more of the wine, not just a further or repeated representation of it. In the case of anything that I judge to be good from the point of view of either mere instrumental (prudential) or pure (moral) practical reason, my judgment is a judgment that the object of my representation ought to exist, thus it is also connected to an interest in the existence of the object.

From the disinterestedness of judgments of taste Kant also infers that they are not based on any determinate concept of their objects, although this would seem properly to entail only that genuine judgments of taste are not based on any concept of their objects *as good for some particular purpose*, whether of consumption (as in the case of the agreeable), or some other prudential or moral purpose (as in the case of judgments of the good). Kant then concludes that "Taste is the faculty for judging an object or a kind of representation through a satisfaction or dissatisfaction **without any interest**," and "The object of such a satisfaction is called **beautiful**"—the object, note, even though the judgment is based solely on the representation of the object.

The second moment of the Analytic of the Beautiful expounds the thesis that "The beautiful is that which, without concepts, is represented as the object of a *universal* satisfaction" (*CPJ*, §6, 5:211) or that "in the judgment of taste nothing is postulated except . . . a **universal voice** with regard to the satisfaction without the mediation of concepts, hence the **possibility** of an aesthetic judgment," that is, according to the first moment, one based on one's own felt pleasure in the representation of an object, "that could at the same time be considered valid for everyone" (§8, 5:216). This last remark is meant to make clear that a judgment of taste is not an empirical assertion that everyone does or will find beautiful what one has oneself found beautiful, but is rather a conditional judgment that if one's own pleasure in an object is in fact a genuine response to its beauty, then everyone else could reasonably be expected to find the object beautiful under optimal circumstances.[6] Kant initially suggests that

---

[6] Kant says that we do not "postulate" the agreement of others in a judgment of taste but only "ascribe" (*ansinnen*) it to them (5:216). This has been interpreted as a statement that others *ought* to agree with my judgment of taste, and has led to the interpretation that judgments of taste impose an *obligation* on others that requires a moral element in them from the outset; see Kenneth F. Rogerson, *Kant's Aesthetics: The Roles of Form and Expression* (Lanham: University Press of America, 1986), pp. 79–91, and numerous

such universal validity—which he calls "subjectively universal validity," because it follows from the non-conceptually determined character of aesthetic judgments that theirs is a validity for all *subjects* responding to a particular object (that is, human beings who might experience and judge it) rather than for all *objects* in some general class, which could only be defined by a determinate concept (§8, 5:215)—follows directly from the disinterestedness of judgments of taste (§6, 5:211). This is a mistake, because a response could be disinterested yet idiosyncratic. But in the final section of the second moment, Kant introduces a positive ground for the imputation of subjectively universal validity to one's pleasure in a beautiful object: his argument there is that such pleasure is due to a special condition of or relation between the cognitive powers of imagination and understanding consisting in a "free play" between them in which "no determinate concept restricts them to a particular rule of cognition" but in which they are pleasurably "facilitated" and "enlivened" (*belebt*) through mutual agreement" (§9, 5:217, 219).[7] This is the core of Kant's aesthetic theory, which he also restates in the Introduction to the whole third *Critique*:

> If pleasure is connected with the mere apprehension (*apprehensio*) of the form of an object of intuition without a relation of this to a concept for a determinate cognition, then the representation is thereby related not to the object, but solely to the subject, and the pleasure can express nothing but its suitability to the cognitive faculties that are in play in the reflecting power of judgment, insofar as they are in play, and thus merely a subjective formal purposiveness of the object. For that apprehension of forms in the imagination can never take place

papers by Hannah Ginsborg, collected in *The Normativity of Nature: Essays on Kant's Critique of Judgement* (Oxford: Oxford University Press, 2015), Part I. In my view, Kant says only much later in his argument that "the feeling in the judgment of taste is expected of everyone *as if* it were a duty" (*CPJ* §40, 5:296, emphasis added), and only on the condition that a moral value can be attached to the experience of beauty *indirectly*, without compromising the original distinction between judgments of beauty and judgments of goodness. On my view whatever "normativity" is expressed in the second moment's claim that we can "ascribe" to others the same pleasure we find in something beautiful is not to be confused with any kind of moral normativity. See my "One Act or Two? Hannah Ginsborg on Aesthetic Judgment," *British Journal of Aesthetics* 57 (2017): 407–19, and Ginsborg's reply in the same issue, pp. 421–35.

[7] For more on my interpretation of Kant's concept of free play, see "The Harmony of Faculties Revisited," in my *Values of Beauty: Historical Essays in Aesthetics* (Cambridge: Cambridge University Press, 2005), pp. 77–109. Here I argue that since according to Kant's own epistemology we are always conscious of an object under some concept, free play must lie in finding unity in some aspect of the appearance of a beautiful object that is left undetermined by the concept or concepts that we recognize to apply to it; I call this the "meta-cognitive" interpretation of Kant's concept, although by this I do not mean that aesthetic experience or the judgment of taste is *about* the possibility of knowledge, just that the aesthetic experience goes *beyond* the unity necessary for ordinary knowledge. The proper interpretation of *CPJ* §9, Kant's "key to the critique of taste," has been debated; see my "Pleasure and Society in Kant's Theory of Taste," in Ted Cohen and Paul Guyer, eds., *Essays in Kant's Aesthetics* (Chicago: University of Chicago Press, 1981), pp. 21–54, and Hannah Ginsborg, "On the Key to Kant's Critique of Taste" (1991), in *The Normativity of Nature*, pp. 32–52; for a recent attempt to split the difference between myself and Ginsborg, see Fiona Hughes, "Feeling the Life of the Mind: Mere Judging, Feeling, and Judgment," in Matthew C. Altman, ed., *The Palgrave Kant Handbook* (London: Palgrave Macmillan, 2017), pp. 381–406. Alexander Rueger interprets free play as lying in a comparison between the form an object actually has and a form the imagination could have imagined for it, in Rueger, "The Free Play of the Faculties and the Status of Natural Beauty in Kant's Theory of Taste," *Archiv für Geschichte der Philosophie* 90 (2008): 298–322, at pp. 300–12, but that approach will require an account of what constraints there are on what the imagination could imagine for a particular object other than those that arise from the concept or concepts of the object.

without the reflecting power of judgment, even if unintentionally, at least comparing them to its faculty for relating intuitions to concepts. Now if in this comparison the imagination... is unintentionally brought into accord with the understanding... through a given representation and a feeling of pleasure is thereby aroused, then the object must be regarded as purposive for the reflecting power of judgment... That object the form of which (not the material aspect of its representation, as sensation) in mere reflection on it (without any intention of acquiring a concept from it) is judged as the ground of a pleasure in the representation of such an object—with its representation this pleasure is also judged to be necessarily combined, consequently not merely for the subject who apprehends this form but for everyone who judges at all.

(*CPJ*, Introduction, Section VII, 5:189–90)

Kant's argument is that a "free play" between imagination and understanding will be pleasurable because it constitutes "subjective formal purposiveness," that is, the satisfaction of every cognitive subject's unintentional aim for harmony among its cognitive powers but without the usual guarantee of such harmony provided through subsumption of the representation of the object under a determinate concept, that is, the determination that an object is entitled to be subsumed under some concept because it presents some "mark" included in that concept, some property corresponding to a predicate included in the concept; the achievement of the goal of harmony despite the lack of any such guarantee is precisely what makes the experience pleasurable (see Section VI, 5:187). Then such a pleasure can be considered "subjectively universally valid" just because everyone's cognitive faculties of imagination and understanding must work the same way.

Kant attempts to support the last step of this inference by the further argument that he calls the "deduction of judgments of taste," the argument, namely, that everyone's cognitive faculties must work the same way in aesthetic contexts because they must work the same way in ordinary cognitive contexts (§§21, 38). Kant claims that this is a synthetic a priori principle. But this deduction is deeply problematic, because it is not obvious, at least not evidently true a priori, that everyone's cognitive faculties must work the same way in ordinary cognition, nor that even if they do so in ordinary cognition, they must also do so in aesthetic contexts.[8] But Kant is deeply invested in the claim that aesthetic judgments are universally valid and thus in this deduction, with consequences that we will see in the sequel.

The passage just quoted from the Introduction to the third *Critique* introduces terms and claims that Kant develops in the third moment of the Analytic of the Beautiful. These are that the free play of imagination and understanding in the experience of beauty is a "subjective formal purposiveness" because it is achieved without the usual condition of subsumption of the represented object under a determinate concept, thus that "nothing other than the subjective purposiveness in the representation of an object without any end (objective or subjective), consequently the mere form of purposiveness in the representation through which an object is **given** to us... can constitute the satisfaction that we judge, without a

---

[8] The soundness of Kant's deduction of aesthetic judgments has been heavily contested. For my criticisms, see *Kant and the Claims of Taste*, chs. 8–10, and "The Psychology of Kant's Aesthetics." *Studies in the History and Philosophy of Science* 39 (2008): 483–94. For a defense, see Allison, *Kant's Theory of Taste*, ch. 8.

concept, to be universally communicable, and hence the determining ground of the judgment of taste" (*CPJ* §11, 5:221). But Kant also claims that this free play, which is "subjective" and "formal purposiveness" in the sense of being achieved without a concept, is formal in the sense of being triggered by and directed at the (represented) *form* of the object, as contrasted to the *matter* of the representation, sensation, on the one hand, and any conceptual *content* or meaning of the object, on the other. Thus Kant goes from the claim that the purposiveness of the free play of the cognitive powers is "formal" to the claim that beauty "should properly concern merely form" (§13, 5:223). It is then in this context that Kant makes his notorious claim that "In painting and sculpture," for example, "indeed in all the pictorial arts,... the **drawing** is what is essential... not what gratifies in sensation," such as "the colors that illuminate the outline" but the outline itself, "merely what pleases through form," and that in music, it is not "the agreeable tones of instruments" but only the "composition," the formal structure of the music, presumably what is captured by the bare notes of the score rather than by the timbres and overtones of any particular instrumentation (§14, 5:225; again, although Kant is still technically analyzing a form of judgment paradigmatically directed toward natural beauty, his examples come from the arts). It is also in this context that Kant makes the claim, quoted at the outset of the previous chapter, that "Taste is always still barbaric when it needs the addition of **charm** and **emotion** [*Reiz und Rührung*] for satisfaction" (§13, 5:223). In §14, Kant specifically connects charm with sensation, saying that the "colors that illuminate the outline" in painting or the "agreeable tones of instruments" have charm (5:225), and we might suppose that some elements that we might consider more formal than material, such as a piece of music being composed in a minor rather than a major key, could also have an emotional impact; but it might be more natural to suppose that the major part of the emotional impact of works of art will be produced by their content, in the case of works that do have content, such as historical or devotional painting, music with text rather than absolute music, and of course most forms of literature, indeed any conceivable to Kant. (In §16, Kant suggests that paradigmatic examples of what he there calls "free" artistic beauties, such as "designs *à la grecque*" and wallpaper "do not represent anything, no object under a determinate concept," and thus have no content; 5:229.) Kant thus derives the exclusion of charm from the proper response to aesthetic objects from the restriction of that response to the form of such objects, and it is natural to suppose that the exclusion of emotion is similarly derived. Kant's view that properties such as color and tone contribute to the mere "charm" rather than genuine beauty of their objects is in clear contrast to Mendelssohn's argument in his review of Meier that such properties make a genuine contribution to beauty.

It is clear that Kant is being moved by a further thought, namely that the response to mere form is universally valid in the way requisite for judgments of taste, but that the response to other possible aspects of aesthetic objects, their material like colors and tones on the one hand and their content (in the case of works of art that may have content) on the other, is not universally valid in the same way. He explicitly states that "it cannot easily be assumed that the agreeableness of one color in preference to another or of the tone of one musical instrument in preference to another will be judged in the same way by everyone" (although he is prepared to concede that *purity* of colors or tones might be a formal feature of the vibrations of light or sound that cause our perceptions of them, and thus properly universal) (*CPJ*, §14, 5:224). And although Kant does not explicitly assert that people vary in their emotional responses to the content of art in the same way that they vary in being charmed by colors or tones, his acceptance of the traditional doctrine of humors (that some people are by nature sanguine, others phlegmatic, and so on) in his early *Observations on the Feeling of the Beautiful and Sublime* (*OFBS* 2:218–25) and anthropology lectures[9] suggests that he would make this assumption as well. In these passages Kant says such things as that "The person of a **sanguine** frame of mind has a dominant **feeling for the beautiful**" (*OFBS* 2:222) and that "Women have a stronger innate feeling for everything that is beautiful, decorative, and adorned" (*OFBS* 62:29) while men are more concerned with the useful on the one hand and the sublime on the other. Concerned as he is with the possibility of consensus in taste, Kant is clearly disposed to exclude as many sources of disagreement from the proper objects of taste as he can. So he could well be moved to exclude charm and emotion from proper aesthetic response because of the danger that they could introduce idiosyncrasy rather than intersubjective validity into aesthetic response and judgment, with the desire to avoid this at all costs.

Kant introduces several further topics in the third moment. First, he takes pains to distinguish his conception of subjective purposiveness as the essence of aesthetic response from any theory that the perfection of objects is the basis of such response. Kant claims that "The judgment of taste is entirely independent from the concept of perfection," because "**Objective** purposiveness can be cognized only by means of the relation of a manifold to a determinate end, thus only through a concept," and from the fact that judgments of taste have as their ground "a merely formal purposiveness" but no concept, it follows that they are not judgments of perfection. Judgments of objective purposiveness could take two forms, being either an "external" judgment of utility, that an object is suited to a specific purpose, or an "internal" judgment of perfection, that an object properly exemplifies its type, but since either sort of judgment depends on the subsumption of the object under a concept, neither is an aesthetic judgment. In particular, although as usual Kant names no names, the account of sensory judgment developed by Leibniz and Wolff and applied to the case of aesthetic judgments by Baumgarten and Meier, that they are "confused" but still conceptual judgments, is rejected by Kant (*CPJ* §15, 5:226–7). We will return to the question of whether this criticism would apply to Mendelssohn as well.

Second, Kant introduces the distinction between "free" and "adherent" beauty or judgments of beauty.[10] Here is where Kant first explicitly complicates his account to

---

[9] See, e.g., *Anthropology Friedländer*, 25:636–48; *Lectures on Anthropology*, pp. 181–92.

[10] See my "Free and Adherent Beauty: A Modest Proposal," *British Journal of Aesthetics* 42 (2002): 357–66, reprinted in *Values of Beauty*, pp. 129–40. See also Eva Schaper, "Free and Dependent Beauty," in her *Sudies in Kant's Æsthetics* (Edinburgh: Edinburgh University Press, 1979), pp. 78–98. Alexander Rueger, "Beautiful Surfaces: Kant on Free and Adherent Beauty in Nature and Art," *British Journal of the History of Philosophy* 16 (2008): 335–57, defends a "conjunctive" account of adherent beauty, in which our response combines a conceptually determined response to the objective perfection of the whole object with a non-conceptually determined, free play in response to the surface appearance of the object. That fits some of Kant's examples, but not those in which our conception of the purpose of the object restricts what

make room for the aesthetic judgment of art, although as we have seen he has in fact been using examples from the realm of art as well as that of nature all along. "Free" beauty is a new name for the beauty that is ascribed to an object by a judgment of beauty made apart from determination by any concept at all, while "adherent" beauty "does presuppose such a concept and the perfection of the object in accordance with it" (*CPJ* §16, 5:229) and is ascribed to the object at least in part on the basis of its subsumption under a concept of its purpose. Judgments that a flower or mollusk is beautiful, according to Kant, take no account whatsoever of the concepts that apply to the object and any purposes and criteria that may be associated with those concepts, but judgments that a building or a horse is do take account of the intended purposes of such objects and criteria for their adequate or perfect satisfaction of such purposes. Kant suggests that in the latter case, that of adherent beauty, the concept functions as a restricting condition on how the object may appear and therefore how we may find it beautiful. "One would be able to add much to a building that would be pleasing in the intuition of it if only it were not supposed to be a church; a figure could be beautified with all sorts of curlicues and light but regular lines as the New Zealanders do with their tattooing, if only it were not a human being" (5:230). These comments need unpacking, but presumably Kant means that there are requirements for being a church, say having a cruciform floor-plan, a western entrance, and a campanile, that are necessary but not sufficient conditions for our finding it beautiful, while the moral dignity of human beings altogether precludes treating their skin as a location for patterns that might be beautiful on an ordinary piece of canvas. (The examples of a horse and a human being show that the category of adherent beauty is not limited to works of art, such as works of architecture, but it includes them. And while a human being is definitely not a work of art for Kant, the status of a horse might be more problematic: of course a horse, or a dog, is an organism that can reproduce itself without human assistance, but a carefully bred animal such as a thoroughbred racehorse or a pedigreed dog might be considered as much a work of human art as of nature.)

Two points about Kant's treatment of adherent beauty should be noted. First, although the previous rejection of perfectionism might be thought to entail that adherent beauty is not genuine beauty at all, Kant does not say that. He says that adherent beauty is not "pure" beauty, which is restricted to natural beauty or to some cases of decorative art or music without words, but he does not deny that it is a kind of beauty. He could not very well have done so without rejecting Hume's claim in that a great number of cases of beauty are in fact beauty of utility or its appearance, but he does not deny this claim.[11] Neither does Kant explain his recognition of adherent beauty as a genuine if not pure kind of beauty, but presumably what underlies his approach is that the restrictions inherent in the concept of some object's purpose, such as those in the concept of a church, as necessary but not sufficient conditions of its beauty, still leave room for the free play of the imagination and understanding

---

we can find beautiful in its form, let alone cases, like the case of tattooing that will shortly be mentioned, in which our judgment of contrapurposiveness in the object blocks any aesthetic appreciation of its surface, patterns, or appearance.

[11] See Hume, *Treatise of Human Nature*, Book II, Part I, Section 8, paragraph 2.

with the appearance of the object. Some possible appearances are excluded altogether by the concept, or by our psychological response to the concept—maybe the form of an incommodious building could be beautiful if we could respond to it in abstraction from its disutility, but the disutility could psychologically block our actual enjoyment of its form, and thus prevent us from finding it beautiful. But a range of other forms or ways of appearing is left open by the conditions necessary to satisfy the intended purpose of the object, and among those some might trigger free play but others not. In the former case but not the latter there will be adherent but genuine beauty. In the case of tattooed Maori, we might have thought that some patterns would be formally beautiful, others not—not every tattoo artist is an artistic genius—but Kant's unexplained view is that something about the dignity of humanity precludes tattooing altogether, and thus, somehow, makes it impossible for us to enjoy free play with any pattern tattooed on human skin.[12]

The second point to note here is that although Kant holds that a failure to distinguish between the two kinds of beauty can be the cause of critical confusion—one person might find an object beautiful while ignoring its purpose, but another might not be able to find it beautiful because she takes its intended purpose into account—and "strictly speaking... perfection does not gain by beauty, nor does beauty gain by perfection"—Kant nevertheless holds that "the **entire faculty** of the powers of representations gains if both states of mind are in agreement" (*CPJ* §16, 5:231). That is, while rejecting straight-out perfectionism, Kant admits that the whole state of mind of a person, presumably including her whole *affective* state, her total state of pleasure or pain, is influenced by both formal properties of an object or the representation of it and recognition of its objective purposiveness, particularly external objective purposiveness, that of utility. So Kant seems to recognize the complexity of our response to many objects of taste. We will come back to the question of how close this brings his view to the conceptual framework within which Mendelssohn found a place for his idea of mixed sentiments.

Kant's final topic in the third moment of the Analytic of the Beautiful is what he calls the "ideal of beauty," a topic that goes back to Sulzer[13] and that was Mendelssohn's topic in the sixty-sixth of the *Letters concerning the Latest Literature*, discussed in the previous chapter. There, it will be recalled, Mendelssohn had argued that the ideal beauty in art, more precisely the ideally beautiful character in art, is not the perfect human being, but the character who is "a mixture of virtues and weaknesses" and who can hereby trigger mixed sentiments in response (*JubA* 5.1:100-1). Kant does not adopt this conception of the ideal of beauty: While agreeing that only human beauty can be a form of ideal beauty, because an ideal must be a *maximum* of some kind and only an "expression of the **moral**" can fix a *maximum* rather than a merely

---

[12] Those of us whose first experience of tattoos was of those on the forearms of concentration camp survivors might understand the tenor of Kant's revulsion even without sharing his apparently general premise that any kind of tattoo is incompatible with the moral vocation of human beings. The Nazis' tattooing of identification numbers on those concentration camp arrivees selected for labor details rather than immediate extermination was doubly offensive, because tattooing of any kind is forbidden in Judaism.

[13] See Johann Georg Sulzer, *Allgemeine Theorie der schönen Künste*, second ed., 4 vols. (Leipzig: Weidmann, 1792-4), entry "Ideal (Schöne Künste)," vol. II, pp. 669-72.

*average* form of beauty, he argues that it must therefore be the outward form of a maximally moral rather than morally imperfect human being that fixes an ideal of beauty (*CPJ* §17, 5:235–6). It might seem surprising that Kant should think there can be any outward, thus aesthetic manifestation of something presumably as inward as morality, and indeed he admits that "The visible expression of moral ideas, which inwardly govern human beings, can of course be drawn only from experience"; but his thought seems to be that it is precisely the leap of imagination that would be required to take an outward form of beauty as an expression of an inward moral condition that makes such expression aesthetic—that there is no rule for the outward expression of morality must mean that it is only by the free play of imagination that an outward form can be recognized as, indeed constituted as, an expression of the moral. But even if this is what Kant means, we should note how he concludes the section:

The correctness of such an ideal of beauty is proved by the fact that no sensory charm is allowed to be mixed into the satisfaction in its object, while it nevertheless allows a great interest to be taken in it, which then proves that judging in accordance with such a standard can never be purely aesthetic, and judging in accordance with an idea of beauty is no mere judgment of taste. (5:235–6)

So one point Kant is eager to make is that a judgment of ideal beauty, whether that be of an actual human form, thus a work of nature, or of an artistic representation of human form, is not a "mere" or pure aesthetic judgment; but as we have already seen, that does not imply that it is not a genuine aesthetic judgment at all, rather only that is a complex rather than a simple case of aesthetic judgment. Mendelssohn's conception of aesthetic judgment as a response to both the perfection of the object, in this case the moral perfection of the object, and to the perfection of the form of the representation of it, would seem to be a framework for what Kant has in mind here. However, Kant might also be distancing himself from Mendelssohn's account, not by disallowing that our response to ideal beauty is a *mixed* sentiment, but by trying to deny that it is *sentiment* at all—"no sensory charm is allowed to be mixed into the satisfaction of its object." We will see that Kant takes a similar position when he finally comes to his direct discussion of the arts.

But first we must complete the discussion of Kant's Analytic of the Beautiful, which is still concerned with all cases of aesthetic judgment, not specifically the judgment of art. Kant's main claim in the fourth moment of the Analytic is that the "modality" of judgments of taste is that of "exemplary necessity," i.e., the "necessity of the assent of all to a judgment that is regarded as an example of a universal rule that one cannot produce" (*CPJ* §18, 5:237). On its face, this feature of judgments of taste does not seem different from the claim to speak with a universal voice analyzed in the second moment. However, Kant's allusion to "a universal rule that one cannot produce" presages a point that Kant will make in his account of genius, which comes later in the work, in his discussion of fine art. There Kant will argue that works of artistic genius cannot be rules for successive artists in the sense of being models to be slavishly followed, but they can nevertheless be exemplars for them, as models of originality and spurs to their own originality. Such works can function as rules in the special sense of expressing the second-order rule that great art must be original, and thus must *not* exactly resemble any previous works, although at the same time, because of the requirement of subjectively universal validity, new examples of successful originality must ideally be accessible to all, thus not "original nonsense" (*CPJ*, §46, 5:308). Since Mendelssohn also thought about the limited role of rules in art, we will come back to this topic momentarily when we consider Kant's account of genius in more detail. But we can conclude this discussion of the fourth moment by noting that Kant devotes its conclusion to his first attempt to prove that if a feeling of pleasure is properly attributed to the free play of the cognitive powers it is attributed to something that must be the same in all ordinary human beings, and thus that judgments of taste are indeed universally valid. I have already hinted at my own reservations about the strength of this deduction.

As already mentioned, Kant holds that the experience of the sublime is produced by nature, not by works of human art. Although he uses the stock examples of St. Peter's Basilica and the Pyramids at Giza[14] to make the point that for an object to trigger the experience of the sublime it must be seen from the right point of view, this is just an analogy, since only mountain ranges and oceans but not even very large human constructions are able to appear big and powerful enough to trigger the experience. Instead, Kant asserts, "if the aesthetic judgment is to be **pure (not mixed up with anything teleological** as judgments of reason) and if an example of that is to be given which is fully appropriate for the **aesthetic** power of judgment, then the sublime must not be shown in products of art (e.g., buildings, columns, etc.) where a human end determines the form as well as the magnitude, nor in natural things **whose concept already brings with it a determinate end** (e.g., animals of a known natural determination), but rather in raw nature...merely insofar as it contains magnitude" (for the case of the mathematical sublime) or power (in the case of the dynamical sublime) (*CPJ* §26, 5:252–3).[15] Kant's objection cannot really be just that judgments of the sublime must be pure while works of art can only give rise to mixed rather than pure aesthetic judgments, for very few works of art (again, there are purely decorative patterns and music without words) give rise to pure judgments of beauty either. The objection must be that works of art, even colossal works of architecture, do not give us the impression of immeasurable size or strength that we need for the experience of sublimity. But whatever Kant's real objection, it is clear that he does not intend his theory of the sublime to be part of his theory of art, so we will leave the sublime aside and turn now directly to the theory of art.

Kant begins his account of fine art without any title to indicate a change of subject from the preceding deduction of judgments of taste and the two ensuing sections on "empirical" and "intellectual interest" in beauty, the latter an important part of Kant's *indirect* connection between aesthetic judgment and morality, to which we will return. Kant begins by distinguishing art from nature as "doing (*facere*) from acting

---

[14] "Thus St. Peter's church at Rome, the great pyramid of Egypt, the Alp towering above the clouds, a great arm of the sea, and above all a clear and serene sky, are grand"; Kames, *Elements of Criticism*, ch. IV; ed. Jones, vol. 1, p. 151.

[15] As I revise this chapter in a hotel room in Shanghai, I can see super-skyscrapers the tops of which become lost in the clouds; they might test Kant's claim that only nature and not art can produce a genuine experience of the sublime.

or producing [*Wirkung*] in general (*agere*)," and the products of art as "**work** (*opus*)" from mere effects (*effectus*) (*CPJ* §43, 5:303). This is to say that art is human or at least intentional production and its products, artifacts. (Kant does not slam the door on Mendelssohn's conception of divine artistry, nor does he acknowledge it.) But art is also distinguished from science, the latter being mere knowledge and theory and the former requiring ability or know-how, and he further distinguishes art from handicraft, art being "liberal" (*frey*) and handicraft undertaken for the sake of remuneration (5:304). He does not explicitly acknowledge the complex but common case in which a work, e.g., an altarpiece, a musical composition, or a monument, might satisfy all the criteria that will eventually be laid out for fine art but also be undertaken on commission. But he does recognize that "in all liberal arts there is nevertheless required something compulsory, or, as it is called, a **mechanism**, without which the **spirit**, which must be **free** in the art and which alone animates the work, would have no body at all and would entirely evaporate (e.g., in the art of poetry, correctness and richness of diction as well as prosody and meter)" (5:304). This remark, which anticipates much of the theory of genius that follows, implies that any fine art uses some medium, whether words or notes, paint or stone, and that there are rules for the successful use of the medium (like "Don't apply fast-drying paint over slow-drying paint, for then your surface is likely to crack"), but that such rules are only necessary conditions for success in that art, true beauty or other artistic success additionally requiring freedom of the spirit—free play of the imagination—in using materials with their rules in ways that cannot be reduced to rules.

Kant also states that art that "has the feeling of pleasure as its immediate aim" can be either "**agreeable** or **beautiful**" art, aiming at mere pleasant sensations in the first case but at pleasure that would "accompany" sensations "as **kinds of cognition** in the second"; in the latter case art "is a kind of representation that is purposive in itself and, though without an end, nevertheless promotes the cultivation of the mental powers for sociable communication" (*CPJ* §44, 5:305–6). The last statement once again needs to be unpacked. It implies that the production of art is intentional, as Kant's original definition required, but also that it be "without an end," which the analysis of genius will reveal to mean that a successful work of art is not produced unintentionally or aimlessly but is never fully determined by the intention or, more typically, multiple intentions that govern its production. The statement also describes the overarching intention that does govern the production of the work of art as that of "promoting the cultivation of the mental powers for sociable communication." This seems to elide a step: Kant's argument in the Analytic of the Beautiful (and in the Deduction of Judgments of Taste; see §36, 5:286–7) has held that all beauty, including both free and adherent beauty, must trigger the free play of our cognitive powers, thus far including imagination and understanding, so art insofar as it is both intentional and aesthetic but not merely agreeable, must *aim* to produce the free play of the cognitive powers, presumably in its audience. Kant has also held that this state of mind is "communicable" or shareable (see especially §9, 5:217–18), so in aiming at the production of the free play of the cognitive faculties the artist is *ipso facto* aiming at the production of a communicable state of those powers. But it is crucial that the artist aim at producing a communicable state of free play, not any other communicable state of the cognitive powers, thus the work cannot realize this aim by simply following any rule. Kant's final statement of the definition of fine art has left that crucial step out. Nevertheless, it is clear both from what has gone before and what is about to come that this is what he means. And the main point in both what he has said about the difference between "mechanism" in art and "spirit" and in what he is about to say about spirit in the following account of genius is that rules in art are necessary but never sufficient conditions for producing beauty—a point that we have seen Mendelssohn has anticipated in his own assessment of the role of rules in the production of art.

Kant begins the discussion of genius with the remark that "In a product of art one must be aware that it is art, and not nature; yet the purposiveness in its form must still seem to be as free from all constraint by arbitrary rules as if it were a mere product of nature" (*CPJ* §45, 5:306). This may sound as if it requires us to believe a contradiction, like "*p* and *not-p*," or at least to be able to take the mental stance that Mendelssohn describes us as holding toward a work of artistic representation, namely, both being emotionally engaged with it as if what it represents were real yet recognizing it to be an illusion but holding those two responses at sufficient distance—aesthetic distance—to retain them both. But Kant does not immediately dispel the appearance of paradox in Mendelssohn's way. Instead, what he argues is that "A product of art appears as nature ... if we find it to agree **punctiliously** but not **painstakingly** with rules in accordance with which alone the product can become what it ought to be, that is, without the academic form showing through, i.e., without showing any sign that the rule has hovered before the eyes of the artist and fettered his mental powers" (5:307). As he proceeds, however, it becomes clear that the artist must not just make his work *look* effortless and unstudied, by fine brushwork for example, and thus like a product of nature rather than of human effort, but that the mechanical rules of art, rules for handling brush and paint for example, and beyond that *any* determinate intentions for the work of art, intentions about its form and also intentions about its content, are never *sufficient* for producing a beautiful work of art: that can be produced only if in addition to following rules the artist can generate a free play of his cognitive powers and express that in his work in a way that in turn triggers a free play of cognitive powers in his audience. Once again Kant puts this metaphorically by saying that "**Genius** is the talent (natural gift) that gives the rule to art ... **Genius** is the inborn predisposition of the mind (*ingenium*) **through which** nature gives the rule to art" (§46, 5:307). Kant still speaks of there being a rule *for* art, because beauty must be exemplary, but this rule cannot be the rules *of* art, rules of prosody or meter or for mixing pigments and so on, because following them alone, even if successfully hiding one's slavish adherence to them, is not sufficient to produce beauty. But what really produces this "rule" will be the free play of the artist's cognitive powers, which however to produce pleasure in beauty in the audience will also have to trigger free play, not slavish adherence to rules, in the audience's mind.

Kant links this to his earlier contrast between mechanism and spirit in art and most fully unpacks his thought in §49, "On the faculties of mind that constitute genius" (5:313). Here he says that a poem, for example, "can be quite pretty and elegant, but without **spirit**," and that "**spirit**, in an aesthetic significance," that which makes a work of art truly beautiful or successful, is "the animating principle in the mind... that which purposively sets the mental powers into motion, i.e., into a play that is self-maintaining and even strengthens the powers to that end." Such spirit, which is genius, is "purposive" in that an artist sets out to produce a beautiful work, and to use certain means or mechanisms to do so, but it also requires a free play, which is precisely a state of mind that cannot be produced according to any rules, which thus goes beyond what can be (and has to be) achieved by following rules. This is the gift of nature. Kant extends his previous account of free play, however, by stating that spirit in art "is nothing other than the faculty for the presentation of **aesthetic ideas**," by which he means such "representation[s] of the imagination that occasion... much thinking without it being possible for any determinate thought, i.e., **concept**, to be adequate to it, which, consequently, no language fully attains or can make intelligible." He continues that "One readily sees that it is the counterpart (pendant) of an **idea of reason**, which is, conversely, a concept to which no **intuition** (representation of the imagination) can be adequate." The ideas of reason he has in mind are intellectual ideas, above all moral ideas, so that "The poet ventures to make sensible rational ideas of sensible beings, the kingdom of the blessed, the kingdom of hell, eternity, creation... envy and all sorts of vices, love, fame, etc." (5:314); in other words, the artistic genius creates an *aesthetic* idea by the free play of his imagination with a *rational* idea:

Now if we add to a concept a representation of the imagination that belongs to its presentation, but which by itself stimulates so much thinking that it can never be grasped in a determinate concept, hence which aesthetically enlarges the concept itself in an unbounded way, then in this case the imagination is creative, and sets the faculty of intellectual ideas (reason) into motion, that is, at the instigation of a representation it gives more to think about that can be grasped and made distinct in it (although it does, to be sure, belong to the concept of the object.

(5:315)

Kant thus assumes that an inspired work of art has content, not just form, that content being some moral idea or ideas, yet that the imagination of the artist presents that idea in a form and by means dictated neither by the idea itself nor by any other rules of art, necessary as those rules are for giving the work of art body, i.e., incorporating it in some durable medium (even the medium of words). Thus art involves a free play between imagination and reason, although since some rules must be followed, rules for conceiving of various sorts of objects given by their concepts as well as the rules of the relevant artistic medium, and rule-following is the characteristic province of the understanding, the artist's state of mind and what is to be communicated to the audience will typically be a free play of imagination, understanding, and reason.[16]

---

[16] On this account, the production and appreciation of works of art involves a free play of cognitive powers, the spirit of works of fine art requires that they have intellectual content, and both requirements can be satisfied by the possibility of free play *with* the intellectual content or *between* the intellectual content and the form of the work. Alexander Rueger and Sahan Evren, in "The Role of Symbolic Presentation in Kant's Theory of Taste," *British Journal of Aesthetics* 45 (2005): 228–47, connect the concepts of free play and aesthetic ideas even more closely by arguing that symbolization of an idea is itself a necessary feature of free play (pp. 241–7), thus the only kind of free play. That supports Kant's statement in *CPJ* §51, 5:319, that *all* beauty involves the presentation of aesthetic ideas, but is inconsistent with Kant's

Kant sums this all up by stating that in genius:

> we find: **first**, that it is a talent for art, not for science, in which rules that are distinctly cognized must come first and determine the procedure in it; **second**, that as a talent for art, it presupposes a determinate concept of the product, as an end, hence understanding, but also a representation (even if in determinate) of the material, i.e., of the intuition, for the presentation of this concept... **third**, that it displays itself not so much in the execution of the proposed end in the presentation of a determinate **concept** as in the exposition or the expression of **aesthetic ideas**... hence the imagination, in its freedom from guidance by all rules, is nevertheless presented as purposive for the presentation of the given concept; finally, **fourth**, that the unsought and unintentional subjective purposiveness in the free correspondence of the imagination to the lawfulness of the understanding presupposes a proportion and disposition of this faculty that cannot be produced by any following of rules... but that only the nature of the subject can produce. (*CPJ* §49, 5:317–18)

That is, genius does not consist in following rules, though rules are necessary conditions for the production of enduring works of art, and the artist must always have some intention for his work, for example, intending to write an oratorio on the theme of faith rather than an operetta on the theme of faithlessness; beyond satisfying conditions of this sort, genius consists in finding imaginative expression for content, typically moral content, that cannot itself be reduced to rules and that instead reflects a free play on the part of the audience and triggers one in the audience. Kant stresses this last point in the case of the influence of the artistic genius on subsequent *artists*, saying that "the product of a genius (in respect of that in it which is to be ascribed to genius, not to possible learning or schooling) is an example, not for imitation (for then that which is genius in it and constitutes the spirit of the work would be lost), but for emulation by another genius, who is thereby awakened to the feeling of his own originality, to exercise freedom from coercion in his art" (5:318); that is, although a student can learn mechanical rules by copying the technique of a genius, e.g., how to handle paint from a Rembrandt or a Pollock or counterpoint from a Bach, he cannot learn how to produce what gives spirit to a work of art by copying a genius, for that is the free play of the genius's cognitive powers and free play is precisely what cannot be produced in accordance with a rule. But this must also apply to the case of the audience, even if we the audience are hardly all geniuses, because what gives pleasure to the *experience* of art, as to any other aesthetic experience, is *our own* free play of imagination and understanding and now, with the typical content of art, reason, so the artist's state of mind, namely *his* free play, cannot simply be triggered, but must rather stimulate *our* free play.

Kant's theory of genius is the heart of his theory of art, but two other aspects of Kant's theory must be mentioned before we reach our goal, the comparison of Kant's

---

own examples of cases of beauty, such as the free beauty of a flower or of a decorative border on wallpaper, that do not clearly have intellectual content. In "Enjoying the Unbeautiful: From Mendelssohn's Theory of 'Mixed Sentiments' to Kant's Aesthetic Judgments of Reflection," *Journal of Aesthetics and Art Criticism* 67 (2009): 181–9, Rueger suggests that in the third *Critique* Kant restricts his earlier generalization of the identity between free play and symbolization to the case of artistic beauty (p. 183); even with that restriction, such a conception of free play is in tension with Kant's examples from the sphere of decorative arts and music without words.

theory to Mendelssohn's. The first is this. We have just seen that in his theory of genius Kant assumes that art (typically) has content, namely ideas of reason, expressed in aesthetic form. But just before giving his full analysis of genius, Kant has also mentioned that (much) art has content in the sense of representing *objects*; presumably, although he does not spell this out, Kant means that art typically expresses rational *ideas* such as those of virtue and vice by representing *objects*, often human beings behaving and speaking in particular ways, but perhaps animals, mountains, clouds and lightning, or whatever. He then states that "Beautiful art displays its excellence precisely by describing beautifully things that in nature would be ugly or displeasing. The furies, diseases, devastations of war and the like can, as harmful things, be very beautifully described, indeed represented in painting" (*CPJ* §48, 5:312). Although Kant does not use Mendelssohn's terminology, this clearly presupposes that we can respond differentially to what is represented and to the representation itself, as Mendelssohn had argued: We can take pleasure in a beautiful representation of something that is not by itself beautiful and that would not by itself produce pleasure, the pleasure in the beauty of the representation presumably outweighing the painfulness of the thought of the represented content. Kant adds that "only one kind of ugliness cannot be represented in a way adequate to nature, without destroying all aesthetic satisfaction, hence beauty in art, namely that which arouses **loathing** [*Ekel*]" (5:312). Mendelssohn had used the same term to say that in spite of the distinction between the perfections of representation and the (im-)perfections of what is represented and the possibility of the pleasure of the former outweighing any displeasure at the latter, there are some things that are beyond the pale of artistic representation. We will see, however, that there is an interesting difference in their explanations of this limitation, and one that might suggest that Kant's explanation was intended as an alternative to Mendelssohn's, his intention signaled by his use of the same word as his target.

But before we do that, a final comment on Kant's sketch of a system of the arts. Kant replaces Mendelssohn's twofold distinction between the "beautiful sciences" of poetry and eloquence and the "fine arts" of painting, sculpture, architecture, music, and dance with a threefold distinction, among (1) the arts of speech, poetry, and rhetoric; (2) the visual (*bildende*) arts, in turn divided into the "plastic" arts of "sensible truth," namely sculpture and architecture, and the art of "sensible illusion," namely painting; and finally (3) the arts of the "**beautiful play of sensations**," namely music and an "**art of colors**" (*CPJ* §51, 5:321–4). Dance does not figure in Kant's initial list of the arts. Two points are noteworthy here. First, Kant does not actually maintain the view that all art involves content, holding rather that the arts of the play of sensation, namely (at least some) music and the (unexplained) art of a mere play of colors, do not have intellectual content—and are lesser arts for that reason. But second, Kant also observes that in the case of those arts that do have intellectual content, there are actually three dimensions of expression:

Thus if we wish to divide the beautiful arts, we can, at least as an experiment, choose no easier principle than the analogy of art with the kind of expression that people use in speaking in order to communicate to each other, i.e., not merely their concepts, but also their sentiments [*Empfindungen*].—This consists in the **word**, the **gesture**, and the **tone** (articulation, gesticulations, and modulation). Only the combination of these three kinds of expression constitutes the speaker's complete communication. For thought, intuition, and sentiment are thereby conveyed to the other simultaneously and united. (*CPJ* §51, 5:320)

Kant subsequently compares the "aesthetic value" of the different arts to one another on the basis of how fully they can exploit these three dimensions, i.e., whether they are able to communicate thought as well as intuition and sensation, or only the latter (§53). Kant borrows this scheme from Charles Batteux, not from Mendelssohn,[17] but there is also a potential link to Mendelssohn here, at least if Kant's word *Empfindungen* should indeed be translated as "sentiments" and not merely "sensations."[18] How the term should be translated is indeed problematic. Kant uses the same word when he comes to the arts of music and the play of colors, and there indeed it seems as if he is talking about what we would call, in contemporary English, mere sensations: hearing sounds of a particular frequency, seeing particular colors, etc. But poetry, for example, will not typically convey sensations in this sense, although perhaps in some cases it can—words in a poem might make us think of the color of a violet or the smell of fresh-turned earth. Yet it would be much more common to think of poetry as communicating what we would now call sentiments, that is, feelings: how someone might *feel about* something, even about a sensation such as the smell of fresh-turned earth. It seems natural to think of Kant's model of "complete" communication as holding that speakers typically communicate both some content, in Kant's terms, thought, to others, through the particular words used, but also how they feel about that content, through their gesture and tone, their gesticulation and modulation—the latter seem better fitted to communicate feelings rather than concepts; thus Kant seems to be suggesting that complete communication, outside the arts but also inside the arts, involves the communication of feelings as well as thoughts—and that the different arts may be graded on how well they can do both of these things.

It would in turn be natural to suppose that *communicating* feelings as well as thoughts requires *stimulating* feelings as well as thoughts in the audience for the communication. This would bring Kant's view into the proximity of Mendelssohn's. Yet Kant does not say this outright. But let's take this question as our signal that it is time to turn to the comparison of the two authors.

---

[17] Charles Batteux, *The Fine Arts Reduced to a Single Principle* (1746), Part III, Section Three, Chapter One; in the translation by James O. Young (Oxford: Oxford University Press, 2015, p. 129. As we previously saw, Batteux's work had been translated into German early, by Ramler. Kant could also have been familiar with the extensively commentated edition, *Einschränkung der Schönen Künste auf einem Grundsatz, aus dem Französichen übersetzt, und mit verschiedenen eignen damit verwandten Abhandlungen begleitet von Johann Adolf Schlegel* (Leipzig: Weidmann, 1770).

[18] As I did translate it, perhaps wrongly, in the Cambridge edition, p. 198.

# 8
# Mendelssohn's and Kant's Aesthetics Compared

As we have just seen, in his discussion of fine art Kant exploits the distinction between our response to what is represented by a work of art and our response to the qualities of the representation itself that is a centerpiece of Mendelssohn's aesthetics. But Mendelssohn framed this distinction in terms of that between objective and subjective perfections, perfections of the represented object and perfections of the representation, the latter in turn understood in terms of the perfections of the representing mind consisting in the improved condition of its cognitive faculties on the one hand and its desiderative and evaluative faculties on the other, all of those in turn connected with the improved condition of the body in aesthetic perception. And Kant rejects perfectionism as a basis for aesthetic theory. Does this mean that he borrows Mendelssohn's distinction between representation and what is represented without accepting any of Mendelssohn's own conceptual framework for this distinction? That would be too strong a conclusion. In fact what Kant rejects is an interpretation of aesthetic judgment as confused perception of *objective* perfections without dismissing anything like Mendelssohn's account of *subjective* perfection, while his own account of aesthetic response as subjective *purposiveness* seems similar in spirit if not in letter to Mendelssohn's. There are at least two important differences between the accounts, namely Kant's greater emphasis on the *free play* of the cognitive faculties in aesthetic response and Mendelssohn's insistence from the outset of his argument that mental capacities for desire and moral judgment as well as cognition are involved. But even here the differences may be more a matter of emphasis than of fundamental disagreement. Mendelssohn's explanation of our pleasure in beauty in terms of subjective perfection and Kant's in terms of subjective purposiveness are closer than Kant lets on.

In his attack upon perfectionism in §15 of the Analytic of the Beautiful, what Kant explicitly rejects is the explanation of our pleasure in beauty as due to a confused perception of the perfection of the beautiful *object*, either the "external" "purposiveness" lying in the utility of the object or the "internal" "perfection" constituted by the object's exemplary exemplification of its type. Kant begins his critique with the statement that "**Objective** purposiveness can be cognized only by means of the relation of the manifold to a determinate end, thus only through a concept" (*CPJ* §15, 5:226), but he never breathes a word against Mendelssohn's idea of subjective perfection or the perfection of the condition of the mind (and body) as the explanation of our pleasure in beauty. He claims that the difference between judgments of beauty and judgments of utility is obvious, although, as we saw, in the very next section (§16) he recognizes the category of adherent beauty, and thus allows that judgments of utility can be *relevant* to aesthetic judgment, at least as *restricting conditions* on our experience of beauty. Perhaps he does not devote more attention to the rejection of utility in §15 precisely because he is going to allow it at least partially back in to aesthetic experience in §16. He devotes more attention to what he specifically calls perfection, namely the internal perfection of objects. This he further divides into two sorts, namely the "**qualitative perfection**" that a thing is judged to have in light of a "concept of **what sort of thing it is supposed to be**" and the "**quantitative perfection**" of a thing "in which **what the thing is supposed to be** is thought of as already determined and it is only asked whether **everything** that is requisite for it exists" (§15, 5:227). Although Kant insists that these two kinds of internal objective perfection are "entirely distinct" from each other, it is difficult to see to what this distinction actually amounts. Perhaps a distinction between the question whether a particular object satisfies all the criteria or in Kant's language "marks" of a sortal concept that is applied to it and the question of whether it satisfies each of these marks to some sort of maximum or high degree might be clearer. But no matter; Kant's fundamental objection against equating aesthetic judgment with any kind of judgment of objective perfection is just that any such judgment presupposes some determinate concept, while an "aesthetic judgment [is] one that rests on subjective grounds, and its determining ground cannot be a concept" (5:228). It is no help, Kant claims, that on the perfectionist approach the recognition of the concept is held to be sensory and confused rather than intellectual and distinct; his position is that the judgment is not aesthetic if it is a judgment that an object satisfies the marks of a determinate concept, whether that judgment is confused or distinct. This position is of course grounded in Kant's general thesis that the distinction between intuitions and concepts, between sensibility and understanding, is a fundamental distinction in kind and role in cognition, not a merely "logical" distinction between confusion and distinctness (*CPR* A 42–5/B 59–63)—or perhaps as we might now say, not a phenomenological distinction.

Although Mendelssohn himself began the letters *On Sentiments* with a criticism of the view that something as negative as mere confusion could explain our pleasure in beauty, such an explanation requiring something positive (Fourth Letter, *PW* 19, *JubA* 1:247), Kant's criticism might still find a target in Mendelssohn's account of the objective perfection or perfections the perception of which contributes to beauty. Mendelssohn's initial account of such perfection is highly formal, "sameness, oneness in a manifold" (Fifth Letter, *PW* 22, *JubA* 1:250; cf. Eleventh Letter, *PW* 48, *JubA* 1:280), and it is not clear that a recognition of such a property requires a concept; perhaps repeating sensory contents of one kind or another, for example colors or tones, could be recognized without a concept. But his fuller description of objective perfection in the "Rhapsody" offers more of a target for Kant. Here Mendelssohn says that "The affirmative marks [*Merkmale*, Kant's word also] of a thing [*Sache*] constitute the elements of perfection, just as its negative marks constitute the elements of its imperfection. For the affirmative marks, insofar as they are in fact affirmative, are in accord with one another... Thus they provide the thing with a manifoldness that harmonizes into something common, i.e., *perfection*. The negative marks on the contrary rob the thing either of its manifoldness or of the harmony of the manifold" ("Rhapsody," *PW* 132–3, *JubA* 1:384–5). Mendelssohn does not say so, but Christian Wolff's account of perfection, which provided the background for his own, clearly states that perfection depends on whether the properties or literally parts of a thing fit together in the way *determined by its concept*, whether that be a concept of its intended function, as in the case of a watch, or just of its characteristic organization, as in the case of an organism. Wolff explicitly applies his conception of perfection to a case from the fine arts, holding that the perfection of a painting consists in its similarity to its object, and supposes that there are rules for producing and recognizing such similarity.[1] The recognition of perfection, so understood, requires the subsumption of the object under a determinate concept, whether the mental recognition of that subsumption be clear or confused. So Mendelssohn's account of the role of objective perfection in the response to beauty, when spelled out, seems subject to Kant's criticism. More concretely, when Mendelssohn comes to the typical content of so much art, namely the virtues and vices of represented human characters and actions, it would seem hard to deny that our response to these could take place without conceptualization of them as the kinds of things and events they are and the kinds of virtues and vices they represent. If Kant's criticism is sound at all, it is sound here.

Then again, when Kant comes to the case of art, it is far from clear that he pays much attention to his own critique of objective perfection. As we saw, he recognizes that we can have a beautiful representation of something, including something morally ugly, such as the devastations of war. The judgment of the latter presumably requires the use of concepts. It might be open to Kant to claim that the recognition of such disvalue, mediated as it must be by concepts, only *detracts* from beauty, while the recognition of positive value, say in an artistic representation of post-war reconstruction, mediated as it is by concepts, does not *add* anything to beauty. Perhaps. But more importantly, Kant's characterization of the content of fine art as aesthetic ideas that are in turn presentations of rational ideas makes it very difficult for him to sustain a view that our response to objective perfections, as his predecessors would have put it, plays no role at all in our response to art. To be sure, Kant insists that the ideas of reason that are presented in aesthetic form are *indeterminate* concepts, concepts that can never be fully spelled out nor fully instantiated in ordinary experience. An idea of reason is "a concept to which no **intuition** (representation of the imagination) can be adequate," while an aesthetic, imaginative presentation of an idea of reason "aesthetically enlarges the concept itself in an unbounded way" (*CPJ* §49, 5:314–15). So there are concepts in the contents of works of art, and it is difficult to believe that these concepts do not color our total aesthetic response, whether positive or negative, to such works. The key point for Kant is that these concepts, as ideas of reason, are indeterminate in a way that ordinary concepts of type or function are not. But this does not seem such a great difference from the perfectionist position that the recognition of concepts in aesthetic

---

[1] See Christian Wolff, *Vernünftige Gedancken von Gott, der Welt, und der Seele des Menschen* ("German Metaphysics"), fourth ed. (Halle: Renger, 1751), §§152, 404.

response is confused, or if it is a difference, it is that Kant puts a positive spin on the indeterminacy of ideas of reason while the concept of confusion sounds pejorative. But that was Mendelssohn's own criticism of the more traditional rationalist aesthetics in Theocles's response to Euphranor. Kant's criticism of objective perfection seems as much in the spirit of Mendelssohn's own criticism of a simpler rationalism as it is a criticism of Mendelssohn.

Whether or not this conclusion is right, it should be clear that there is considerable affinity between Mendelssohn's conception of the *subjective perfections* of the mind in aesthetic experience and Kant's conception of the *subjective purposiveness* of aesthetic response. Kant's language almost signals that he is accepting this half of Mendelssohn's account even if he takes himself to be rejecting the objective half. Again, Theocles's response to Euphranor was that "the pure gratification of the soul must be grounded in the positive powers [*Kräften*] of the soul and not in its incapacity [*Unvermögen*], not in the limitation of these original powers" (Fourth Letter, *PW* 19, *JubA* 1:248), and in the "Rhapsody" Mendelssohn had expanded upon this point by arguing that "perceiving and recognizing" are not merely responses to the objective perfections or imperfections of things but are "affirmative determinations" of the soul, powers of it the exercise of which we enjoy in its own right. He had claimed that "every representation, at least in relation to the subject, as an affirmative predicate of the thinking entity, must have something about it that we like," and he had accommodated the case of the artistic representation of evil actions and other forms of disvalue by supposing that we like the exercise our faculty of approving and disapproving on those objects even if we do not like the objects themselves ("Rhapsody," *PW* 133, *JubA* 1:385–6). Some pages further, Mendelssohn used verbs for mental activity in claiming that in "the mind's projection, the movement and stirring which is produced in the soul by unpleasant representations cannot be anything else but pleasant," and called these "movements of the mind" (*Gemüthsbewegungen*) (*PW* 137, *JubA* 1:389).[2] The subjective perfection of the mind thus consists in its own activity, one in which multiple faculties of the mind are brought into play together, but Mendelssohn does not claim that the mind must have any concept *of* its own activity in order to enjoy it. Kant, meanwhile, characterizes the condition of the mind in aesthetic response as subjective "purposiveness" rather than "perfection," but he similarly places great emphasis on the *activity* of the mind as the source of our pleasure. This is evident in the conclusion of the second moment of the Analytic of the Beautiful, when Kant states that "The animation [*Belebung*] of both faculties (the imagination and the understanding) to an activity that is indeterminate but yet, through the stimulus of the given representation, in unison, namely that which belongs to a cognition in general, is the sensation"—of pleasure—"whose universal communicability is postulated by the judgment of taste" (*CPJ* §9, 5:219); and then in the third moment he characterizes

---

[2] Anne Pollok also stresses that Mendelssohn's conception of the perfection of the mind in aesthetic experience is an active one—*Vervollkommnung* and not mere *Vollkommenheit*—one on which there is *Harmonisierung* of mental faculties, in which "sentiments and cognitions are brought into concord, although each domain preserves its own identity"; *Facetten des Menschen: Zur Anthropologie Moses Mendelssohns* (Hamburg: Felix Meiner Verlag, 2010), pp. 241–2.

our feeling of pleasure in beauty as "The consciousness of the merely formal purposiveness in the play of the cognitive powers of the subject... because it contains a determining ground of the activity of the subject with regard to the animation of its cognitive powers" (§12, 5:222). The formal or as he also calls it "subjective purposiveness" (§11, 5:221) of the mind in aesthetic experience is nothing other than the pleasurable consciousness of the mind's activity, just as it is in Mendelssohn's account of subjective perfection.[3] In this case there does not seem to be much difference between "purposiveness" and "perfection."

Thus Kant's core conception of aesthetic experience seems deeply Mendelssohnian. To be sure, there are noticeable differences between the two accounts. These are hinted at in the passages just quoted, in which Kant has emphasized that the mental activity in aesthetic experience is *free play* and has also *restricted* it to the mental powers of imagination and understanding. Yet on the first point, one might still ask whether the difference between the two is as great as initially seems. On the one hand, Mendelssohn does not use the phrase "free play," although his friend Lessing comes close at least once in his *Laokoön*, when he says that the representation of the battle of the gods over the fate of the Trojans in the *Iliad* (Book XXI, line 385) as invisible "gives the imagination free rein to enlarge the scene and envisage the persons and actions of the gods on a grander scale than the measure of ordinary man."[4] But on the other hand, Kant's own usage of the phrase is deeply metaphorical, perhaps derived from but by no means denoting the same as "play" (*Spiel*) in such contexts as children's play, playing sports, a play in the theater, etc. What Kant means by free play has to be cashed out, and the only way in which it is plausible to cash it out is as a harmony between imagination and other cognitive powers arrived at without the ordinary use of concepts or rules.[5] Since Mendelssohn so clearly stresses that the perception of beauty involves cognitive harmony, the question then becomes whether there is a significant difference between them on the governing role of concepts or rules in aesthetic experience.

We have just argued that the first question comes down to whether Kant's allowance of the role of *indeterminate* concepts in the content of art is a significant departure from Mendelssohn. On the question of the role of rules, we saw that Mendelssohn allowed only a limited role for rules in art, as "preparations by means of which the poet [or other artist] should be putting himself and the object to be worked over into a state where the beauties are shown in their most flattering light," but which should not "disturb" the "virtuoso" "in the heat of the work itself" (Fourth Letter, *PW* 18, *JubA* 1:246–7). As Kant does with his characterization of rules as the mere "mechanism" of art, Mendelssohn suggests that rules can never be more than necessary, not sufficient conditions for the creation of beauty (and presumably,

---

[3] For an approach to Kant's aesthetics that emphasizes aesthetic pleasure as the "feeling of life," see Ross Wilson, *Subjective Universality in Kant's Aesthetics* (Bern: Peter Lang, 2007), chapter 4, pp. 109–46.
[4] Gotthold Ephraim Lessing, *Laocoön: An Essay on the Limits of Painting and Poetry*, trans. Edward Allen McCormick (Indianapolis: Bobbs-Merrill, 1962), Chapter Twelve, p. 66.
[5] See Paul Guyer, "The Harmony of the Faculties Revisited," in Rebecca Kukla, ed., *Aesthetics and Cognition in Kant's Critical Philosophy* (Cambridge: Cambridge University Press, 2006), pp. 162–93, reprinted in Paul Guyer, *Values of Beauty: Historical Essays in Aesthetics* (Cambridge: Cambridge University Press, 2005), pp. 77–109.

*mutatis mutandis*, for the reception of it). More concretely, Mendelssohn describes a number of ways in which artists exercise their imaginations, and, again presumably, the imaginations of their audiences in response to their work. In a not entirely fair criticism of Batteux, who did not in fact think otherwise, Mendelssohn argues that an artist does not simply imitate nature, but "must accordingly elevate himself above common nature, and, since beauty is his sole, final purpose, he is free to concentrate this beauty everywhere in his works so that it might move us all the more intensely" ("Main Principles," *PW* 176, *JubA* 1:435).[6] "Nature has perhaps never had to produce a human character such as Charles Grandison, but the poet takes the trouble to portray him as, in keeping with the prevailing will of God, the human being would have had to become. He set up an ideal beauty as a standard..." (*PW* 177, *JubA* 1:436).[7] Since humans have no direct knowledge of the will of God, such a creation of an ideal is clearly an act of imagination. The creation of such an ideal in art does not seem to differ much from what Kant has in mind when he talks about the aesthetic presentation of an idea of reason, such as that of virtue (in the case of Sir Charles Grandison) or vice, which must involve the imagination in order to find a sensory way to present an idea that is not directly sensory. The difference seems to be chiefly that Kant foregrounds the word "imagination" (*Einbildungskraft*) while Mendelssohn uses it more sparingly. This difference is not trivial, since Kant states more clearly than Mendelssohn does that the free play of imagination is the *sine qua non* of all aesthetic experience and of the creation and reception of art, while Mendelssohn does not. Still, their theories are not entirely different in kind.

The second question raised was whether Kant's account of the faculties involved in his conception of subjective purposiveness as the free play of the mental powers is more restrictive than Mendelssohn's conception of the positive powers of the mind involved in its subjective perfection. On first glance, this must be the case: Kant repeatedly says that the free play is between imagination and understanding, while Mendelssohn says that the positive powers of the mind involved in the experience of beauty are the "mental powers of knowing and desiring" or the powers of knowing and approbation or disapprobation (*Billigung* and *Mißbilligung*) ("Rhapsody," *PW* 133, *JubA* 1:35-6). Mendelssohn's power of knowing would seem to include the faculty of reason, which Kant does not initially mention on his list, and the powers of desire and approbation or disapprobation are not obviously cognitive powers at all. But we saw that when Kant came to the case of adherent beauty, he had to allow concepts of function and thus the faculty of empirical practical reason into his mix, and when he came to the case of art, he allowed the ideas of reason and thus the faculty of pure practical reason into his model; so the initial restriction of the faculties involved in free play to imagination and understanding is clearly relaxed over the course of Kant's exposition, perhaps having served its purpose of allowing Kant to introduce the idea of free play with the simplest case of beauty, that of the pure

---

[6] That Batteux's own conception of the "imitation" of nature is actually a model of the idealization of nature in the form of "*la belle nature*," see Batteux, *The Fine Arts Reduced to a Single Principle*, Part I, Chapter 3, pp. 11–14, and Part II, Chapter Two, pp. 32–4.

[7] The reference is to Samuel Richardson, *The History of Sir Charles Grandison* (London: Hitch and Hawes *et al.*, 1754).

beauty of natural objects such as flowers and seashells, before moving on to the more complex cases of adherent and artistic beauty.

Nevertheless, there does appear to be a significant difference with Mendelssohn in Kant's restriction of the proper objects of taste to such versions of form as design in painting and composition in music in the second moment of the Analytic of the Beautiful. Mendelssohn criticized Meier and Baumgarten for, at least as he saw it, focusing entirely on the "thoughts" expressed in works of art at the cost of recognizing the sensible features of representations that we can find pleasing. In Mendelssohn's words, "*The first part of Meier's First Principles deals with the different kinds of beauty in sensory cognition.* Only one finds nothing other than the *beauty of thoughts* mentioned. Not a syllable is devoted to *figures, lines, movement, tones, and colors*, and all the doctrines and principles are expounded as if these beauties could make no claim to such status."[8] Mendelssohn tasks Meier and through him Baumgarten with having neglected the entire range of sensory properties in their account of beauty, both what would be called from a Kantian point of view formal properties, such as line, figure, and perhaps movement, and material properties (in Kant's sense in which sensation is the matter of perception; CPR A 20/B 34, A 165/B 207), such as color and tone. Mendelssohn clearly holds that the whole range of material, formal, and intellectual properties of representations can properly enter into our experience of beauty. Kant, however, seems to go to the opposite extreme from Mendelssohn, allowing that only such formal properties as line and figure are proper objects of taste, thus not more material sensory qualities such as color and tone on the one hand and intellectual properties—concepts—on the other (see again CPR §14, 5:225). Kant's free play seems to be limited to a play with form, while Mendelssohn's conception of the activity of the positive powers of the mind is limited in no such way.

We have already seen that over the course of his exposition, Kant clearly relaxes his initial exclusion of conceptual content from the aesthetically significant properties of art, so this difference between him and Mendelssohn gradually disappears. But what about their difference on the matter of colors and tones? Here things are murkier. Kant concedes that *pure* colors and tones may be proper objects of the experience of beauty, but only because he allows that the uniform vibrations of light or air that produce such experiences may be considered to be forms and to be apprehended by us, even if subconsciously, as forms. At least in the third edition of the third *Critique* he allows that this hypothesis of Euler may be correct (*CPJ* §14, 5:224). But that seems a narrow concession. Later on in the text, he suggests that different colors might have different, "higher," moral meanings, as the "white color of the lily seems to dispose the mind to ideas of innocence," red to the ideas of sublimity, blue to the idea of modesty, and so on (§42 5:302), and presumably colors may play such a role in works of art, as the use of blue for the cloak of the mother of Jesus signifies her virginity or yellow in Chinese art signifies imperial authority. Perhaps Kant is anticipating his subsequent discussion of aesthetic ideas and allowing that the use

---

[8] Review of G.F. Meier, *Auszug aus den Anfangsgründen aller schönen Künste und Wissencahften*, in *Bibliothek der schönen Wissenschaften und der freyen Künste*, 3. Band, 1. Stuck (June, 1758): 130–8, JubA 4:196–201, at pp. 199–200.

of colors may be one of the ways in which the imagination presents rational ideas, but he does not mention this possibility in his later discussion of aesthetic ideas, focusing instead on how the imagination uses such "attributes" as Jupiter's eagle and Juno's peacock to present ideas of their power and dignity imaginatively (§49, 5:315)—in other words, he recognizes the importance of iconography in art, but not explicitly the importance of sensations such as colors and tones. Only in the case of the arts of the "**beautiful play of sensations,**" namely "**music and the art of colors,**" does he seem to allow that combinations of tones or colors might be beautiful on their own. But even here he hedges his bets, first again raising the possibility that it must actually be something formal to which we are responding in these cases, such as "the rapidity of the vibrations of the light" if such arts are to be genuinely "**beautiful**" rather than merely "**agreeable**" (§51, 5:324–5), and also suggesting, if simply by the third place of these arts in his list of the arts, that the expressive potential of these arts falls far short of that of the literary and pictorial arts. In the end, one can only conclude that Kant's recognition of the contribution of "material," sensory qualities such as color and tone to the aesthetic impact of the arts was very limited, in historical terms that his position was ultimately closer to that of Baumgarten and Meier, and that on this issue Mendelssohn should be awarded the palm. No more than Kant did Mendelssohn foresee paintings, for example, that might be deeply moving as much in virtue of the relations among their colors as those among their forms, such as the paintings of Josef Albers or Mark Rothko, but he certainly left the door open to a much wider contribution of such properties as color and tone to the overall effect of art than did Kant.

But the even more important question about the restrictiveness of Kant's conception of the proper objects of taste in comparison to Mendelssohn's concerns *Empfindungen*—always translated as "sentiments" in Mendelssohn and sometimes, as already argued, correctly so translated in Kant. I suggested in the previous chapter that late in his work Kant does at least leave the door open for counting sentiments— meaning the large range of ordinary emotions, such as joy and fear, admiration and contempt, sympathy and disdain, and so on—as proper parts of aesthetic response, at least of the response to art, in his enumeration of word, gesture, and tone as parts of expression in general and of artistic expression. Of course words often carry an emotional charge and are not properly understood without understanding that charge, which we might think in turn requires *feeling* the relevant emotion to some degree; but even when the specific words spoken, by a character or in the persona of the author, do not carry an explicit emotional charge, the gesture and tone with which they are spoken, or which is otherwise suggested by the work of art, will certainly communicate emotion (*mutatis mutandis* for other kinds of signifiers in other media). And it is natural to suppose that not only understanding but also feeling such emotion is a normal part of properly apprehending the entire expression. But only in the case of music does Kant explicitly suggest that emotions might be part of the normal response to art, and then only under the abstract term "affects" without mentioning any particular garden-style emotions.

Thus, in the "Comparison of the aesthetic value of the beautiful arts with each other" that follows the classification of the arts (after an intervening section "On the combination of the beautiful arts in one and the same product," §52, in which Kant acknowledges such forms as opera, oratorio, and dance), Kant praises poetry for its "fullness of thought to which no linguistic expression is adequate, and thus elevates itself aesthetically to the level of ideas."

It strengthens the mind by letting itself feel its capacity to consider and judge of nature, as appearance, freely, self-actively, and independently of determination by nature, in accordance with points of view that nature does not present by itself in experience either for sense or for the understanding, and thus to use it for the sake of and as it were as the schema of the supersensible. (*CPJ* §53, 5:326).

One might initially think that what no linguistic expression can adequately capture would be the emotional concomitants of the thought articulated by a verbal sign, but that is not what Kant goes on to suggest. His claim is rather that poetry is uniquely suited to convey *thoughts*, that is, intellectual content, concepts, that cannot be determinately *articulated*, namely, thoughts of the supersensible. On Kant's usual account of our only permissible thoughts of the supersensible, that would mean thoughts of God, human freedom, and human immortality. But Kant says nothing at all about the emotions that might ordinarily be thought to accompany or be stirred by such ideas, although most people would think such emotions to be a normal part of entertaining such ideas, and the aim of stirring them to be a normal part of the artistic expression of such ideas. Kant seems to be describing what it might be like to read Milton's *Paradise Lost* or Klopstock's *Messias* as a purely intellectual but not an emotional experience. The same seems to be true in Kant's previous description of aesthetic ideas. He says:

The poet ventures to make sensible rational ideas of invisible beings, the kingdom of the blessed, the kingdom of hell, eternity, creation, etc., as well as to make that of which there are examples in experience, e.g., death, envy, and all sorts of vices, as well as love, fame, etc., sensible beyond the limits of experience, with a completeness that goes beyond anything of which there is an example in nature, by means of an imagination that emulates the precedent of reason in attaining to a maximum; and it is really the art of poetry in which the faculty of aesthetic ideas can reveal itself in its full measure. This faculty, however, considered by itself alone, is really only a talent (of the imagination). (§49, 5:314).

Kant breathes not one word of the emotions that might be thought naturally to accompany such ideas. He talks only of the way in which through aesthetic ideas, that is, the aesthetic presentation of a theme through characters, attributes, and so on, the imagination emulates reason's motion toward "a maximum," that is, an *intellectual* expansion beyond the ordinary limits of sensibility. Contrast this with Mendelssohn's description of the effect of the presentation of a sublime character in his essay "On the Sublime and Naïve in the Fine Sciences": "We wish, hope, and fear for the object of our love or our sympathy and admire his or her great soul that is beyond hope and fear... These, then, are the most distinguished sorts of awe which can spring from the object itself without its being necessary to draw the perfections of the artist into consideration as well" (*PW*, 198–9, *JubA* 1:462). Here Mendelssohn leaves aside our admiration for the skill of the artist to focus on the range of our emotional reactions to the content of works of art, depicted characters, and their noble actions. The kingdoms of heaven and hell, vices and virtues, would likewise seem to be ideas destined to produce a similar range of emotions (including negative ones triggered by thoughts of hell, vice, etc.). Kant's silence on this side of aesthetic experience is so deafening that it is hard to read it except as an explicit rejection of Mendelssohn's more natural position.

As I said, Kant does acknowledge that music arouses "affects." Thus he says that "every expression of language has, in context, a tone that is appropriate to its sense; that this tone more or less designates an affect of the speaker and conversely also produces one in the hearer, which then in turn arouses in the latter the idea that is expressed in the language by means of such a tone; and that...the art of tone," namely music, "puts that language into practice for itself alone...namely as a language of the affects, and so, in accordance with the law of association, universally communicates the aesthetic ideas that are naturally combined with it" (*CPJ* §53, 5:328–9). Two things should be noted about this passage. First, although Kant now concedes that affects or emotions are naturally associated with aesthetic ideas, he emphasizes that music uses such associations to suggest ideas rather than the other way around. He thus plays down the importance of the arousal of affects: it is a mere means to the end of conveying ideas. This may be a reasonable thing to say about music without text, which could not otherwise directly convey abstract ideas of virtue and vice and the rest. But it also suggests that communicating emotions, if it is a legitimate aim of art at all, is of only subsidiary importance. And, second, Kant makes perfectly clear the lesser status of music insofar as it does aim at producing affects. He says that music comes close to poetry only "**if what is at issue is charm and movement of the mind**" (5:328)—"charm" being the very word Kant had earlier used in connection with taste that is still "barbaric" (§13, 5:223). Music "does not, like poetry, leave behind something for reflection"; "it moves the mind in more manifold and, though only temporarily, in deeper ways"—perhaps that refers to its emotional impact—"but it is, to be sure, more enjoyment than culture (the play of thought that is aroused by it in passing is merely the effect of an as it were mechanical association)" (§53, 5:328). Kant cannot fail to notice the emotional impact of music, but he speaks of it in terms that come close to contempt. If "one estimates the value of the beautiful arts in terms of the culture that they provide for the mind and takes as one's standard the enlargement of the faculties that must join together in the power of judgment for the sake of cognition, then to that extent music occupies the lowest place among the arts" (5:329).

Mendelssohn's attitude toward music is very different because he ranks the communication and arousal of sentiment so highly among the aims or "perfections" of art. To be sure, he argues that because poetry uses the artificial signs of language while music uses natural signs, that is, tones and combinations naturally rather than conventionally linked with various emotions, "All things, possible and actual," can be expressed by poetry and "The poet can express everything of which our soul can have a clear concept," while "Music, the expression of which takes place by means of inarticulate sounds, cannot possibly indicate the content of a rose, a poplar tree, and so on," except of course by being linked to a verbal text ("Main Principles," *PW* 178–9, *JubA* 1:438). But this is not to rank poetry as aesthetically more valuable than music. On the contrary, Mendelssohn argues, although in considering the specific case in which the arts of poetry and music are combined in complex works, such as ancient tragedy, modern opera, and so on, one art might have to bend its rules in favor of the other depending on the overall aim of the work. In live performances of music, he writes, "The voice must sometimes be raised, sometimes lowered in the expression of sentiments, inclinations, and passions," but what might be desirable from the musical point of view, for the maximal expression of sentiment, might have to be tempered "as long as music is only used to give a greater emphasis to the arbitrary signs of poesy" (*PW* 185, *JubA* 1:445). But it is also possible for the "intense, lively, and moving" even if "indeterminate" "expression of sentiment" in music to be the main objective of a work, "in which case all exceptions must take place on the side of poetry" and particular rules of poesy such as "the unity of place, time, and action" can be relaxed if that "happens to be what is best as far as the music is concerned," that is, if that is what is necessary to maximize the emotional impact of the music. In this case the poet "must sketch the sentiments, images, and all musical beauties only, as it were, in outline and provide music with the opportunity of elaborating them and giving the sentiments their true fire, the images life, and the comparisons their similarity" (*PW* 187, *JubA* 1:447–8). This possibility presupposes that the expression and communication of sentiment or emotion can be at least as important an aim of art as the communication of thoughts or intellectual content.

Neither Kant nor Mendelssohn devotes as much attention to the rank of the pictorial or visual arts (*bildende Künste*) relative to the other arts as they do to the relative merits of poetry and music. Kant mentions pictorial art only in passing in his comparison of the value of the various arts, but associates it more closely with poetry than with music. The pictorial arts "far surpass" music, he holds, "for while they set the imagination into a free play that is nevertheless also suitable for the understanding, at the same time they conduct a business by bringing about a product of the understanding as an enduring and self-recommending vehicle for its unification with sensibility and thus as it were for promoting the urbanity of the higher powers of cognition" (*CPJ* §53, 5:329). Kant says nothing about the possible emotional impact of painted or sculpted images, but stresses only their potential contribution to the "business" of the understanding and to the "urbanity" of the *higher* powers of cognition, that is, understanding and reason but certainly not emotion. Mendelssohn, however, in a passage closely connected to the argument of Lessing's *Laokoön*, perhaps indeed the source for Lessing's famous thesis, argues that if a painter correctly chooses the single moment of an action that he can represent, then "When we view such a painting with due attentiveness, our senses are all at once animated, all the capabilities of our soul suddenly become lively, and the imagination can fathom the past from the present while reliably anticipating the future." Painting need not "occupy itself merely with the sort of objects that are visible in and for themselves," on the contrary "Even the subtlest thoughts, the most abstract concepts, can be expressed on canvas," but neither is painting limited in its appeal to our strictly cognitive or intellectual capacities—it can appeal to *all* our faculties, including not just our senses for color and tone, but also, clearly, for sentiment or emotions ("Main Principles," *PW* 180–1, *JubA* 1:440). Perhaps "The expression of inclinations and passions in painting is...not as lively and moving as in music, yet it is nevertheless more distinct and definite" (*PW* 189, *JubA* 1:449). But for Mendelssohn, the expression and communication of inclinations and passions remains as important an aim of art as the communication of distinct and definite ideas.

So while Mendelssohn recognizes the centrality of the expression of emotion in our experience of art, Kant either ignores it where it would seem natural to acknowledge it, or downgrades it where he cannot avoid acknowledging it. What explains this difference between theories that we have seen are otherwise more alike than not? One point has already been mentioned, namely that Mendelssohn is not as obsessed with the universal subjective validity of judgments of taste upon which Kant insists and would not be tempted to eliminate sentiments from the proper response to art because allowing them in might introduce a potential source of disagreement in aesthetic judgment. But no doubt a deeper reason for the difference lies in the way that Kant downplays the role of emotion in *moral motivation* while Mendelssohn takes emotion to be a central part of moral motivation. This is not the place for an extensive contrast between the moral philosophies of the two authors, and indeed, as I mentioned in the Prologue, Mendelssohn never fully developed a moral philosophy after his brief treatment of the subject in his prize essay. So a few points will have to suffice here.

At some point after completing his own prize essay in 1762, Kant became determined to establish that the content of the fundamental *principle* of morality cannot be determined by any form of sentiment, even love of fellow human beings. In the *Groundwork for the Metaphysics of Morals*, the first of his main works on moral philosophy but the only one that Mendelssohn could have read before his death, he argued that the only morally worthy *motivation* is that of respect for the moral law itself, which might express itself at the level of experience in terms of a distinctive *feeling* of respect, but a feeling which is itself "self-wrought" by reason, that is, an "effect" of the "determination of the will by means of the [moral] law" (G 4:401n.), which he will eventually explain takes place at the noumenal level—the choice of the moral law is a free choice of the will as it is in itself, not a determined choice of the will as it appears in space and time—and is not a matter of feeling at all. As early as in his notes in his own copy of his 1764 *Observations on the Feeling of the Beautiful and Sublime* Kant states that, for example, "About compassion it is only to be noted that it must never rule, but must rather be **subordinated** to the capacity and the rational desire to **do** good" (Rischmüller 46, NF No. 16, p. 8), and as late as the 1797 *Metaphysics of Morals* he says that while moral motivation is a matter of will, "Love is a matter of *feeling*, not of willing, and I cannot love because I *will* to, still less because I *ought* to" (MM DV Introduction, section XII.c, 6:401). So love in the ordinary sense of feeling cannot be the basis of moral motivation, let alone of the moral principle, although love in the ordinary sense, what Kant calls "pathological" love, not to express contempt about it but just to indicate that it is a matter of feeling, may as a matter of empirical fact come about as an *effect* of continued "practical" love, that is, beneficence toward others exercised out of principle rather than mere feeling (*MM* DV, §25, 6:449–50).

So when Kant says, in his remark following the completion of the two Analytics of the Beautiful and Sublime, that "The beautiful prepares us to love something, even nature, without interest; the sublime, to esteem it, even contrary to our (sensible) interest" (*CPJ* General Remark following §29, 5:267), it seems most natural, given the works in moral philosophy that he had just completed and was still to write, to interpret him as meaning that aesthetic judgment teaches us to *evaluate* our feelings rather than simply to *have* certain feelings, and to avoid judging immediately upon the basis of first feelings, which might lead simply to judgments of agreeableness in the case of what should be judged to be beauty and to judgments of fearfulness in the case of what should be judged to be sublime. And learning to evaluate and judge our own feelings so as to avoid immediate action upon them is surely a necessary step in learning to act on our feelings only when so doing is consistent with the fundamental principle of morality, which is not itself given by feeling. Kant's remark does not have to be taken to encourage the cultivation of aesthetic feelings because feelings can play an indispensable role in moral judgment or moral evaluation.

Mendelssohn is much friendlier to the role of feelings in moral motivation. After the section on morality in his early prize essay, Mendelssohn never wrote directly on moral theory, nor is moral theory a major subject of the aesthetic essays. There is a discussion of suicide that extends over several of the letters *On Sentiments*, but Mendelssohn's aim in introducing that topic seems to be just to emphasize that what may be effective and permissible on the stage may not be such in real life, thus in providing a concrete illustration of the idea of aesthetic distance that he introduces more formally in the essay on the "Main Principles." But there is one passage in the "Rhapsody" added to the original letters in the editions of 1761 and 1771 that is of interest in the present context. Here Mendelssohn is arguing that the instinct to communicate our feelings is itself one of the perfections of the soul, "implanted in the soul as much as the instinct to preserve oneself." He continues:

No love, no friendship can exist without the benign reproduction of itself. Love is a readiness to take pleasure in someone else's happiness. That means, if one reduces the concepts of happiness and pleasure to their elements, that love is the readiness to regard another's progress to a higher level of perfection as an increase in our own perfection... In the case of the general love of humanity, this takes place to a lesser degree; but in the case of friendship this readiness grows into the inclination to put ourselves completely in the position of our friend and to feel everything that affects him as though it affected us ourselves... Far from cancelling the mutual interest of moral beings [*Wesen*] or even weakening it in the slightest, the basic principle of perfection is instead the source of universal sympathy, of this brotherhood of spirits, if I may be allowed this expression, which engulfs and entwines each person's own interest and the common interest... ("Rhapsody," *PW* 152-3, JubA 1:406-7)

Mendelssohn does not argue that such sentiments as love and sympathy can determine what is right without any principle of reason, but he does argue that these sentiments can lead to moral action toward others, actions that contribute toward the perfection of others. They are also perfections in oneself, and insofar as the fundamental principle of morality for a follower of Wolff and Baumgarten is to maximize the perfection of oneself and others while minimizing their imperfection, the cultivation of such sentiments is itself commanded by the fundamental principle of morality. Insofar as the capacity for sentiment is itself one of the positive powers of the soul, its cultivation would seem to be commanded by morality as a form of maximizing self-perfection; if we can assume that the cultivation of such sentiments in our experience of art contributes to their strengthening for purposes of friendship and brotherhood towards others, then their cultivation would also be commanded by morality as a form of maximizing the perfection of others. Either way, Mendelssohn's conception of morality hardly calls for the suppression of the importance of sentiment in our experience of art.

Perhaps Kant somewhat grudgingly accepted the potential value of the cultivation of sentiments in moral conduct in his final work on the subject, the Doctrine of Virtue of the *Metaphysics of Morals*. As we already saw, in this work he continues to maintain that feelings cannot be commanded and so cannot be the direct object of any moral command, and argues that the feeling of love ought to follow the practice of beneficence, not precede it. Nevertheless, Kant does recognize that, at least at the phenomenal level, "Every determination of choice proceeds *from the representation of a possible action to* the deed through the feeling of pleasure or displeasure, taking an interest in the action or its effect" (*MM* DV, Introduction section XII.a, 4:399) or, presumably, an aversion in the case of a displeasure. If we take the feeling of pleasure and displeasure here to be a generic term covering a range of sentiments, or if we take the phrase to refer to the affective dimension of a variety of emotions, Kant's argument would be that even though the fundamental principle of morality must come from pure reason and even though at some level the will must be determined by pure reason, what this means in practice is that feelings that can promote the performance of morally appropriate actions must be cultivated—cultivated and strengthened, Kant says, because, again, we cannot simply have feelings on command, but we can take steps to strengthen dispositions to feeling that we naturally have (6:400). Kant specifically mentions "love of human beings" and "self-esteem" in this context, and although in his discussion of the former (section XII.c, 6:401–2) he again repeats his argument that to do good to others is a duty and that pathological love for them will follow doing good to them, not precede it, in his subsequent fuller discussion under the rubric of "duties of love" of feelings of *sympathy* he makes it clear that such feelings must be cultivated and strengthened so they can be effective when beneficent action is required (*MM* DV, §§34–5).

However, Kant does not say much about *how* such feelings are to be cultivated. He says that "moral feeling" in general can be cultivated "through wonder at its inscrutable source" (*MM* DV, Introduction, section XII.a, 6:400), but not much more. In particular, he does *not* say that moral feeling or its specific varieties can be cultivated through arousal of them in the experience of art, as Mendelssohn clearly thought. Here one might only conclude that it might have been well had Kant been able to revise his aesthetic theory in light of his eventual revision of his conception of the role of feelings in moral motivation. Then the distance between him and Mendelssohn could have been narrowed without having been entirely effaced.

Mendelssohn is supposed to be the rationalist and Kant the philosopher who attempts to synthesize rationalism and empiricism. But in aesthetics and to some extent in moral philosophy as well, Mendelssohn tends to be more responsive to the full range of human experience, particularly to the weight of sentiments or emotions in the human experience of art and of morality itself. Kant may have had a clearer conception of the role of imagination in the creation and reception of art and of reason in morality, but that tends to come at the cost of his acknowledgment of the emotional dimension of human experience. In particular, his single-minded focus on the possibility of consensus in taste, and on the necessity and universality of the moral law, may push him to deemphasize both sensations and sentiments in aesthetic experience and moral experience, as potential sources of disagreement. At the very least, Kant's acknowledgement of the role of emotions in our experience of art is grudging and conflicted: as we saw in our discussion of his view of music, he cannot suppress the role of "affects" or emotions in our experience of that art, but precisely because of the prominence of those affects in our experience of music he compares it unfavorably to other art forms, above all poetry. And while emphasizing that poetry does involve the moral ideas that are most important to human beings, thus ideas that we would expect to be closely associated with powerful emotions, the experience of which would be a significant part of the point of our engagement with art, Kant gives no emphasis to this fact. We did not linger over Kant's theory of our experience of the sublime, in his view a response to nature rather than art, but in that case too, although Kant cannot deny the emotional nature of the experience, he rushes past it to emphasize the intellectual significance of such experience. Thus throughout his aesthetics, Kant attempts to keep the emotions at arms' length, while Mendelssohn—truer, I dare say, to the experience of most people—foregrounds the emotional dimension of aesthetic experience. As we turn now, in the final part of this study, to a comparison of the two philosophers' views about religion in human society and history, we shall see that here too there are some ways in which Kant is the more extreme rationalist and Mendelssohn produces a more realistic synthesis of empiricism and rationalism.

# PART III
# Religion, Politics, and History

This Part will examine Mendelssohn's and Kant's views on enlightenment, religious liberty, and the relation between church and state, and the possibility of moral progress on human history. In 1784, both Kant and Mendelssohn published essays on the question "What is Enlightenment?" in the *Berlinische Monatsschrift*, although Kant states that he had not yet seen Mendelssohn's paper in the September issue when he wrote his own, published later that year. So Kant's essay is not a reply to Mendelssohn's, but the comparison of the two is instructive. For while Mendelssohn treats enlightenment as both a theoretical and practical matter, Kant's essay makes it clear that he regards it as primarily moral, political, and religious. In particular, he connects enlightenment to "complete freedom" in "religious matters." This leads us to one of the central topics of Mendelssohn's *Jerusalem*, published the year before in 1783, which begins with an argument for the exclusion of coercion in the relation of the state to churches of all denominations but also from the internal affairs of churches. We will then see that while Kant clearly had read *Jerusalem* and his *Religion within the Boundaries of Mere Reason* of 1793 is a response to Mendelssohn on a number of important issues, it does not itself include any argument for the freedom of religion from state interference. This is not because Kant's commitment to the separation of church and state has weakened in the years since the essay on enlightenment, however, but because unlike Mendelssohn's argument, which uses a religious premise, Kant's argument is based on strictly secular, moral premises, and is therefore stated in his works on politics, not on religion. In my discussion of these two works I will also argue that Mendelssohn shows a greater commitment to the cause of religious pluralism than does Kant. This is hardly surprising given Mendelssohn's position as a member of a despised religious minority, but I will argue that it also shows his deeper empiricism, or, as we might say using one of his own favorite terms, his greater common sense when it comes to the question of the enduring role of historical religions in human life. Finally, this Part will conclude with a brief chapter on the two philosophers' views on the prospects for moral progress in human history. This chapter will focus on Kant's response in yet another work of 1793, his essay on "Theory and Practice," to a passage in *Jerusalem* in which Mendelssohn had argued against his own friend Lessing that there can be moral progress in individual human lives but that precisely because of the freedom of individual human beings it is unrealistic to expect continuous moral progress in the human species as a whole. I will suggest that this position fits better with Kant's own commitment to the radical nature of individual freedom in his *Religion* than does the position he defends against Mendelssohn. Here is another point at which Mendelssohn's common sense seems more plausible than Kant's ultimately Leibnizian optimism.

# 9
# Mendelssohn, Kant, and Enlightenment

## 1. Introduction

In September, 1784, Mendelssohn published an essay "On the Question: What is Enlightenment?" in the *Berlinische Monatsschrift*.[1] The essay was based on a paper that he presented to a regular circle of Berlin intellectuals, the Wednesday Club, on May 16 of that year, which in turn was a response to one presented in January by Johann Friedrich Zöllner (1753–1804), a preacher at the Marienkirche in Berlin and later a member of the *Oberkonsistorium*, the supervisory board for the Lutheran church throughout Prussia; Zöllner would also publish a book-length response to Mendelssohn's *Jerusalem* in 1784.[2] Zöllner had initially formulated the question in an essay "Is It Advisable to Sanction Marriage through Religion?" in the December, 1783, issue of the journal, where he asked:

*What is enlightenment?* The question, which is almost as important as the question *What is truth?* should be answered before one begins to enlighten others. And yet I have never found it answered anywhere.[3]

On September 30, 1784, Kant completed an essay with the same title as Mendelssohn's that was published in the December issue of the same journal.[4] He too may have been stimulated by Zöllner's question; since he states at the end of his essay that upon completing it he had seen only the announcement of Mendelssohn's essay but had not yet seen that number of the *Berlinische Monatsschrift*, Kant's essay could not have been formulated as a response to Mendelssohn's. As Kant put it, if he had known of Mendelssohn's essay sooner, then he "should have held back the present essay, which may now stand only in order to find out to what extent chance may bring about agreement in thoughts" (*WIE?*, 8:42). In fact, while both essays offer

---

[1] For the context as well as content of Mendelssohn's essay, see Altmann, *Moses Mendelssohn*, pp. 653–64, and "Das Menschenbild und die Bildung des Menschen nach Moses Mendelssohn," in Altmann, *Die trostvolle Aufklärung: Studien zur Metaphysik und politischen Theorie Moses Mendelssohns* (Stuttgart-Bad Canstatt: Frommann-Holzboog, 1982, pp. 11–27; and Pollok, *Facetten des Menschen*, pp. 426–68.

[2] Johann Friedrich Zöllner, *Ueber Moses Mendelssohn's Jerusalem* (Berlin: Friedrich Maurer, 1784).

[3] Quoted from editor's introduction to the translation of Kant's "What is Enlightenment?," in Kant, *Practical Philosophy*, ed. Mary J. Gregor (Cambridge: Cambridge University Press, 1996), p. 13.

[4] For other contributions to the debate, see James Schmidt, *What Is Enlightenment? Eighteenth-Century Questions and Twentieth-Century Answers* (Berkeley and Los Angeles: University of California Press, 1996).

powerful arguments for freedom of thought and inquiry, there are subtle differences between them, which reveal subtle differences between the standpoints of the two spokesmen for the Enlightenment. In this chapter, I will first compare the two essays on enlightenment, which reveal both similarities and characteristic differences between the philosophical positions of Mendelssohn and Kant, and then turn to Kant's 1786 essay on "What Does It Mean to Orient Oneself in Thinking?" in which he responds to the famous debate between Mendelssohn and Friedrich Heinrich Jacobi of the previous year. As Kant saw matters, the ultimate issue between Mendelssohn and Jacobi was whether belief in the existence of God could be founded on reason or only on faith, what Jacobi called a *salto mortale* or what Søren Kierkegaard later called a "leap" of faith. Kant would take Mendelssohn's side in arguing that faith must itself be founded on reason, but would criticize Mendelssohn by arguing that this must be practical, not theoretical reason.

## 2. What is Enlightenment?

Kant's critique of Mendelssohn in 1786 is founded on his position in the debate over enlightenment of 1784, for the fundamental distinction between Mendelssohn's answer to the question "What is enlightenment?" and Kant's is that for Mendelssohn enlightenment is a matter of theoretical knowledge while for Kant it lies in the development of practical reason unhindered by external coercion or by the internal coercion of "self-incurred immaturity" (Kant, WIE?, 8:35).

Mendelssohn starts with the premise that "education, culture, and enlightenment" (*Bildung, Kultur*, and *Aufklärung*) are "modifications of social life; the effects of diligence, and the efforts of people to better their social condition" (*JubA* 6.1:115). One thing that is immediately striking is that there is not much emphasis on individual responsibility for enlightenment in Mendelssohn's approach, while although Kant will nod in the direction of the social character of enlightenment, there is more emphasis on individual responsibility in Kant's treatment of the subject, as of course there is throughout Kant's moral philosophy—although as we will see in the final chapter of this study, when it comes to the question of the possibility of moral progress on human history, it is in fact Mendelssohn who places more emphasis than Kant on the individuality of moral choice. I will argue there, however, that in the essay on theory and practice, where Kant criticizes Mendelssohn on the possibility of moral progress in history, Kant is actually departing from his own best-considered view. On the issue of progress, the two philosophers will once again not be so far apart as Kant pretends.

Having introduced three terms, Mendelssohn next reduces them to two by stating that "Education divides itself into *culture* and *enlightenment*." He says that the former "seems to be directed more toward the *practical*" and the latter "to be related more to the *theoretical*," but culture does not seem to be concerned directly with the moral, as it would be if the "practical" with which it is concerned were Kant's pure practical reason. Rather, Mendelssohn glosses the practical as "goodness, refinement, and beauty in handicrafts, arts, and social customs (objectively), and readiness, diligence, and skillfulness in those, and inclinations, drives, and habits (subjectively)." Enlightenment, on the contrary, concerns itself with "rational cognition" (*theoretische Erkenntniß*). To be sure, both "subjective" culture and "objective" enlightenment are aimed at the "vocation of mankind" (*Bestimmung des Menschen*), which for Mendelssohn, unlike for Johann Joachim Spalding, the originator of the phrase,[5] comprises the development of the full range of human perfections, including but not limited to moral perfections. Thus, enlightenment and culture together—*Bildung*—aim "at rational cognition (objective) and readiness (subjective) for rational reflection, on the things of human life, in proportion to their importance and their influence in the vocation of mankind" (6.1:115). But Mendelssohn's view is at bottom that the vocation of mankind calls for the perfection of a variety of human capacities, that there is theoretical knowledge about how these perfections are to be realized, and that enlightenment is the social acquisition of this special knowledge; of course individuals need the disposition to acquire and act upon such knowledge and have to cultivate such a disposition, in the form of "culture."[6] Mendelssohn concludes the opening of his essay by stating that "Enlightenment is related to culture as in general theory is related to practice, as cognition to morality [*Sittlichkeit*], as critique to virtuosity. Considered in and for themselves (objectively) they stand in the closest connection, although subjectively they can very often be separated" (*JubA* 6.1:116). That is, the knowledge required to realize the vocation of humankind and the dispositions to act upon this knowledge are two different things, each of which has to be acquired in its own way. Although realization of the vocation of mankind depends upon both, it is all too easy for only one or the other—or, needless to say, neither—to be acquired.

Kant's moral philosophy in the 1780s tends to assume that theory and practice cannot come apart in the same way, and only with the distinction between *Wille* and *Willkür*, the former as pure practical reason and the latter as the faculty of choice, in *Religion within the Boundaries of Mere Reason* of 1793, thus nearly a decade after the death of Mendelssohn, does Kant clearly allow that, in Mendelssohn's terms, enlightenment and culture can come apart. This recognition was eventually forced upon Kant by a debate that began with Johann Heinrich August Ulrich's *Eleutheriologie* ("Theory of Freedom") of 1788,[7] so it does not seem to have been a belated response to Mendelssohn's distinction between enlightenment and culture in 1784. But a striking similarity as well as difference between the two philosophers' approaches to enlightenment appears in the next section of Mendelssohn's essay. For what Mendelssohn next does is to "divide the vocation of mankind into (1) the vocation of the human being as *human being* and (2) the vocation of the human being as *citizen*" (*JubA* 6.1:116). His idea is that there are certain perfections required of all

---

[5] For discussion of Spalding, see Chapter 4.

[6] On the social aspect of Mendelssohn's conception of Enlightenment, see especially Pollok, *Facetten des Menschen*, pp. 429–41, 453–7.

[7] Johann August Heinrich Ulrich, *Eleutheriologie, oder über Freyheit und Nothwendigkeit* (Jena: Cröker, 1788). Kant wrote notes for a possible review of this volume, preserved at 23:79–81; these notes appear to have been used by a student of Kant, Christian Jacob Krause (1753–1826), who published a review of Ulrich's book in the *Allgemeine Literatur-Zeitung* for 25 April 1788, which appears at 8:451–60 and is translated in *Practical Philosophy*, pp. 123–31. For an introduction to this debate and further references, see my "The Struggle for Freedom: Freedom of Will in Kant and Reinhold," in Eric Watkins, ed., *Kant on Persons and Agency* (Cambridge: Cambridge University Press, 2018), pp. 120–37.

people simply as moral agents and other perfections required of them by their specific social "status [*Standes*] and profession" (6.1:117).⁸ Properly fulfilling one's general moral duties as well as one's specific social and professional duties each requires appropriate theoretical knowledge and thus enlightenment. The danger is that in an imperfect state the demands of citizenship and the demands of morality in general can collide: "Human enlightenment and civil enlightenment can come into conflict" (6.1:117). Then:

> Unhappy is that state, that must concede that in it the essential vocation of the human being does not harmonize with the essential vocation of the citizen, that the enlightenment that is indispensable for the human being cannot extend itself to all statuses in the realm without the constitution being in danger of collapsing. Here the philosopher places his hand over his mouth! Necessity may here prescribe laws, or forge the shackles that are to be placed upon humanity in order to bend it and keep it under constant pressure! (6.1:117)

The danger is that if the demands of the state are incompatible with the demands of morality, experts in statecraft will use their expertise to bend their subjects to their will, and morality itself will suffer—in other words, the danger is Machiavellianism.⁹ To prevent this, "laws must be determined according to which exceptions" to the *civil* laws can be made and "collisions avoided" with the demands of *morality*. But Mendelssohn does not make clear *who* will make such laws and *who* will put them into place and enforce them, so it remains a pious hope on his part that conflicts between the demands of the state and the demands of morality can be resolved.

Mendelssohn's distinction between civil and more general moral enlightenment seems to anticipate the distinction between the private and the public use of reason that Kant would make two months later.¹⁰ But the difference is that Kant makes his distinction precisely in order to suggest a mechanism by which the conflicts between imperfect states and genuine morality can ultimately be overcome, namely, the difference between the private and the public use of reason and the argument that anyone, no matter what their civil status or profession, is entitled to make public use of reason, that is, address the public in his own voice rather than that of his position. As Kant will make clear in other writings, no one has the right to take the law into his own hands, so actual reform of government—in Mendelssohn's terms, reconciliation of the civil laws with the general conditions of the moral vocation of mankind—will have to come from duly empowered rulers responding to the public use of reason; but

---

⁸ See also Pollok, *Facetten des Menschen*, pp. 453–7. This was actually a standard trope in Wolffian moral philosophy; the fifth volume of Geogr Griedrich Meier's *Sittenlehre* (1764) is devoted entirely to the duties associated with particular positions of responsibility, such as parent, official, etc.

⁹ Friedrich II, "Frederick the Great," had himself published a book entitled *Anti-Machiavel*.

¹⁰ Following Norbert Hinske, Pollok suggests that both Mendelssohn's distinction between "professional" and "extra-professional" (*Außerberufsgeschäfte*) uses of reason and Kant's between the "private" and "public" use of reason were based upon an anonymous contribution, from the "Wednesday Society" in Berlin of which Mendelssohn was a part, in the *Berlinische Monatsschrfit*, Teil III (1784): 312–20; see Pollok, *Facetten des Menschen*, pp. 454–5, and Norbert Hinske,"Mendelssohns Beantwortung der Frage: Was ist Aufklärung? oder über die Aktualität Mendelssohns," in Hinske, *Ich handle mit Vernunft: Moses Mendelssohn und die europäische Aufklärung* (Hamburg: Felix Meiner Verlag, 1981), pp. 85–117. As previously noted, however, the distinction between general duties of humankind and duties associated with specific positions was well established in German thought of the time.

at least the public use of reason might prompt rulers to reform. To be sure, Mendelssohn hardly asserts that by virtue of their status and profession, anyone has lost the right to address the republic and call for reform, but neither has he asserted that regardless of status and profession everyone has this right.[11]

Turning from Mendelssohn's essay to Kant's, the first thing that strikes one is that Kant's is addressed to the individual: each individual has the responsibility to enlighten herself, and the enlightenment of humankind as a whole can only come from the efforts of individuals to enlighten themselves:

Enlightenment is the human being's emergence from <u>his self-incurred</u> immaturity [*Unmündigkeit*]. Immaturity is inability to make use of <u>one's own</u> understanding without being led by another. This immaturity is self-incurred when its cause lies not in lack of understanding but in lack of resolution and courage to use without being led by another. *Sapere aude!* Have courage to make use of <u>your own</u> [*dich deinen eigenen*] understanding! is thus the motto of enlightenment. (*WIE?*, 8:35, emphasis added)

The second-person address of this opening, using the intimate *dich* to go straight to the heart of the individual, is a radical departure from Mendelssohn's language. Kant's term *Unmündigkeit* also implies individual responsibility. Mary Gregor translated it as "minority," which connotes not being responsible and needing supervision by another but also suggests that this is simply because of youth. However, Kant's term literally means not being able to speak for oneself, and speaking for oneself is the mark of maturity. Suffering from immaturity, "self-incurred" (*selbst verschuldet*) also implies, is not a matter of age, but a matter of will, more precisely of lacking the will to speak for oneself. Conversely, speaking for oneself is also a matter of will. Thus from the outset, Kant also suggests that the key to enlightenment is not expert knowledge, but the exercise of will.

Kant's next remarks might appear to weaken the connection between enlightenment and individual responsibility with which he has begun. He says that "it is difficult for any single individual to extricate himself from the immaturity that has become almost nature to him," that he has even "grown fond of... but that a public should enlighten itself is more possible; indeed this is almost inevitable, if only it is left its freedom" (*WIE?*, 8:36). This suggests that the public rather than the individual can institute enlightenment. On Mendelssohn's approach, where enlightenment consists in knowledge, and knowledge might be accumulated socially, this might make sense. But Kant's next remark undercuts any impression that enlightenment might be instituted by society as a whole but not by individuals: "For there will always be a few independent thinkers, even among the established guardians of the great masses, who, after having themselves cast off the yoke of immaturity, will disseminate the spirit of a rational valuing of one's own worth and of the calling of *each* person to think *for himself*" (8:36, emphasis added). That is, only individuals can enlighten

---

[11] Pollok observes that Mendelssohn's "reference to the responsibility for the public use of reason is not a satisfactory program for the defense of the vocation of humankind in a dictatorial state" (*Facetten des Menschen*, p. 459). It could certainly be argued that Kant's insistence on the right to freedom in the public use of their reason by those who hold offices and the duty of governors to reform their governments is also powerless in the face of a dictatorial government. But Kant is clearer about the moral responsibility of governors to heed criticism of their regimes, even if they fail to do so.

themselves, but, Kant optimistically assumes, the example of some individuals will inevitably, even if slowly, serve to stimulate others to self-enlightenment.[12] Society cannot do something that individuals cannot do for themselves, but if some individuals enlighten themselves that will gradually move others to do so as well.

All of this raises two questions. First, note that Kant says that for enlightenment individuals must *think* for themselves, not *know* something special; why does he assume that merely *thinking* for oneself will be sufficient for enlightenment? Second, *how* are individuals to think for themselves when various social positions, indeed precisely most of those positions involved in the exercise of civil power—the positions of jurists and soldiers, for example—seem to militate against thinking for oneself?

The answer to the first question is that in Kant's view morality is not aimed at the realization of some perfections, which requires expert knowledge, but simply at the equal freedom of all; and *thinking* about the worth of one's own freedom, that is, thinking *rationally* about one's own freedom, thinking in *universal* terms, will lead directly to the principles of morality, including those of a morally rightful state.[13] This is why Kant can say that "For this enlightenment...nothing is required but freedom, and indeed the least harmful of anything that could even be called freedom, namely, freedom to make public use of one's reason in all matters" (*WIE?*, 8:36). Of course, not any use of freedom is moral, not, for example, the use of one's own freedom to deny or destroy the freedom of another who is not aiming to do that to you; but Kant's assumption is that genuinely free thinking about freedom, thinking that is not itself coerced by another or by one's own inclinations, will be rational, and that rationality will tell you that it is a contradiction to deny freedom wherever it exists, whether in yourself or in any other, or that the worth that lies in your own freedom lies in everyone else's as well.[14] So enlightenment as thinking for oneself is bound, without any special knowledge that can only be accumulated by society, to lead to the moral law to act only on universalizable maxims and to what Kant will eventually call the Universal Principle of Right, that an action as the external use of one's choice is right only "if it can coexist with everyone's freedom in accordance with a universal law, or if on its maxim the freedom of choice of each can coexist with everyone's freedom in accordance with a universal law" (*MM*, DR, Introduction, section C, 6:230). A state is rightful only insofar as it is governed in accordance with this principle and promotes right so defined. Kant's argument throughout his essay on enlightenment is based upon the assumption that individuals have an innate right

---

[12] Kant would famously express a similar hope, at the level of states, that France's self-transformation into a republic would set an example for other states to undertake the same self-transformation (*CF* 7:85–6).

[13] For this reason, Ian Hunter's unqualified alignment of Kant with what he regards as the "intellectualist," "metaphysical" ethics of Leibniz and Wolff, as contrasted to the "civil" tradition of Pufendorf and Thomasius, in his *Rival Enlightenments: Civil and Metaphysical Philosophy in Early Modern Germany* (Cambridge: Cambridge University Press, 2001), has always struck me as wrong-headed; as usual, Kant is trying to find a way between two schools of thought recognized as opposed in his time—as he is doing with rationalism and empiricism themselves (and as is Mendelssohn).

[14] For the full development of this interpretation of Kant, see my *Kant on the Rationality of Morality* (Cambridge: Cambridge University Press, 2019).

to freedom and that the function of the state is nothing less and nothing more than to make this right and all the rights that follow from it in the particular conditions of human existence determinate and secure.[15]

But this brings us to the second question, how can individuals, particularly those in positions of authority, be free to enlighten themselves and to set the example of enlightenment for others, if their roles in currently existing and no doubt less than fully rightful states conflict with morality and right? Mendelssohn said that in such a case better *laws* must avoid such conflicts, but Kant addresses the question how such laws can ever come to be made. And his answer is that even though in their "private" use of reason, that is, in their use of their intellectual capacities in their official positions, individuals must follow existing law—soldiers must follow their orders, doctors must comply with the licensing regulations of the Department of Health, ministers must preach at least consistently with the doctrines of their church—all individuals, including such officials or officially licensed ones, retain the freedom to think and publish "as a scholar who by his writings addresses a public in the proper sense of the word" and thereby the freedom to "argue without thereby harming the affairs assigned to him in part as a passive member" of a civil status or profession (*WIE?*, 8:37–8). Kant's insistence upon a scholarly form of address is meant to make clear that not *any* form of self-expression is permitted—not inflammatory speech that is akin to yelling "Fire!" in a crowded theater when there is none—but of course that is a restriction on all freedom of speech, not just the freedom of speech of public officials. The main point is that in the public use of their freedom rather than in the discharge of their official positions—as we might be more likely to say, inverting Kant's usage, in their private use of reason rather than in their public positions—officials and licensees of the state have just as much freedom of speech as anyone else, and can use it for any otherwise permitted purpose, including calls for reform of the state itself.

As Kant famously argues nine years later, in the essay "On the Common Saying: That Might be Correct in Theory but it is of no Use in Practice" (1793), the freedom of *all* subjects in a state extends *only* to freedom of speech, that is the freedom to criticize their state and call for its reform, and it is up to the rulers of the state to hearken to those calls for reform and not up to citizens to take matters into their own hands in the form of rebellion. That is another matter, not in dispute with Mendelssohn. The present point is just that Mendelssohn does not say where the laws reconciling civil society with morality will come from, but Kant does say where they will come from, namely from citizens, including officials but in the public rather than private use of their reason, addressing their rulers and calling for reform. That is to say that the laws must come from the rulers—in Kant's account of a rightful republic, from the legislators, not from the executive, although Kant's cloud of terms for the rulers of a state (such as *Oberbefehlshaber*) may have been designed to obscure

---

[15] See, among other, Guyer, "The Twofold Morality of *Recht*," *Kant-Studien* 107 (2016): 34–63. For another interpretation of Kant's political philosophy that also stresses his recognition of the need of the state to make provisional claims to right conclusive in these dual senses of being determinate and secure, see Arthur Ripstein, *Force and Freedom: Kant's Legal and Political Philosophy* (Cambridge, Mass.: Harvard University Press, 2009).

his message for his Prussian kings—but the *ideas* for the laws that will bring the actual condition of the state closer to the ideal of justice can come from any citizen exercising his or her freedom of speech, including officials.

The last main point to note about Kant's essay on enlightenment is that the chief example of a subject for the public use of reason is that of religion, thus that his essay "What is Enlightenment?" is above all an essay on religious liberty. While it could not have been a direct response to Mendelssohn's own essay on enlightenment, which as we saw Kant learned of only on the day he finished his own essay, Kant's "What is Enlightenment?" may thus be a response to Mendelssohn's argument for religious liberty in *Jerusalem*, published the year before the two enlightenment essays. I will argue more fully in the next two chapters that Kant's position on religious liberty is grounded entirely on his moral and political principles, and unlike Mendelssohn's does not depend on any premise that is itself religious in nature; let us see now how Kant first suggested this approach in 1784.

At first, Kant just mentions the freedom of clergymen alongside that of military officers and taxpayers (not exactly officials, to be sure, but citizens in a particular civil status, to use Mendelssohn's terminology) without any suggestion of a special argument about the case of religious freedom. A military officer must obey his superiors, in the private use of his reason, but "cannot fairly be prevented, as a scholar, from making remarks about errors in the military service and from putting these before his public for judgment," and a citizen must pay his taxes but "does not act against the duty of a citizen when, as a scholar, he publicly expresses his thoughts about the inappropriateness or even injustice of" those taxes (*WIE?*, 8:37–8). Likewise, "a clergyman is bound to deliver his discourse to the pupils in his catechism class and to his congregation in accordance with the creed of the church he serves, for he was employed by it on that condition... But as a scholar he has complete freedom and is even called upon to communicate to the public all his carefully examined and well-intentioned thoughts about what is erroneous in that creed and his suggestion for a better arrangement of the religious and ecclesiastical body" (8:38). As with any other official, the obedience to ill-considered rules that a clergyman must suffer in the private use of reason should not abridge his full freedom in his public use of reason. "Thus the use that an appointed teacher makes of his reason before his congregation is merely a *private use*," but "as a scholar, who by his writings speaks to the public in the strict sense, that is, the world—hence a clergyman in the *public use* of his reason—he enjoys an unrestricted freedom to make use of his own reason and to speak in his own person" (8:38). Of course, to speak in one's own person is precisely what it is to be mature, *mündig* rather than *unmündig*, and if one does truly speak in one's own voice, a voice not distorted by external forces or even by one's own inclination, then one will advocate equal freedom for all, for that is all that reason, one's "proper self" (*G*, 4:457) can advocate.

But the clergyman is not just one more example of an official who does not lose the freedom for the public use of his reason by the constraints on his freedom in the private use of his reason. The case of the clergyman is Kant's special concern and no doubt his real motivation for writing the essay. For the remainder of Kant's "What is Enlightenment?" concerns entirely what he calls "matters of religion" (*WIE?*, 8:41). And these are arguments parallel to, perhaps even influenced by, some in

Mendelssohn's *Jerusalem*, but subtly different as well. First, Kant argues that clergymen cannot be bound by oaths to a synod "to a certain unalterable creed," because a contract among clergymen "concluded to keep all further enlightenment from the human race forever, is absolutely null and void, even if were ratified by the supreme power, by imperial diets and by the most solemn peace treaties" (*WIE?*, 8:39). As we will see, Kant's formulation of his point in terms of restrictions on what can be the proper subject of a contract or oath may well be influenced by Mendelssohn's approach to the restriction of the state from interference in religious matters in *Jerusalem*, but his specific argument that to hold firm to a given creed no matter what the further progress of human reason might turn up is nothing less than a violation of the freedom of thought, one of the essential elements of humanity's innate right to freedom (see *MM*, DR, Introduction, 6:237), and thus can never be rightfully enforced, is very much his own way of putting things, based entirely on his conception of maximal but equal freedom for all as the essence of right commanded by morality itself. A prohibition of enlightenment is a prohibition of freedom, which is always itself prohibited. Again, a synod may have the right to require conformity to its present rules in the official acts of its subordinate clergymen, but it cannot rightfully bind itself or any of its subordinates to forego their freedom of thought and inquiry in the public use of their reason. "[T]o renounce enlightenment, whether for [one's] own person or even more so for posterity, is to violate the sacred right of freedom and trample it underfoot" (8:39)—the sacred right to freedom including freedom of both thought and its expression in what seems to one appropriate religious practice. (In *Jerusalem*, Mendelssohn had argued against the rightfulness of oaths, but had gone further than Kant in arguing against internal governments of religious institutions at all, thus against the very existence of synods in the first place. He did not mention this in his essay on enlightenment, but as I said, perhaps Kant had *Jerusalem* in mind in writing his own.)

"But," Kant adds, "what a people may never decide upon for itself, a monarch may still less decide upon for his people; for his legislative authority rests precisely on this, that he unites in his will the collective will of the people" (*WIE?*, 8:39–40)—who can only will their own freedom, including their freedom of thought. That is, not only can there be no coercion within the quasi-governmental structure of religious institutions; government in the ordinary sense—in eighteenth-century Prussia, of course, a monarch exercising legislative as well as executive functions—has no right to prohibit religious inquiry and coercively enforce any particular religious dogma. Kant's further language on this subject is clearly influenced by the founding text of so much thought about religious liberty in the eighteenth century, namely John Locke's 1689 *Letter concerning Toleration*,[16] for he economically sums up Locke's two main points: the business of government is "civil order," not "salvation," and therefore no governmental interference in religious matters is legitimate except to preserve civil order, in which case the religious intent of action earns it no special privilege. In Kant's terms, as long as the ruler:

---

[16] John Locke, *Epistola de Tolerantia/A Letter on Toleration*, edited by Raymond Kilbansky and translated by J.W. Gough (Oxford: Clarendon Press, 1968).

sees to it that any true or supposed improvement is consistent with civil order, he can for the rest leave it to his subjects to do what they find necessary for the sake of their salvation; that is no concern of his, but it is indeed his concern to prevent any of them from forcibly hindering others from working to the best of their ability to determine and promote their salvation.

(*WIE?*, 8:40)

For Kant, enlightenment is not special expertise but the exercise of freedom; the first part of freedom is the innate freedom of the human being; the first part of innate freedom is freedom of thought; and the primary subject for freedom of thought is religion. Coercive enforcement of particular religious dogma and practice is the chief enemy of enlightenment. The duty to refrain from such coercion is the duty of rulers, whether of governments or quasi-governmental churches. The right and the duty to enlightenment is the duty of all individuals, even though as citizens their right is to exercise the public use of their reason and to call for reform, not the right to rebel or take government into their own hands. Enlightenment is thus not a matter of theoretical but of practical reason.

Much of this would be spelled out by Kant in later essays and treatises, but the core of his theory of rightful government and of religious liberty from governmental and other forms of coercion is present *in nuce* in his essay on enlightenment. As we will see shortly, Mendelssohn too is influenced by Locke's *Letter on Toleration*, but by what is in fact a religious argument for religious liberty, and though he has criticisms of Locke to make he does not criticize this style of argument. But let us defer further discussion of religious liberty for a moment, however, and before completing this chapter turn to Kant's direct intervention in the debate between Jacobi and Mendelssohn in his essay on "orientation" in thinking.

## 3. What Does It Mean to Orient Oneself in Thinking?

In 1785, as we saw in Part I, Mendelssohn published his *Morning Hours, or Lectures on the Existence of God*, which was to be his final major work. The book was hastened by the dispute that had broken out between Mendelssohn and Friedrich Heinrich Jacobi, who had asserted that Gotthold Ephraim Lessing, Mendelssohn's lifelong friend, had avowed Spinozism to him, Jacobi, something Lessing had never done to his best friend. Spinoza's view that both extension and thought are but modes of the one substance, God, was held to be pantheism, and a charge of pantheism was in turn tantamount to a charge of atheism, since it denied any ontological distinction between finite beings and God. One might have thought that it could have been taken as tantamount to blasphemy because it denied any distinction between God and finite creatures, and in the ensuing "pantheism controversy" Mendelssohn in fact tried to defend his friend by ascribing to him at most a "refined pantheism," in which the distinction between God and finite beings is not obliterated because even though finite beings are held to be contained in God as modes they are not held to exhaust his modes or his nature (which was in fact Spinoza's own position). Mendelssohn left his house on New Year's Eve, 1785, to deliver his next piece in the controversy, "To the Friends of Lessing," to his publisher, and caught a cold and died five days later. In this crude way, Jacobi seemed to have triumphed over Mendelssohn, and since Jacobi had argued that Spinozism and thus atheism was the only consistent conclusion of rationalism and that the only alternative to that was sheer faith in the existence of a God separate from His creation (Jacobi can be considered a forerunner of Søren Kierkegaard), friends of the Enlightenment who believed in a rational basis for religion were aghast. Kant was thus pressed by the liberal editor Johannn Erich Biester (1749–1816) to enter into the fray, and in October, 1786, he published an essay, also in Biester's *Berlinische Monatsschrift*, entitled "What Does it Mean to Orient Oneself in Thinking?" This essay explicitly comments on both Mendelssohn and Jacobi, and to that extent is certainly a response to Mendelssohn.[17] But Kant used the occasion mainly as a platform to promote his own conception of rational faith, *Vernunftglaube*, which he had briefly laid out in the "Canon of Pure Reason" in the *Critique of Pure Reason* five years earlier and which he would defend at length in the *Critique of Practical Reason* that he would compose the following year.[18] This is the doctrine that we can and must assert the theoretical propositions that the human will is free, the human soul immortal, and God omniscient, benevolent, and just, but only on practical grounds, as necessary conditions of the rationality of striving to fulfill the demands of morality, that is, conditions without which, in Kant's view, the full realization of the objectives of morality would not even be possible. Kant thus wanted to argue that his own position provided a middle way between the extremes of Mendelssohn, who had held that these doctrines could be established by theoretical reason alone, and Jacobi, who held that they could not be established by any kind of reason but only by groundless faith: Kant wanted to argue that the core truths of religion could be established by reason, but by the practical rather than theoretical use of reason.[19] Once he had completed his more narrowly professional mission of establishing the possibility of synthetic a priori cognition, establishing what he called the postulates of pure practical reason was the broader mission that most concerned Kant in his final years, so it is no surprise that he took the occasion of the pantheism controversy to advertise his own view.

In his controversy with Mendelssohn, Jacobi had appealed to the authority of Kant, maintaining that Kant's conception of "moral faith" in the *Critique of Pure Reason* supported his own position that it can only be faith *rather* than reason that can support a non-heterodox affirmation of the existence of God. Kant thought that Jacobi's position was mere "enthusiasm," indeed nothing but "humbug" (*Gaukelwerk*).[20] Kant mentioned in a letter to Marcus Herz in April, 1786, that he might write an essay for the *Berlinische Monatsschrift* to this effect, and the editor of the journal, Biester, appealed to Kant for such a piece. However, when Kant's essay

---

[17] See Altmann, *Moses Mendelssohn*, pp. 750–2; Beiser, *The Fate of Reason*, pp. 113–18; Kuehn, *Kant*, pp. 305–13; and Bourel, *Moses Mendelssohn*, pp. 553–62.

[18] Altmann regards this essay as having taken the wind out of Jacobi's sails and signally contributed to the increased influence of Kant's own philosophy (*Moses Mendelssohn*, p. 752). He does not look as far ahead as to the recrudescence of Jacobi's conception of faith in Kierkegaard half a century later.

[19] See also Beiser, *The Fate of Reason*, pp. 115–17. In his words, "Armed with [his] concept of rational faith, Kant walks down his middle path between Mendelssohn's dogmatism and Jacobi's mysticism" (p. 117).

[20] See editor's introduction to "What Does It Mean to Orient Oneself in Thinking?" (*WOT?*), in Kant, *Religion and Rational Theology*, p. 5.

appeared in October, 1786, under the title "What Does It Mean to Orient Oneself in Thinking?" it made only one reference to Jacobi's "destructive way of thinking" (*WOT?*, 8:134). Instead, while being generally supportive of Mendelssohn's side in the controversy, Kant took the occasion to distinguish carefully his own foundation of religion on *practical* reason from Mendelssohn's attempt to ground it upon *theoretical* reason. It seems natural to see Kant as taking the occasion of the Mendelssohn-Jacobi controversy to prepare the public for the full-blown defense of his own *moral* theology in the imminent *Critique of Practical Reason* and, as it turned out, the *Critique of the Power of Judgment* that would follow.

Kant saw Mendelssohn as having attempted to argue for the existence of God on theoretical grounds in *Morning Hours* but as also having attempted to buttress his theoretical arguments with an appeal to "*common sense* or *healthy reason*" (*WOT?*, 8:133). However, he thought that Mendelssohn had failed in "the task of purifying the common concept of reason of its contradictions, and defending it against its *own* sophistical attacks on the maxims of healthy reason" (*WOT?*, 8:134). In other words, he brought against Mendelssohn the charge that he always brought against Wolff and his followers, namely that he had not subjected reason itself to the critique that is necessitated by the fact that the uncritical use of theoretical reason lands itself in contradictions. As he puts it, Mendelssohn, who "recommended" the "Wolffian" "scholastic method," "probably did not think about the fact that *arguing dogmatically* with pure reason in the field of the supersensible is the direct path to philosophical enthusiasm, and that only a critique of this same faculty of reason can fundamentally remedy this ill" (*WOT?*, 8:138n). If Mendelssohn had subjected theoretical reason to the necessary critique, no doubt he would have realized that religion can only be founded on practical, not theoretical reason. Kant puts the point in this essay by saying that an "extended and more precisely determined concept of *orienting oneself* can be helpful to us in presenting distinctly the maxims healthy reason uses in working on its cognition of supersensible objects" (*WOT?*, 8:134), those being, of course, the free and immortal human soul and God.

Kant then launches into a discussion of orientation that does not seem very helpful in the present context. He spends several pages explaining how our "feeling" of the difference between right and left is necessary to orient or locate ourselves in space because a purely *conceptual* description of any spatial shape or relation is incomplete and insufficient to distinguish, say, between our right and left hands (*WOT?*, 8:134-7). This argument, which goes back to Kant's 1768 paper on "The Differentiation of Regions in Space" and the 1770 inaugural dissertation on "The Form and Principles of the Sensible and Intelligible Worlds" does not seem relevant to the dispute between Kant and Mendelssohn, because Kant himself will not allow *feeling* a *foundational* role in our knowledge of the moral principle, upon which his further practical argument for the existence of God will depend. So let us turn directly to Kant's argument that not theoretical reason but practical reason can ground rational religious belief.

Kant introduces this argument thus:

Yet through...the mere concept, nothing is settled in respect of the existence of this object [God] and its actual connection with the world (the sum total of all objects of possible

experience). But now there enters *the right* of reason's *need*, as a subjective ground for presupposing something which reason may not presume to know through objective grounds, and consequently for *orienting* itself in thinking, solely through reason's own need, in that immeasurable space of the supersensible, which for us is filled with dark night.
(*WOT?*, 8:137)

Both Mendelssohn and Kant may be taken to agree that some presupposition is needed to "orient" reason in the otherwise open realm of metaphysical speculation about the supersensible, without any reference to the details of Kant's particular theory of orientation in space. The difference between them will now emerge, however, in Kant's distinction between a merely theoretical "presupposition" of reason and practically grounded rational "belief" in the existence of God (and the free and immortal human soul). Kant puts the distinction in terms of his own philosophy. He concedes that we have a theoretical urge for completeness in the determination of all particular objects, and that we "presuppose reality as given for the possibility of all things," considering "the differences between things only as [different] limitations arising through the negations attaching to them" (*WOT?*, 8:138n). This is the argument for God as the ground of all possibilities and thus as the condition for the complete determination of all actualities that Kant had advanced in his 1763 book *The Only Possible Basis for a Demonstration of the Existence of God* and had *criticized* in the *Critique of Pure Reason* as a mere "idea" of reason, as we saw in Part I. In the "Orientation" essay, Kant puts his criticism by suggesting that the theoretical urge for completeness in determination that leads to the posit of the existence of God as the ground of all possibility is *conditional* or *optional*: "one sees very well that it is only conditioned, i.e., we must assume the existence of God *if we want to judge* about the first cause of everything contingent, chiefly in the order of ends which is actually present in the world" (*WOT?*, 8:139). *But apparently we do not have to want to judge about the first cause of everything contingent*. However, when it comes to morality and *its* presuppositions, there is nothing optional. We *have to act as morality commands*—its imperatives are categorical—and therefore *we have to assume the actuality of whatever the conditions of the possibility of morality are*. That is, Kant argues, the existence of God would be a condition of the possibility of completing the task of theoretical reason, but completing those tasks is optional, so theoretical reason leaves the existence of God unproven, a mere presupposition; the existence of God would also be a condition of the possibility of completing the task imposed by morality, but there is nothing optional about attempting to complete that task, we must believe it is possible to complete it, and therefore we must believe in the existence of God, although on practical rather than theoretical grounds. In the moral case, "we are necessitated to presuppose the existence of God not only if we *want* to judge, but because we *have to judge*" (*WOT?*, 8:139).

The argument turns on the claim that morality commands the realization of the highest good, assumes that it would be irrational to attempt to accomplish that which we cannot believe to be possible, and concludes that only the existence of God can make the realization of the highest good possible—so we must believe in the existence of God, although only on the ground of this argument from practical reason. Kant will attempt to work out the details of this argument in the *Critique of Practical*

*Reason*, where he will repeat the argument against the merely conditional necessity of belief in the conditions of the possibility of morality in response to the criticism, by Thomas Wizenmann (1759–87),[21] that his postulates of pure practical reason are basically just wish-fulfillment (CPracR, 5:143–4). He will still be trying to work them out properly in the 1790 *Critique of the Power of Judgment* and in the 1793 essay on "Theory and Practice." Perhaps he never settled on a completely definitive version of the argument, although it seems to have been more important to him than anything else. Be that as it may, in the essay on "Orientation" he contents himself with a brief statement of the argument, and we can too:

> [T]he pure practical use of reason consists in the precepts of moral laws. They all lead, however, to the idea of the *highest good* possible in the world insofar as it is possible only through *freedom*: morality; from the other side, these precepts lead to what depends not merely on human freedom but also on *nature*, which is the greatest *happiness*, insofar as it is apportioned to the first. Now reason *needs* to assume, for the sake of such a *dependent* highest good, a supreme intelligence as the highest *independent* good; not, of course, to derive from this assumption the binding authority of moral precepts or the incentives to observe them (for they would have no moral worth if their motive were derived from anything but the law alone, which is of itself apodictically certain), but rather only in order to give objective reality to the concept of the highest good, i.e., to prevent it, along with morality, from being taken merely as a mere ideal, as it would be if that whose idea inseparably accompanies morality should not exist anywhere. (WOT?, 8:139)

Thus Kant concludes that it is "not *cognition* but a *felt need* of reason" (even though literally "Reason does not feel") that grounds our belief in the existence of God and that "oriented" Mendelssohn himself in his "speculative thinking" even if he did not realize it (WOT?, 8:139–40).

The details of Kant's argument are and would remain obscure, but some of his general claims are clear. First, we do not need God to tell us what is right and wrong nor do we need a promise of divine reward and/or threat of divine punishment to motivate us to do what is right. Pure reason alone suffices for that, although Kant hardly explains how here—that will be the first task of the *Critique of Practical Reason*. But, second, in some way also not explained here, morality itself will be unsatisfied if our attempts to be moral are not accompanied by the natural condition of happiness, or perhaps morality even commands that we realize happiness, not for ourselves but for all, not perhaps for its own sake but as the inevitable outcome of treating all as ends in themselves. (This is the line that Kant suggests in "Theory and Practice," 8:278–9). Either way, to suppose that morality will either be accompanied with or lead to happiness requires that we presuppose that nature is compatible with morality, thus that there be an author of nature who is also cognizant of and

---

[21] Beiser discusses Wizenmann's intervention in the Mendelssohn-Jacobi affair at *The Fate of Reason*, pp. 109–13, and his criticism of Kant's conception of practical faith or postulates of pure practical reason at pp. 118–21. Beiser offers a mostly sympathetic account of Kant's reply to Wizenmann that practical faith is justified only by the necessary and universal demand of morality, not by any old wish, and that it justifies only a specific belief in the existence of God defined by moral predicates, and immortality, but he weakens Kant's position by characterizing the belief in the possibility of the highest good thereby made possible as an "incentive" for being moral rather than as a condition for the rationality of acting to achieve the object that morality commands (p. 121).

committed to the moral law, and also that the author of nature makes sure that all those who are moral are ultimately granted happiness—in other words, that there be God as creator and judge. (Kant never explicitly argues that we must believe that God punishes the immoral with unhappiness.) This argument, Kant claims, is neither a matter of "rational insight" nor "rational inspiration," but is "rational belief or faith" (*WOT?*, 8:140). It is not located anywhere on the spectrum of assertion on theoretical grounds ranging from mere opinion to knowledge, but "rests on a need of reason's use with a *practical* intent, [and] could be called a *postulate* of reason—not as if it were an insight which did justice to all the logical demands for certainty, but because this holding true (if only the person is morally good), is not inferior in degree to knowing, even though it is completely different from it in kind" (*WOT?*, 8:141–2).[22]

Apart from the details of Mendelssohn's arguments for the existence of God and Kant's critique of them, which we examined in Part I, Kant's most fundamental critique of Mendelssohn is that he tried to accomplish by means of the theoretical use of reason what in Kant's view can be accomplished only by the practical use of reason. This was hardly a ground for Kant to scorn Mendelssohn; on the contrary, he thought Mendelssohn's efforts were worthy of respect:

> ...need is taken for insight. Just as it is here, so it is with all the proofs of the worthy Mendelssohn in his *Morning Hours*. They accomplish nothing by way of demonstration. But they are not for that reason by any means useless. For not to mention the fine occasion which such acute developments of the subjective conditions of the use of our reason provides for the complete cognition of this faculty of ours, of which they are lasting examples, a holding of something true on the subjective grounds of the use of reason—if we lack objective ones and are nevertheless necessitated to judge—is always of great importance; only we must not give out what is in fact only a necessary *presupposition* as it if were a *free insight*; otherwise we needlessly offer the opponent with whom we are *arguing dogmatically* weaknesses which he can use to our disadvantage. (*WOT?*, 8:138n)

That is, in spite of the merits of his presentation of the theoretical proofs of the existence of God as a stimulus for critique, in Kant's view Mendelssohn had himself opened the door to Jacobi's alternative, mere enthusiasm or the "leap of faith." Mendelssohn did as well as anyone could in defending the theoretical arguments for the existence of God, but Kant would explain why they can never work and why the practical argument is preferable.

But for all Kant's concern with defending his practical rather than theoretical theology, it is striking that "What Is Orientation in Thinking?" concludes with a discussion of a very different issue: like the essay on enlightenment, it concludes with a defense of freedom of religion, that is, the freedom of each to think about and practice religions as he or she thinks best. The transition to this topic is abrupt: Kant seems to worry that the proponents of enthusiasm, his term for a faith in the truth of

---

[22] This statement reprises Kant's section on "On having an opinion, knowing, and believing" in the "Canon of Pure Reason" in the "Doctrine of Method" of the *Critique of Pure Reason* (A 820–31/B 848–59), and anticipates his sections "On the kind of affirmation involved in a moral proof of the existence of God" and "On the kind of affirmation produced by means of a practical faith" in the "Doctrine of Method" of the "Critique of the Teleological Power of Judgment" in the *Critique of the Power of Judgment* (§§90–1, 5:461–74).

religion, like Jacobi's, that is held independently of any rational argument at all, presuppose that they have the freedom to think as they want about religion but may also put that freedom in danger by their enthusiasm, by their eagerness to undermine their opponent, or at the very least that they do not trouble to defend it. But without "preserving inviolate" their "freedom to think," their own "free flights of genius would soon come to an end" (WOT?, 8:144). Kant then makes the following interesting point:

> The freedom to think is opposed first of all to *civil compulsion*. Of course it is said that the freedom to *speak* or to *write* could be taken from us by a superior power, but the freedom to *think* cannot be. Yet how much and how correctly would we *think* if we did not think as it were in community with others to whom we can *communicate* our thoughts, and who communicate theirs with us! Thus one can very well say that this external power which wrenches away people's freedom publicly to *communicate* their thoughts also takes away from them the freedom to *think*—that single gem remaining to us in the midst of all the burdens of civil life, through which alone we can devise means of overcoming all the evils of our condition.
> (WOT?, 8:144)

As in the essay on enlightenment of two years earlier, Kant has not yet worked out the details of his conception of the rightful state or civil condition as the one that does no less and no more than make freedom in every other-regarding form determinate and secure. But this passage is interesting because even though it just presupposes the freedom of thought, it makes clear that such freedom cannot exist in isolation from freedom of action in the form of unhindered communication with other thinkers. Kant would cast doubt on any strict metaphysical dualism between mind and body, exploiting the resources of his transcendental idealism, in the "Paralogisms of Pure Reason" in the *Critique of Pure Reason*, especially in the second edition, on which he was working in the same year as the composition of "What is Orientation?." We do not need to go into that argument here. Instead, we might content ourselves with the remark that from the standpoint of his own empirical realism, Kant recognizes that thought is not something that proceeds, or proceeds very well, in isolation; it flourishes in conversation with others. This is as true for thought about religion as well as about anything else. If anyone's thinking about religion is to flourish—which of course for Kant means to progress to a clear recognition of the rational grounds and limits of religious belief—it can do so only in free conversation with others. Woe to anyone, including supposed friends of religion, whether governments or enthusiasts, who would hinder that freedom. Thus the essay on orientation ends up at the same place as the essay on enlightenment, with a defense of the freedom of religious thought and discourse.

This had been a major topic of Mendelssohn in *Jerusalem*, and perhaps it is no accident that the freedom of religious thought and action from interference by the state became such a prominent theme for Kant just after he read Mendelssohn's book. As we will see in the next two chapters, religious freedom would continue to be—pardon the expression—a crusade for Kant until the end of his career. But as I have suggested, for all of Mendelssohn's possible influence on Kant's recognition of the importance of this issue, there are also subtle differences between their positions. The fundamental difference between the two philosophers on the conditions of enlightenment is that while for Mendelssohn it depends above all upon knowledge, for Kant it depends above all on the exercise of freedom. Kant is clearer than Mendelssohn on the theoretical significance of freedom. However, we will also see that Mendelssohn may have deeper insight into what the practice of religious freedom really means than Kant does. Kant is the better theoretician of religious liberty, Mendelssohn the better practitioner. So let us turn to the similarities and differences between our two philosophers' defenses of religious liberty now in their further writings on religion, Mendelssohn's *Jerusalem* and Kant's *Religion within the Boundaries of Mere Reason* but also his fundamental political text, the "Doctrine of Right" of the *Metaphysics of Morals*.

# 10

# Freedom of Religion in Mendelssohn and Kant

## 1. Introduction

Both Mendelssohn and Kant argued for intimate connections between religion and morality but for strict separation between religion and the coercive power of the state. In the view of both, the state could claim no authority to privilege one religion or sect over any other, nor any power to require religious belief or practice on the parts of its citizens at all. Yet because of underlying differences in their conceptions of the foundations of morality, and thus in their conceptions of the relations of morality to the state on the one hand and religion on the other, their arguments for the separation of church and state could not be exactly the same. Each approach has both its strengths and weaknesses. On the one hand, Kant provides a more secure theoretical basis for freedom of religious belief and practice or even freedom from religious belief and practice than does Mendelssohn. On the other hand, Mendelssohn, perhaps from his politically underprivileged but epistemically more privileged position as a member of a barely tolerated religious minority in eighteenth-century Prussia, provides a more convincing account of what the practice of religious liberty could be like than Kant does: Mendelssohn recognizes the pluralism of historical religious faiths as a fact of human existence, while Kant seems to fancy that at some point all historical faiths will fall away, leaving only the core doctrines of the religion of pure reason. Based as it is only on a moral and political premise and not on any specifically religious doctrine, Kant's argument for religious liberty comes closer to satisfying the requirement that such an argument appeal only to what John Rawls called "public reason," but Mendelssohn's recognition that religious pluralism is not going to simply fade away is a triumph of empiricism and common sense over excessive rationalism. Both positions have crucial contributions to make to thought about religious liberty in the contemporary world, but Kant's rationalism needs to be tempered by Mendelssohn's empiricism on this issue.

Mendelssohn's great plea for freedom of religion, his 1783 book *Jerusalem, or on Religious Power and Judaism*,[1] begins with one explicit criticism of John Locke's

---

[1] Moses Mendelssohn, *Jerusalem, or on Religious Power and Judiasm*, translated by Allan Arkush, introduction and commentary by Alexander Altmann (Hanover: University Press of New England, 1983), hereafter "*J*."

pathbreaking *Epistola de tolerantia* of 1689,[2] and his argument that not only should the state have no coercive power to enforce any particular religion but even religious institutions themselves should not have the power to enforce conformity of belief or practice in the form of excommunication of offenders is also clearly directed against Locke. Although Locke looms large in Kant's conception of the project of the *Critique of Pure Reason* and a critique of Locke's labor theory of property is central to Kant's own account of the right to private property, he is nowhere mentioned in Kant's published writings or his main surviving lecture course on philosophy of religion.[3] But it is hard to imagine that Kant was not familiar with Locke's argument for religious toleration, and his own position is close to Locke's although with one key difference. It may thus be useful to precede the direct comparison of the views of Mendelssohn and Kant with a brief account of Locke's argument, since contrasts to it will help illuminate both of the subsequent positions.[4] This chapter will then compare Mendelssohn's and Kant's views on religious freedom. The next chapter will interpret Kant's defense of the uniqueness of Christianity as an historical forerunner of the pure religion of reason as a critique of Mendelssohn's defense of religious pluralism and of Judaism as a genuine religion within the plurality of such religions.

## 2. Locke

Locke, born in 1632, came of age during the English Civil War of the 1640s and the Protestant Commonwealth of the 1650s, and the question of the toleration of Roman Catholicism or even the threat of its re-establishment persisted throughout the Stuart Restoration until the Glorious Revolution of 1688.[5] The question of religious liberty was thus the central question of British politics for most of Locke's life, and it was a central question of his own intellectual career as well. Locke began writing on the question of toleration as early as 1659,[6] and an "Essay concerning Toleration" from

---

[2] [John Locke,] *Epistola de tolerantia* (Gouda: Justus ab Hoeve, 1689); John Locke, *Epistola de tolerantia/A Letter on Toleration*, Latin text edited with a preface by Raymond Klibansky, English translation by J.W. Gough (Oxford: Clarendon Press, 1968), henceforth "*LT*."

[3] Kant's chief publication on philosophy of religion is *Religion within the Boundaries of Mere Reason* ("*RBMR*") from 1793, translated by George di Giovanni in Kant, *Religion and Rational Theology*, edited and translated by Allen W. Wood and George di Giovanni (Cambridge: Cambridge University Press, 1996). In what follows, I will also cite Kant's main work on political philosophy, the Doctrine of Right of the 1797 *Metaphysics of Morals* ("*MM*, *DR*"), from Kant, *Practical Philosophy*, edited and translated by Mary J. Gregor (Cambridge: Cambridge University Press, 1996).

[4] On the relation between Locke's and Mendelssohn's arguments, see Alexander Altmann, "The Philosophical Roots of Moses Mendelssohn's Plea for Emancipation," in his *Die trostvolle Aufklärung*, pp. 217–28, at pp. 222–3; Allan Arkush, *Moses Mendelssohn and the Enlightenment* (Albany: State University of New York Press, 1994), pp. 121–3; Cord-Friedrich Berghahn, *Moses Mendelssohn's "Jerusalem": Ein Beitrag zur Geschichte der Menschenrechte und der pluralistischen Gesellschaft in der deutschen Aufklärung* (Tübingen: Max Niemeyer Verlag, 2001), pp. 223–6; and Björn Pecina, *Mendelssohns diskrete Religion* (Tübingen: Mohr Siebeck, 2016), pp. 249–59.

[5] On Locke's life, see Maurice Cranston, *John Locke: A Biography* (London: Longmans, Green and Co., 1957), and Roger Woolhouse, *Locke: A Biography* (Cambridge: Cambridge University Press, 2007).

[6] See *LT*, Introduction, pp. 3–4.

1667 also survives;[7] but the work that became best known during his life and since, although it was published anonymously and Locke did not acknowledge it until shortly before his death in 1704, was the *Epistola de tolerantia*, written during his Dutch exile in 1685 and published in 1689, only after Locke's return to England in the aftermath of the ascension of the Dutch William of Orange as the husband of Mary, the actual heiress to the throne as the daughter of the deposed James II.

The argument of the *Letter on Toleration* is straightforward. Locke begins by arguing that true Christianity lies not in particular doctrines and rituals, but in "charity, meekness, and goodwill towards all mankind, even towards those who do not profess the Christian faith" (*LT*, p. 59). This prepares the way for the argument that there is a rational core of Christianity independent of any more particular beliefs and revelations that Locke will develop in *The Reasonableness of Christianity* of 1695,[8] and that will be expanded into the view that there is a rational and minimal core to *all* religions by later Enlightenment thinkers such as Mendelssohn and Kant. Locke presupposes that it is only through internal commitment to charity, meekness, and good will to all grounded upon conviction of the value of these attitudes that anyone can earn salvation. He then separates the aims of the state from the aims of religion: "the commonwealth" is "a society of men constituted only for preserving and advancing their civil goods [*bona civilia*]," namely "life, liberty, bodily health, and freedom from pain, and the possession of outward things, such as lands, money, furniture, and the like," while religion aims at salvation, which Locke supposes can be consequent only upon the individual's belief or conviction, thus "It is faith that gives force and efficacy to the true religion that brings salvation" (*LT*, pp. 65–7). The institution of the state is necessitated by the fact that people can interfere with each other's freedom and security in their life and possessions, a danger that can be remedied only through the establishment and enforcement of laws by a magistrate who must answer to the interests of all, but salvation is the private business of each:

Since men are so dishonest that most of them prefer to enjoy the fruits of other men's labour rather than work to provide for themselves; therefore, to protect their possessions, their wealth and property, and also their liberty and bodily strength, which are their means of livelihood, they are obliged to enter into society with one another, so that by mutual assistance and combined forces each man may have secure and private possession of the things that are useful for life. Meanwhile the care of his eternal salvation is left to each individual, since the attainment of it cannot be assisted by another man's industry, nor can the loss of it turn to another man's prejudice, nor the hope of it be taken from him by any force... This being settled, it is easy to understand the ends that determine the magistrate's prerogative of making laws, that is, the public good in earthly or worldly matters, which is the sole reason for entering society and the sole object of the commonwealth once it is formed; and on the other hand the liberty that is left to private men in matters concerning the life to come; namely that each may do what he believes to be pleasing to God, on whose good pleasure man's salvation depends.

(*LT*, pp. 125–7)

---

[7] See John Locke, *An Essay concerning Toleration and Other Writings on Law and Politics 1667–1683*, ed. J.R. Milton and Philip Milton (Oxford: Clarendon Press, 2006), pp. 267–302.

[8] John Locke, *The Reasonableness of Chistianity, As delivered in the Scriptures*, ed. John C. Higgins-Biddle (Oxford: Clarendon Press, 1999), and *Vindications of the Reasonableness of Christianity*, ed. Victor Nuovo (Oxford: Clarendon Press, 2012).

Locke draws a fundamental distinction between the ends and means of the commonwealth or state on the one hand and of religion on the other. The end of the state is the security of each of its members in their freedom of action including use of their possessions, and the means to the realization of this end is the promulgation of laws that define the rights of each and the coercive enforcement of these laws when necessary. The end of religion is the salvation of individual souls, and this can be secured only by the faith, belief, or conviction of each, which cannot be secured by any external, let alone coercive means at all. The coercive means of enforcement available to a state might determine outward behavior, such as the utterance of certain words or performance of certain rituals, but this cannot reach inward to belief: "whatever profession you make, to whatever outward worship you conform, if you are not fully persuaded in your own mind that it is both true and well pleasing to God, far from being any furtherance, it is an obstacle to salvation" (*LT*, p. 67). Locke also puts this point by stating that "It is useless for an unbeliever to assume the outward appearance of morality; to please God he needs faith and inward sincerity" (*LT*, 99), from which it follows that it is also useless for the state to compel the outward appearance of morality or any particular religious practice, since that cannot in turn produce "faith and inward sincerity." Even more generally, "To believe this or that to be true is not within the scope of our will," so nothing could be "gained by enjoining by law what a man cannot do," namely believe in some prescribed manner, "however much he may wish to do it" (*LT*, p. 121).

Locke's argument is thus that the state has neither the *right* nor the *means* to control the belief or faith of its members, thus that any attempt by the state to establish any particular religion or to give one preference over any other would in the first instance be unjustified and in the second doomed to failure, able to affect at best the outward behavior but not the real beliefs of anyone. People may join churches, as "free and voluntary" societies "for the public worship of God in such manner as they believe will be acceptable to the Deity for the salvation of their souls" (*LT*, p. 71). Because they involve public worship, the state *could* effectively interfere with the freedom of churches, as contrasted to the freedom of internal belief of individuals, but it still has no *right* to do so. The rights of the state arise only from individuals' concession of their own power to protect the security of their lives, freedom of action, and use of goods for the sake of the more efficient collective protection of those rights, and the state has no rights that extend beyond that. Further, even though churches are associations of individuals, because they are associations with the aim of helping each of their members toward salvation, and salvation can be earned only through "inward sincerity," churches or religions as outward institutions "may employ as many exhortations and arguments" as they please, "but all force and compulsion must be forborne, and nothing be done for the sake of dominion. Nobody is obliged in this matter to obey the admonitions or injunctions of another further than he himself chooses" (*LT*, p. 125). Thus there is no place for civil interference in the practices of churches, but there is also no place for the use of coercive methods *within* the practices of churches either. They can only attempt to persuade or, more broadly, educate their members. However, Locke does claim that although *magistrates* (his term for those who exercise the power of the state) have neither right nor means to try to enforce any doctrinal orthodoxy, as voluntary associations, *churches* do have the right to control their own membership, in particular to exclude opponents of their views. The means available to create orthodoxy within a church are "exhortations, admonitions, and advice," but "If by these means offenders will not be reclaimed, and those who go astray brought back to the right path," which every church has the right to define for itself, then "nothing further remains to be done but that such stubborn and obstinate persons...should be separated and cast out from the society" (*LT*, p. 77). Thus Locke grants the power of excommunication to churches, though he is careful to insist that no *civil* penalties should be attached to excommunication from any particular church.

But Locke places several restrictions on this apparently absolute exclusion of the civic use of coercion in religious matters. The first exception follows by *modus tollens* from the premise that "laws are not concerned with the truth of opinion, but with the security and safety of the commonwealth and of each man's goods" (*LT*, p. 123), that is, his civic goods in the broad sense including life and liberty: its charge being to secure civic security, the state does have the right to prohibit "doctrines, incompatible with human society, and contrary to the good morals which are necessary for the preservation of civil society" (*LT*, p. 131). Of course the state cannot prohibit inward conviction of doctrines any more than it can coerce such conviction, so this must mean that the state has the right to prohibit outward expression of and most importantly action upon such doctrines. Second, Locke argues that one sect cannot arrogate privileges to itself that are not granted to others, in particular, that members of no sect can claim the privilege of breaking faith with "heretics," since each sect will "declare all who are not of their communion to be heretics" (*LT*, p. 133), and thus such a privilege would lead to a complete breakdown of civil order, which depends upon keeping faith with contracts, those among all citizens as well as those between citizens and their magistrate. Third, "That church can have no right to be tolerated by the magistrate which is so constituted that all who enter it *ipso facto* pass into the service and allegiance of another prince" (*LT*, p. 133). This clause was of course aimed at the continuing exclusion of Roman Catholics from British public life, on the ground that they owed their fealty not to the British crown and state but to the Papacy as a temporal power—as indeed it was in gradually decreasing degrees until 1929, although whether anyone in any country who practiced Catholicism "*ipso facto*" owed allegiance to the Pope as a temporal power is another matter. Finally, Locke claimed that "those who deny the existence of the Deity are not to be tolerated at all," because "Promises, covenants, and oaths, which are the bonds of human society, can have no hold upon or sanctity for an atheist" (*LT*, p. 135). Since no atheist can be trusted to keep a contract or a promise if he thinks he can get away with breaking it, no atheist can be trusted to maintain the security of civil society, which depends upon the security of promises or contracts.

Locke's first restriction is part of every reasonable account of freedom of religion, or of freedom of speech more generally. It continues in secular form in John Stuart Mill's recognition that even in the name of free speech no one has the right to start a panic by yelling "Fire!" in a crowded theater that is not in fact on fire—that is just an unacceptable injury to the safety of the public. Locke's second and third restrictions likewise arise from the magistrate's right and duty to maintain public security by regulating the external behavior but not internal beliefs. Locke's final claim, that atheists can be excluded from society because they cannot be trusted to keep compacts, depends upon what we might regard as a pre-Enlightenment conception of the basis of moral motivation, namely that it must lie ultimately in the hope of divine rewards for the fulfillment of moral obligations and the fear of divine punishments for their breach—a conception of moral motivation that Locke's own student and a patron saint of the Enlightenment and significant influence upon Moses Mendelssohn among many others, namely Anthony Ashley Cooper, the Third Earl of Shaftesbury, would decry just a few years after Locke's *Letter* as "mercenary."[9]

## 3. Mendelssohn

With this account of Locke's argument for toleration and its restrictions in place, let us now turn to Mendelssohn's *Jerusalem*. While Mendelssohn maintains Locke's firm distinctions between the *means or methods* of coercion and instruction, he does not correlate this with a strict distinction between the *goals* of state and religion; in our subsequent comparison between Mendelssohn and Kant, we will see that Kant returns to a stricter separation between the goals of state and religion, although not exactly to Locke's version of that distinction. Mendelssohn also firmly rejects the right of churches to excommunication of their own members and the necessity of oaths as the foundation of civic order. These arguments are clearly directed against Locke although Mendelssohn does not repeat Locke's name in connection with them. Kant will not repeat Mendelssohn's arguments on these points, although he provides no grounds for rejecting them. His main argument with Mendelssohn, as we will see, is on an altogether different point.

*Jerusalem* begins with the claim that finding the correct balance between "state and religion—civil and ecclesiastical constitution—secular and churchly authority" remains an unsolved problem, in spite of the centuries of effort devoted to it. He is worried about civil interference in properly religious matters, religious interference in properly civil matters, but also about excessive cooperation between church and state, "for they seldom agree but for the purpose of banishing from their realms a third moral entity, *freedom of conscience*, which knows how to derive some advantage from their disunity" (J, p. 33, JubA 8:103).[10] Mendelssohn then reprises Locke's distinction between the goals of state and of religion in the following way: on his interpretation of Locke, "*A state is a society of men who unite for the purpose of collectively*

---

[9] See Anthony Ashley Cooper, Third Earl of Shaftesbury, *Inquiry into Virtue and Merit* (1699) and *The Moralists* (1709), both included in his *Characteristicks of Men, Manner, Opinions, Times* of 1711; the best modern edition is ed. Philip Ayres, 2 vols. (Oxford: Clarendon Press, 1999). Reservations about the morality of atheists would continue, indeed can be found as late as Kant's *Critique of the Power of Judgment* of 1790, thus a century after Locke's *Letter*, although Kant's reservation is not that the atheist can have no *initial* motivation to be moral but that he could not *sustain* his motivation to be moral in the absence of any promise of an afterlife in which happiness can accompany virtue even if it does not do so in the moral agent's natural lifespan; see Kant, *Critique of the Power of Judgment*, §87, 5:452–3.

[10] I have changed Arkush's translation of *Freyheit* from "liberty" to "freedom" both to foster terminological consistency with the translations of Kant that will subsequently be used, but also because "liberty" in the English linguistic tradition including Hobbes, Locke, and Hume might connote *external* freedom of action while "freedom" is a more general term that can include *internal* freedom of belief. "Conscience" should certainly connote the latter even though it may also be meant to include the former.

*promoting their temporal welfare*," and "From this it follows, quite naturally, that the state is not to concern itself at all with the citizens' convictions regarding their eternal happiness,[11] but is to tolerate everyone who conducts himself well as a citizen, that is, who does not interfere with the temporal happiness of his fellow citizens" (J, pp. 37-8, JubA 8:107). His first criticism of Locke is then that a distinction between temporal and eternal happiness cannot be applied rigidly to the case of religion, because true religion also concerns temporal happiness and further eternal happiness is to be earned only through contribution to the temporal happiness of one's fellows, not through any other putative service of God. And conversely, he does not see a need to "restrict the purpose of society solely to the *temporal*": "If men *can* promote their eternal happiness by public measures it should be their natural duty to *do* so" (J, p. 38, JubA 8:107). Mendelssohn believes that in principle both state and church can work toward the perfection and therefore the happiness of human beings, the state by influencing human actions and religion by influencing human convictions. He writes:

Hence actions and convictions belong to the perfection of human beings, and society should, as far as possible, take care of both by collective efforts, that is, it should direct the action of its members toward the common good, and cause convictions [*Gesinnungen*][12] which lead to these actions. The one is the *government*, the other the *education* of social human beings. To both the human being is led by *reasons* [*Gründe*], to actions by *motivating grounds* and to convictions by *grounds of truth*. (J, p. 40, JubA 8:110)

Underlying Mendelssohn's rejection of Locke's distinction between the goals of state and religion is a fundamental difference in moral and therefore political theory. Locke in the *Letter* grounds his argument upon the assumption that the aim of government is the security of "civil goods," above all the *freedom* of all to use their natural endowments and their rightfully acquired property, even their lives, as they think best; for Mendelssohn, a philosopher working within the perfectionist tradition of Gottfried Wilhelm Leibniz, Christian Wolff, and Alexander Baumgarten, the moral goal is the *perfection* of human capacities, one's own and that of others, with *happiness* as the natural consequence of perfection. Thus Locke can separate the goal of the state as essentially negative, preserving the freedom of each from undue interference by others, from the positive goal of religion, salvation, while no such separation is possible for Mendelssohn. Both state and religion are to contribute to the perfection of the human condition. And further, while there might seem to be a separation between the perfection of human capacities in the natural or "temporal" lifespan of human beings and the continued perfection of human beings in a non-natural, non-temporal or eternal existence, and in this way still a separation between the goals of state and religion, Mendelssohn does not want to separate temporal and eternal perfection in this way, so religion, like the state, remains concerned with temporal perfection, and indeed eternal perfection—Mendelssohn does not speak of salvation, which is a specific conception of perfection presupposing original sin, and

---

[11] Here I have changed Arkush's translation of *Glückseligkeit* from "felicity" to "happiness," again to preserve terminological consistency with the translation of Kant.

[12] This could also be translated as "dispositions," as it often is in Kant translations.

thus not part of any conception of human perfection general enough to include Judaism under its umbrella[13]—can be founded only on temporal perfection.

Nevertheless, Mendelssohn still wants to keep the state from either establishing or interfering with religion, and indeed, as we will see, he clearly targets some of the restrictions on the separation of church and state that Locke had allowed: he rejects the idea that oaths that ultimately require a religious foundation should be required as a condition of citizenship as well as the idea that churches should have the right to excommunicate their members. On what ground does he do so? Not by a distinction between the *ends* of the state on the one hand and religion on the other, but by a distinction in their *means*. He argues that the state can use coercion to enforce at least some of its laws, namely those that protect the fully determinate or perfect rights of citizens by imposing determinate or perfect duties upon others, even though in such cases the state will have to be "content, if need be, with mechanical[14] deeds, with works without spirit, with conformity of action without conformity in thought" (J, p. 44, JubA 8:113), that is, with outward compliance with its laws even in the absence of inward commitment to or conviction of the validity of those laws; but that in other cases, the state, and in all cases religion, can use only *persuasion* or *education*, what Locke had called "exhortations and arguments" for "faith and inward sincerity." "The state has *physical power* and uses it when necessary," Mendelssohn writes; "the power of religion is *love* and *beneficence*." "In one word, civil society, viewed as a moral person, can have the *right of coercion*, and, in fact, has actually obtained this right through the social contract. Religious society lays no claim to the *right of coercion*, and cannot obtain it by any possible contract" (J, p. 45, JubA 8:114). Thus it is impermissible for the state to apply coercive means to religious ends, for example to establish one religion or to give one religion preferences over others, and it is impermissible for religions themselves to apply coercive means, for example to excommunicate members, even without civil penalties, as Locke had argued, let alone with civil penalties, which would violate the first prohibition. Actually, the argument for this conclusion ought to proceed in two steps: first, coercive means *cannot* achieve the end of modifying inward convictions, beliefs, or dispositions, only the end of modifying external behavior, so it is irrational for any institution, state or religion, to attempt to use external means for this end; second, even if such modification of belief and not just behavior by external means were possible, no reasonable person would agree to allow it, or contract to do so, because only a concession of some external control of action by each is necessary to preserve as much security of freedom of action as is possible for all. Thus any use of coercion by the state would lie outside the pale of that to which reasonable persons could contractually agree.

Mendelssohn allows that the state may employ educational means to promote the perfection and happiness of its citizens in ways that go beyond what can properly be

---

[13] The Göttingen professor of "oriental" languages and defender of Christianity Johann David Michaelis got this exactly right in his review of *Jerusalem* when he wrote that the Jews "could become blessed without Messiah, according to their religion he has not come *to make his people blessed from their sins*, but merely for their hopes of a future, brilliant earthly happiness"; Michaelis, *Orientalische und Exegetische Bibliothek* 22 (1783): 59–99, cited from *JubA* 22:229–54, at p. 254.

[14] Mendelssohn actually writes *todten*, literally "dead."

enforced by coercive means. (He does not raise issues concerning the legitimacy of compulsory public education, which did not exist in the Prussia of his time.) But his fundamental claim about religious institutions is that they can use only educational, not coercive means; and his argument against Locke's allowance of the right of excommunication to churches is based on his conception of the educational mission of religion. This point is part of a larger series of inferences that he draws from his basic premise. The argument begins with the claim that the church—that is, any institution for public worship and instruction, regardless of denomination—"is founded upon the relationship between God and man," but since God, as a perfect being, "is not a being who needs our benevolence, requires our assistance, or claims any of our rights for his own use" (J, p. 57, JubA 8:126), we have no direct duties of service to him; we have only our duties to preserve and promote our own perfection and that of others in his name. "All of men's duties are obligations toward God" while none of them are obligations solely to God: rather, "We ought, from love of God, to love ourselves in a rational manner, to love his creatures; just as we are bound, from a rational love of ourselves, to love our fellow men" (J, p. 58, JubA 8:127). The last step relies upon Mendelssohn's reasonable assumption that human beings cannot perfect themselves by themselves, but only in society, with the assistance of others, which requires that each be prepared to assist others. "A human being cannot be happy without *beneficence*, not without *passive*, but also not without *active* beneficence. He cannot become perfect except through mutual assistance, through an exchange of service and reciprocal service, through active and passive connection with his fellow human" (J, p. 47, JubA 8:116). Mendelssohn sees what God requires of us as nothing less and nothing more than our service toward the perfection of ourselves and others—religion "only gives those same duties and obligations a more exalted *sanction*" (J, p. 58, JubA 8:127)—and on this basis he rejects the traditional but "erroneous" and "inconsistent" trifold division of duties into those toward God, self, and others found in Pufendorf, Wolff, Baumgarten, and others. Kant likewise rejects the idea of a separate category of duties to God, from the lectures on ethics delivered before the publication of *Jerusalem* to the *Religion within the Boundaries of Mere Reason* published a decade later.

But it is the premise that the sole task of religion is to promote human perfection by influencing the inward dispositions of human beings, or through broadly educational means—"to admonish, to instruct, to fortify, to comfort" (J, p. 59, JubA 8:128)—that furnishes the basis for Mendelssohn's exclusion of any coercive powers of churches or of the state upon churches. First he claims that the church owes its members duties of education towards perfection, but that they have no obligations back to the church, thus it has no "right to goods and properties" that can conflict with those of its members, and that because the church has no claim upon the property of its members there is also no contract between its members and a church. Thus no "compulsory duty toward it [can] ever be imposed upon its members" (J, p. 59, JubA 8:128), "Nor has the church any right to reward or punish actions" (J, p. 60, JubA 8:128). These are the lemmata for Mendelssohn's more specific restrictions on the use of coercion in religion.

First, if the church has no claims to property, its teachers can have no claim to payment (although Mendelssohn allows that the state may compensate individuals, not for their service to their church, but for their loss of time available for other occupations.) This restriction is accompanied with the empirical claim that payment would undermine the educational and exemplary efficacy of the teacher of religion: "What influence can the teacher of wisdom and virtue hope to have when he teaches for pay and is for sale to the highest bidder?" (J, p. 60, 8:128).

Second, Mendelssohn infers that churches have no need for any form of government (*Regierungsform*), because if a church has no "rights and claims" against its members, it has no need for laws, judgments, and penalties, thus no need for a legislature, judiciary, and executive (J, p. 62, *JubA* 8:130). Of course, disputes over rights and claims may arise between members of a church, as between any persons, but since these cannot be specifically religious rights and claims, there being none, they can be handled by ordinary civil authority. (This was part of Mendelssohn's long-running argument that ordinary disputes among Jews should be handled by civil rather than rabbinical courts, which hardly endeared him to contemporary rabbis.)

Third, a church cannot rightly restrict inquiry or freedom of opinion or impose orthodoxy, "For it evidently acts contrary to its own purpose [*Endzweck*] when it directly forbids inquiry, or allows disputes to be decided in any other manner than by rational arguments" (J, p. 63, *JubA* 8:131). For Mendelssohn, the model of the appropriate attitude of a church toward doctrinal disagreement is obviously not a claim of papal infallibility (the right to which would in any case not be asserted for another century) but that of free-spirited dispute among rabbis, themselves understood not as officers of a church but simply as especially learned but open-minded scholars and thinkers.

And fourth, "Excommunication and the right to banish, which the state may occasionally permit itself to exercise"—for the state represents the contract among its members to enforce their rights, and those who do not wish to bear the costs of a contract may rightly be excluded from its benefits—"are diametrically opposed to the spirit of religion. To banish, to exclude, to turn away the brother who wishes to take part in my edification and lift up his heart to God in beneficial union together with me" is simply incompatible with the educational mission of any church (J, p. 73, *JubA* 8:140). Presumably, a member who would disrupt the meetings of the church might have to be separated from those meetings, as an unruly student may have to be taken out of the classroom, but just as such a student should not simply be expelled from school but rather needs to receive extra educational efforts to accomplish the mission of the school, so the disruptive church member needs extra educational efforts, not the outright denial of such benefits by means of excommunication. Or in the rhetorical figure that Mendelssohn uses, "To exclude a dissident, say a worthy clergyman of this city, to expel a dissident from the church is like forbidding a sick person to enter a pharmacy" (J, p. 74, *JubA* 8:141)—the sick person is the one who needs the pharmacy the most.

Mendelssohn's rejection of the permissibility of oaths also comes in his series of exclusions of coercive methods within religious institutions.[15] This is because it is in

---

[15] For a discussion of Mendelssohn's rejection of oaths and an argument that Kant's "What is Enlightenment?," which we discussed in the previous chapter, defends them, see J. Colin McQuillan,

the first instance a rejection of the permissibility of demanding oaths from "teachers and priests...that they subscribe to certain doctrines of the faith" (J, p. 63, JubA 8:131). The rationale for this exclusion is that, first, there is only a very small body of beliefs essential to any church, namely belief in the existence of God, providence, and immortality, and second, that it is *inward belief* in these essentials that matters; the outward expression of commitment to these essentials is just "empty sound, words," neither necessary nor sufficient for internal conviction. And adding the formula of some oath, adding the words "I swear that..." to some pronouncement of belief, like adding the words "It is true that..." to an otherwise unadorned utterance of a sentence on a deflationary theory of truth, is just adding words to words, which the swearer of the oath "tosses into the air at no greater cost to himself than is required by a simple assurance" (J, p. 64, JubA 8:131-2). If you cannot trust the unadorned utterances of a speaker to convey sincerely his inmost beliefs or intentions, you cannot trust his more adorned utterances either.

Since this argument is made within the framework of Mendelssohn's argument against the use of coercion within religion, it is not specifically aimed at Locke's rejection of toleration for atheists in civil society on the basis of the argument that the security of the social contract depends upon the oaths of the contractors but atheists will refuse to give oaths and could not be trusted if they did. Mendelssohn's point that adding the form of an oath to the expression of a commitment is just to add more words, which does not by itself add anything to the strength of the commitment, which is either inwardly there or not regardless of what words are uttered, would apply outside the religious context as well. If I am sincere, simply saying that I will keep my end of a bargain is enough; if I am insincere, adding that I swear to God that I will do so will not change that. To be sure, Locke did not place his hope for fulfillment of the social contract on the sheer sincerity of the contractors, but on their fear of divine punishment if they broke an oath to God; but Mendelssohn has no room for that model of moral motivation within or without religious institutions.

The conclusion of the first half of *Jerusalem* is thus that "according to principles of sound reason, the divinity of which we must all acknowledge, neither state nor church would be authorized to assume any right in matters of faith other than the right to teach, any power other than the power to persuade, any discipline other than the discipline of reason and principles" (J, p. 77, JubA 8:145). No church has the right to use coercion against its members, thus within any church, "all ecclesiastical coercion will be unlawful," and no state has the right to use coercion whether against or in behalf of any church, or for or against any individual on account of religious beliefs, thus "all external power in religious matters will be violent usurpation" (J, p. 78, JubA 8:145). The sole restriction on this broad prohibition is Locke's proviso that the state may regulate the external actions of churches or their members if these threaten the civil order that is the *raison d'être* of the existence of the state itself; this is so obvious that Mendelssohn does not bother to state it until the very end of the book, where he concludes "Let everyone be permitted to speak as he thinks, to invoke

"Oaths, Promises, and Compulsory Duties: Kant's Response to Mendelssohn's *Jerusalem*," *Journal of the History of Ideas* 75 (2014): 581–604.

God after his own manner or that of his fathers, and to seek eternal salvation where he thinks he may find it, as long as he does not disturb public happiness and acts justly toward you and his fellow citizens" (J, p. 139, JubA 8:204).[16]

In the second half of the book, Mendelssohn takes up the objection, which had been brought against him in an anonymous pamphlet entitled "The Search for Light and Right in a Letter to Mr. Moses Mendelssohn," in fact written by a Berlin writer and satirist named August Friedrich Cranz, but presented to suggest that it had been written by Joseph Sonnenfels, a distinguished Habsburg civil servant who was a converted Jew, that Mendelssohn's prohibition of ecclesiastical law was inconsistent with his continued acceptance of the "sacred authority of the Mosaic religion," because "What are the laws of Moses but a system of religious government, of the power and right of religion?" (J, p. 84, JubA 8:154).[17] To this was added a question by an army chaplain, Daniel Ernst Mörschel, concerning Mendelssohn's commitment, as a Jew, to revelation (J, pp. 87–9, JubA 8:154–6)—a wedge to the further question, why Mendelssohn should not accept the revelation of the New Testament if he accepted that of the Old? Mendelssohn's answer to these challenges was a broad interpretation of the function of the commandments of the Jewish religion and of religious language and symbols more generally. This constitutes an essential and distinctive elements of his account of religious freedom.

The first part of his answer is that he, speaking on behalf of Judaism, "*recognize[s] no eternal truths other than those that are not merely comprehensible to human reason but can also be demonstrated and verified by human powers*" (J, p. 89, JubA 8:156). Judaism requires no belief in doctrines that could be revealed to humans only by a message from the divine, through a spokesman such as Moses; it requires only belief in the existence of God, providence, and the immortality of the human soul, all of which can be established by human reason alone, as Mendelssohn, as we have already seen, attempted to establish at length in his final extended work, the *Morning Hours*. Moses brought down from Sinai "no doctrinal opinions, no saving truths, no universal propositions," and Judaism requires no conviction of any such beyond the truths accessible to all human reason (J, p. 90, JubA 8:157). "Among all the prescriptions and ordinances of the Mosaic law, there is no single one which says: *You shall believe or not believe*" (J, p. 100, JubA 8:166). Instead, what Moses did bring

---

[16] Previously in the text Mendelssohn had recognized the Lockean proviso that the state may regulate actions even in the name of religion if they would injure public order by endorsing the remark of Isaak Iselin that "With respect to civil rights, the members of all religions are equal, with the sole exception of those whose opinions run counter to the principles of human and civil duties." Iselin made this remark in his review of Mendelssohn's earlier Preface to Menasseh ben Israel's *Defense of the Jews* (*Vindiciae Judaeorum*, 1782), JubA 8: 3–25, translated in Micah Gottlieb, ed., *Moses Mendelssohn: Writings on Judaism, Christianity, and the Bible* (Waltham: Brandeis University Press, 2011), pp. 40–52. As cited by Mendelssohn, Iselin's review appeared in *Ephemerides* Number 10 (October, 1782), p. 429; see J, pp. 78–9n.

[17] On the circumstances leading to the composition of *Jerusalem*, see Altmann, *Moses Mendelssohn*, pp. 502–13; Altmann's introduction to *Jerusalem*, ed. Arkush, pp. 7–13; Arkush, *Moses Mendelssohn and the Enlightenment*, pp. 158–61; Bourel, *Moses Mendelssohn*, pp. 395–401; and Micah Gottlieb, *Faith and Freedom: Moses Mendelssohn's Theological-Political Thought* (New York: Oxford University Press, 2011), p. 34. Partial translations of Cranz's tract and Mörschel's postscript can be found in Michah Gottlieb, ed., *Moses Mendelssohn on Judaism, Christianity, and the Bible* (Waltham: Brandeis University Press, 2011), pp. 53–69.

down from Sinai was a "divine *legislation*—laws, commandments, ordinances, rules of life, instructions in the will of God as to how the [Jews] should conduct themselves in order to attain temporal and eternal happiness" (which as we have already seen he did not rigorously separate as Locke had done) (J, p. 90, *JubA* 8:157). "They all say: *You shall do or not do*" (J, p. 100, *JubA* 8:166).[18] And about these commandments of types of actions rather than beliefs, Mendelssohn has three things to say.

First, in spite of what the penultimate reference to attaining temporal and eternal happiness might suggest, the point of performing the commanded actions—prayer at appointed times of the day, week, and year, the binding of the forehead with *tefilim*, the placement of the *mezzuzah* upon the doorpost, and so on—is not to earn reward, which would be mercenary, but to encourage reflection upon the fundamental truths of religion that are accessible to reason. Human beings do have reason, but they are also sensory creatures, and need sensory stimulation to trigger their use of reason. Mendelssohn makes a general claim that the eternal truths of religion are not merely accessible to pure reason, but also taught by God not through words but "through creation itself, and its internal relations, which are legible and comprehensible to all men." God does not confirm the eternal truths "by miracles, which affect only historical belief" (Mendelssohn gives no example, but one might be the miracle that a day's supply of oil burned for eight can remind later Jews of the resistance of their ancestors to their Alexandrian oppressors), "but He awakens the mind, which He has created, and gives it an opportunity to observe the relations of things, to observe itself, and to become convinced of the truths which it is destined to observe here below" (J, pp. 93–4, *JubA* 8:160). The further argument is then that commanded *practices*, as physical actions performed in the natural world, such as putting on *tefilim* or circumcising a male infant, can work the same way, "awakening the mind"[19] and leading it to reflect upon and become convinced of the eternal truths of religion. "Prescribed actions, each practice, each ceremony" can be "an occasion for a man in search of truth to reflect on... sacred matters or to seek instruction from wise men" (J, p. 119, *JubA* 8:184).

The last remark is important for Mendelssohn's next idea as well. The reason why reflection upon the eternal truths of religion should be stimulated through actions rather than through specific words is that words present themselves as having fixed meanings even though the historical circumstances of their speakers and hearers inevitably change, thus words are all too likely to create an *illusion* of stable meaning that could seem to obviate the need for reflection every time they are used, whereas actions obviously call for interpretation from the outset, because their intentions are not self-evident, and thus stimulate rather than suppress reflection. Fixed verbal formulas seem to "spare us the effort of penetrating and searching," while actions and practices are not "like hieroglyphic script" which "could lead to idolatry through abuse or misunderstanding," and further "also have the advantage over alphabetical

---

[18] Of course this interpretation of the character of Judaism was and remains deeply controversial, or in the words of Allan Arkush, "highly dubious" (*Moses Mendelssohn and the Enlightenment*, p. 181, see further pp. 186–94). See also Bourel, *Moses Mendelssohn*, pp. 427–36.

[19] That is presumably, the minds of the elders at the time of the circumcision, and the mind of the child only much later!

signs of not isolating the human being, of not making him to be a solitary creature, poring over writing and books," but "impel him rather to social intercourse, to imitation, and to oral, living instruction" (J, pp. 118–19, JubA 8:184), the best path toward human perfection and happiness. Mendelssohn accompanies this line of thought with the observation that *discussion* is essential to Jewish education, "living, spiritual instruction, which can keep pace with all changes of time and circumstances, and can be varied and fashioned according to a pupil's needs, ability, and power of comprehension" (J, p. 102, JubA, 8:168–9). This thought can be linked to his argument against excommunication in the first part of *Jerusalem*: the proper response to a resistant student is not to throw him out of school, but to find the way of putting the point at hand that will ultimately reach that particular student. Thus, Mendelssohn's idea is that words by themselves all too easily become "dead letter" (J, p. 103, JubA 8:169), and "The spirit of truth, which was to have been preserved in them, [can evaporate], and the empty vehicle that remain[s] behind [can turn] into a pernicious poison" (J, p. 115, JubA 8:181); words can lead to genuine reflection only if accompanied by conversation, and actions can lead to genuine reflection, no doubt calling for conversation as well.[20]

The point that conversation tailored to the particular student can lead to reflection and insight in a way that mere formulaic words cannot leads to Mendelssohn's third idea, a foundation for his resistance to those who pressed him to convert to Christianity or at least justify his continuing adherence to Judaism. His argument that instruction must be tailored to the individual student is connected to a larger argument that the mentalities of not only individuals but also peoples at different places and times in human history are different, thus that modes of presentation of religious ideas, even if the underlying ideas are the same, must differ for different audiences if they are to be effective. One size does not fit all. Mendelssohn puts this argument in a framework that disturbs Kant, as we will see in the last chapter, for he claims that there may be moral progress in individual lives but that "it does not seem to me to have been the purpose of Providence that mankind as a whole advance steadily here below and perfect itself in the course of time… Now as far as the human race as a whole is concerned, you will find no steady progress in its development that brings it ever closer to perfection. Rather do we see the human race in its totality slight oscillate" (J, p. 96, JubA 8:163). As we will see in the final chapter of this study, Kant took these remarks as an expression of what he called "Abderitism," or pessimism about the possibility of human improvement over the course of history, a belief that Kant thought would all too easily provide an excuse for not trying very hard to improve the human moral and political condition. But in context, Mendelssohn's point is more limited: his claim is that while individual humans

---

[20] Mendelssohn's views on language, script, and conversation have recently attracted a great deal of commentary and analysis. See Bruce Rosenstock, *Philosophy and the Jewish Question: Mendelssohn, Rosenzweig, and Beyond* (New York, Fordham University Press, 2010), pp. 73–5; Gideon Freudenthal, *No Religion without Idolatry: Mendessohn's Jewish Enlightenment* (Notre Dame: University of Notre Dame Press, 2012); Grit Schorch, *Moses Mendelssohns Sprachpolitik* (Berlin and Boston: Walter de Gruyter, 2012), pp. 220–31; and Elias Sacks, *Moses Mendelssohn's Living Script: Philosophy, Practice, History, Judaism* (Bloomington: Indiana University Press, 2017).

may develop in a somewhat predictable fashion, with one way of putting religious ideas thus being most suitable for the child, another for the adolescent, and yet another for the adult, humankind as a whole does not develop as a single individual, with one mode of religious presentation—say the Old Testament—being suitable for it at one stage, another—say the New Testament—being suitable for it at another. Rather, humankind consists of different groups, with different histories, who cannot be compared to each other on some single scale of progress, and for whom different outward forms of religion may be and remain suitable. Since conviction of the few central, eternal truths of religion cannot in any case be guaranteed by the repetition of any particular formulaic liturgy, there is no need for uniformity across all human groups. And even if it makes sense for a group to hold some particular set of *practices* constant, as Mendelssohn sees the Jews as having done so since the time of Moses, this does not contradict the claim just made, because the practices are only stimuli for reflection, which must be alive for each individual as well as generation and carried on in its own way by each.

This line of thought leads to the argument with which Mendelssohn concludes *Jerusalem*. He argues that an attempt to bring about "a union of faiths...could have but the most unfortunate consequences for reason and liberty of conscience," because all it could do would be to stifle individual thought without effectively producing unity of belief: "The agreement, therefore, could lie only in the words, in the formula" (J, p. 137, JubA 8:202). Human beings are by nature simply too diverse to be led to a single set of convictions by any single set of words. But beyond this, Mendelssohn makes what we might regard as the aesthetic point that human diversity is interesting and ought to be pleasing to any enlightened thinker. In the context of *Jerusalem*, to be sure, Mendelssohn puts this point in religious or we might say teleological rather than purely aesthetic terms: he says "let us not feign agreement where diversity is evidently the plan and purpose of Providence" (J, p. 138, JubA 8:202). If human diversity is the plan of providence, then clearly we ought to recognize it, and if the plan of providence is ultimately to yield human happiness, then recognizing and contemplating human diversity ought to be part of human happiness. We ought to enjoy our differences, including our differences in religious practice, rather than trying to suppress them, undergirded in any case by the recognition that at the very most fundamental level the essential beliefs of all religions are the same. In the end, then, Mendelssohn's argument is that diversity of religious belief ought not to be merely tolerated, because no individual and therefore no state has the right to try to forcibly enforce any orthodoxy; such diversity ought to be *celebrated* as part of the pleasing diversity of humanity itself. Or as Micah Gottlieb has put the point, within the conceptual framework of both Mendelssohn's perfectionism and his theory of the relation between church and state, "Mendelssohn considers the very fact of religious diversity a way of promoting individual perfection. In opposing state religion and defending the value of multiple forms of religious practice in a single state, Mendelssohn stakes out a position opposed to both Maimonides and Spinoza."[21]

---

[21] Gottlieb, *Faith and Freedom*, p. 54.

Or as Bruce Rosenstock sees it, Mendelssohn has found the basis of diversity within Judaism itself: "Judaism raises its dissident voice in the name of the ineradicable heterogeneity in the very heart of humanity. The fact that 'God has stamped everyone, not without reason, with his own facial features' is a sign that to seek after unanimity of expressed belief... is 'deliberately to contravene our calling, our vocation in this life and the next'."[22] And as Alexander Altmann implies, Mendelssohn's argument is a double-edged sword: it is an argument to the Christian majority that they can accept the Jews as their civil equals without worrying that the Jews will attempt to undermine the majority religion, but also "an appeal to the Jewish community not to sacrifice Jewish identity on the altar of emancipation."[23] Of course, that was the path subsequently taken by many Jews in Germany, including most of Mendelssohn's own children.

Mendelssohn's argument that Judaism itself celebrates religious diversity might be hard to square with the Biblical claim that God made the Jews a chosen people and commanded them to conquer neighboring peoples, although it is easier to reconcile with the non-proselytizing character of the religion. But whether the acceptance or even celebration of religious diversity has its basis in a particular religion, in the metaphysics of perfectionism, or in aesthetic preference, it seems to be an inescapable fact of history and of contemporary life. Kant, as we will see in the following chapter, thinks of the diversity of historical religions as something to be superseded, but Mendelssohn's acceptance of such diversity seems the more reasonable response to its empirical reality.[24] Yet the risk in Mendelssohn's hanging his argument for religious freedom on the premise that the coercive means of the state neither can nor should be used to enforce conformity to any favored doctrine is another matter. One contemporary reviewer recognized the strength of Mendelssohn's commitment to the principle of religious freedom but also the risk of defending it as he did:

Nothing is more illuminating than the grounds with which Mr. M. has disputed *coercion of conscience* in this important text, and there is no doubt that this book will remain a defense of freedom of conscience as long as people can still think and write about religion...

But if positive religion is necessary for the perfection of the commonwealth, then the state cannot concede that anyone could be a citizen or a subject who does not at least externally confess to some positive religion... And thus the state in accordance with all right of reason can connect the right of citizenship to the condition of confession to a religion.

And from this I can draw the conclusion, *that in accordance with the law of reason there are rights to persons and things that are connected to doctrines, insofar as these constitute a part of the external service of God, and are preserved through consensus in these... and that external religion is grounded on the relation of people to people.*[25]

---

[22] Rosenstock, *Philosophy and the Jewish Question*, p. 77, quoting from *J*, p. 138, *JubA* 8:203.
[23] Altmann, "The Philosophical Roots of Moses Mendelssohn's Plea for Emancipation," *Die trostvolle Aufklärung*, p. 225.
[24] And so this recognition, although without reference to Mendelssohn, became the basis of "reasonable pluralism" in John Rawls, *Political Liberalism* (New York: Columbia University Press, 1993).
[25] Johann Christian Loßius, review of *Jerusalem*, *Übersicht der neuesten Litteratur der Philosophie* 1 (1784): 27-47, cited from *JubA* 22:255-6.

This argument is that if the "perfection" of the state, even the perfection of its security, requires conformity in the outward practice of religion, then it is permissible to enforce that, and if that should in turn bring with it conformity in doctrine (*Lehrmeynungen*)—well, that might then be possible and there would be no ground to object to it. This was the central issue in Zöllner's otherwise quite friendly response to *Jerusalem* as well. He put the issue of whether beliefs can really be separated cleanly from actions and thus whether certain beliefs might not inevitably lead to actions threatening to the security of the state in terms of a contemporary dispute over whether Mennonites who would not serve in the military should be allowed to remain in Prussia's Rhenish territories: "Whether for example the doctrine [*Lehrbegriff*] of the Mennonites be true or false, whether it contains many or few or no errors at all would be able to be a matter of indifference to the King of Prussia as long as their opinions are nothing more than opinions. But if a number of his subjects in West Prussia adopt this doctrine, and on this account except themselves from a civil duty that is necessary in our state, that of military service, then their religious opinion becomes a matter for the state."[26] The argument that matters of conscience have a special status that can never be the concern of the state may be problematic. In that case, it would be better to defend freedom of conscience with an argument that presupposes neither that the state has no means nor no right to enforce opinions or convictions. This is exactly what Kant attempts to do, by deriving the inviolability of freedom of conscience directly from the moral and political imperative to restrict only the *external* use of freedom and that only insofar as it is necessary to guarantee the equal external use of freedom by all. Anything, whether belief or its expression in speech or other action, is exempt from state control as long as it does not by itself constrain the freedom of others, but anything, not just action but belief, might, indeed must be subject to regulation if it does necessarily impact the freedom of others. Such an argument will not presuppose any special status for belief, but puts a burden of proof on any limitation of freedom, that of showing that it is necessary to preserve the greatest equal freedom for all.

## 4. Kant on the Separation of Church and State

Kant's position on the separation between church and state is crystal-clear. On the basis of a model of the state that is closer to Locke's conception of it as a mechanism for the collective assurance of rights than to Mendelssohn's conception of it as a partner with churches in the promotion of human perfection and felicity, he concludes without reservation that the state has no right to institute or endorse any religious practices. He suggests no limits on religious liberty other than the Lockean proviso that religious practice not upset public peace. His position on religious pluralism, however, is more complicated. He believes that there is a religion of reason common to all humankind, specifically that the moral law and what it commands, the highest good, stand grounded in reason independent of any divine command, but that it leads to rational belief in the fundamental ideas of religion, namely the

---

[26] Zöllner, *Ueber Moses Mendelssohn's Jerusalem*, p. 127.

existence of God and human immortality as the conditions of the realizability of the highest good, the maximal combination of virtue and happiness as the complete object of morality, without belief in which it would be irrational for us to act, as the moral law commands us, to try to bring this about. He also believes that the rational ideas central to morality and religion need presentation in forms accessible to human beings who are sensible as well as rational, thus need what he calls "aesthetic" presentation, that is, presentation in the forms of metaphors, symbols, and the like. He goes further and argues that human beings need social organizations, churches, to advance in morality, and that these in turn need foundational texts, that is, scriptures. Unlike, Mendelssohn, however, he sees no intrinsic value in historical traditions, and rather than holding that different forms for the sensible presentation of the fundamental beliefs of religion may be valid for different people and peoples, he clearly believes that the central ideas of Christianity, even though they are only metaphors or symbols, are better representations of morality than any others. He thus holds that different religious practices should be protected like any other exercises of freedom, but finds no special value in religious pluralism for its own sake. Further, he also seems to believe that the need for visible churches practicing historical faiths will someday disappear from human history altogether, so that the plurality of visible churches and their practices will be replaced by a single, invisible church with no special practice except that of morality itself. For this reason he does not seem to take religious pluralism as seriously as does Mendelssohn. On this issue, a dream of reason may carry Kant beyond the evidence of human experience.

Kant's *Religion within the Boundaries of Mere Reason*, published when Kant was already under significant pressure from the conservative Prussian regime of Friedrich Wilhelm II, is as complex, even convoluted a work as he ever wrote, in part no doubt because of the rush in which he wrote as he saw the end of his own days approaching but in part perhaps to make it difficult to pin his views down.[27] The first two parts of

---

[27] Kant's *Religion* has recently received considerable commentary, including Pablo Muchnik, *Kant's Theory of Evil: An Essay on the Dangers of Self-love and the Aprioricity of History* (Lanham: Lexington Books, 2009); James J. DiCenso, *Kant, Religion, and Politics* (Cambridge: Cambridge University Press, 2011) and *Kant's Religion within the Boundaries of Mere Reason: A Commentary* (Cambridge: Cambridge University Press, 2012); Christopher J. Insole, *Kant and the Creation of Freedom: A Theological Problem* (Oxford: Oxford University Press, 2013); Lawrence J. Pasternak, *Routledge Guidebook to Kant on Religion within the Boundaries of Mere Reason* (London: Routledge, 2014); and Stephen R. Palmquist, *Comprehensive Commentary on Kant's Religion within the Boundaries of Mere Reason* (Chichester: Wiley, 2016). There have also been a number of collective volumes, including Chris L. Firestone and Stephen R. Palmquist, eds., *Kant and the New Philosophy of Religion* (Bloomington: Indiana University Press, 2006); Chris L. Firestone and Nathan Jacobs, *In Defense of Kant's Religion* (Bloomington: Indiana University Press, 2008); Sharon Anderson-Gold and Pablo Muchnik, eds., *Kant's Anatomy of Evil* (Cambridge: Cambridge University Press, 2010); Benjamin J. Bruxvoort Lipscomb and James Krueger, eds., *Kant's Moral Metaphysics* (Berlin and New York: Walter de Gruyter, 2010); and Otfried Höffe, ed., *Immanuel Kant: Die Religion innerhalb der Grenzen der bloßen Vernunft* (Berlin: Akademie Verlag, 2011). Much of this work, as several of the titles suggest, focus on the topic of radical evil and Kant's theory of human (and, in the case of Insole's book, divine) freedom; and since, as I am about to argue, Kant does not address the topic of religious freedom in his *Religion* but in his political works, little of it focuses on this question. In spite of its title, DiCenso's 2011 book is devoted mostly to the bearing of Kant's epistemology and moral philosophy on matters of religion, although he does emphasize that "questions concerning the meaning and function of religion are deeply intermeshed with ethical-political considerations" (p. 17) and discusses Kant's conception of enlightenment (pp. 48–62). Allen Wood writes on "Ethical Community,

the work, in which he argues that the freedom of the human will entails human responsibility for evil but also the possibility of human conversion from evil to good without divine intervention (Part One) and then interprets the Christian imagery of Christ and God as symbols of this freedom (Part Two), are clear. The argument becomes more involuted in the last two parts of the work, in which, like Mendelssohn, he clearly argues that the only rational conception of service to God is service to mankind in the form of morality, but argues more obscurely for the unique suitability of Christianity as a sensible form of religion, and then suggests that even that will be superseded by the pure religion of reason within human history. There will be no room here to follow all the twists and turns of Kant's argument, but I will try to address its main points.

The basis of all of Kant's thought, of course, is the Enlightenment idea that morality does not derive its force from divine command, but from human faculties,[28] in Kant's case that of pure reason, to which he adds his own argument that morality nevertheless grounds rational belief in the existence of human freedom, the existence of God, and the immortality of the soul—his version of Mendelssohn's three fundamentals of the religion of reason, the existence of God, providence, and immortality. The Preface to the *Religion* stated Kant's basic view clearly enough to have guaranteed his subsequent difficulties with the regime:

So far as morality is based on the conception of the human being as one who is free but who also, just because of that, binds himself through his reason to unconditional laws, it is in need neither of the idea of another being above him in order that he recognize his duty, nor, that he observe it, of an incentive other than the law itself. At least it is the human being's own fault if such a need is found in him; but in this case too, the need could not be relieved through anything else: for whatever does not originate from himself and his own freedom provides no remedy for a lack in his morality.—Hence on its own behalf morality in no way needs religion... (*RBMR*, 6:3)

As Kant had argued in previous works, the moral law is simply the expression of any pure practical reason, thus of our own pure practical reason, the application of reason's characteristic requirement of non-contradiction to our choice of ends and actions, and our consciousness of reason's own demand to act only in light of its requirement also entails our freedom to do so. We do not need theoretical belief in

---

Church and Scripture" in Höffe, *Religion*, pp. 131–5, touching upon Kant's "prophecy" that historical religion will ultimately be superseded by the pure religion of reason at pp. 148–50.

[28] This is the position stated so clearly at the outset of the century by Shaftesbury's *Inquiry concerning Virtue, or Merit*, originally published in 1699, when he writes "For whoever thinks there is a GOD, and pretends formally to believe that he is *just* and *good*, must suppose that there is independently such a thing as *Justice* and *Injustice*, *Truth* and *Falsehood*, *Right* and *Wrong*; according to which he pronounces that *God is just, righteous,* and *true*" (*Inquiry* I.iii.2, *Characteristicks*, vol 1, p, 213), and that Christian Wolff more cautiously implied, though not cautiously enough to spare him from the wrath of the Halle Pietists, when he wrote that the non-theistic Chinese could not be faulted because they "practiced good actions because they precisely considered their inner goodness...the same thing that God considered, when he commanded certain actions and forbade others," in his rectoral address on "The practical philosophy of the Chinese," *Oratio de Sinarum philosophica practica/Rede über die praktische Philosophie der Chinesen*, ed. Michael Albrecht (Hamburg: Felix Meiner Verlag, 1985), p. 61.

the existence of God to ground the moral law, nor do we need theoretical belief in divinely granted grace to ground our belief in our own freedom to be moral, although the *Religion* does clarify an unclarity in Kant's previous works by insisting that our freedom can only be understood as the freedom to choose *either* good *or* evil, and still to choose one even if we have previously chosen the other.[29] Kant will subsequently make room for the images of a divine lawgiver and grace, but on his account grace can never be granted except in response to the moral exercise of human freedom. He further argues that in virtue of reason's second main idea, that of the "unconditioned," morality itself gives rise to the idea of its complete object, "the idea of an object that unites within itself the formal condition of all such ends as we ought to have (duty) with everything which is conditional upon ends which we have and which conforms to duty (happiness proportioned to its observance), that is, the idea of a highest good in the world," and that to coherently believe in the realizability of such an end we must "assume" or "believe" (*glauben*) in the existence of "a higher, moral, most holy, and omnipotent being who alone can unite the two elements of this good" (*RBMR*, 6:5). In the *Critique of Practical Reason*, Kant had also argued that belief in the possibility of the highest good requires belief in personal immortality, to give infinite time for the perfection of individual virtue; but as was already argued in Chapter 4, the new interpretation of freedom in the *Religion* actually undercuts that argument by making conversion from evil to good in the choice of fundamental principle or maxim—whether to subordinate morality to self-love, or self-love to morality (*RBMR*, 6:36)—completely available to the human being *at any time*, and therefore has to offer a more subtle interpretation of the function of the idea of immortality.

After this brief statement of the principles of the religion of reason, the Preface to *Religion* continues with an equally brief statement of the freedom of philosophical theology from censorship by biblical theology (*RBMR*, 6:8–9) that prefigures the more extensive argument a few years later, in *The Conflict of the Faculties* (1798), that the responsibility of the philosophical faculty even within a state-supported university (the only kind that Kant knew) is a no-holds-barred search after truth even if that of the theological faculty is to train ministers of a particular religion, in the terms of his essay on enlightenment, in the "private" rather than "public" use of their reason. This seems to allow for the institution of a particular religion by the state even if the state's own philosophers are to be exempted from any censorship or constraint on their research. This might well appear to be a less strict separation between church and state than Mendelssohn or Locke had previously advocated. However, Kant might just have been limiting which fight he wanted to have in the *Religion* and *Conflict*, because his position on the impermissibility of state endorsement or institution of any particular church is just as clear and forceful as those of Locke

---

[29] This was the issue that was raised by Ulrich in 1788, and that was addressed by Carl Christian Erhard Schmid in his *Versuch einer Moralphilosophie* (1790), Karl Leonhard Reinhold in the Second Series of his *Letters on the Kantian Philosophy* (1792), and by Kant himself in Part One of the *Religion* (also 1792). The literature on this issue is too voluminous to be listed here; I have touched upon it in "The Struggle for Freedom: Freedom of the Will in Kant and Reinhold," and will go into more detail in a subsequent book.

and Mendelssohn in the work that comes between the *Religion* and the *Conflict*, namely the *Metaphysics of Morals* of 1797. Here is where Kant argues that freedom of belief and its expression is simply an intrinsic part of the "innate right" of freedom due to the "humanity" in each of us.

Like both Locke and Mendelssohn, Kant distinguishes public institutions, including churches, from religion proper, "which is an inner disposition lying wholly beyond the civil power's sphere of influence." Like both of them, Kant also accepts that the state does have one "right with regard to churches," namely the "*negative* right to prevent public teachers from exercising an influence on the *visible* political commonwealth that might be prejudicial to public peace" (*MM*, DR, General Remark C, 6:327). Unlike Mendelssohn, Kant does not argue that state and church share the end of promoting human perfection, but that since the improvement of human convictions which this end ultimately requires can only be accomplished by instruction, not coercion, the state has no right to try to coerce conviction either on its own or through its control of religious institutions. Like Locke, Kant instead separates the goals of state and church, arguing that the state is concerned chiefly with the preservation of security in person and property while the church is concerned with something else. Unlike Locke, however, Kant does not separate church and state by distinguishing between the temporal and the eternal—the this-worldly and the other-worldly—or even between the sphere of politics and the sphere of morality proper. Rather, he distinguishes between the functions of church and state by limiting the function of the state to the coercive enforcement of a small *part* of morality, namely the prohibition of injury to the freedom of external action of others, leaving the enforcement of all the rest of morality, our perfect duty not to injure our own freedom and our imperfect duty to promote our own perfection and the happiness of others, to the inward motivation of respect for the moral law itself, or the phenomenal form of such respect, namely virtue as "free self-constraint" (*MM*, DV, Introduction, section II, 6:383). Churches, as Kant will define them in *Religion*, are communal associations or institutions meant to support individuals in the development of their own virtue. Their concern is thus promotion of the fulfillment of all of the non-coercibly enforceable parts of morality, not some other-worldly salvation, or even of all of morality, since Kant holds that even though the state is required by the undeniable fact that people do not always act morally out of respect for morality alone and must sometimes be coerced to act at least in outward compliance with morality, although it is morally permissible to do this only for a subset of what morality demands, they *could* be motivated to comply with *all* the demands of morality out of respect for morality alone (*MM*, Introduction, section IV, 6:219). But the aims of the state remain distinct from those of churches, the former being only to enforce the small part of morality that is consistent with coercive enforcement, the latter being to foster fulfillment of all of morality by promotion of the proper inward disposition. The means at the disposal of the state, namely coercive enforcement, have no place in religion or in the institution or administration of churches—on this Kant agrees with Mendelssohn.

Here is the core of Kant's argument. Morality in general requires consistency in all uses of freedom, those affecting only oneself as well as those affecting others and those that potentially enhance the range of freedom of others as well as those that could infringe upon the latter.[30] The "Universal Principle of Right," which defines the proper sphere of the state, concerns only those actions that potentially infringe upon the freedom of action of others, and states that "An action is *right* if," that is, *only* if, "it can coexist with everyone's freedom in accordance with a universal law, or if on its maxim the freedom of choice of each can coexist with everyone's freedom in accordance with universal law" (*MM*, DR, Introduction, section C, 6:230). That is, any and all actions are rightful as long as they are compatible with the possibility of the free action of others as long as *those* actions observe the same constraint, that is, are also compatible with the free actions of others as long as they too observe this constraint. The Universal Principle of Right thus requires a distributed maximization of freedom of action in the form of as much freedom of action for each as is compatible with an equal freedom of action for all.[31]

Now the essence of the state, for Kant and other thinkers in his tradition, is the rightful threat and when necessary use of coercion for the enforcement of its laws; or, in Kant's terminology, right, as the domain of the state, is "connected with an authorization to use coercion," or more precisely "strict right can also be represented as the possibility of a fully reciprocal use of coercion that is consistent with everyone's freedom in accordance with universal laws" (*MM*, DR, Introduction, sections D and E, 6:231–2). That is a matter of definition, but it has to be shown that the exercise of right so defined is morally permissible. This Kant proposes to do by means of a very short argument:

Resistance that counteracts the hindering of an effect promotes this effect and is consistent with it.

That is a general claim, perhaps best understood as a causal claim.

Now whatever is wrong is a hindrance to freedom in accordance with universal laws.

This is the moral definition of wrong.

But coercion is a hindrance or resistance to freedom.

That is the definition of coercion.

Therefore, if a certain use of freedom is itself a hindrance to freedom in accordance with universal laws (i.e., wrong), coercion that is opposed to this (as a *hindering of a hindrance to freedom*) is right.

That is the conclusion of the argument, combining the definition of coercion with the moral requirement that freedom be preserved rather than hindered. Kant's gloss on this conclusion, namely:

Hence there is connected with right by the principle of contradiction an authorization to coerce someone who infringes upon it,

---

[30] See, for this kind of formulation, Kant's *Lectures on Ethics*, e.g., the Collins transcription, at 27:344–6.
[31] I have here presented Kant's Universal Principle of Right as if it obviously follows from the fundamental principle of morality. I have defended this interpretation from objections by Allen Wood, Thomas Pogge, and Marcus Willaschek in "Kant's Deductions of the Principles of Right," in Mark Timmons, ed., *Kant's Metaphysics of Morals: Interpretative Essays* (Oxford: Oxford University Press, 2002), pp. 23–64, reprinted in my *Kant's System of Nature and Freedom* (Oxford: Clarendon Press, 2005), pp. 198–242, and "The Twofold Morality of *Recht*: Once More Unto the Breach," *Kant-Studien* 107 (2016): 34–63.

may make it sound as if the entire argument is a matter of definition or analytic, but in fact the argument depends upon both the moral premise that preservation of maximal compossible freedom is morally right and injury to such freedom is wrong as well as the definition of coercion as hindrance to freedom; then it is supposed to follow that although *ceteris paribus* the hindrance of freedom is wrong, the hindrance to the hindrance of freedom is by contrast right. So coercion is justified when it is a necessary means to a hindrance of the hindrance of freedom (as well as a sufficient means—that is the significance of the first premise of the argument), and given that freedom must be preserved coercion is not merely morally permissible but morally necessary under such conditions, although not under any others.

Of course, not every free action falls under the protection of the Universal Principle of Right and earn the right to coercive enforcement. My unprovoked act of shooting you might be, considered in isolation from its effect on you, an exercise of my freedom, but it is one that would destroy your freedom, and is, again *ceteris paribus* (acting in self-defense might be a different case), prohibited under the Universal Principle of Right and thus liable to coercive prevention or punishment, at least under a deterrence theory of punishment aimed at the prevention of further such acts. But it is only such acts that are infringements upon the freedom of others that are prohibited and coercible under the Universal Principle of Right, and Kant makes it clear that *belief* and the *expression of belief in speech* or otherwise is not suitable for coercion under the Universal Principle of Right. He does this in his exposition of the "only innate right...belonging to every human being by virtue of his humanity," namely "*Freedom* (independence from being constrained by another's choice), insofar as it can coexist with the freedom of every other in accordance with a universal law" (*MM*, DR, General Division, B, 6:237). This is just a restatement of the Universal Principle of Right: if what the Principle declares to be right is all exercise of freedom that is in accordance with universal law, then what it protects is all exercise of freedom in accordance with universal law. But now Kant specifies three "authorizations" of more specific forms for the exercise of freedom that cannot injure others and therefore do not require consent by others to fall under the Universal Principle of Right—unlike what he calls "acquired right," that is, the assertion of property claims which do take away from what others might control or use and therefore do require some form of assent by others before they can be protected by the Principle. These authorizations, which simply spell out what it means to have freedom equal to the freedom of others, are "*equality*, that is, independence from being bound by others to more than one can in turn bind them"; "being *beyond reproach*, since before [one] performs any action affecting rights he has done no wrong to anyone";[32] and finally,

---

[32] This sounds like what is called in the Anglo-American tradition the presumption of innocence before any court. However, that is a procedural principle determining that the prosecution has the burden of proof, to establish guilt, rather than the defendant, to prove innocence. Kant's principle is a substantive, moral principle, that no one should be punished except for actually having committed a crime, however that is to be proved. Leslie A. Mulholland has called this Kant's "deed principle"; see his *Kant's System of Rights* (New York: Columbia University Press, 1990), pp. 224–5. B. Sharon Byrd and Joachim Hruschka do not make this distinction in their comment on this passage in *Kant's Doctrine of Right: A Commentary* (Cambridge: Cambridge University Press, 2010), pp. 82–3.

freedom of thought and speech, "merely communicating [one's] thoughts to [others], telling or promising them something, whether what he says is true and sincere or untrue and insincere; for it is entirely up to them whether they want to believe him or not" (6:237–8). The right to free belief and expression of belief is based on the premise that "one is authorized to do to others anything that does not in itself diminish what is theirs, so long as they do not want to accept it," which is simply the converse of the principle that one is prohibited from doing to others anything that does diminish "what is theirs," that is, even before we consider acquired rights to property, simply their own freedom of their person, *their* right to believe and say whatever they want as long as *they* do not limit the freedom of others. The great assumption that Kant is making, of course, is that simply believing something oneself or expressing it to others does not force others to believe it or do anything further, thus does not compromise their freedom in any way. Brainwashing, if such a thing exists, or planting electrodes in the head of another to modify their beliefs would not be permitted under Kant's principle, and yelling "Fire!" in a crowded theater may be speaking to people under circumstances in which they cannot retain their ordinary freedom to decide what to believe. Perhaps how we speak to or educate children or other especially impressionable persons also requires special scrutiny. But Kant's assumption is that in general, competent adults retain the freedom to make up their own minds about their beliefs regardless of what is said to them, so there can be no right to constrain what is said to them in any way. Even lies and false promises, Kant argues, are juridically permissible as long as those to whom they are addressed retain their freedom to make up their own minds whether to believe them, although they are certainly morally objectionable, for telling a lie violates a duty to *oneself* to perfect one's own capacity for truthful communication (6:238n).[33]

From this general argument for free belief and speech Kant derives the specific claim that there can be no right to coerce religious belief and expression or coercively prevent religious inquiry, thus there is no right to such coercion that could be transferred to and enforced by the state. Kant's account of the state, or what he calls "public right," is premised on the thesis that it can only take over rights and duties that belong to the people as a whole, which are defined by the Universal Principle of Right. This is reflected in his view that the people are sovereign, with their sovereignty expressed in a legislature and with executive and judicial powers delegated to agents of the legislature (*MM*, DR, §46)—a radical doctrine in eighteenth-century Prussia, indeed in Germany before 1945, where even during the best years of the second *Reich* parliamentary power was conceived as delegated from the Crown rather than executive power flowing from the people in parliament to their designated agent. Perhaps to obscure how radical his doctrine of sovereignty is, Kant often speaks of the power of the state being exercised by a "supreme commander" (*Oberbefehlshaber*), a turn of phrase that might allow a monarch exercising

---

[33] The right to freedom of opinion and speech as the third component of the innate right to freedom are briefly discussed by Arthur Ripstein in *Force and Freedom: Kant's Legal and Political Philosophy* (Cambridge, Mass.: Harvard University Press, 2009), p. 51, and Bryd and Hruschka, *Kant's Doctrine of Right*, pp. 83–4.

the role of the executive to believe that he is the real source of sovereignty rather than a mere agent of the real sovereign, the people. Be that as it may, Kant says that rights belong to the "supreme commander" only "*indirectly*, that is, insofar as he has taken over the duty of the people" (*MM*, DR, General Comment C, 6:325). He then applies this to the case of churches. Here is where he provides the definition of churches as "institutions for public *divine worship*" aimed at fostering "an internal disposition" to morality "lying wholly beyond the civil power's sphere of influence." He then says, as was quoted earlier, that the state does have the negative right to regulate churches but solely for the sake of "public peace": "Its right is therefore that of policing, of not letting a dispute arising within a church or among different churches endanger civil harmony." This statement, Kant's version of the Lockean proviso, *presupposes* that different churches are rightfully permitted within a single state, thus that the state does not have the right to institute a single church.

Kant observes that for "the supreme authority to say that a church should have a certain belief, or to say which it should have or that it must maintain it unalterably," would inevitably involve the state in the doctrinal squabbles to which churches as human institutions are liable and would be "*beneath its dignity*," perhaps even compromising its authority by "put[ting] itself on a level of equality with its subjects." But most importantly, Kant argues that the state has no right to intervene in the beliefs of churches because no individual and therefore no public as a whole has any right to try to interfere with the beliefs of individuals or with their attempts to improve their beliefs—these are exercises of the innate right to freedom of individuals that do not compromise the freedom of others. As Kant puts it:

> The supreme authority has no right to prohibit internal reform of churches, for what the whole people cannot decide upon for itself the legislator also cannot decide for the people. But no people can decide never to make further progress in its insight (enlightenment) regarding beliefs, and so never to reform its churches, since this would be opposed to the humanity in their own persons and so to the highest right of the people. So no supreme authority can decide on this for the people. (6:327–8)

There are actually several steps in Kant's argument. First, no individual can morally attempt somehow to block *her own* further inquiry into religious matters, because that would be an unnecessary restriction of *her own* freedom. Second, no individual can rightfully attempt to block the freedom of inquiry of any *other*, including inquiry into religious matters, because that would be an impermissible constraint on the freedom of others, impermissible because it is unnecessary to prevent any injury to the freedom of oneself and others—each remains free to believe what he wants no matter what others, in the exercise of their own freedom of inquiry, come to believe. Finally, because no individual has any right to block freedom of religious inquiry, no state or its "supreme commander" can have any such right, because the state has only rights transferable from individuals.

Kant does not refer to a social contract in this argument, but his basic idea is similar to but stronger than that underlying the contractualist thought of Locke and Mendelssohn: not only is there no need for any individual to bargain away the right to freedom of belief and further inquiry into reasonable belief, but it would actually be morally wrong for any individual to bargain away this right.[34] Kant draws a firmer distinction between the realms of state and church than Mendelssohn does, not resting the impermissibility of state interference in religion solely on the premise that there can be only instruction and not coercion in matters of belief. And unlike Locke, he does not distinguish the concerns of state and church as those of public order and eternal salvation, but instead makes the concern of religion morality in general while severely restricting that part of morality that is the business of the state. Kant thus has a powerful argument in his political philosophy for the separation of church and state and for the toleration of as many churches within a state as is compatible with public order. This argument depends solely on his conception of the innate right to freedom due to every human being and not on any specific psychological doctrine such as that beliefs *could* not be affected by state coercion or religious doctrine that actions are well-pleasing to God only if they derive from inward conviction and are not coerced. He may not disagree with these, particularly with the latter, but they are no part of his argument for religious freedom.

---

[34] Kant uses the *idea* of a social contract to test the legitimacy of proposed legislation (*MM* DR §47, 6:315), but it is misleading to associate him too closely to the social contract tradition, because whereas for Hobbes or Locke entering into the social contract to establish a state is a matter of prudence, for Kant it is a moral obligation in any situation in which we cannot otherwise avoid conflict with other human beings, which is to say pretty much in any known circumstances of human life whatever. John Rawls was fond of calling Kant the best representative of the social contract tradition, but that is only because Kant actually transcended it (as did Rawls himself, for whom the idea of contracting in an original position was only a "device of representation" for determining the principles of justice that are morally required by our nature as free and equal persons; see *A Theory of Justice*, §40).

# 11

# Judaism, Christianity, and the Religion of Pure Reason

So much for the direct relation between religion and the state. In *Religion within the Boundaries of Reason Alone*, however, something more is going on. This is a complex argument—at least to some extent aimed at (the now deceased) Mendelssohn—in three parts. First, Kant presents the central images of Christianity as making the truths of the religion of reason accessible to the human senses. Second, he argues that Christianity is *uniquely* well-suited to do this, particularly in contrast to Judaism, which Kant does not consider a genuine religion at all, although he is equally clear that individual Jews are as capable of recognizing the religion of reason as any other human beings. But finally, perhaps taking back with one hand what he has just given with the other, Kant argues that *all* historically based, "ecclesiastical" faith must ultimately be superseded by the religion of reason alone. Kant presents this last point so obscurely that he may have intended to obscure it from the Prussian authorities, although the royal prohibition of his further publishing on matters of religion suggests that they were not fooled. Moreover, such a view may be just as implausible as the Marxist view that the state will ultimately wither away, and we might conclude that Mendelssohn's argument for toleration and governmental non-interference with any religion compatible with civic order remains a more plausible premise for politics than a vain hope that organized religion will someday simply go away.

Let us now consider the three steps in this argument.

(i) *Christian Symbols*. After having presented his argument in Part One of *Religion* that our freedom of will makes us responsible for the evil that we do but also makes it possible for us to undertake our own conversion from evil to good (RBMR 6:35–7), Kant shows in Part Two how central images of Christianity symbolize the key ideas of this doctrine. The three central ideas of morality as Kant has expounded them in the *Critique of Practical Reason* are human freedom, which is the source of the moral law even if we know our freedom only *through* our consciousness of moral law (the "fact of reason"), and the existence of God and of human immortality as the conditions for the realization of the complete object of morality, namely the highest good, immortality being the condition for the possibility of completing our virtue and the existence of God the condition of the possibility of our enjoying happiness proportionate to our virtue. These ideas have undergone subtle and not fully acknowledged modifications in *Religion*. As I argued in Chapter 4, Kant's clarification that our freedom of the will is always the freedom to undertake a complete change of heart from evil to good, from the subordination of morality to self-love to the contrary, actually obviates the need for immortality for the perfection of virtue, but Kant will continue to find a role for the *idea* of immortality. And the role of God becomes more that of an epistemic agent who can be sure of the change of heart of which we ourselves can never be sure, than that of a guarantor of happiness in proportion to virtue. But in some form, Christianity provides sensibly accessible images of human freedom and immortality and of the existence of God.

Kant begins Part Two with the radical claim that "That which alone can make the world the object of divine decree and the end of creation is *humanity* (rational being in general in worldly form) *in its full moral perfection*, from which happiness follows in the will of the Highest Being directly as from its supreme condition" (*RBMR*, 6:60). Instead of claiming that the goal of the divine will is to create the best of all possible worlds even if we cannot understand beyond an abstract formula (maximal variety combined with maximal unity) what makes it the best, as did Leibniz, or reducing the role of humanity to that of a spectator of the divine glory, as did Christian Wolff, Kant makes humanity's own realization of morality, in its intrinsic and unconditional value, the only thing that could possible give a point to the creation of the world (see also *CPJ* §84),[1] and then tacks on the realization of the complete happiness that would follow from the complete realization of morality as part of the divine purpose. To many this would surely seem an extreme form of anthropocentrism. Kant's radical interpretation of the figure of Jesus Christ, which is of course what most distinguishes Christianity from other faiths, is equally anthropocentric. For Kant, Christ is essentially just a symbol of the human freedom to be moral. Reason presents us with "our universal human duty to elevate ourselves to [the] ideal of moral perfection," and the figure of Christ is a "prototype of moral disposition in its entire purity...for our emulation" (*RBMR*, 6:60-1). "From the practical point of view," Kant continues, the moral law and the idea of our freedom to comply with it completely "has complete reality within itself[, f]or it resides in our morally-legislative reason" (6:62), but because of our sensible as well as rational nature, "an experience must be possible in which the example of such a moral being is given" (6:63), one who fully complies with morality, with no reservations and at the cost of the ultimate sacrifice of his own life for others. This is Christ, but if he is to play the role of exemplifying the extent of our own freedom to us, then he must be understood not as a god in his own right, but as "a human being of... truly divine disposition." If he is to work as a symbol for us, we must "have no cause to assume in him anything else except a naturally begotten human being"; "from a practical point of view" any other "presupposition" would be of "no benefit to us (6:63). As Kant puts it, "we always need a certain analogy with natural being in order to make supersensible characteristics comprehensible to us" (6:65n): *our own* freedom is a supersensible, that is, noumenal characteristic, but in order to represent it we need to do so in natural, that is, phenomenal form. That is the essential function of the figure of Christ: he represents our own freedom. This will in turn imply that if Christ is our

---

[1] For commentary, see my "From Nature to Morality: Kant's New Argument in the 'Critique of Teleological Judgment'," in Hans-Friderich Fulda and Jürgen Stoltzenberg, eds., *Architektonik und System in der Philosophie Kants* (Hamburg: Felix Meiner Verlag, 2001), pp. 375-404, reprinted in my *Kant's System of Nature and Freedom*, pp. 314-42.

savior, then it is only our own freedom that can save us from (our own) evil. An "appropriation of" the disposition of Christ "for the sake of our own must be possible, provided that ours is associated with the disposition of the prototype, even though rendering this appropriation comprehensible to us is still fraught with great difficulties" (*RBMR*, 6:66).

Kant further details the symbolic functions of the idea that Christ is the son of God born of a virgin woman. God as lawgiver is an image of the unconditional value of the moral law within ourselves; God as the father who gives his only son for the salvation of the human race is a symbol of his "love for the human race" (6:65n); and Christ's virgin birth is a symbol of "the possibility of a person free from innate propensity to evil" (6:80n), although of course in fact we can only *free ourselves from* our propensity to evil, never hoping simply to be born without it. Here Kant indulges in a remarkable reconciliation of the idea of a virgin birth with the issues of eighteenth-century embryology that had fascinated him in the *Critique of the Power of Judgment*.[2] Since we inevitably think of sex as something animal and shameful, he supposes, "the idea of the birth, independent of any sexual intercourse (virginal), of a child untainted by moral blemish is well suited to [the] obscure representation" of the freedom to become morally pure. But such a birth cannot be understood as "epigenesis," which explains the embryo as a mixture of elements from both parents, for in that case Christ would still carry the taint of his mother's own natural conception. The alternative to epigenesis is preformation, on which the embryo is fully formed in one parent and just nourished by the contribution of the other. But the version of preformation on which the embryo is fully formed in the mother will not do, for then the embryo will still be tainted with her own natural origin. The only alternative is that "since the male side has no part in a supernatural pregnancy, this mode of representation could be defended as theoretically consistent with the idea" of virgin birth. That is, only if Christ is represented as fully preformed in God, not Mary, can he be represented as free of all evil—yet he must also still be represented as fully human in order to be an exemplar for us. In the end, and wisely enough, Kant sets all such speculation aside with the rhetorical question, "What is the use of all this theorizing *pro* or *contra* when it suffices for practical purposes to hold the idea itself before us as a model, as symbol of humankind raising itself above temptation to evil (and withstanding it victoriously)?" (6:80n). After all is said and done, Christ can work as a symbol of our own freedom only if he is represented as fully human. Insofar as he has a kind of divinity, it is one to which we can all aspire—that of overcoming all temptation to become fully committed to the moral law.

No doubt this radical humanization of Christ would have been enough to earn Kant his royal rescript. His interpretation of the idea of immortality is also radical, and intertwined with an account of the function of the idea of God. In the second *Critique*, Kant had argued that the postulation of immortality is necessary to allow for "an *endless progress* toward that complete conformity" with the moral law that is required as the first component of the highest good (*CPracR*, 5:122). But with the

---

[2] See Philippe Huneman, *Métaphysique et Biologie: Kant et la Constitution du Concept d'Organisme* (Paris: Éditions Kimé, 2008), pp. 113–41.

*Religion*'s argument that freedom is the noumenal capacity to choose either the fundamental maxim of evil or that of good, the need for an infinite amount of time to effect complete moral conversion is obviated: on Kant's doctrine of transcendental idealism, the noumenal, therefore noumenal choice, is not supposed to take place in time at all, but from a phenomenal point of view the freedom of noumenal choice means that the phenomenal agent is free to become fully moral *at any time*, and that it does not *take any time*, let alone endless time, to make the moral law one's fundamental maxim. Yet precisely because the moral change of heart can only be noumenal, it must also be empirically unknowable by us whether we have actually performed it. Empirically, our only evidence for our moral disposition is our actions, but actions are intrinsically defective evidence of underlying disposition, because any particular action could be performed from genuine inward commitment to morality or from merely outward compliance with it for the sake of self-love, and any particular number of actions could still be performed out of self-love although in outward compliance with morality.[3] So we allow ourselves the thought that we can complete an "infinite progression of the good toward conformity with the law," as if we could then finally know for sure that we had really converted from evil to good. Of course, we do not really have infinitely extended lives, and we can never complete the synthesis of an infinite manifold, so we cannot really rest our hopes of becoming certain of our moral conversion on a postulate of immortality. So we also form the image of God as a judge who can know our hearts even if we cannot. These are the ideas that lie behind this complex passage:

> According to our mode of estimation, unavoidably restricted to temporal conditions in our conceptions of the relationship of causes to effect, the deed, as a continuous advance *in infinitum* from a defective good to something better, always remains defective, so that we are bound to consider the good as it appears in us, i.e., according to the *deed*, as *at each instance* inadequate to a holy law. But because of the *disposition* from which it derives and which transcends the senses, we can think of the infinite progression of the good toward conformity with the law as being judged by him who scrutinizes the heart (through his pure intellectual intuition) to be a perfected whole even with respect to the deed (the life conduct). And so notwithstanding his permanent deficiency, a human being can still expect to be *generally* well-pleasing to God, at whatever point in time his existence be cut short. (*RBMR*, 6:67)

Our existence *is* cut short in time, whether in a few years or many. And our actions can never be a conclusive indication of our underlying moral disposition, hence of our change of heart, because our real disposition is noumenal and inscrutable to us. But we allow ourselves the idea of God as a judge of hearts to allow for the possibility of some knowledge of our fundamental maxim after all—for what Kant means by "*generally* well-pleasing to God" is not that *enough* of our actions are moral—some sufficient percentage of them—but that our *fundamental maxim* is moral and can be

---

[3] At G 4:407 Kant famously writes that we are good at hiding our motives from ourselves or self-deceit as if this were an empirical fact (which of course it is), but that actions are intrinsically defective evidence of our fundamental motivation or disposition follows from the fact that the same action could be performed in the same circumstances from different motives combined with the implication of transcendental idealism that our choice of fundamental maxim is noumenal rather than phenomenal.

known to be so, by God if not by ourselves, even though no number of actions is adequate evidence for such knowledge for us.

There are other aspects of Kant's account of our image of God, but there is not space here to follow all the convolutions of his thought. At this point I will turn to the second stage of Kant's argument, his suggestion that the symbols of Christianity are not only well-suited to make sensible the fundamental ideas of morality but are also uniquely well-suited to do so. This is the stage of his argument that represents a rejection of Mendelssohn's empirically motivated position that different historical religions are suitable for different peoples, and includes a clear rejection of Mendelssohn's interpretation of the function of commandments in Judaism.

(ii) *The Uniqueness of Christianity.* The complex argument of Part Three of *Religion*[4] holds that the only true religion is completely universal commitment to and communal support for morality, but that historical Christianity is the only possible starting point for such a religion, yet that in turn historical Christianity must be superseded. This argument was no doubt the final straw for the Prussian authorities.

Kant's argument begins with the observation that since the "causes and circumstances" of immorality are social, the presence of others triggering the temptation to privilege oneself over others, so "the dominion of the good principle is not otherwise attainable, so far as human beings can work toward it, than through the setting up and the diffusion of a society in accordance with, and for the sake of, the laws of virtues—a society which reason makes it a task and a duty of the entire human race to establish in its full scope" (*RBMR*, 6:94). Kant's premise cannot be that the presence of others is *sufficient* to *cause* anyone to become evil, for that would be inconsistent with his doctrine of the radical freedom of the human will. It can only be that the *temptation* to evil presented by the presence of others can and should be counteracted by the creation of a community dedicated to fostering rather than undercutting the virtue—strength of commitment to morality—of each of its members.

Kant next distinguishes the idea of an "ethical community" from that of a "political community." This distinction is grounded on the claim that a political union requires the possible use of coercion, while "it would be a contradiction... for the political community to compel its citizens to enter into an ethical community, since the latter entails freedom from coercion in its very concept" (*RBMR*, 6:95). Here Kant assumes that the ethical community is above all a community of disposition, or conviction, and that the coercive means available to the political community might modify outward behavior but cannot reach people's convictions. On this point Kant is on common ground with Mendelssohn, since as we have seen, Mendelssohn also accepts this assumption. Kant also observes that "the duties of virtue concern the entire human race" and thus the "concept of an ethical community always refers to the ideal of a totality of human beings" (6:96), while, as he argues in his political philosophy,

---

[4] See Allen W. Wood, *Kant's Ethical Thought* (Cambridge: Cambridge University Press, 1999), pp. 309–21; Philip J. Rossi, S.J., *The Social Authority of Reason: Kant's Critique, Radical Evil, and the Destiny of Humankind* (Albany: State University of New York Press, 2005), pp. 87–112; Pasternack, *Kant on Religion*, pp. 174–214; and Palmquist, *Comprehensive Commentary*, pp. 249–376.

geography and human history entail an inevitable multiplicity of political communities or states; the idea of a single world-state is a dangerous illusion, a peaceful *federation* of separately sovereign states instead being the only possible route to perpetual peace, "the entire final end of the doctrine of right within the limits of mere reason" (*MM*, DR, Conclusion, 6:355; see also §61, 6:350). On this point too Kant might seem to share some ground with Mendelssohn, recognizing as he does the inevitable historical diversity of nations. From this, the inevitable and insuperable diversity of religious practices might seem to follow, which should then—given the arguments we earlier examined—be tolerated.

However, Kant infers from his idea of the ethical community that true religion should aim at a *single* "church invisible" comprising all human beings even though any "church visible," an "actual union of human beings into a whole that accords with this ideal," seems inevitably limited to some part of the total human population. The true religion of reason aims at the church invisible, and thus the "requisites for a true church," enumerated according to Kant's favorites scheme for categories, namely quantity, quality, relation, and modality, are (1) "*Universality*, whence its numerical unity... universal union in a single church (hence, no sectarian schisms), (2) "*purity*: union under no other incentives than moral ones (cleansed of the nonsense of superstition and the madness of enthusiasm," (3) "*Relation* under the principle of *freedom*: the internal relation of its members among themselves as well as the external relation of the church to the political power," and finally, as (4) "*modality*," the "*unchangeableness* of its *constitution*," because the only real constitution of the church invisible, as opposed to the administration of churches visible, which can always be improved, is the moral law itself, "expressed in secure principles within itself *a priori*" (*RBMR*, 6:101–2).

Kant's vision here is certainly similar to Mendelssohn's. He describes true religion as aiming at the moral treatment of the entire human community, as motivated only by morality, and as governed only by the moral law, and explicitly infers that there must be freedom in the relation of the church to political authority and also in the relation of the church to its members, Mendelssohn had made the first point when he asserted that "According to the concepts of true Judaism, all the inhabitants of the earth are destined to felicity" (*J* p. 94, *JubA* 8:161), and the last point by means of his argument for the separation of church and state and his argument that religious instruction should always take the form of free discussion. Kant further emphasizes the point that true religion requires only morality by his extended argument that "steadfast zeal in the conduct of a morally good life is all that God requires of [human beings] for them to be his well-pleasing subjects in his Kingdom," that "it is absolutely impossible to serve [God] more intimately in [any] other way" than by fulfilling our "duties to human beings"—even though "human beings are not yet easily persuaded" of this (*RBMR*, 6:103). As a perfect being, God has no needs of his own, but only expects us to respect and help satisfy the needs of each other. Kant expands upon this point at great length in Part Four of *Religion*, emphasizing that "*Apart from a good-life conduct, anything which the human being supposes that he can do to become well-pleasing to God is mere religious delusion and counterfeit service of God*" (*RBMR*, 6:170–1). On this point, Kant is entirely at one with Mendelssohn.

Further, Kant seems to be agreeing with Mendelssohn when he again apparently concedes that diversity of visible churches is inevitable. They may aim at universality of moral concern, but apparently will never do it through a union of all human beings in a single visible institution. Kant writes:

> The sublime, never fully attainable idea of an ethical community is greatly scaled down under human hands, namely to an institution which, at best capable of representing with purity only the form of such a community, with respect to the means for establishing a whole of this kind is greatly restricted under the conditions of sensuous human nature. But how could one expect to construct something completely straight from such crooked wood? (*RBMR*, 6:100)

Kant had previously used the image of crooked timber in his essay "On the Idea of Universal History from a Cosmopolitan Point of View" to explain the necessity of government: people can always know what is right but in some circumstances have to be forced into doing it, as trees can be forced to grow straight in a closely packed grove (*IUH*, Sixth Proposition, 8:23);[5] here the suggestion is that even though a single visible church would be the ideal incarnation of a single invisible church, under the natural conditions of human existence only a multiplicity of churches can be expected. Kant further seems to agree with Mendelssohn when he argues that even though "The distinguishing mark of the true church is its *universality*... historical faith (which is based on revelation as experience)," revelation, Kant adds, reported in a text or scripture, "has only particular validity, namely for those in contact with the history on which the faith rests... This faith can therefore indeed suffice as an ecclesiastical faith (of which there can be several); but only the pure faith of reason, based entirely on reason, can be recognized as necessary and hence as the one which exclusively marks out the *true* church" (*RBMR*, 6:115). Kant's conclusion seems to be that although there is only one pure religion, that of pure reason, thus one ultimate content for ecclesiastical faiths, that is faiths organized into particular churches, those churches will inevitably differ, because of their histories, the differences of their purported revelations, and thus their scriptures, presumably therefore also differing in their liturgies, practices, and so on. This seems to be an inevitable consequence of the human condition but no bar to true religion, which is nothing other than pure morality.

But that is not the end of Kant's argument. Instead, now breaking from Mendelssohn, he argues that there is something in Christianity as an historical ecclesiastical faith uniquely suited to lead the way to the one true religion, and he specifically rejects Mendelssohn's claims that Judaism is an equally good conduit to true religion. Kant's position has two parts: his suggestion that Christianity is the ecclesiastical faith uniquely suited to make the religion of reason accessible to us and to bring about progress toward adherence to it, and his argument against the suitability of Judaism for that end. Both his defense of Christianity and his critique of Judaism are tempered, however, the former with the claim that once early Christianity became institutionalized "its history, so far as the beneficial effect

---

[5] See my "The Crooked Timber of Mankind," in Amélie Oksenberg Rorty and James Schmidt, eds., *Kant's Idea for a Universal History with a Cosmopolitan Aim: A Critical Guide* (Cambridge: Cambridge University Press, 2009), pp. 129–49.

which we rightly expect from a moral religion is concerned, has nothing in any way to recommend it" (*RBMR*, 6:130), and the latter with the observation that although *Judaism* contains *nothing* of the true religion of reason there is no reason to believe that individual *Jews* throughout history have had any less commitment to the fundamental tenets of true religion, that is, morality itself, than anyone else. In any case, Kant's argument is ultimately that *all* historical, ecclesiastical faith is ultimately to be overcome. I will come back to these points.

Kant's argument (on the one hand) that original Christianity was a superior embodiment of the true religion of reason is based on his further interpretation of Jesus as "a teacher for whom the story ... has it that he was the first to advocate a pure and compelling religion, one within the grasp of the whole world (i.e., a natural religion) and of which the doctrines, as preserved for us, we can therefore test on our own; [that he did so] publicly and even in defiance of a dominant ecclesiastical faith, oppressive and devoid of moral scope" (that would be Pharisaical Judaism); so "if we find that he made this universal religion of reason the supreme and indispensable condition of each and every religious faith ... then, despite the accidentality and arbitrariness of what he ordained to this end, we cannot deny to the said church the name of the true universal church" (*RBMR*, 6:158). In other words, Jesus himself, who did not make any claim to his own divinity but simply presented himself as a reforming teacher of the moral truth, had no intention of founding a new ecclesiastical faith but simply meant to bring out what "is inscribed in the heart of all human beings" and thereby found "the first true *church*" (6:158). Kant presents Jesus not as advocating "the observance of external civil or statutory ecclesiastical duties" but as teaching in plain terms the moral truths of pure religion: that "only the pure moral disposition of the heart can make a human being well-pleasing to God"; "that sins in thought are regarded in the eyes of God as equivalent to the deed" (which might be thought to twist Kant's own view that purity of motivation is a *necessary* condition of moral worth into the view that impurity of motivation is a *sufficient* condition for moral unworthiness); "that holiness is above all the goal for which the human being should strive" (which might be taken as a statement of the *necessity* of purely moral motivation for moral worth), and so on—the list of examples continues for two more pages (*RBMR*, 6:159–61). At the end of his illustration of Jesus's purely moral teaching, Kant says that "even when the teacher of the Gospel speaks of a recompense in the world to come, he did not mean thereby to make this recompense an incentive of actions but only (as an uplifting representation of the consummation of divine goodness and wisdom in the guidance of the human race) an object of the purest admiration and greatest moral approval for a reason which passes judgment upon human destiny as a whole" (*RBMR*, 6:162). Even at the risk of undercutting his own position that immortality is, as a condition of the possible realization of the highest good, a necessary postulate of pure practical reason itself (which, as I have argued, is already undercut by *Religion*'s argument for the always present possibility of change of heart), Kant interprets Jesus's promise of immortality as a colorful statement of the fact that knowing that one has attempted to do the right thing for the right reason is all the reward the truly moral person needs. Kant's argument in behalf of genuine Christianity is thus that even though he did not intend to found a new visible church, Jesus was the first to enunciate plainly the universal truths of morality.

We saw Kant say that Jesus was the first to put the "pure and compelling religion" of reason in a form "within the grasp of the whole world," but he says nothing of Jesus's tendency to speak in parables, which might have been part of an argument that Christianity puts the truths of morality in a form uniquely accessible to empirical human beings. He does argue that "the universal true religious faith is faith in God (1) as the almighty creator of heaven and earth, i.e., morally as a *holy* lawgiver; (2) as the preserver of the human race, as its *benevolent* ruler and moral guardian; (3) as the administrator of his own holy laws, i.e., as *just* judge" (RBMR, 6:139), and that the Christian conception of the trinity of father, son, and holy ghost represents what is actually the "threefold power" of "a people regarded as a community," that is, of the potential *human* ethical community (6:140). Kant further explains that from a moral point of view we should represent the "supreme lawgiver" not as "indulgent" but as giving laws "directed at the holiness of the human being," his goodness as consisting not in mere "unconditional *benevolence*" but in his seeing to "the moral constitution" of human beings "through which they are *well-pleasing* to him," and his justice not as "*generous* and *condoning*" but as "restricting his generosity to the condition that human beings abide by the moral law," and thus that "In a word, God wills to be served as morally qualified in three specifically different ways, for which the designation of different (not physically, but morally) personalities of one and the same person is not a bad expression" (6:141). However, Kant is also clear that "if this very faith (in a divine Trinity) were to be regarded not just as the representation of a practical idea, but as a faith that ought to represent what God is in himself, it would be a mystery surpassing all human concepts" (6:142). In other words, just as clearly as in the three *Critiques*, Kant insists that our idea of God provides no theoretical knowledge, but may be affirmed only for practical purposes. There is no concession to any conception of religion as theoretical cognition in Kant's *Religion*. And mostly he simply maintains that Jesus taught pure morality. In this regard, Kant's approach to religion is more radical than Mendelssohn's—perhaps why Mendelssohn called him the *Allzermalmender*, the one who destroys all, after the publication of the *Critique of Pure Reason*, long before the *Religion*: Mendelssohn's view is that all religion involves reflection upon the objective truth of the existence of God, providence, and immorality, while Kant's view is that these ideas are of the greatest practical import but have no theoretical claim to truth.

Kant's basic view is thus that Jesus himself was purely a teacher of morality. Kant then argues that as an ecclesiastical faith, indeed a collection of sects, Christianity gradually fell away from this moral purity, burdening itself with "mystical enthusiasm in the life of hermits and monks," with the celebration of celibacy, with belief in miracles, splitting into "bitter parties over opinions on matters of faith," and more (RBMR, 6:130). However, he maintains that despite its dispiriting history, "the fact still clearly enough shine[s] forth from its founding that Christianity's true first purpose was none other than the introduction of a pure religious faith, over which there can be no dissension of opinions" (6:131) because it is nothing other than morality itself; and he claims that in his own time Christianity is recapturing its original spirit and promise of leading directly to the religion of reason or pure morality.

Should one now ask, Which period of the entire church history in our ken up to now is the best? I reply without hesitation, *The present*. I say this because one need only allow the seed of the true religious faith now being sown in Christianity—by only a few, to be sure, yet in the open—to grow unhindered, to expect from it a continuous approximation to that church, ever uniting all human beings, which constitutes the visible representation (the schema) of the invisible Kingdom of God on earth. (*RBMR*, 6:132)

The last part of this statement, I take it, suggests that what true religion actually leads to is an ethical community *on earth*, the realization of the moral kingdom of ends in the phenomenal world, not the postponement of the realization of the highest good to some supernatural condition but the transformation of the natural world into a moral world, to borrow Kant's terms from the first *Critique* (A 809–10/B 837–8). This could be inferred from the use of his term "schema": a schema is not a *symbol*, hence not an earthly symbol of some super-earthly condition, but the means by which an abstract concept is applied to concrete, intuitable reality. The church that unites all human beings is the schema through which the abstract idea of the Kingdom of God is applied to our earthly condition, the means by which the kingdom of ends is actually realized in human life. Of course, this realization may take place in the form of a "world that is future for us" (*CPR*, A 811/B 839) in the sense of lying in the future of the particular human beings living *now*, in 1781, or 1793, or 2020, but still lying somewhere in the actual future of humankind, not in personal immortality.

Perhaps it is already clear that what Kant is saying is that Christianity is a uniquely privileged ecclesiastical faith because it is actually destined to return to its original condition of not being an ecclesiastical faith at all, but a pure religion that just enunciates the fundamental truths of morality. But before we consider that point further, we need to look at Kant's critique of Judaism. Here Kant clearly repudiates central arguments of Mendelssohn's interpretation of the commandments and practices of Judaism, although, ten years after the publication of *Jerusalem* and seven years after the death of its author, he may have been prompted to make this argument by a more recent work, the theologian Johann Salomo Semler's *Leztzes Glaubensbekenntnis* ("Final Confession of Faith") of 1792.[6] Mendelssohn's central argument had been that the numerous (613) commandments (*mitzvot*) of Judaism had not been intended to enforce particular doctrinal beliefs, but to give members of the faith occasions for reflection on and discussion of the fundamental truths of religion, those themselves being understood as accessible to human reason but needing constant reflection and discussion. Kant stands by the position, going back to Spinoza but repeated by Semler, that "The *Jewish faith*, as originally established, was only a collection of merely statutory laws supporting a political state" and that "whatever moral additions were *appended* to it, whether originally or only later, do not in any way belong to Judaism as such." "Strictly speaking," he continues, "Judaism is not a religion at all, but simply the union of a number of individuals

---

[6] A point stressed some time ago by Josef Bohatec, in *Die Religionphilosophie Kants in der "Religion innerhalb der Grenzen der bloßen Vernunft"* (Hamburg: Hoffmann und Campe, 1938). Semler's work (the last of his well over one hundred books) is *Letztes Glaubensbekenntniß über natürliche und christliche Religion* (1792), ed. Dirk Fleischer (Nordhausen: Verlag Traugott Bautz, 2012).

who, since they belonged to a particular stock, established themselves into a community under purely political laws, hence not into a church" (*RBMR*, 6:125).[7] The "moral additions" made to political statutes, whether in Biblical times or later, are due to the fact that individuals Jews are just as much rational human beings as any others, "for it can hardly be doubted that the Jews subsequently produced, each for himself, some sort of religious faith that they added to their statutory faith, yet such a faith was never an integral part of the legislation of Judaism" (6:126–7). Thus, the principles of morality are as accessible to Jews as anyone else, and there is no reason to think that Jews are morally worse (or better) than anyone else, but Judaism as such is pure politics, not morality.

Kant's argument that Judaism is the statutory faith of a now-vanished political community rather than a religious faith is that "all its commandments are of the kind which even a political state can uphold and lay down as coercive laws, since they deal only with external actions" (*RBMR*, 6:126). This is based on the premise that Kant shares with Mendelssohn, that the possibility of coercive enforcement is an essential condition of juridical law and that such law can concern only what is susceptible to such enforcement, thus external actions. But it simply sidesteps Mendelssohn's argument that the performance of the commandments of Judaism is intended only as the occasion for reflection and discussion. It also does not address Mendelssohn's point that there is no obvious juridical penalty for the failure to comply with the commandments. Mendelssohn, who was of course familiar with Spinoza's position, puts this point in historical form, conceding that as long as the Jewish state and its temple existed the commandments were also statutory laws, but holding that once the temple ceased to exist, the rabbis themselves—now teachers, not officers or priests in a theocratic state—"expressly state that...*all corporal and capital punishments, and, indeed, even monetary fines*...*have ceased to be legal.*" Mendelssohn claims, as much of Judaism as of any other religion, that "religion, as religion, knows of no punishment, no other penalty than the one the remorseful sinner *voluntarily* imposes on himself" (*J*, p. 130), that is, remorse itself. The Jewish commandments may once have *also* been statutory laws, but even without a state, they still have their function as occasions for reflection, which they must always have had. And it is Mendelssohn's view that religious belief cannot be coercively enforced which is the premise for his argument that all churches, including Jewish communities, have no right to excommunicate members of the community.

Kant does not address Mendelssohn's general argument against the penal enforcement of religious duties or his specific argument against excommunication. He does concede that "the Ten Commandments would have ethical validity for reason even if they had not been publicly given," but he still denies that they are genuinely moral laws "because in that legislation they are given with no claim at all on the *moral disposition* in following them ... but were rather directed simply and solely to external observance" (6:126). This seems a particularly unfair argument for Kant to make. It is true that some of the commandments command outward actions. The canonical

---

[7] This was a standard view, going back at least to Spinoza's *Theological-Political Treatise* (1670), Preface; in *The Collected Works of Spinoza*, ed. and trans. Edwin Curley, vol. II (Princeton: Princeton University Press, 2016), p. 72.

version (Exodus 20:1–17, Deuteronomy 5:4–21) commands "Thou shalt not make...any graven image," "Thou shalt not kill," "Thou shalt not commit adultery," among others, all of which certainly prohibit outward actions. The version at Exodus 24:1–28 commands some further, even more specific actions, such as "Celebrate the Festival of Unleavened Bread," "Do not cook a young goat in its mother's milk," which is the basis of all the rules of *kashrut*, and more. But some of the commandments do command what might be regarded as inner states rather than, or along with, outer actions, such as "Honor thy father and mother," for honoring would seem to be a matter of attitude as well as action, and the prohibition of coveting one's neighbor's wife or house also addresses, though by prohibiting rather than commanding, an inner state rather than outward action. Moreover, while Kant's own categorical imperative, most obviously in its first formulation, directly addresses inner states—what maxims one may adopt—it certainly also commands or prohibits actions, namely actions performed on the basis of commanded or prohibited maxims. Further, although what Kant might really have in mind is that the Jewish commandments do not explicitly command the performance of the relevant actions out of respect for the moral law, neither does his own categorical imperative or the specific duties derived from it. Being motivated by the moral law is the necessary condition of *moral worth*, but it is not explicitly commanded by the categorical imperative—it is the attitude we should take *toward* the categorical imperative. If the duty to act out of that motivation is a duty at all, it is a duty in addition to the specific duties of right and virtue: it is the duty to be virtuous rather than a specific duty of virtue.[8] Given the absence of a direct reference to moral motivation in Kant's own standard formulation of the categorical imperatives and our specific duties, Kant's criticism of Judaism seems unfair.

Kant makes the further argument that Judaism is not a genuine religion because it does not include "faith in a future life," although once again "It can hardly be doubted that, just like other peoples, even the most savage, the Jews too must have had faith in a future life" as rational human beings, independent of their political statutes.[9] In this too, Kant is dismissing one of Mendelssohn's claims, for Mendelssohn had not only argued for the rationality of belief in immortality in his secular work *Phaedo* (1767) but had also included it among the articles of the religion of reason on which Jews are prompted to reflect by their practices. That Jews are not *commanded* to believe in immortality by their commandments is not to the point, for on Mendelssohn's interpretation belief can never be commanded, and the Jewish *mitzvot* are not commands to believe but commands to act in a way that can prompt reflection on and discussion of belief. Again, Kant does not address this interpretation.

Kant's conclusion is that "We cannot...begin the universal history of the Church (insofar as this history is to constitute a system) anywhere but from the origin of

---

[8] See Guyer, "The Obligation To Be Virtuous: Kant's Conception of the *Tugendverpflichtung*," *Social Philosophy and Policy* 27 (2010): 206–32, reprinted in Guyer, *Virtues of Freedom: Selected Essays on Kant* (Oxford: Oxford University Press, 2016), pp. 216–34.

[9] As we saw in Chapter 4, this is a highly controverted matter in the history of Jewish philosophy, with many prayers in traditional liturgy and Jewish philosophers over the centuries supporting a belief in immortality, although certainly never with bodily resurrection.

Christianity, which, as a total abandonment of the Judaism in which it originated, grounded on an entirely new principle, effected a total revolution in doctrines of faith" (*RBMR*, 6:127). Insofar as this is based on the premise that Judaism never was a genuine religion, that is, one with the articles of the religion of reason as its ultimate content, it is far from convincing. But in any case, his argument in behalf of Christianity is problematic, for Kant's real point is that any organized religion or ecclesiastical faith must not just include the religion of reason, but must ultimately be superseded by a pure religion of reason. The difference between Christianity and any other ecclesiastical faith is just that Christianity supersedes itself, or contains the seeds of its own supersession.

(iii) *The self-supersession of Christianity.* The argument that Christianity as an institutionalized church will ultimately fade away is buried in the larger argument of Part Four of *Religion*, which emphasizes the less radical point, fully shared with Mendelssohn, that the only service acceptable to God is moral service to human beings, not purported service to God himself in the form of rituals in accordance with the statutes of any church. "*Apart from a good life-conduct, anything which the human being supposes that he can do to become well-pleasing to God is mere religious delusion and counterfeit service of God*" (*RBMR*, 6:170). If what true religion really commands is simply morality, then the true demands of religion can be satisfied only by being moral.

This position, however, calls for an interpretation of the meaning of Christian practices and sacraments that is similar in spirit to Mendelssohn's interpretation of the function of the Jewish *mitzvot* even though Kant had rejected Mendelssohn's interpretation in the case of Judaism. Speaking of "private prayer," "public assembly on days legally consecrated thereto... (church-going)," "baptism" as the "reception of new members joining the fellowship of faith," and "communion" as "public formalities which stabilize the union of its members into an ethical body," Kant says that "these formalities have from antiquity been found to be good sensible intermediaries that serve as schemata for the duties, thus awakening and sustaining our attention to the true service of God" (*RBMR*, 6:193). As Mendelssohn had argued that observance of the Jewish commandments was intended only to occasion reflection on and discussion of the true nature of God and his requirement that humans serve him only by serving each other, so Kant holds that the Christian "formalities" are meant to awaken and sustain our attention to the true service of God, that is, morality. He does not explicitly add Mendelssohn's point that these formalities stimulate discussion, between teacher and student, parent and child, and co-practitioners, but his emphasis on the social character of church-going and communion could make a similar point, especially since he is denying any special role for priests as intermediaries between church-members and God and suggesting instead that church-goers simply communicate their faith to each other, no doubt in good part through their words. While clearly rejecting Mendelssohn's defense of Jewish practice, Kant silently appropriates it in behalf of Christian practice.

In spite of his argument on behalf of the distinctive suitability of Christian symbolism, as in the case of the Trinity itself, and his appropriation of a Mendelssohnian approach for a defense of Christian practices, Kant also subtly undermines the enduring necessity of Christianity as an organized church. The following passage undercuts his own claims in behalf of the suitability of Christianity as a universal institutional or in Kant's term ecclesiastical faith, but goes beyond this to suggest that all statutory faith is problematic, running the risk of counterfeit rather than genuine service to God:

> The one true religion contains nothing but laws, i.e., practical principles, of whose unconditional necessity we can become conscious and which we therefore recognize as revealed through pure reason. Only for the sake of a church, of which there can be different and equally good forms, can there be statutes... Now to deem this statutory faith (which is in any case restricted to one people and cannot contain the universal world religion) essential to the service of God in general, and to make it the supreme condition of divine good pleasure toward human beings, is a *delusion of religion*, and acting upon it constitutes counterfeit service, i.e., a pretension of honoring God through which we act directly contrary to the true service required by him. (*RBMR*, 6:168)

Considering this passage in conjunction with Kant's previous argument, his position seems to be that although Jesus did indeed teach a truly universal religion, namely morality itself, *any* institutionalization of even his religious teaching into a church is bound, first, to take on a form suitable only to one particular people, or to people at some particular time and place, and, second, to run the risk of encouraging counterfeit service to the rituals and priests of such a particular institution rather than genuine service to God, namely, morality toward human beings. To be sure, "Christianity has the great advantage over Judaism of being represented as coming *from the mouth of the first teacher* not as a statutory but as a moral religion" (6:167), but even so it had to be initially presented in a form accessible to its original audience, and that inevitably runs the risk that means of presentation suitable to that time and place will be ossified into statutes that transform historical contingencies into pseudo-necessities. "The appeals which we find here to older (Mosaic) legislation and prefiguration, as though these were to serve the teacher as authentication, were not given in support of the truth of the teachings... but only for their introduction among people who, without exception and blindly, clung to the old" (6:162). But surely it was not just the Jews of first-century Palestine who had a tendency to cling to the old, but human beings of every time and place are subject to such a tendency, thus change always meets with resistance and even when it is accepted then it itself becomes entrenched. So what was meant to ease the acceptance of the purely moral teaching of Jesus by its first audience, namely an assimilation of his new teaching to the commandments of traditional Judaism, inevitably leads to the ossification of those new teachings into forms not equally suitable for other or later audiences. Thus although, as Kant continues, "no one should be disconcerted to find an exposition, which accommodated itself to the prejudices of the times, now enigmatic and in need of careful exposition," that nevertheless "lets a religious doctrine shine forth, and often even points to it explicitly, which must be comprehensible to every human being and must convince without expenditure of learning" (6:162–3), still, there will be an overwhelming tendency to transform what were mere accommodations to one audience into statutes and counterfeit services for other and later generations. Mendelssohn's confidence that commandments can function as a "living script" that will serve to maintain "the spirit of living conversation" (J, pp. 102–3) for every generation under changing circumstances does not seem to be shared by Kant. Further, Kant rejects Mendelssohn's argument that religious *practices* are immune from corruption into mere idolatry in a way that religious *symbols* are not: for Kant, the human predisposition to radical evil, which is nothing but the fact of complete freedom, makes it possible for us to pervert *anything*, practices as well as words or symbols. It is always possible for human beings to:

> place their service of God in something (faith in certain statutory articles, or the observance of certain arbitrary practices) which cannot by itself constitute a better human being. Only those whose intention is to find this service solely in the disposition to good life-conduct distinguish themselves from those others by crossing over into an entirely different principle, one exalted far above the other, namely the principle whereby they profess themselves members of a (invisible) church which encompasses all right-thinking people within itself and alone, in virtue of its essential composition, can be the true church universal. (RBMR, 6:176)

In fact, this passage suggests not only that anything, practices as well as statutory articles, symbols, or anything else, can become the subject of false service to God, but since true service to God requires nothing else, indeed is nothing else, than genuine morality, aimed at all human beings and motivated solely by respect for the moral law, anything that divides people can be seen as an obstacle to true morality and true religion. Adherence to the practices of a particular historical, visible church, whatever they are, can be an obstacle to the realization of the invisible church.

That Mendelssohn is a, if not the, target of this argument is made clear in a lengthy note in which Kant responds to Mendelssohn's objection to those who would have him convert to Christianity that for him to repudiate Judaism would be like tearing down the first floor of a building while trying to preserve the second story (J, p. 87, JubA 8:154). Kant writes:

> Mendelssohn very ingeniously makes use of this weak point of the customary picture of Christianity to preempt any suggestion of religious conversion made to a son of Israel. For, as he said, since the faith of the Jews is, according to the admission of the Christians, the lower floor upon which Christianity rests as the floor above, any such suggestion would be tantamount to asking someone to demolish the ground floor in order to feel at home on the second. His true opinion, however, shines through quite clearly. He means to say: first remove Judaism from your *religion* (though in the historical teaching of faith it may always remain as an antiquity) and we shall be able to take your proposal under advisement. (In fact nothing would then be left over, except pure moral religion unencumbered by statutes.) Our burden will not be lightened in the least by throwing off the yoke of external observances, if another is imposed in its place, namely the yoke of a profession of faith in sacred history, which, for the conscientious, is an even more onerous burden. (RBMR, 6:166n.)

Kant goes on to say that the "sacred books" of the Jews have a unique value not for religion but for scholarship, as the oldest credible works of human history (although many of his contemporaries had already criticized the age and reliability of the books of the Bible). But this concession hardly blunts his charge that the particular practices of the Jews can stand in the way of a truly universal choice. Of course, his charge is a two-edged sword, or he is saying "a pox on both your houses": the Christians too would need to remove all particularizing creeds and rites from their religion too for it to become truly universal—and then nothing would remain "except pure moral religion unencumbered by statutes." Kant's argument is directed as much against historical Christianity as against historical Judaism.

Moreover, Kant does not merely seem to think that the historical faiths of humankind *ought* to be transcended; he actually seems to think that in the fullness of time they *will* be. He seems to think that humankind will inevitably progress toward a truly universal practice of morality, with the mutual support to be expected from an invisible church, without the further necessity of any visible, statutory, ecclesiastical church. This will obviate the enduring necessity of the Jewish commandments for Jewish individuals, but will equally obviate the enduring necessity of any visible Christian church. What began as a purely moral teaching will end as purely moral insight and practice that can be shared by any and all human beings. Or so at least Kant seems to suggest when he states:

It is therefore a necessary consequence of the physical and, at the same time, the moral predisposition in us—the latter being the foundation and at the same time the interpreter of all religion—that in the end religion will gradually be freed of all empirical grounds of determination, of all statutes that rest on history and unite human beings provisionally for the promotion of the good through the intermediary of an ecclesiastical faith. Thus at last the pure faith of religion will rule over all... The leading-string of holy tradition, with its appendages, its statutes and observances, which in its time did good service, becomes bit by bit dispensable, yea, finally, when a human being enters upon his adolescence [*Jünglingsalter*], turns into a fetter. (*RBMR*, 6:121)

By *Jünglingsalter*, Kant seems to mean precisely the period of life in which, in the terms of his essay on enlightenment, someone may pass from *Unmündigkeit* to *Mündigkeit*, from having to have someone else—like a priest in an organized religion—speak for him to being able to think and speak for himself. The historical faiths of mankind are thus part of its immaturity. Further, Kant writes:

Thus the principle in an ecclesiastical faith which rectifies or prevents every religious delusion is this: ecclesiastical faith must contain with itself, beside the statutory articles which it yet cannot quite dispense with, another principle as well, of bringing about the religion of good life conduct as its true goal, in order at some future time to be able to dispense with statutory articles altogether. (*RBMR*, 6:175)

On the principle that ought implies can, to which Kant appeals throughout the *Religion*, the principle that human beings *ought* to work toward a future fully exemplifying good life-conduct without any statutory articles implies that they *can* realize such a condition. Kant's initial vision of an ethical community, "the dominion of the good principle... so far as human beings can work toward it... through the setting up and the diffusion of a society in accordance with, and for the sake of, the laws of virtue—a society which reason makes it a task and duty of the entire human race to establish in its full scope" (*RBMR*, 6:94)—must be realizable at some point in human history without any remnant of the statutory articles of any particular ecclesiastical faith.

This seems to be the conclusion to which Kant's argument must lead. What he has given with one hand by arguing for the superiority of Christianity as an ecclesiastical faith over any other he has taken away with the other by arguing that the supersession of all statutory religion by the true religion of pure morality must be possible in the history of humankind. Or has he? One passage still in Part Three must give pause. First Kant says that "The teacher of the Gospel manifested the Kingdom of God on earth to his disciples only from its glorious, edifying, and moral side, namely in terms of the merit of being citizens of a divine state" (*RBMR*, 6:134), in which "the very form of a church is dissolved" and "the vicar on earth enters the same class as the human beings who are now elevated to him as citizens of Heaven, and so God is all in all" (6:135). This is consistent with the suggestion of our first passage, from earlier in Part Three, as well as with Kant's statement in Part Four that even Christianity as a statutory religion should be superseded and therefore must be able to be superseded. But then Kant takes a breath (paragraph break), and replies to himself:

This representation in a historical narrative of the future world, which is not itself history, is a beautiful ideal of the moral world-epoch brought about by the introduction of the true universal religion and *foreseen* in faith in its completion—one which we do not see *directly* in the manner of an empirical completion but *have a glimpse of* in the continuous advance and approximation toward the highest possible good on earth (in this there is nothing mystical but everything proceeds naturally in a moral way), i.e., we can make preparation for it.

(*RBMR*, 6:135–6)

What exactly is Kant doing here? Is he trying to raise a cloud about his real intention, obfuscating his real conviction that Christianity must eventually fade away with the disingenuous suggestion that maybe this is just a beautiful dream? Or is he revealing a genuine realism about human progress, arguing that we must hold out the possibility of complete morality as a regulative ideal for our individual and collective action, our goal in all our moral deliberation, but also believe that no matter how much progress we make toward the realization of our moral aims, human conduct will never be perfect?[10] As we will see in the next and final chapter, this would be consistent with the position he took in response to Mendelssohn in the essay on "Theory and Practice," which is that human *progress* rather than oscillation is inevitable, but which is not to say that human progress is ever *completed*. It would also, it might be noted, undercut the argument of his earlier works that *individual* human immortality is a necessary postulate of morality; it would require only the postulation of the possibility of unending *collective progress* toward morality as the presupposition of true religion. But then again, as I argued in Chapter 4, Kant's doctrine of individual freedom for moral conversion in Part One of the *Religion* has already undercut his previous postulate of individual immortality—and thereby also undercut his argument that Judaism was never a genuine religion because it allegedly did not include a belief in personal immortality.

---

[10] In his brief treatment of the issue, Allen Wood just suggests that Kant's conception of a religion of reason is a valuable ideal to be hung onto in the face of real-world conflicts without trying to settle the question of whether Kant believed the historical emergence of a religion of reason alone is a genuine necessity, a mere possibility, or even a genuine possibility. See Wood, "Ethical Community, Church, and Scripture," in Höffe, *Kant: Die Religion*, pp. 148–50.

I will briefly draw up the balance sheet comparing Mendelssohn's and Kant's philosophies of religion as expounded over the last two chapters. Both agree that the state should use its coercive means to regulate religion only in order to preserve civic order. But their arguments for this conclusion differ. Mendelssohn holds that both state and religion have the goal of human perfection, but that part of human perfection requires belief in the existence of God, providence, and immortality, and since conviction cannot be produced by coercion, the state cannot use its means of coercion to try to bring such conviction about, nor can it apply its coercive means to religion, which should attempt to bring about conviction only by instruction and discussion, stimulated in different religions by different signs, texts, and practices. But the state could use its own instruction to try to bring about conviction; at least there is nothing in Mendelssohn's premises that blocks that. Kant argues for a stricter separation between state and religion. Morality aims at human freedom, or the perfection of human freedom, but not human perfection in general. The state aims only at the preservation of conditions of equal freedom in external, other-affecting actions, and does not concern itself with the inner motivation or more generally moral state of its subjects. Its interest is only in enforcing that small part of morality outward compliance with which can effectively and permissibly be enforced by external, aversive incentives. Morality concerns itself with the rest of human duties and with the inward motivation of human beings, and that in the end that is all that religion concerns itself with as well. Thus the state has no business with religion, unless mere statutory faith, which is in any case not genuine religion at all, should disturb justice or public peace. Nor should the state use non-coercive means to try to bring about the ends of morality and, therefore, religion. Kant is insistent that compliance with the laws of justice could be motivated by the commitment to morality (*MM*, Introduction, section IV, 6:318), but that is not to say that the means available to the state—coercion—could ever bring about moral motivation.

On the relation between Christianity and Judaism, Mendelssohn's position is straightforward, Kant's less so. Mendelssohn argues that the commandments of Judaism serve just to occasion reflection and discussion on the ultimately entirely moral truths of religion, and are as good for Jews for that purpose as the practices of any other religions are for their communicants. Kant rejects Mendelssohn's interpretation of the Jewish commandments, but silently re-deploys it for his own interpretation of Christian practices. More generally, Kant argues for the superiority of Christian symbolism over Judaism, and insists that Christianity espouses a universal morality that individual Jews may well do but that Judaism as the statutes of a historical particular state did not. But then he argues that Christianity as a visible church must ultimately be superseded by Christianity as a purely moral and therefore universal, invisible church, or at least that humanity must make unending progress toward that goal. Kant's critique of Judaism remains unabated, but his argument for the superiority of Christianity is tempered by his argument for the necessity of its own supersession. In the end, Kant's argument against Judaism may be submerged in his larger argument for the disappearance of statutory religion altogether.

It would be hard to disprove Kant's conviction that the historical faiths of humankind someday will or even could disappear. But while participation in organized religious observance may be at an all-time low in some European countries, there is hardly any evidence that organized religion is disappearing from the United States or many other regions of the world, and in some, such as post-Communist Russia, it surely seems to be resurgent. Kant's conviction that pure reason will supersede historical religion seems implausible, while Mendelssohn's acceptance of the plurality of historical religions can strengthen the conviction that whatever one thinks of the ultimate value and fate of organized religion, we had better make sure that our actual governments are dedicated to safeguarding the conditions for religious pluralism for the foreseeable future. Here Mendelssohn's empiricism seems more plausible than Kant's dreamy rationalism.

# 12
# Mendelssohn, Kant, and the Possibility of Progress

## 1. Abderitism or Chiliasm?

Is the progress of humankind from a condition less compliant with the demands of morality to one that is more compliant inevitable and irreversible, or not? In the essay on "An Old Question Raised Anew: Is the Human Race Constantly Progressing?," which was published in 1798 as the Second Section of *The Conflict of the Faculties*, Kant puts this question by asking which is true: *chiliasm*, that humankind exists "in perpetual *progression* toward improvement in its moral vocation [*Bestimmung*]," or *abderitism*, "eternal stagnation in its present stage of moral worth among creatures (a stagnation with which eternal rotation in orbit around the same point is one and the same)" (*CF*, section II, 7:81)?[1] Kant affirms moral chiliasm against abderitism (a term coined with reference to the inhabitants of ancient Abdera, renowned for their supposed vacillation). Five years earlier, in his 1793 essay "On the Common Saying: That May Be Correct in Theory but It Is of No Use in Practice," he had accused Moses Mendelssohn of having held abderitism in his *magnum opus* of ten years earlier, *Jerusalem, or on Religious Power and Judaism*, although in "Theory and Practice" Kant is more specifically concerned with what he calls in *Religion within the Boundaries of Mere Reason* "*philosophical chiliasm*, which hopes for a state of perpetual peace based on a federation of nations united in a world-republic" rather than "*theological chiliasm*, which awaits for the completed moral improvement of humankind" (*RBMR*, 6:34). In "Theory and Practice" he thus defends the thesis that the condition for perpetual peace and thus perpetual peace itself is inevitable against Mendelssohn's abderitism on the same issue. However, Kant thereby talks past Mendelssohn, whose position in *Jerusalem* was moral, thus "theological" abderitism, not "philosophical" or what we might better call political abderitism. Further, carefully considered, Kant's own position on the question of the inevitability of *moral* progress is not so different from Mendelssohn's. And finally, closely read, Kant's own promise of the inevitability of perpetual peace is carefully qualified. Thus on the issue of philosophical or political chiliasm, Kant's position is not so far from

---

[1] In *CF*, Kant distinguishes a third possibility besides chiliasm and abderitism, namely "moral terrorism," the possibility that humankind "exists in continual *retrogression* toward wickedness" (*CF*, 7:81). He argues that if this were the case, then humankind would at a certain stage destroy itself. This is not a complete argument without the additional premise that if moral terrorism were true we must, *per impossibile*, already have reached this stage; but Kant does not further consider this possibility in the texts I will discuss, and neither will I.

the corresponding version of abderitism as initially appears. On some issues, as we have seen, the difference between Kant and his respected counterpart in Berlin is significant, but sometimes not as great as it at first seems. On the issue of abderitism, I will argue, the development of Kant's theory of human freedom in the 1790s, particularly in *Religion within the Boundaries of Mere Reason*, should have undercut his criticism of Mendelssohn.

Here is what Kant says about Mendelssohn in "Theory and Practice." Although the third section of the essay is entitled "On the Relation of Theory to Practice in the Right of Nations Considered from a Universally Philanthropic, that is, Cosmopolitan Point of View," thus pointing us toward the question about the inevitability of perpetual peace that he will discuss in the conclusion of the section, Kant initially poses his question in more general, that is, moral terms. He asks "Is humankind[2] as a whole to be loved, or is it an object such that one must regard it with vexation...?" and says that the answer to this question depends on the answer to the further one, "Are there in human nature predispositions from which one can gather that the species will always progress toward what is better and that the evil of present and past times will disappear in the good of future times?" He then states that Mendelssohn held the opposite, that is, that the evil of present and past times will not disappear, and thus that one must regard mankind with vexation. He writes:

Moses Mendelssohn was of the latter opinion (*Jerusalem*, Section II), which he opposed to his friend Lessing's hypothesis of a divine education of humankind.[3] It is, to him, a fantasy, "that the whole, humanity here below, should in the course of time always move forward and perfect itself." "We see," he said, "the human race as a whole make small oscillations, and it never takes a few steps forward without soon afterward sliding back twice as fast into its former state... An individual makes progress, but humanity constantly vacillates between fixed limits; regarded as a whole, however, it maintains in all periods of time roughly the same level of morality, the same measure of religion and irreligion, of virtue and vice, of happiness (?) and misery." He introduces these assertions by saying: "Do you want to guess what sort of purposes providence has for humanity? Forge no hypotheses (he had earlier called these 'theory'); just look around at what is actually happening, and if you can take an overview of all past ages, look at what has happened from time immemorial. This is fact, this must have belonged to that purpose, must have been approved within the plan of wisdom or at least adopted along with it."

I am of another opinion... I shall therefore be allowed to assume that, since humankind is constantly advancing with respect to culture (as its natural end) it is also to be conceived as progressing toward what is better with respect to the moral end of its existence, and that this will indeed be *interrupted* from time to time but will never be *broken off*. I do not need to prove this presupposition; it is up to its adversary to prove his case. (*TP*, section III, 8:307–9)

---

[2] I am changing the translation of *menschliches Geschlecht* from "the human race" to "humankind" because Kant is here considering human beings as a single group or "species" (*Gattung*) without any consideration of the question of whether this is divided into biologically distinctive populations or "races" (*Rasse*), although as is well known he elsewhere takes a position on that issue.

[3] Kant refers here to Lessing's piece "The Education of the Human Race," the first half of which was published in 1777 and the whole in 1780, the year before Lessing's death; see Gotthold Ephraim Lessing, *Philosophical and Theological Writings*, ed. H.B. Nisbet (Cambridge: Cambridge University Press, 2005), pp. 217–40. For discussion of Lessing's piece, see Henry E. Allison, *Lessing and the Enlightenment* (Ann Arbor: University of Michigan Press, 1966), pp. 148–61. On Mendelssohn's response to Lessing and Kant's to Mendelssohn, see Altmann, *Moses Mendelssohn*, pp. 541–2.

Here is the passage from *Jerusalem* from which Kant quotes:

On balance, men's doings and the morality of their conduct can perhaps expect just as good results from the crude mode of conceiving things as from these refined and purified concepts. Many a people is destined by Providence to wander through this cycle of ideas, indeed, sometimes it must wander through it more than once; but the quantity and weight of its morality may, perhaps, remain, on balance, about the same during all of these various epochs.

I, for my part, cannot conceive of the education of humankind as my late friend Lessing imagined it under the influence of I don't know which historian of mankind. One pictures the collective entity of the human race as an individual person and believes that Providence sent it to school here on earth in order to raise it from childhood to manhood. In reality, humankind is—if the metaphor is appropriate—in almost every century, child, adult, and old man at the same time, though in different places and regions of the world... Progress is for the individual man, who is destined by Providence to spend part of his eternity here on earth. Everyone goes through life in his own way. One man's path takes him through flowers and meadows, another's across desolate plains, or over steep mountains and past dangerous gorges. Yet they all proceed on their journey, making their way to the felicity [*Glückseligkeit*] for which they are destined. But it does not seem to have been the purpose of Providence that mankind as a whole advance steadily here below and perfect itself in the course of time. This, at least, is not so well settled nor by any means so necessary for the vindication of God's providence as one is in the habit of thinking.

That we should again and again resist all theory and hypotheses, and want to speak of facts, to hear of nothing but facts, and yet should have the least regard for facts precisely where they matter most! You want to divine what designs Providence has for mankind? Do not frame hypotheses; only look around you at what actually happens and, if you can survey history as a whole, at what has happened since the beginning of time. This is fact, this must have been part of the design; this must have been decreed or, at least, admitted by Wisdom's plan. Providence never misses its goal. Whatever happens must have been its design from the beginning, or part of it. Now, as far as humankind as a whole is concerned, you will find no steady progress in its development that brings it ever closer to perfection. Rather do we see humankind in its totality slightly oscillate; it never took a few steps forward without soon afterwards, and with redoubled speed, sliding back to its previous position. Most nations of the earth live for many centuries at the same stage of culture, in the same twilight, one which seems much too dim for our pampered eyes. Now and then, a dot blazes up in the midst of the great mass, becomes a glittering star, and traverses an orbit which now after a shorter, now after a longer period, brings it back again to its starting point, or not far from it. Individual man advances, but mankind continually fluctuates within fixed limits, while maintaining on the whole, about the same degree of morality in all periods—the same amount of religion and irreligion, of virtue and vice, of felicity and misery... of all these goods and evils as is required for the passage of the individual many in order that he might be educated here below, and approach as closely as possible the perfection which is apportioned to him and for which he is destined. (J, pp. 95–7, JubA 8:162–4)[4]

Kant's quotations from Mendelssohn, we can see, are accurate (although we have two different translations before us). But there is a great deal going on in Mendelssohn's text that is not reflected in Kant's quotations from it.

---

[4] As in my quotations from Kant, I have translated *menschliches Geschlecht* as "humankind" rather than "the human race," for the reason previously given.

For one, Mendelssohn is not discussing the possibility of perpetual peace at all; rather this passage is part of his larger argument that the moral truths of the religion of reason always are and always have been available to all people, thus that Christianity should not be regarded as a more progressive religion than Judaism that automatically brings its adherents closer to moral perfection and should be universally adopted for that reason. On the contrary, the principles that need to be adopted in order to realize moral perfection are and always have been just as available to Jews (and Muslims) as to Christians, although individual Jews (and Muslims) have no more uniformly lived up to these principles than have individual Christians. As we have just seen, in *Religion within the Boundaries of Mere Reason*, Kant argued that while all historical religions are only symbolic representations of the true religion of reason, the Christian symbols are better than any others, although he allowed that individual Jews or others are just as capable of discovering what morality requires and doing it as is anyone else. But the alleged superiority of Christianity as a step towards the pure religion of reason, which brings Kant's position closer to that of Lessing, is not at issue in "Theory and Practice" itself and I will not discuss this point further here.

Another point that Kant does not mention is that Mendelssohn does not *need* to posit the actual moral perfection of all human beings in their earthly existence because he remains committed to their eternal existence beyond their earthly life spans and thus to the possibility or actuality of the moral perfection of all in their afterlife rather than their natural life. Mendelssohn had firmly held this position in his *Phaedo*, no doubt before, and through the end of his life; and while Kant seems to have agreed with it in the postulate of immortality in the *Critique of Practical Reason*, as I argued in Chapter 4 he had surrendered it in the *Religion* and thus at the time of "Theory and Practice" in favor of the view that complete conversion from evil to good is possible for every individual at any and every time of their natural life. I will come back to this decisive point.

But for now, what I want to stress is that for Mendelssohn moral good and evil is a matter of individual choice and character, although that can be favorably affected by religion as a strictly *educational* institution, and that the question of whether moral progress in the natural lives of human beings is destined can only be settled empirically. On this matter the distance between Mendelssohn and Kant is not as great as Kant makes it appear. Kant scorns Mendelssohn's rejection of "theory," that is, a priori reasoning, on the question of moral progress, but Mendelssohn's position seems as much driven by common sense and empirical observation as by theory, while Kant's rejection of Mendelssohn's "abderitism" is actually undermined by his own a priori theory, that is, his commitment to his transcendental idealist theory of free will with its implication that the "change of heart" from evil to good or vice versa is available to everyone all the time. Further, when Kant turns from the question of moral chiliasm to that of philosophical or political chiliasm, he too relies on empirical rather than a priori arguments. In spite of Kant's rejection of Mendelssohn's empiricism on the question of the moral progress of the human species in favor of his own a priori assurance of the inevitability of such progress, Kant's transcendental theory of freedom actually complements Mendelssohn's own conviction that human history is nothing but a sum of individual choices.

I have already mentioned what is in fact the main point of Part II of *Jerusalem*. The argument of Part I, as we saw in Chapter 10, is that government has no business preferring one religion over any other, because while religion is concerned with the education of people to compliance with duty out of inward love of virtue and God, insofar as government is concerned with the enforcement of rights by external means, it has no business establishing any religion at all. This distinction in turn assumes that motivation is always a matter of the determination of the individual will, although precisely because individuals need to be educated in the proper determination of their will, to the fulfillment of duty out of love of virtue, this individual determination of the will takes place in a social context and can be helped or hindered by better or worse education. Given Mendelssohn's equation of religion with moral education, this means that there might be better or worse religions, but it does not imply that there is necessarily a single religion that offers a better moral education than any other; and in any case, the efficacy of religious education to virtue on individuals will vary, as Mendelssohn's example of the recalcitrant student has made clear—he made no suggestion that even extra educational attention to any particular student will necessarily bring him around. In light of this background, what the passage before us argues is that Lessing's reification of mankind or any group of people, e.g., any nation, into a single moral entity is a mistake; moral agents are individuals, it is individuals who act out of their individual motivations, and individuals are not merely the agents but the loci of moral progress, or not. Thus Mendelssohn asserts that moral "progress is for the individual man." The moral progress of any society will only be a sum of the moral progress of the individuals that comprise it. One might be tempted to reify the educational system of a society, to treat its religion as if it at least were an entity; but there too Mendelssohn is, or at least should be, committed to what we might call, in later terminology, methodological individualism: the educational or religious institutions or system of a society or nation is no more than, and no better or worse than, the sum of the educational or religious practices of its members.

And to all of this, Mendelssohn applies an empirical rather than a priori epistemology: at least as far as the moral development of individuals during their natural life spans is concerned, its pattern is determined by experience, not by any a priori theory, and what experience tells us is that although the rational core of morality is accessible to all, some individuals make progress in realizing that during their lives, others do not. But further, since the moral development of societies depends on the moral development of individuals, and since experience tells us both that at any moment different individuals are at different stages of their own development—for the simple reason that at any moment there are individuals of all different ages, not a single generation—and that at any given time some individuals are making moral progress but others not, experience then tells us that society as a whole does not make moral progress. In principle, it could, if all or at least most of its members were making progress at the same time; but in fact, since they are not, society does not make moral progress since it is nothing but a sum of individuals some of whom are making moral progress but some of whom are not. That is why "Individual man advances, but mankind continually fluctuates within fixed limits." Again, any given society may be more or less conducive to the moral development of its members, but society as a whole is not a single moral subject, thus not a potential agent of moral progress apart from its individual members.

Finally, Mendelssohn can accept this result because he does not believe that the natural life span of individuals is the limit of their existence. As Mendelssohn puts it, "the individual man... is destined by Providence to spend part of his eternity here," but only part of it. And in *Phaedo*, fifteen years earlier, Mendelssohn had argued— and this was obviously "theory," a priori rather than empirical argument—that a benevolent Providence would not have given the human being capacities it did not intend him to develop, if not in his natural life span of three score and ten (plus or minus), then in his eternal life. The key to Mendelssohn's argument, not to be found in Plato's dialogue which is his model, is that we cannot have been given powers that we are not destined to develop fully, or that are destined to disappear without a trace, like "foam upon water or the flight of an arrow through the air" (*JubA* 3.1:106–7). Rather, Mendelssohn argues we can be confident that our powers are destined to reach their goals or at least to make unending progress toward them, thus "we can assume with good ground that this progress toward perfection, this increase, this growth in inner perfection, is the destiny [*Bestimmung*] of rational beings, thus also the highest final goal [*Endzweck*] of creation" (*JubA* 3.1:114). Mendelssohn's Socrates waxes eloquent:

> Is it fitting for wisdom, to bring forth a world in which the spirits that it places there... could be happy and... yet to withdraw eternally from these spirits the capacity for contemplation and happiness?... Oh no, my friends! providence has not given us a longing for eternal happiness in vain; it can and will be satisfied... Thus here below we serve the regent of the world by developing our capacities; thus we will also in that [eternal] life continue under his divine protection to practice in virtue and wisdom continually making ourselves more perfect and industrious in fulfilling the series of divine aims that stretch before us into the infinite.
>
> (*JubA* 3.1:115)

Mendelssohn is actually arguing that we can be confident in the ultimate realization of what Kant will call the highest good, namely the perfection of the virtue of each human being and of the happiness of all, just not in the natural life span accessible to empirical observation. But for that very reason he can afford to be relaxed about the fact that experience does not prove the moral progress of humankind within what is accessible to it, that is, the natural history of humankind. With the argument for immortality as the necessary condition of moral perfection in the background, moral abderitism as an empirical observation is nothing to worry about.

What I now want to show is that in spite of his scorn, Kant actually shares key elements of Mendelssohn's position.

## 2. Kant's Moral Abderitism

My first point is that Kant's own mature theory of the freedom of the will, carefully considered, does not allow him to say more than that the choice of good over evil is always in the power of any individual, but then again, so is the choice of evil over good, so throughout life there is always at least the possibility of oscillation between good and evil. Moral progress in individuals, and therefore in the species as a whole, is always possible, but cannot be inevitable. This remains true even if individuals receive the strongest possible support to choose good from their educations or their churches, visible or invisible. Second, this remains true even for individuals in a position of political power, so even the best ordered system of government, a republic in both formal structure and actual governance, can be subverted by the free choice of those individuals. So the *possibility* of both moral abderitism for individuals and therefore for humankind as a whole as well as political abderitism is entailed by Kant's theory of freedom of the will, whether he likes it or not.

This is not the place for a complete review of Kant's mature theory of the freedom of the will.[5] For present purposes, suffice it to say that in spite of suggestions in his earlier works that a free will can act only in accordance with the moral law (e.g., G 4:446), Kant was sufficiently chastened by the objection of J.A.H. Ulrich in his 1788 *Eleutheriologie*[6] that this would make responsibility for immoral action impossible that in Part One of his own *Religion*, first published in 1792,[7] he firmly distinguished between *Wille* as the source of the moral law, thus identical to pure practical reason, and *Willkür*, the faculty of choice, which is always free to choose between subordinating self-love to the moral law or subordinating acting on the moral law to self-love. Kant's key claim is that "if a propensity to" subordinating morality to self-love "does lie in human nature," as experience clearly shows, "then there is in the human being a natural propensity to evil," but that it is not such a natural propensity but the free choice to act upon it that makes a human being actually evil, for if "this propensity itself" is to be "morally evil ... it must ultimately be sought in a free power of choice [*Willkür*], and hence is imputable. This evil is *radical*, since it corrupts the ground of all maxims," that is, all the particular maxims of an evil person are chosen under the general policy of subordinating morality to self-love. Yet if the choice of evil is genuinely free, then "it must equally be possible to *overcome* this evil, for it is found in the human being as acting freely" (*RBMR*, 6:37). That is, since evil is the product of free choice, the free choice of the fundamental maxim of always subordinating morality to self-love, but free choice is nothing less than the power to choose between good and evil, even the person who has freely chosen evil must also always be free to choose good, no matter what she has previously chosen. By the same token, however, if the choice of good is a free choice, then even the person who has chosen good remains free to choose evil, to undo her conversion from evil to good. The free will is not restricted to a single choice, since it is the basis of Kant's theory that it can undo its own free choice of evil, so must be capable of at least two free choices; but then there is no reason to stop at two. Moral backsliding is always a possibility: thus the threat of moral abderitism at the individual level is a consequence of Kant's theory of freedom, and with that in turn comes the possibility of generic moral

---

[5] Among other discussions, see my *Kant*, second edition (London: Routledge, 2014), chapter 6, pp. 245–65.
[6] Johann August Heinrich Ulrich, *Eleutheriologie, oder über Freyheit und Nothwendigkeit* (Jena: Cröker, 1788).
[7] Kant, "Of the radical evil in human nature," *Berlinische Monatsschrift* (1792); published as Part One of *Religion within the Boundaries of Mere Reason* in 1793 with the additional title" Concerning the indwelling of the evil principle alongside the good" (6:18).

abderitism, that is, moral abderitism for the whole of humankind, because at any time any of its members can undertake the conversion from evil to good but also backslide from good to evil.

The claim that the person who has chosen evil nevertheless remains free to choose good might seem surprising against the background of Kant's transcendental idealist defense of freedom of the will (*Willkür*), that is, his claim that the possibility of choice free from determination by antecedent events beyond the current control of the agent is secured by the timeless and therefore non-deterministic character of the noumenal ground of such choice. For the timelessness of noumenal choice or the noumenal ground of choice might seem to imply that there is no room for a *sequence* of choices, thus for a multiplicity, thus to imply that each agent gets to make only a single choice of fundamental maxim. Kant's transcendental idealism was understood in this way by Arthur Schopenhauer, for example, who argued precisely that because the real choice of character is noumenal, the character of each individual must be fixed, that is, each individual gets only one choice of character in life.[8] But Kant clearly rejected that inference in his supposition that conversion from evil to good is possible, and moreover he was right to do so. For to suppose that we get to make only a single choice at the noumenal level would also be to import a temporal characterization of choice where it does not, according to transcendental idealism, belong. All that follows from the denial of temporality to the noumenal and thus to noumenal choice is that we cannot *represent* the room for a multiplicity of choices there in our ordinary, temporal terms, as taking place sequentially, not that there is no room for multiplicity of choice there. To be sure, from a *theoretical* point of view, we have no more ground for imputing the possibility of multiple choices to the noumenal level than we have for restricting it to a single choice, for from a theoretical point of view we have no basis for saying anything about the noumenal at all beyond that it exists and that it is the ground of the phenomenal. But as Kant constantly stresses, our basis for making any further claims about the noumenal is *practical*, not theoretical, and we can rationally believe (*glauben*) about the noumenal whatever, but only whatever morality requires us to believe about it (for one example among many, see *RBMR*, 6:117–18). And morality requires us to believe that we are free, thus that we are free to choose good even if we have already chosen evil, but also free to choose evil even if we have already chosen good. Of course, because of the temporal character of our sensibility and therefore our imagination, we have no other way to *picture* this freedom and thus to *talk* about it except sequentially. So we have no choice but to *say* that even once we have chosen evil, we always remain free to choose good, but even having chosen good, we still remain free to choose evil once again.

All of this is why I insist that Kant himself is committed to the *possibility* of moral progress at the individual level, but also to the *possibility* of individual moral abderitism, that is, in plain language, of individual moral backsliding. And it is clear that Kant thinks of the locus of moral choice, thus either moral progress or

---

[8] See Arthur Schopenhauer, *Prize Essay on the Basis of Morals*, §10; in *The Two Fundamental Problems of Ethics*, translated and edited by Christopher Janaway (Cambridge: Cambridge University Press, 2009), p. 173.

moral abderitism, as the individual. Even passages from Part Three of the *Religion*, in which he is arguing that because there is a social basis for the *temptation* to choose evil, social support for the choice of good in the form of a church, ultimately a universal, invisible church committed only to the rational, moral core of religion is necessary, still stress that the actual choice between good and evil is always individual. This is evident in Kant's general argument that the "God-man" Christ cannot be understood as actually remitting our sins for us but only as a "prototype lying in our reason" of our own possibility of moral conversion (*RBMR*, 6:119), which is itself a necessary premise for his argument that there is a truly universal rational religion inherent in Christianity (but only in Christianity). And it is clear in particular statements, such as this attack upon the historical form that Christianity has taken:

> The degrading distinction between *laity* and *clergy* ceases, and equality springs from true freedom, yet without anarchy, for each indeed obeys the law (not the statutory one) which he has prescribed for himself, yet must regard it at the same time as the will of the world ruler as revealed to him through reason, and this ruler invisibly binds all together, under a common government, in a state inadequately represented and prepared for in the past through the visible church. (*RBMR*, 6:122)

We may represent the moral law as the will of a single law-giver, but we must each also legislate it for ourselves and in any case each choose for ourselves whether or not to obey it. Only our several individual choices of the moral law over self-love can bind us together into an invisible church, free of historical trappings and a clergy. Kant further adds:

> We cannot expect to draw a *universal history* of humankind from religion on earth (in the strictest meaning of the word); for, inasmuch as it is based on pure moral faith, religion is not a public condition; each human being can become conscious of the advances which he has made in this faith only for himself... the *church universal* begins to fashion itself into an ethical state of God and to make progress toward its fulfillment, under an autonomous principle which is one and the same for all human beings and for all times. (*RBMR*, 6:124)

Again, Kant's position is that each individual must make her own choice in behalf of morality, although the moral law, the "autonomous principle," is "one and the same for all human beings." The morality of mankind as a whole can only be the product of the individual human beings who comprise mankind, and if they themselves can oscillate between good and evil, then *a fortiori* so can mankind as a whole. On this point there is actually little difference between Kant's position and Mendelssohn's, in spite of Kant's protest.

Having reached this point, I should now turn to its implications for the topic of Kant's political chiliasm, the actual topic of his criticism of Mendelssohn although not of Mendelssohn's own argument. But before I do that, I want to spend another moment on the topic of individual moral progress, because Kant's various comments on this topic may be confusing. In his *Phaedo*, Mendelssohn, as we saw, argued that we need to assume an eternal life for the perfection of both our virtue and our happiness—the vocation of mankind can be fulfilled only in eternal life. In the *Critique of Pure Reason*, Kant had agreed that we need to "assume" (*annehmen*) a "world that is future for us" for the realization of the "two presuppositions that reason imposes on us in accordance with principles of that very same reason"

(A 811/B 839), that is, the perfection of both virtue and happiness as the components of the highest good, his version of the vocation of mankind, while in the *Critique of Practical Reason*, Kant had argued that we must "postulate" an "endless progress toward...complete conformity of the will with the moral law" that in turn is "possible only on the presupposition of the *existence* and personality of the same rational being continuing *endlessly* (which is called the immortality of the soul)" (*CPracR*, 5:122), leaving the realization of happiness to take place in nature, although one authored by God. Either way, Kant's departure from Mendelssohn's argument for the immortality of the soul seemed to be more in its epistemic status than anything else, that is, in his change of the key of the argument from a theoretical proof to a practical postulate—as indeed Kant suggested in 1786 in his essay on orientation in thought. But in the *Religion* Kant seems to walk back from this argument, instead treating the idea of endless progress toward the good and thus immortality merely as our way of *representing* in our sensible terms the gap between our own kind of will, which even if it chooses to be moral always has to overcome temptations toward self-love, and a truly holy will, which does not (and which therefore, one might interject, should not really count as a will at all). The passage I have in mind, partially cited earlier but now cited in full, is this:

The distance between the goodness which we ought to effect in ourselves and the evil from which we start is...infinite, and, so far as the deed is concerned—i.e., the conformity of the conduct of one's life to the holiness of the law—is not exhaustible in any time. Nevertheless, the human being's moral constitution ought to agree with this holiness... And this is a change of heart which must itself be possible because it is a duty.—Now the difficulty lies here: How can this disposition count for the deed itself, when this deed is *every time* (not generally, but at each instant) defective? The solution rests on the following: According to our estimation [*Schätzung*], [to us] who are unavoidably restricted to temporal conditions in our conceptions of the relationship of cause to effect, the deed, as a continuous advance *in infinitum* from a defective good to something better always remains defective, so that we are bound to consider the good as it appears in us, i.e., according to the *deed*, as *at each instant* inadequate to a holy law. But because of the *disposition* [*Gesinnung*] from which it derives and which transcends the senses, we can think of the infinite progression of the good toward conformity to the law as being judged by him who scrutinizes the heart (through his pure intellectual intuition) to be a perfected whole even with respect to the deed (the life conduct). And so not withstanding his permanent deficiency, a human being can still expect to be *generally* well-pleasing to God, at whatever point in time his existence be cut short. (*RBMR*, 6:66–7)

Being noumenal, our choice of fundamental maxim and thus our conversion from evil to good, if indeed that takes place, is inaccessible to us, and we can only judge our choice of maxim from our deeds. And that is an inadequate basis for judgment, for several reasons: As Kant suggests, there is always some element of self-love in us, so no particular action can prove complete commitment to the moral law; more generally, the same type of outward action can always be performed from different motives and maxims; and even if it were determinate what motive and maxim has led to a particular action, that is no guarantee that our choice of that maxim is an enduring one. But none of these are problems for God, who can (should he exist) recognize our choice of fundamental maxim directly, without an inference from the outward appearance of our deeds or even from our more particular maxims; and since he can do that *at whatever point our existence be cut short* it follows that the choice of fundamental maxim must be complete at any point at which our existence can be cut short, that is, in our natural, finite life spans, although at the noumenal level, rather than only in some supposed endless progress possible only in immortality. The idea of endless progress toward morality is only an image; we do not need endless time to perfect our morality because we can do it at any time—or not, in which case more time will not help, that is, will not guarantee that we will convert from evil to good (and not revert). Kant's theory of freedom of choice yields no guarantee that we must ever choose morality, nor any guarantee of endless progress toward morality; it leaves room for individual moral abderitism.

One last text does not change this picture. In the essay "The End of All Things," which followed the *Religion* by one year, Kant talks again about eternity, namely the eternity that should follow a final day of judgment, and further seems to suggest that our moral disposition is "unalterable," which would seem to belie the possibility of a multiplicity of choices even at the noumenal level that leaves Kant himself open to the possibility of moral abderitism. But Kant is very clear that the idea of an unalterable eternity following a day of judgment is once again only a sensible image by means of which we can impress upon ourselves the fact that there will come for each of us a real time after which it will no longer be possible to change our moral disposition, so "it is wise to act *as if* another life—and the moral state in which we end this one, along with its consequences in entering upon that other life—is unalterable" (*EAT*, 8:330). This does not imply that before our actual, natural deaths we cannot change our moral dispositions, thus convert from evil to good if we have already chosen evil, but neither does it imply that having once converted from evil to good we cannot revert to evil. It just impresses upon us that in our natural lives there will come a point at which we can no longer change, and that since none of us knows when that will be, each of us ought always to act as if any moment could be our last, thus make every effort as soon as we can to convert from evil to good and to remain committed to the moral law rather than backsliding. But of course this presupposes rather than precluding the possibility of any one of us never converting in the first place, or of backsliding—so it is entirely consistent with the possibility of individual moral abderitism.

With this conclusion in place, let us now finally turn to the question whether Kant is entitled to assert a "philosophical" or political chiliasm, that is, a guarantee that the conditions for perpetual peace must be realized in human history, the point that he wanted to press against Mendelssohn in "Theory and Practice" even though it is not what Mendelssohn had explicitly denied.

## 3. Kant's Political Abderitism

Here I want to make three points. First, Kant's argument that a worldwide federation[9] of republics would generate perpetual peace turns on an assumption about the

---

[9] I assume here that at least in *Toward Perpetual Peace* and the Doctrine of Right of the *Metaphysics of Morals* Kant's thesis is that perpetual peace can be secured by a *federation* of sovereign republics and not by a single world-state armed with its own coercive force. This of course has been the topic of considerable

effects of the self-love of citizens that can only be known empirically and that can only yield an increased probability of world peace over any other government, not a certitude. Second, republics, like any other kind of government, must be instituted and maintained by individual human beings with free wills, and these individuals are just as liable to moral abderitism as anyone else, thus the states that they rule are also liable to institutional abderitism. For both of these reasons, then, thus third, Kant's argument cannot yield a guarantee of perpetual peace, but at most a guarantee of its *possibility*. Since Mendelssohn never denied that the moral progress of mankind or its political progress is *possible*, the difference between Kant's position and his may ultimately be more rhetorical than anything else.

First, then, the basis of Kant's argument for the claim that perpetual peace will arise when and only when the "civil constitution in every state" is "republican" is that "When the consent of the citizens is required in order to decide whether there shall be war or not (and it cannot be otherwise in this constitution), nothing is more natural than that they will be very hesitant to begin this game, since they would have to decide to take upon themselves all the hardships of war," whereas "under a constitution in which subjects are not citizens of the state, which is therefore not republican," deciding upon war "is the easiest thing in the world; because the head of state is not a member of the state but its proprietor and gives up nothing at all" (PP, 8:350). Both sides of this argument turn on assumptions about self-love or self-interest, not about morality: republican citizens will, Kant supposes, decide against war because it is against their self-interest, promising them more costs—"doing the fighting and paying the costs of the war from their own belongings"—than benefits, while non-republican rulers can easily decide that war is in their self-interest, since the costs will be borne by their subjects but, Kant supposes, any profits will accrue to themselves. If this were not clear enough, Kant makes it explicit that the argument from republicanism to perpetual peace actually turns on self-interest in the essay on progress in the *Conflict of the Faculties*, when he says that "progress toward the better" will yield humanity "Not an ever growing quantity of *morality* with regard to intention, but an increase of the products of *legality* in dutiful actions whatever their motives," because "There will arise in the body politic" under republican government "perhaps more charity and less strife in lawsuits, more reliability in keeping one's word, etc.," where "eventually this will also extend to nations in their external relations toward one another up to the realization of the cosmopolitan society... partly out of love of honour, partly out of well-understood self-interest... without the moral foundation in humanity having to be enlarged in the least" (CF, 7:91–2).

These are empirical claims yielding probabilities, not necessities, just as Mendelssohn's argument for abderitism was also an empirical argument yielding probabilities. And the *Conflict of the Faculties* makes it clear that this is an empirical argument: "we have only *empirical data* (experiences) upon which we are founding

---

dispute. For my position, see "The Possibility of Perpetual Peace," in Luigi Caranti, ed., *Kant's Perpetual Peace: New Interpretative Essays* (Rome: LUISS Press, 2006), pp. 161–81. There has been an extensive debate whether Kant advocates a league of nations or a single world-state; for review of this debate, and an intermediate position, see Pauline Kleingeld, *Kant's Cosmopolitanism* (Cambridge: Cambridge University Press, 2012).

this prediction, namely, the physical cause of our actions as these actually occur as phenomena; and not the moral cause—the only one which can be established purely *a priori*—which contains the concept of duty with respect to what ought to happen" (*CF*, 7:91). That is, it is an a priori claim, indeed the pinnacle of the concept of justice, that all should seek world-wide peace, but it is empirical claim, not an a priori claim, that citizens motivated by self-interest will be averse to war and monarchs motivated by self-interest will not be; and as empirical claims these can only be confirmed within the general, inductive limits of confirmation for empirical claims—which yield probability, not certainty. Kant's language in *Toward Perpetual Peace* also makes this perfectly clear, for what he says there is that nothing is *more natural* than that self-interested citizens will not want to make war while for non-republican monarchs deciding upon war is the *easiest* thing in the world. But neither "more natural" nor "easiest" means necessary or certain. Citizens operating as rational economic agents may generally be averse to war, but sometimes even such citizens might think it in their self-interest to start a war—the pickings might seem so easy—and we also know perfectly well that even rationally self-interested citizens are not always purely *economic* agents. Further, as Albert Hirschman famously argued, and as history all too often proves, politics is driven by "passions" as well as "interests,"[10] and Kant himself has alluded to "love of honour" as well as "well-understood self-interest." Passions can be inflamed and honor offended, leading to actions that conflict with merely economic self-interest. Rational economic self-interest might make the decision in favor of war less likely than it is in any other form of government, but it cannot make it impossible.

Second, even republican governments need to be instituted and maintained by ordinary human beings, and those who have such responsibilities are just as free as any other human beings, thus free to be moral but also free not to be. Kant is famous for his image of human beings as crooked timber, who, like trees in a well-maintained forest, can be forced to grow straight by external constraints when their internal constraint of respect for the moral law does not suffice. Such external constraints could include more than appeals to their economic self-interest, so it might seem that the previous problem could be overcome with threats of punishment or promises of reward appealing to other but still non-moral motives. However, Kant also makes it clear that those in power are themselves potentially crooked timber who, however, cannot be forced to govern properly by yet further external constraints—for that would lead to an infinite regress—but only by their own respect for morality—a motive, as we have seen Kant to argue in the *Religion*, that cannot be guaranteed to be efficacious. Kant makes this point bluntly in the 1784 essay on the "Idea for a Universal History" by saying that "the human being is an *animal* which, when it lives among others of its species, *has need of a master*," but that the master too can come from "Nowhere else but from the human species" yet is then "exactly as much an animal who has need of a master." The only solution to this is find leaders who have "correct concepts of the nature of a possible constitution, great experience practiced through many courses of

---

[10] Albert Hirschman, *The Passions and the Interests: Political Arguments for Capitalism before its Triumph* (Princeton: Princeton University Press, 1977).

life, and beyond this a good will that is prepared to accept" a correct constitution (*IUH*, Sixth Proposition, 8:23). But there is nothing that can guarantee that a free will is always a good will, so nothing that can guarantee that even the most carefully chosen leaders will do the right thing. Even the best institutions only make justice possible, not necessary—the human will can pervert anything.[11]

In his writings from the 1790s, Kant emphasizes that the *inauguration* of republican government depends on the good will of non-republican rulers, that is, monarchs or aristocrats who decide of their own free will to transform their autocratic governments into republics. In *Perpetual Peace*, he takes the existence of autocratic government as the default position, and then, having argued as he already did in "Theory and Practice" that there is no right to rebellion, he has to argue that the transformation to republican government can only be effected by the good will of "moral politicians," prodded no doubt by the rightful freedom of the pen of citizens who protest against current wrongs. That is, moral politicians will undertake to reform their non-republican governments into republics: A moral politician in a state that "by its present constitution...possesses a despotic *ruling power*...will make it his principle that, once defects...are found within the constitution of a state or in the relations of states, it is a duty, especially for heads of state, to be concerned about how they can be improved as soon as possible, and brought into conformity with natural right, which stands before us as a model in the idea of reason" (*PP*, 8:372). Likewise, in the *Conflict of the Faculties* Kant argues that "Progress toward the better can be expected...not by the movement of things *from bottom to top*, but *from top to bottom*," but that what can be "expected and exacted" from the top is still to be expected and exacted "from *human beings*," and is thus still liable to the "infirmity of human nature as subject to the contingency of events" (*CF*, 7:92–3). The dependence of political progress on individual wills could not be clearer. Further, although Kant does not make this equally explicit, even once a republic is in place, it must still be administered and maintained by ordinary human beings, again with their inscrutable freedom of the will to choose evil as well as good. Kant partly addresses this problem by insisting that the executive in a government, who has a monopoly of coercive force, is only an "agent" of its legislature, who can rightfully be deposed or reformed by that legislature if he is violating his brief in the enforcement of the laws legislated by the latter (*MM*, DR, §49, 6:317); but since Kant has banned violent revolution, the legislature has no clear recourse if the unjust executive refuses to be deposed or reformed, and in any case the legislature itself is comprised of ordinary human beings, for whom the concept of the general will of the people as expressed in a social contract is an "idea...in terms of which alone we can think of the legitimacy of a state" (*MM*, DR, §47, 6:315)—so once again there can be no guarantee that an actual legislature, comprised of ordinary human beings, will govern even a properly formed republic in a genuinely republican way. The involvement of free and fallible human beings at every level of government means that no mere form of government can guarantee completely rightful governance.

---

[11] For a fuller development of this point, see my "The Crooked Timber of Mankind," in Rorty and Schmidt, *Kant's Idea for a Universal History*, pp. 129–49.

But how can Kant acknowledge this? Throughout *Perpetual Peace*, until its Appendix on moral politicians, Kant speaks of the "guarantee (surety)" of the ultimate institution and preservation of peace that is to be afforded by the "great artist *nature*... from whose mechanical course purposiveness shines forth visibly, letting concord arise by means of the discord of human beings even against their will" (*PP*, 8:360–1); and his critique of Mendelssohn, as we saw, is that while the latter has not made his doubts about the possibility of progress "quite certain" Kant himself can safely assume that the progress of humankind toward the "moral end of its existence... will indeed be *interrupted* from time to time but will never be *broken off*" (*TP*, 8:308–9). But Kant's objection to Mendelssohn needs to be read carefully, as does all talk of a guarantee in *Perpetual Peace*. Here is what Kant actually says in support of his assumption:

I do not need to prove this presupposition; it is up to its adversary to prove [his] case. For I rest my case on my innate duty, the duty of every member of the series of generations—to which I (as a human being in general) belong and am yet not so good in the moral character required of me as I ought to be and hence could be—so to influence posterity that it becomes always better (the possibility of this must, accordingly, also be assumed)... It does not matter how many doubts may be raised against my hopes from history, which, if they were proved, could move me to desist from a task so apparently futile; as long as these doubts cannot be made quite certain I cannot exchange the duty... for the rule of prudence not to attempt the impracticable... and however uncertain I may always be and remain as to whether something better is to be hoped for from humankind, this cannot infringe upon the maxim, and hence upon its presupposition, necessary for practical purposes, that it is practicable. (*TP*, 8:309)

Kant appeals to his premise that "ought implies can," and argues that unless Mendelssohn can prove "cannot," that is, prove (a priori) that humans *cannot* progress under any circumstances, then "ought" is not overturned, that is, humans remain under the obligation to work towards moral progress (in the form of perpetual peace) no matter what interruptions and disappointments they encounter. But Mendelssohn did not attempt any a priori proof that progress is impossible, and for his own part Kant has not attempted any proof that it is inevitable. What he has done throughout his discussions from the "Idea of a Universal History" through the *Conflict of the Faculties* is to argue that there are mechanisms in nature—in human nature, thus in human self-interest—that make it *possible* for humans to achieve the moral end of their existence *if they freely choose to use them for that purpose*, or which maybe even make it *likely* that humans will achieve their moral end *if they do not freely choose to subvert them*, as in their personal lives they can freely choose to subvert their natural predispositions to the good (see *RBMR*, 6:26–8)—but which never make it *necessary* or inevitable that humans, individually or collectively, will fulfill their moral vocation. In other words, Kant proves the *possibility* of moral progress and perpetual peace, not their *necessity*; even Kant argues only that "ought implies can," not that "ought implies does" or "ought implies must do."[12] And

---

[12] Yirmiahu Yovel, *Kant and the Philosophy of History* (Princeton: Princeton University Press, 1980), takes Kant to have advanced over the "Idea of a Universal History" by making the "cunning of nature" a regulative rather than constitutive principle in the *Critique of the Power of Judgment* (p. 141). This does not address the fact that in *Toward Perpetual Peace* Kant remains torn between a "constitutive" and a "regulative" view of historical progress toward a morally necessary political goal.

nothing in Mendelssohn's argument proves or seems intended to prove that moral progress is *impossible*.

To be sure, Kant's argument is not simply that Mendelssohn has not proven the *logical* impossibility of progress, so that he himself remains free to appeal to the merely logical possibility of progress in order to maintain his moral principle that we ought to seek progress. Logical possibility, that is, the mere absence of self-contradiction in a concept, comes too cheaply for Kant; he always wants real possibility. We might then interpret his argument that there are mechanisms in nature that can lead to political (if not strictly moral) progress as long as we do not abuse our freedom to subvert them as the demonstration of the real rather than merely logical possibility of progress. But even real possibility is still just possibility: as long as it remains possible for us to subvert any natural mechanism, including the peaceable tendencies of republics, there can be no absolute guarantee of perpetual peace.

So in the end, the difference between Mendelssohn and Kant seems more rhetorical than substantive. Mendelssohn makes the glass sound half empty, and Kant tries to make it sound more than half full. But his own conception of free will means that there can be no guarantee that any human being will always do the right thing, and thus he cannot preclude moral aberitism at the individual level; and Kant's clear-eyed recognition of the dependence of even the best-designed form of government on the good will of individual human beings means that no form of government can evade the fact of human freedom, for better or worse. All that Kant can properly argue, against Mendelssohn or anyone else, is that human beings are *capable* of morality and justice, but not that nature can force them to be moral and just.

## 4. Conclusion

In commenting on Kant's response in "Theory and Practice" to Mendelssohn's position on progress in *Jerusalem*, Alexander Altmann said that Mendelssohn was "perhaps more of a realist than Kant," although he added, referring to a passage which have quoted from the *Conflict of the Faculties*, that there Kant "took a more cautious view, for "What was increasing, he now said, was the quantity of legality, not morality."[13] Since Kant held that any individual's fundamental motivation is inscrutable, the most that Kant could ever have said, if even that were true, is that the quantity of legality, not morality, is known to be increasing. Given his transcendental idealism, perhaps Kant should not have picked a fight with Mendelssohn over whether the quantity of individual or collective morality is actually increasing; at the most, he should have held that we must be able to believe that individual moral and social political progress are *possible*, because it would be irrational for us to work toward either if we could not believe that. More generally, the tension in Kant's writings between the idea that progress is an inevitability or only a possibility reveals the tension between rationalism and empiricism in his thought. Neither Mendelssohn nor Kant, as we have seen throughout this study, can be simply put

---

[13] Altmann, *Moses Mendelssohn*, p. 542.

into the box of either rationalism or empiricism. Each is trying in his own way to combine the two properly. Sometimes Kant seems to do better in this project than Mendelssohn, as when he insists that the empirical conditions for knowledge preclude theoretical knowledge of the existence of God, freedom, and immortality but leave room for practical belief in these ideas. Sometimes rationalism seems to get the better of Kant, as when he convinces himself, or at least toys with the idea, that a pure religion of reason is inevitable in human history. Sometimes Mendelssohn's rationalism gets the better of him, as when he holds tenaciously to the ontological argument. But sometimes Mendelssohn strikes the better balance between rationalism and empiricism, as when he makes room for emotion within the framework of rationalist aesthetics and recognizes that moral progress is individual rather than collective. But both their successes and their failures in balancing rationalism and empiricism show that Kant and Mendelssohn were alive to the complexity of human experience and thought: both reason and experience have indispensable contributions to make to the human representation of both self and the rest of the world and to human decisions about how to attempt to change the world, and the attempt to determine precisely what these dual contributions are is a permanent struggle for, but also the lifeblood of, philosophy. The history of the lifelong interaction of Immanuel Kant and Moses Mendelssohn, with all its fruitful agreements as well as misunderstandings and missed opportunities, is but a part of the larger history and on-going life of philosophy.

# Bibliography

## 1. Primary Sources: Mendelssohn and Kant

Kant, Immanuel. *Kant's gesammelte Schriften.* Edited by the Royal Prussian (later German, then Berlin-Brandenburg) Academy of Sciences. 29 vols. Berlin: Georg Reimer (later Walter de Gruyter & Co.), 1900–.

Kant, Immanuel. *Bemerkungen in den "Beobachtungen über das Gefühl des Schönen und Erhabenen."* Edited by Marie Rischmüller. Kant-Forschungen, Band 3. Hamburg: Felix Meiner Verlag, 1991.

Kant, Immanuel. *Theoretical Philosophy 1755–1770.* Translated by David E. Walford in collaboration with Ralf Meerbote. Cambridge: Cambridge University Press, 1992.

Kant, Immanuel. *Practical Philosophy.* Edited and translated by Mary J. Gregor. Cambridge: Cambridge University Press, 1996.

Kant, Immanuel. *Religion and Rational Theology.* Edited and translated by Allen W. Wood and George di Giovanni. Cambridge: Cambridge University Press, 1996.

Kant, Immanuel. *Lectures on Ethics.* Edited by J.B. Schneewind and Peter Heath, translated by Peter Heath. Cambridge: Cambridge University Press, 1997.

Kant, Immanuel. *Critique of Pure Reason.* Edited and translated by Paul Guyer and Allen W. Wood. Cambridge: Cambridge University Press, 1998.

Kant, Immanuel. *Correspondence.* Edited and translated by Arnulf Zweig. Cambridge: Cambridge University Press, 1999.

Kant, Immanuel. *Critique of the Power of Judgment.* Edited by Paul Guyer, translated by Paul Guyer and Eric Matthews. Cambridge: Cambridge University Press, 2000.

Kant, Immanuel. *Theoretical Philosophy after 1781.* Edited by Henry Allison and Peter Heath, translated by Gary Hatfield, Michael Friedman, Henry Allison, and Peter Heath. Cambridge: Cambridge University Press, 2002.

Kant, Immanuel. *Notes and Fragments.* Edited by Paul Guyer, translated by Curtis Bowman, Paul Guyer, and Frederick Rauscher. Cambridge: Cambridge University Press, 2005.

Kant, Immanuel. *Anthropology, History, and Education.* Edited by Günter Zöller and Robert B. Louden, translated by Mary Gregor, Paul Guyer, Robert B. Louden, Holly Wilson, Allen W. Wood, Günter Zöller, and Arnulf Zweig. Cambridge: Cambridge University Press, 2007.

Kant, Immanuel. *Lectures on Anthropology.* Edited by Allen W. Wood and Robert B. Louden, translated by Robert R. Clewis, Robert B. Louden, G. Felicitas Munzel, and Allen W. Wood. Cambridge: Cambridge University Press, 2012.

Gotthold Ephraim Lessing, Moses Mendelssohn, and Friedrich Nicolai. *Briefwechsel über das Trauerspiel.* Edited by Jochen-Schulte-Sasse. Munich: Winkler Verlag, 1972.

Mendelssohn, Moses. *Gesammelte Schriften: Jubiläumsausgabe.* Begun by Ismar Elbogen, Julius Guttmann, and Eugen Mittwoch in collaboration with Fritz Bamberger, H. Borodianski, Simon Rawidowicz, Bruno Strauss, Leo Strauss, and Werner Weinberg, continued by Alexander Altmann, Eva J. Engel, Michael Brocke, and Daniel Krochmalnik. 25 vols. Stuttgart-Bad Canstatt: Friedrich Frommann Verlag—Günther Holzboog, 1929–.

Mendelssohn, Moses. *Manasseh Ben Israel, Rettung der Juden. Aus dem Englischen übersetzt. Nebst einer Vorrede von Moses Mendelssohn. Als ein Anhang zu des Hrn. Kriegsraths Dohm Abhandlung: Ueber die bürgerliche Verbesserung der Juden.* Berlin and Stettin: Friedrich Nicolai, 1782; JubA 8:1–71.

Mendelssohn, Moses. *Jerusalem, or on Religious Power and Judaism*. Translated by Allen Arkush, Introduction and Commentary by Alexander Altmann. Hanover: Published for Brandeis University Press by University Press of New England, 1983.

Mendelssohn, Moses. *Philosophical Writings*. Translated and edited by Daniel O. Dahlstrom. Cambridge: Cambridge University Press, 1997.

Mendelssohn, Moses. *Phaedon oder über die Untersblichkeit der Seele, in drey Gesprächen*. Berlin and Stettin: Friedrich Nicolai, 1767. In Mendelssohn, *Ausgewählte Werke: Studienausgabe*, Band I: *Schriften zur Metaphysik und Ästhetik 1755–1772*, edited by Christoph Schulte, Andreas Kennecke, and Grażyna Jurewicz. Darmstadt: Wissenschaftliche Buchgesellschaft, 2009.

Mendelssohn, Moses. *Morning Hours: Lectures on God's Existence*. Translated by Daniel O. Dahlstrom and Corey Dyck. Dordrecht: Springer, 2011.

Mendelssohn, Moses. *Writings on Judaism, Christianity, and the Bible*. Edited by Micah Gottlieb, translations by Curtis Bowman, Elias Sacks, and Allen Arkush. Waltham: Brandeis University Press, 2011.

Mendelssohn, Moses. *Last Works*. translated by Bruce Rosenstock. Urbana: University of Illinois Press, 2011.

## 2. Primary Sources: Others

Addison, Joseph and Richard Steele, *The Spectator* (1711–12). Edited by Donald F. Bond. 5 volumes. Oxford: Clarendon Press, 1965.

Akenside, Mark. *The Pleasures of Imagination: A Poem in Three Books*. London: R. Dodsley, 1754.

Batteux, Charles *The Fine Arts Reduced to a Single Principle* (1746). Translated by James O. Young. Oxford: Oxford University Press, 2015; *Einschränkung der Schönen Künste auf einem Grundsatz, aus dem Französichen übersetzt, und mit verschiedenen eignen damit verwandten Abhandlungen begleitet von Johann Adolf Schlegel*. Leipzig: Weidmann, 1770.

Baumgarten, Alexander Gottlieb. *Meditationes philosophicae de nonnullis ad poema pertinentibus/Philosophische Betrachtungen über einige Bedindungen des Gedichtes* (1735). Edited by Heinz Paetzold. Hamburg: Felix Meiner Verlag, 1983.

Baumgarten, Alexander Gottlieb. *Metaphysica* (1739); *Metaphysics*. Translated by Courtney D. Fugate and John Hymers. London: Bloomsbury, 2013.

Baumgarten, Alexander Gottlieb. *Aesthetica* (1750–58), *Ästhetik*. Edited by Dagmar Mirbach. 2 volumes. Hamburg: Felix Meiner Verlag, 2007.

Baumgarten, Alexander Gottlieb. *Anfangsgründe der praktichen Metaphysik* (1760), Latin and German texts. Translated by Alexander Aichele. Hamburg: Felix Meiner Verlag, 2019.

Baumgarten, Alexander Gottlieb. *Elements of First Practical Philosophy*. Edited and translated by Courtney D. Fugate and John Hymers. London: Bloomsbury, 2020.

Berkeley, George. *The Works of George Berkeley, Bishop of Cloyne*. Edited by A.A. Luce and T. E. Jessop. 9 vols. London: Thomas Nelson and Sons, 1948–57.

Burke, Edmund. *A Philosophical Inquiry into the Original of Our Ideas of the Subime and Beautiful* (1757, 1759). Edited by Paul Guyer. Oxford: Oxford World's Classics, 2015.

Descartes, René. *Oeuvres de Descartes*. Edited by Charles Adam and Paul Tannery. Revised edition. 12 vols. Paris: Vrin/CNRS, 1964–76.

Descartes, René. *The Philosophical Writings of Descartes*. Translated by John Cottingham, Robert Stoothof, and Dugald Murdoch. 3 volumes. Cambridge: Cambridge University Press, 1984–91.

Dohm, Christian Wilhelm. *Ueber die bürgerliche Verbesserung der Juden*. Berlin and Stettin: Friedrich Nicolai, 1781.

Dohm, Christian Wilhelm. *Über die bürgerliche Verbesserung der Juden: Kritische und kommentierte Studienausgabe.* Edited by Wolf Christoph Seifert. 2 volumes. Göttingen: Wallstein Verlag, 2015.

Eberhard, Johann August. *Preparation for Natural Theology* (1781). Translated by Courtney D. Fugate and John Hymers. London: Bloomsbury, 2016.

[Garve, Christian, edited by Johann Feder]. "*Critique of Pure Reason* by Immanuel Kant. 1781." *Zugabe zu den Göttingschen Anzeigen von gelehrten Sachen* (January 19, 1782): 40–8; translation from Brigitte Sassen, editor. *Kant's Early Critics: The Empiricist Critique of the Theoretical Philosophy*. Cambridge: Cambridge University Press, 2000. Pp. 53–8.

Gerard, Alexander. *An Essay on Taste, with Three Dissertations on the same Subject by Mr. De Voltaire, Mr. D'Alembert, and Mr. De Montesquieu.* London and Edinburgh: A. Millar, A. Kincaid, and J. Bell, 1759; third edition (1780), with *Observations concerning the Imitative Nature of Poetry.* Edited by Walter J. Hipple, Jr. Delmar, NY: Scholars' Facsimiles and Reprints, 1963.

Herz, Markus [Marcus]. *Betrachtungen aus der spekulativen Weltweisheit* (1771). Edited by Elfriede Conrad, Heinrich P. Delfosse, and Birgit Nehren. Hamburg: Felix Meiner Verlag, 1990.

Home, Henry, Lord Kames. *Elements of Criticism, in Three Volumes.* London and Edinburgh: A. Millar, A. Kincaid, and J. Bell, 1762); sixth edition (1785), ed. Peter Jones, 2 vols. Indianapolis: Liberty Fund, 2005; Heinrich Home, *Grundsätze der Kritik, aus dem Englischen übersetzt*, 3 vols. Leipzig: Dyck, 1763–6.

Hume, David. *A Treatise of Human Nature* (1739–40). Edited by David Fate Norton and Mary J. Norton. 2 volumes. Oxford: Clarendon Press, 2007.

Hume, David. *Enquiry concerning Human Understanding* (1748). Edited by Tom L. Beauchamp. Oxford: Clarendon Press, 2000.

Hume, David. *Essays Moral, Political, and Literary.* Edited by Eugene F. Miller. Revised edition. Indianapolis: Liberty Fund, 1987.

Hutcheson, Francis. *An Inquiry into the Original of Our Ideas of Beauty and Virtue* (London, 1726). Edited by Wolfgang Leidhold. Revised edition. Indianapolis: Liberty Fund, 2008.

Leibniz, Gottfried Wilhelm. *Philosophical Papers and Letters.* Edited by Leroy E. Loemker. Second edition. Dordrecht: D. Reidel, 1969.

Leibniz, Gottfried Wilhelm. *New Essays on Human Understanding* (1765). Translated and edited by Peter Remnant and Jonathan Bennett. Cambridge: Cambridge University Press, 1981.

Leibniz, Gottfried Wilhelm. *Philosophical Essays.* Translated by Roger Ariew and Daniel Garber. Indianapolis: Hackett Publishing Co., 1989.

Lessing, Gotthold Ephraim. *Laocoön: An Essay on the Limits of Painting and Poetry.* Translated by Edward Allen McCormick. Indianapolis: Bobbs-Merrill, 1962.

Lessing, Gotthold Ephraim. *Philosophical and Theological Writings.* Edited by H.B. Nisbet. Cambridge: Cambridge University Press, 2005.

Locke, John. *An Essay concerning Toleration and Other Writings on Law and Politics 1667–1683.* Edited by J.R. Milton and Philip Milton. Oxford: Clarendon Press, 2006.

Locke, John. *Epistola de Tolerantia/A Letter on Toleration* (1689). Edited by Raymond Kilbansky, translated by J.W. Gough. Oxford: Clarendon Press, 1968.

Locke, John. *An Essay concerning Human Understanding* (1690). Edited by P.H. Nidditch. Oxford: Clarendon Press, 1975.

Locke, John. *The Reasonableness of Chistianity, As delivered in the Scriptures* (1695). Edited by John C. Higgins-Biddle. Oxford: Clarendon Press, 1999.

Locke, John. *Vindications of the Reasonableness of Christianity* (1696–7). Edited by Victor Nuovo. Oxford: Clarendon Press, 2012.

Maimon, Salomon. *Essay on Transcendental Philosophy* (1790). Translated by Nick Midgley, Henry Somers-Hall, Alistair Welchman, and Merten Reglitz. London: Continuum, 2010.

Meier, Georg Friedrich. *Anfangsgründe aller schönen Wissenschaften*. 3 volumes. Halle: Renger, 1748–50.

Meier, Georg Friedrich. *Excerpt from the Doctrine of Reason* (1752). Translated by Aaron Bunch. London: Bloomsbury, 2016.

Meier, Georg Friedrich. *Allgemeine praktische Weltweisheit*. Halle: Carl Herman Hemmerde, 1764.

Meier, Georg Friedrich. *Frühe Schriften zur ästhetischen Erziehung der Deutschen*. Edited by Hans-Joachim Kertscher and Günter Schenk. 3 volumes. Halle: Hallescher Verlag, 2002.

Plato. *Complete Works*. Edited by John M. Cooper, Associate Editor D.S. Hutchinson. Indianapolis and Cambridge: Hackett Publishing Co., 1997.

Reinhold, Karl Leonhard. *Versuch einer neuen Theorie des menschlichen Vorstellungsvermögens* (1789). Edited by Ernst-Otto Onnasch. 2 volumes. Hamburg: Felix Meiner Verlag, 2012.

Reinhold, Karl Leonhard. *Briefe über die Kantische Philosophie, Zweyter Band*. Leipzig: Georg Joachim Göschen, 1792.

Richardson, Samuel. *The History of Sir Charles Grandison*. London: Hitch and Hawes et al, 1754.

Royce, Josiah. *The Religious Aspect of Philosophy: A Critique of the Bases of Conduct and Faith*. Boston: Houghton, Mifflin, 1885.

Schmid, Carl Christian Erhard. *Versuch einer Moralphilosophie*. Jena: Cröker, 1790.

Schopenhauer, Arthur. *The Two Fundamental Problems of Ethics*. Translated and edited by Christopher Janaway. Cambridge: Cambridge University Press, 2009.

Schopenhauer, Arthur. "On the Basis of Morality," in *The Two Fundamental Problems of Ethics*, translated and edited by Christopher Janaway. Cambridge: Cambridge University Press, 2009.

Semler, Johann Salomo. *Letztes Glaubensbekenntniß über natürliche und christliche Religion* (1792). Edited by Dirk Fleischer. Nordhausen: Verlag Traugott Bautz, 2012.

Shaftesbury, Anthony Ashley Cooper, Third Earl of. *Characteristicks of Men, Manner, Opinions, Times* (1711). Edited by Philip Ayres. 2 volumes. Oxford: Clarendon Press, 1999.

Spalding, Johann Joachim. *Die Bestimmung des Menschen*. Edited by Wolfgang Erich Müller. Waltrop: Hartmut Spenner, 1997.

Spinoza, Baruch. *The Collected Works of Spinoza*. Edited and translated by Edwin Curley. 2 volumes. Princeton: Princeton University Press, 1985–2016.

Sulzer, Johann Georg. *Kurzer Begriff aller Wissenschaften und andern Theile der Gelehrsamkeit*. Second edition. Leipzig: Langenheim, 1759.

Sulzer, Johann Georg. *Allgemeine Theorie der schönen Künste* (1771–4), second edition, 4 vols. Leipzig: Weidmann, 1792–4.

Ulrich, Johann August Heinrich. *Eleutheriologie, oder über Freyheit und Nothwendigkeit*. Jena: Cröker, 1788.

Vallée, Gérard, editor. *The Spinoza Conversations between Lessing and Jacobi: Text with Excerpts from the Ensuing Controversy*. Lanham: University Press of America, 1988.

Wolff, Christian. *Oratio de Sinarum philosophica practica/Rede über die praktische Philosophie der Chinesen* (1723). Edited by Michael Albrecht. Hamburg: Felix Meiner Verlag, 1985.

Wolff, Christian. *Preliminary Discourse on Philosophy in General* (1728). Translated by Richard J. Blackwell. Indianapolis: Bobbs-Merrill, 1963.

Wolff, Christian. *Vernünftige Gedanken von der natürlichen Dinge*. Die andere Auflage. Frankfurt and Leipzig: Renger, 1726.

Wolff, Christian. *Vernünftige Gedanken von Gott, der Welt, und der Seele des Menschen*. Neue Auflage. Halle: Renger, 1751.

Wolff, Christian. *Vernünfftige Gedancken von der Menschen Thun und Lassen, zu Beförderung ihrer Glückseeligkeit*. Fourth edition. Frankfurt and Leipzig: n.p., 1733.
Zöllner, Johann Friedrich. *Ueber Moses Mendelssohn's Jerusalem*. Berlin: Friedrich Maurer, 1784.

## 3. Secondary Sources

Abela, Paul. *Kant's Empirical Realism*. Oxford: Clarendon Press, 2002.
Allais, Lucy. *Manifest Reality: Kant's Idealism and his Realism*. Oxford: Oxford University Press, 2015.
Allison, Henry E. *Lessing and the Enlightenment*. Ann Arbor: University of Michigan Press, 1966.
Allison, Henry E. "Transcendental Idealism: A Retrospective." In Allison, *Idealism and Freedom: Essays on Kant's Theoretical and Practical Philosophy*. Cambridge: Cambridge University Press, 1996. Pp. 3–26.
Allison, Henry E. *Kant's Theory of Taste*. Cambridge: Cambridge University Press, 2001.
Allison, Henry E. "Transcendental Realism, Empirical Realism, and Transcendental Idealism." In Allison, *Essays on Kant*. Oxford: Oxford University Press, 2012. Pp. 67–83.
Altmann, Alexander. *Moses Mendelssohns Frühschriften zur Metaphysik*. Tübingen: J.C.B. Mohr (Paul Siebeck), 1969.
Altmann, Alexander. *Moses Mendelssohn: A Biographical Study*. Alabama: University of Alabama Press, 1973.
Altmann, Alexander. "Moses Mendelssohn's Proofs for the Existence of God." In Altmann, *Essays in Jewish Intellectual History*. Hanover: University Press of New England, 1981. Pp. 119–41.
Altmann, Alexander. "Das Menschenbild und die Bildung des Menschen nach Moses Mendelssohn." In Altmann, *Die trostvolle Aufklärung: Studien zur Metaphysik und politischen Theorie Moses Mendelssohns*. Stuttgart-Bad Canstatt: Frommann-Holzboog, 1982. Pp. 11–27.
Altmann, Alexander. "The Philosophical Roots of Moses Mendelssohn's Plea for Emancipation." In Altmann, *Die trostvolle Aufklärung*. pp. 217–28.
Ameriks, Karl. "Reinhold and the Short Argument to Idealism." In *Proceedings of the Sixth International Kant Congress*. Edited by Gerhard Funke and Thomas Seebohm. Washington, 1989. Vol. 2, part 2, pp. 441–5.
Ameriks, Karl. "Kant, Fichte, and Short Arguments to Idealism." *Archiv für Geschichte der Philosophie* 72 (1990): 63–85.
Ameriks, Karl. "Kant and Short Arguments to Humility." In Ameriks, *Interpreting Kant's Critiques*. Oxford: Clarendon Press, 2003. pp. 135–57.
Anderson-Gold, Sharon, and Pablo Muchnik, editors. *Kant's Anatomy of Evil*. Cambridge: Cambridge University Press, 2010.
Anscombe, G.E.M. *Intention*. Oxford: Blackwell, 1957.
Arkush, Allan. *Moses Mendelssohn and the Enlightenment*. Albany: State University of New York Press, 1994.
Atlas, Samuel. *From Critical to Speculative Idealism: The Philosophy of Salomon Maimon*. The Hague: Martinus Nijhoff, 1964.
Beck, Lewis White. *Early German Philosophy: Kant and His Predecessors*. Cambridge, Mass.: Harvard University Press, 1969.
Beiser, Frederick C. *The Fate of Reason: German Philosophy from Kant to Fichte*. Cambridge, Mass.: Harvard University Press, 1987.

Beiser, Frederick C. *German Idealism: The Struggle against Subjectivity, 1791–1801*. Cambridge, Mass.: Harvard University Press, 2001.

Beiser, Frederick C. *Diotima's Children: German Aesthetic Rationalism from Leibniz to Lessing*. Oxford: Oxford University Press, 2009.

Bennett, Jonathan. *Kant's Dialectic*. Cambridge: Cambridge University Press, 1974.

Berghahn, Cord-Friedrich. *Moses Mendelssohn's "Jerusalem": Ein Beitrag zur Geschichte der Menschenrechte und der pluralistischen Gesellschaft in der deutschen Aufklärung*. Tübingen: Max Niemeyer Verlag, 2001.

Bohatec, Josef. *Die Religionphilosophie Kants in der "Religion innerhalb der Grenzen der bloßen Vernunft."* Hamburg: Hoffmann und Campe, 1938.

Bourel, Dominique. *Moses Mendelssohn: Begründer des modernen Judentums*. Translated by Horst Brühmann. Zürich: Ammann Verlag, 2007.

Bruxvoort Lipscomb, Benjamin J. and James Krueger, editors. *Kant's Moral Metaphysics*. Berlin and New York: Walter de Gruyter, 2010.

Bullough, Edward. "'Psychical Distance' as a Factor in Art and as an Æsthetic Principle." *British Journal of Psychology* 5 (1912): 87–118, reprinted in Bullough, *Æsthetics: Lectures and Essays*. Edited by Elizabeth M. Wilkinson. Stanford: Stanford University Press, 1957.

Byrd, B. Sharon, and Joachim Hruschka. *Kant's Doctrine of Right: A Commentary*. Cambridge: Cambridge University Press, 2010.

Callanan, John. "Mendelssohn and Kant on Mathematics." *Kant Yearbook* 6 (2014): 1–21.

Cranston, Maurice. *John Locke: A Biography*. London: Longmans, Green and Co., 1957.

Crawford, Donald W. *Kant's Aesthetic Theory*. Madison: University of Wisconsin Press, 1974.

Dahlstrom, Daniel O. "Truth, Knowledge, and 'the Pretensions of Idealism': A Critical Commentary on the First Part of Mendelssohn's *Morning Hours*." *Kant-Studien* 109 (2018): 329–51.

di Giovanni, George. *Freedom and Religion in Kant and His Immediate Successors: The Vocation of Humankind 1748–1800*. Cambridge: Cambridge University Press, 2005.

DiCenso, James J. *Kant, Religion, and Politics*. Cambridge: Cambridge University Press, 2011.

DiCenso, James J. *Kant's Religion within the Boundaries of Mere Reason: A Commentary*. Cambridge: Cambridge University Press, 2012.

Dyck, Corey W. "Turning the Game against the Idealist." In Rainier Munk, editor. *Moses Mendelssohn's Metaphysics and Aesthetics*. Dordrecht: Springer, 2011. Pp. 159–82.

Emundts, Dina. "The Refutation of Idealism and the Distinction between Phenomena and Noumena." In Paul Guyer, editor. *The Cambridge Companion to Kant's Critique of Pure Reason*. Cambridge: Cambridge University Press, 2010. Pp. 168–89.

Erdmann, Benno. *Kant's Kriticismus in der ersten und in der zweiten Auflage der Kritik der reinen Vernunft: Eine historische Untersuchung*. Leipzig: Leopold Voss, 1878.

Feiner, Shmuel. *Moses Mendelssohn: Sage of Modernity*. Translated by Anthony Berris. New Haven: Yale University Press, 2010.

Firestone, Chris L. and Stephen R. Palmquist, editors. *Kant and the New Philosophy of Religion*. Bloomington: Indiana University Press, 2006.

Firestone, Chris L. and Nathan Jacobs. *In Defense of Kant's Religion*. Bloomington: Indiana University Press, 2008.

Franks, Paul. *All or Nothing*. Cambridge, Mass.: Harvard University Press, 2005.

Freudenthal, Gideon. *No Religion without Idolatry: Mendelssohn's Jewish Enlightenment*. Notre Dame: University of Notre Dame Press, 2012.

Friedlander, Eli. *Expressions of Judgment: An Essay on Kant's Aesthetics*. Cambridge, Mass.: Harvard University Press, 2015.

Ginsborg, Hannah. *The Normativity of Nature: Essays on Kant's Critique of Judgement*. Oxford: Oxford University Press, 2015.

Gottlieb, Micah. *Faith and Freedom: Moses Mendelssohn's Theological-Political Thought.* New York: Oxford University Press, 2011.
Gregor, Mary J. "Baumgarten's *Aesthetica.*" *Review of Metaphysics* 37 (1983): 357–85.
Guyer, Paul. *Kant and the Claims of Taste.* Cambridge, Mass.: Harvard University Press, 1979; second edition, Cambridge: Cambridge University Press, 1997.
Guyer, Paul. "Pleasure and Society in Kant's Theory of Taste." In Ted Cohen and Paul Guyer, editors. *Essays in Kant's Aesthetics.* Chicago: University of Chicago Press, 1981. Pp. 21–54.
Guyer, Paul. "Kant's Intentions in the Refutation of Idealism." *Philosophical Review* 92 (1983): 329–83.
Guyer, Paul. *Kant and the Claims of Knowledge.* Cambridge: Cambridge University Press, 1987.
Guyer, Paul. "The Rehabilitation of Transcendental Idealism?" In Eva Schaper and Wilhelm Vossenkuhl, editors. *Reading Kant: New Perspectives on Transcendental Arguments and Critical Philosophy.* Oxford: Basil Blackwell, 1989. Pp. 140–67.
Guyer, Paul. "Reason and Reflective Judgment: Kant on the Significance of Systematicity." *Nous* 24 (1990): 17–43; reprinted in Guyer, *Kant's System of Nature and Freedom: Selected Essays.* Oxford: Clarendon Press, 2005. Pp. 11–37.
Guyer, Paul. "The Transcendental Deduction of the Categories." In Paul Guyer, editor. *The Cambridge Companion to Kant.* Cambridge: Cambridge University Press, 1992. Pp. 123–60.
Guyer, Paul. "The Unity of Reason: Pure Reason as Practical Reason in Kant's Early Conception of the Transcendental Dialectic." In Guyer, *Kant on Freedom, Law, and Happiness.* Cambridge: Cambridge University Press, 2000. Pp. 60–95.
Guyer, Paul. "From Nature to Morality: Kant's New Argument in the 'Critique of Teleological Judgment'." In Hans-Friderich Fulda and Jürgen Stoltzenberg, editors. *Architektonik und System in der Philosophie Kants.* Hamburg: Felix Meiner Verlag, 2001. Pp. 375–404; reprinted in Guyer, *Kant's System of Nature and Freedom.* Pp. 314–42.
Guyer, Paul. "Free and Adherent Beauty: A Modest Proposal." *British Journal of Aesthetics* 42 (2002): 357–66; reprinted in Guyer, *Values of Beauty.* Cambridge: Cambridge University Press, 2005. Pp. 129–40.
Guyer, Paul. "Kant's Deductions of the Principles of Right." In Mark Timmons, editor. *Kant's Metaphysics of Morals: Interpretative Essays.* Oxford: Oxford University Press, 2002. Pp. 23–64: reprinted in Guyer, *Kant's System of Nature and Freedom.* Pp. 198–242.
Guyer, Paul. *Kant's System of Nature and Freedom: Selected Essays.* Oxford: Clarendon Press, 2005.
Guyer, Paul. "The Harmony of Faculties Revisited." In Guyer, *Values of Beauty: Historical Essays in Aesthetics.* Cambridge: Cambridge University Press, 2005. Pp. 77–109.
Guyer, Paul, 2006. "The Possibility of Perpetual Peace," in Luigi Caranti, ed., *Kant's Perpetual Peace: New Interpretative Essays.* Rome: LUISS University Press. Pp. 161–81.
Guyer, Paul. "The Crooked Timber of Mankind." In Amélie Oksenberg Rorty and James Schmidt, editors. *Kant's Idea for a Universal History with a Cosmopolitan Aim: A Critical Guide.* Cambridge: Cambridge University Press, 2009. Pp. 129–49.
Guyer, Paul. "The Deduction of the Categories: The Metaphysical and Transcendental Deductions." In Paul Guyer, editor. *The Cambridge Companion to Kant's Critique of Pure Reason.* Cambridge: Cambridge University Press, 2010. Pp. 118–50.
Guyer, Paul. "The Obligation To Be Virtuous: Kant's Conception of the *Tugendverpflilchtung.*" *Social Philosophy and Policy* 27 (2010): 206–32; reprinted in Guyer, *Virtues of Freedom: Selected Essays on Kant.* Oxford: Oxford University Press, 2016. Pp. 216–34.
Guyer, Paul. "Mendelssohn's Theory of Mixed Sentiments." In Rainier Munk, editor. *Moses Mendelssohn's Metaphysics and Aesthetics.* Dordrecht: Springer, 2011. Pp. 259–78.
Guyer, Paul. *A History of Modern Aesthetics.* 3 volumes. Cambridge: Cambridge University Press, 2014.

Guyer, Paul. *Kant.* Second edition. London: Routledge, 2014.
Guyer, Paul. "The Twofold Morality of *Recht.*" *Kant-Studien* 107 (2016): 34–63.
Guyer, Paul. *Virtues of Freedom: Selected Essays on Kant.* Oxford: Oxford University Press, 2016.
Guyer, Paul. "Kantian Perfectionism." In *Virtues of Freedom.* Pp. 70–86.
Guyer, Paul. "Kantian Communities: The Realm of Ends, the Ethical Community, and the Highest Good." In *Virtues of Freedom.* Pp. 275–302.
Guyer, Paul. "Transcendental Idealism: What and Why?" In Matthew C. Altman, editor. *The Palgrave Kant Handbook.* London: Palgrave Macmillan, 2017. Pp. 71–90.
Guyer, Paul. "One Act or Two? Hannah Ginsborg on Aesthetic Judgment." *British Journal of Aesthetics* 57 (2017): 407–19.
Guyer, Paul. "The Infinite Given Magnitude and Other Myths about Space and Time." In Ohad Nachtomy and Reed Winegar, editors. *Infinity in Early Modern Philosophy.* Cham, Switzerland: Springer, 2018. Pp. 181–204.
Guyer, Paul. "The Struggle for Freedom: Freedom of Will in Kant and Reinhold." In Eric Watkins, editor. *Kant on Persons and Agency.* Cambridge: Cambridge University Press, 2018. Pp. 120–37.
Guyer, Paul. *Kant on the Rationality of Morality.* Cambridge: Cambridge University Press, 2019.
Guyer, Paul. "Kant's Reformed Teleology." In Jeffrey McDonough, editor. *Teleology,* in *Oxford Philosophical Concepts.* New York: Oxford University Press, 2020. Pp. 186–218.
Heidemann, Dietmar. *Kant und das Problem des metaphysischen Idealismus.* Berlin: Walter de Gruyter, 1998.
Henrich, Dieter. *Der Ontologische Gottesbeweis.* Revised edition. Tübingen: J.C.B. Mohr (Paul Siebeck), 1960.
Hinske, Norbert. "Mendelssohns Beantwortung der Frage: Was ist Aufklärung? oder über die Aktualität Mendelssohns." In Hinske, *Ich handle mit Vernunft: Moses Mendelssohn und die europäische Aufklärung.* Hamburg: Felix Meiner Verlag, 1981. Pp. 85–117.
Hirschman, Albert. *The Passions and the Interests: Political Arguments for Capitalism before its Triumph.* Princeton: Princeton University Press, 1977.
Höffe, Otfried, editor. *Immanuel Kant: Die Religion innerhalb der Grenzen der bloßen Vernunft.* Berlin: Akademie Verlag, 2011.
Hogan, Desmond. "Three Kinds of Rationalism and the Non-Spatiality of Things in Themselves." *Journal of the History of Philosophy* 47 (2009): 355–82.
Hughes, Fiona. "Feeling the Life of the Mind: Mere Judging, Feeling, and Judgment." In Matthew C. Altman, editor. *The Palgrave Kant Handbook.* London: Palgrave Macmillan, 2017. Pp. 381–406.
Huneman, Philippe. *Métaphysique et Biologie: Kant et la Constitution du Concept d'Organisme.* Paris: Éditions Kimé, 2008.
Hunter, Ian. *Rival Enlightenments: Civil and Metaphysical Philosophy in Early Modern Germany.* Cambridge: Cambridge University Press, 2001.
Insole, Christopher J. *Kant and the Creation of Freedom: A Theological Problem.* Oxford: Oxford University Press, 2013.
Jackson, B. Darrell. "The Theory of Signs in *De Doctrine Christiana.*" In R.A. Markus, editor. *Augustine: A Collection of Critical Essays.* Garden City: Doubleday, 1972. Pp. 92–147.
Kinkel, Walter. "Moses Mendelssohn and Immanuel Kant." *Kant-Studien* 34 (1929): 391–409.
Klemme, Heiner F., editor. *Die Schule Immanuel Kants: Mit dem Text von Christian Schiffert über das Königsberger Collegium Fredericianum.* Kant-Forschungen, Band 6. Hamburg: Felix Meiner Verlag, 1994.

Koch, Gertrud. *Die Wiederkehr der Illusion: Der Film und die Kunst der Gegenwart.* Berlin: Suhrkamp, 2016.

Koller, Aaron. "Mendelssohn's Response to Burke on the Sublime." In Reinier Munk, editor. *Moses Mendelssohn's Metaphysics and Aesthetics.* Dordrecht: Springer, 2011. Pp. 329–50.

Kuehn, Manfred. *Kant: A Biography.* Cambridge: Cambridge University Press, 2001.

Loeb, Louis E. *From Descartes to Hume: Continental Rationalism and the Development of Modern Philosophy.* Ithaca and London: Cornell University Press, 1981.

Macor, Laura Anna. *Die Bestimmung des Menschen (1748–1800): Eine Begriffsgeschichte.* Stuttgart-Bad Canstatt: Frommann-Holzboog, 2013.

Madonna, Luigi Cataldi. "The Eighteenth-Century Rehabilitation of Sensitive Knowledge and the Birth of Aesthetics: Wolff, Baumgarten and Mendelssohn." In Rainier Munk, editor. *Moses Mendelssohn's Metaphysics and Aesthetics.* Dordrecht: Springer. Pp. 279–97.

Markus, R.A. "St. Augustine on Signs." *Phronesis* 2 (1957): 60–83, reprinted in R.A. Markus, editor. *Augustine: A Collection of Critical Essays.* Garden City: Doubleday, 1972. Pp. 61–91.

McQuillan, J. Colin. "Oaths, Promises, and Compulsory Duties: Kant's Response to Mendelssohn's Jerusalem." *Journal of the History of Ideas* 75 (2014): 581–604.

Muchnik, Pablo. *Kant's Theory of Evil: An Essay on the Dangers of Self-love and the Apriority of History.* Lanham: Lexington Books, 2009.

Mulholland, Leslie A. *Kant's System of Rights.* New York: Columbia University Press, 1990.

Munk, Reinier, editor. *Moses Mendelssohn's Metaphysics and Aesthetics.* Dordrecht: Springer, 2011.

Munk, Reinier. "'What is the Bond?' The Discussion of Mendelssohn and Kant 1785–1787." In Munk, editor. *Moses Mendelssohn's Metaphysics and Aesthetics.* Pp. 183–202.

Nadler, Steven. "Theodicy and Providence." In *The Cambridge History of Jewish Philosophy* (vol. 1): *From Antiquity through the Seventeenth Century.* Edited by Steven Nadler and T.M. Rudavsky. Cambridge: Cambridge University Press, 2009. Pp. 619–58.

Palmquist, Stephen R. *Comprehensive Commentary on Kant's Religion within the Bounds of Bare Reason.* Chichester: Wiley Blackweel, 2016.

Pardey, Ulrich. "Über Kants Widerlegung des Mendelssohnschen Bewieses der Beharrlichkeit der Steele." *Kant-Studien* 90 (1999): 257–84.

Pasnau, Robert. *After Certainty: A History of Our Epistemic Ideals and Illusions.* New York: Oxford University Press, 2017.

Pasternak, Lawrence J. *Routledge Guidebook to Kant on Religion within the Boundaries of Mere Reason.* London: Routledge, 2014.

Paton, Herbert James. "Is the Transcendental Deduction a Patchwork?". *Proceedings of the Aristotelian Society* in 1930, reprinted in H.J. Paton. *In Defence of Reason.* London: Hutchinson, 1951. Pp. 65–90.

Pecina, Björn. *Mendelssohns diskrete Religion.* Tübingen: Mohr Siebeck, 2016.

Pollok, Anne. *Facetten des Menschen: zu Anthropologie Moses Mendelssohns.* Hamburg: Felix Meiner Verlag, 2010.

Pollok, Anne. "Beautiful Perception and its Object: Mendelssohn's Theory of Mixed Sentiments Reconsidered." *Kant-Studien* 109 (2018): 270–85.

Rawls, John. *A Theory of Justice* (1971). Revised edition. Cambridge, Mass.: Harvard University Press, 1999.

Rawls, John. *Political Liberalism.* New York: Columbia University Press, 1993.

Ripstein, Arthur. *Force and Freedom: Kant's Legal and Political Philosophy.* Cambridge, Mass.: Harvard University Press, 2009.

Rogerson, Kenneth F. *Kant's Aesthetics: The Roles of Form and Expression.* Lanham: University Press of America, 1986.

Rosenstock, Bruce. *Philosophy and the Jewish Question: Mendelssohn, Rosenzweig, and Beyond.* New York, Fordham University Press, 2010.

Rossi, Philip J., S.J. *The Social Authority of Reason: Kant's Critique, Radical Evil, and the Destiny of Humankind.* Albany: State University of New York Press, 2005.

Rovira, Rogelio. "Mendelssohn's Refutation of Kant's Critique of the Ontological Proof." *Kant-Studien* 108 (2017): 401–26.

Rudavsky, T.M. *Jewish Philosophy in the Middle Ages: Science, Rationalism, and Religion.* Oxford: Oxford University Press, 2018.

Rueger, Alexander. "Beautiful Surfaces: Kant on Free and Adherent Beauty in Nature and Art." *British Journal of the History of Philosophy* 16 (2008): 335–57.

Rueger, Alexander. "The Free Play of the Faculties and the Status of Natural Beauty in Kant's Theory of Taste." *Archiv für Geschichte der Philosophie* 90 (2008): 298–322.

Rueger, Alexander. "Enjoying the Unbeautiful: From Mendelssohn's Theory of 'Mixed Sentiments' to Kant's Aesthetic Judgments of Reflection." *Journal of Aesthetics and Art Criticism* 67 (2009): 181–9.

Rueger, Alexander and Şahan Evren. "The Role of Symbolic Presentation in Kant's Theory of Taste." *British Journal of Aesthetics* 45 (2005): 228–47.

Sacks, Elias. *Moses Mendelssohn's Living Script: Philosophy, Practice, History, Judaism.* Bloomington: Indiana University Press, 2017.

Schaper, Eva. *Sudies in Kant's Æsthetics.* Edinburgh: Edinburgh University Press, 1979.

Schmidt, James. *What Is Enlightenment? Eighteenth-Century Questions and Twentieth-Century Answers.* Berkeley and Los Angeles: University of California Press, 1996.

Schorch, Grit. *Moses Mendelssohns Sprachpolitik.* Berlin and Boston: Walter de Gruyter, 2012.

Smith, Norman Kemp. *A Commentary to Kant's "Critique of Pure Reason."* Second edition. London: Macmillan, 1923.

Smith, Norman Kemp. *The Philosophy of David Hume.* London: Macmillan, 1941.

Sorkin, David. *Moses Mendelssohn and the Religious Enlightenment.* Berkeley and Los Angeles: University of California Press, 1996.

Stroud, Barry. *Hume.* London: Routledge & Kegan Paul, 1977.

Vaihinger, Hans. "The Transcendental Deduction in the First Edition of the *Critique of Pure Reason*" In Vahihinger, *Philosophische Abhandlungen* (Halle, 1902), partially translated in Moltke S. Gram, editor. *Kant: Disputed Questions.* Chicago: Quadrangle Books, 1967. Pp. 13–61.

Warda, Arthur. *Immanuel Kants Bücher.* Berlin: Martin Breslauer, 1922.

Willaschek, Marcus. *Kant on the Sources of Metaphysics.* Cambridge: Cambridge University Press, 2018.

Williams, Thomas. "Gaunilo." In *Encyclopedia of Philosophy*, second edition. Edited by Donald M. Borchert. 10 volumes. Farmington Hills: Thomson-Gale, 2006. Vol. 4, pp. 33–4.

Wilson, Ross. *Subjective Universality in Kant's Aesthetics.* Bern: Peter Lang, 2007.

Wood, Allen W. *Kant's Rational Theology.* Ithaca: Cornell University Press, 1978.

Wood, Allen W. *Kant's Ethical Thought.* Cambridge: Cambridge University Press, 1999.

Wood, Allen W. "Ethical Community, Church, and Scripture." In Höffe, *Kant: Die Religion.* Pp. 148–50.

Woolhouse, Roger. *Locke: A Biography.* Cambridge: Cambridge University Press, 2007.

Yolton, John W. *John Locke and the Way of Ideas.* Oxford: Clarendon Press, 1956.

Yovel, Yirmiahu. *Kant and the Philosophy of History.* Princeton: Princeton University Press, 1980.

# Index

For the benefit of digital users, indexed terms that span two pages (e.g., 52-53) may, on occasion, appear on only one of those pages.

Abbt, Thomas 207
Abderitism 289-90, 321-2, 326-36
Addison, Joseph 210-11
aesthetic ideas 236-7, 243-4, 249-50
aesthetics 25-6, 73-5, 254-5
   Mendelssohn's. 22-3, 127-9, 205-23
   Kant's 22-3, 203-11, 215, 221-42
   Mendelssohn's and Kant's, compared 218, 221-5, 238-55
Akenside, Mark 210-11
Alsace 20-1
Altmann, Alexander 290-1, 336-7
analytic and synthetic judgment, Kant's distinction between 11, 18-19, 111
Anscombe, Gertrude Elizabeth Margaret 127
Antinomy of Pure Reason 104-5, 129-30
   fourth 110, 112-15
   Mendelssohn on Kant's fourth 132
apperception, transcendental unity of 49-50
approbation, faculty of, in Mendelssohn 127-9, 131, 210-11, 246-7
Aristotle 5-7, 57
arithmetic 175-6, 196-7
artistry 215-17

Basedow, Johann Bernhard 127-9
Batteaux, Charles 222
Baumgarten, Alexander Gottlieb 4, 11, 13-14, 26, 45-7, 53-4, 59, 67-8, 81-3, 93, 107, 180-1, 185-7, 192-4, 196, 203-6, 213-15, 225-6, 282-4
beauty 210-11, 225-33, 252-3
Ben-Israel, Menasseh 20-1
Bernhard, Isaac 8-9
Berkeley, George 5, 94-5, 168-9, 185-6, 198-200
Biester, Johann Erich 268-70
Bonnet, Charles 15-16
Burke, Edmund 8-11, 210-11, 221-2

Cambridge Platonists 5
Canon of Pure Reason 118-23, 145-6, 151-3, 268-9
Charles V 69-70
chiliasm 321-2, 329-30
Christianity 276-8, 289-90, 292-4, 302-20
Clarke, Samuel 5, 34-5
*cogito* 11, 49-50, 52-3, 85, 188

common sense 3, 194-5, 270
conscience, freedom of 22-3
consequentialism 65-6
cosmological argument 11, 44, 52-3
   Kant on 96-7, 103-4, 109-10, 112-16, 129-30
   Mendelssohn on 81-5, 93, 96-7, 112-13, 129-37
Cranz, August Friedrich 20-1, 287
Cromwell, Oliver 20-1
Crusius, Christian August 143-4
Cudworth, Ralph 5

Dahlstrom, Daniel 53-4
Descartes, René 5, 11, 45-7, 49, 75, 80-2, 85, 89-90, 134-5, 137-8, 186-8, 190, 199-200
design, argument from 19-20, 52-5 *See also* physico-theological argument
   Kant on, 97-9, 103-4
   Mendelssohn on 85-6, 98-9, 101-2, 117-18
Dessau 7-9
disinterestedness 225-6
Dohm, Christian Wilhelm 20-1
dualism 192-4

education, Mendelssohn on 260-1, 283-4, 314, 324-5
embryology 304
emotions 210-12, 228-9, 248-55
empiricism 4-5, 26, 28-9, 33-5, 42-3, 254-5, 336-7
enlightenment 259-68
Ephraim, Benjamin Veitel 16
epistemology 74
Euclid 63
Euler, Leonhard 247-8
excommunication 20-1, 285
existence, not a predicate 89-92, 111-12, 139

Feder, Johann Georg Heinrich 168-9, 179-80, 185-6
fine art(s)
   Kant on 234-40
   Mendelssohn on 206-7, 219-22
form, aesthetic 228-30
Formey, Samuel 12-13, 28
Francis I 69-70
Fränkel, David 8-9
Frederick II, "The Great," 5-9, 99-100

free play of imagination and understanding 226–9, 245–7
Frege, Gottlob 175–6
freedom
  as postulate of pure practical reason 143–4
  of speech 274, 280–1, 285–7 See also will, freedom of
Friedländer, David 16, 22
Friedrich Wilhelm II 293–4

Galileo, Galilei 189–90
Garve, Christian 5–7, 164, 168–9, 185–6
genius
  Kant on 233–40
  Mendelssohn on 217–18
Geometry 175–6
  Kant's treatment of 35–7, 170–1, 196–7
  Mendelssohn's treatment of 29–35, 37
Gerard, Alexander 221–2
Giza 234
God
  arguments for existence of 11, 15–16, 25–6, 29–30, 32, 75, 140–1
  and time 182–3, See also cosmological argument; design, argument from; Kant on; Mendelssohn on; ontological argument; physico-theological argument; possibility
Gottlieb, Micah 290–1
Gregor, Mary 263
Gumpertz, Aaron 8–9

happiness, in highest good 120–2, 151–6
Henry II 20–1
Herz, Marcus 14–15, 17, 20–1, 130, 176, 179–80
highest good 118–22, 151–6, 158–9, 271–3, 292–3, 302–5, 329–30
Hirschman, Albert 332–3
Hobbes, Thomas 86–7
holiness 153–4, 156, 159
Hume, David 4–7, 19–20, 26, 43, 57, 64–5, 79–80, 86, 172–3, 187–91, 221–2, 231–2
Hutcheson, Francis 26, 32, 68–70, 206
Huysum, Jan van 216

ideal of beauty 232–3
Ideal of Pure Reason 48, 78–9, 104–9, 114
idealism 5, 25–6, 34–5, 50, 101, 167–201
  Mendelssohn on 184–96
  transcendental 13–15, 86–7, 124–5, 143–4, 167–9, 185–6, 194–202
ideas of pure reason 104–5
imagination
  Mendelssohn on 208, 245–6
  See also free play of imagination and understanding
immortality 15, 25–6, 49–50, 77–8, 105–6, 121–2, 127–9, 140–66, 302–6, 309, 313, 318

imperatives, Kant on 66–7
intuition 49–50, 93, 169–70, 172–4

Jacobi, Friedrich Heinrich 2, 5–7, 23–5, 103, 123–4, 184–5, 259–60, 268–70, 273
Jesus Christ 303–5, 309–11
Jews, civil rights for 20–1
  See also Judaism
Judaism 15–16, 22–3, 142–3, 287–92, 302, 308–9, 312–13, 315–17, 319–20

Kames, Henry Home, Lord 205–6
Kant, Immanuel
  on aesthetic ideas 236–7, 243–4, 249–50
  on aesthetics 203–12, 215, 224–40
  on anthropology 61, 224–5
  on arguments for existence of God 77–9, 81, 86–99, 103–23
  comments on *Morgenstunden* 1–4, 273
  on Christianity 292–4, 302–20
  on church invisible 307–8
  on color 247–8
  on enlightenment 262–8, 317
  on ethical community 306–7, 311, 317
  on faith 269–70
  on fine art 206–7, 234–40, 243–4
  on free and adherent beauty 230–2
  on free play of imagination and understanding 226–30, 245–7
  on freedom of speech 273–4
  on freedom of the will 60–2, 261–2, 326–8
  on genius 233–40
  on highest good 118–22, 151–6, 158–9, 271–3, 292–3, 302–5, 329–30
  on idealism 51, 167, 169–86, 194–202
  on immortality 121–3, 142–7, 149–66, 302–6, 309, 313, 318
  on Jesus Christ 303–5, 309–11
  on Judaism 302, 308–9, 312–13, 315–17, 319–20
  life of 7–8, 10–25
  on mathematical method 35–7, 70–1, 80–1
  meeting with Mendelssohn 16–17
  moral theology of 118–23, 271–3
  on morality 56–7, 59–72, 206–7, 252, 254, 261–2, 294–300, 310
  on perfectionism 68
  on practical grounds for belief 53–4, 118–23
  on progress 321–3, 326–37
  on religion of reason 291, 294, 314–18
  on religious liberty 266–8, 276–7, 281, 292–301, 319
  response to *Jerusalem* 22–3, 312–18, 321–37
  on sacraments 314
  on the sublime 211–12, 234
  support for Basedow 127–9
  on time 167–84

Kant's works
  Conflict of the Faculties 295–6, 321–2, 332–6
  Critique of Practical Reason 23–5, 60, 77, 103, 119, 122–3, 140–1, 144, 146, 150–5, 157, 268–9, 271–3, 294–5, 302–3, 329–30
  Critique of Pure Reason 2, 7, 14–17, 19–20, 23–6, 43, 47–50, 54–5, 71, 73–4, 77–81, 85–7, 96–7, 102–3, 145–8, 150–3, 164, 168–75, 177, 181–6, 194–203, 241–2, 268–70, 274, 276–7, 329–30
  Critique of the Power of Judgment 5–7, 22–3, 73–4, 77, 86–7, 122–3, 151, 157–8, 163, 205, 224–42, 244–5, 248–52, 259–60, 269–70, 303–4
  Dreams of a Spirit-Seer 12–14
  "End of All Things," 155–6, 162, 331
  "False Subtlety of Four Syllogistic Figures," 10–11
  Groundwork for the Metaphysics of Morals 56, 60–1, 67–8, 119, 151, 176–7, 194–5, 252
  "Idea for a Universal History from a Cosmopolitan Point of View," 23–5, 73–4, 146, 162–3, 308, 333–6
  Inquiry concerning the Distinctness of the Principles of Natural Theology and Morality (prize essay) 5–7, 12–13, 25–6, 28, 30, 35–7, 40–3, 51–2, 66–7
  "Introduction of Negative Quantities into Philosophy" 10–11
  lectures on anthropology 205–6
  lectures on ethics 151–2
  letter to Schütz 1
  Meditation on Fire 7–8
  Metaphysical Foundations of Natural Science 189–90
  Metaphysics of Morals 19–20, 56, 60, 151, 176–7, 252, 254, 264–5, 274–5, 296–300, 306–7, 334
  New Exposition of the First Principles of Metaphysical Cognition 7–8, 25–6, 40, 78–9, 86–90, 134–5, 143–4
  Observations on the Feeling of the Beautiful and Sublime 10–11, 203, 205–6, 230, 252
  "On the Common Saying: That Might be Correct in Theory but it is of no use in Practice," 5–7, 25–6, 144, 151, 164, 265–6, 272–3, 318, 321–2, 334–5
  "On the Differentiation of Regions in Space," 270
  On the Form and Principles of the Sensible and Intelligible World (inaugural dissertation) 13–14, 80–1, 168, 169–76, 270
  Only Possible Basis for a Demonstration of the Existence of God 5–7, 11, 13–14, 47–8, 51–2, 54–5, 71, 78–9, 85–7, 90–104, 116–17, 134–5, 137, 271
  Opus postumum 102
  Physical Monadology 7–8
  Prolegomena to Any Future Metaphysics 168–9, 184–6, 196–7, 200–1
  Religion within the Boundaries of Mere Reason 5–7, 15, 19–20, 22–6, 73–4, 143–4, 146–7, 151–2, 155–64, 201–2, 257–8, 261–2, 274–5, 293–6, 302–18, 321–2, 324, 327–8, 333–4
  Towards Perpetual Peace 146–7, 165–6, 331–2, 334–5
  True Estimation of Living Forces 7–8
  Universal Natural History and Theory of the Heavens 5–8
  "What Does It Mean to Orient Oneself in Thinking?" 2–4, 23–6, 45–6, 103, 117–18, 140–1, 259–60, 268–74
  "What is Enlightenment?," 257–60, 263–8, 295–6
  "What Progress Has Metaphysics Made in German since the Times of Leibniz and Wolff?," 118

kashrut 312–13
Kierkegaard, Søren 23–5, 268–9
Kiesewetter, Johann Gottfried Karl Christian 200–1
Klopstock, Friedrich Gottlieb 249
knowledge, Mendelssohn's theory of 125–6, 186–94
Knutzen, Martin 7–8
Königsberg 7–8, 16, 20–1, 200–1
Kypke, David 20–1

Lambert, Johann Heinrich 5–7, 12–15, 176–84
Laplace, Pierre-Simon 7–8
Lavater, Johann Caspar 7, 15–16
Leibniz, Gottfried Wilhelm 4–9, 13–14, 26, 28–9, 34–5, 43, 46–7, 75–6, 99–100, 134–5, 143–4, 174–5, 203–4, 282–3, 303–4
Lessing, Gotthold Ephraim 8–9, 23–5, 123–4, 134–5, 184–5, 203, 207, 212–13, 245, 268–9
Lewald, August 16
liberty, religious 266–8, 273–301
Locke, John 5–9, 26, 28–9, 43, 75–6, 79–80, 89–90, 172–3, 186–8, 190–1, 267–8
  on toleration 276–83, 286, 292–3, 296, 300–1

Maimon, Salomon 177
Maimonides 10–11, 290–1
Malebranche, Nicolas 5
Mary, the Virgin 304
Mary II 277–8
mathematics, method of 11, 27–8, 70–1, 80–1
  Kant on 30, 35–7
  Mendelssohn on 29–35
maxims 63–4, 305–6, 330–1

Meier, Georg Friedrich 53–4, 205–6, 213–15, 247
Memel (Klaipeda) 16
Mendelssohn, Joseph 23–5, 124
Mendelssohn, Moses
  on aesthetics 53–4, 203, 222–3
  on arguments for existence of God 32, 38, 40, 44–55, 76–88, 96–7, 103, 107, 117–18, 123–41
  on education 260–1, 283–4, 314, 324–5
  on enlightenment 259–66
  on excommunication 285
  on fine arts 219–22
  on freedom of the will 61–2
  on genius 217–18
  on idealism 50–1, 167–9, 178–9, 181–94, 201–2
  on immortality 142–50, 155–6
  on Judaism 287–92, 311–13, 319, 324
  on justice 38–9
  Kant's comments on 1
  Kant's relations with 5–7, 16–17
  Kant's response to *Jerusalem* 22–3, 312–17
  on Kant on time 176–84
  life 7–25
  on mathematical method 31–5, 37, 80–1
  on maxims 63–4
  on mixed sentiments 232
  on *mitzvot* 312–14
  on morality 32, 55–71, 307–9
  on oaths 285–6, 319
  on philosophical method 37–41
  on progress 321–2, 324–6, 335–7
  on religious liberty 276–7
  on representation 212–15
  response to *Critique of Pure Reason* 17–19, 23–5, 123–41
  review of Kant's *Only Possible Basis* 99–102, 107–8
  on separation of church and state 281–4
  on signs 219–21
  on the sublime 211–12
  on Sulzer 210–11, 217
  on tragedy 212–13
Mendelssohn's works
  "Essay on Evidence," 5–7, 11, 28–35, 37–40, 44–51, 56–9, 61–4, 76–7, 79–86
  *Jerusalem, or on Religious Power and Judaism* 7, 17, 20–3, 25–8, 73–4, 164, 201–2, 257–9, 266–7, 274–7, 281–91, 307, 312, 315–16, 321–5, 336–7
  *Letters concerning the Latest Literature* 78–9, 99–102, 210–11, 217, 232–3
  *Letters on the Sentiments* 8–9, 203, 205–10, 242–6
  *Morning Hours* 1–2, 15–17, 19–20, 23–6, 58–9, 71, 73–4, 76–7, 79, 86–7, 98, 101–2, 123–41, 167–9, 184–95

"On the Main Principles of the Fine Arts and Sciences," 203, 205–6, 208–9, 213–16, 219–22, 245–6, 250–1, 253
"On the Sublime and the Naïve in the Fine Sciences," 205–6, 211–12, 217–18, 250–1
*Phaedo* 15, 49–50, 73–4, 77–8, 140–1, 145–50, 153, 164, 313, 324, 326, 329–30
*Philosophical Dialogues* 8–9
*Philosophical Writings* 8–9, 203, 205–6, 224–5
"Pope a Metaphysician!" 8–9
review of Batteux 222
reviews of Kant 10–13
"Rhapsody," 205–6, 208–10, 242–7, 253
*To the Friends of Lessing* 23–5, 268–9
Translation of Maimonides's *Logical Terms* 10–11
"What is Enlightenment?," 257–63
Mendelssohn, Felix-Bartholdy 23–5
Mennonites 292
metaphysics, method of
  Kant on 30, 40–3, 71
  Mendelssohn on 29–30, 37–41, 71
Mill, John Stuart 20–1, 280–1
Milton, John 99–100, 249
moral theology, Kant's 118–23
morality
  fundamental maxim of 58–61
  method of 55–70
  *See also* Kant, on morality; Mendelssohn, on morality
Mörschel, Daniel 20–1, 287
music 219–20, 241, 250–1

Newton, Isaac 42, 189–90
Newtonians 174–5
Nicolai, Friedrich 8–9, 23–5, 203, 207, 212–13
novelty 210–11

ontological argument 11, 44–7, 71, 75–9, 81, 108–12, 116–17
  Kant on 81, 86–94, 103–4
  Mendelssohn on 29–30, 81–4, 99–100, 137–41

*Pantheismusstreit* 2, 23–5, 268–9
Paralogisms of Pure Reason 5–7, 15, 49–50, 104–5, 145–8, 183, 199–200, 274
patchwork theory 18
Peirce, Charles Sanders 77–8
perfectionism 11, 58–60, 68, 72, 282–3
  in aesthetics 208–10, 215, 230, 241–54
phenomena 171
physico-theological argument 103–4, 116–18
  *See also* argument from design
poetry, Mendelssohn on 220

possibility
   Kant's argument for existence of God as ground of 11, 76–7, 93–6, 103–4
   Mendelssohn's review of Kant's argument 76–7, 99–102, 107–9
practical reason 57–8
practical syllogism 57–8, 63–4
pre-established harmony 13–14
progress 23–6, 146, 162–6, 321–37
Prussian Academy of Sciences 5–7, 27–8
Pufendorf, Samuel 283–4

Ramler, Wilhelm 222
rationalism 4–5, 10–11, 26, 28–9, 56, 254–5, 336–7
Rawls, John 276
reason, theoretical vs. practical 3–4, 45–6
   *See also* practical reason
Refutation of Idealism
   Baumgarten's 192–3
   Kant's 49–50, 124–5, 168–9, 173–4, 185–6, 198–202
   Mendelssohn's 184–6, 193–4
Right, Universal Principle of 296–9
Rosenstock, Bruce 290–1
Rousseau, Jean-Jacques 8–9
Russell, Bertrand 175–6

St.Peter's Basilica 234
Schütz, Christian Gottfried 1
Semler, Johann Salomo 311–12
sentiment (*Empfindung*) 45, 248, 253–5
   mixed 212
separation of church and state 22–3, 273–301
   Locke on 278–81, *See also* Kant, on religious liberty; Mendelssohn, on religious liberty
Shaftesbury, Anthony Ashley Cooper, third Earl of 26, 63, 134–5
signs, natural vs. artificial 219–21
silent decade, Kant's 13–14
skepticism 168–9
Socrates 147–50, 153, 216
Sonnenfels, Joseph 287
space
   as infinite given magnitude 108
   transcendental ideality of 14–15, 124–5, 130–1, 143–4, 168–9, 174–6, 196–7

Spalding, Johann Joachim 12–13, 145–6, 154–6, 160–1, 260–1
Spinoza, Baruch 8–9, 22–5, 27, 86–7, 123–4, 184–5, 268–9, 290–1
Spinozism 134–5, 184–5, 268–9
sublime, the
   Kant on 211–12, 234, 252
   Mendelssohn on 211–12, 249–50
sufficient reason, principle of 48–9, 85–6, 133
Sulzer, Johann Georg 5–7, 12–15, 27, 54–5, 176–7, 181–2, 210–11, 217–18, 232–3
Swedenborg, Emmanuel 12–13
symbols, Kant on Christian 302–6

taste
   Kant on judgments of 226–30
   Mendelssohn on 221–2
   universal validity of 226–30
teleology 86–7
time, transcendental ideality of 14–15, 143–4, 168–83
tragedy 206, 212–13
Transcendental Aesthetic 172, 196–8
Transcendental Deduction 145–6, 149
Transcendental Dialectic 104–23, 145–6
transcendental idealism. *see* idealism

Ulrich, Johann Heinrich August 261–2, 327–8
utilitarianism 69–70

visual arts 251

Wessely, Bernhard 23–5
will, freedom of 15, 59, 61–2, 104–5, 144, 261–2, 326–8
William II (of Orange) 277–8
Witzenhausen, Simon Veit 23–5
Wizenmann, Thomas 271–2
Wolff, Christian 4, 8–9, 26–9, 43, 59–60, 67–8, 74, 81–2, 96–7, 117–18, 185–7, 205, 242–3, 282–4, 303–4

Zöllner, Johann Friedrich 259, 292

The manufacturer's authorised representative in the EU for product safety is Oxford University Press España S.A. of El Parque Empresarial San Fernando de Henares, Avenida de Castilla, 2 – 28830 Madrid (www.oup.es/en or product.safety@oup.com). OUP España S.A. also acts as importer into Spain of products made by the manufacturer.

Printed in the USA/Agawam, MA
November 5, 2025

895578.037